Universal Microservices Architecture

Device-Independent Modeling for Distributed Systems Using WebAssembly

Enrico Piovesan

Apress®

Universal Microservices Architecture: Device-Independent Modeling for Distributed Systems Using WebAssembly

Enrico Piovesan
Golden, BC, Canada

ISBN-13 (pbk): 979-8-8688-2793-8 ISBN-13 (electronic): 979-8-8688-2794-5
https://doi.org/10.1007/979-8-8688-2794-5

Managing Director, Apress Media LLC: Welmoed Spahr
Acquisitions Editor: Anandadeep Roy
Editorial Assistant: Jessica Vakili

Cover designed by eStudioCalamar

Cover image designed by Pixabay

Distributed to the book trade worldwide by Springer Science+Business Media New York, 1 New York Plaza, New York, NY 10004. Phone 1-800-SPRINGER, fax (201) 348-4505, e-mail orders-ny@springer-sbm.com, or visit www.springeronline.com. Apress Media, LLC is a Delaware LLC and the sole member (owner) is Springer Science + Business Media Finance Inc (SSBM Finance Inc). SSBM Finance Inc is a **Delaware** corporation.

For information on translations, please e-mail booktranslations@springernature.com; for reprint, paperback, or audio rights, please e-mail bookpermissions@springernature.com.

Apress titles may be purchased in bulk for academic, corporate, or promotional use. eBook versions and licenses are also available for most titles. For more information, reference our Print and eBook Bulk Sales web page at http://www.apress.com/bulk-sales.

Any source code or other supplementary material referenced by the author in this book is available to readers on GitHub. For more detailed information, please visit https://www.apress.com/gp/services/source-code.

If disposing of this product, please recycle the paper

To the women who shape my world.

To my wife, my partner through every long day, week, and year of this journey. Your support and belief in me have made all of this possible.

To my daughters Millie and Charlie, who give me a reason every single day to do more and be better.

And to my Chief Architect and VP, who has never let me settle, always pushed back, always questioned, and in doing so made me grow.

Table of Contents

About the Author

Enrico Piovesan is a software architect at Autodesk with over 20 years of experience designing distributed, event-driven, and modular systems across cloud, edge, and client environments. His work has focused on scalability, performance, developer experience, and long-term system design.

Over the past few years, he has been working on new architectural models focused on portability, contracts, and runtime-independent execution.

Before that, he co-founded startups in education, travel, and payments, focusing on turning new ideas into working systems. He is passionate about system design, platform thinking, team autonomy, and architecture that evolves with scale.

Book website: `https://www.universalmicroservices.com`

Code repository: `https://github.com/enricopiovesan/UMA-code-examples`

Author website: `https://enricopiovesan.com`

About the Technical Reviewer

Tarun Telang has over 20 years of experience working with leading tech firms, including Microsoft, Oracle, BlackBerry, and SAP. He has worked in the development of flagship enterprise products and platforms, including SAP HANA, Oracle Industry Cloud, SharePoint, and OneDrive in Microsoft 365. His contributions have helped improve the scalability, reliability, and performance of these platforms for millions of customers worldwide. Through these experiences, he has developed deep expertise in designing, building, and operating complex software systems at scale. He specializes in solving challenging engineering problems and architecting reliable, high-performance platforms that support evolving business needs.

Tarun was recognized as a DZone Core Member, SAP Mentor, and Community Influencer for his thought leadership and technical contributions to the developer community. He regularly publishes blogs and articles focusing on microservices, cloud architecture, AI prompt engineering, and career roadmaps for software engineering leaders.

Tarun authored the official *MicroProfile API Tutorial*, maintained by the Eclipse Foundation, and actively contributes to advancing open standards for cloud-native Java development. As a technical educator, he has created video training content for O'Reilly Media on Java, JVM internals, Jakarta EE, .NET, and GraalVM, as well as interactive courses on Udemy and Educative.io covering PostgreSQL, regular expressions, YAML, and other software engineering topics. He has also authored books on YAML and DNS fundamentals.

He is the author of *Beginning Cloud Native Java Development with MicroProfile, Jakarta EE, and Kubernetes*. He is also the co-author of *Java EE to Jakarta EE 10 Recipes: A Problem-Solution Approach for Enterprise Java* (Apress, 2022), *Learn Microservices with Spring Boot 3: A Practical Approach Using Event-Driven Architecture, Cloud-Native Patterns, and Containerization* (2023), and *Practical Microservices Architectural Patterns: Build Highly Scalable Distributed Applications with Spring Boot 3 and Spring Cloud* (2025).

Tarun has presented at various technical conferences in North America, Europe, and India, including SAP TechEd and the Great Indian Developer Summit (GIDS). He regularly shares his expertise in cloud-native architectures, distributed systems, and software engineering best practices.

He is passionate about mentoring developers, architects, and managers through writing, technical training, open-source contributions, and public speaking. Having previously worked in Canada and Germany, Tarun now resides in Hyderabad, India, with his wife, Nikita, and their son, Vihan.

Tarun enjoys connecting with software engineers, architects, technology leaders, and learners at all levels. You can connect with him through the following channels:

LinkedIn: `https://linkedin.com/in/taruntelang`

Blogs: `https://taruntelang.medium.com/`, `https://substack.com/@devskills`

YouTube: `https://youtube.com/@dev-skills`

Website: `https://practicaldeveloper.com`

X (formerly Twitter): @taruntelang

PART I

The Architecture We Need Now

CHAPTER 1

Introduction

The Changing Location of Software

In the past, software usually ran in stable and predictable environments. Early systems used mainframes, where all the computing happened in one place and users connected through terminals. This setup naturally led to centralized architectures.

With client-server computing, workloads were spread across several machines. Clients handled some of the logic, while servers took care of data and main processing. This change brought new challenges like network communication, keeping data in sync, and managing data across different systems.

The rise of the web brought another big change. Applications were now split between browsers and servers. Browsers became powerful enough to run application logic. As web apps grew, more logic moved into the browser, while servers focused on providing APIs and services.

Mobile computing added yet another place for software to run. Now, systems had to work not just on desktops and servers, but also on mobile devices with different speeds, connections, and ways users interact. Architects started to consider problems like unreliable connections. Cloud computing then changed server operations by offering flexible infrastructure, distributed storage, and on-demand execution. Systems could now scale as needed, and infrastructure became programmable. More recently, edge computing has made it possible to process data closer to users and devices, spreading workloads across many locations. Code can now run in browsers using portable formats, on serverless platforms that execute functions, and on edge runtimes between clients and the cloud. Technologies like WebAssembly help run the same logic in different places with little change.

With all these changes, software is no longer tied to just one place. The same system might run in a browser, on a mobile device, at the edge, and in the cloud at the same time. Logic, data, and execution can move between these environments. Still, most software architectures are designed for specific deployment setups, not for what the software actually does.

E. Piovesan, *Universal Microservices Architecture*, https://doi.org/10.1007/979-8-8688-2794-5_1

In the past, software architecture focused on where code would run. As more environments appear, this way of thinking is becoming less useful.

The Problem We Didn't Solve

Over the past decades, software engineering has solved many difficult problems. We learned how to build systems that scale to millions of users. We learned how to distribute computation across clusters and regions. We learned how to package and deploy software using containers and automated pipelines. We standardized communication through APIs, messaging systems, and event-driven architectures. We built platforms that allow systems to grow, scale, and evolve.

Modern software systems can do a lot. They are distributed, scalable, resilient, and well-connected. From an infrastructure and operations point of view, many of the toughest problems have already been solved.

But one problem remains: making behavior portable. When a system needs to work in different places—like browsers, mobile, edge, and cloud—the same feature often gets built more than once. Logic for things like data validation, request processing, or rule evaluation is rewritten for each runtime, language, or framework. Even if services talk through APIs, the behavior behind those APIs is still linked to the environment where the service runs.

Because of this, many organizations end up maintaining several versions of the same feature: one for backend services, one for web apps, one for mobile devices, and sometimes another for edge or embedded systems. These versions might share ideas and interfaces, but they are still separate codebases that need to be built, tested, deployed, and maintained on their own.

This fragmentation isn't mainly due to bad engineering. It happens because of how software architecture is set up. Services are usually designed along with the runtime they'll use. Choices about language, framework, deployment, and infrastructure are often made before the service's boundaries and behavior are fully worked out. So, behavior gets tied to the environment right from the start.

Even though we've gotten good at building distributed systems, true portability of behavior is still missing. This is an important difference. Distributed systems let parts run in different places, but portable behavior means the same feature can run anywhere without being rebuilt. A system can be distributed but still need several versions of the same logic.

As software spreads to browsers, mobile devices, edge platforms, and the cloud, this problem stands out even more. The more runtimes and environments there are, the more expensive it gets to keep up with duplicated behavior.

What's missing isn't another deployment model or framework. What's missing is an architectural model where behavior is defined separately from the environment it runs in.

How This Book Came to Be

Like many engineers, I started out working on monolithic systems, where the main challenge was making them scale. As these systems grew, it became harder to scale both the software and the teams working on it. Monolithic architectures made it tough for large teams to work independently, and changes in one part often affected the rest of the system.

When microservices became popular, they seemed to solve many of these problems. Systems could be broken into smaller services, teams could work more independently, and different parts could scale independently. This worked well for a while. But over time, many organizations found that microservices brought new challenges. Systems became more distributed, operations got more complex, and the number of services grew so much that managing and understanding the system became hard.

This pattern is common in software architecture. New ideas come along to solve big problems, catch on quickly, and then their limits show up. The industry adjusts, and more balanced methods emerge. Trends often swing between extremes before finding a middle ground.

A few years ago, I ran into a different problem while working on a system with tough performance limits. We had a big client-side app with complex business logic and data processing that was too much for the client to handle well. Even after breaking up the app, adding lazy loading, and using standard techniques for large client apps, performance was still not good enough.

The practical solution then was to move the heavier business logic into a separate layer running in a different environment, while the client handled interaction and presentation. The client would call this layer for more complex tasks. At the time, this seemed like a sensible way to solve the performance problem.

Later, I realized this solution had a bigger architectural impact. The business logic was no longer stuck in the client environment. Instead, it became a separate feature that could run somewhere else and be used by the client when needed. Where the logic ran was now just a detail, not a key part of the system's design.

Over time, I saw this pattern in different situations. Systems became more distributed. Over time, I noticed this pattern in other projects as well. Systems were spread out across clients, servers, edge environments, and the cloud. Often, similar features were built more than once for different environments—they shared logic but had different implementations. This made me ask, why do we have to decide where logic runs in advance? What if a feature were defined by what it does, and the runtime could change as needed? This question is at the heart of this book. I'm not trying to invent a new architecture but to look at a common pattern: behavior is still closely tied to where it runs, which makes it hard for systems to evolve as environments change. The Universal Microservices Architecture came from the need to separate these concerns. It's a model that defines behavior separately from the environment, with a runtime that manages execution across different places. This book explains the model, how its parts work together, and how systems can be built around portable features instead of fixed deployments.

> **Universal Microservices Architecture separates what a service does from where it runs.**

Traditional software architecture usually defines a service along with its environment. A service might be designed as a web service, a backend service, a mobile backend, a serverless function, or an edge service. The behavior of the service and the environment are usually decided together, and over time, the implementation becomes tied to that environment.

Universal Microservices Architecture suggests a different approach. In UMA, a service is defined by what it does, not where it runs. The service's behavior is described using contracts, interfaces, and metadata that define its capabilities, inputs, outputs, and constraints. The implementation is packaged so it can run on different runtimes, instead of being locked to a single platform.

In this model, systems are seen as collections of capabilities, not just deployments. Each capability is a unit of behavior that can run when needed, in the environment that makes the most sense at the time. The runtime's job is to load, execute, and coordinate these capabilities based on their contracts and the current context.

Separating behavior from environment changes how systems are designed. Instead of building services just for the browser, the edge, or the cloud, architects define capabilities that can work across all these environments using a consistent execution model. The environment becomes just a parameter for execution, not what defines the service.

Recent advances in portable runtimes and standardized execution environments have made this approach more practical. Technologies like WebAssembly and other portable runtime models let you package service logic so it can run the same way on different platforms. UMA isn't tied to any one technology; it's an architectural model that can use different runtimes as they develop.

The objective of Universal Microservices Architecture is not to supplant existing architectural styles but to provide a framework for designing systems in which behavior is portable, capabilities are discoverable, and execution can occur across diverse environments without necessitating system redesign for each runtime change.

The Layered System Model

To understand Universal Microservices Architecture, it is useful to think of the system as a set of layers, each with a specific responsibility. These layers separate concerns that are often combined in traditional architectures, such as execution, communication, and decision-making.

At the foundation of the system are the environments in which software can run. These environments include browsers, mobile devices, edge runtimes, and cloud platforms. Each environment provides different capabilities, performance characteristics, and constraints. In traditional architectures, services are usually designed specifically for one of these environments. In UMA, the environment is treated as a location where capabilities can execute rather than as a defining characteristic of the service itself.

Above the environment layer is the execution layer, which is responsible for loading and running capabilities. This layer is the UMA runtime. Its responsibility is to execute services in accordance with their contracts, manage dependencies, handle events, and coordinate communication among capabilities. The runtime ensures that capabilities behave consistently regardless of where they are executed.

Above the runtime layer is the contract and metadata layer. This layer describes what each capability does, what inputs it expects, what outputs it produces, what dependencies it has, and under which conditions it can operate. These descriptions allow capabilities to be discovered, validated, and executed without requiring prior knowledge of their internal implementation.

Above the contract layer is the discovery and interaction layer. In this book, this role is represented by the Model Context Protocol. This layer makes capabilities discoverable and queryable, allowing systems and agents to find available capabilities, understand how to use them, and invoke them in a structured way.

At the top of the model is the reasoning layer. This layer includes agents or other decision-making components that determine which capabilities to use and in what sequence to achieve a specific objective. Instead of relying entirely on predefined workflows, systems can construct processes dynamically by selecting and composing capabilities based on the current context.

When these layers are viewed together, the system can be understood as a flow: capabilities are described through contracts and metadata, discovered through a protocol layer, selected by reasoning components, and executed by a runtime in the most appropriate environment.

This layered model separates execution, description, discovery, and decision-making into distinct concerns. This separation makes it possible to design systems in which capabilities are portable, discoverable, and composable across different environments.

The diagram below illustrates this conceptual model.

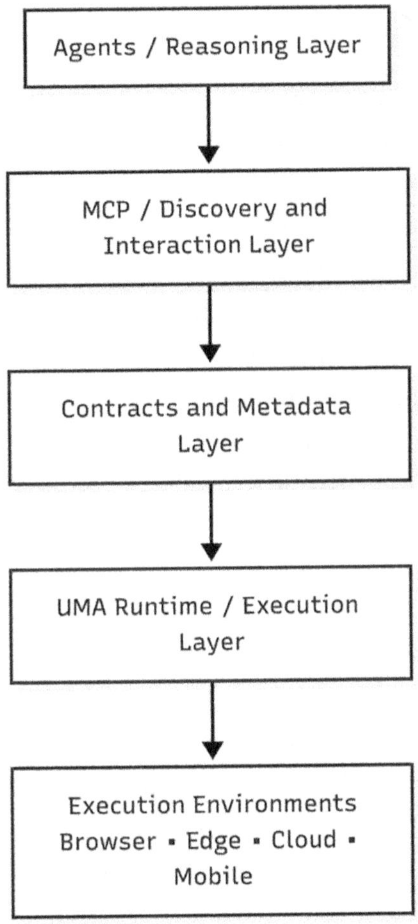

Figure 1-1. *The UMA layered system model. Capabilities are described through contracts and metadata, exposed through a discovery layer, selected by reasoning components, and executed by a runtime across different environments*

This model separates concerns that are frequently combined in traditional architectures. Contracts and metadata specify what a capability does. The discovery layer exposes capabilities to other systems. The runtime executes capabilities according to their contracts. The environment supplies the resources and context for execution. At the top of the model, reasoning components such as agents select and compose capabilities to achieve specific objectives. By dividing these responsibilities into layers, systems can evolve, scale, and operate across different environments without requiring architectural redefinition each time the runtime changes.

Why This Matters Now

For many years, software systems were designed around a small number of stable execution environments. Most business logic ran on servers, user interfaces ran on desktop applications or browsers, and communication occurred between well-defined tiers. Under these conditions, designing services specifically for a particular environment was a reasonable and effective approach.

Today, this assumption no longer holds. Modern systems operate across a wide range of environments, including browsers, mobile devices, edge runtimes, and cloud platforms. Each of these environments can execute meaningful parts of an application, and the boundary between client and server is no longer fixed. Logic can move closer to the user for performance reasons, closer to the data for efficiency, or into centralized systems for large-scale processing.

At the same time, execution models have become more flexible. Serverless platforms allow code to run on demand without dedicated infrastructure. Edge runtimes allow computation to be placed geographically closer to users. Browsers have evolved into full application runtimes capable of executing complex logic. Portable binary formats and standardized runtime interfaces make it increasingly feasible to execute the same code across different environments with consistent behavior.

These changes have an important architectural consequence. The environment in which a capability runs is no longer a fixed design decision made once during development. It can become a runtime decision based on latency, cost, data locality, security, or availability. A capability might execute in the browser in one scenario, at the edge in another, and in the cloud in a third.

When execution location becomes dynamic, architecture can no longer be tightly coupled to a single runtime. Systems must be designed so that behavior can move without requiring the system to be redesigned each time the execution environment changes.

This is one of the key reasons why portability is becoming a primary architectural concern. Portability is no longer only about moving applications between servers or cloud providers. It is about moving behavior across different types of environments while maintaining consistent contracts, interactions, and outcomes.

Technologies such as WebAssembly and other portable runtime models are important not because they introduce a new programming language, but because they make it practical to package behavior in a way that is less dependent on a specific operating system, language runtime, or infrastructure platform. These technologies do not define the architecture, but they make new architectural models possible.

Universal Microservices Architecture is based on the idea that software should be designed for this multi-environment reality. Instead of assuming a fixed deployment location, the architecture assumes that capabilities may execute in different environments and focuses on defining behavior, contracts, and execution rules in a way that remains consistent across those environments.

Why This Matters Next

While portability across environments is an important driver for this architectural model, it is not the only one. Another shift is happening in parallel, and it changes how software systems are used and how they interact with each other.

Traditionally, software systems have been designed primarily for human users. Interfaces were built for people, and developers predefined integrations between systems through APIs and workflows. The structure of the system and how its capabilities were used were mostly decided during development.

However, software is increasingly interacting with other software in more dynamic ways. Systems discover services at runtime, integrate through standardized protocols, and react to events produced by other systems. More importantly, a new class of software components is emerging that does not simply follow predefined workflows but also makes decisions about which capabilities to use to achieve a goal.

These components are often described as agents. Regardless of the specific technology used to implement them, their role is to interpret a request, determine which capabilities are available, select the appropriate ones, and compose them into a process that produces a result. Instead of executing a fixed sequence of steps, the system constructs the process dynamically based on context and available capabilities.

For this type of interaction to work, systems must be able to describe themselves in a way that other systems can understand. Capabilities must be discoverable. Their inputs, outputs, constraints, and effects must be defined in a structured, machine-readable way. Execution must be predictable and governed by clear contracts so that a capability can be invoked safely by a system that did not originally implement it.

This is where the layered model described earlier becomes particularly important. In this model, capabilities are defined through contracts and metadata, exposed through a discovery layer, and executed by a runtime that enforces their constraints. Reasoning components, including agents, interact with the system through the discovery layer, selecting and composing capabilities to achieve specific objectives.

In this context, Universal Microservices Architecture is not only a model for portability across environments. It is also a model for making software capabilities discoverable, composable, and executable in ways that enable systems to collaborate and construct processes dynamically.

This shift changes the role of architecture. Instead of defining only how components are deployed and how they communicate, the architecture must also define how capabilities are described, discovered, and safely executed by other systems.

As systems become more distributed, more dynamic, and more autonomous in their operation, the ability to define portable, discoverable, and contract-driven capabilities becomes increasingly important. Universal Microservices Architecture is an attempt to provide a model for designing systems that operate in this way.

How This Book Is Structured

This book is organized into several parts, each focusing on a different aspect of Universal Microservices Architecture. The structure progresses from architectural motivation to system design and finally to runtime behavior and future system models.

Part I: The Architecture We Need Now

This part examines the declining stability of traditional assumptions regarding runtime, deployment, and system boundaries. It introduces the concept of device independence and discusses the growing importance of portability and runtime flexibility as primary architectural considerations.

Part II: Designing UMA Systems

This part introduces the core elements of Universal Microservices Architecture. It explains how universal services are structured, how contracts and metadata define behavior, how the runtime layer operates, and how portability across environments can be achieved.

Part III: Deploying, Securing, and Scaling

This part focuses on operating UMA systems in real environments. It covers deployment models, security and trust boundaries, scalability, observability, and strategies for adopting UMA in existing systems.

Part IV: Operating and Evolving UMA Systems

This part explores how capabilities can be exposed and discovered through protocols such as the Model Context Protocol and how reasoning components, such as agents, can dynamically discover and compose capabilities. This part connects the UMA execution model with systems that construct processes at runtime rather than relying entirely on predefined workflows.

Part V: Realizing UMA Systems

The final part of the book follows a complete system from start to finish. It shows how capabilities are discovered, selected, executed, and combined across multiple runtimes to produce a result. The goal of this part is to demonstrate how the concepts introduced throughout the book work together as a complete system.

Although the book is organized in this sequence, readers are not required to read it from beginning to end. Some may be primarily interested in the runtime model, while others may focus on contracts, portability, or discoverability. However, the central idea is best understood when the parts are read together, as each part addresses a distinct layer of the same architectural model.

This book prioritizes architectural concepts and system design over specific tools or frameworks. Nonetheless, practical demonstration enhances understanding. Accordingly, a set of code examples and a reference implementation are available in the public repository accompanying this work. These examples demonstrate the implementation and composition of UMA services, contracts, runtimes, and discovery components within a functional system. The repository serves as a reference for the architectural model described herein, rather than as a production-ready framework.

Forward-Looking

Software systems are no longer confined to a single environment, a single runtime, or a deployment model. They operate across devices, networks, regions, and platforms, often simultaneously. Execution can move closer to the user, closer to the data, or into centralized systems, depending on the needs of the moment. As this flexibility increases, the assumptions that shaped traditional software architecture become less reliable.

In this environment, architecture can no longer be defined primarily by infrastructure boundaries or deployment targets. It must be defined by behavior, contracts, and the rules that govern how capabilities are executed and interact. Systems must be designed so that capabilities can move, be discovered, and be composed without redefining the system each time the runtime environment changes.

Universal Microservices Architecture is an attempt to describe a model for this type of system. It is based on the idea that software should be organized around portable capabilities, defined by contracts and metadata, executed by a runtime, and discoverable through standardized interfaces. This approach allows systems to evolve across environments while maintaining consistent behavior and interaction models.

As systems become more distributed and dynamic, and as software increasingly interacts with other software rather than only with human users, the ability to consistently describe, discover, and execute capabilities becomes more important. Architecture begins to define not only how systems are built and deployed but also how they are understood and used by other systems.

The goal of this book is to describe this architectural model, explain how its components work, and show how systems can be designed using these principles across client, edge, and cloud environments.

The question that motivated this work is simple:

> **What if software were not built for a specific environment, but for any environment?**

The chapters that follow explore one possible answer to that question.

Author's Note

This book was written in a personal capacity. The ideas, models, examples, and reference implementations presented here are based on independent research, personal experience, and publicly available information. They do not represent the views of any employer, past or present, and are not associated with any specific company, product, or proprietary system.

No confidential, proprietary, or non-public information has been used in the preparation of this book. All architectural concepts described are vendor-neutral and are presented as general software architecture patterns and models.

Any references to technologies, platforms, or tools are provided only as examples of possible implementation approaches and do not constitute endorsements of any particular product or vendor.

A set of code examples and a reference implementation accompanying this book is available in a public repository. This repository is provided for educational and illustrative purposes only and is intended to demonstrate the architectural concepts described in this book. It is not an official product and is not intended to represent a production-ready platform.

Reference implementation and code examples: `https://github.com/enricopiovesan/UMA-code-examples`

The purpose of this book is to present and explore an architectural model for building portable, discoverable, and composable software systems across multiple runtimes and environments and to contribute to the broader discussion around software architecture in distributed and multi-environment systems.

CHAPTER 2

Why Device Independence Matters

From Platform Silos to Portability by Design

The Pain Was Always There

I still remember the first time I felt truly misled by the software I had written. It was sometime in the early 2000s, during what we now call the AJAX era, a period roughly between 2004 and 2008 when Asynchronous JavaScript and XML (AJAX) made it possible for web pages to fetch data and update their content without a full page reload when Web 2.0 (the shift from static, read-only web pages to interactive, user-generated-content platforms) was more of an aspiration than a movement. Internet Explorer dominated the market, Firefox was still new, and Facebook didn't yet exist. I had built what I thought was a clean, interactive web interface. It worked beautifully in Firefox. But when I opened it in Internet Explorer, everything fell apart. Layouts shifted, buttons failed to respond, and event handling broke in subtle and confusing ways.

It wasn't just frustrating; it felt like something deeper had gone wrong. I hadn't done anything wrong. I had followed the standards, reused code where possible, and even adopted early modular practices. But behind each small utility function and layout choice were invisible assumptions about the runtime, the browser APIs, and even the user's operating system. Those assumptions were never declared; they were simply embedded in the code, ready to betray me if the environment changed.

For instance, a utility function that formatted dates assumed the browser would supply a Intl.DateTimeFormat API available in Firefox at the time but was absent in Internet Explorer 6. Another helper cached user preferences in sessionStorage, an API that IE6 simply did not expose. Neither assumption was documented anywhere in the code; both surfaced only at runtime, in production, for users on the wrong browser.

E. Piovesan, *Universal Microservices Architecture*, https://doi.org/10.1007/979-8-8688-2794-5_2

Back then, cross-platform development involved making a single webpage work similarly across two browsers, which was quite challenging. Opera and Safari introduced their own rendering quirks, but Internet Explorer was especially unpredictable. It lacked reliable support for modern CSS, handled JavaScript events inconsistently, and often needed fragile workarounds to address rendering inconsistencies. At that time, our focus wasn't on solving architectural challenges but on constantly addressing compatibility problems.

The dream persisted: reuse, modularity, building once and fixing in one place to use everywhere—an aspiration that Java had already enshrined in its motto "write once, run anywhere" (WORA), introduced with the Java Virtual Machine in the mid-1990s. We initially believed that portability wasn't just a code feature but depended on how well we defined *boundaries.* We assumed that by keeping things generic, everything else would naturally fall into place. However, this wasn't the case. Unknowingly, we were already linking behavior to execution context, the specific runtime environment (browser, operating system, device, or server) in which a piece of code actually runs. We had built abstractions (simplified models that hide complexity behind a clean interface) and relied on generalization (writing logic broadly enough to cover multiple cases), but we had never explicitly defined the boundaries (the lines separating what a component is responsible for from what it assumes the environment will provide).

And then mobile arrived.

In 2008, Apple launched the inaugural iOS SDK. I remember it vividly. The iOS SDK (Software Development Kit) was a package of tools, APIs, and programming interfaces that allowed third-party developers to build native applications for the iPhone. Before it existed, Apple had expected developers to build web apps that ran inside Mobile Safari. The SDK changed everything: it opened the device's hardware camera, accelerometer, and GPS to developers; established the App Store distribution model; and set the expectation that mobile software was a separate discipline from web software, with its own languages, conventions, and performance constraints. During my first trip to the United States, I purchased my first programming book in English. Although I wasn't very familiar with Objective-C, I sensed a significant change on the horizon. Mobile development was about to change, not just due to screen size or battery limits, but because the entire stack, from UI to deployment, was built on its own set of assumptions.

At the time, I was working primarily on web-based applications. When the iPhone SDK was released, it seemed natural to try porting existing web projects to mobile platforms. After all, we already had logic and interfaces running within the browser, so it could likely be adapted. However, mobile development brought a different kind of challenge.

The assumptions embedded in our web code were no longer valid. We assumed a persistent network connection; mobile apps had to work offline or in low-signal environments. We assumed a large screen with a mouse and keyboard and mobile required touch targets, gesture navigation, and portrait/landscape switching. We assumed localStorage and sessionStorage for state; iOS enforced stricter privacy rules around browser storage from the start. And we assumed the browser runtime itself and mobile apps ran in Objective-C (later Swift) on iOS, completely outside any web engine.

UI conventions were strict, performance constraints were tighter, and debugging was, at best, a guess-and-check process with limited tools.

Teams reacted as usual: they divided. One team focused on the web, another on iOS, and soon Android would require a third team. We split our codebase, recreated the same features repeatedly, and rationalized the duplication as essential for "platform consistency." This approach also led to duplicated bugs, tests, and CI pipelines (the automated workflows that build, test, and deploy software) and increased the maintenance workload. In practice, it meant that every bug fix had to be applied two or three times, every feature had to be estimated and staffed independently per platform, and the cost of a single product decision multiplied with every new runtime that had to implement it.

When Android emerged a year later, the gap between the platforms grew wider. The Android SDK was still immature, the device ecosystem was fragmented, and its tools lagged years behind Apple's offerings. Developing cross-platform applications became more complex, not just because it involved two different programming languages (Objective-C for iOS and Java for Android) and two separate build toolchains (Xcode on macOS for iOS; Ant, then Gradle, for Android), but because developers had to navigate two radically different environments: varying memory architectures, hardware capabilities, and privacy rules. Each abstraction layer behaved differently depending on the platform it was running on.

By then, teams had begun developing coping strategies. Internal frameworks appeared. Design systems, shared libraries of reusable UI components (buttons, forms, typography rules, color tokens) that enforce visual and interaction consistency across a product, were forked and customized for each client. Shared libraries were created in multiple languages to promote reuse. However, most of these efforts only deepened the core issue: we were still making assumptions about the platform when writing the code. Additionally, we weren't considering how those assumptions might be exposed, challenged, or invalidated later.

This pattern occurred everywhere. Every abstraction we created was shaped by the environment in which it was born. And as soon as we tried to extend it across different contexts, it became fragile. Sometimes it was a third-party library that relied on undocumented browser APIs. Other times, it was an internal module that worked perfectly on iOS but never quite matched on Android. The surface area of incompatibility kept growing, along with the cost of reuse. A typical example: a team on the web platform built a session-management utility that stored authentication tokens in the browser's localStorage. The logic was clean and well-tested. When the iOS team was asked to reuse it, they discovered it had a hard dependency on the window global object, a browser concept that does not exist in a native iOS app. The utility had to be rewritten entirely. The business logic, storing and retrieving a token, was identical. But the execution environment was not, and the abstraction had never made that dependency explicit.

What we were pursuing wasn't wrong; we aimed for consistency. We tried to define capabilities once and apply them everywhere. But we believed we could achieve this by controlling the code rather than the underlying assumptions.

This book is built on that distinction: failure doesn't come from reuse being too limited but from reuse without clear boundaries, contracts, or architectural intent. The next section will explore how this issue resurfaced strongly as mobile use expanded, platforms multiplied, and the challenge of making solutions work across multiple environments reemerged in a bigger way.

The Platform Explosion

If the early 2000s were dominated by browser wars and the illusion of shared standards, the subsequent years introduced a more difficult challenge to overlook: platform fragmentation on a large scale. It began gradually. The iPhone was released in 2007, followed by the first iOS SDK in 2008.

Android was announced that same year, with the first commercial device, the HTC Dream, released a few months later. Within two years, mobile had shifted from a niche experiment to a core part of software development. And this time, it wasn't just about screen size or pixel density. It was about entirely new runtime environments with their own memory models, threading models, deployment pipelines, permission systems, and user expectations.

Mobile broke more than just our code; it disrupted our entire development model. Logic that once comfortably resided on the server was now being shifted to the client. Offline capability became a default requirement. Network reliability had to be assumed to be spotty. Caching was no longer just a performance optimization; it became a necessity. Suddenly, each client wasn't just a view layer; it was a complete execution environment with real responsibilities.

At the architectural level, this transformation had a profound impact. Previously, server logic was centralized and enforceable, but now it has been duplicated and adapted across various platforms. For example, authentication, which used to reside solely in a centralized backend, has now been extended to every client. Mobile applications had to cache tokens, refresh them proactively, handle expired sessions, and recover from partial failures, all using libraries or SDKs of varying maturity levels, often maintained by different teams.

This pattern was consistent everywhere: the same capability was reinvented three times. Then came tablets, smart TVs, wearables, embedded browsers, and hybrid apps inside native shells. Later, desktop runtimes bundled Electron or WebViews. Each new wave expanded the range of devices, brought new constraints, and increased the challenge of maintaining consistency.

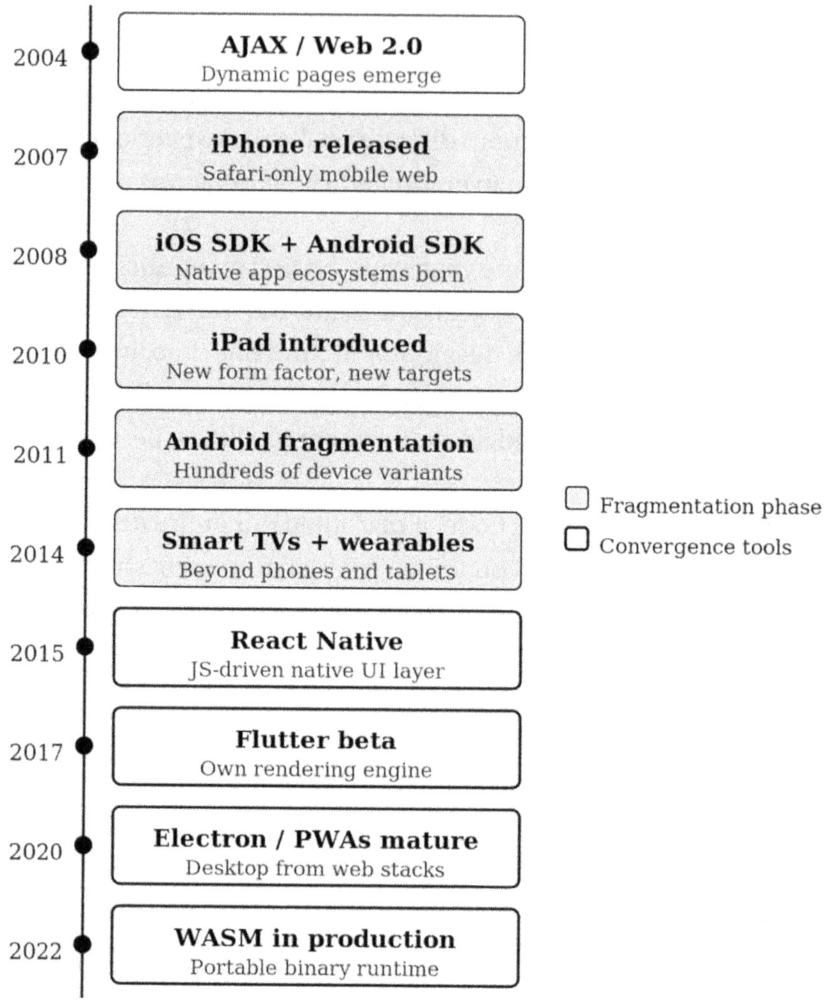

Figure 2-1. *Platform Fragmentation Over Time (2004–2022)*

The Architectural Fallout Before

The real cost wasn't just the engineering time. It was architectural drift.

Each team developed its own view of the product. The web team prioritized responsiveness and keyboard navigation. The iOS team concentrated on gesture accuracy and low-latency animations. The Android team is tailored for a wide range of hardware, including low-end devices requiring careful memory management. Each team made logical decisions, but those decisions led to different versions. Users didn't experience a single product across devices; instead, they encountered three distinct interpretations, each influenced by platform constraints and team goals.

The backend struggled to keep up. Every client had slightly different expectations for API contracts, payload formats, performance latency, and error handling. Over time, endpoints evolved not around product design but around client-specific quirks. New query parameters were added to fix bugs on one platform. Authentication flows were adjusted to address token-handling bugs in another. Logic that should have been unified became conditional, wrapped in flags, and cluttered with version-specific paths.

Attempted Solutions and Their Limits

Developers responded with the only tool they had: reuse. SDKs were built. Shared libraries were created. Design systems were designed in Figma (a browser-based visual design and prototyping tool widely used by product teams to create and share UI component libraries) and handed off with the promise of consistency. However, the reuse was seldom straightforward. Most libraries were written by one team for a single platform and then hastily adapted for others. Assumptions ingrained in the original implementation, such as access to local storage, synchronous API calls, or native sensors, often became liabilities when ported.

Worse, these efforts were rarely staffed for long-term success. Teams built reusable SDKs with good intentions but lacked the operational budget or abstraction discipline to treat them as full products. Documentation was limited. Upgrade paths were unclear. Maintenance costs were shifted onto the teams that used them. Reuse became a liability instead of an advantage.

Even when teams invested in centralization, the results were mixed. Suppose a platform team developed authentication SDKs for four different programming languages: JavaScript (used for web frontends and Node.js backends), Swift (the primary language for iOS development), Kotlin (the modern standard for Android development), and C++ (used for performance-critical native modules and cross-platform game engines). On paper, this seemed successful: the logic was unified. However, behind the scenes, the business rules needed to be rewritten in four different languages. Small implementation differences appeared. Error-handling strategies varied. And in some cases, critical decisions like how to refresh a token depended on platform-specific APIs that worked well in one environment but failed silently in another.

Portability wasn't just hard. It was structurally unsound.

Developers eventually sought a more fundamental solution: cross-platform framework toolkits that allow a developer to write application code once and have it compile to, or run on, multiple target platforms (iOS, Android, web) from a single codebase. Options like React Native, Flutter, Xamarin (officially deprecated by Microsoft in May 2024 in favor of .NET MAUI), Cordova (still maintained but with declining adoption as PWAs and native webviews improved), and Ionic offered many promises. Write your app once, and it runs everywhere, reducing fragmentation and speeding up deployment. Initially, it was effective. Creating a small app in one language and having it run seamlessly on both iOS and Android felt almost magical. Teams eagerly embraced these tools, with initial projects shipping rapidly, costs decreasing, and time-to-market improving.

But the magic didn't last.

As applications became more complex, the abstraction began to leak. Performance lagged on older devices. UI responsiveness wasn't quite native. Debugging cross-platform bugs became more difficult than fixing them natively. Most importantly, the same assumption failures reoccurred. A library that worked well on Android didn't behave the same on iOS. Custom native modules had to be created for edge cases. Teams ended up maintaining forked code within a shared shell. Eventually, the cost of alignment exceeded the cost of separation.

Some organizations handled this well. React Native and Flutter still support production apps in many large companies. But success came with a price: dedicated teams, strict design discipline, and accepting the limitations these frameworks impose. These aren't magical solutions. They are limited tools, and their usefulness depends entirely on how well their constraints fit your problem.

The myth of "just one stack" didn't disappear; it simply shifted. It stopped focusing on browsers and instead centered on mobile shells. However, the architectural challenge remained unchanged: our systems lacked a means to express, isolate, and reason about the assumptions each runtime carried.

From the outside, it appeared that the issue was platform diversity. However, the more profound truth is that we never created a language to describe *where* code should run, *what* capabilities it expects, or *how* it should behave when those assumptions are violated. Instead, we relied on organizational strength, team coordination, manual QA, and makeshift policies for versioning, testing, and deployment. Portability wasn't engineered; it was brute-forced.

This landscape is what UMA, Universal Microservices Architecture, a framework for designing portable, contract-defined business capabilities that can run across any runtime environment, was created to address. However, before we determine the solution, it's important to examine another failure pattern: the illusion of reuse. Shared logic can become problematic when it lacks proper structure, leading developers to abandon reuse not due to unwillingness, but because what they are asked to share no longer matches the structure needed at runtime.

False Promises of Frameworks

I still remember a team I worked with that rebuilt their internal dashboard app using React Native. They were excited. Within weeks, they achieved 90% feature parity across iOS and Android, with a shared codebase and unified design. Leadership regarded it as a success. Velocity metrics increased. Releases were happening more quickly.

Then came the edge cases.

They needed to create custom animations on Android. Animations that already functioned on iOS but weren't supported natively in the shared framework. The team tried to patch them with plugins, then rewrote parts in native Java. It worked, but now they had a fragmented animation system.

Then came performance complaints on older devices. After that, a plugin they depended on became unmaintained. Next, an OS update introduced gesture conflicts. Each problem took more time to debug than if it had been handled natively from the start.

None of these issues were showstoppers, but they accumulated. The productivity gains they had celebrated began to decline. Eventually, parts of the app were replatformed, migrated away from the cross-platform framework, and rewritten using the native SDK for that specific platform. The cost of reuse had caught up with them.

By the time most organizations recognized the costs of fragmented codebases, the tooling ecosystem had already started to adapt. New frameworks emerged with strong promises: Write once, run anywhere; reuse your team's skills; shorten time to market; and create native-like experiences without the need to maintain multiple platforms.

It felt like an answer.

The developer blogosphere lit up with tutorials and benchmarks. New frameworks emerged each quarter, each with a pitch that echoed the last but hinted at a missing piece finally solved. JavaScript became the common language of portability. You didn't need to learn Swift, Java, or platform-specific build tools. You could develop with React Native, Flutter, Ionic, or some newer compile-to-native variation and deploy to iOS, Android, and the web all at once.

It was easy to believe this time would be different.

And for a while, it was.

You could prototype more quickly. You could share more logic. You could demo a working app across devices in days instead of weeks. But as soon as teams moved beyond prototypes and began scaling toward production, the cracks appeared. Familiar ones.

The "Hello World" Trap

Every cross-platform framework works well for "Hello World." That's intentional. Demos are designed for simplicity and enjoyment. They demonstrate how easy it is to build a screen, navigate between views, connect to a service, and deploy. They provide quick feedback, clear messaging, and a sense of progress.

But production software doesn't live in the world of demos.

It exists in edge cases, device-specific APIs, platform UI norms, and CI/CD pipelines (the automated workflows that build, test, and deploy code on each change). third-party dependencies, performance limits, accessibility audits, and regulatory constraints. When these factors come into play, the framework's abstraction begins to leak.

Suddenly, the runtime-specific behavior you thought you had abstracted away starts asserting itself again. Gesture handling breaks subtly on older Android devices. Scroll performance lags on lower-end iPhones. Fonts render inconsistently between web and native. And the deeper you go into product development, the more you realize that no framework can fully flatten the platform beneath it.

You don't escape fragmentation. You just delay the moment you're forced to deal with it.

Cost of Reuse at the Wrong Level

Frameworks promise reuse, which is their main appeal. However, most frameworks focus more on code reuse than on contract isolation, the practice of explicitly defining and enforcing the boundaries between a component and the rest of the system, specifying what inputs it accepts, what outputs it produces, what side effects it may have, and what runtime capabilities it requires. When a component is contract-isolated, a different platform can adopt it without needing to understand its internal implementation. They encourage you to create shared components without clearly defining what should be shared, extended, replaced, or versioned.

This works until it doesn't.

Consider a shared UI component like a date picker. It works well in your design system until one platform needs a different localization format. Or an accessibility review requires platform-native behavior. Or legal compliance mandates jurisdiction-specific variants.

Now that the shared component has become a liability, you can't change it without impacting every user. You can't fork it without duplicating business logic, and you can't isolate the platform-specific parts because they were never clearly defined to start with.

What started as a win for speed turns into a long-term maintenance burden.

Worse, because most frameworks don't enforce capability boundaries, developers often combine reusable logic with platform-specific assumptions. A shared module might import a library that depends on browser APIs, expect access to the filesystem, or assume synchronous execution models. These assumptions remain hidden until you try to run that module in a different context and it fails.

The code was reusable in theory. But the contract was never portable.

Platform Assumptions That Hard-Coded the Future

One of the most subtle and harmful effects of adopting a cross-platform framework is how it solidifies platform assumptions in your architecture. For example, when you choose Flutter, you inherit its rendering pipeline, layout model, and plugin ecosystem. You also inherit its constraints.

Some teams learned this lesson the hard way. They built large-scale applications using a framework still under active development, only to find that performance issues on low-end devices couldn't be fixed without native extensions. Others encountered obstacles when trying to upgrade to newer OS versions or comply with new accessibility standards, only to discover that the framework was falling behind or moving in a different direction entirely.

One real pattern: teams building media-heavy apps in Flutter discovered that the framework's custom rendering engine, which draws every pixel itself rather than delegating to native OS components, meant that platform-native accessibility features (like iOS VoiceOver's ability to read screen elements in a specific order) required manual re-implementation. For apps with regulatory accessibility requirements, this became a significant unplanned cost. The framework had not hidden that constraint in its documentation, but teams had not evaluated it during adoption because the initial demos had no accessibility requirements.

These issues aren't the fault of the framework maintainers. Every abstraction has tradeoffs. But what matters is whether those tradeoffs were visible at the time of adoption. In many cases, they weren't because the tooling encouraged speed and unification, not introspection and isolation.

When you choose a framework at the core of your stack, you're not just picking a collection of libraries. You're adopting a specific worldview. That perspective might be helpful initially, but when it no longer meets your needs, the cost of switching becomes steep.

And in software, few things are more dangerous than a dependency you can't outgrow.

When Reuse Becomes a Trap

It's important to recognize that many teams achieved some level of success with cross-platform frameworks. They shipped products. They served millions of users. They reached parity across platforms. However, even in those success stories, the cost of reuse was never without expense.

Teams needed to maintain expertise in the framework and underlying platforms. They had to develop bridges and plugins. They needed to split their QA pipelines. They also had to train developers on debugging hybrid stacks. When issues occurred, they often happened at the intersection of those boundaries.

Reuse is only beneficial when it lowers long-term entropy, the tendency of software systems to accumulate disorder over time as each change adds complexity, conditional logic, undocumented assumptions, and subtle inconsistencies that make the codebase progressively harder to understand, modify, and extend. If your abstraction hides the important differences, it creates more work later. If your shared module can't be versioned separately or adapted without duplication, it will become a bottleneck. If your framework restricts you to a specific build toolchain or runtime model, it reduces your flexibility.

Actual reuse starts with boundaries, not just in code but in capability definition. Frameworks rarely offer that.

They prioritize short-term productivity over long-term resilience.

The Mirage of Universal UI

One of the most ambitious promises of the cross-platform era was the concept of a universal UI layer, the idea that with proper abstraction, you could write code once and have it render seamlessly across web, mobile, desktop, VR, and embedded devices.

This promise still comes up often. It sounds nice, but it overlooks the basic truth that UI is about more than just pixels. It includes affordances (the visual or tactile cues that signal to a user how an element can be interacted with; for example, a raised button affords pressing, and a draggable card affords swiping), gestures, conventions, latency expectations, and accessibility standards. It's how users interact with and interpret software in its context.

No abstraction can completely unify that diversity. What functions well as a responsive web layout might seem overgrown on mobile. What works in a native app might feel abrupt in a web view. What appears fast on a desktop might seem slow on a smart TV interface.

And the moment you try to account for these differences, you're forced to poke holes in the abstraction. You add conditional logic. You detect device types. You override styles. You fork components. And soon, your universal UI starts to resemble the very fragmentation it was meant to solve.

The only difference is that now it's harder to reason about.

Reframing the Problem

None of this argues against reuse. It argues against **unstructured** reuse, reuse without contracts, and architecture that assumes sameness instead of modeling difference.

If you define reuse as shared code, you're forced to make early decisions about what should be shared, how, and with whom. However, if you define reuse based on capability boundaries and learn contracts that specify inputs, outputs, behaviors, and constraints, you create a system where different runtimes can adopt, extend, or override behavior without collapsing the architecture.

This shift isn't just technical; it's cultural. It requires teams to think in terms of interfaces instead of inheritance, isolation rather than inheritance, and composition rather than coupling. It involves resisting the urge to fix everything in one place and instead focusing on modularity.

It also means accepting that some duplication is strategic. That you might want different UIs for different devices, even if they use the same capabilities. That you might prefer to use native performance where it matters and shared logic where it doesn't. That true unification comes not from writing everything in one stack but from exposing clear contracts that enable each stack to collaborate safely.

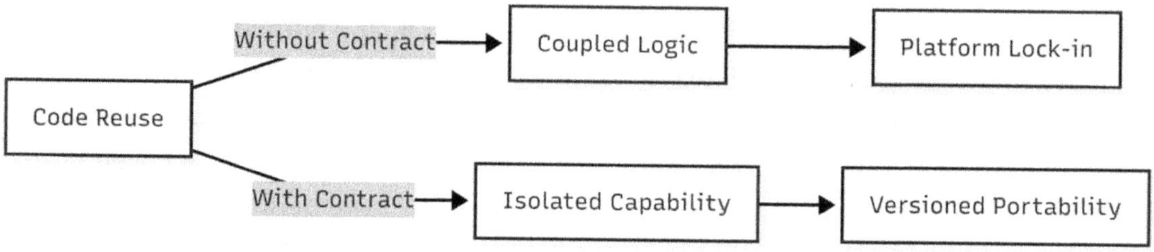

Figure 2-2. *Code reuse without boundaries leads to coupling. Capability contracts enable isolation and extensibility*

A positive example of this in practice: Stripe's payment UI. The core payment capability, capturing a card number, validating it, and tokenizing it, is defined as a contract: a specific set of inputs (card number, expiry, CVC), a guaranteed output (a single-use payment token), and a clear security constraint (the raw card data never touches the merchant's servers). The implementation differs per platform: a JavaScript element on the web, a native SDK on iOS, an Android SDK, and a server-side API for automated billing. But the contract is identical. Consuming teams do not need to know which implementation they are calling; they only need to know the contract. That is what structured reuse looks like.

Frameworks gave us hope, but they also provided a chance to understand the boundaries of abstraction.

Now it's time to design with those lessons in mind.

Why Reuse Keeps Failing

Reuse is among the oldest goals in software engineering. It offers speed, consistency, and efficiency. Write code once, use it everywhere. Tackle the hard parts once, and gain benefits repeatedly.

But in large, long-lived systems, especially those spread across multiple runtimes, reuse fails more often than it succeeds.

And it tends to fail in just three ways.

1. **Shared SDKs** promise logic reuse across runtimes but leak assumptions and break at the edges.
2. **Design systems** promise visual and interaction consistency but become either too rigid or too generic to reuse effectively.
3. UI + logic bundles, such as micro frontends (independently deployable frontend applications that can be composed together to form a larger product; think of each feature area as its own mini-app, mounted into a shared shell) or widgets (self-contained UI components that include both their visual layer and the business logic needed to operate, deployable as a single embeddable artifact), promise drop-in functionality but often become black boxes that can't evolve.

Let's look at each of these more closely.

SDKs: When Business Logic Reuse Breaks Down

The most common and optimistic reuse story starts like this:

A backend team develops a strong feature, like user authentication, and realizes it could be turned into an SDK. That SDK gains internal visibility, other teams start using it, and suddenly it becomes the "standard" across the organization.

But the SDK was never designed for reuse across different platforms. It assumes synchronous I/O (input/output operations that block the program's execution until they complete; the code stops and waits for the result before moving on, as opposed to asynchronous I/O, which lets the program continue doing other work while waiting) and relies on platform-specific storage. It provides interfaces that mimic the workflows of the original product. Over time, other teams begin wrapping, polyfilling, or patching it just to make it usable.

Then one of them forks it.

> ***Example:***
>
> *A team ships a JavaScript authentication SDK built on browser APIs. It uses window.fetch and localStorage and relies on the global window context, all browser-specific APIs that exist only in a web browser environment and have no equivalent in Node.js or native*

> *mobile runtimes, for session propagation. Another team tries to adopt it in a Node environment. It fails immediately. They create a wrapper package using undici and an in-memory session store, but now there are two implementations of the same logic, drifting over time. When a security patch is needed, only one gets fixed.*

This kind of reuse begins with a good idea: extracting logic and reducing duplication. However, without contracts, it becomes impossible to isolate assumptions about the environment, behavior, or side effects. The result isn't shared infrastructure; it's tangled risk.

Design Systems: The UI Reuse Illusion

If SDK reuse fails in code, design system reuse fails in pixels.

Design teams seek consistency. Therefore, they create a library of buttons, cards, modals, and inputs. Developers are responsible for implementing these in real environments: React, Vue, SwiftUI, and Jetpack Compose.

The problem is that UI is never just UI. It's accessibility, latency, gesture semantics, form factors, and cultural expectations.

Over time, most organizations swing between two failure modes:

- Components that are too **generic**: atomic primitives that require engineers to reassemble every pattern from scratch
- Components that are too **rigid**: massive "kitchen sink" widgets that only work in very narrow conditions

> ***Example:***
>
> *A team ships a unified form input component with 20 props. It manages date pickers, phone numbers, country selectors, and password strength. It works well on the web, but mobile developers can't integrate native inputs without rewriting the component. Localization teams report that the layout breaks in right-to-left languages such as Arabic and Hebrew, where the entire reading direction and UI layout direction are mirrored, elements that appear on the left in English must appear on the right, and the flow of text reverses entirely. The result? Two forks of the same element, both drifting and violating the design system's intent.*

At that point, reuse turns into a liability. Teams lose trust in the system. They rebuild what they need, even if it duplicates logic or breaks visual guidelines.

It's not because they're lazy. It's because the component failed to support real-world variation. It was never designed to be modularly reusable, meaning it could not be broken into smaller, independently adoptable pieces that different teams could extend, override, or version separately without affecting each other. It was designed only for visual consistency: ensuring the same colors, fonts, and spacing appeared across the product. Consistency is a presentation goal; modularity is an architectural one. The two are not the same.

Widgets and Micro Frontends: The Coupling Trap

To avoid code duplication and UI divergence, some organizations ship complete capabilities as embeddable widgets or micro frontends.

Think:

- Drop-in account settings panels
- Pre-built checkout flows
- Embedded search experiences

These bundles often include both logic and UI. They seem like a win: low integration cost and no need to duplicate validation rules or endpoint wiring. Just include a script and you're finished.

Until you need to customize something.

> ***Example:***
>
> *A team adds an embeddable widget that manages password resets. However, they need to include one new step in the process: a security question after the email input. The widget doesn't support custom steps and lacks an extension point. They contact the owning team, who are overwhelmed with feature requests. Weeks go by. Eventually, the consuming team forks the widget and rewrites the flow from scratch. Now, there are two versions, with duplicated API logic (the code that constructs HTTP requests, handles authentication headers, parses server responses, and manages error states for calls to the backend) and inconsistent UI behavior.*

The close coupling of UI and business logic makes these components fragile. They can't be easily recomposed. They can't be updated separately. Plus, they often can't be audited for compliance or security because the logic is hidden deep within the UI.

What started as the easiest way to share capability ends up being the most complex system to evolve.

So Why Does This Keep Happening?

Each of these traps is different in shape. But they all share the exact root cause.

Reuse fails when it's based on code, not on contract.

When we extract code without setting capability boundaries, we make consumers accept not only the functionality but also all its assumptions.

Assumptions about

- Runtime environment
- UI expectations
- Side effects
- Performance constraints
- Security model

Even worse, most reuse strategies lack the following:

- **Versioning Semantics:** A formal system for communicating what kind of change a new version represents. Semantic Versioning (SemVer) uses a MAJOR.MINOR.PATCH scheme:
    - MAJOR version bump signals a breaking change (consumers must update their code).
    - MINOR adds new capabilities without breaking existing ones.
    - PATCH fixes bugs. Without this, consumers cannot safely update a shared library.
- **Compatibility Guarantees:** An explicit commitment about which versions of a dependency work together. For example: "This SDK is compatible with iOS 15 and above" or "This API version will remain stable until December 2025." Without guarantees, every upgrade is a gamble.

- **Observability and Metrics:** The ability to measure how a shared component is being used, where it is failing, and how it performs across different environments. For example, logging which version of the authentication SDK each platform is using, and tracking the error rate per version, makes it possible to detect divergence before it becomes a crisis.

Over time, each shared asset turns into a risk. Teams either add defensive code, fork it entirely, or replace it with a simpler abstraction they manage. As a result, the dream of reuse often falls back into local duplication.

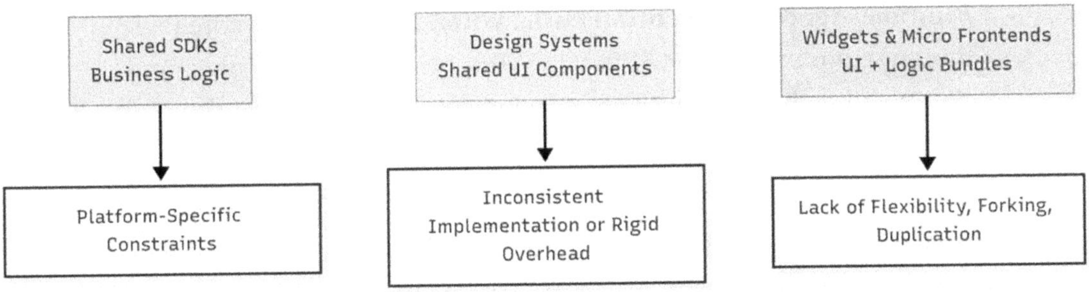

Figure 2-3. *Three reuse strategies, three failure patterns. Without capability contracts, reuse breaks under change*

The Way Out: Contract-First Reuse

The lesson here isn't to stop reusing code. It's to be deliberate about **what** gets reused and **how**.

Reuse should be grounded in

- **A Clear Capability Contract:** A machine-readable definition of what a component does, what inputs it requires, what outputs it produces, and what side effects it may have. Benefit: any team on any platform can implement or consume the capability correctly without needing to read the source code or ask the original authors.
- **Versioned Interfaces:** The contract is published with a version number, and breaking changes require a major version increment (see Versioning Semantics above). Benefit: platform teams can upgrade on their own schedule without fear of silent breakage.

- **Separation of UI and Logic:** The visual presentation layer is decoupled from the business rules. Benefit: the iOS team can render a native UIDatePicker while the web team renders an HTML input, and both satisfy the same underlying date-capture contract.
- **Isolation of Side Effects**: Actions that affect state outside the component (network calls, storage writes, event emissions) are declared in the contract, not hidden inside the implementation. Benefit: consuming teams can mock or replace side effects in tests without understanding the component's internals.
- **Runtime-Agnostic Execution Paths When Possible:** The core logic does not import browser APIs, iOS SDKs, or any platform-specific module directly; it depends only on interfaces that each runtime can implement. Benefit: the same business logic can run in a browser, a Node.js service, and a WASM module without modification.

These aren't just theoretical ideals. They enable modular, multi-runtime systems to develop safely over time. Without them, reuse is risky. With them, reuse becomes part of the architecture.

> *Reuse is not a shortcut. It's a design decision. If you don't get the boundaries right, you're just scaling your next rewrite.*

The Coordination Bottleneck

At some point, reuse isn't even the biggest problem. Alignment is.

As teams expand, platforms diversify, and runtimes diverge, the real bottleneck shifts from technology to coordination. Even when teams generally agree on what to develop, daily execution starts to break down. What gets released for the web isn't always what makes it to iOS, and Android falls behind by a quarter, trying to catch up with a slightly different backend.

In any mid- to large-scale product organization, this pattern is common. Someone submits a ticket: "Add feature X." The backend team creates a flag, while the web team develops a UI flow. The mobile teams check for stability. Someone notices the flag isn't documented. The endpoint sends different payloads depending on the caller. The Android lead, absent from the sync meeting, incorrectly implemented the fallback.

Each step compounds the misalignment. Everyone is working hard, yet the outcome is fragmented.

This isn't about team velocity. It's about architecture failing to support scale.

Parity Isn't a Roadmap; It's a Mirage

The idea of platform parity, the goal of delivering the same features, behaviors, and user experience across all supported platforms simultaneously, sounds great during planning meetings. But it rarely turns out that way in practice. Different platforms have varying capabilities, constraints, and levels of staffing or expertise.

What often happens is reactive catch-up.

Consider the example of a new login experience with passkeys. The iOS team integrates it using Apple's biometric APIs. The backend sets a temporary flag for the feature. The Android team is busy with a release and defaults to PIN-based login. The web team doesn't support passkeys at all and repurposes an existing form.

Three versions of the same feature ship in production.

The analytics team begins seeing inconsistent metrics. Customer support is unsure how to troubleshoot the problem. The backend adds conditionals to manage three client types. And the codebase, once again, bears the cost of misalignment.

Parity was promised. But parity was never clearly defined, scoped, or enforced.

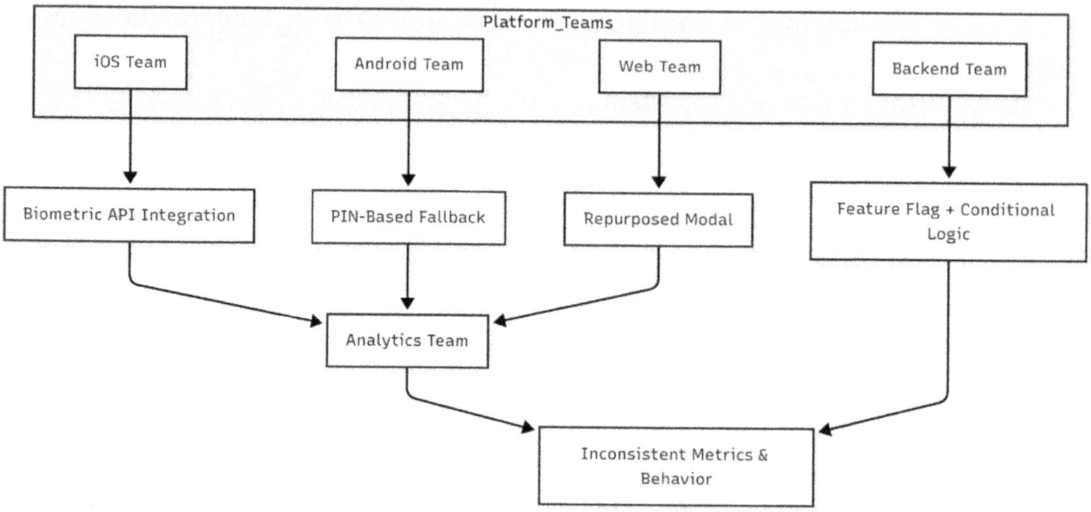

Figure 2-4. *A single feature request results in divergent implementations across iOS, Android, web, and backend. Each team delivers a working solution, but without shared contracts or boundaries, coordination failures accumulate and behavior fragments*

Tribal Knowledge Is Not an API

In most large product stacks, what gets built is often based more on memory than on metadata. Teams depend on tribal knowledge, an undocumented, informal understanding of how a system works that lives only in the minds of long-tenured team members, passed on through conversations rather than written specifications to know which endpoints to use, what headers to send, and what side effects to expect.

This system worked when teams were small and collocated. It breaks down as platforms and services scale independently.

A product manager might have a document outlining the flow. An architect might have a diagram from a past design review. The backend lead remembers which feature flags to flip, configuration switches that allow a feature to be enabled or disabled for specific users, platforms, or environments without deploying new code, commonly used to roll out changes gradually or test behavior in production. None of that is visible to the team implementing the feature on a new platform for the first time.

The result is delays, incorrect implementations, and fragmented telemetry.

Without machine-readable contracts, structured definitions of a capability's interface that tools can parse, validate, and generate code from, such as an OpenAPI specification for a REST API, a GraphQL schema, a Protocol Buffer (.proto) file, or a JSON Schema document, and clearly defined capability models, there is no dependable source of truth. A machine-readable contract means a CI/CD pipeline can automatically verify that a backend change does not break any registered client without a human needing to read documentation or attend a sync meeting. Each team interprets the product specifications differently, and the more decentralized the system, the more problematic this becomes.

The Cost of Endpoint Drift

Endpoint drift is the gradual divergence of an API endpoint's behavior from its original specification, with fields added for one client, query parameters patched for another, and response shapes adjusted to fix a mobile bug until the endpoint no longer has a single clean contract but a tree of conditional behaviors. Backend systems are often where misalignments go unnoticed the longest because the backend is shared and each client-specific patch appears to be a local fix rather than a systemic problem. Since they're shared, any inconsistency is quietly patched over. A new field is added only for Android. A flag is checked only if the request comes from the web. A second endpoint is created with a slightly different shape for a specific client version.

Eventually, the backend manages not just one API but also a tree of conditional behaviors customized for each platform and version. Developers add branches because removing them would break a team they don't own.

The system calcifies. Adding new features becomes harder. Reuse becomes dangerous.

This isn't just about API design. It's about architectural intent. If you don't maintain the separation between capability and implementation, the backend becomes a dumping ground for hacks and workarounds.

You can't sustain velocity, or predictability, across platforms when the backend bears the burden of misalignment. Velocity is how fast a team ships; predictability is how accurately they can estimate when something will ship. Both suffer when the backend is a maze of undocumented conditionals that every new feature must navigate.

Meetings Don't Scale; Contracts Might

To address these issues, organizations often hold more meetings. Weekly syncs among web, iOS, Android, and backend leads of cross-functional teams. Shared roadmaps. Design review rituals.

These are well-intentioned. But they don't scale.

The more meetings you schedule, the more time teams spend aligning instead of shipping. And the alignment rarely holds. As soon as one platform updates, the others fall out of sync again.

Documentation isn't the answer either. Most teams don't trust documentation, because it's rarely up to date and never fully reflects edge cases or tradeoffs made during implementation.

What does scale mean in architecture?

Architecture can define capability boundaries, explicit rules that specify which components own which behaviors, what inputs and outputs cross component borders, and what no component is permitted to assume about another component's internal state. In practice this might mean a decision that "all date formatting logic lives in the date-capability module" combined with a contract that specifies the module's interface so that the iOS team, the Android team, and the web team each implement or consume it within those defined limits rather than reimplementing it differently in each codebase. It can establish reusable contracts. For example, an organization defines a "user-authentication" capability contract that specifies the expected inputs (username, credential), the outputs (session object with expiry), the error states (invalid credential, account locked, network timeout), and the security constraints (tokens must be signed, credentials must not be logged). Every team that implements authentication, web, iOS, Android, backend, work on this same contract. The contract is versioned; when requirements change (e.g., adding multi-factor authentication as a required output field), all teams receive a breaking-change notification and can plan the upgrade on their own schedule. The architecture is doing the coordination work that would otherwise require recurring cross-team meetings. It can enforce constraints that prevent divergence before it occurs. But only if it becomes the definitive source of truth, not just an artifact of a past decision.

To enhance coordination, you must make intent clear to both humans and machines. This requires structured metadata that details the shape, behavior, and constraints of each capability. Return to the date picker. Its structured metadata might look like this: capability name: date-input; input: ISO 8601 date string or null; output:

ISO 8601 date string; localization: must respect the user's configured locale and display format; accessibility: must expose a date value to screen readers via the platform's native accessibility API; platforms: web (HTML input type=date), iOS (UIDatePicker), Android (MaterialDatePicker). This metadata is not a comment in a README; it is a structured document that a build tool can validate, a test framework can use to generate compliance tests, and a new platform team can use to implement the capability correctly without consulting the original authors. You also need versioning that reveals any drift. Additionally, contracts are essential to distinguish what a platform requires from how it functions.

When architecture becomes declarative, coordination becomes distributed.

In concrete terms: imagine an authentication capability defined as a contract, input: credentials; output: a signed session token; side effects: an audit log entry; runtime requirement: a secure credential store. Each platform team reads the contract and implements it independently. The iOS team uses Keychain Services as the secure credential store. The Android team uses the Android Keystore. The web team uses an HTTP-only cookie. No meeting was needed to decide these details; each team made the platform-appropriate choice within the boundaries the contract defined. The contract replaced the meeting.

When You Don't Own the Whole Thing

In modern organizations, no one owns the entire product. Ownership is intentionally broken up. Platform teams handle their own delivery. Product managers are responsible for roadmaps. Backend teams manage their own services. QA takes ownership of regression testing.

But features cut across all of them.

So, who is responsible for maintaining parity of a feature across iOS, Android, and web? Who owns the telemetry strategy? The rollout sequence? The deprecation plan?

Most organizations punt these questions to the process. That's why coordination becomes a bottleneck.

What's missing is a capability model, a structured representation of what a feature does, what it requires, and how it should behave, treated as a first-class architectural artifact independent of any specific implementation. Think of it as the feature's specification written in a format that both humans and tools can read. In the passkey login example, the capability is "authenticate user"; the model defines the inputs (user identifier, biometric challenge response, or PIN); the expected outputs (session token);

the acceptable fallback behaviors (PIN if biometric unavailable); and the platforms each implementation targets. Instead of each team reverse-engineering the feature from a Confluence page, they read the model. If each capability had a contract, a shape, and a runtime behavior spec, teams could align without centralizing. They could operate independently but stay within boundaries.

This is the foundation needed to scale software as a system, not just as a set of platforms.

When coordination is distributed through architecture rather than centralized through meetings, teams gain several concrete advantages. Autonomy: Each team can make platform-specific decisions (which storage API, which rendering approach) without seeking approval because the contract defines the boundaries within which they are free to choose. Parallel delivery: iOS, Android, and web teams can build the same capability simultaneously from the same contract, rather than waiting for a reference implementation on one platform to be complete. Verifiable parity: automated tests can check each implementation against the contract, producing a clear yes/no answer about whether a platform is compliant; no manual QA matrix is needed. Safer evolution: when a capability must change, the contract is updated with a version increment, and only teams whose current version is incompatible need to act. Teams running a compatible version are unaffected.

The Coordination Bottleneck Isn't a People Problem

It's tempting to treat misalignment as a communication failure. But it's not.

It's a system design failure, one that occurs when architecture fails to clearly define the boundaries between feature logic, platform execution, and service integration.

You can't scale coordination by asking humans to remember what the system forgot to model.

When Centralization Isn't Enough

One of the most common mistakes in software architecture is confusing centralization with portability. A team notices duplication across products or platforms and chooses to centralize the logic into a shared library. It appears clean, abstract, and well-documented. It promises to "unify" how a capability is implemented across platforms.

But it doesn't work. At least not the way people expect.

You centralize the logic, but you don't eliminate the assumptions. You move it into an SDK, but you still carry the same platform-specific bias.

A concrete example: a team extracts their user-profile fetching logic into a shared TypeScript package. The logic is correct and tested. But internally it uses the Fetch API with credentials: "include," a browser-specific behavior that relies on cookies and the browser's session model. When a Node.js microservice tries to use the same package for server-to-server calls, the cookie-based session model does not exist. The SDK compiles and installs without error but fails silently at runtime because it was written with a browser mental model baked in. The platform-specific bias was not in the business logic; it was in the invisible assumption about how sessions work.

You avoid duplication in code, but not in behavior.

And sooner or later, it breaks.

Code Is Not the Abstraction

The core issue is that code, by nature, is never neutral. Even the most straightforward business logic contains hidden dependencies. The language you select. The libraries you include. The runtime features you depend on unknowingly. Every decision impacts the execution surface.

Let's say you build a shared library in TypeScript. You keep your logic functional and modular. You even write tests. But you use fetch() for network calls because you're building for the web. That same package can't run in a Node worker (a Worker Thread in Node.jsa, a separate JavaScript execution context running in the same process, used for CPU-intensive work without blocking the main event loop) without shims. It can't run in a browser worker (a Web Worker, a script that runs in a background thread in the browser, isolated from the main page's JavaScript context and without access to the DOM or window object) without manually exposing APIs. It definitely can't run in a serverless edge runtime without polyfills or rewrites.

The business logic didn't change. The assumptions did.

Business logic is the set of rules that define what the software does: how it calculates a result, validates an input, or sequences a workflow. Execution assumptions are beliefs about the environment in which that logic will run: that fetch() exists, that the file system is accessible, and that environment variables are injected at startup. When you move code between runtimes, the business logic is portable; the assumptions are not. The failure always lives in the gap between them.

This isn't hypothetical. It occurs in every large stack where someone attempts to extract shared logic into a central SDK. Once it makes assumptions about the runtime, it begins to break down.

Clean ≠ Portable

It's easy to confuse clean code with reusable code. They often appear similar, especially in the early stages. Clean code is modular, tested, and easy to read. It adheres to best practices, minimizes coupling and repetition, and is crucial for maintainability. However, portability concerns boundary control.

Portable code isn't just about avoiding repetition. It also avoids assumptions. It defines what it needs without dictating how to obtain it. It separates its execution context from its behavior. Often, achieving this requires a level of design discipline that isn't reflected in a linter.

Most central SDKs are designed cleanly but lack portability, which is why they don't scale.

The Import That Breaks Portability

In fast-paced teams, developers make small trade-offs every day. Use this library instead of creating a wrapper. Import this utility because it's already in use. Call this helper because it's been proven in battle.

These decisions make sense in context. They save time. They reduce friction.

But they carry hidden costs.

The third-party library utilizes DOM APIs. The internal helper depends on window.localStorage. The utility includes 300 KB of unused code. The abstraction leaks, and you don't realize it until you try to use the code elsewhere.

By then, it's too late. The code is coupled. The logic is contaminated. And the only way to fix it is a rewrite.

The same goes for mobile. A Swift SDK that uses Keychain Services (Apple's platform-specific API for securely storing credentials, certificates, and cryptographic keys available only on iOS, macOS, watchOS, and tvOS) depends on an Apple runtime. An Android module relying on Room DB (Google's persistence library for Android that provides an abstraction layer over SQLite available only within the Android runtime) won't run in a web worker. Portability isn't lost because of business logic but due to these bindings.

This isn't a unique problem. It's what happens when architecture fails to define transparent contract surfaces between logic and execution.

A positive counterexample: the WHATWG Fetch Standard. The fetch() function has a precisely defined contract; its inputs (URL, options object), outputs (a Promise resolving to a Response object), error states (network failure, CORS rejection), and behavior across environments are all documented in a public specification. Because the contract is transparent and machine-verifiable, implementations exist for browsers (native), Node.js (node-fetch, then native from Node 18), and edge runtimes (Cloudflare Workers, Deno), all satisfying the same contract. Teams can write code using fetch() and have reasonable confidence it will behave consistently across runtimes, precisely because the contract was defined before the implementations.

You build quickly, but the cost appears later.

Portability isn't free. But it's cheaper to design for than to retrofit.

The Trap of Shared Codebases

There's a related trap that's even more subtle: using the same codebase for multiple platforms and assuming that means reuse has been solved.

In reality, most "shared" codebases are simply co-located. They include logic for various targets, often with branching conditionals, runtime checks, and platform-specific overrides. The business logic becomes scattered across folders and files, with little true portability between them.

A developer changes one flow and breaks iOS. Another change to the backend dependency breaks the web. Tests pass in CI but fail on mobile. Each target drifts, and the codebase becomes a minefield.

Centralization hides the problem. It doesn't solve it.

What's missing is a clear boundary between capability and implementation. It should specify here's what this logic does, what it needs, and what it returns. Not just in code, but in a way that runtime tools, build pipelines, and platform-specific layers can understand and respect.

Without that, your shared code is just code that happens to live in the same place.

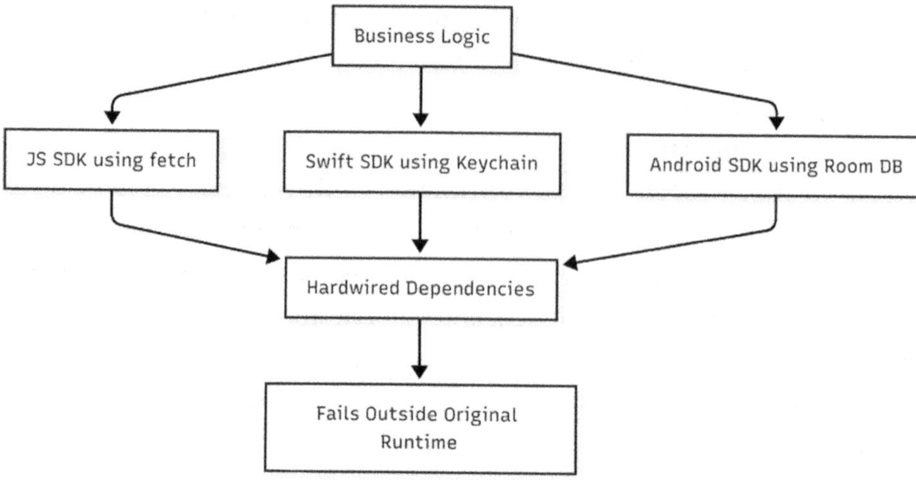

Figure 2-5. *Even clean business logic can become runtime-bound when embedded in platform-specific SDKs. Without runtime boundaries, portability fails*

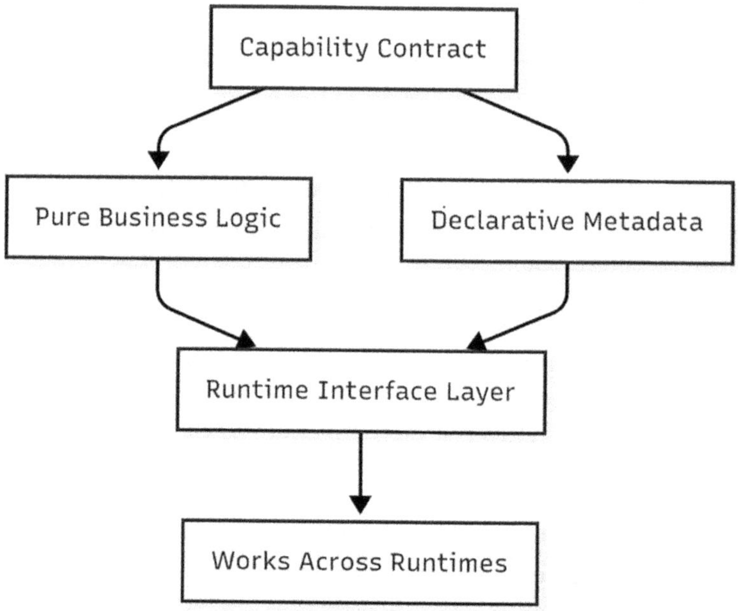

Figure 2-6. *Capability contracts isolate business logic from execution. Paired with a runtime interface layer, this approach enables safe reuse across platforms*

You Can't Refactor Your Way to Portability

Many teams try to resolve these issues through better code discipline, cleaner abstractions, more consistent patterns, wrapper libraries, monorepos (single version-control repositories that contain multiple projects or packages, for example, a single Git repository holding the web app, the iOS shared logic, the Android shared logic, and the backend API, making it easier to share code and enforce consistent tooling across them), and type-safe interfaces (contracts between components expressed in a statically typed language like TypeScript, so that the compiler catches mismatches at build time rather than at runtime).

These practices are helpful, but they don't address the main problem.

The issue isn't code quality; it's the absence of runtime-agnostic boundaries architectural lines that define what a component does without specifying how or where it runs. A runtime-agnostic boundary for a logging component would define that it accepts a structured log event as input and delivers it to a log sink; the interface to the log sink is an abstraction, not a concrete implementation. The Node.js runtime provides a file-based sink; the browser runtime provides a console sink; a serverless runtime provides a managed logging service sink. The component's logic does not change only the sink implementation. The boundary is agnostic to the runtime because it depends on the abstraction, not the implementation.

You need a way to define logic that isn't tied to its current execution environment. You need metadata that describes the contract, not just the function signature. You need a model that allows capabilities to run in different locations without needing rewriting for each one.

That doesn't come from refactoring. It comes from rethinking what software boundaries actually mean in a multi-platform, multi-runtime world.

Centralization Without Contracts Is a Dead End

If you centralize logic without contracts, you're just shifting the problem. You decrease visible duplication but increase hidden coupling. You standardize APIs but lock them to a single runtime. You align teams but also anchor them to shared fragility.

This is where most large software organizations get stuck. A common version of this trap: a platform team centralizes authentication into a shared service, one endpoint, one token format, and one session model. It works well initially. But as products expand internationally, the session model doesn't support regional data residency requirements.

As mobile clients mature, the token expiry behavior doesn't match iOS's background refresh constraints. As the web app adds single-page-application routing, the session invalidation timing conflicts with the SPA's client-side state. Each team asks for a small adjustment. Over eighteen months, the "centralized" authentication service accumulates twenty-three conditional branches, each one handling a specific client's quirk. The center held, but it became the most fragile part of the system. Centralization without contracts produced exactly the coupling it was meant to eliminate, just in one place instead of many. They try to scale through reuse, but their reuse isn't portable. They attempt to simplify through centralization, but their center can't handle the load.

To move forward, we need a different model. One that treats capabilities as contract-defined units. One that makes boundaries clear and behavior declarative. One that allows code to move between runtimes without carrying the past along.

That model is what this book will define.

But first, we need to understand what reuse actually needs to work.

It Was Never Just About Code

There was never a single moment of clarity. No groundbreaking keynote or incident report that suddenly revealed the entire picture. When I wrote the UMA white paper (`https://bit.ly/UMA-White-Paper`), it was the result of years spent observing the same problems resurface across runtimes, across teams, and across generations of software.

But only recently did the deeper pattern become clear: we have been pursuing the wrong abstraction.

For years, we viewed code as the main unit of reuse. If a piece of logic worked well, we'd extract it into a library, publish an SDK, and tell other teams to integrate it. That approach worked when platforms were relatively stable and requirements changed slowly. But that's not how modern development works.

Today, code runs everywhere. It powers mobile apps, browser extensions, cloud functions, edge devices, embedded systems, and even autonomous agents. It's triggered by humans, UIs, models, cron jobs, and background services. It often runs in contexts the original developers never expected or imagined.

Requirements are equally dynamic. A capability established last quarter might soon need to accommodate new privacy regulations, different form factors, or real-time triggers. Business logic is no longer a fixed asset; it must be explainable, testable, discoverable, and portable not only across various environments but also through time.

A useful positive reference is the Stripe SDK ecosystem. Its core payment-processing logic is explainable: every API operation is documented with the exact inputs, outputs, and error codes in a public reference. It is testable: Stripe provides a dedicated test mode with synthetic card numbers that simulate every failure scenario, allowing teams to write deterministic tests without real transactions. It is discoverable: the API reference, changelog, and SDK documentation are indexed and searchable, so a new team member can find the right capability without tribal knowledge. And it is portable: the same logical operation (charge a card) is available via a REST API, a JavaScript SDK, a Python library, a mobile SDK, and a CLI, all satisfying the same contract. The capability travels with its definition.

In this context, clean code isn't enough. What we actually need is a way to define, describe, and reuse **capabilities**.

Capability, Not Computation

A capability is more than just a block of logic. It's a declaration that explains what a service does, what it requires, and what guarantees it offers. It defines the interface and the constraints, making the assumptions behind its design clear.

Traditionally, these assumptions are invisible. They reside in the minds of developers or spread across comments in various files. But when code runs on new environments, those hidden assumptions often emerge as bugs or failures.

Imagine a simple function to calculate tax. It works flawlessly in your US-based web app. But try to reuse it in an EU mobile app, and the logic silently breaks. The function had no understanding of regional policies. It assumed state-based rates, USD currency, and no VAT. None of that was encoded, typed, or declared. The logic wasn't wrong; it just wasn't portable.

This isn't an isolated case. It's the norm. And it's not just about tax rates. It occurs in SDKs that depend on fetch in the browser or Keychain in iOS. It also happens in services that assume AWS IAM (Amazon Web Services Identity and Access Management, Amazon's service for controlling who can access which AWS resources and under what conditions) or in functions that expect environment variables to be injected by CI/CD tools (such as GitHub Actions, GitLab CI, CircleCI, or Jenkins systems that automatically build, test, and deploy code whenever a change is pushed to the repository). Code that appears "clean" can still be closely tied to its original environment.

We need to elevate the definition of capability to match the level of logic. It's not just about how code runs; it's about how behavior is described.

From Source Code to Source of Truth

Software architecture has steadily evolved from implicit wiring to explicit structure. Consider the shifts we've already embraced:

- From imperative scripts to declarative infrastructure, instead of writing step-by-step shell scripts that say "create a server, then install this package, then configure this port," teams now write configuration files (using tools like Terraform, Pulumi, or AWS CloudFormation) that declare the desired end state: "I want three servers of this type with this network configuration," and the tooling figures out the steps.
- From monolithic logic to service interfaces
- From undocumented APIs to schema-driven contracts instead of APIs whose shape you only discover by reading the source code or calling them and seeing what comes back, teams now publish formal schemas (OpenAPI for REST, GraphQL SDL, Protocol Buffers) that describe the exact structure of every request and response. These schemas can be used to auto-generate client SDKs, validate requests at the gateway, and run contract tests to catch breaking changes before they reach production.

Each shift made our systems more observable, automatable, and composable. The next one is about **making capabilities explicit and portable**.

Observable: The system's internal state can be understood from its external outputs, logs, metrics, and traces, which provide visibility into what is happening without requiring access to the source code. Automatable: machines can reliably trigger, configure, test, and operate the system without human intervention at each step. Composable: independent components can be combined in new arrangements to build larger capabilities, because their interfaces are well-defined enough that they can be connected without each component needing to know the internals of the others.

This means defining behavior not just by what it computes, but by how it behaves and what it relies on. What context does it need? What policies does it respect? What latency, scale, or region assumptions does it bake in? Instead of starting from code and wrapping documentation around it, we begin from intent and design downward. From purpose to contract to logic to implementation. The goal is not to remove code but to make behavior understandable and adaptable before code is even written.

Beyond Interfaces: Describing Meaning, Not Just Shape

Type systems and interfaces define structure. But they don't capture meaning.

An interface might tell you that a function takes a string and returns a boolean. However, it does not specify that the string must be a signed token, nor does it indicate that the boolean signifies a user's biometric authentication status. Such context is rarely included, yet it determines how safely and effectively that logic can be reused.

This is what I call the metadata gap: the absence of structured, machine-readable information that describes a component's intent, constraints, behavioral guarantees, and environmental assumptions. The metadata gap is the space between what the code does and what other teams need to know in order to safely reuse it. Most reuse failures are not caused by wrong code. They occur because the code is misunderstood, since its behavior, intent, and assumptions are hidden.

The result is fragile systems: functions that seem generic until used outside their native environment. At that point, everything can break; inputs might become incompatible, behavior could change, side effects may occur, or compliance might be violated.

If you don't specify a capability, you can't coordinate it, test it, or expand it across platforms.

And if you can't describe it, you can't reuse it.

UMA Starts Here

The Universal Microservices Architecture starts with the understanding that **portability depends on defining capability boundaries**.

Code reuse remains fragile until behavior is clearly defined by contracts. This isn't about a new SDK, runtime, or framework. It's about redefining how software behavior is modeled, validated, and reused across platforms that change faster than any codebase.

This chapter has outlined the failures that brought us here: from platform divergence to false promises of reuse, from coordination bottlenecks to centralization that failed to deliver. Each layer reveals the same core flaw: code alone is insufficient.

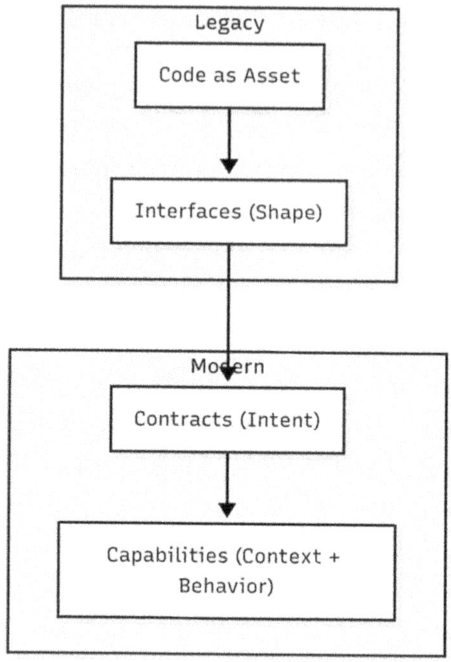

Figure 2-7. *The evolution of abstraction boundaries. Code and interfaces focus on execution and shape. Contracts and capabilities expose intent, constraints, and behavioral context, making logic portable, observable, and automatable*

To create software that lasts, scales, and adapts, we need a new abstraction.

Portability is not about moving code.

It's about moving understanding.

That's where UMA begins.

CHAPTER 3

What Is Universal Microservices Architecture (UMA)?

From Concept to Blueprint: Defining the Architecture for a Device-Independent Future

Introduction

The Expanding Gap Between Platforms

It's important to remember how young many of our platforms remain. Two decades ago, engineers talked about "write once, run anywhere." In practice, we joked it was "write once, debug everywhere" as browser engines and operating systems behaved differently. Back then, the most significant differences were between Windows and Linux or Internet Explorer and Firefox. Creating a web app that worked in those environments sometimes required script adjustments, compatibility fixes, and rendering refinements for Safari or Opera, but the gap was comparatively narrow.

Fast forward to today, and that gap has become a chasm. A single product may be expected to run as

- A web application in multiple browsers, each with its own JavaScript engine and security policies
- A mobile app on both iOS and Android, each with a different SDK (Software Development Kit), the collection of platform-specific APIs, tools, and libraries used to build native applications for that environment), lifecycle model (the sequence of states an

E. Piovesan, *Universal Microservices Architecture*, https://doi.org/10.1007/979-8-8688-2794-5_3

app transitions through from launch and foreground activity to background processing, suspension, and termination, each with different rules about what code can run and for how long), and UI framework

- A desktop application, either native or wrapped in Electron (a framework that packages a web application's HTML, CSS, and JavaScript into a standalone desktop app by bundling it with the Chromium browser engine and a Node.js runtime), with different APIs for file access, GPU rendering, and background tasks
- An edge application running on constrained hardware with strict power and memory budgets, for example, a quality-inspection system on a factory production line, a real-time route optimizer in a delivery vehicle, a predictive maintenance sensor in a wind turbine, or a fraud-detection module on a point-of-sale terminal
- A cloud-hosted service that must scale to thousands of concurrent requests while meeting strict latency targets

Each environment has its own APIs, performance quirks, and failure modes. Teams end up splitting their attention across multiple code paths and domain knowledge. The result is a higher barrier to innovation and rising costs: features take longer to reach all users; bug fixes often require multiple redevelopments; an optimization that helps one platform might break another. Every new device or runtime becomes a separate branch in the development plan and increases maintenance.

Over time, this tax builds up. Teams stop trying new approaches because each experiment requires support across multiple platforms. Roadmaps become cluttered with compatibility tasks. Systems that begin modern and flexible gradually become patchworks of fragile codebases that cost more and more to keep running.

To see how these challenges manifest, consider a straightforward request we once received. In one project, product management asked us to add offline support for a data-heavy form so users in remote areas could still submit entries. On paper, this looked simple: cache the form data locally and sync when a connection is available.

The initial version of the desktop client was finished in a week. The local cache was just a file-based store, and the sync logic integrated with the existing network layer, making the process relatively simple.

Next came the web version. Browser storage APIs seemed straightforward at first, but slight differences between Chrome, Firefox, and Safari increased our workload. Chrome's quota system for IndexedDB (a browser-native, low-level key-value database built into modern browsers for storing large amounts of structured data client-side) offered ample space; Firefox imposed stricter limits that disrupted large uploads; Safari's aggressive local data clearing during low-storage situations silently deleted our test entries. We spent an extra 2 weeks developing platform-specific guards and fallbacks.

On iOS, we faced another challenge. Background sync was heavily throttled, causing queued submissions to remain unsent for hours unless the user reopened the app. We had to move the sync trigger into short-lived background tasks and redesign how we store in-flight data to prevent corruption when iOS terminates the app. On Android, device manufacturers had their own "battery optimization" strategies that unpredictably killed background services. This required another redesign of the data layer and a switch to push-based sync when possible.

By the time we shipped that same feature to all platforms, more than 3 months had passed. Over half of that time was spent not on building the feature but on adapting the same business logic to each environment's quirks. Every bug fix after launch needed four separate pull requests, and each performance optimization had to be re-benchmarked for each platform because assumptions that worked in one runtime failed in another.

This is not an isolated experience. Many teams find that the feature itself is rarely the hard part. The fragmentation of runtimes, APIs, and lifecycle rules turns "ship everywhere" into "fix everywhere," and maintenance costs only go up. Instead of focusing on improving the user experience, we end up translating and re-translating the same concepts into slightly different platform dialects.

When "Ship Everywhere" Turns into "Fix Everywhere"

In a project I was involved in, we received a straightforward request from product management: add offline support for a data-heavy form so users in remote areas could still submit their entries. On paper, it looked like a small task: store the form data locally and then sync it once a connection is available.

The initial version of the desktop client was finished in a week. The local cache was just a file-based store, and the sync logic was integrated with the existing network layer, making the process relatively simple.

Then the web version was next. Browser storage APIs seemed straightforward initially, but slight differences between Chrome, Firefox, and Safari increased our workload. Chrome's quota system for IndexedDB offered ample space, Firefox imposed stricter limits that disrupted large uploads, and Safari's aggressive local data clearing during low-storage situations silently deleted our test entries. We spent an extra 2 weeks developing platform-specific guards and fallbacks.

On iOS, we faced another challenge. Background sync was heavily throttled, causing queued submissions to remain unsent for hours unless the user reopened the app. We had to move the sync trigger into short-lived background tasks and redesign how we store in-flight data (requests that have been initiated but have not yet received a confirmed response—data that is partway through the submit-and-sync cycle) to prevent corruption when iOS terminates the app. On Android, device manufacturers had their issues with "battery optimization," which unpredictably killed background services. This required another redesign of the data layer and a switch to push-based sync when possible.

In a push-based sync model, the server initiates contact and delivers data to the client the moment it is available, rather than waiting for the client to periodically ask (polling) or for a specific user action to trigger a request (event-triggered sync). This is more power-efficient and reduces background wakeups, an important consideration given by Android manufacturers' aggressive battery optimization policy.

By the time we shipped the "same" feature to all platforms, over 3 months had gone by. More than half of that time was spent not on developing the feature but on adjusting the same business logic to fit each environment's quirks. Every bug fix after launch required four separate pull requests, and each performance optimization had to be re-benchmarked for each platform because assumptions that worked in one runtime failed in another.

This isn't an isolated experience. It's common for many teams: the feature itself is rarely the most challenging part. The fragmentation of runtimes, APIs, and lifecycle rules turns "ship everywhere" into "fix everywhere," and the maintenance costs only increase over time. Instead of focusing on improving the user experience, we spend too much time translating and re-translating the same concepts into slightly different platform dialects.

From Fragmentation to a Unified Model

Universal Microservices Architecture starts with a simple but consistent observation: the most challenging part of multi-platform development isn't the variety of programming languages but the inconsistency of runtime environments. Each platform manages execution based on its own rules regarding process lifecycles, resource limits, network access, and security boundaries. These differences are subtle enough to go unnoticed during early design phases but significant enough to cause major divergence in production.

UMA considers these environmental differences top priorities, not afterthoughts. Instead of requiring each team to modify business logic for every runtime's quirks, UMA packages services into portable units with a consistent contract. This contract details how the service functions under load, what resources it needs, how it communicates, and how it should degrade when resources are limited. Significantly, the contract is enforced by runtime adapters (thin software layers that translate between the capability's abstract contract interface and the specific APIs, security model, and resource mechanisms of a given execution environment), enabling the same service binary to run in a browser tab, at an edge node, or within a cloud data center without reimplementation.

In practice, the thumbnail generator from our earlier example could be written once, tested against a consistent set of performance and reliability standards, and deployed everywhere without the costly process of re-tuning for each platform. The business logic would not need to know whether it is running in a Chromium browser, an AWS Lambda function, or an on-premises edge gateway. The runtime adapter manages that translation.

Table 3-1. *The UMA model removes most of the repetitive, platform-specific work by enforcing uniform behavior through service contracts and adapters*

Aspect	Traditional Multi-Platform Development	UMA-Style Portable Services
Codebase	Separate code per platform	Single binary per service
Runtime adaptation	Manual per environment	Automatic via runtime adapter
Performance tuning	Repeated for each platform	Done once, enforced everywhere
Testing complexity	Separate test suites per platform; bugs found only on specific runtimes; QA pipelines duplicated	Single capability validated against its contract across all runtimes; one test suite covers all environments
Failure handling	Platform-specific logic	Uniform policies in the service contract
Deployment	Multiple pipelines	One pipeline, multiple runtimes (browsers, mobile devices, edge gateways, serverless functions, VMs, and cloud containers)
Team silos	Standard due to different stacks	Reduced through shared contract and tooling

Introducing Universal Microservices Architecture

Universal Microservices Architecture is not a new programming language, nor is it a single framework. It is an architectural approach designed to make services portable, modular, and runtime-agnostic from the start. At its core, UMA defines a service as a self-contained unit of logic packaged together with a declarative contract. This contract specifies how the service should be executed, how it communicates, and how it behaves when conditions change.

The idea is simple: a service should work anywhere without needing to be rewritten, recompiled, or reconfigured beyond what the contract allows. Whether run in a browser, on an edge device, or in a cloud region, the service should provide consistent behavior, performance guarantees, and failure modes.

While this book will explore UMA in depth, it is helpful at this stage to highlight the core principles that shape it.

Table 3-2. *The six principles of UMA provide a consistent foundation for building portable, adaptable systems across heterogeneous environments*

Principle	Description
Portability	Services are packaged as portable binaries that can execute in different runtimes without code changes.
Modularity	Each service is autonomous, with well-defined boundaries and no hidden dependencies on the hosting environment.
Declarative Contracts	Execution, resource, and communication policies are defined in a contract that is enforced by the runtime adapter.
Event-Driven Coordination	Services communicate through events and messages, reducing tight coupling and enabling distributed execution.
Edge-Native Execution	UMA assumes that some workloads will run closest to the user, making low-latency and offline-friendly execution first-class concerns.
Governance by Design	Contracts, metadata, and policies form an auditable record of service behavior, aiding compliance and operational governance.

Hands-On Takeaways: When Portability Arrives Too Late

In large-scale systems, portability is often ignored until it's necessary. Teams usually begin with a familiar single-stack setup, trusting that their chosen runtime will stay stable for years. However, the reality is different. Platform updates, security requirements, and new device types can force sudden migrations. By the time these pressures happen, systems are usually heavily reliant on their original runtime, making changes expensive and risky.

In my experience, I've seen projects where portability was seen as a "later" problem. They performed well early on, with quick iterations and little abstraction, but faced issues when expanding to new environments. One example was a high-traffic analytics service designed specifically for a specific Linux distribution and x86 hardware. When the company's new edge initiative required ARM support, the team had to rewrite large parts of their pipeline under tight deadlines, leading to regressions and instability. The technical debt was present not only in the code but also in the assumptions built into architecture, deployment, and operations.

This is why UMA prioritizes portability as a core design goal, not an afterthought. It views the ability to run on various runtimes and devices as a fundamental requirement, rather than a feature to add later.

Defining Universal Microservices Architecture

Why a Definition Matters

Every significant architectural movement tends to go through a hype phase where the label becomes popular before its actual meaning is understood. Service-oriented architecture experienced this phase, as did microservices. Even "cloud-native" once became a catch-all term for nearly anything outside one's own data center. The danger is that, without a precise definition, the term becomes so flexible that it loses its usefulness. Teams may think they are working on the same concept, but in fact, their end goals can be very different.

When definitions drift, three problems appear almost immediately:

1. **Patterns stop being portable.** If my "UMA service" looks different from yours in how it's packaged, discovered, or governed, the patterns I document might not apply to you. That defeats the purpose of creating a shared architecture style.

2. **Tooling becomes fragmented.** Vendors or internal platform teams start addressing different assumptions.

3. **Tooling becomes fragmented**. Vendors or internal platform teams start addressing different assumptions. One CLI or SDK interprets UMA as "WASM everywhere with service workers," while another treats it as "containerized microservices with a shared schema registry." Neither is wrong within its own frame, but they are incompatible in practice.

4. **Lessons learned lose their usefulness.** Postmortems, scaling tips, and best practices rely on a shared baseline. Without it, advice becomes situational folklore that can't be applied to other projects or companies.

Universal Microservices Architecture is particularly vulnerable to this drift because it combines various architectural approaches: microservices, serverless, portable binaries, event-driven systems, and edge computing. Without a shared definition, teams will each apply their familiar approach to UMA, creating a patchwork that cannot expand beyond isolated successes.

A clear definition serves two primary purposes. First, it acts as a **contract** for the community: here's what qualifies as UMA and what doesn't. Second, it provides a **framework** for decision-making: when you face a trade-off, you can ask whether the option aligns with UMA's principles of portability, modularity, and independence from any single runtime.

If we misunderstand the definition or let it become vague, we risk repeating the history of other architectural movements that started with promise but ended up with too many conflicting ideas.

How UMA Extends the Microservices Model

Microservices, as most developers understand them, are small, independently deployable components that contain a single business function within a defined boundary. They provide a powerful solution to monolithic architectures, allowing teams to work in parallel, scale selectively, and deploy without requiring coordination across the entire system.

But microservices, as practiced initially, came with implicit assumptions that made sense in their early context:

- **They lived in a specific runtime stack.** A "Java microservice" ran in a JVM, a "Node.js microservice" in V8, and moving between them meant rewriting or wrapping.
- **They were often tied to a specific hosting model.** You picked containers, serverless functions, or VMs and optimized for those environments.
- **They assumed a stable, networked backend.** This left the left edge, offline, or highly heterogeneous environments as afterthoughts.

Universal Microservices Architecture preserves the benefits of microservices such as modularity, bounded contexts, and independent deployment, while removing runtime and environment constraints.

In UMA:

1. **Runtime independence is a first-class property.** Services are packaged as portable binaries (often via WASM or similar) so they can execute in a browser, at the edge, or in the cloud without modification.

2. **Contracts replace runtime assumptions.** A service declares its capabilities, inputs, outputs, and policies in a platform-neutral format. The hosting environment adapts to the service, not the other way around.

3. **Event-driven coordination is baked in.** UMA services are designed to participate in distributed workflows where events, not synchronous API calls, are the default glue.

4. **Edge-native thinking is the default, not an afterthought.** UMA assumes workloads might execute as close to the user or device as possible, then shift dynamically based on latency, cost, or policy.

The result is not "microservices with a twist," but a more adaptable model that treats location, runtime, and deployment target as variables rather than fixed points. This flexibility enables UMA systems to endure platform changes without costly rewrites and to grow from a single device to a global network without changing their core design.

Bounded Contexts Still Matter in UMA

Removing runtime and platform constraints does not eliminate the need for clear service boundaries. In fact, in UMA, these boundaries become even more critical because services may operate in very different environments yet still need to work together without interfering with each other.

This is where **Domain-Driven Design (DDD)** provides a fundamental foundation. DDD introduced the idea of a **bounded context**: a mental boundary that defines the scope of a service's vocabulary, rules, and responsibilities. Within a bounded context, terms have a precise and clear meaning. Outside of it, they can mean something entirely different.

In traditional microservices, bounded contexts prevent tight coupling between teams or domains. In UMA, they also prevent **environmental coupling**. If your "pricing" service depends on database schemas or runtime libraries from your "checkout" service, you are forcing them into the same execution model, which reduces their runtime independence.

Key principles for bounded contexts in UMA:

- **One Service, One Context:** No shared domain models across services. Translation at boundaries is intentional and explicit.
- **Ownership of Data and Schema:** The service that defines a schema owns it, controls its evolution, and is the only one allowed to persist or query its data directly.
- **Context Mapping Remains Explicit:** Context mapping is the practice of documenting how different bounded contexts relate to each other, which terms are shared, which are translated at the boundary, and which services act as upstream or downstream dependencies. In UMA, context mapping is expressed through contracts that describe how one service's outputs map into another's inputs, especially when bridging runtime boundaries.

Why this matters:

- **Without bounded contexts, runtime independence becomes fragile**. A service that is "portable" but relies on shared data structures or implicit behaviors from another service is not truly portable.
- **UMA systems are designed to evolve**. Boundaries make it possible to replace or move services, say, from the cloud to the browser, without re-architecting dependent services.
- It also enables **independent scaling**: the "checkout" service might need more edge instances during peak traffic, while the "inventory" service runs mainly in the cloud with batch updates. Clear boundaries make this operational flexibility possible.

Service Ownership of Data and Schema

In UMA, portability is more than just moving code between different runtimes; it involves transferring **full capability**. To keep that capability consistent across environments, the service must carry not only its logic but also its data definitions and the rules that govern them.

When a service owns its schema, it

- Controls how that schema evolves over time.
- Ensures that any changes to data representation are intentional and do not break consumers.
- Can maintain backward compatibility through explicit contract versions, rather than silently altering shared data models.

Why This Is Crucial for UMA:

1. **Prevents Hidden Dependencies:** If two services rely on a shared schema file or database table, any change in one causes a ripple effect in the other. In UMA, this ripple can cross runtime boundaries, increasing complexity and risk. By maintaining strict ownership, you ensure that any change has a clear point of control.
2. **Enables True Runtime Independence:** A service might run in a browser, at the edge, or in the cloud. If it needs to fetch data, it should do so through its own defined contract, not by assuming access to another service's database or in-memory structures. This is the only way to guarantee consistent behavior across environments.
3. **Supports Independent Scaling and Deployment:** When data ownership is clear, services can be deployed, upgraded, or moved without needing to coordinate database migrations or schema changes with unrelated teams. This is crucial when scaling certain services differently based on runtime requirements.

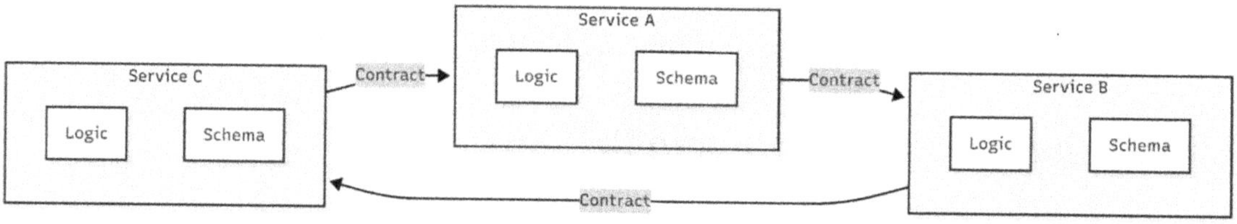

***Figure 3-1.** Context Ownership Diagram. Each service contains its own logic and schema. All interactions happen through explicit contracts, avoiding shared databases*

Portability Beyond the Stack

A common misconception about microservices is that they are inherently portable because of their small size and independent deployability. In fact, many microservices remain tightly coupled to their host environment. For instance, a Java service might depend on the JVM's classloader system, a .NET service might rely on CLR-specific libraries, or a Node.js service might depend on the peculiarities of its event loop. Even when housed in containers, these services continue to rely on the container runtime and the orchestration platform that oversees them.

UMA recognizes this as a key challenge to address. The unit of portability is now a **runtime-agnostic service binary rather than a container image**. This binary includes not only the logic but also its contract, metadata, and minimal runtime interface. When paired with the appropriate host adapter, the same binary can operate in the browser, at an edge node, or in a cloud data center without requiring recompilation or environment-specific setup. This shift changes how teams approach deployment boundaries. Instead of customizing a service for Kubernetes in production and creating a separate in-browser build for client-side execution, the UMA binary now acts as the single artifact. Portability is not just a side effect of container tooling; it is an architectural feature built into the service itself.

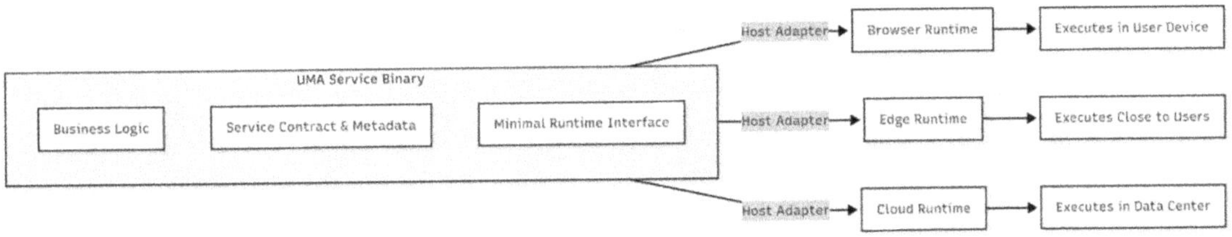

***Figure 3-2.** A single UMA service binary runs unchanged across browser, edge, and cloud by pairing with the appropriate host adapter*

Event-Driven Coordination As a Core Principle

UMA not only enables services to be portable but also facilitates effective coordination in highly distributed environments. Conventional microservices typically rely on synchronous request-response interactions. Although suitable for controlled data center environments, this method becomes fragile when services are distributed across devices, edge nodes, and multiple cloud regions, especially where network conditions are inconsistent and latency spikes occur unavoidably.

Connecting two services via synchronous calls means that a delay in one can cause failures in the other. This is especially problematic in UMA's scenarios, where system components may run on a user's laptop browser, a nearby edge server, or a remote cloud region. Relying on instant responses increases risk. Event-driven coordination changes this dynamic. Instead of direct API calls, UMA promotes communication through asynchronous, immutable events that describe occurrences rather than issuing immediate commands. This approach eliminates temporal dependency, allowing services to function even when some parts are offline, and supports patterns like eventual consistency, buffering, and replay. In UMA, events are **self-describing** with schemas, version info, and context metadata, enabling any runtime, whether in a browser, at the edge, or in the cloud, to process them without centralized translation. For instance, a service in a WebAssembly sandbox in the browser can generate an event that a cloud-based AI analytics service can consume directly, without custom adapters.

This design has several concrete benefits:

- **Resilience**: A temporary outage in one part of the system does not halt the rest.
- **Scalability**: Events can be fanned out to multiple subscribers without overloading the producer.
- **Flexibility**: New consumers can be added without changing existing producers.
- **Edge-First Workflows**: Local nodes can react instantly to events, applying policies or optimizations before sending data upstream.

From an operational perspective, UMA views event coordination as **a fundamental runtime feature**. It is not just a pattern that developers can choose to implement but a crucial part of the architecture supported by all runtimes.

Edge-Native Design in UMA

In UMA, the edge serves as a primary execution target instead of a secondary deployment zone. This architecture expects services to run on gateways, in-vehicle processors, industrial controllers, or other devices with constraints significantly different from those in cloud data centers.

Running at the edge shapes service design in three ways:

1. **Autonomy:** An edge-deployed universal microservice must keep functioning even if connectivity is lost. This requires designing logic and contracts so the service can make decisions locally and reconcile state later when the network becomes available.

2. **Adaptation to Constraints:** Edge hardware might have limited CPU, memory, or power resources. UMA addresses this by ensuring that services are portable in form factor, allowing a developer to select the appropriate binary target and resource profile without changing the service's logic or breaking its contracts.

3. **Local Event Responsiveness:** In many edge cases, the key factor isn't raw throughput but predictable, low-latency responses to local events. UMA's event-driven coordination enables an edge node to process and react to stimuli directly, without waiting behind distant cloud services.

This approach does not attempt to replicate the cloud at the edge. Instead, it develops a service model that scales down intelligently, preserving key capabilities while respecting the unique operational environment.

What the Edge Changes, and How UMA Responds

- **Connectivity is variable.** UMA services include enough logic and policy in the package to act locally and then reconcile later. Contracts specify which actions can be taken offline and which must be deferred.

- **Resources are limited.** UMA considers resource budgets as part of the contract. The same service can specify smaller memory and time limits at the edge without altering its logic.

- **Latency budgets are tight.** UMA favors event handling close to the source. Local handlers react immediately, while longer workflows use events to continue in nearby or central runtimes.

- **Hardware is heterogeneous.** UMA packages logic as a portable binary plus a minimal host interface so that the same artifact can run across diverse chipsets with consistent behavior.
- **Operational access is limited.** UMA assumes constrained observability and remote control. Services emit compact, structured signals and are designed to roll forward or back atomically.

Edge Realities and UMA Design Responses

Table 3-3. *Mapping typical edge constraints to UMA's architectural responses*

Edge Reality	UMA Design Response
Intermittent network	Local autonomy with later reconciliation is described in the contract
Small CPU and memory budgets	Resource limits declared and enforced uniformly across runtimes
Need for predictable latency	Event handling locally, long paths decoupled via messages
Diverse hardware and OS mixes	Portable binaries with a minimal, stable host interface
Limited ability to intervene	Atomic updates, clear fallbacks, compact telemetry

Edge-Native Design in UMA

UMA considers the edge as a primary execution environment, not just a smaller version of the cloud. The architecture is based on the idea that services may need to run on devices ranging from industrial controllers and in-vehicle processors to mobile gateways and remote field units. These environments have very different operational realities compared to central data centers.

The key design responses are

- **Local Autonomy:** UMA packages include all the logic and contracts needed to operate independently when network access is unreliable or unavailable, with mechanisms for reconciling state once connectivity returns.

- **Resource Adaptation:** The same service logic can be packaged into binaries tuned for constrained devices, with resource budgets declared in the contract and enforced consistently across runtimes.
- **Latency-Driven Event Handling:** UMA allows events to be processed and acted on locally, ensuring predictable responses for scenarios where cloud round-trip times are impractical or unsafe.
- **Hardware Diversity Support:** By abstracting platform capabilities and relying on portable binaries, UMA enables the same service to run consistently across heterogeneous processors and operating systems.
- **Minimal Operational Footprint:** UMA assumes that remote maintenance and debugging will be limited. Services are designed to emit compact telemetry, support atomic updates, and roll back gracefully.

With the edge functioning as a primary runtime, UMA guarantees that services are not just theoretically portable but also practically deployable in environments where achieving portability is most challenging.

Interplay of the Three Pillars

UMA's strength isn't just in service modularity, portability, or event-driven coordination individually. Each principle tackles a specific problem, but its real value emerges when they are integrated.

- **Service modularity** ensures that functionality is defined in small, well-bounded units with clear contracts.
- **Portability** guarantees those units can run without modification across cloud, edge, and client environments.
- **Event-driven coordination** lets those units interact without coupling, allowing the system to adapt dynamically to where and how each service runs.

When these pillars are combined, a UMA system can seamlessly transfer workloads across different environments based on the situation. For example, an analytics service might run in the cloud during normal conditions, shift to the edge when low latency is essential, and work with client-side services using the same event contracts. The service logic stays the same; only its placement and coordination change. This integration allows UMA to deliver the long-promised "write once, run anywhere' capability without the compromises of earlier approaches.

Imagine a logistics platform that handles deliveries in both urban and rural areas. It features separate UMA services like route optimization, inventory checking, and vehicle tracking, each managed by its own contract. These services are portable: the vehicle tracker can operate on in-vehicle hardware in areas with poor connectivity, while in urban zones, it runs in the cloud to gather data from multiple sources. Both setups use the same binary and contract. When a vehicle approaches a delivery point, the tracker triggers an event that prompts the inventory checker to act locally at the edge, confirming the package's readiness without waiting for cloud confirmation. This modular, portable, and event-driven design allows the platform to adapt smoothly to changing network conditions and operational needs, avoiding the need for code rewrites or architectural changes. These three pillars enable the system to adjust to different network environments and operational demands as a cohesive whole, rather than a patchwork of environment-specific solutions.

What UMA Is (and Is Not)

Universal Microservices Architecture (UMA) isn't just a rebranding of existing models. Although it draws from service-oriented architecture, microservices, and serverless computing, it doesn't fit neatly into any single category. UMA is defined by its ability to package services as portable binaries that can run across multiple environments without changes and coordinate via event contracts that remain consistent regardless of location. It's not simply "microservices everywhere," since it doesn't assume a single dominant runtime or a fixed deployment topology. Neither is it "serverless on the edge," as it doesn't rely on opaque, provider-specific infrastructure that limits control. Finally, UMA isn't just "WebAssembly with contracts" because it also emphasizes orchestration, governance, and lifecycle management alongside execution formats.

UMA is both a design philosophy and an implementation framework. It aims to help teams define a capability once and deploy it anywhere, ensuring predictable coordination without requiring runtime-specific rewrites or glue code. Built on years of architectural experimentation, UMA is tailored to modern distributed systems where cloud, edge, and client are considered peers rather than separate tiers. Its core principles, service modularity, portability, and event-driven coordination, along with its suitability for edge environments, create a solid architectural foundation. UMA isn't just about adding another tool or framework but about redefining how capabilities are designed, packaged, and deployed to operate seamlessly across any runtime. Introducing these concepts early allows the rest of the book to focus on how the model is built, operated, and evolved in real systems.

Service Modularity Without Stack Boundaries

In UMA, modularity starts with the capability, not the codebase. The ability is the smallest unit of meaningful work that can be executed, verified, and reused across any runtime environment without rewriting its logic. This contrasts with traditional microservices or service-oriented architectures, where boundaries are often determined by the stack, language, framework, or infrastructure used.

Breaking from Stack-Defined Boundaries: In conventional microservices, the "shape" of a service is usually dictated by the deployment environment. A team might design an API service around specific web framework limitations or structure modules to align with a cloud provider's serverless platform. While practical locally, these choices tie the service to that environment. Moving it to an edge gateway, browser sandbox, or different cloud often requires significant rework or a complete rewrite.

UMA rejects these restrictions. Instead of asking, *"How do we build for this stack?"*, the focus shifts to *"What is the smallest, stable capability we can define, and what contract describes it?"* The runtime becomes an adaptor layer, not a design starting point. This approach improves portability and encourages more explicit responsibility definitions.

The "what" and the "how" are applicable concepts to differentiate. The "what" refers to the capability: the defined outcome, its inputs, outputs, guarantees, and resource constraints. The **"how"** describes the execution strategy, including scheduling, concurrency, and runtime-specific optimizations. In UMA, the *"what"* is fixed by the contract, ensuring consistency, while the *"how"* can vary based on the environment without violating that contract. This flexibility allows the same "document parser" to operate at high throughput in the cloud, be memory-optimized at the edge, and run incrementally in the browser, all without altering its core logic.

Eliminating Design Drift

One of the hidden costs in distributed systems is design drift: the gradual, often invisible divergence of supposedly identical capabilities implemented in different stacks. It happens when the same business rule, say, how a discount is calculated or how a session token is validated, is implemented independently by multiple teams, each making small, locally reasonable decisions. Over months, those decisions compound into meaningfully different behaviors: one platform rounds differently, another handles expired tokens differently, and a third has a stricter validation rule. No single change was wrong; the accumulated difference is the problem. Over time, these differences cause inconsistent behavior, uneven feature sets, and operational surprises. In many organizations, this occurs because each environment evolves independently and under different constraints. UMA addresses this by making the capability, not the environment, the authoritative unit of design. Any runtime-specific differences are contained in adapters, leaving the capability definition consistent and intact across all environments.

Stable boundaries, adaptable runtimes. Since UMA boundaries are defined around outcomes rather than frameworks, they stay consistent even as runtimes evolve. When a new edge runtime emerges, the capability can be deployed with just an adapter update. If the cloud provider's API changes, the core logic of the capability remains unaffected. This stability minimizes regression risk, decreases testing costs, and enables teams to adopt new environments proactively rather than reactively.

From Modularity to Orchestration

This stack-agnostic modularity also streamlines orchestration. When each capability has a clear contract, services can be easily assembled, replaced, or relocated without risking hidden dependency issues. This predictability is vital in UMA because orchestration is frequently event-driven and can involve clients, edges, and cloud runtimes within a single workflow. Without contract-based modularity, such a system would more likely turn into a fragile network of environment-specific assumptions.

A Unifying Effect on Teams: Finally, stack-independent modularity changes how teams collaborate. In many organizations, frontend, backend, and edge teams work in silos, each defining and owning their own "versions" of similar functionality. UMA provides a single, unified definition of a capability that all teams can work with, regardless of their preferred runtime. This reduces duplication, encourages reuse, and aligns quality expectations across the system.

By using capability boundaries instead of stack boundaries, UMA delivers services that are naturally portable, stable, and consistent. These qualities make large, distributed systems more predictable and more straightforward to develop and adapt.

The Single-Responsibility Principle, Reframed for UMA

The single-responsibility principle has been a staple in software engineering for many years, yet in many organizations, it is still closely tied to the specific technology stack in use. For example, one team might define "responsibility" as a module that fits within a particular framework, while another might scope it by the limits of a database schema. These definitions are fragile because they tend to shift with changes in the stack and often do not transfer well when moving between different runtime environments.

UMA offers a different perspective. Instead of defining responsibility by code structure or hosting constraints, it is based on a capability's capacity to achieve a **single, clear, verifiable outcome.** This outcome should be delivered within an agreed-upon **quality level** and **resource budget**. The three components, outcome, quality tier, and resource budget, form the service's contract. They remain consistent regardless of where the service is deployed.

An **outcome** describes what the capability does in the simplest terms. It should be a statement that can be verified: "Validate an invoice," "Compress an image to 50KB," or "Return the shortest driving route given a set of constraints." An outcome should be singular. If you find yourself adding "and" to the description, you are likely combining responsibilities that should be separated into different capabilities.

A **quality tier** defines how well the service must achieve that outcome. It may include accuracy thresholds, availability targets, throughput expectations, or latency guarantees. In UMA, quality tiers are explicit, not assumed. This allows the same capability to operate in different environments with varying quality tiers without losing its core identity.

A **resource budget** sets the practical limits within which the capability must function. This could mean memory limits for edge devices, CPU quotas in a shared environment, or execution time limits for latency-sensitive tasks. Declaring these budgets is not just about optimization; it's about ensuring the capability can run predictably wherever it is deployed.

Together, these three elements establish the meaning of "single responsibility" in UMA. They enable capabilities to be designed once, tested against a consistent contract, and deployed anywhere without changing their purpose or guarantees. This is what enables portability and consistency in a diverse runtime environment.

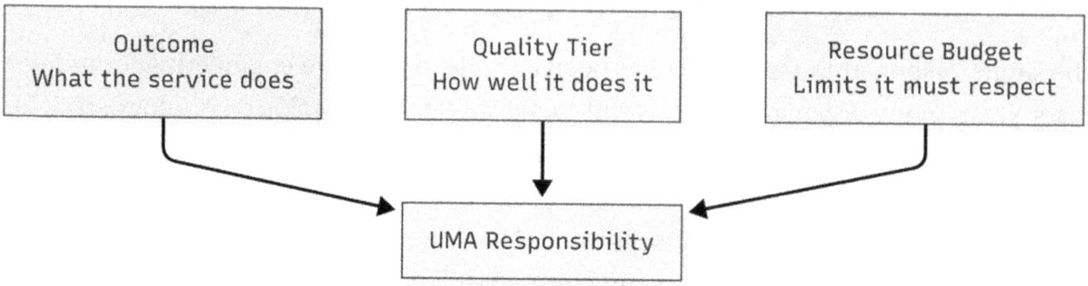

Figure 3-3. *UMA defines a capability's responsibility as the intersection of its outcome, quality tier, and resource budget, ensuring the definition is stable across all runtimes*

Determining Boundaries: From Theory to Heuristics

Once a capability's responsibility is clearly defined, the next step is to determine its boundaries, where it begins and ends. In UMA, these boundaries must work across multiple environments without needing to be redrawn when the hosting context changes. Boundaries are not set to match the specifics of a framework, deployment pattern, or a team's preferred tools. Instead, they are chosen to keep each capability cohesive, stable, and predictable, whether it runs in a data center, on an edge gateway, or within a client application.

A key principle is to aim for a single, stable outcome. This outcome should retain its meaning even as technology evolves or user needs change. For example, "payment authorization" is a capability likely to remain relevant for years, despite changes in payment methods and security protocols. Conversely, a capability like "process this specific vendor's payment API" is fragile, requiring frequent redefinition and retesting as external dependencies evolve. In UMA, the preference is for the former, as it safeguards the service from instability caused by external fluctuations.

The stability of the core domain concept is closely linked to the next factor: change pace. Some parts of a system evolve quickly, driven by experimentation or user input. Others change slowly, perhaps due to regulatory rules or established, proven processes. Combining fast-changing and slow-changing concerns within the same capability creates friction. It requires redeploying the stable logic each time the fast-changing part updates. Separating them allows for rapid innovation without destabilizing long-lasting components.

Data ownership is another key indicator for boundary placement. In UMA, the capability that owns a dataset should also be responsible for setting the rules governing its access, modification, and sharing. Splitting these responsibilities across multiple services can cause race conditions, conflicting laws, and inconsistent states when data moves between environments. Keeping data logic close to its owner also simplifies compliance, security, and auditing.

Failure domains often reveal where boundaries should be set. If a capability fails, its impact should be limited to the work it directly handles. A routing service should not turn off order processing, and an image compressor should not halt the entire content pipeline. This isolation enhances resilience and makes troubleshooting easier without causing cascading failures across unrelated workflows.

Resource budgets are equally important. Capabilities with significantly different performance characteristics should not be grouped together. A capability needing low latency might require aggressive caching and optimized I/O patterns, while a batch processor for analytics might be tuned for throughput and cost savings. Keeping them separate allows each to be deployed and scaled independently, avoiding unnecessary compromises.

The scope of the state also affects boundaries. Stateless capabilities are easier to move between environments, but when state is necessary, it should be well-defined and confined within a capability's scope. Mixing unrelated states across boundaries creates tight coupling and makes migration more complex.

Latency class adds another layer for separation. A real-time fraud detection service and an overnight reconciliation job may both process financial transactions, but their latency expectations are incompatible. Keeping them in different capabilities ensures each can meet its own performance goals without being limited by the other's requirements. Trust levels and team ownership are also key considerations. Capabilities handling sensitive personal data may need extra review, restricted deployment environments, and stronger access controls. If a capability requires specialized governance, isolating it reduces the security risks for the rest of the system. Likewise, defining capability boundaries aligned with clear team ownership prevents operational conflicts. When a team wholly owns a capability from development through deployment, changes are quicker, accountability is more transparent, and coordination is simpler.

In UMA, these heuristics work best when considered together rather than as a sequential checklist. A well-bounded capability often emerges where multiple factors intersect, such as a stable domain concept with a clear data owner, consistent change cadence, and specific performance and trust requirements. The resulting boundaries are durable, portable, and adaptable, making them far easier to maintain across heterogeneous runtimes.

Example: Defining the "Real-Time Shipment Tracker" Capability

A logistics platform must offer real-time shipment tracking through a browser-based customer portal, a mobile driver app, and edge gateways situated in regional warehouses. The initial thought might be to develop a large "Shipment Management" service that oversees tracking, route optimization, inventory updates, and customer alerts. In UMA, this approach would cause unnecessary coupling and reduce portability. Using the heuristics results in a more precise approach and result.

- **Stable Outcome:** The long-term goal is to show the shipment's current status and location in real time, regardless of how location data is collected or displayed.
- **Change Cadence:** Tracking logic changes often due to evolving GPS and telemetry devices, while inventory checks and notification templates change more slowly. Keeping tracking separate avoids redeploying the slower-changing parts.
- **Data Ownership:** The tracking service owns location and timestamp data. Other services can read but not overwrite it.
- **Failure Domain:** If tracking fails due to network issues, order processing and inventory management continue unaffected.
- **Resource Budget:** Frequent, lightweight updates require low-latency processing and efficient memory usage.
- **State Scope:** Maintains short-lived state for active shipments, with long-term archival handled by another capability.
- **Latency Class:** Real-time requirements mean updates must appear within seconds.

- **Trust Levels and Team Ownership:** Sensitive location data demands security controls and clear ownership by the telemetry integration team.

Resulting Boundary: *Ingest shipment location updates and deliver the current location and status to authorized users within seconds, meeting specified accuracy and availability targets while operating within resource constraints suitable for real-time processing.* This single capability can be packaged once and deployed across cloud, warehouse edge gateways, and browser runtimes without altering its scope or guarantees.

Hands-On Takeaways

A few years ago, we collaborated with a team to build a complex supply chain platform. Initially, they combined real-time shipment tracking, route optimization, and notifications into a single large "Shipment Management" service. It was quick to develop, and on paper, it seemed like they were saving time by reusing a lot of shared code. However, the first time they rolled out an update to the GPS parsing logic for a new fleet device, things went wrong. Deploying this update also required redeploying route optimization and notification logic, even though those had not changed. In the cloud, this caused only a brief delay, but at warehouse edge nodes, the restart created minute-long gaps where location updates stopped reaching customers. When they finally separated the tracking logic into its own component, the difference was immediate. GPS updates could be deployed independently of the rest of the shipment system, edge gateways stayed online, and teams could work on their parts separately. It reminded everyone that having clear boundaries isn't just an architectural goal; it directly impacts uptime, team productivity, and user trust.

Trade-Offs of Granularity in UMA

Granularity is highly debated in service design. While dividing functionality into smaller, dedicated capabilities can enhance clarity and adaptability in theory, there is a point where the operational costs of managing numerous components surpass the benefits of finer granularity. UMA highlights this trade-off, as each capability must operate across various runtimes. Smaller, focused capabilities are simpler to port and test individually, but increasing their number also raises the complexity of packaging, deployment, and coordination across environments. This challenge is particularly evident at the edge and on client devices, where deployment pipelines and event orchestration are often more limited than in cloud settings.

On the **benefit side**, detailed capabilities enhance functional clarity. Each unit has a clearly defined outcome, quality level, and resource budget, making it easier to test and understand. This lowers the risk of scope creep and makes incremental changes safer. Smaller capabilities also enable more independent deployment, allowing teams to move quickly without waiting on unrelated code changes.

On the **cost side**, each capability incurs overhead. Contracts need to be maintained and versioned, monitoring and telemetry pipelines require configuration, deployment scripts must be updated, and runtime orchestration must be tested. These costs are steady per capability, so the more granular the system, the more these costs accumulate.

Granularity also influences **runtime performance**. UMA aims to reduce the cost of cross-capability communication, but splitting a tightly coupled workflow too finely can introduce network or messaging delays. This is especially important in edge deployments, where bandwidth and processing power are limited. A shipment tracking system that works well in the cloud might start missing update windows if location processing is divided into too many capabilities on an edge device.

Team structure also plays a key role. Highly granular systems require obvious ownership boundaries. Without these, teams risk getting stuck in endless coordination meetings and negotiating contract changes. Conversely, overly coarse capabilities can become bottlenecks, with multiple teams competing to make changes to the same codebase. The optimal point is often where boundaries correspond to both the functional cohesion of the capability and the structure of the teams responsible for it. The ideal level of granularity depends on the **maturity of the operational environment**. Early in a project, slightly coarser capabilities help reduce deployment complexity and enable faster delivery of value. As the system matures and tooling improves with automated contract testing, streamlined CI/CD, and runtime orchestration, teams can safely divide capabilities into smaller units where the benefits justify the costs.

Anti-patterns That Undermine Modularity

Even with clear boundaries and carefully chosen granularity, recurring mistakes can weaken UMA's benefits over time. These anti-patterns often emerge when teams are pressured to deliver quickly or when habits from monolithic or single-runtime architectures resurface. They rarely cause instant failure but gradually increase friction, making it more difficult to port capabilities, slower to test, and costlier to evolve. A common mistake is over-granularity: while dividing a system into small capabilities might seem to improve clarity and separation, each capability still needs to be built, deployed, monitored, versioned, and validated across all supported runtimes. Adding a few capabilities might not be burdensome, but many can overload deployment pipelines and strain operational resources. This issue is more evident in UMA because every capability must ensure the same portability and contract guarantees across browsers, edges, and cloud environments. What appears simple on an architecture diagram can become a logistical challenge when scaled across different environments.

Another subtle but harmful anti-pattern is hidden coupling through shared databases. In many organizations, services that seem independent in code are actually writing to the same set of tables in a shared database. This bypasses the service's contract and makes the database an implicit point of integration. In UMA, the impact is even worse because moving one capability to another runtime often involves moving the database too, which removes the portability benefit. True modularity requires each capability to own its data fully, exposing it only through its established contract.

A close relative to shared databases is the overuse of shared utility libraries. Reuse is generally good, but when those libraries contain business logic or runtime-specific dependencies, they become a hidden coordination point. Updating the library forces coordinated redeployments of multiple capabilities, even if only one needs the change. In UMA, where capabilities are meant to run independently across different runtimes, this can lead to complex dependency chains that reduce agility. Utility libraries should be lightweight, focused on generic functions, and free of runtime-specific logic.

Leaky contracts are another form of hidden coupling. A well-designed contract hides implementation details so that internal changes do not affect consumers. A leaky contract does the opposite, exposing too much of the internal model or process. Once consumers depend on those details, changing the capability without breaking compatibility becomes nearly impossible. This undermines UMA's promise of independent evolution and runtime flexibility.

Duplicated capability logic is an anti-pattern that often occurs when teams work separately. Without a shared contract repository or effective governance, different teams may reimplement the same logic in slightly different ways. Over time, these slight differences lead to inconsistent behavior between capabilities running in various environments. UMA reduces this risk with its contract-first approach, but protection only works if contracts are considered the authoritative source and are reviewed with portability in mind.

Finally, embedding runtime-specific optimizations into the core logic can lock a capability to a single environment. For example, adding low-level hardware calls for a specific edge device inside the main processing code may boost short-term performance but will prevent cloud deployment without significant rewriting. In UMA, runtime-specific adaptations should go into an abstraction or adapter layer, leaving the core logic portable. This separation ensures that the same capability can operate with different performance profiles depending on the environment without needing rewrites.

These anti-patterns share a common trait: they create hidden dependencies that tie capabilities together, either technically or operationally. In a UMA system, avoiding them is not just about cleaner code but also about maintaining the ability to run, test, and update capabilities independently across diverse environments.

Hands-On Takeaway

The Edge Rollback That Never Happened

A logistics provider adopted UMA to unify its cloud and warehouse edge workloads. One capability processes incoming shipment scans on edge gateways to reduce cloud latency. Another capability, running in the cloud, generates daily compliance reports from the same data. On paper, they appeared as independent services. In reality, both wrote to the same relational database tables, an early shortcut to avoid duplicating schemas.

When the edge team made a minor change to the analytics capability, a simple schema tweak to support a new barcode type, they assumed the cloud reports wouldn't be affected. However, the report generator relied on the old schema, and the first nightly job failed. Worse, the database migration was automatic across all edge nodes, meaning the only rollback option was to revert both edge and cloud capabilities simultaneously. Doing so would have reversed 3 weeks of unrelated cloud-side improvements.

The fix took 2 weeks, involved creating an emergency staging database, and required multiple after-hours deployments to realign the environments. The lesson was costly but straightforward: in UMA, shared write access to a database between capabilities destroys portability and independence. After this incident, the team shifted to a model where each capability manages its own storage and publishes events instead of writing directly into another service's tables.

The Library That Halted the Release Train

A fintech startup built its UMA platform with a focus on code reuse. Two teams collaborated on a shared library containing math utilities, shared DTOs, and convenience functions for currency conversion. Over time, the currency conversion logic became more sophisticated, including real-time exchange rate retrieval, formatting rules for specific markets, and compliance checks. Six months later, a subtle bug in the conversion logic caused rounding errors for certain high-value transactions. Fixing the bug was easy, requiring just a few lines of code. However, since the logic was in the shared library, every service that used it had to be redeployed; this included unrelated services like the customer notification system and an edge-based analytics processor, both with different deployment schedules and testing pipelines. Coordinating these cross-runtime redeployments halted the entire release process for a week. Edge deployments had to be staggered due to limited on-site access at some data centers, and cloud pipelines faced additional compliance checks before going live. After this costly delay, the team restructured the library so that shared code remained strictly generic and runtime-independent, keeping business logic within each individual capability where it appropriately belongs.

The Leaky Contract That Wouldn't Stay Quiet

A retail media platform had a UMA capability dedicated to handling image uploads from advertisers. For convenience, the service returned the exact storage path and file naming convention in its API responses, believing this would save consumers an extra lookup. The naming convention included timestamp-based folders and internal UUID sequences that were simply implementation details.

Over time, downstream capabilities started relying on these exact naming patterns. The image processing system used them to group thumbnails, the ad-serving engine used them to prefetch assets, and even the front-end web application had code that assumed this structure when building image URLs.

When the image team later optimized their storage system to cut costs by switching from a timestamp-folder model to a hash-based structure, they thought the change was internal and safe. Within minutes of deployment, the ad-serving engine began serving broken images, the front-end displayed 404 errors, and the thumbnail generator failed to find its source files. Restoring the old naming format required rolling back across multiple runtimes, including client apps that had already been shipped.

The postmortem led to a stricter contract review policy. Any proposed change now had to pass a "consumer impact" test, ensuring no internal details were exposed in public contracts. The incident became a textbook example for the team: in UMA, leaky contracts can turn runtime independence into a tightly coupled trap.

The Role of Contracts in Sustaining Modularity

If service boundaries are the skeleton of a UMA system, then contracts are the connective tissue that holds it together. Without them, even the most elegant modular design will gradually weaken under the strain of shortcuts, implicit dependencies, and uncoordinated changes. In UMA, contracts are not just interface definitions. They are explicit agreements that specify what a capability promises to deliver, the quality level it will meet, and the resource budget it will consume, regardless of any specific runtime. A well-designed contract protects consumers from changes to internal implementation. This allows a capability to evolve, improve, and even shift between runtimes without requiring coordinated updates across the system. For instance, a capability might begin as a cloud-hosted service and later transition to an edge runtime to reduce latency. As long as its contract remains the same, consumers never need to know where it runs. This captures UMA's portability goal: to make deployment location and runtime an implementation detail, rather than an integration risk.

Contracts also serve as a safety boundary for team autonomy. In multi-team UMA projects, different groups own different capabilities. Without strong agreements, changes in one service can easily ripple across others, creating coordination overhead that slows delivery. A clear, enforceable contract allows a team to release improvements at its own pace, confident that it will not break downstream consumers. Another essential function of contracts is in governance and versioning. In UMA, capabilities are validated against their contracts during build and deployment, often automatically. This enforces consistency and prevents unintentional contract drift, where subtle changes in logic or structure gradually alter expected behavior. A strict contract policy also simplifies managing multiple versions of a capability simultaneously, which can be critical when rolling out changes gradually across cloud, edge, and client runtimes.

Contracts are also the antidote to hidden coupling. As we saw in the anti-pattern stories, sharing databases, embedding business logic in shared libraries, or leaking internal details all create dependencies that can sabotage portability. A proper contract ensures that any data exchange or functional integration happens through an explicit, well-defined channel, making it possible to test, monitor, and evolve those integrations without surprises.

Finally, contracts provide teams with a safety net for portability. When testing a capability in a new runtime, the first question isn't "does it run?" but "does it still meet its contract?" This shifts the focus from technical implementation to functional correctness, ensuring portability doesn't sacrifice reliability or quality. The stakes are high. Without strong contracts, the system's modularity begins to weaken in subtle ways. Capabilities that appear independent on a diagram become intertwined through hidden dependencies. A change intended for one runtime spills over into others, forcing coordinated redeployments that negate the benefits of portability. Testing shifts from proactive validation to reactive firefighting. The operational costs of even small changes rise, and over time, the architecture drifts back toward the same fragile, tightly coupled state UMA was designed to avoid.

The real danger is that this erosion often goes unnoticed until a critical moment: a high-traffic event where scaling fails because a hidden dependency slows down deployment, or a migration stalls because capabilities cannot be moved without breaking consumers. In those moments, the absence of strong contracts turns a portable, adaptable system into a fragile one that resists change. In contrast, a system with well-governed contracts treats such events as routine operations instead of existential risks.

Hands-On Takeaway: The Migration That Could Have Caused Major Problems. A global retailer chose to shift one of its order-processing capabilities from the cloud to edge nodes inside distribution centers. The goal was to reduce latency for inventory updates during peak shopping seasons. In many architectures, this type of migration would have required coordinated changes across payment services, fraud detection, and the customer notification system. In this case, none of those downstream teams even knew the move had happened until after it was complete.

The reason was straightforward: the order-processing capability had a stable, versioned contract that had not changed in years. The migration team managed to package the same capability for the edge runtime, verify it against the existing contract, and deploy without involving any consuming services. No rewrites. No emergency war rooms. No unexpected outages.

What could have been a months-long, high-risk project was completed in less than 2 weeks, entirely within the scope of one team's delivery cycle. For the retailer, it proved that in UMA, strong contracts are not just an architectural detail but the key difference between fearless change and operational paralysis.

Summary and Transition

Service modularity in UMA is both a design discipline and an operational commitment. It begins with defining capabilities that each deliver a single, meaningful outcome, under a clear quality tier and resource budget, and extends to ensuring that those capabilities can be deployed, moved, and evolved without entangling the rest of the system.

The boundaries we draw in UMA are not symbolic. They protect autonomy at the code, data, and team levels. When those boundaries are respected, a capability can be re-implemented, relocated to a different runtime, or optimized for a specific performance profile without requiring a synchronized release across unrelated parts of the platform. This freedom makes UMA practical in environments where the same service might need to run in a browser, on an edge device, or in the cloud without changing its behavior.

The cost of ignoring modularity is high. Overly granular capabilities can flood the system with orchestration overhead. Hidden coupling through shared databases or business logic in utility libraries can quietly weaken independence. Leaky contracts reveal internal details that become dependencies for consumers, locking you into brittle patterns that are difficult to change. Embedding runtime-specific optimizations directly into core logic can make a capability effectively immovable. Each of these anti-patterns reduces portability, increases coordination costs, and raises the risk of failure during migrations or scaling events.

The unifying safeguard against this erosion is the contract. A firm, enforceable contract is more than an API specification; it is a durable agreement that defines what a capability is, what it delivers, and how it can be trusted, regardless of where it runs. Contracts preserve independence by ensuring that all interactions happen through explicit, testable channels. They enable incremental change, allowing teams to iterate at their own pace without destabilizing the broader system.

The role of contracts in maintaining modularity cannot be overstated. In UMA, they are a difference between a system that embraces change and one that resists it. They turn architectural diagrams from aspirational models into operational reality. They give teams the confidence to make bold moves, whether shifting workloads to the edge for latency gains or consolidating cloud deployments for cost efficiency, knowing those moves won't destabilize the rest of the platform.

Once the principles of modularity are established, the next step is to understand how these capabilities come to life in a running system. In the following chapter, we transition from designing independent services to the mechanics of how UMA's runtime layer loads, orchestrates, and coordinates them across different environments. This is where contracts, capability boundaries, and runtime abstractions come together in practice, ensuring that portability is not just feasible but operationally smooth.

Portable Binaris and Runtime-Agnostic Logic

Why Portability Needs More Than Just Containerization

For many teams, "portability" has become equated with containerization. Packaging the application in a container, running it on any host with the appropriate runtime, and calling it portable is common. However, in reality, containers address a narrower issue: they standardize the environment at the operating system level. While this is valuable, it does not resolve the portability challenges UMA aims to address.

UMA's objective is runtime-agnostic execution. A capability should be able to run in a browser, on an edge device, within a serverless function, or inside a containerized microservice, all without altering its internal logic. Containers can assist in some of these environments, but they are not always available, desirable, or efficient. Edge devices might lack a container runtime altogether. Browsers certainly do. Even in the cloud, a containerized workload may experience cold start delays or resource overheads that make it unsuitable for latency-sensitive capabilities.

Another drawback of relying solely on containers is that they tend to carry the entire environment with them, including the operating system and all dependencies. This makes them heavier to move and slower to start compared to a portable binary or bytecode module. In UMA, the portability target is smaller and more precise: the core capability itself, stripped of environmental baggage, capable of plugging into any runtime that can execute it.

Containerization also creates gaps in cross-runtime consistency. A capability built with OS-specific system calls will work properly in a container for that OS but fail to run in a runtime that lacks those calls entirely, such as a WebAssembly sandbox in the browser. The only way to achieve true portability is to separate capability logic from runtime-specific concerns at design time, making runtime bindings replaceable without modifying the core implementation.

Example 1: The Edge Device Without Docker

A manufacturer wanted to run a predictive maintenance capability on industrial IoT gateways in a factory. The devices had just enough storage and memory for a lightweight runtime and could not run Docker or any container engine. By building the capability as a portable WebAssembly module, they deployed exactly the same binary to those devices and to a cloud batch-analysis environment, without creating a separate "edge" codebase.

Example 2: The Browser That Doesn't Care About Your Container

A logistics platform needed to shift the route optimization logic from a cloud container to the browser to reduce latency for real-time route planning. Since browsers cannot run containers, the team compiled the core capability to WebAssembly, maintaining the same contract and logic while only replacing the runtime binding.

Example 3: The Cold Start That Breaks the SLA

An e-commerce company's fraud detection system ran in a serverless container environment but experienced cold start delays during traffic surges. Switching to a portable binary executed in the platform's WebAssembly runtime cut startup latency from hundreds of milliseconds to under 50ms, with no changes to business logic.

These scenarios illustrate why UMA considers containers just one deployment option among many, not the sole standard of portability. They are helpful for packaging and orchestrating capabilities in certain situations, but UMA's architecture focuses on a smaller, more flexible portability unit that performs well even in environments where containers are too heavy, too slow, or simply unavailable.

Separating Capability Logic from Runtime Infrastructure

The first step toward true portability in UMA is separating the core logic of the capability from the runtime infrastructure that hosts it. This is not just a packaging task; it is an architectural commitment that ensures the logic remains independent, testable, and reusable across any execution environment.

In UMA terms, a capability has two layers:

- **Capability Core:** The pure functional logic that produces the defined outcome within its quality tier and resource budget. This part contains no runtime-specific calls, no direct OS dependencies, and no hard-coded integrations. It is expressed entirely in terms of the contract so that it can be executed in any compliant runtime.
- **Capability Envelope:** The runtime-specific bindings, adapters, and optimizations required to integrate the core into a specific environment. This may include handling I/O, platform APIs, hardware access, or orchestration hooks. The envelope can vary for each deployment target without modifying the core.

This separation means that when you need to transfer a capability from one runtime to another, you don't modify the business logic. Instead, you replace or recompile the envelope for the target environment while keeping the core unchanged.

Example: Real-Time Translation Across Runtimes

A real-time translation feature was initially deployed in the cloud, where the envelope connected to a managed speech-to-text service, handled the translation in the core, and then sent the output to a text-to-speech API. When the same feature was later moved to a wearable device, the core remained unchanged. Only the envelope was replaced, now connecting to the device's on-board microphone, local speech model, and Bluetooth output. The same contract was maintained, and the same validation tests passed in both deployments.

This model also makes testing easier. The core capability can be tested alone with mock inputs and outputs to ensure accuracy, no matter where it is deployed. Each envelope can then be tested separately for specific runtime concerns, such as API rate limits, hardware constraints, or security policies. This helps prevent runtime issues from affecting the core and causing problems in other environments.

Finally, the separation enables performance tuning without sacrificing portability. For example, an edge deployment might utilize a GPU-accelerated envelope to speed up certain operations, while the browser version employs a WebAssembly-optimized path. Both produce the same functional output under the same contract, but the envelope adapts to the strengths of the target platform. In UMA, this pattern is essential. Without it, capabilities quickly become tied to their original deployment environment, making future migrations costly and prone to errors. With it, the architecture can seamlessly shift workloads between runtimes as performance requirements, cost considerations, or user experience goals evolve.

The Role of WebAssembly and Other Portable Formats

Separating capability logic from runtime infrastructure is only part of the solution. To achieve true portability, the capability core must be packaged into a form that can operate across diverse environments, including browsers, mobile devices, serverless functions, and embedded gateways. This packaging must be lightweight, secure, and consistent across different runtimes. In UMA, this process produces a **portable binary** or bytecode module, accompanied by the capability's contract, allowing it to be loaded and executed wherever the contract is supported.

Portability Without Lock-In: Choosing a binary format is a technical decision, not an architectural commitment. UMA's architecture ensures that the binary format is simply an output of the build pipeline. If a better format emerges in the future, capabilities can be rebuilt for it without modifying their core logic or contracts. This is a key difference from traditional application stacks, where code often becomes inseparable from the runtime it was initially built for. In UMA, the core is designed to be runtime-agnostic, and the format is merely a delivery mechanism.

Why WebAssembly Is Strong Today

Currently, WebAssembly (WASM) is one of the most capable and widely adopted portable formats. Initially created for browsers, it has expanded into serverless platforms, edge computing runtimes, and even desktop environments. WASM provides

Cross-Runtime Execution: The same binary can run in the browser, on an IoT edge device, inside a cloud worker, or within a containerized service.

Security by Default: WASM binaries operate in a sandbox with explicitly granted permissions, making them safer to deploy in untrusted environments.

Predictable Performance and Quick Startup: This helps meet latency demands in time-sensitive applications, such as fraud detection or real-time translation.

In UMA, WASM is often the preferred choice for capabilities that need the widest runtime support. The same core capability can be compiled into WASM and combined with runtime-specific wrappers that interface with the system's APIs or hardware.

Beyond WASM: A Broader Toolbox

WASM is not the only option, and UMA does not assume it will always be the best one. Other formats are often better suited for specific performance profiles or target platforms:

- **Native shared libraries** (`.so`, `.dll`, `.dylib`) for maximum performance in fixed OS environments, compiled per architecture.
- **Java bytecode or .NET IL,** where the execution environment already standardizes on those runtimes.
- **GPU-specific binaries** such as CUDA PTX, Vulkan SPIR-V, or Metal Shading Language for capabilities that are heavily parallelized.
- **Interpreted formats** like Python `.pyc` or Lua bytecode for rapid iteration in script-friendly runtimes.

Because UMA capabilities are defined by their contract, not their binary format, different capabilities within the same system can use other formats, as long as they comply with the same interoperability rules.

Example: The Multi-format Media Pipeline

Consider a video encoding capability that needs to run in four places:

1. **Browser** for in-page previews without server roundtrips
2. **Mobile apps** for local encoding during video capture
3. **Edge gateways** for live TV signal processing.
4. **Cloud pipelines** for large-scale batch encoding.

The capability core is written in C++ with no runtime-specific code. The build pipeline outputs:

- WASM for browser and serverless use
- Native ARM and x86 shared libraries for mobile apps
- CUDA binaries for GPU-rich edge nodes
- POSIX binaries for general-purpose cloud workers

Every output conforms to the same contract. Each runtime uses an envelope to bind the binary to its local APIs, whether that means Web APIs, native device calls, or GPU driver interfaces.

Future-Proofing the Binary Decision: By maintaining the **core logic ➤ portable binary ➤ contract ➤ runtime binding** pipeline intact, UMA avoids tying the architecture to a single technology trend. If a new format emerges that combines WASM's portability with GPU-native performance, capabilities can be rebuilt for it without changing their logic or contracts. This separation makes adopting new execution models an incremental change instead of a system-wide migration.

In UMA, the actual portability unit is not the container, the binary format, or the runtime. It is the capability core plus its contract. Everything else, whether WASM, native code, or something yet to be invented, is just a delivery mechanism. This perspective is what allows UMA systems to evolve over decades, not just technology cycles.

Abstracting Platform Capabilities Without Losing Performance

Portability often comes with a hidden cost: performance. When you try to run the same logic on multiple platforms, the temptation is to hide each platform's differences behind a single uniform interface. While this makes code easier to port, it often forces you to ignore platform-specific optimizations. The result is an application that runs everywhere but not particularly well anywhere.

UMA is designed to avoid this trap. Its architecture keeps capabilities portable while still allowing them to exploit the full performance potential of each runtime. The key is **how** platform abstractions are designed: at the **contract boundary** and not buried inside the capability core.

Why "Lowest Common Denominator" Portability Fails

In many cross-platform systems, the abstraction layer only exposes features available on **every** target platform. For instance, if some environments have GPU acceleration but others do not, the abstraction layer may exclude GPU access entirely. This maintains portability, but it also prevents capabilities that could operate much faster from being utilized. This "lowest common denominator" approach leads to long-term stagnation. When new platform capabilities appear, such as dedicated AI accelerators in mobile devices or hardware codecs in edge gateways, they are ignored unless the abstraction layer is updated. By the time that update happens, the technological advantage may already be lost.

UMA's Contract + Envelope Model

UMA solves this by separating the **capability core** from its **capability envelope**.

- The **core** contains the portable logic that fulfills the capability's contract. It is runtime-agnostic and does not know about platform-specific features.
- The **envelope** is responsible for binding the core to the platform APIs, selecting the best available implementation path, and taking advantage of specialized hardware or services when possible.

The **contract** outlines the minimum requirements: which inputs are accepted, what outputs are produced, the expected quality level, and the resource budget. The scope can go beyond these requirements, for example, by delivering the same results more quickly using GPU acceleration, as long as it still meets or exceeds the contract guarantees.

Diagram: Capability Core and Envelope Abstraction

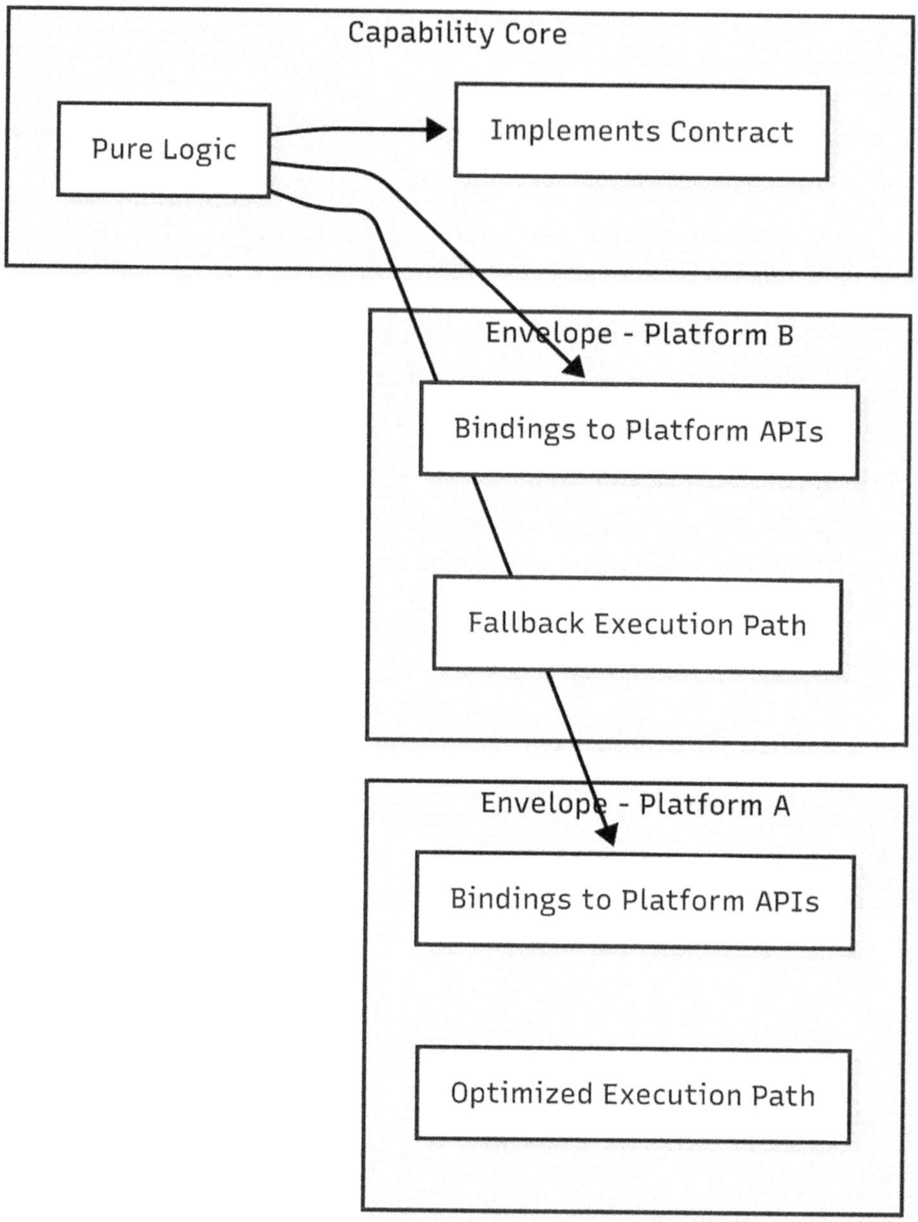

Figure 3-4. *In UMA, the capability core is identical for every deployment. Each platform uses its own envelope to bind the core to its APIs, allowing optimized and fallback paths without altering the logic*

Real-World Examples

Example 1: Adaptive Video Encoding in Media Streaming

A live streaming platform needs a video encoding capability that guarantees 1080p resolution at 30 frames per second within a 500 ms processing window. On a GPU-rich cloud node, the envelope binds the core to NVIDIA NVENC hardware acceleration, delivering the output in under 150 ms. On a CPU-only edge node, the envelope falls back to a multithreaded software encoder, still meeting the 500 ms SLA. The viewer experience is identical, but the GPU deployment uses less compute and scales more efficiently.

Example 2: AI Inference Across Browsers and Edge Devices

A real-time image classification system must operate on both browsers and IoT gateways. In the browser, the envelope uses WebGPU to send image data directly to the WASM core without unnecessary memory copies. On the gateway, the envelope interfaces with a dedicated neural accelerator through a vendor SDK. Both meet the same confidence threshold outlined in the contract, but each uses the most suitable path available.

Example 3: Financial Transaction Processing Across Regions

A fraud detection system operates in areas with different legal requirements. In some regions, the envelope connects to a low-latency in-memory database. In others, it uses a slower but compliant on-disk storage API. The core remains the same, but the envelopes meet both performance and legal standards.

Avoiding Common Abstraction Pitfalls

Pitfall 1: Over-Marshalling Data. When data is unnecessarily copied or reformatted between layers, it increases latency. UMA envelopes are designed to pass data in the most direct, runtime-native form possible, converting only when required by the contract.

Pitfall 2: Embedding Platform Logic in the Core. If the core directly calls platform APIs, portability is lost. UMA enforces a strict separation so that platform logic exists only in the envelope.

Pitfall 3: Assuming Optimizations Will Always Be Present. UMA envelopes always provide a compliant fallback path. If the optimization isn't available, for example, if a GPU driver is missing the capability, it still runs at the defined quality tier.

The Long-Term Payoff

Because the envelope is specific to runtime and replaceable, UMA systems can leverage new platform features without rewriting core logic. When a new hardware accelerator, cloud API, or browser standard becomes available, only a new or updated envelope is needed. The core remains unchanged, and the contract remains valid. This is how UMA achieves both **portability** and **performance,** two goals often seen as mutually exclusive in traditional architectures.

Security Implications of Cross-Runtime Execution

When a capability can run in a browser, on an edge gateway, in a cloud function, and on a mobile device without modification, it inherits the security challenges of all those environments. Cross-runtime execution increases the attack surface. A capability deployed to a tightly controlled cloud data center faces very different threats than one running on an untrusted edge device in a remote location.

UMA is designed to make portability secure by treating security as a primary architectural concern, not an afterthought added during deployment.

In a traditional system where code runs only in one environment, security controls can be closely aligned with that environment's assumptions. A server-based service might assume its host OS is secure, its network perimeter is monitored, and its filesystem is private. Moving that same code to a browser or IoT device breaks these assumptions. The filesystem may be exposed, the network may be hostile, and the execution environment might be evident to the user. UMA prevents these assumption leaks by enforcing security boundaries through the capability contract and envelope design.

The capability contract in UMA does more than define functional behavior. It also sets security guarantees and trust boundaries. These may include what data the capability can access or store, whether the capability runs in a dedicated sandbox or a shared environment, execution limits like timeouts and memory caps, and input validation rules for handling malformed or malicious input.

These rules are enforced regardless of the runtime, ensuring that even if the underlying platform has vulnerabilities, the capability still operates within safe boundaries. The envelope implements the runtime-specific security settings. In a browser, the envelope might enforce same-origin restrictions and block access to local storage unless the contract explicitly allows it. On an edge device, it may restrict filesystem access to a specific directory or require signed firmware checks before execution. In the cloud, it might use the platform's IAM policies to limit API access to only what is necessary. By managing security enforcement within the envelope, UMA guarantees that each deployment adheres to the contract and adapts to the specific requirements of its runtime environment.

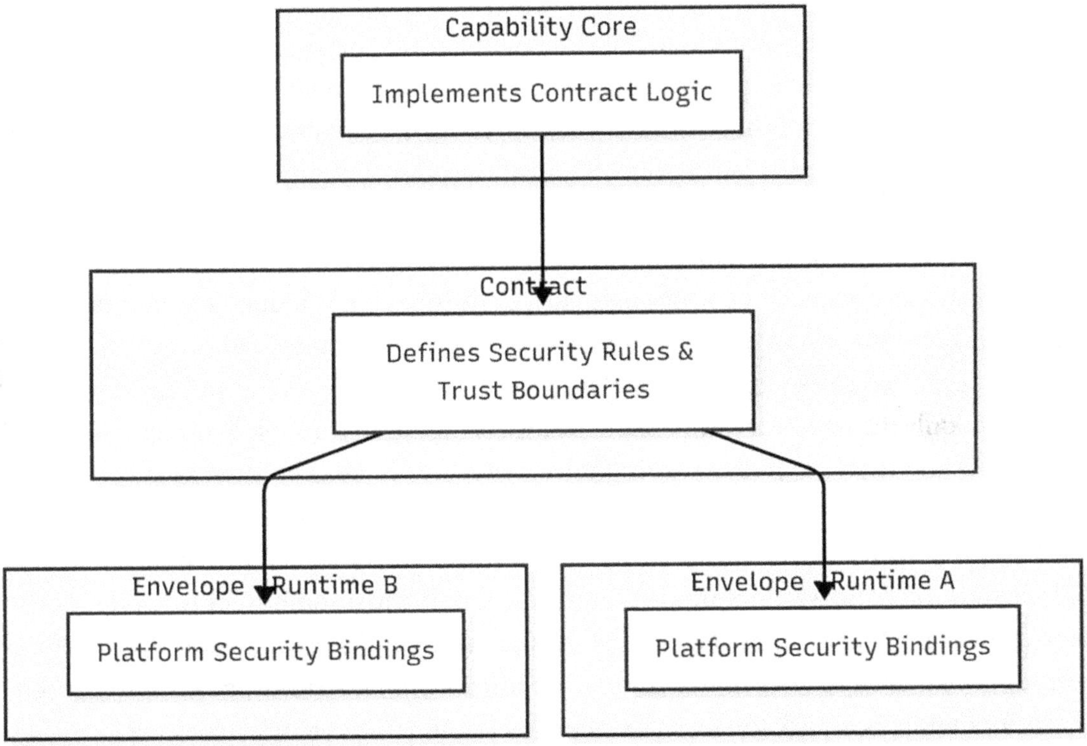

Figure 3-5. *In UMA, security rules live in the contract, while runtime-specific enforcement lives in the envelope. The core remains unchanged but always runs within the declared security boundaries*

For example, a payment authorization feature might operate in retail point-of-sale terminals, mobile apps, and cloud payment gateways. The contract specifies that it never stores raw card data and always uses tokenized transactions. The browser envelope ensures encryption before data is transmitted. The edge terminal envelope employs a hardware security module to safeguard tokens. The cloud envelope integrates with PCI DSS-compliant (Payment Card Industry Data Security Standard, a global set of security requirements that any organization storing, processing, or transmitting payment card data must comply with, covering encryption, access control, and audit logging) storage APIs. The logic remains the same, and the guarantees are consistent, but the enforcement adapts to the runtime environment.

Another example is telemetry ingestion in mixed networks. A capability on a factory floor IoT device signs all outgoing data and sends it over TLS 1.3 (Transport Layer Security version 1.3, the current standard cryptographic protocol for securing data in transit over a network, providing encryption, authentication, and integrity checking between communicating systems). The cloud version verifies the signature before accepting it, ensuring that only trusted devices can transmit telemetry.

Even document rendering can pose security risks. If a capability runs in both secure intranet environments and public SaaS applications, the contract may specify that embedded scripts are never executed. The SaaS deployment's envelope can add extra sanitization to protect against browser vulnerabilities.

UMA's model also tackles common threats. Code injection is reduced by compiling capability cores into portable binary formats with no dynamic code loading unless explicitly permitted in the contract. Privilege escalation is prevented by limiting envelope bindings to only the necessary APIs. Data leakage is managed through contract-defined data scopes and strict I/O policies within the envelope. Side-channel attacks are countered by controlling resource usage and masking timing differences in sensitive operations.

By separating security definitions in the contract from enforcement in the envelope, UMA avoids the typical failure mode where developers must remember to "add security later" for each platform. The rules are established once and automatically enforced in every runtime, even as new environments are introduced. If a runtime is compromised or a vulnerability is found, the fix can usually be implemented at the envelope level without rebuilding or retesting the capability core. This quick response is essential in a world where security threats change daily.

Observability and Diagnostics Across Runtimes

A capability operating across multiple runtimes will inevitably face different operational conditions in each environment. Cloud deployments may have access to detailed system metrics, centralized logs, and advanced tracing tools. In contrast, browser-based deployments rely on console logs, in-memory diagnostics, and limited client-side telemetry. Edge devices often fall somewhere in between, with intermittent connectivity and constrained storage.

For UMA to function effectively at scale, it must hide these differences from the monitoring teams. Operators should access consistent key metrics, traces, and error reports, regardless of the runtime environment. This necessitates integrating observability into the architecture from the outset, rather than treating it as a deployment-specific issue.

The capability contract specifies what must be observable, including operational metrics like request rates, latency distributions, error counts, and domain-specific metrics reflecting the capability's performance. For instance, a translation feature might report average confidence scores per session, while a fraud detection function could provide the percentage of flagged transactions. These observability requirements are embedded in the contract, ensuring all runtimes provide consistent reporting even if their underlying mechanisms differ.

The envelope translates these observability needs into the native features of the runtime. In the cloud, it might send metrics to Prometheus or CloudWatch. In the browser, it could send periodic telemetry beacons to a collection endpoint. On an IoT device, it may batch metrics locally and only send them when the network is available. The main point is that the shape and meaning of the metrics remain consistent, even if the way they are transported and stored changes.

Another vital aspect is consistent logging. UMA capabilities should generate logs in a structured, machine-readable format so they can be indexed, filtered, and analyzed without guesswork. The envelope determines how these logs are stored or transmitted, but the contract ensures the log schema stays the same across deployments.

Imagine a global health monitoring platform equipped with blood oxygen measurement capability for patients worldwide. In well-resourced hospitals, this system runs on cloud servers, processing continuous data streams from patient monitors and integrating results into electronic health records. In rural clinics with limited connectivity, the same system operates on battery-powered edge devices, storing readings locally and transmitting updates only when the network becomes available. For home monitoring, it functions within a browser-based telemedicine app that connects to Bluetooth oximeters. Without UMA's approach, the monitoring team would have to navigate three incompatible dashboards, each with different formats and missing fields. In UMA, the system's contract clearly defines which observability data must be generated: patient ID, timestamp, device ID, reading value, confidence score, and metrics such as average reading interval and number of device connection errors. The data envelopes adapt to local conditions while maintaining the data's structure and meaning. The cloud streams data in real time, the edge devices buffer and upload periodically, and the browser sends encrypted telemetry beacons every 30 seconds. This creates a unified view in which ICU readings from hospitals can be directly compared to rural clinic data, supporting consistent alert thresholds and global trend analysis.

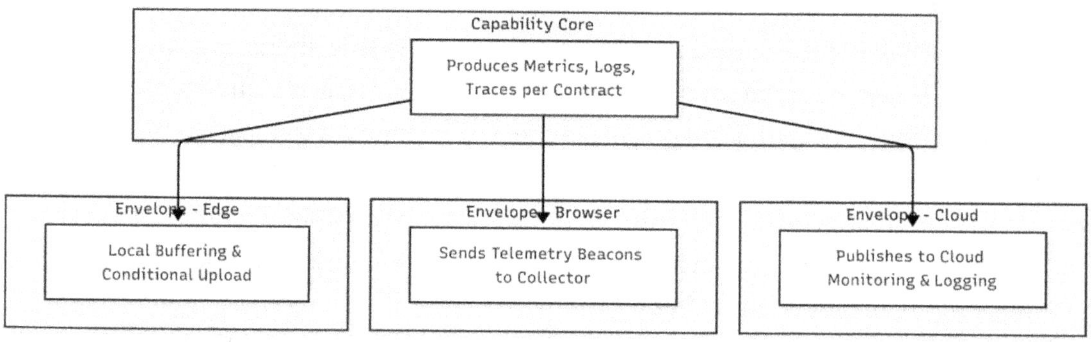

Figure 3-6. *The capability core produces observability data in a consistent format. Each envelope adapts the output to the runtime's available infrastructure*

Real-world examples outside healthcare follow a similar pattern. A video analytics capability running in the cloud may emit detailed GPU utilization metrics. The same capability running in the browser cannot access GPU hardware counters, so it estimates performance based on frame processing times and memory usage. Both sets of metrics adhere to the contract, providing operators with comparable data without sacrificing portability. Another example is predictive maintenance, where an anomaly detection capability on an industrial edge device logs both regular readings and detected anomalies. The edge buffer stores logs locally and transmits them only when the network is stable. In the cloud version, logs are streamed in nearly real-time to a central dashboard. The contract guarantees that both environments produce identical alert formats so downstream alerting systems do not need special-case logic.

Diagnostics follow the same pattern. If a capability fails, the diagnostic information must be structured uniformly across all runtimes so automated tools can process it. In UMA, the envelope might gather additional runtime-specific details, like stack traces in the browser or container logs in the cloud, but the core diagnostic payload is always consistent. This enables cross-runtime troubleshooting without specialized tools for each environment.

By making observability a contract-level concern, UMA ensures that monitoring and diagnostics stay consistent and reliable no matter where the capability runs. This consistency lowers operational risk, accelerates incident response, and helps teams measure performance and quality confidently across an increasingly diverse set of runtimes.

Versioning and Backward Compatibility

Versioning in UMA is not just a release engineering task; it is a crucial part of maintaining system integrity across multiple runtimes and deployment scenarios. In a traditional single-stack application, a new version typically replaces the old one entirely, and backward compatibility is managed in code or overlooked if the upgrade process is tightly controlled. UMA operates in a very different environment. A single capability may be running in a browser for one group of users, on an edge device for another, and in a cloud function for yet another. These deployments are not always upgraded simultaneously. Some may be offline for extended periods, others might be constrained by regulatory validation cycles, and still others may be deliberately delayed for A/B testing. Without a clear versioning strategy, updating one deployment could lead to silent failures in another.

This is why UMA makes versioning an explicit part of the capability contract. Every contract includes a version identifier and compatibility guarantees. The version isn't just a label; it signals to other capabilities or clients how to interpret the contract and what changes to expect. UMA promotes a semantic versioning approach.

- **Major version** changes indicate breaking changes to the contract that require consumers to update.
- **Minor version** changes add backward-compatible functionality or data fields.
- **Patch version** changes fix bugs or make internal improvements without affecting the contract's external behavior.

With semantic versioning, teams can quickly determine if a new capability version is safe to use without code modifications or if a coordinated rollout is needed. This is important in UMA because capabilities are not just internal modules; they are independently deployable, runtime-portable units that may be managed by different teams or third parties.

Backward compatibility in UMA is protected by contract evolution rules. These include:

- Never remove or rename required fields in inputs or outputs.
- Making new fields optional and providing sensible defaults.
- Retaining deprecated behaviors until all dependent capabilities have migrated.
- Documenting changes in a machine-readable format so automation can enforce compatibility rules during build and deployment.

The **reason** is apparent: without these guarantees, cross-runtime deployments would be fragile. Imagine a cloud capability sending data to an edge device that still runs a 6-month-old version. If the new version silently changes a field name, the edge device might reject the data or misinterpret it, leading to operational errors. With UMA's approach, this scenario is avoided because the versioning rules make changes visible and enforce safe fallbacks.

The envelope plays a key role in easing transitions. Since it adapts the capability to the runtime, the envelope can mediate differences between versions during rollout. For example, a browser envelope can transform the output of a newly upgraded cloud capability into the older format expected by the current browser client. This allows upgrades to be staged gradually, rather than requiring all runtimes to switch at once.

Consider a logistics platform with a route optimization capability. It runs on truck-mounted edge devices, warehouse cloud systems, and driver mobile apps. If a new version introduces real-time traffic data into the output, the contract specifies that if this data is unavailable or unused in older deployments, the capability must still return a valid route. The envelopes for older runtimes insert a placeholder value for the traffic field, ensuring the data structure remains intact. This means the new cloud deployment can go live immediately without breaking the edge devices that will not be upgraded for weeks.

Another example comes from a financial trading platform. A market data processing feature adds a new "market volatility" field. Minor versioning indicates this is an additive, backward-compatible change. Clients who do not recognize the field simply ignore it. Older envelopes remove the field entirely before passing data downstream, preventing unexpected parsing errors in legacy systems. This approach also enables safer rollouts and faster rollbacks. Multiple versions can run concurrently for testing. Because compatibility rules are machine-readable, automation can prevent deploying a breaking change to a runtime still depending on an older version. Rollbacks become simpler because the capability contract clearly states which earlier versions remain valid and supported. In UMA, semantic versioning and strict contract evolution rules are not just best practices; they are the foundation of safe, incremental system evolution. They allow capabilities to improve without breaking trust, letting the entire system evolve at the pace of its slowest, most constrained runtime without hindering innovation in the faster ones.

Governance and Policy Enforcement Across Runtimes

In a traditional application running on a single stack, governance typically relies on coding standards, code reviews, and internal deployment checklists. In UMA, where capabilities operate across browsers, edge devices, and cloud infrastructure, governance must be more explicit, portable, and enforceable. A policy effective in one runtime should be reliably applied across all others without dependence on runtime-specific tools or manual enforcement.

Governance in UMA is articulated through the capability contract and enforced both at build time and runtime. This contract specifies not just functional behavior but also rules concerning security, compliance, performance, and operational visibility. These rules are machine-readable, enabling automated validation within the delivery pipeline. This approach minimizes reliance on tribal knowledge or ad hoc processes, ensuring every capability, wherever it runs, adheres to consistent standards.

This is crucial because the variety of runtimes in UMA presents both opportunities and risks. For instance, a capability deployed in the browser might need to comply with privacy regulations like GDPR by anonymizing user data before transmission. The same capability in the cloud could require additional encryption standards for data at rest. The capability contract can specify both requirements, while the envelopes for each runtime guarantee their implementation. Automated validation prevents any runtime-specific shortcuts from bypassing these rules.

The reason is simple: without runtime-agnostic governance, organizations risk drifting into inconsistent practices, where some deployments meet critical requirements and others do not. This inconsistency could lead to data breaches, compliance violations, or degraded performance, which may be hard to diagnose if it only occurs in specific runtimes. UMA's approach embeds governance directly into the architecture, ensuring policy compliance is not optional or reliant on human oversight.

Consider a healthcare imaging platform that processes X-ray scans. The same image analysis capability operates on hospital servers, portable diagnostic devices in rural clinics, and as part of a browser-based remote consultation tool. Governance rules in the capability contract specify that all patient-identifiable metadata must be removed from the image before analysis and that diagnostic results must be digitally signed. The envelopes for each runtime enforce these rules automatically: the hospital server strips metadata and signs results before sending them to the medical records system; the portable device does the same before uploading to the central review platform; and the browser tool applies the same steps before transmitting to the consulting physician. Policy compliance is not left to each development team's discretion; it is built into the system.

Governance also extends to performance and reliability requirements. A media streaming capability might have a contract requirement for a maximum startup latency of 200 milliseconds and a minimum throughput threshold. The browser envelope might meet this by prefetching resources, while the edge device envelope might use a local cache. The governance layer checks that these thresholds are met in every runtime, preventing a deployment from going live if it cannot meet the agreed performance contract.

Policy enforcement can be proactive or reactive. Proactive enforcement occurs at build time, where automated tools validate the capability's code and configuration against the governance rules. Reactive enforcement happens at runtime, where the envelope monitors actual behavior and halts or limits execution if the policy is violated. For example, a data export capability might be automatically suspended if it exceeds its allocated bandwidth budget, preventing runaway costs or service degradation.

Codifying governance in contracts and automating enforcement, UMA eliminates the reliance on manual oversight, reduces the risk of policy drift between runtimes, and ensures operational, compliance, and performance standards are consistently applied across the entire deployment spectrum. This makes it possible to innovate rapidly without sacrificing control and to expand into new runtimes or markets without re-engineering governance from scratch.

Self-Describing Contracts

Interfaces vs. Contracts

In software engineering, the term "interface" refers to nearly any boundary, from a Java interface to an HTTP API. In strongly typed languages, an interface is a compile-time feature that defines the methods or fields a component must have for communication with another element. Interfaces assist developers in detecting errors early, improving tooling, and making refactoring safer within a single codebase. They are crucial for teams building software in one language and runtime. However, once execution crosses process, runtime, or organizational boundaries, these guarantees no longer hold. For example, a TypeScript interface provides no protection once a request leaves the browser and reaches a Java-based service. Similarly, a gRPC interface specifies message structure but cannot ensure the service meets performance, security, or logging standards. Interfaces are static; they do not verify themselves or enforce governance at runtime.

UMA's **contracts** function at a different level. A contract is a machine-readable, runtime-verified agreement that specifies *how* a capability must behave, not just *what* its method signature looks like. A contract includes the operational truth of the capability, such as

- The whole structure and meaning of inputs and outputs
- Error models, including enumerated error codes and recovery strategies
- Version identifiers and backward compatibility guarantees
- Execution metadata such as latency expectations, throughput guarantees, and resource usage limits
- Security, compliance, and governance rules that the capability must meet in every runtime

Contracts are **active metadata** that travel with the capability as part of their package. Any runtime capable of executing that capability, whether a browser, edge device, container, or serverless function, can load the contract, validate it, and enforce its constraints. This is why UMA treats contracts as first-class citizens: they are not a side document but the definitive runtime truth. Why does this matter? Because UMA's goal is portability without hidden dependencies. If all you have is an interface, portability ends where the compiler's reach does. The runtime using it might have no idea about performance budgets, governance rules, or data handling requirements until it fails in production. With contracts, all that information is explicit, machine-readable, and enforceable before and during execution.

Consider a few examples:

- **Payment Processing**: An interface might define `processPayment(amount, currency, cardDetails)`. The contract specifies that transactions under $500 must complete within 200 ms, that card details must be encrypted using AES-256 (Advanced Encryption Standard with a 256-bit key, the current gold standard for symmetric encryption, chosen for its resistance to brute-force attacks and its adoption by governments and financial institutions worldwide as the minimum acceptable standard for sensitive data at rest and in transit), that certain fraud checks must run, and that every transaction must be recorded in an immutable audit log. Without the contract, a payment service running in an edge runtime might unknowingly skip encryption or miss latency targets.
- **Video Streaming**: An interface may expose `getStream(videoId)`. The contract defines minimum bitrates, fallback rules for degraded network conditions, regional content restrictions, and DRM enforcement (Digital Rights Management technical controls that restrict how digital content can be copied, shared, or accessed, used by media companies to enforce licensing agreements and prevent unauthorized redistribution). This guarantees that the same capability functions reliably whether it runs in a smart TV app, a browser tab, or an edge CDN node.
- **IoT Sensor Data**: An interface might define `getTemperature()`. The contract specifies acceptable error margins, reporting intervals, calibration requirements, and behavior when data is unavailable. This allows a runtime in a factory gateway to validate that incoming readings from a sensor are within tolerances before trusting them.

- **Translation Service**: An interface might define `translate(document, targetLanguage)`. The contract adds latency limits per document size, fallback behavior when a language model is unavailable, rules for handling unsupported characters, and privacy requirements for temporary storage.

The difference becomes even more evident when considering **governance and portability together**. In UMA, a capability can be deployed in a new runtime without custom wiring because the contract explicitly defines what the runtime needs to do, such as validating inputs, allocating resources, enforcing security, and adhering to operational constraints. Without an agreement, these responsibilities are scattered across tribal knowledge, wiki pages, and ad hoc runtime configurations, all of which are susceptible to drift and human error. Interfaces are crucial for building capabilities. Contracts are vital for running them safely, predictably, and portably across any runtime. UMA is built around the understanding that, in a heterogeneous, cross-runtime system, the latter is even more critical.

Elements of a UMA Contract

A UMA contract is more than an API description. It is a complete specification of how a capability behaves in any runtime and under any allowed operating condition. Each element of the contract exists for a reason, either to enable safe interoperability, to make performance predictable, or to guarantee compliance and governance across environments.

1. **Input and Output Types**

   Every contract clearly specifies the exact structure and meaning of the data it takes in and outputs. This is similar to an interface but extends further by defining constraints that can be checked during runtime. For example, a route-planning feature might accept a list of waypoints with latitude and longitude in WGS84 format and could reject any request with more than 200 waypoints. The output might include an array of route segments, each with an estimated travel time, cost, and reliability score. These rules are embedded in the contract, so any runtime can verify them before running, preventing wasted resources on invalid requests.

2. **Error Models**

   UMA contracts list all expected error conditions and their meanings. Instead of just returning an error code, the contract explains the error's cause, whether it can be recovered, and which retry or fallback actions are suitable. For example, a machine learning inference capability might define `MODEL_NOT_AVAILABLE` as a temporary error with a recommended retry after 30 seconds, while `INVALID_INPUT` is a permanent error that should never be retried. This enables envelopes to handle the mistakes intelligently without hardcoding logic for each runtime.

3. **Version Compatibility**

   Each UMA contract includes a version field along with compatibility guarantees. This might use semantic versioning to indicate whether changes are backward-compatible, breaking, or additive. For example, a contract might guarantee that a new optional field will not disrupt existing clients, but a change to an existing field's data type will require a significant version increment. This is crucial in UMA because capabilities may be upgraded in one runtime while older versions continue running elsewhere.

4. **Execution Metadata**

   Contracts specify non-functional requirements essential for runtime orchestration. This includes expected latency, throughput, memory consumption, CPU needs, and trust level (e.g., whether the capability can operate in an untrusted browser environment or requires a secure enclave). For example, a financial risk calculation capability might need at least 2 GB of RAM and must complete within 500 ms. A runtime scheduler uses this data to determine whether to execute the capability locally, offload it to the edge, or send it to the cloud.

5. **Governance and Compliance Rules**

   Contracts define operational policies that must be enforced during runtime. These include encryption standards, data residency restrictions, or logging requirements. For example, a health record analysis feature might require that all processing take place within the EU and that no personally identifiable information be stored permanently. This ensures compliance regardless of where the feature is deployed.

6. **Optional x-Extensions**

   UMA supports custom contract fields through `x-`extensions. These enable teams to add domain-specific metadata without disrupting interoperability. For example, a retail recommendation capability might include an `x-seasonality` field indicating the relevant seasons or events (e.g., holiday sales) for which it is optimized or an `x-ml-model-version` to specify the exact model in use.

In UMA, each of these elements is machine-readable, validated at runtime, and discoverable without reviewing source code or external documentation. This ensures capabilities are portable while maintaining control, as every runtime can reliably determine what a capability requires, what it will produce, and how to interact with it safely.

The Contract Schema Format

If a UMA contract is the agreement, then its contract schema is essentially the language used to define it. Each capability within UMA articulates its contract through a structured, machine-readable format, enabling any runtime, tool, or governance process to parse, validate, and act on it automatically, without needing custom integrations. UMA's contract schema leverages well-established standards like JSON Schema for type validation and uses OpenAPI-like conventions (OpenAPI is an industry-standard specification format formerly known as Swagger for describing REST APIs in a machine-readable way, defining endpoints, request/response schemas, authentication methods, and error codes in a single structured document that tools can use to generate client SDKs, documentation, and validation logic automatically) to describe operations. It also extends these standards with additional features to suit its specific needs, runtime-specific and governance-specific metadata that most API description formats leave out.

At its core, the schema captures the elements:

- **Inputs and Outputs**: Defined with JSON Schema type declarations, including constraints such as value ranges, array lengths, and required fields
- **Error Models**: Enumerated with clear codes, categories (recoverable or not), and recommended handling strategies
- **Versioning**: Semantic version identifiers and compatibility guarantees
- **Execution Metadata**: Structured fields for latency expectations, CPU/memory requirements, concurrency limits, and trust classifications
- **Governance Rules**: Data residency, encryption, logging, and other compliance constraints

Beyond these, UMA contracts support **custom `x-`extensions**. These are namespaced fields that allow teams to embed domain-specific metadata without breaking interoperability. For example:

- `x-ml-model-version` to indicate the specific machine learning model used by an inference capability.
- `x-energy-profile` for a capability running on IoT devices, indicating its average and peak power consumption.
- `x-business-priority` to help orchestrators schedule high-priority capabilities ahead of non-critical ones.

These extensions are not just comments. They are parsed, stored, and available for orchestration, monitoring, or governance automation. If a new runtime type emerges, such as a secure execution environment with specialized APIs, teams can add an `x-runtime-binding` section without changing the core schema specification.

One of UMA's schema format strengths is its **separation of core and environment-specific metadata**. The logic for the capability is described once, and runtime bindings are contained in an envelope or in x-sections that can evolve independently. This allows UMA to remain flexible with current deployment models. WebAssembly may be a primary portability target now, but if a new universal runtime format emerges, contracts will stay valid with minimal adjustments.

An example from a real-world scenario helps illustrate this. Imagine a **parcel tracking capability** used by logistics companies worldwide. Its contract might define

- **Input**: `trackingId` (string, format: UUID), `locale` (string, ISO 639-1).
- **Output**: `status` (enum: "in transit," "delivered," "delayed"), `lastUpdated` (date-time), and optional `location` (lat/long).
- **Error Models**: `NOT_FOUND` (permanent), `TEMPORARY_UNAVAILABLE` (retry after 60 seconds).
- **Execution Metadata**: Latency ≤ 150 ms, memory ≤ 128 MB.
- **Governance**: Must comply with GDPR (General Data Protection Regulation, the European Union's comprehensive data privacy law that gives individuals rights over their personal data and requires organizations to handle it lawfully, transparently, and securely; it applies to any system processing data of EU residents, regardless of where the system is hosted) when handling customer addresses.
- **Extensions**: `x-partner-carrier-code` for integrations with regional carriers, `x-cache-policy` for specifying how long results may be cached at the edge

Because the schema is machine-readable and standardized, a runtime at an edge distribution center can load the same contract as a cloud orchestrator in another country and execute the capability with consistent guarantees. The schema format makes UMA contracts **self-sustaining**: they are not just documentation but the operational blueprint. They enable UMA's "write once, run anywhere" vision to be viable across different runtimes.

Semantic Versioning and Contextual Changelogs

Capabilities in UMA are designed to operate across multiple environments: browsers, edge devices, cloud runtimes, and sometimes even offline or intermittently connected settings. This creates a unique challenge for evolution. A change made to a capability in one environment can affect dozens of others, some of which may still be running older versions. Without a disciplined approach to versioning and change communication, compatibility issues are likely.

Semantic versioning (semver) provides a shared language for expressing the impact of changes. In UMA, every contract carries a version identifier in the form `MAJOR.MINOR.PATCH`, where

- **MAJOR** increments signal breaking changes that require consumers to update their integrations.
- **MINOR** increments add functionality in a backward-compatible way.
- **PATCH** increments fix bugs or make internal changes without altering the contract's behavior.

For example, a payment capability moving from `1.3.2` to `1.4.0` might add a new optional field for `customerEmail`. Consumers who do not use this field can continue working without changes. However, a move from `1.4.0` to `2.0.0` might alter how errors are reported, requiring all consumers to update their handling logic. While semantic versioning addresses the *what* of change impact, UMA also needs the *why* and *how;* this is where **contextual changelogs** come in. A contextual changelog is machine-readable metadata that explains

- Which contract elements changed
- Whether the change is additive, breaking, or internal
- Which runtime environments or bindings are affected
- Migration guidance for consumers

This is crucial because not every change has the same impact in every runtime. Adding a new optional parameter to an HTTP binding might be backward compatible for web clients but could break an IoT runtime with a fixed request payload format. Contextual changelogs enable orchestrators and governance systems to evaluate whether a capability upgrade is safe in a specific environment before deployment.

Consider a **parcel tracking capability** used globally:

- **Version `1.2.0`**: Adds a `carrierName` field to the output. Backward-compatible in all runtimes.
- **Version `1.3.0`**: Adds real-time GPS tracking. Backward-compatible in browsers and mobile apps, but requires an additional permission in IoT gateways.

- **Version `2.0.0`**: Changes the `status` field from a free-text string to a fixed enum. This is a breaking change everywhere and requires migration before rollout.

Because UMA contracts are self-describing and carry these contextual changelogs, an orchestrator can automatically

1. Detect that `carrierName` is safe to roll out immediately
2. Delay real-time GPS tracking in IoT until permissions are updated Block deployment of version `2.0.0` until all dependent systems are updated to handle the new enum type

This level of version intelligence ensures that UMA's portability does not compromise stability. Capabilities can develop, but their development remains transparent, intentional, and tailored to the realities of diverse runtime environments.

Contracts As Active Metadata

Most software systems treat API specifications or interface definitions as static documentation that describes behavior without any runtim*e* action. In contrast, UMA adopts a different strategy. Its contracts are not just passive references but **active metadata** that engage directly in execution, orchestration, and governance. An active contract is machine-readable, discoverable, and enforceable in real time. It is loaded into the runtime along with the capability, validated before execution, and used by orchestration layers to inform decisions. This approach shifts the contract from a simple design-time artifact to a flexible runtime control mechanism. Because UMA operates across diverse environments, this change is crucial. A browser runtime might need to determine if a capability can run within a 100 ms latency budget. An IoT gateway should confirm that a capability will not exceed its 256 MB memory limit. A serverless platform should schedule capabilities in a way that respects both their concurrency limits and their trust classifications. All of these decisions rely on the information contained in the contract.

Practical Implications of Active Contracts in UMA

- **Dynamic Discovery**: Runtimes can query a contract registry to find capabilities that meet specific criteria, such as "image classification, runs in less than 200 ms, and can execute in untrusted environments." This allows the creation of new workflows without manual integration.

- **Policy Enforcement**: Contracts include governance rules (e.g., encryption requirements, data residency) that can be automatically validated before execution. If a capability's contract states it can only store data in the EU, a scheduler in North America can prevent its deployment.
- **Runtime Adaptation**: Because execution metadata is explicit, runtimes can adjust behavior on the fly. For example, if a capability's contract states that it can switch to a lower quality mode under heavy load, the orchestrator can make that switch without developer intervention.
- **AI-Assisted Composition**: When capabilities describe themselves in a structured way, AI systems can reason about compatibility. An AI orchestrator could analyze multiple UMA contracts and figure out how to connect capabilities to achieve a higher-level goal, all without human-written glue code.

Imagine a logistics company building a same-day delivery workflow. Using UMA contracts as active metadata, their orchestrator can

1. Discover a **parcel tracking** capability that meets latency requirements for real-time updates
2. Pair it with a **traffic analysis** capability that can run on an edge node near the customer
3. Add a **delivery ETA prediction** capability that respects privacy laws in the destination country
4. Validate that all three capabilities' contracts are compatible in terms of data formats, error models, and latency budgets

This occurs without a single developer manually verifying the integration rules. The contracts themselves *serve* as the integration rules. By making contracts executable within the runtime's decision-making process, UMA transforms them into a dynamic layer of the system. They are no longer just a shared understanding between teams; they become the operational DNA that allows a heterogeneous, cross-runtime system to behave predictably and evolve safely.

Governance Practices for Contracts

In UMA, contracts are not just static documents stored in a repository; they are dynamic agreements that define how capabilities behave across every runtime they operate in. Because these contracts are active metadata, their quality and consistency directly influence system stability, portability, and compliance. Without proper governance, contracts can drift, become inconsistent, or fail to accurately reflect the actual behavior of the capability, leading to runtime failures, security gaps, or regulatory violations.

Why governance matters in UMA? In a traditional microservices setup, a contract mismatch between services might cause a failed API call or break a feature. In UMA, the stakes are higher because a single capability could be deployed in dozens of runtimes, each enforcing its contract rules automatically. If a contract is wrong or incomplete, that error will be propagated and implemented across the entire ecosystem.

Core Governance Practices in UMA

1. **Contract Registries:** UMA depends on centralized or federated registries where all contracts are published and versioned. These registries are machine-readable and accessible to both humans and automation tools. They facilitate discovery, compatibility checks, and automated validation before deployment. In many cases, they also serve as the source of truth for AI-assisted orchestration.

2. **Contract Stewards:** Each contract has an owner or steward responsible for its accuracy, completeness, and alignment with organizational standards. The steward ensures that updates follow semantic versioning rules, that contextual changelogs are maintained, and that runtime metadata remains accurate. This role is vital in multi-team or multi-organization environments where contract drift can occur quickly.

3. **Cross-Team Review Boards:** In larger UMA ecosystems, governance involves formal review boards that assess new or updated contracts before they are published. These assessments focus on backward compatibility, compliance with security and privacy policies, and alignment with established performance and reliability standards. This is especially important when capabilities are exposed across organizational boundaries.

4. **Automated Diffing and Validation:** UMA governance workflows include automated tools that diff contract versions and flag changes for review. These tools check for:
    - Breaking changes are not reflected in the version number.
    - Missing or inconsistent execution metadata.
    - Alterations that violate compliance rules (e.g., removing encryption requirements).
    - Automated diffing ensures that human reviewers focus on high-impact changes rather than manually scanning for every field difference.
5. **Lifecycle Management:** Governance processes also cover the entire lifecycle of a contract, including deprecation policies, sunset timelines, and automated notifications to dependent systems. For example, if a capability is scheduled for retirement, its contract might include an `x-deprecation-date` field to help orchestrators plan migration well in advance.

Example: Why Governance Prevents Systemic Risk

Imagine a **real-time translation** capability deployed in browsers, mobile apps, and call center servers. If its contract is updated to require a GPU without proper governance review, mobile runtimes without GPU acceleration might fail silently or degrade service quality. With UMA's governance practices:

- The automated diff would flag the GPU requirement as a new runtime constraint.
- The review board would determine its impact on mobile deployments.
- The steward could create an alternate contract variant for non-GPU environments or delay rollout until compatible runtimes are ready.

In UMA, governance is not an afterthought; it is the mechanism that keeps a distributed, cross-runtime system aligned and predictable even as capabilities evolve. Contracts may be the operational DNA, but governance is the quality control system that ensures that DNA remains healthy.

Hands-On Takeaways

A few years before UMA was officially established, I was involved in a project for a national retail chain that aimed for a unified analytics view across all its sales channels. The goal was straightforward: gather transaction data from in-store POS systems, the e-commerce backend, and several third-party marketplaces, then create dashboards for regional managers and headquarters. We developed it the way most teams did at the time: define some REST APIs, document them in a wiki, agree on formats in a few meetings, and begin coding. The integration worked perfectly in our controlled staging environment. But once it went live, reality set in.

The "Before UMA" Reality

- The in-store POS terminals were running on an older, vendor-locked runtime. When we added a new `discountCode` field to the transaction schema, those devices silently dropped it, causing reconciliation mismatches.
- The e-commerce platform team rolled out a new error code, `PAYMENT_TIMEOUT`, without warning. Our marketplace integration gateway didn't recognize it, so it retried aggressively until it hit partner API rate limits, ironically causing *more* failures.
- A cloud analytics component assumed timestamps were UTC, while POS terminals were sending them in local time without offsets. That one bug corrupted quarterly sales figures for two regions before it was caught.
- Changes often arrived "in surprise style." By the time a problem appeared, it had already propagated across three different environments, making rollbacks painful and expensive.

We spent more time firefighting than improving the system. Every "small change" felt like a new risk.

The first UMA-based project we did in that environment was an **inventory optimization feature**. The goal was different, but the technical challenge was the same: to run in all those environments without breaking when something changed.

The difference was that this time we started with a UMA contract, which meant

- **Strict Input/Output Schemas**: Each field had a defined type, allowed range, and business meaning. The contract validation layer in every runtime rejected invalid data before it reached the capability logic.
- **Error Models with Recovery Guidance**: Instead of ad hoc status codes, every error was categorized (recoverable, permanent, policy violation) and included an action plan. This enabled the orchestrator to retry only when appropriate and fail fast otherwise.
- **Execution Metadata**: The contract specified latency budgets, CPU/memory requirements, and supported runtime classes. If POS terminals couldn't handle a new forecasting model locally, the orchestrator sent that workload to the cloud without human intervention.
- **Contextual Changelogs**: Each version update included machine-readable notes explaining what changed, which runtimes it affected, and migration steps. When adding "predictive replenishment" to the inventory model, the orchestrator knew to roll it out to the cloud and newer store kiosks first, leaving older terminals on the stable branch until they were patched.

The Outcome:

- The rollout was predictable. No runtime tried to run a capability it couldn't handle.
- Failures were rare, and when they happened, the cause was clear because the contract defined both expected inputs and failure conditions.
- The capability could evolve in weeks instead of months. We could release a new feature to the cloud, pilot it in high-traffic stores, and hold it back from legacy devices without creating forks in the codebase.

The Lesson: Self-describing contracts in UMA eliminate the guesswork from integration. They enable systems to communicate without relying on shared assumptions. They make changes a controlled process, not a risk. And once you experience the stability and speed this provides, the old way seems reckless.

Event-Driven Coordination (≈ 5–6 Pages)

What Event-Driven Architecture Means in UMA

Event-Driven Architecture (EDA) isn't a new concept, but in UMA, it takes on a more intentional role. Fundamentally, EDA involves systems communicating via events indicating that something has occurred rather than through direct, synchronous calls. Instead of one service calling another and waiting for a reply, it emits an event and continues. Other services interested in that event can react, but the producer doesn't need to know who they are or how they operate.

In UMA, EDA fits naturally because capabilities are built to be loosely coupled, portable, and composable across various runtimes. If every interaction were a direct call, changes in a capability's location, runtime, or availability could cascade through the system. With events, these dependencies are reduced: a producer only needs to publish according to its **event contract**, and any compatible consumer, whether in a browser, on an edge node, or in the cloud, can respond.

The basic roles remain familiar:

- **Producers** publish events when something of interest happens, such as "inventory depleted," "payment authorized," or "forecast model updated."
- **Consumers** subscribe to events and perform actions in response, like restocking an item, shipping an order, or refreshing a dashboard.
- **Routers or brokers** handle the delivery of events from producers to consumers, often with filtering, transformation, or buffering.

What changes in UMA are the **contract-driven nature** of these roles. Every event type is defined by a machine-readable contract that specifies its schema, meaning, allowed values, error handling, and runtime characteristics. This makes events discoverable, versioned, and governed in the same way as service capabilities.

For example, an "orderPlaced" event in UMA is not just a JSON blob sent over a message queue; it is a versioned, documented product in the event catalog. Any runtime that knows how to interpret that contract can consume it safely, even if it is using a completely different messaging broker than the producer.

Why Asynchronous Events Improve Scalability and Maintainability

Asynchronous eventing is more than just a design choice in UMA; it is an essential architectural requirement for enabling cross-runtime coordination at scale. In environments where capabilities might run in browsers, edge devices, serverless platforms, or containerized clusters, the ability to decouple execution in time and space is what distinguishes a responsive system from a fragile one.

Scalability Without Choke Points

Synchronous calls create a dependency chain: the producer must wait for the consumer, and the consumer might in turn be waiting for another service. This serializes work and increases delays. With asynchronous events, producers emit and move on, freeing themselves from the consumer's speed, availability, or runtime type. Consider an online retail promotion that triggers **tens of thousands of orders** in minutes. In a synchronous design, the payment process would have to wait for inventory checks, fraud detection, loyalty program updates, and shipment creation, all within the same execution flow. Any slowdown in one stage delays the entire process. In UMA's async model, each step is a separate capability responding to the "orderPlaced" event independently. The payment confirmation can be sent to the customer in milliseconds, while inventory restocking and loyalty points updates happen in parallel, possibly on completely different runtimes.

Maintainability in a Heterogeneous Runtime Ecosystem

In traditional systems, service changes often require updating both sides of the interaction. In UMA's asynchronous model, producers and consumers are linked by **event contracts** rather than direct code dependencies. As long as the contract remains valid, either side can modify its implementation, location, or scaling profile without the other needing to adapt. For example, replacing a cloud-hosted "recommendation engine" capability with a new on-device inference model for mobile apps is simple: both versions use the same "userSessionStarted" event. The change is invisible to the producers and any other consumers.

Enabling Parallel Evolution

Asynchronous eventing allows capabilities to develop independently, which is crucial when dealing with mixed release schedules. In UMA, a browser-based capability might be updated weekly, while an embedded edge capability only receives updates quarterly due to certification standards. Async delivery and contract stability ensure both can coexist without blocking each other's roadmaps.

Operational Resilience Through Decoupling

Failures in synchronous chains often cascade if one call fails; upstream services must handle the failure immediately, often in the middle of a user request. With async events, the broker can buffer messages, and consumers can retry on their own schedules. In UMA, this is especially important for edge deployments that may operate in **environments with intermittent connectivity**, such as ships at sea, rural IoT gateways, or mobile workforces. Events can be queued locally and delivered once connectivity is restored, without forcing upstream components to stall or retry aggressively.

The Stake If You Ignore Async

Without asynchronous eventing, a UMA system becomes more fragile and more complex to move. Runtimes with inconsistent performance may cause bottlenecks, scaling becomes more complicated and depends on tight coordination between teams, and upgrades risk disrupting entire workflows. Over time, the architecture drifts toward the very "big ball of mud" UMA aims to prevent.

Introducing the Event Contract Catalog Architecture (ECCA)

In UMA, events are not just messages; they are durable, reusable assets. That is why we sometimes use a model called the **Event Contract Catalog Architecture (ECCA)**, which can be seen as a reference design for managing events with the same level of rigor as services. ECCA isn't the only possible approach, but it is a clear example that illustrates the principles UMA promotes: ownership, discoverability, governance, and runtime neutrality.

Why ECCA Exists

In most event-driven systems, event definitions are usually informal. Schemas might be stored in a wiki, a shared repository, or within code comments. Often, there is no single location to view all available events, identify their owners, or track their change history. When multiple teams and runtimes are involved, as is common in UMA, this lack of structure can lead to silent failures, unclear responsibilities, and duplicated effort. UMA's contract-first philosophy also applies here. Just as capabilities have **self-describing service contracts**, events should have **self-describing event contracts** that make them safe to evolve and easy to consume across different runtimes.

The ECCA Model

ECCA proposes that events be treated as products in their own right, with

- **Ownership**: A named steward or owning team responsible for keeping the event contract accurate and up to date.
- **Rich Metadata**: Not just a schema, but also delivery guarantees, latency expectations, retention policies, and security classifications.
- **Versioning Discipline**: Breaking changes increment the major version, backward-compatible changes increment the minor version, and metadata-only updates increment the patch version.
- **Discoverability**: A central, machine-readable catalog where all events are listed, searchable by name, version, tags, and capabilities they relate to.
- **Governance Hooks**: Automated checks that prevent a producer from emitting an event that violates its contract and prevent consumers from subscribing to incompatible versions.

Example: Before and After

Before ECCA, a logistics platform had a simple "shipmentDispatched" event. Over time, different teams extended it, adding fields for `carrierCode`, `estimatedArrival`, and `priorityLevel`. Some of these fields were added without documentation, and others used different types (`priorityLevel` as a number in one producer and a string in another). Consumers built workarounds that were brittle and environment-specific.

With ECCA in place, the same event became a governed product:

- The event contract clearly defined each field, its type, meaning, and valid range.
- Metadata specified that estimatedArrival must be in ISO 8601 UTC format (e.g., 2024-11-15T14:30:00Z, where the T separates date from time, and the trailing Z indicates UTC timezone, a globally unambiguous representation that avoids the timezone confusion that plagues informal date formats).
- The owning team controlled version increments and documented every change in the catalog's machine-readable changelog.
- Consumers could query the catalog to see all compatible versions and register their subscriptions automatically.

Not the Only Path

ECCA is a pattern, not a strict rule. UMA can employ lighter approaches in smaller systems or leverage existing catalog tools like AsyncAPI (an open specification for describing event-driven APIs; it is to asynchronous messaging what OpenAPI is to REST, providing a standard format for documenting event schemas, channels, and delivery protocols), CloudEvents (a CNCF-backed specification that defines a common, vendor-neutral format for event metadata, making events from different systems interoperable without custom parsing), or schema registries integrated with platforms such as Confluent or AWS EventBridge. The key point is the **principle**: in UMA, events are portable, governed assets with clear contracts, regardless of which broker or runtime they pass through. By adopting an event catalog, whether ECCA or another UMA system, organizations can safely evolve their event ecosystem even when producers and consumers are spread across browsers, edge devices, serverless functions, and long-lasting cloud services.

Event Contracts and UMA's Runtime Agnosticism

One of UMA's main promises is that a capability can operate in any suitable runtime environment, such as a browser, edge node, container, or serverless function, without altering its core logic. This promise also applies to events. In many event-driven systems, the event broker is a strict dependency: producers and consumers are explicitly designed for Kafka, RabbitMQ, NATS, AWS EventBridge, or another broker. Switching the broker involves changing the code.

UMA prevents this lock-in by making the event contract the stable boundary and using adapters to connect to specific broker implementations. The capability never interacts directly with Kafka APIs (Apache Kafka is a high-throughput, distributed event streaming platform widely used for real-time data pipelines and stream processing) or relies on RabbitMQ-specific routing rules (RabbitMQ is a message broker that implements the AMQP protocol, commonly used for task queues, work distribution, and reliable point-to-point or publish-subscribe messaging). Instead, it communicates through an event abstraction layer defined by the contract.

- The schema describes the event payload.
- Metadata specifies delivery guarantees of at-least-once (the message will be delivered but may be duplicated if a failure occurs mid-delivery; consumers must handle duplicates), exactly-once (the message is delivered precisely once, regardless of failures, the strongest and most expensive guarantee), or at-most-once (the message is sent once and not retried; some events may be lost) along with ordering requirements and performance targets.
- The runtime adapter handles the translation between this abstract definition and the specific broker's API or protocol.

Why This Matters

- **Portability**: A "paymentAuthorized" event produced in a browser using a WebSocket adapter can be consumed by a service running in AWS Lambda through an SNS/SQS adapter without either side knowing what the other is using.
- **Migration Safety**: If a team decides to move from RabbitMQ to Kafka, they only need to swap the adapter in the deployment configuration, not rewrite the event producer or consumer.
- **Experimentation**: Teams can test different brokers in staging without impacting production capabilities.

Example Scenario

An IoT monitoring system for industrial equipment needs to send "temperatureThresholdExceeded" events. In the factory, these events are transmitted via MQTT (Message Queuing Telemetry Transport, a lightweight publish-subscribe messaging protocol designed for constrained devices and low-bandwidth, high-latency networks; it is widely used in IoT deployments because it is efficient enough to run on microcontrollers with minimal power consumption) over a local network. In the cloud, they are processed via Kafka for real-time analytics. With UMA's event abstraction, the same capability contract works in both environments: the edge runtime uses an MQTT adapter, and the cloud runtime uses a Kafka adapter. The core capability logic for validating temperature readings and generating alerts remains unchanged.

The Role of Shadow Mode and Telemetry

Because UMA separates event definition from the broker, it can also run shadow consumers, additional subscribers that receive the same events as production consumers and process them in parallel, but whose outputs are discarded rather than acted upon that subscribe to events simultaneously without disrupting the central processing. Shadow consumers are a safe testing pattern: they let you validate that a new consumer implementation, adapter version, or schema change behaves correctly under real production traffic before switching it live. This enables testing new adapters, evolving schemas, or adding new brokers without risking live workflows. Telemetry from these shadow consumers feeds back into the event catalog, providing maintainers with concrete data on performance, schema compliance, and usage patterns before making a production switch. This adapter-driven approach ensures that UMA systems stay truly runtime-agnostic, not just in theory but in daily operation. Event portability becomes as practical as capability portability, both enforced by contracts and not broker-specific code.

Shadow Mode Validation and Telemetry in UMA Eventing

In UMA, event contracts are not fixed agreements. They evolve as the business grows, new features are added, and performance targets shift. UMA systems are diverse, with an event possibly being consumed by a browser-based dashboard, a serverless workflow, an edge device in a factory, and an analytics job in the cloud all at once. Any change to the event schema or delivery method can risk disrupting one or more of these consumers. That's where shadow mode becomes essential.

Shadow mode lets you introduce changes without requiring an immediate switch-over. When a producer emits an event like shipmentCreated, it continues sending the current version to all production consumers while also sending a second copy, possibly with new fields or a modified schema, to a set of shadow consumers. These consumers behave like production services except that their results are not used in live workflows. Their purpose is to test whether the proposed change will work under real-world conditions.

The benefit of this approach is that it tests actual performance, not just theory. A schema validator can confirm whether a payload is formally correct, but only a shadow consumer running in the browser, with spotty 3G connectivity, can reveal whether the payload size has become too large for the page to render promptly. In UMA, shadow mode is often used before upgrading to a new schema version, switching broker technologies, or changing delivery guarantees.

Consider a financial trading platform adding a broker commission field to the tradeExecuted event. Without shadow mode, this change would require coordinating updates across all consuming services, some with strict release cycles or maintained by third parties. Using shadow mode, the platform emits both v1 (the current schema) and v2 (the new schema with the commission field) simultaneously. Shadow consumers in browser dashboards, serverless analytics functions, and risk analysis systems process v2 exactly as they would in production, but their outputs are discarded. Over days or weeks, their logs show whether they can parse the new field, handle its data type, and meet performance targets.

This process is effective only if supported by detailed telemetry. UMA's runtime instrumentation captures metrics for every shadow event: payload size, broker delivery latency, retry counts, schema compliance, and processing results. These metrics are stored alongside the event contract in the catalog, creating a time-stamped record of how the event performs across various environments and conditions. For event owners, this becomes a decision-making tool: they can see, for example, that 98 percent of consumers are ready for the change, while the remaining 2 percent are tied to an older mobile runtime needing a different adaptation strategy.

In UMA, shadow mode with telemetry is not optional; it's part of the release process. By the time a new event version is published in the catalog, it has already been tested across all critical runtimes, under the same network conditions, data loads, and broker setups it will encounter in production. This method provides event owners with confidence that when they update the contract, the system will continue functioning as expected: no surprises, no firefighting, just a well-informed, steady evolution.

Bringing It All Together

Event-driven coordination in UMA is not just a single feature but a collection of practices that support each other. Events are defined as contracts, making them explicit, versioned, and discoverable. Cataloging ensures that anyone building a capability can see what events exist, who owns them, and how to use them safely. Runtime-agnostic adapters free producers and consumers from broker lock-in, allowing the same contract to work across MQTT, Kafka, or serverless queues without rewriting the core logic. Shadow mode and telemetry provide the operational safety net, enabling teams to develop events openly without risking the live system.

Together, these elements transform event handling from an informal message exchange into a disciplined part of the architecture. Producers focus on emitting meaningful facts, consumers subscribe with confidence in what they will receive, and governance becomes an ongoing process rather than a post-event correction. This is how UMA can coordinate work across browsers, edge devices, and cloud runtimes without creating fragile dependencies.

When implemented this way, event-driven coordination transcends a mere technical choice. It becomes a shared language for the system, an approach to expressing change that remains independent of where the code runs or which technologies are currently in use. This is one of the reasons UMA can support a truly universal service layer, where capabilities stay portable even as the runtime landscape evolves.

Hands-On Takeaways

During the rollout of a smart-city traffic management system, a team using UMA needed to integrate new "incidentReported" events from roadside sensors into multiple consuming systems: a live public dashboard, an AI-based traffic flow optimizer, and a historical data warehouse. In a traditional setup, this would have required broker-specific APIs, tight coupling to the message bus, and a high-risk migration window. With UMA's event coordination approach, the team registered the new event in the catalog, defined its schema and ownership, and published it in shadow mode to validate that each consumer could parse and process it correctly. The dashboard consumed the event through a WebSocket adapter, the optimizer via Kafka, and the warehouse via an S3 event bridge, none of them aware that others used different brokers. Telemetry revealed that the optimizer struggled with payload size on specific routes, leading to a minor contract update before the event was fully promoted to production. By the time the event went live, every consumer had already been tested in real conditions. No rewrites were needed, no outages occurred, and the city's new traffic incident workflow was up and running without a single emergency patch.

Edge-Native Design

Definition of Edge

Edge computing is a term many in tech feel familiar with, but when asked to define it, opinions range widely. In meetings, some say it's about IoT devices; others define it as anything outside the cloud. At conferences, vendors might describe a small regional data center as "the edge." The term has been stretched to mean nearly anything outside hyperscale data centers.

In reality, edge computing is more specific and intriguing. It involves running workloads closer to where data is generated or where users interact with the system, instead of sending everything to a central cloud. The key is proximity, reducing the time, network hops, and dependencies between an event and the system's response. This proximity improves response times, conserves bandwidth by processing data locally, and allows systems to operate even if cloud connectivity is unstable.

This concept isn't new. It has existed for decades under various names. In the 1970s and 1980s, factories used programmable logic controllers (PLCs ruggedized, industrial computers designed to reliably automate machinery and processes in harsh environments; unlike general-purpose computers, PLCs are purpose-built for real-time control tasks such as reading sensor values, opening valves, starting motors, and triggering alarms) to read sensors and operate machinery directly on-site. Waiting for a remote mainframe to decide whether to shut a valve was unthinkable; decisions had to be made immediately and locally. These early embedded systems represented pure edge computing close to the source, reliable, and independent of distant infrastructure.

By the late 1990s, a new form of "edge" emerged in the internet era. Serving websites from a few centralized servers resulted in frustrating delays for users on the other side of the world. Content Delivery Networks appeared, scattering caches of data around the globe so that the content was physically closer to users. Although the technology and purpose were different from industrial PLCs, the principle was the same: move the processing and data as close as possible to where it is needed.

The 2010s marked a pivotal shift. Billions of connected devices started generating continuous streams of data, from factory sensors to autonomous vehicles. Initially, it was assumed that all data could be sent to the cloud for processing. This was a straightforward mental model: devices collected data, the cloud handled intensive processing, and results were returned. However, reality proved otherwise. Bandwidth costs increased. Latency made real-time control difficult. Network outages caused system failures. It became clear that not all processing should occur in the cloud. Some decisions needed to happen near the source, for example, a drone in flight, a surgical device during operation, or a point-of-sale terminal. This renewed emphasis on local processing is what most people now associate with "edge computing." Today, the edge isn't just a technical detail but an architectural principle. Its modern scope includes everything from processing directly on the device to local infrastructure supporting multiple devices to regional facilities closer to the source than the nearest cloud server. The goal remains the same: reduce the distance between event and response. The specific form the edge takes depends on the problem. For example, a camera on a production line may need to detect defects instantly, without waiting for cloud communication. A hospital might process imaging scans locally for quicker diagnosis. A wind farm might analyze turbine performance onsite at a control center, avoiding the costs and delays of transmitting raw sensor data over a wide-area network.

It is also essential to be clear about what the edge is not. It is not a single product that can be bought and installed. It is not synonymous with IoT, even though IoT often benefits from it. Also, it is not automatically small-scale; an edge deployment can be as minimal as a microcontroller or as significant as a rack of servers, depending on the need. Misunderstanding this can lead to poor designs, such as treating edge nodes as if they must replicate every feature of the cloud or, conversely, assuming they are only helpful for niche sensor applications.

In UMA, the edge is not a special case that must be handled differently from other runtimes. It is treated as a peer to the cloud, the browser, and the data center. The same capability can run on an industrial camera, in a store server, or in a regional cluster without any changes to its internal logic. The runtime-specific bindings that enable it to work in each environment are isolated by contracts, not scattered throughout the code. This approach allows deciding where to run a capability based on operational needs, latency, connectivity, and cost without redesigning or rewriting it for each scenario.

Understanding the edge in these terms, rooted in its history, grounded in its purpose, and free of marketing distortion, sets the stage for why it is so important in modern architecture. It also explains why, in UMA, the edge is simply another place where the same code can run, not an entirely different kind of system. In the next section, we will examine closely why pushing computation to the edge is sometimes not just a performance choice but a fundamental requirement for the system to function at all.

Why Push Computation to the Edge

The motivation for moving computation to the edge often begins with a simple, stubborn fact: distance takes time. Each hop across a network adds latency, and in some systems, even tens of milliseconds can mean the difference between a smooth experience and a malfunction. This isn't just about speed for speed's sake; it's about enabling entire classes of applications that can't tolerate the round trip to a centralized cloud.

Imagine an autonomous delivery robot navigating a crowded sidewalk. If it had to send every camera frame to a data center for object detection and wait for a response before deciding to brake, it would be unsafe and unusable. The same applies to a drone inspecting power lines, a point-of-sale terminal processing a card payment, or an industrial robot adjusting its grip on a part. The closer the processing occurs to the source, the faster the system can respond in real time.

Latency isn't the only concern. Bandwidth is another critical factor. Many edge scenarios generate enormous amounts of data, far more than makes sense to send upstream. A single high-resolution video stream from a security camera can use tens of megabits per second. Multiply that by dozens or hundreds of cameras, and the cost of moving all that raw data to the cloud becomes prohibitive. Processing at the edge enables you to analyze the data locally, detect events, extract features, and compress summaries so only the most valuable information needs to be transmitted.

Connectivity is the third key factor. Not all environments provide a stable connection to the cloud. Ships at sea, rural farms, underground mines, and hospitals with strict network segmentation can all experience disconnections. In those times, cloud-dependent systems cease to function. Edge-computing systems, however, can keep functioning by storing data locally and syncing once connectivity is restored. AI emphasizes these issues. Many current AI applications, like real-time video analysis, predictive maintenance, and natural language interfaces, require high processing power and low latency. Relying solely on the cloud works for batch tasks or less time-sensitive scenarios, but immediate feedback needs make the cloud a bottleneck. For example, an AR headset waiting 200 milliseconds for remote AI to identify objects may feel laggy. Similarly, a factory system relying on cloud-based detection in under 50 milliseconds can fail due to network delays. Deploying AI models at the edge allows meeting these strict constraints, provided they are optimized for limited compute, memory, and power. Privacy and compliance are also growing concerns. Regulations in healthcare, finance, and public safety may restrict certain data from leaving premises. Edge AI can process such sensitive information locally, sharing only anonymized or aggregated data. This reduces compliance risks and builds user trust, as customers prefer AI services when their raw data stays on-site. In UMA, moving computation to the edge does not mean creating a separate "edge version" of services. The same capability, with its contracts and runtime bindings, can be deployed in the cloud, browser, or edge without modification. The choice of where to run depends on operational needs: minimizing latency, bandwidth use, ensuring independence from constant connectivity, or complying with local data regulations. AI highlights the urgency of this decision, being especially demanding for compute and immediacy. Designing with the edge in mind shifts the view from it being a fallback to a primary environment handling critical and data-heavy tasks. Pairing this approach with UMA's ability to run the same service anywhere allows placing workloads optimally, where they best fit.

Constraints of Edge Environments

If the cloud is a wide, paved highway with limitless lanes, the edge can feel more like a winding mountain road. It gets you closer to your destination, but it also requires you to drive differently. You cannot simply take a service built for the cloud and expect it to thrive at the edge. The constraints are real and shape how capabilities must be designed.

The first constraint is hardware. Edge devices range from microcontrollers with kilobytes of RAM to industrial gateways and powerful regional clusters. Even at the higher end, you rarely have the same headroom as a cloud instance that can scale CPU and memory on demand. Many edge CPUs are optimized for low power consumption rather than peak throughput, and thermal limits often prevent sustained heavy workloads. An AI model that runs effortlessly on a cloud GPU may choke an edge device processor unless it is pruned (pruning removes neurons, layers, or connections in a neural network that contribute little to accuracy, reducing

Browser runtimes are an environment of their own. Even on modern laptops, JavaScript and WebAssembly share CPU resources with other browser activities like rendering pages, decoding videos, and handling input. A single tab might only get a fraction of available cores in practice. Memory is also limited: browsers typically restrict WebAssembly memory to around 2–4 GB, depending on the platform and configuration, with many mobile browsers offering even less. For example, Mobile Safari can enforce limits as low as a few hundred megabytes before reclaiming memory aggressively, meaning large in-memory datasets or AI models must be carefully optimized to fit.

Mobile devices running native apps have their own limitations. High-end phones may have multi-core ARM processors exceeding 2 GHz, but these numbers hide the fact that sustained heavy computation will trigger thermal throttling within minutes. Memory is shared across the device, and background apps can cause sudden reclamation of what you thought was available. Even with 8 GB of RAM, your app might only be allowed a fraction of it before the OS terminates it. UMA's contract-based resource budgets help set clear expectations so deployment tools can reject configurations unlikely to survive under real-world limits.

Storage and state management are equally limited. Edge nodes, whether a browser, mobile device, or embedded gateway, often have strict quotas on local storage. IndexedDB in the browser, for example, is often limited to a small percentage of available disk space, and some platforms clear it without warning under pressure. On mobile, persistent storage may be slower than expected, with high-latency writes making naive database use impractical for time-sensitive operations.

Hardware heterogeneity increases these challenges. At the edge, you may encounter dozens of CPU architectures, instruction set quirks, and different operating system versions. That's why UMA keeps runtime bindings as isolated, swappable components. The same capability can adapt to a rugged ARM-based gateway, a desktop-class regional server, or a browser tab without changing its core logic.

Environmental constraints add another layer. An edge workload might run inside a hot warehouse, on a moving vehicle, or within a sealed medical device. These conditions influence cooling, power availability, and the stability of compute performance. AI workloads, in particular, must consider these limits, as sustained inference can be CPU- and memory-intensive. UMA's portability allows the same AI capability to run locally in a trimmed form when needed but scale to a more powerful backend when conditions permit.

These constraints are not obstacles to be ignored; they are design considerations. The systems that succeed at the edge are those that acknowledge these limits and make them explicit in their architecture. UMA embeds that discipline, ensuring any capability running in the cloud is already prepared by contract and design for the realities it will face at the edge.

Real-World Examples and Challenges

Edge computing ceases to be just a theory the moment you attempt to run a real workload outside the cloud. Hardware limitations like limited CPU, strict memory caps, and unpredictable connectivity quickly undermine the assumptions built into many traditional architectures. UMA was designed with those realities in mind. The following examples show what happens when these constraints meet business needs and how UMA's principles enable meeting those needs without splitting the codebase into environment-specific versions.

Industrial IoT: Defect Detection at the Gateway

Manufacturing plants are filled with embedded compute nodes, often powered by low-power industrial gateways. A typical example is real-time defect detection on a production line. Cameras capture each unit as it moves along the conveyor, and an AI model classifies it as pass or fail.

The issue: that gateway might have a dual-core ARM processor running at 1.2 GHz, 1 GB of RAM, and a minimal embedded Linux system. The high-accuracy model trained in the cloud could be hundreds of megabytes in size, requiring multiple gigabytes of RAM for inference. Shipping that model "as is" to the gateway would lead to constant swapping or failure to load.

In a UMA deployment, the *capability* is defined once its inputs, outputs, and accuracy expectations are part of the contract. The runtime adapter detects the edge constraints and chooses a quantized, pruned version of the model. It may also batch frames for inference to maximize throughput without exceeding the latency limits. The key point is that the core logic remains unchanged; only the runtime packaging adjusts. The same capability can operate in the factory gateway and in a cloud analytics cluster, delivering equivalent results within an agreed accuracy tier.

Aviation: Predictive Maintenance in Flight

Aircraft generate a continuous flow of sensor data, including engine vibrations, cabin pressure, and hydraulic system status. Predictive maintenance models can identify anomalies early, helping to reduce costly unplanned downtime. However, airborne hardware is selected for its reliability and certification, not raw performance. CPUs may be a decade old, memory is limited, and sustained high loads can cause components to overheat. Cooling systems are intentionally minimal. With UMA, the anomaly detection capability is set once. On the aircraft, it runs in a lightweight configuration with fewer model parameters, optimized to fit strict resource limitations. After landing, the same raw sensor data can be processed with a high-fidelity model in a cloud environment, providing more detailed diagnostics. Since both outputs follow the same contract, they are compatible, making it easy to merge or compare results. This approach avoids the "two separate codebases" problem and keeps in-flight and post-flight analyses aligned.

Retail: Offline Point-of-Sale Transactions

Retail chains cannot risk downtime at checkout. A point-of-sale terminal must approve transactions even if the connection to headquarters fails. Many POS systems are built on small embedded CPUs with limited memory and storage in the megabytes. If payment validation logic is embedded in a single backend service, these terminals become useless when offline. In a UMA design, the payment validation is portable. Offline, it runs directly on the terminal, applying basic fraud rules and queuing transactions. The contract sets acceptable latency and resource limits, ensuring the terminal's UI stays responsive even under load. When connectivity is restored, queued transactions are sent to a more advanced cloud validation service that runs the same logic in a higher-tier setup. The process is identical; only the runtime environment changes.

Agriculture: Drone-Based Crop Analysis

Drones used in precision agriculture capture high-resolution images to identify crop stress, pests, or disease. Processing this imagery onboard enables immediate action, but onboard computing is limited by size, weight, and power constraints. Every watt used for processing reduces flight time. A UMA capability for stress detection can be deployed at varying levels of fidelity. While in flight, the drone runs a compact model that flags areas of interest in real time, using lightweight image processing and an 8-bit quantized AI model. This allows it to keep up with the camera feed without draining the battery. Once back at base, the flagged images are sent to the same capability running in a cloud environment with full-fidelity model weights. The outputs are integrated seamlessly because the contract specifies the result schema and quality tiers.

Healthcare: Imaging in Air-Gapped Networks

Hospitals often operate critical imaging equipment like MRI or CT scanners on isolated networks for compliance and security reasons. These devices might be restricted to specific OS versions and CPU architectures, with no internet access at all. UMA allows the same diagnostic capabilities to run in both the air-gapped scanner and a research lab's HPC cluster. The contract specifies resource needs, latency requirements, and output formats so that the scanner's runtime adapter can enforce strict memory limits and local storage policies. When results are transferred to the research environment, they remain identical in format and meaning, making them immediately usable in larger studies without extra translation or reconciliation.

Logistics and Automotive: Safe Onboard Routing

Fleet tracking and autonomous vehicle systems need to calculate routes in real time. Onboard computing may be shared with infotainment, driver-assist, and safety systems. If the routing engine consumes too many CPU cycles, it can impair safety-critical performance. With UMA, the routing capability specifies a maximum CPU usage and latency budget in its contract. In limited onboard environments, it operates in a reduced mode, offering fewer route options and less detailed traffic data to stay within that budget. When connected to a nearby edge server or the cloud, it can run at full fidelity. The capability logic remains the same, but the runtime can adjust its inputs and processing depth to match available resources.

SaaS with Large, Complex Products

Large SaaS platforms like CRMs or ERPs often turn into sprawling monoliths. Adding real-time, near-user processing, for example, lead scoring in the browse, becomes a nightmare if it requires rewriting logic in a different language. UMA capabilities prevent this problem. The same scoring logic can run as a WebAssembly module in the browser, as a native binary on a regional edge node, or as a containerized microservice in the cloud. The contract guarantees consistent inputs, outputs, and performance standards across all deployments. This allows computation to be brought closer to the user for faster speed, without losing consistency or increasing maintenance efforts.

AI-Native Systems

AI-native products where inference is central to the user experience are susceptible to edge constraints. A corporate AI assistant might need to run locally to keep sensitive data in-house or in regulated industries where cloud inference is not allowed. UMA enables the same inference capability to operate with a smaller model and reduced context locally and a full-sized model in the cloud. The contract specifies not only input/output schemas but also latency expectations and model quality tiers, clarifying what to expect in each runtime. This predictability is essential for AI workloads, where uncontrolled variation can undermine trust in the system.

Gaming

Games are increasingly complex distributed systems. Multiplayer synchronization, AI NPC behavior, and real-time content streaming all require logic that can operate across diverse environments. A UMA capability for NPC decision-making could run entirely on a console for instant response or on a low-latency edge server for large multiplayer worlds where NPCs interact across sessions. The contract ensures behavior remains deterministic within a given configuration, preventing desyncs when capabilities shift between runtimes. These examples across heavy industry, healthcare, SaaS, AI products, and gaming emphasize the same truth: edge environments challenge assumptions. UMA's approach of portable, contract-governed capabilities makes it possible to treat the edge as just another runtime, without cutting corners or maintaining divergent code paths.

UMA Strategies for Edge Deployment

Designing for the edge isn't about taking what works in the cloud and forcing it onto smaller hardware. It's about creating capabilities that are naturally resilient to the realities of limited compute, unpredictable connectivity, and operational diversity. UMA enables this through strategies that turn edge constraints from afterthoughts into fundamental architectural considerations.

An offline-first mindset forms the foundation. Many systems still treat offline operation as an exception, a temporary failure to be tolerated rather than a state to be designed for. In UMA, a capability can specify in its contract which parts of its logic are self-contained and which rely on external services. This makes it possible to test, verify, and deploy an offline mode as an intentional operating tier, not just a fallback.

For example, a maintenance tool for wind turbines might keep diagnostics local, even generating repair suggestions without cloud access. When a connection is available, it can synchronize logs, update models, or send aggregated insights upstream. In AI workloads, this can extend to partial model fine-tuning locally, with weight updates sent to the cloud later for overall merging. Without an explicit offline mode, every network outage risks becoming a service outage, which is simply unacceptable in industries like retail, healthcare, or aviation.

Local control loops with eventual synchronization address the fact that many edge decisions cannot afford the latency of cloud feedback. In an industrial robot arm, the decision to stop due to an obstacle must be made within milliseconds. In a fleet routing system, traffic conditions need to update driver instructions instantly, even if the cloud is unreachable. UMA makes this safe and consistent by treating the control loop as a standalone capability that can operate entirely from local data. Synchronization occurs in the background, sending summarized decisions, sensor logs, or higher-resolution requests to the cloud once conditions permit. This prevents the risky pattern of relying on network availability for safety- or mission-critical operations, while still ensuring that global insights enhance local decision-making over time.

Deterministic resource budgets are essential in edge environments. While resource use in the cloud is flexible, in the edge it is limited by physical constraints and fixed provisioning. UMA contracts enable a capability to specify its CPU usage, memory limit, storage size, and latency class in measurable terms. This allows an orchestrator to determine precisely which runtime can support it. Without this discipline, a capability might perform well in the lab but cause cascading failures in production by starving nearby workloads of CPU or RAM. For instance, in an automotive setting, this could mean an infotainment update that unintentionally delays sensor fusion processes for driver assistance, posing safety risks. Deterministic budgets ensure predictable performance, prevent resource starvation, and enable operators to model and test worst-case scenarios before deployment.

Progressive fidelity is UMA's way of acknowledging that quality is not simply on or off. A capability should have different levels of operation that match available resources, rather than a single "all or nothing" approach. For example, a drone surveying farmland could run a lightweight plant health model in real time during flight to flag areas for closer inspection. Once on the ground, the same capability could reprocess the data with the full-resolution model on a powerful workstation. Since both levels follow the same contract, they provide consistent output formats, metadata, and semantics, making the transition between them smooth. This approach is especially useful in AI systems, where a smaller model can give quick feedback, and a larger model can refine results later, keeping the user experience fast while allowing for more detailed analysis when additional resources are available.

Runtime-agnostic execution ties all these strategies together. It ensures that capabilities are not locked to a particular runtime, broker, or platform. A WebAssembly-based capability could run in a browser today, inside an embedded device's sandbox tomorrow, and in a secure enclave in the future without rewriting its core logic. This separation of capability from runtime bindings means you can design once and deploy anywhere. It also means investments in edge readiness will carry forward as new execution environments emerge. This is crucial in fast-moving domains like AI inference, where dedicated accelerators, model formats, and runtime APIs evolve quickly. By keeping execution portable, UMA ensures that your edge strategy remains adaptable rather than brittle.

These strategies are essential, not optional extras. Ignoring them often results in brittle, single-environment designs that can't scale across various edge contexts. A retail POS system without offline-first capability will simply cease functioning when the network goes down. An AI-native application lacking progressive fidelity will feel slow and unresponsive on mobile devices. A fleet management system without deterministic resource budgets risks unpredictable latency spikes that can compromise driver safety. UMA's approach addresses these risks by integrating edge strategies into the core architecture, rather than treating them as afterthoughts to be added at deployment time.

Regulatory and compliance requirements add another layer. In healthcare, finance, or defense, data may be restricted from leaving the device or local network. This rules out architectures that rely on sending raw data to the cloud for processing. UMA enables running the same capability in both constrained and unconstrained environments through adaptive runtime bindings while maintaining consistent input/output schemas and quality tiers. This allows an AI model to operate entirely within a regulated hospital network using the same logic and contracts as its cloud version.

For **AI-native systems**, these constraints become even sharper. Model size, inference latency, and memory footprint are critical, especially when working with GPUs (Graphics Processing Units processors with thousands of small, parallel cores optimized for the matrix multiplications that underpin neural network inference; originally designed for rendering graphics, they have become the primary compute hardware for AI workloads) or NPUs (Neural Processing Units dedicated AI accelerator chips designed specifically for running neural network operations efficiently, found in modern smartphones such as Apple's Neural Engine and Qualcomm's Hexagon DSP, as well as edge AI devices like the Google Coral and NVIDIA Jetson) with fixed VRAM. A model that functions perfectly in a data center might be unusable in a mobile browser due to memory limitations. UMA's approach of defining model tier options and latency budgets in the contract guarantees that the appropriate version is deployed in the correct runtime without guesswork.

UMA Principles Applied to Edge

The edge is where UMA's principles are most rigorously tested. Every constraint discussed earlier, such as limited compute, constrained memory, diverse hardware, and intermittent connectivity, serves as a testing ground for whether an architecture is truly portable, maintainable, and resilient. UMA's strength at the edge comes from applying its core principles consistently, ensuring that the same service design can succeed both in a data center and on a sensor-rich field device.

Portability in UMA is not just about compiling for a different target; it's about maintaining functional equivalence across different runtimes. A capability that runs in a cloud container should also run in a browser tab, an embedded industrial gateway, or a battery-powered AI camera without needing to rewrite its logic. This is achieved through strict separation of capability logic from runtime bindings, enforced by contracts. In practice, this means an AI-powered quality inspection service might run on a GPU-accelerated workstation in a factory, then be deployed as a WebAssembly module in a browser for remote monitoring, all while maintaining the same input/output schemas and latency guarantees.

Contract governance is equally essential. At the edge, the risks of breaking a contract are greater. A change to an event schema in the cloud can be quickly detected and rolled back, but on a remote edge device with limited connectivity, that exact change could cause silent failures for days. UMA's governance model, which includes versioned contracts, compatibility graphs, and automated diffing, ensures that deployments are intentional and that any change to a capability is evaluated for its impact across all edge contexts before deployment. In heavily regulated sectors like healthcare and aviation, this isn't just a best practice; it's a compliance requirement.

Event-driven coordination also naturally suits edge environments when applied with UMA's principles. Instead of forcing all processing into a synchronous request/response cycle, UMA allows capabilities to subscribe to relevant events and act when they occur, even offline. For instance, an intelligent irrigation system at the edge can respond to soil moisture readings locally, opening valves instantly without waiting for cloud validation. When connectivity is restored, it publishes a summary event upstream, keeping global systems informed without adding unnecessary delay.

The principle of progressive fidelity becomes a practical necessity at the edge. UMA's approach of defining multiple quality tiers within a single capability enables developers to design for resource-aware execution from the beginning. An AI-based object recognition capability might run at low resolution for real-time detection on a drone's onboard system, then reprocess footage at higher resolution once uploaded to a regional edge cluster. Because these tiers are specified in the contract, they are discoverable and predictable, allowing orchestrators to make smart deployment decisions automatically.

Finally, UMA's focus on observability ensures that edge deployments remain transparent despite their isolation. Edge capabilities publish telemetry according to their contracts, including latency metrics, error counts, and resource usage. This facilitates proactive maintenance and adaptation, which are critical in environments where debugging is costly or impossible on-site. An agricultural cooperative using UMA-based monitoring could detect increased CPU load on edge nodes before it affects crop analysis, enabling an optimized capability update in advance.

What makes UMA effective at the edge is not a special "edge mode" but its design as a runtime-agnostic architecture. The same patterns that enable safe, scalable deployments in the cloud, such as clear contracts, event-driven coordination, and resource budgeting, translate directly to the edge because they are not tied to a specific environment. The key difference is that at the edge, there is far less margin for error, making UMA's principles not just advantageous but essential.

Hands-On Takeaways

A small but high-stakes embedded system project involved creating an AI-assisted inspection tool for industrial turbines. The aim was to provide technicians with a portable device that could scan a turbine, identify wear patterns, and recommend maintenance actions instantly. The device was a rugged ARM-based unit running a minimal Linux distribution with 2 GB of RAM and no GPU. The company also wanted the same logic accessible via a browser dashboard for supervisors and in a C++ desktop tool used for detailed analysis at the office.

Initially, the team developed separate versions: a native C++ build for the device, a Node.js backend for the browser dashboard, and a more extensive desktop version with proprietary extensions. Each version gradually diverged. Bug fixes applied in one environment often needed to be reimplemented in the others. Even more, the embedded device's AI model was smaller and optimized differently from the browser's, resulting in inconsistent detection results.

The switch to UMA changed the dynamic entirely.

The inspection logic became a **self-contained capability** written in C++, compiled for various targets, including WebAssembly for browsers and native binaries for embedded devices. The capability's contract specified its input schema (sensor data format), output schema (detection list with confidence scores), CPU and memory limits, and a low-fidelity execution tier for constrained hardware. On the device, it ran locally without relying on any cloud calls. In the browser, it operated within a WebAssembly sandbox, using the same core logic as the embedded version. On the desktop, it functioned as a native C++ plugin within the analysis application. Because the runtime bindings were separated from the logic, all three environments produced identical detection results from the same input data.

Event-driven coordination was introduced so the device could operate even with intermittent connectivity. Detection events were processed locally, cached, and then uploaded to the supervisor dashboard once the network was available. This prevented the problem where the device would stall mid-inspection, waiting for a server round-trip.

Progressive fidelity was a game-changer. The embedded unit ran a smaller, distilled AI model that could complete inference within CPU and memory limits. The browser and desktop runtimes could opt to run the higher-precision model when resources allow. Both tiers were defined in the UMA contract, ensuring predictable outputs and no hidden discrepancies.

Contract governance maintained stability. When the output schema for detection results changed to include severity levels, UMA's compatibility checks flagged that the embedded runtime didn't support the new field yet. This prevented a field update from bricking inspection devices during active maintenance.

Telemetry was integrated from the start. Each runtime published metrics like average inference time, CPU load, and memory usage. This helped detect a memory leak in the embedded build early, preventing midday crashes in the field.

Within months, the company retired the old, fragmented codebase. Updates were shipped to all runtimes from a single source, and field technicians reported that inspections became more consistent, faster, and more reliable, even in remote locations with no connectivity. UMA's runtime-agnostic approach enabled the unification of embedded C++, browser JavaScript, and desktop builds without sacrificing accuracy or maintainability.

Non-functional Design Constraints

Introduction

In most software systems, non-functional requirements such as availability, resilience, scalability, and resource discipline are often documented vaguely in a separate section of the design specification. They tend to sound like aspirations: "should handle 10,000 concurrent requests," "should respond within 200 ms," and "should recover gracefully from failures." While technically correct, these statements are often inert; they exist on paper rather than code, are rarely enforced during runtime, and when the system drifts from its original constraints, there is usually no mechanism to detect or correct the issue.

Encoding these constraints directly into the contract solves two chronic problems. First, it forces the design team to confront operational realities early. A capability that must run in a constrained edge device will have very different CPU, memory, and startup budgets than one running in a well-provisioned cloud environment. By declaring these limits from the start, you design with them in mind rather than retrofitting optimizations after performance issues arise. Second, it provides orchestration systems and runtime adapters with the necessary information to act proactively. They can adjust scheduling, apply concurrency caps, or activate backup plans automatically when approaching resource limits.

The key advantage of UMA's approach is that these constraints are **runtime-agnostic**. The same contract can inform a WebAssembly sandbox in a browser, an embedded C++ runtime on an industrial controller, and a containerized deployment in a cloud cluster. The enforcement mechanisms differ, such as fuel counters in WASM, cgroup quotas in Linux, or requestIdleCallback in browsers, but the definition of the constraint remains the same. This consistency ensures that a capability behaves predictably regardless of where it operates, reducing surprises when transitioning between environments.

By shifting non-functional requirements from an afterthought to an integral part of the system's core, UMA bridges the gap between what is promised and what is delivered. The upcoming sections will explore how these policies are expressed, enforced, and tested and how they enable teams to deploy capabilities across diverse operational profiles confidently.

Policy Blocks for Budgets and Limits

In UMA, a contract is considered complete only when it clearly defines what the service can consume and the conditions for its operation. These boundaries are formalized as **policy blocks,** which exist alongside the functional descriptions of a capability. They specify non-functional requirements like CPU time, memory limits, execution deadlines, concurrency restrictions, and quality-of-service levels. A policy block isn't an afterthought or hidden in a wiki page; it's a machine-readable component of the capability's contract that the runtime can interpret and enforce. This allows adapters in browsers, edge device orchestrators, or cloud schedulers to apply consistent rules without guesswork or undocumented assumptions.

Budgets come in several dimensions. A CPU budget might declare that a capability should not exceed 200 milliseconds of total computation per invocation. A memory budget might set a maximum of 150 MB for active data structures. A wall-clock budget might require that results be returned within 1.5 seconds from the time a request is received, regardless of CPU time consumed. When the runtime sees these constraints in the contract, it can proactively prevent violations by yielding in a WASM sandbox, throttling in a browser, or terminating long-running processes in the cloud before they cause cascading delays.

Concurrency limits are equally important. If a capability declares a maximum of three concurrent executions per runtime instance, the UMA runtime ensures that no more than three run at the same time, queuing or rejecting excess requests according to the contract's stated preference. This is critical in environments like embedded devices or browsers, where opening too many parallel executions can freeze the interface or starve other processes.

Quality-of-Service (QoS) classes provide added flexibility. A capability can offer multiple modes, such as "standard" for general requests, "premium" for latency-sensitive tasks, and "low-priority" for background processing. The policy block sets the performance target for each class along with the resource budget it is willing to use. This allows orchestrators to schedule work intelligently based on priority without having to guess the needs or capabilities.

Failover preferences are also included in the policy block. A capability can specify whether it prefers to fall back to cached results, a lower-fidelity algorithm, or a redundant instance in another region when the primary execution path is unavailable. Since this preference is part of the contract, failover behavior becomes predictable and testable before deployment.

The real power of policy blocks is their portability. The same CPU budget, concurrency limit, and failover preference are understood by a WASM runtime in a browser, a containerized service in the cloud, and a bare-metal process on an edge gateway. While each environment may enforce these limits differently, the intent remains consistent, making the behavior predictable regardless of where it runs.

In practice, policy blocks help prevent common resource-related failures before they occur. They turn vague non-functional requirements into enforceable rules that guide runtime behavior. This approach shifts the mindset from reactive firefighting to proactive control, ensuring capabilities stay fast, stable, and predictable even when deployed across diverse runtimes.

Enforcing Budgets Across Runtimes

Declaring budgets in a contract is only the first step. For them to be useful, they must be enforced in a way that works across different runtimes with vastly different execution models. UMA's approach is to standardize the **definition** of the budget, such as how much CPU time, memory, or wall-clock time a capability is allowed to consume while letting each runtime enforce it using mechanisms suitable for its environment. In a **WebAssembly** runtime, enforcement often relies on yield points and fuel counters. A yield point is a deliberate check in the capability's execution path where the runtime can pause, abort, or switch context if a budget threshold has been reached. Fuel counters go a step further by assigning a finite number of "execution credits" to a capability when it starts running. Each instruction consumes a small amount of fuel. When the counter reaches zero, the runtime halts execution gracefully. This model offers deterministic control over CPU usage and protects the host environment from runaway workloads. For example, an edge device running multiple WASM capabilities can ensure that one intensive task will not starve the others by exhausting CPU resource cycles.

In **cloud environments**, the equivalents are often **cgroup quotas** and resource control policies at the container or VM level. A cgroup can limit the total CPU shares, memory allocation, or even network bandwidth available to a process. When paired with UMA's contract, the orchestration layer can read the declared budget and automatically apply the correct cgroup settings. If the contract specifies a 200 MB memory limit, the container is started with that exact cap, ensuring it cannot exceed it even if the underlying machine has more resources. These controls work with cloud schedulers to make scaling decisions; if one capability needs more CPU time than its budget allows, the orchestrator can spin up another instance instead of breaking its own rules. In **browser runtimes**, the tools differ but serve the same purpose. Since browsers are single-threaded, long-running tasks can freeze the UI. UMA adapters for browsers use APIs like requestIdleCallback to schedule work during idle periods, breaking long tasks into smaller units that yield back to the event loop between steps. This ensures that even CPU-heavy capabilities respect the user's experience budget, keeping the interface responsive. Memory budgets are enforced by tracking heap usage through performance APIs and triggering early cleanup or fidelity reduction before the garbage collector causes visible lag. The main challenge is ensuring that the same **budget definition** feels consistent everywhere. A "200 ms CPU budget" should seem the same whether you're running in Chrome, on a Raspberry Pi, or inside a Kubernetes pod. UMA addresses this by treating the contract as the single source of truth for limits and calibrating each runtime's enforcement layer to map those limits to the local enforcement mechanism. This calibration accounts for differences in measurement granularity, scheduling delays, and platform quirks, so the user's practical experience of the limit remains consistent. The mapping between a UMA-defined budget and the local enforcement mechanism demonstrates the architecture's portability. A 200 ms CPU budget or a 300 MB memory limit means the same across all environments, even though enforcement varies in a WASM sandbox, a cloud container, or a browser tab. Calibration inside each runtime adapter ensures these budgets feel consistent, considering differences in measurement, scheduling, and platform quirks. For developers, this consistency eliminates a common frustration: having to rewrite or retune a capability for each environment. The contract sets the limit once, and every runtime respects it according to its rules. The orchestration layer can then make intelligent scheduling and scaling decisions based on these shared constraints, without sacrificing predictability in how the capability behaves.

Concurrency and Backpressure Management

Before diving into UMA's approach, it helps to define the two terms in this section title. Concurrency refers to the number of tasks a system executes or appears to execute simultaneously. High concurrency means many requests or operations are in progress at the same time, which can exhaust CPU, memory, or network resources if not bounded.

Backpressure is the mechanism by which a system signals to its upstream producers that it is struggling to keep up with the incoming load, effectively asking them to slow down or queue it. It prevents a fast producer from overwhelming a slow consumer, which is a common cause of cascading failures in distributed systems.

Even if a capability stays within its CPU or memory limits, it can still strain the system if too many instances run at once. UMA employs concurrency constraints and backpressure techniques to keep workloads manageable and avoid system degradation. In UMA, concurrency is more than just a technical setting; it's part of the capability's agreement. This contract may specify, for example, that a capability allows up to ten concurrent executions in a single runtime or processes only one request at a time on a resource-constrained edge node. These restrictions help the orchestration layer plan effectively and prevent overloads before performance suffers.

Enforcement varies depending on the environment. Inside a WebAssembly runtime, concurrency limits are often managed using lightweight semaphores embedded in the module wrapper, ensuring that no more than the permitted number of executions can enter critical sections simultaneously. This prevents starvation of other capabilities sharing the same runtime. In cloud or server environments, concurrency policies can be enforced through adapters utilizing token-bucket schedulers or priority queues, where incoming requests are assigned tokens and queued based on their importance. When the bucket is empty, new requests either wait or fail immediately, depending on the policy. Backpressure plays a crucial role in preventing cascading failures. When a capability is under sustained load, UMA adapters can slow down incoming requests via fairness delays, prioritizing higher-priority work for resource access while allowing lower-priority work to wait or be shed. In browser runtimes, where user interaction is the priority, backpressure might involve deferring heavy computations until the next idle period to keep the UI responsive. The fundamental difference with UMA is that these concurrency and backpressure rules are declared once, within the capability's contract, and then consistently interpreted across all runtimes. A limit of five concurrent executions has the same operational meaning whether enforced by a semaphore in a WASM module, a priority queue in a Node.js adapter, or an API gateway in a cloud deployment. This alignment reduces the need for environment-specific tuning and minimizes the risk of inconsistent behavior across platforms. When properly designed, these controls transform concurrency from an invisible operational variable into a predictable system feature. The result is a platform that remains stable under load, allocates resources to critical work, and gracefully sheds excess demand instead of failing unpredictably.

Resilience Patterns Across Runtimes

Resilience in UMA ensures that a failure in one part of the system doesn't spread to others. Since capabilities can operate in very different environments from browsers and edge devices to server clusters, resilience patterns must be portable, enforceable through contracts, and adaptable to local conditions. A typical example is the circuit breaker, a resilience pattern borrowed from electrical engineering, where a breaker "trips" to cut power when a fault is detected, preventing damage to the rest of the system. In software, a circuit breaker monitors calls to a downstream dependency and "opens" (stops sending requests) after a defined number of consecutive failures, allowing time for recovery instead of flooding a struggling service with further requests. In a UMA capability, the agreement can specify that if a downstream service fails more than three times within a rolling one-minute window, the circuit should open, and future requests should fail quickly until a cooldown period passes. This prevents the capability from wasting resources on calls unlikely to succeed, freeing capacity for other tasks. The enforcement layer might be a WASM wrapper maintaining a simple failure counter or a cloud API gateway applying the same logic through configuration. Another pattern is the idempotency key. Idempotency is the property of an operation that can be applied multiple times without changing the result beyond the first application. In other words, retrying an idempotent operation is safe. For example, submitting a payment twice should not charge a customer twice. When a capability performs actions with side effects ... the same request should not cause duplicate results if retried. In UMA, idempotency is declared in the contract along with the scope and retention period of the keys. An edge deployment might store these keys in lightweight local storage for minutes, while a cloud deployment keeps them in a distributed cache for hours. The core principle remains the same: retries should not produce unintended duplicates.

Bulkheads are also crucial in a multi-runtime environment. They isolate failure domains by dividing resources so that the failure of one capability or dependency cannot consume the entire runtime's capacity. In UMA, a bulkhead might be a dedicated thread pool or memory partition for a high-risk capability, configured based on its contract's risk classification.

To address tail latency, the phenomenon where a small percentage of requests (typically the slowest 95th, 99th, or 99.9th percentile) take dramatically longer than the median, often because they hit a loaded server, triggered garbage collection, or encountered a slow disk, UMA supports hedged requests**,** which send the same request to multiple endpoints and use the first successful response. This can involve a hedge between two cloud regions or between local edge execution and a fallback cloud service. The contract specifies whether hedging is allowed, how many parallel requests are permitted, and the timeout threshold before they are triggered.

Retries with backoff and jitter complete the pattern set. UMA contracts can define retry policies at a detailed level, specifying maximum attempts, base delays, and jitter (randomization added to retry wait times; for example, instead of all failed clients retrying after exactly 5 seconds, they retry after a random interval between 3 and 7 seconds). Jitter is important because without it, a wave of simultaneous failures causes a synchronized retry storm: all clients retry at the same moment, flooding the already-struggling service with a traffic spike precisely when it is least able to handle it. Randomizing the delay spreads that traffic out, giving the service time to recover. These policies are then applied consistently, whether the capability runs as a WebAssembly module, a cloud function, or an embedded service in a field device.

Resilience in UMA is not left to chance. Each pattern is explicitly modeled in the contract, enabling predictable, cross-environment behavior. This means a capability can fail fast, retry smartly, or reroute around problems in a way that is consistent from the smallest sensor to the largest data center deployment.

Failover Strategies and QoS Knobs

Quality of Service (QoS) in the context of distributed systems refers to the set of policies and mechanisms that prioritize certain types of traffic or workloads over others, ensuring that latency-sensitive operations (such as real-time payment authorization) receive resources ahead of background tasks (such as nightly analytics batch jobs) and that the system degrades gracefully under load rather than treating all requests equally until everything fails.

Failover in UMA is not an afterthought applied to a single runtime; it is integrated into the capability's contract so that the same strategy applies regardless of where the capability is running. The goal is to maintain service continuity even when the primary execution path is unavailable or underperforming. The simplest and most effective enabler is **statelessness**. A stateless capability can be redeployed instantly to another runtime without concerns about migrating in-memory data or session context. In UMA, the contract can specify whether a capability is fully stateless or stateful with synchronization requirements. Stateless capabilities are the most flexible for failover; they can shift from edge to cloud or between regions with minimal coordination. Failover often involves having **multiple endpoints** ready for the same logical capability.

In a cloud deployment, this might mean two or more areas running identical services; in an edge deployment, it could be a local instance paired with a central fallback. UMA contracts enable defining these endpoints along with their priority and selection criteria. Some failover patterns actively combine multiple execution paths. An example is **hedging between edge and cloud;** a capability may start executing locally for low-latency response but send a parallel request to the cloud if local execution is expected to exceed a certain threshold. If the cloud responds first, its result is used; if the edge finishes first, the cloud request is discarded. This approach is beneficial for AI inference workloads, where local execution is faster in good conditions but can degrade under heavy load.

Quality-of-service controls make failover more adaptable. UMA contracts can specify how fidelity should be adjusted when resources are limited or when the system is operating in degraded mode. For instance, a real-time analytics feature might lower sampling rates or compress data more efficiently during failover, maintaining essential functionality while consuming less bandwidth or CPU. In an AI-native system, QoS adjustment might involve switching to a smaller, faster model if the primary model becomes unavailable or too slow to meet latency goals.

Observability and Testing

In UMA, observability is not an optional add-on; it is a contractual responsibility. Each capability outlines the signals it will emit, the formats those signals will follow, and the points in its execution where they will be captured. This ensures runtime behavior is measurable consistently across all environments, from a WebAssembly module in the browser to a high-throughput service in the cloud.

Structured logs form the foundation. Instead of free-form text, UMA contracts specify fields such as event type, reason code, capability ID, runtime ID, and execution phase. When a request fails, it doesn't just log "error," but emits a reason code like `timeout`, `downstream`, or `validation.schemaMismatch` that can be analyzed automatically. This accuracy enables automated monitoring and AI-driven diagnostics to respond to events without human intervention.

Timing data is equally crucial. UMA capabilities record queue wait time, service execution time, and total response time separately, enabling the differentiation between delays caused by load and those due to slow execution. In a browser runtime, this might reveal that a capability spends 80% of its budget waiting for the main thread to free up. In a cloud deployment, it could expose a specific dependency as the bottleneck.

Testing practices in UMA extend beyond just unit and integration tests. Since capabilities are portable, they need to be tested across every target runtime. Contract tests verify that the declared inputs, outputs, error models, and resource budgets behave consistently in a WASM sandbox, an edge node, and a containerized cloud service. These tests run during development and continuous integration, catching environmental drift before it reaches production.

Fault injection and chaos engineering are integral to this lifecycle. UMA supports injecting controlled failures such as dropping network calls, corrupting payloads, and simulating slow dependencies based on contract parameters. This enables teams to observe how resilience patterns and failover strategies perform under real stress. For instance, an AI-native capability can be tested to determine if it gracefully switches to a smaller model when GPU memory is artificially limited.

The key is that observability and testing in UMA focus on building an evidence trail of runtime behavior that is reproducible, analyzable, and trustworthy. When an incident occurs, structured telemetry and consistent contract-driven tests allow precise root cause identification without guesswork, whether the capability runs in a warehouse, on a mobile device, or within a browser tab.

Governance and Best Practices

Introduction

In any distributed architecture, governance is often viewed as a burden that slows delivery and creates friction in the creative process. However, in UMA, that view needs to shift. Governance is the discipline that allows multiple teams across diverse environments to evolve their capabilities without interfering with each other's work. It acts as the invisible backbone that maintains system coherence amid constant movement. UMA's setting intensifies this challenge; a single capability might be used by a browser app developed by one team, an edge workflow managed by another, and a cloud service maintained by a third. These users may belong to different departments, companies, or industries and might never communicate directly. Yet, they share a common dependency: the contract outlining how the capability functions. Without robust governance, small changes can cause unpredictable ripple effects across this network, undermining trust and raising operational risks. The goal isn't to centralize control or hinder progress. Instead, UMA treats governance as a catalyst for productivity. When contracts are effectively managed, teams can act faster, confident in the guarantees these contracts offer. They know a change will be compatible or will clearly indicate necessary adjustments. It becomes easier to discover capabilities without hunting for documentation, and automated checks can catch inconsistencies before they reach production. In UMA, good governance balances technical and cultural aspects, building habits, treating contracts like code, maintaining visibility and reviewability of changes, making specifications easily discoverable, and designing for compatibility from the outset. Ultimately, this leads to a system where stability and agility support each other, rather than remaining in constant conflict.

Best Practices for Maintaining Contracts Across Teams

In UMA, it emphasizes that a contract is not just a static document stored on a wiki that becomes outdated. Instead, it is an active, versioned artifact that evolves with the capability it describes. Treating it as a first-class citizen in the development process is essential to maintaining its trustworthiness when multiple teams depend on it.

The first habit is to **treat contracts as code**. This means storing the contract file in the same version control repository as its implementation. A change to the implementation that affects the contract should be made in the same commit or pull request, making the relationship explicit and reviewable. When contracts are kept separate, they tend to diverge, leading consumers to guess which version is authoritative.

Semantic versioning is the language UMA uses to communicate changes. A patch version indicates a fix or non-breaking improvement, a minor version signifies new functionality that remains backward-compatible, and a major version signals a breaking change. Semantic versioning only works if teams apply it consistently; cutting corners here can cause unexpected runtime failures.

Every version should include a **contextual changelog**, not just a list of file diffs. A good changelog explains the purpose behind a change, the scenarios it impacts, and any suggested migration steps. This is especially important in UMA's cross-runtime environment, where a change might behave differently in a browser sandbox than in a cloud container.

For breaking changes, UMA recommends **that consumers sign off** before release. This is not just a formal approval but an explicit acknowledgment from downstream teams that they understand the change and are prepared to handle it. In environments with automated contract validation, this process can be supported by CI pipelines that identify incompatible updates and block them until all affected consumers have adapted.

By adopting these practices, contracts cease to be static references and become living agreements that teams can rely on. The hurdles of governance are replaced by confidence born from knowing everyone is working from the same verified source of truth.

Contract Registries and Signed Contracts

In UMA, discoverability isn't a luxury but a fundamental requirement. A capability's usefulness depends heavily on its ability to be located, understood, and trusted by potential users. This underscores the importance of contract registries, which serve as the definitive source for all deployed contracts covering synchronous API calls, event payloads, or execution budgets.

A **contract registry** is more than just a repository; it acts as a searchable index enabling teams to find capabilities by name, domain, version, or supported input/output types. In advanced UMA setups, the registry supports schema introspection, allowing developers to browse or query the exact data shapes a capability accepts and returns. This accelerates onboarding and minimizes errors caused by assumptions.

When capabilities span organizational or trust boundaries, the registry also functions as a trust anchor. UMA facilitates **signed contracts**, where the contract file is cryptographically signed by the publishing team. This enables runtime systems to verify that a contract hasn't been altered and originates from the legitimate source. The exact process can validate that an executing capability aligns with its stated contract, bridging the gap between static specifications and actual runtime behavior.

Registries can be centralized, federated, or hybrid. A centralized model is easier to manage but may not scale across independent business units or partner organizations. A federated registry, where multiple nodes synchronize their published contracts, can work better for multi-company ecosystems or regulated environments where data residency matters. UMA's architecture does not mandate a specific registry topology, but it requires that the registry be treated as the single source of truth for contract definitions within its domain. By integrating the registry and its trust mechanisms into the operational framework, UMA ensures that capabilities are not only portable and well-defined but also reliably discoverable and verifiable across different runtimes and teams.

Automated Validation and Multi-version Support

Governance in UMA would collapse under its own weight if it relied solely on manual reviews. Automated validation is essential for keeping contracts honest at scale, catching issues well before they cause production incidents.

The first layer is **linting**. Contracts are parsed and checked for structural correctness, such as invalid JSON, missing required fields, and inconsistent type definitions, before they can be committed. Linting rules go beyond syntax, enforcing naming conventions, field order, and the presence of key metadata like version numbers and error models.

Next is **diffing**. When a contract changes, automated tools compare the new version to the previous one, classifying the change as breaking, non-breaking, or additive. This classification can trigger downstream workflows: for example, a breaking change might automatically open tickets for dependent teams, while a non-breaking change might simply be flagged in a shared update feed.

Validation continues into runtime with **example tests**. These are minimal input/output samples included in the contract that can be executed in CI pipelines against the actual capability implementation. Running these tests across all target environments, browser sandbox, edge device, and cloud container, confirms that the implementation behaves as specified in every environment UMA supports.

Contract changes that pass validation can still fail subtly when deployed at scale, which is why UMA advocates for **runtime canarying**. A new contract version can be deployed to a small group of consumers or environments, with telemetry monitoring for anomalies in latency, error rates, or resource usage. If issues arise, rollback is immediate and contained. Multi-version support is sometimes necessary. A single capability may need to support an older contract for a large consumer base while rolling out a new one for early adopters. UMA recommends isolating these versions at the adapter layer rather than allowing version logic to creep into the core of the capability. This keeps the implementation clean and makes removal of the old version straightforward once it is retired. When automated checks and version isolation are used together, teams can evolve their contracts confidently, knowing they have safety nets both in development and in production.

Federated Contribution Models and Drift Detection

In UMA's ecosystem, no single team owns all capabilities. Large systems are built through the combined efforts of many contributors, often spread across different departments, subsidiaries, or partner organizations. A federated contribution model allows these groups to collaborate without funneling all changes through a single bottleneck.

In a federated model, each team manages its own set of contracts and capabilities but follows shared governance rules. This ensures compatibility without restricting autonomy. A core architecture group might define naming conventions, schema fragments, and error code standards, while individual teams remain free to design their contracts as needed within those boundaries. This mirrors how open-source projects maintain coherence even when hundreds of contributors work in parallel.

Federation only works if the ecosystem can detect and address **drift,** the gradual divergence between a contract and its implementation. Drift is inevitable over time: a capability may gain optional fields that never make it into the contract, or a contract may describe error conditions that the implementation no longer produces. Left unchecked, drift erodes trust in the registry and forces consumers to compensate for inconsistencies.

To prevent issues, UMA employs automated **drift detection tools**. These tools test the implementation against the contract's own sample inputs and outputs, comparing actual behavior with the declared specifications. Any differences trigger alerts, which can be triaged like any other defect. In more advanced setups, drift checks run continuously in staging environments and prevent deployments if the contract and implementation no longer match. This combination of shared ownership and ongoing validation creates a healthy balance: teams have the freedom to innovate, but they cannot silently break shared agreements. It's a balance of independence and accountability that allows UMA ecosystems to grow without collapsing under the burden of integration failures.

Cross-Team Standards

Even in a federated environment, some rules must be universal. Without shared standards, the registry becomes a patchwork of incompatible styles that hinder discovery and integration. Cross-team standards in UMA focus more on eliminating unnecessary friction than on restricting creativity.

One of the simplest yet most impactful areas is **naming conventions**. When capabilities, fields, and events follow consistent naming rules, they are easier to search for and understand instantly. A developer moving from one project to another should not have to guess whether a customer identifier is called `customerId`, `cust_id`, or `CID`. Standardizing on a single pattern benefits both tooling and human understanding.

Schema fragments are another vital shared asset. Many capabilities need to represent common concepts such as addresses, currencies, timestamps, or user identities. Defining these once as reusable schema components prevents duplication and guarantees consistency. It also allows validators to enforce rules across multiple contracts automatically; for example, if the "currency" fragment requires a three-letter ISO code, that requirement applies everywhere it is used.

For error handling, UMA benefits from **standardized error codes**. Instead of relying on free-form messages, capabilities map errors to predefined codes that carry specific meanings. This enables automated routing, categorization, and even translation of mistakes without needing to parse unpredictable text strings.

Finally, UMA uses **policy profiles** to bundle non-functional requirements. A profile might specify latency targets, resource budgets, retry behavior, and QoS class for a category of capabilities. Assigning a profile to a contract makes these requirements clear and machine-readable, allowing enforcement tools to act on them consistently across runtimes.

Cross-team standards like these do not eliminate the need for creativity in capability design but remove the noise resulting from avoidable inconsistency. They give UMA systems a shared language, one that both humans and machines can understand.

Closing Thoughts on Governance

Governance in UMA is integrated into the architecture itself, not an afterthought added later. The contracts, registries, validation pipelines, and shared standards are all technical expressions of a core principle: stability and agility can coexist, but only with active maintenance. In many organizations, governance is seen as a barrier to speed, but in UMA, it encourages confidence. The stronger the governance framework, the freer teams are to innovate, experiment with new runtimes, and respond to changing needs, knowing that automated safeguards and transparent processes prevent accidental errors. Over time, the benefits accumulate. A well-governed UMA ecosystem is easier to extend, audit, and integrate into new environments. Contracts remain accurate, users trust the registry, and potential issues are caught early. Even when capabilities span browsers, edge devices, and cloud services, the rules for change stay precise and predictable. Good governance isn't a one-time setup but an ongoing practice that evolves with the architecture. As UMA grows more complex and widely adopted, its governance must evolve by adding validation rules, refining standards, and learning from real-world incidents. This flexibility helps keep the architecture healthy long-term. When governance is viewed as a tool to boost productivity rather than just control, it quietly supports scale. It enables diverse teams to work seamlessly as if they're one, despite differences in runtimes, locations, and organizations. In UMA, such unity is no accident; it results from intentional and disciplined design.

Case Studies and Lessons

Introduction

Theory alone can make architecture appear deceptively tidy. On paper, all capabilities connect seamlessly, contracts are flawlessly upheld, and runtime systems perform exactly as planned. However, real-world scenarios are more chaotic. Hardware can fail, networks can deteriorate, requirements can change midway through a project, and decisions made under stress can have long-lasting ripple effects. Case studies dispel this idealized view by illustrating what happens when UMA principles are applied to actual problems, sometimes effectively, other times through valuable lessons learned. These anonymized examples, drawn from deployments in various industries, showcase different constraints from bandwidth-limited rural classrooms to high-speed payment systems at retail counters. The purpose isn't to promote UMA as a perfect solution but to demonstrate how concepts like capability contracts, portable modules, resource budgets, quality tiers, and failover strategies perform under real operational conditions. They also highlight the importance of observability and governance in helping teams respond when things go wrong, often preventing minor issues from escalating into costly outages.

By exploring scenarios in education, travel, payments, automotive, healthcare, logistics, and energy, we observe recurring architectural patterns that appear in different forms. A portable rendering engine for lesson plans has more in common with an in-vehicle update service than it might initially seem. An event contract catalog for airline itineraries offers lessons for fleet logistics. These patterns serve as the connective tissue of UMA, demonstrating that the architecture is versatile and can adapt across various runtimes, industries, and regulatory environments.

The following sections are not hypothetical exercises. They showcase the architecture in action, transforming abstract diagrams into real-world constraints, where success hinges on aligning design principles with the limitations and opportunities of the deployment environment.

Education: Distributed Learning Platform at the Edge

In many regions, delivering high-quality educational content is not just a matter of software; it is a fight against unreliable infrastructure. One deployment involved a national program aimed at modernizing classrooms in rural and semi-urban areas. The vision was to give students access to interactive science modules, video lectures, and adaptive assessments, all without relying on constant internet connectivity.

The first challenge was **hardware diversity**. Some schools had decade-old desktop PCs running outdated operating systems, while others had newer tablets with limited storage and modest CPUs. There was no realistic way to standardize the hardware fleet before launch. The second challenge was **network unreliability**. In many locations, the network was down for hours at a time, and when it was up, bandwidth was often too low for real-time streaming.

The UMA solution centered on **portable capability modules** that could render lesson content locally. Each module was packaged to run on any of the target environments: browser, native desktop, or low-cost Linux thin client without rewriting its internal logic. A **capability contract** specified the content formats supported, the rendering latency budget (to ensure snappy classroom use), and the maximum memory footprint to avoid crashing older machines.

An **offline-first synchronization pattern** was essential. Content and student progress data were cached locally and only synchronized back to the central system when bandwidth was available. The sync process was incremental, meaning only changes were transmitted, which reduced bandwidth use. Resource budgets were enforced at runtime so modules could adjust quality levels based on available CPU or memory, shifting from animated simulations to static diagrams when needed.

One unexpected benefit of the UMA approach was easier integration with external educational tools. Because lesson rendering and student tracking were defined in contracts, third-party content providers could package their material as UMA-compliant modules. This avoided the complex process of custom integrations and allowed the program to expand its library rapidly.

Lesson Learned: In constrained, heterogeneous environments, portability is not just a convenience; it is a vital survival feature. UMA's ability to run the same capabilities on old PCs, new tablets, and offline browsers without forking the codebase transformed a fragile pilot into a scalable national program.

Travel: Real-Time Itinerary Updates Across Devices

In the travel industry, timing and consistency are crucial. One primary transportation provider received recurring customer complaints: itinerary details displayed on the mobile app, airport kiosks, and in-flight entertainment systems often conflicted. Sometimes, a gate change would update on one channel but be delayed by minutes or hours on another. For connecting passengers, those minutes could mean missing a flight.

The main challenge was **maintaining consistency across multiple channels amid constant updates**. Flight schedules, gate assignments, and seat allocations could change dozens of times per hour, especially during disruptions. The system had to send updates instantly to various devices, including mobile apps, kiosk terminals, airline partner portals, and onboard systems, all with limited bandwidth.

The UMA implementation started with **capability contracts** for itinerary services. These outlined the structure of an itinerary update event, the expected latency for delivery, and the acceptable staleness of cached data. Instead of each device platform connecting directly to the airline's central scheduling system, they subscribed to an **event-driven coordination layer**.

A catalog of event contracts served as the single source of truth for what each update contained and how it should be interpreted. This enabled routing the same update through different adapters: JSON over WebSockets for mobile apps, a compact binary format over satellite links for in-flight systems, and direct API calls for kiosks. UMA's runtime-agnostic modules allowed the same event processing logic to operate seamlessly across all environments.

The system also implemented **multi-endpoint failover**. If the primary event broker became unreachable, edge adapters in kiosks or aircraft could request incremental updates from a backup source. Resource budgets in UMA contracts ensured that large, unexpected payloads (like updated seat maps) were handled smoothly, preventing crashes in memory-limited environments.

One key insight came from observability. UMA's structured telemetry made it clear where delays were creeping in. In one incident, a specific in-flight system firmware update introduced extra parsing latency. With UMA's contract-based monitoring, this was identified within hours, not days, and patched before passengers noticed widespread issues.

Lesson Learned: When information must be accurate across multiple runtimes in near real time, a single authoritative event contract with portable, runtime-agnostic logic can transform a fragmented integration into a unified experience without forcing every channel to share the same stack.

Payments: Low-Latency Transaction Processing

In retail payments, every millisecond matters. A point-of-sale (POS) system for a major chain needed to process card authorizations in less than 300 milliseconds during peak hours. This was not just about improving the customer experience; payment processors also imposed penalties for prolonged transaction times, and delays could directly impact revenue. The challenge was that network conditions varied across locations. Urban stores with fiber connections could quickly reach the central payment gateway. In contrast, rural or pop-up locations often relied on shared, high-latency links. At significant events, some mobile POS setups experienced intermittent connectivity, especially when cell towers were overloaded. The UMA solution relied on **local decision loops, with** each POS terminal running a portable capability module that pre-validated transactions using cached rules, risk thresholds, and card network metadata. This allowed many transactions to be approved or denied locally within tens of milliseconds, while still queuing them for settlement with the central system when connectivity permitted.

The capability contract for the payment module specified:

- **Resource budgets** to ensure the decision process is completed within 50 milliseconds under typical load.
- **Latency classes** to differentiate between immediate approvals and deferred settlements.
- **Failover strategies** to route to an alternate payment processor if the primary one exceeds a timeout threshold.

For locations with stable connections, UMA's runtime-agnostic approach enabled the same validation logic to run inside a containerized microservice at the edge of the payment processor's infrastructure. For offline or resource-constrained environments, the same module could operate in a browser-based POS or on an embedded terminal running a lightweight Linux OS. Observability was crucial. UMA's structured logs tagged each decision with a reason code such as local approval, network fallback, or processor failover, allowing the payment operations team to fine-tune the rules over time. This setup enabled them to push updated capability modules without modifying the underlying POS application code.

Lesson Learned: In latency-sensitive domains, the ability to run identical logic at multiple points, including edge, browser, and cloud, without code divergence is crucial for meeting SLAs and avoiding lost transactions. UMA's contract-driven portability transformed what was once a fragile, single-path workflow into a resilient, multi-path system that can continue processing even when the network fails.

Automotive: Predictive Maintenance and OTA Updates

In the automotive sector, software is no longer just an accessory; it has become central to vehicle safety, performance, and user experience. One manufacturer needed a system to deliver predictive maintenance insights and over-the-air (OTA) software updates to vehicles across multiple regions. These vehicles ranged from the latest models with powerful onboard computers to older platforms with modest embedded processors and limited storage.

The challenge comprised two main issues. First, **hardware differences** meant that a single binary or update image would not work across all models. Second, **connectivity was inconsistent**. Some vehicles had a constant LTE connection; others only connected when visiting a service center or via a driver's mobile hotspot. Pushing a significant update without addressing these limitations could leave a vehicle in an incomplete or unsafe state.

UMA's approach began with **portable update modules** rather than monolithic firmware packages. Each update capability was described in a contract that included:

- Target hardware compatibility matrix
- Expected install time under the given CPU and memory budgets
- Rollback procedures in case of failure
- Resource usage profiles for both installation and operation

This contract-driven design allowed the update service to determine, at runtime, whether a vehicle could accept an update, needed a degraded version, or should defer installation until resources were available.

Policy profiles were used to categorize the fleet into tiers. Premium infotainment systems could handle high-resolution assets, while older units received lighter builds. UMA's runtime-agnostic modules ensured that diagnostic and maintenance capabilities could also operate in both the vehicle's embedded environment and the manufacturer's cloud analytics platform, using the same core logic for consistency.

A key safety feature was the **failover strategy between the edge and cloud**. If a vehicle started an update and lost connection, it could continue using a locally cached package, verifying integrity against a signed contract before applying changes. In predictive maintenance, onboard UMA modules gathered sensor data, used local health models, and triggered service recommendations, sending summaries to the cloud once connectivity was restored.

Lesson Learned: In safety-critical fields like automotive, combining precise compatibility metadata, staged rollouts, and runtime-agnostic modules isn't just operationally efficient; it's essential to prevent failures that could endanger both the vehicle and the brand's reputation. UMA's model guaranteed that the same capability could be trusted whether operating in the cloud, on a high-end infotainment system, or on a basic embedded controller.

Healthcare: Diagnostic Workflow in Constrained Environments

In healthcare, time and accuracy directly influence patient outcomes. A hospital network serving remote areas needed to quickly process diagnostic imaging and lab results, often in facilities with limited bandwidth and older equipment. Delays in delivering results to doctors could delay treatment decisions, especially for urgent cases. The main challenge was **balancing performance with compliance**. Medical data is protected by strict privacy laws, and in some regions, patient information cannot leave the facility without encryption or anonymization. At the same time, clinicians required AI-assisted analysis of imaging scans to accelerate diagnosis, especially in areas lacking specialists.

UMA provided a **portable diagnostic capability module** that could run in three modes:

1. **Local AI inference** on a hospital workstation or imaging device, using a smaller, resource-optimized model.

2. **Hybrid processing**, where preliminary results were computed locally and the complete analysis was run in a compliant cloud environment.

3. **Cloud-only mode** for facilities with sufficient bandwidth and regulatory approval.

The module's **capability contract** specified:

- Required input formats and metadata (DICOM for images, HL7 for lab data)
- Latency classes for urgent vs. routine cases
- CPU and GPU usage budgets to avoid impacting other hospital systems
- Security policies, including mandatory encryption at rest and in transit

In facilities with unreliable internet, UMA's **offline-first approach** enabled AI models and diagnostic logic to operate entirely on-site. When connectivity was restored, results were synchronized, and the cloud service verified the outputs against updated models, highlighting discrepancies for review. This setup not only ensured compliance but also kept critical workflows running even during network outages.

An important aspect was **observability linked to compliance**. UMA's structured logs included policy compliance markers and anonymization status, facilitating automated audits without manual data searches. This reduced the effort needed to prove regulatory compliance while maintaining operational speed.

Lesson Learned: In regulated, latency-sensitive domains, UMA's capability to package logic into portable, policy-aware modules allowed hospitals to deploy the same diagnostic workflows across very different environments without sacrificing compliance, performance, or the ability to incorporate AI where it added the most value.

Logistics: Multi-modal Fleet Coordination

In large-scale logistics operations, even minor inefficiencies can lead to significant delays. A global shipping and delivery company faced the challenge of managing a mixed fleet of trucks, ships, rail, and last-mile delivery vans across multiple regions. Each mode had its own tracking systems, connectivity profiles, and operational limitations.

The main issue was **fragmented visibility**. Drivers in rural areas often worked offline for hours. Ships depended on satellite links with limited bandwidth. Trains sent periodic bulk updates rather than continuous streams. This situation made it difficult to provide customers with accurate ETAs and to reroute shipments dynamically when disruptions happened.

The UMA solution started with **event-driven coordination features** packaged as portable modules. These features subscribed to standardized **movement update events** defined in a shared capability contract. The contract outlined the minimum required fields (vehicle ID, location, status, cargo details), optional enrichments (weather, traffic), update frequency expectations, and the maximum acceptable latency for synchronization.

Because the modules were runtime-agnostic, the same event-processing logic could run in

- A cloud control center, integrating updates from all fleets
- Onboard gateways in trucks and ships, processing data locally and sending summarized updates
- Last-mile delivery devices, including ruggedized tablets running browser-based UMA modules offline

A **local control loop** pattern was vital. When offline, edge modules used routing rules locally to change delivery sequences or reassign loads, then synchronized these changes once connectivity was restored. For instance, a delivery van stuck in traffic could swap drop-off orders without needing central approval, as long as the capability contract's SLA rules were satisfied. A significant achievement was in **progressive fidelity**. In low-bandwidth conditions, modules sent only essential data such as position and ETA updates, buffering full telemetry for later. This method kept customer-facing ETAs accurate even when backend systems worked with partial data. Observability across this diverse environment was achieved through UMA's structured logging and **compatibility graphs**. These tools showed when specific fleet segments were lagging in updates, enabling targeted fixes like prioritizing bandwidth for critical vehicles.

Lesson Learned: UMA's portable, contract-driven event processing transformed a collection of disconnected tracking systems into a coordinated fleet. By maintaining consistent logic and rules across runtimes, the company improved ETA accuracy, reduced rerouting delays, and handled disruptions more smoothly, even when entire fleet segments were offline for hours.

Energy: Grid Monitoring and Demand Response

In modern power grids, real-time monitoring and response to fluctuations are essential for maintaining stability and efficiency. A regional energy provider needed a comprehensive system for grid monitoring and demand management across a diverse area, including urban, industrial, and rural zones. The environment was highly heterogeneous, with smart meters, industrial sensors, and control systems from various vendors operating on different systems and communication protocols. The main challenge was to deliver low-latency responses without overloading the central control system. During peak demand, delays in load adjustments could cause blackouts or expensive emergency power procurement. Additionally, regulatory standards required detailed traceability of every change, ensuring that no consumer's service was unfairly affected.

UMA addressed the problem with **distributed capability modules** deployed both at the edge inside substations, industrial controllers, and smart meters and in the cloud. These modules implemented the same decision logic for

- Detecting over-threshold consumption or under-frequency conditions
- Triggering localized demand reduction (e.g., cycling HVAC systems or shifting industrial loads)
- Reporting state changes back to the central grid operator

The **capability contracts** set the latency limits for detection and response, as well as the maximum CPU and memory usage for embedded devices, along with compliance metadata for audit logging. This guarantees that even on low-power or legacy hardware, the modules can run reliably without interfering with other critical systems.

A **progressive fidelity** approach allowed the modules to operate in three tiers:

1. **Immediate local action** based on the last known policy, without waiting for central confirmation
2. **Regional coordination** via substation controllers to balance loads across neighborhoods
3. **Central orchestration** when bandwidth allowed, aligning local actions with grid-wide priorities

This design considerably shortened the time-to-action during demand spikes from several seconds to under 200 milliseconds in most cases, while still maintaining a complete audit trail for regulatory review. UMA's **runtime-agnostic modules** enabled the same demand response logic to run in cloud simulations, field devices, and even browser-based control panels used by operators in remote monitoring centers.

Lesson Learned: In critical infrastructure, speed and consistency must coexist with governance and auditability. UMA's ability to push decision logic to the edge, while ensuring it matched cloud-based orchestration, created a system that was fast enough to prevent blackouts and transparent enough to pass regulatory scrutiny.

Patterns That Survive the Real World

Across industries as diverse as education, travel, payments, automotive, healthcare, logistics, and energy, the same UMA principles appear in slightly different forms. The environments differ, constraints shift, and priorities change, yet certain patterns consistently distinguish success from failure. Portable, runtime-agnostic capabilities enable teams to write logic once and deploy it in the cloud, at the edge, or in constrained embedded environments without rewriting core functionality. Contracts rich in metadata, clear about constraints, and carefully versioned provide every system participant with a transparent and enforceable understanding of how a capability should behave. Resource budgets, quality tiers, and policy profiles ensure that capabilities operate reliably regardless of deployment location. Event-driven coordination allows loosely coupled systems to remain responsive under fluctuating connectivity and scale pressures. Observability and governance transform what could be chaotic, multi-runtime sprawl into a system that is measurable, testable, and predictable. The case studies also reveal a common truth: **UMA's success depends as much on discipline as on technology**. The most advanced architecture will fail if teams bypass contracts, ignore resource budgets, or allow coupling through shortcuts. Conversely, even modest capabilities can deliver outsized value if they respect these constraints from the start. These real-world examples demonstrate that UMA is not just an abstract design. It is a set of practices, patterns, and tools that adapt to the physical, operational, and regulatory realities of the industries they serve. The architecture's value comes not from promising that nothing will ever go wrong, but from ensuring that when issues arise, the system can bend without breaking and recover without guesswork.

Trade-Offs and When UMA Might Not Fit

Introduction

Universal Microservices Architecture is designed to address specific issues such as portability across runtimes, consistency in distributed execution, and governance at scale. In the right context, it can revolutionize how capabilities are developed, deployed, and maintained. However, like any architectural approach, it is not a magic solution.

Treating UMA as the only solution risks applying it where the trade-offs outweigh the advantages. Microservices of any kind introduce complexity: they require a certain level of organizational discipline, mature DevOps capabilities, and a culture comfortable with distributed systems. Without these foundations, the overhead of managing contracts, enforcing budgets, and maintaining multi-runtime deployments can quickly outweigh the benefits UMA aims to provide.

A good architect views UMA as one tool among many, to be employed when the problem aligns with its strengths. It works best when systems need to operate across diverse environments, when portability provides a competitive edge, and when consistent governance is crucial for scaling. In simpler situations, or with teams lacking the skills to handle its operational demands, other patterns might offer a better balance of simplicity and value.

The Cost of Complexity

UMA is designed to manage the complexity of running capabilities across browsers, edge devices, and cloud environments with consistent contracts, budgets, and governance. However, this strength brings operational challenges.

In a UMA system, each capability is its own independently deployable unit. It has a contract that must be defined, versioned, tested, and published. It runs within a specified budget for CPU, memory, and execution time that must be enforced across various runtimes. It may require adapters for multiple brokers, databases, or event formats. Additionally, it needs to be observable from the outside, with logs, metrics, and traces collected and correlated regardless of where it executes.

This is not just a tooling problem. It's a skill and culture problem. A UMA-ready team needs the following:

- **Engineering discipline** to keep logic runtime-agnostic, respecting contract boundaries without "just this once" shortcuts.
- **Operational maturity** to run automated CI/CD pipelines, resource quota enforcement, and runtime validation across heterogeneous environments.
- **Governance capability** to track versions, manage compatibility, and enforce quality tiers without slowing delivery.

Without these foundations, UMA's moving parts can overwhelm the team. Developers might spend more time battling cross-runtime bugs than delivering features. Operations could get buried under the complexity of managing and monitoring multiple deployment targets. Governance may become a bottleneck instead of an enabler. The truth is that UMA's benefits scale with the size, diversity, and longevity of the system. In small, uniform, short-lived projects, the cost of this complexity often outweighs the benefits.

When UMA Is Overkill

There are many situations where UMA's complexity isn't necessary. If the problem doesn't require runtime-agnostic execution, strict governance, or multi-runtime observability, then UMA is like using a cargo ship to carry a single box.

- **Small, simple applications** such as personal blogs, informational websites, or internal tools for a handful of users rarely require the portability and runtime diversity UMA addresses. For these, the extra contracts, orchestration layers, and observability frameworks would add unnecessary maintenance overhead without creating business value.
- **Short-lived projects** are another case. A proof-of-concept, hackathon project, or short campaign landing page might be better served by a simple monolith or minimal microservice setup. UMA's up-front investment in defining and governing contracts only pays off when the system has to live and evolve over time.

- **Single-platform products** also often fall outside UMA's sweet spot. A native desktop app, an embedded C++ application for a specific device, or an iOS-only product can be built with full optimization for its target platform. Adding a runtime-agnostic abstraction layer here would likely make the code more complex and less performant without unlocking any real portability.
- Finally, there are **hard real-time or ultra-low-latency systems,** such as firmware for industrial robots, audio DSP engines (Digital Signal Processing engines specialized hardware or software systems that perform real-time mathematical operations on signals such as audio, video, or radio waves; audio DSPs power noise cancellation, equalization, and codec processing in headphones, hearing aids, and broadcast equipment, often requiring sub-millisecond deterministic processing that cannot tolerate abstraction overhead), or high-frequency trading systems. These systems require strict control over hardware, memory, and execution cycles. UMA's abstraction layers and budget enforcement mechanisms could interfere with the precise control these systems need.

The point is not that UMA is "too heavy" in a strict sense, but that every architecture involves trade-offs. If portability, governance, and cross-runtime deployment are not key concerns, then the simplest, most straightforward solution is usually the best.

Partial Adoption Patterns

Even when a full UMA deployment isn't suitable, many of its principles can still provide value when applied selectively. The key is to identify where portability, governance, or consistency can meaningfully enhance a system and to adopt only those elements. One common approach is **using contracts without full portability**. For example, a team developing a set of cloud-only microservices might still benefit from having machine-readable contracts with defined inputs, outputs, error models, and resource expectations. This enhances discoverability, supports automated validation, and allows consumer teams to integrate with confidence even if all services run on the same platform.

Another approach is **introducing UMA runtime principles to a select group of services**. A large SaaS product may have dozens of backend services, but only a few need to run both in the cloud and on customer-managed edge appliances. By applying UMA's portability and budget enforcement only to those capabilities, the team avoids adding unnecessary complexity to services that don't require it.

Selective adoption also works for **device-specific products that occasionally need to operate across different environments**. For example, a medical imaging device might perform most processing locally but periodically send workloads to the cloud for advanced analysis. In this case, only the cloud-facing capabilities would be wrapped in UMA's runtime-agnostic execution model.

In all of these cases, the goal is to leverage the **governance and consistency benefits** of UMA, such as contract validation, observability standards, and quality tiers, without the full overhead of multi-runtime deployment. This "pick and choose" approach can also serve as a stepping stone toward full UMA adoption later, enabling teams to develop skills and infrastructure gradually.

The Maturity Path

For teams considering UMA, the journey to full adoption rarely happens with a single leap. Most successful implementations grow gradually, starting with practices that offer immediate value and building a foundation for more advanced capabilities over time.

The first phase typically involves **contract discipline**. Even if services are not yet portable across runtimes, establishing clear, machine-readable contracts improves interoperability and creates a common language among teams. This step also encourages habits like semantic versioning, compatibility testing, and maintaining contextual changelogs, which are essential for UMA.

The next phase is **selective runtime abstraction**. Teams start separating business logic from platform-specific bindings so that the core capability can, in theory, operate across multiple environments. This stage may also include developing a small adapter layer for one alternative runtime, such as running a service both in the cloud and a local container for offline use.

From there, teams can progress to **multi-runtime deployment**. This is when UMA's full advantages begin to surface, but also when its complexity increases. Capabilities are now deployed to browsers, edge devices, and cloud runtimes under the same contract, with consistent resource budgets, quality tiers, and governance. Observability and orchestration must work seamlessly across all environments, and operational practices need to adapt for the expanded scope.

The final stage is **governed by large-scale UMA**. At this point, contracts are not merely static agreements but active metadata that drives automated composition, compatibility analysis, and AI-assisted orchestration. Multiple teams can contribute capabilities confidently, knowing they will work across runtimes without regression.

This maturity path enables teams to develop into UMA gradually, avoiding early overwhelm. It also offers natural checkpoints to evaluate if the architecture is providing the expected value before progressing further.

Next Steps

Universal Microservices Architecture isn't just a theoretical idea. It offers a practical solution to the increasing fragmentation of runtimes, devices, and execution environments that modern systems must handle. At its essence, UMA views capabilities as portable, contract-based units that can operate anywhere, within set budgets, and with predictable behavior.

Over the course of this book, we've examined why portability is essential, how UMA's principles function in real-world scenarios, and what it takes to implement them across diverse platforms. We've explored the role of self-describing contracts, the significance of event-driven coordination, and strategies that enable edge-native design. We've seen how governance, observability, and resource management turn an abstract architecture into an operational setup.

For teams ready to start, the following steps don't require a complete overhaul. You can begin small: introduce machine-readable contracts, establish consistent budget definitions, or deploy a single capability to both an edge device and a cloud runtime. Each step helps build the habits and tools needed for full UMA adoption when it's the right choice.

The main lesson is that architecture decisions should reflect business and technical realities, not trends. UMA is powerful because it addresses specific issues of cross-runtime portability, governance, and consistency that are increasingly relevant as systems integrate cloud, edge, and client execution. However, as we've discussed, it's just one of many tools, and it works best when used intentionally.

In the coming years, the lines between devices, runtimes, and services will continue to blur. AI-native systems will need to coordinate capabilities across unpredictable environments. Developers will expect the same service to run in the browser for quick interactions, at the edge for local decisions, and in the cloud for large-scale processing, all without rewriting core logic. UMA offers a framework to meet this challenge, and for those who adopt it, the benefits go beyond the technical elegance; they provide a genuine strategic advantage.

Summary and Transition

Introduction

Before diving into the practical steps for building services within a Universal Microservices Architecture, let's pause to review what we've covered so far. A summary isn't just a recap; it helps link the concepts into a clear mental model. Reflecting back ensures our foundation is solid before adding the complexities of implementation.

So far, we've examined UMA from various perspectives: its definition and purpose, how contracts, logic, and runtime are separated, how service boundaries are set, and how these services can be made portable and resilient in diverse environments. We've discussed event-driven coordination, edge-native constraints, governance, and the trade-offs involved in choosing UMA.

The aim of this chapter is to synthesize these ideas into key takeaways that will steer the upcoming content. With the core principles in place, the following chapters will focus on the practical aspects of runtime abstractions, service packaging, and transforming these concepts into operational, deployable capabilities.

Core Concepts Recap

At its core, Universal Microservices Architecture (UMA) outlines a way to design and operate capabilities that are portable, contract-governed, and consistent across different runtimes. Portability isn't just about moving code; it's about separating concerns so that business logic remains isolated from runtime bindings and execution environments. This separation enables the same capability to run in a browser, at the edge, or in the cloud without rewriting the core logic.

We started by defining UMA itself and its purpose: to address the fragmentation of modern computing environments and to provide a framework for deploying services across diverse platforms. This led to the principle of separating contract, logic, and runtime. Contracts serve as machine-readable agreements detailing inputs, outputs, error models, performance expectations, and resource limits. Logic encompasses the core business rules, free from platform-specific dependencies. Runtime bindings manage adaptation to specific environments.

Next, we examined how to define service boundaries that maintain modularity and minimize unintended coupling. This involved considering outcomes, domain stability, change frequency, data ownership, failure domains, and trust levels when deciding where one capability ends and another begins.

Portability was explored in depth, from portable binaries and runtime-agnostic execution to how event-driven coordination allows services to remain loosely coupled. The Event Contract Catalog Architecture demonstrated how event metadata, ownership, and governance can simplify the operation of large-scale asynchronous systems.

We also examined edge-native design, taking into account the limitations of limited CPU, memory, intermittent connectivity, and diverse hardware. Strategies like offline-first processing, progressive fidelity, and deterministic resource budgets demonstrated how UMA adapts to these conditions.

Governance was positioned as a productivity enhancer, not a bureaucratic hurdle, ensuring that contracts stay trustworthy, discoverable, and versioned while enabling automated validation and cross-team collaboration. Finally, we considered non-functional aspects such as availability, resilience, scalability, and quality of service, along with the trade-offs that influence when UMA should and should not be applied.

Benefits in Practice

The ideas discussed throughout this book are not just academic concepts; they directly translate into tangible advantages when building and operating modern systems. UMA's design principles offer benefits that accumulate over time, making it easier to adapt to new environments, incorporate emerging technologies, and maintain system quality as complexity increases.

One of the most immediate advantages is **reusability**. Because capabilities are designed with a clear separation between contract, logic, and runtime, the same core module can be deployed in multiple contexts without changes. A data transformation capability, for example, could run in a serverless cloud function for batch processing, in a browser for client-side filtering, and at the edge for low-latency decisions without any branching logic or environment-specific hacks.

Testability improves alongside. With well-defined contracts, capabilities can be tested against the same scenarios regardless of the runtime. This enables uniform automated testing, where a single test suite validates a module across different environments, reducing the risk of runtime-specific bugs going unnoticed.

Deployment agility is another key benefit. When capabilities are small and portable, teams can release updates independently of a platform's deployment cycle. This makes it easier to address security issues, optimize performance, or implement feature requests without waiting for monolithic releases.

Finally, UMA establishes a foundation for **AI-assisted orchestration**. Because contracts are machine-readable and include detailed metadata such as performance budgets, latency classes, and error handling rules, AI systems can reason about how to compose, optimize, and route capabilities dynamically. This enables orchestration decisions that adapt to shifting load, network conditions, or device capabilities in real time, without human intervention.

Looking Ahead

With the core concepts and benefits of UMA now clear, the next step is to move from theory to practice. The upcoming chapter will focus on how to actually build UMA-compliant services, translating the architectural principles into tangible implementation steps. We will start with **runtime abstraction layers**, the foundation that enables a single capability to function in different environments without changing its core logic. From there, we will examine **service packaging** and how to bundle logic, contracts, and metadata into a portable unit that can be deployed across browsers, edge devices, and cloud platforms. The chapter will also cover the practical aspects of **tooling, build pipelines, and deployment patterns** that support UMA's goals. This includes strategies for automated testing across runtimes, ensuring consistent enforcement of resource budgets, and integrating governance into daily development workflows. By the end of the next chapter, the reader will have a step-by-step guide for creating their first UMA service, packaging it for multiple runtimes, and verifying that it performs consistently across them. In short, we will transform the ideas that so far exist in diagrams and examples into real-world implementations.

CHAPTER 4

The Road to UMA: From SOA to Metadata

How the Evolution from SOA to Edge Computing Shaped the Foundations of UMA

The Promise of SOA and ESBs

The Dream of Reuse in the Early 2000s

When service-oriented architecture (SOA) emerged in the early 2000s, it was a genuine breakthrough. After years of building massive monoliths, the concept of defining services as modular units, communicating through standard protocols, and reusing logic across different domains seemed transformational. Vendors claimed that with an enterprise service bus at the center, everything would just work.

It is worth pausing on what those standard protocols actually were. SOAP (Simple Object Access Protocol) was the messaging format: it wrapped data in XML for transmission between services. WSDL (Web Services Description Language) was the contract file that described what a service accepted and returned in machine-readable form. XML (eXtensible Markup Language) was the underlying data format that tied both together. Together they formed a stack that was verbose and ceremonial but for the first time gave teams a shared language across organizational boundaries.

The ESB (Enterprise Service Bus) sat at the center of this model. It was a middleware layer, a piece of infrastructure software that connected applications and handled routing, transformation, and orchestration of messages between them. The appeal was that application teams no longer needed to know how to talk to each other directly. They connected to the bus, and the bus managed the complexity. In the hospitality industry, for example, booking systems, payment services, loyalty programs, and customer profile

E. Piovesan, *Universal Microservices Architecture*, https://doi.org/10.1007/979-8-8688-2794-5_4

management could all be exposed as services connected through the bus. An airline could expose seat inventory as one service, fare calculation as another, and check-in processing as a third, each consumed by multiple channels without rebuilding the underlying logic. These are representative examples from one domain; SOA promised similar gains across healthcare, banking, retail, and logistics.

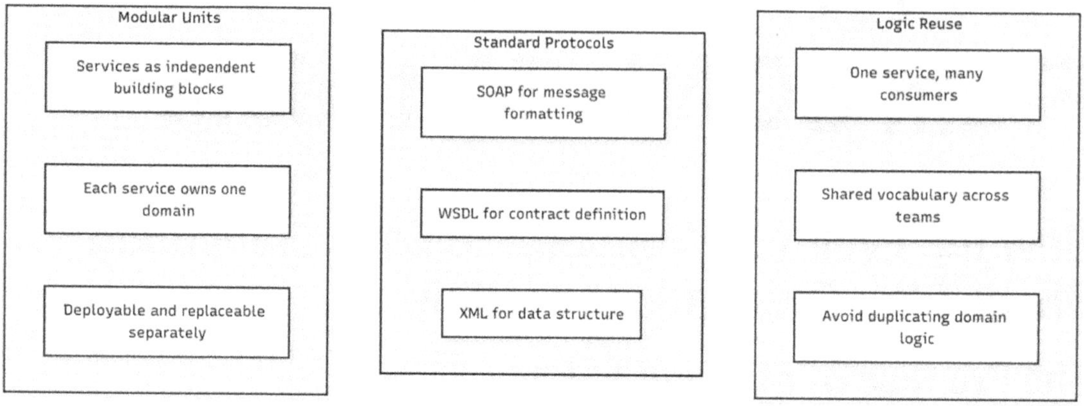

Figure 4-1. *The three foundational ideas of SOA, each valuable in isolation, but combined under a heavy ESB, created as many problems as they solved*

SOA did not entirely live up to its promise, but it is worth crediting what it got right before examining what went wrong. For the first time, contracts were taken seriously. WSDL files (the machine-readable contract format) and XML schemas (formal definitions of the structure, data types, and constraints of an XML document, used to validate that messages matched the agreed format) were cumbersome to write and maintain, but they created a shared language across teams. A developer joining a project could open a WSDL, read what a service accepted and returned, and write code against it without consulting the original authors. A schema acted as a contract enforced at the wire level: if a service sent a message that violated the schema, the ESB could reject it before it reached the consuming service. Service boundaries became clearer, and the idea of reuse stopped being a fantasy and became something teams could plan around.

But in practice, the promise did not hold. I saw this firsthand while working on a booking system that was supposed to combine inventory, payments, and customer profiles into one platform. The architecture looked impressive on paper: SOAP services defined for each domain, an ESB handling calls between them, and XML schemas ensuring consistency. Yet in practice, every step exposed the weight of the model.

Technically, SOAP contracts (which wrap every message in XML, including a mandatory envelope structure around even the simplest data payload) were verbose and fragile. Updating a single field in a booking record meant updating multiple WSDLs, generating new client stubs (auto-generated code that allows a consuming application to call a remote service as if it were a local function, produced by tools that read the WSDL and write the boilerplate communication code), and retesting serialization across services. XML schemas added another layer of overhead, and what seemed like a small change in business terms often led to days of adjustments across dependent schemas.

Organizationally, the ESB (the central middleware layer) became a bottleneck. A central team controlled it, and every integration had to pass through them. Adding something as simple as a loyalty points field to a booking was not a quick task; it triggered a series of approvals, contract updates, and regression tests that stretched timelines. Teams started designing around the ESB, not around the business.

This is the textbook definition of tight coupling: when one part of a system becomes so entangled with another that changing either requires coordinating both. The ESB had promised to decouple services from each other, but in practice it created a new, central coupling point. Every service was coupled to the ESB, which meant every service was indirectly coupled to every other service through it.

What struck me most during that project was how little of our energy went into improving the customer experience. Most of it was consumed by the mechanics of keeping the ESB and SOAP contracts satisfied. The architecture had promised reuse and agility, but what we got was complexity, bloat, and slowness. SOA gave us contracts and service boundaries, but it also showed me how fragile those promises become when the architecture itself is too heavy to evolve.

Microservices: Freedom at a Cost

The Rise of Microservices

The frustrations with SOA and ESBs naturally led to the search for a simpler model. As containers and cloud-native tools started to become popular through the late 2000s and into the early 2010s, the industry was ready for change. Microservices emerged as the answer, gaining real momentum around 2012 to 2014 as Docker matured and cloud infrastructure made independent deployment practical at scale.

Several technologies came together to enable this transformation. Docker simplifies packaging and running services consistently across different environments. REST APIs

(Representational State Transfer, an architectural style for building web services that uses standard HTTP methods and simple URLs rather than complex SOAP envelopes) and JSON (JavaScript Object Notation, a lightweight, human-readable data format that replaced XML for most service-to-service communication) replaced SOAP and XML as the primary means of communication between services, reducing the overhead caused by contracts that previously slowed projects down. Continuous delivery pipelines (automated workflows that build, test, and deploy code to production with minimal manual intervention, enabling teams to ship changes daily or even hourly rather than monthly) allowed teams to push changes into production quickly, avoiding the long release cycles of the SOA era.

The independence was broad. Teams could choose their own programming language and runtime: one team might build in Java, another in Node.js, and a third in Go. They could pick their own databases, their own testing tools, and their own deployment cadence. A new feature no longer requires negotiations with a central integration team or waiting weeks for approval. If a booking service needed to add loyalty points, the responsible team could implement the change, deploy it, and expose a new endpoint without disrupting the rest of the system. That freedom, after years of centralized SOA governance, felt genuinely liberating.

These services are typically communicated through synchronous REST calls over HTTP. One service called another and waited for a response before continuing. This worked well for simple workflows but created dependency chains: if service A called service B, and B was slow or unavailable, A would stall waiting for it. The synchronous default made the system feel responsive in good conditions and fragile under load.

When Freedom Became Fragmentation

At this startup, microservices meant something broader than the typical backend-only interpretation. Because the product had to run natively across iOS, Android, the web, and a backend, we applied the same principle of independent, platform-optimized units to every layer of the stack. Each platform was its own vertical team, with its own codebase, its own tooling, and its own deployment. The parallels to backend microservices are direct: small teams, independent delivery, and no central bottleneck. The difference was that our services ran on clients and devices, not just servers.

But even in those early days, cracks started to show. Freedom meant more services, and more services meant more moving parts. Each team optimized for its own goals, often reimplementing similar business logic in slightly different ways.

Orchestration quickly became its own bottleneck. Connecting dozens of independently deployed services into a coherent workflow was often harder than building the services themselves. When a user request touched six services in sequence, and something went wrong, the logs for each service lived in a different location, were formatted differently, and had no shared trace identifier linking them. Reproducing a bug often required coordinating engineers from multiple teams, each inspecting their own service in isolation, with no single view of what the whole request had done. The freedom that made microservices attractive also made the system much harder to understand as a whole.

Service sprawl increased the pressure. Every new feature seemed to justify launching another service, and soon the architecture map looked more like a web of dependencies than a clean design. Each service had its own APIs, deployment schedule, and quirks. Some services evolved quickly while others lagged behind, leading to unstable and unpredictable integration points.

A Java microservice was locked to the JVM (the Java Virtual Machine, the runtime that executes Java bytecode). A Node.js service was locked to V8 (the JavaScript engine used by Node.js and Chrome). Moving core logic from one to the other did not mean copying a file; it meant rewriting the code in a different language, with different idioms, different library ecosystems, and different failure modes. Portability within a runtime was real. Portability across runtimes remained a myth.

What Microservices Taught Me

Yet that freedom carried a hidden cost. What had once been centralized in the ESB was now duplicated across dozens of services. Consistency was no longer dictated by middleware, but it was also no longer guaranteed.

As we saw with the vector maps project (explored in depth in the section "Fragmentation in Practice: The Vector Maps Project"), early platform independence felt liberating. The costs only became visible as the system scaled and the same business logic needed to produce consistent results across fundamentally different environments.

What I learned during this period was that microservices addressed some of the pains of SOA but did not solve the core challenge of portability. Logic was portable within a container but not across different runtimes. Each platform still needed its own version of the same rules, and without a way to maintain consistency, those rules gradually drifted apart. Autonomy gave teams room to innovate, but it also made it more difficult to trust the system as a whole.

The bigger lesson was that architecture cannot stop at freedom. Autonomy without coherence ultimately collapses under its own weight. Speed and independence alone are not enough. True portability requires that business logic stays consistent, discoverable, and adaptable wherever it runs. Without this foundation, fragmentation ultimately erodes the benefits that microservices provide.

Serverless: Agility Meets Hidden Coupling

The Arrival of Serverless and Its Early Appeal

By the mid-2010s, teams were moving at a faster pace than ever before, but they were also starting to feel the strain of managing orchestration, monitoring, and deployment overhead. With each new service came more pipelines to maintain and more infrastructure to manage. Developers who once relished their independence were spending a growing portion of their time just keeping the system up and running.

It was in this context that AWS Lambda emerged in 2014. Lambda, along with the serverless platforms that followed, conveyed a simple yet radical idea: stop thinking about servers altogether. Instead of building and managing entire services, developers could write a single function, upload it, and let the platform determine how to execute, scale, and bill for it.

Three characteristics defined how serverless functions behaved. They were stateless: each invocation started with no memory of previous calls, making them easy to scale horizontally but requiring state to be stored externally in databases or caches. They were event-driven: a function ran only in response to a trigger, such as an HTTP request, a file upload, or a message on a queue, and was idle the rest of the time. And they were reactive: the platform handled scheduling and provisioning automatically, scaling from zero to thousands of concurrent executions without any configuration from the developer.

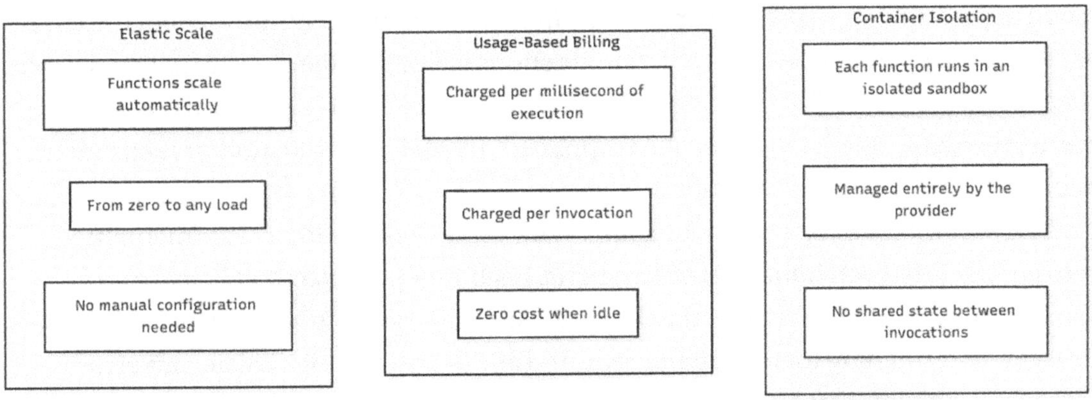

***Figure 4-2.** The three enabling factors that made serverless economically and operationally viable in the mid-2010s*

The appeal was immediate. Small yet critical tasks that had always been cumbersome to implement with larger services became straightforward. Processing an uploaded image, cleaning up database records, and sending notifications when an event occurred were perfect fits for serverless functions. Prototypes that once took weeks could be built in days or even hours. Costs tracked neatly against usage, and integrations could be wired together almost instantly.

Connecting a function to an event source was effortless, at least on the surface. The cloud provider handled the wiring, but the event payloads that arrived at a function were raw JSON blobs in a format specific to that provider. An S3 upload event in AWS looked nothing like a Cloud Storage event in GCP. There was no governed schema, no version identifier, and no contract describing what a consumer could rely on. As long as the function worked today, no one worried about what would happen when the provider changed the payload format in a future update.

The Hidden Costs

As experiments turned into production systems, the hidden costs of serverless began to surface. The first and most visible problem was cold starts. Every time a serverless function was called after being idle, the platform had to provision the environment before executing it.

This delay was a direct consequence of the stateless, event-driven model. Because functions held no state in memory and only existed in response to a trigger, the platform had no reason to keep them running between calls. An HTTP request, a database update signal, or a message arriving on a queue would wake the function from a cold state, requiring the environment to be initialized from scratch: the runtime loaded, the code parsed, and dependencies resolved. For functions called frequently, the platform could keep instances warm. For those called rarely or in unpredictable bursts, the cold start was unavoidable. For latency-sensitive applications such as navigation or real-time interactions, this was unacceptable.

The second challenge was debugging. With serverless, the logic was fragmented across dozens or even hundreds of functions. Each function executed in isolation, leaving little trace of the context that had triggered it. Logs were scattered across multiple services, and stitching them together required additional tooling. Tracing an error through a workflow was like following a conversation in which every sentence was spoken by someone new in a different room.

Vendor lock-in became another cost that grew over time. To stitch serverless functions into coherent workflows, teams leaned on provider-specific orchestration tools: AWS Step Functions to sequence Lambda calls, Azure Durable Functions to manage stateful workflows, and Google Cloud Workflows for multi-step pipelines. The event buses that triggered functions, such as AWS EventBridge or Google Pub/Sub, used proprietary schemas and routing rules. What had seemed portable at the level of a function was actually deeply bound to its environment.

The highest cost was the fragmentation of business logic. Serverless encouraged developers to decompose logic into the smallest possible units. Taken to its extreme, this became what practitioners call the nanoservice antipattern: dividing logic into functions so small that each one does almost nothing meaningful on its own, but together they form a web of tiny dependencies with no clear owner. Business rules were spread across multiple functions, sometimes duplicated, sometimes slightly inconsistent. The problem had changed shape but not disappeared.

Why Agility Was Not Enough

Serverless served as a reminder that removing servers from view does not eliminate architectural issues. It offered speed but lacked coherence. It provided agility at the level of individual functions but did not ensure portability across different environments.

What serverless made clear is that infrastructure efficiency alone is not enough. Cold starts and debugging headaches were frustrating, but they were symptoms, not root causes. The real problem was fragmentation. Business logic was still being rewritten, duplicated, or split into pieces that drifted apart over time. Without a way to ensure consistency, every new generation of architecture carried forward the same weakness in a new form.

Serverless was both a success and a disappointment. It proved that the industry was ready to think differently about infrastructure, but it also revealed that the pursuit of true portability was still ongoing. The way forward required a model that provides not only speed and elasticity but also coherence across environments. That realization drove me to think beyond functions and toward the foundations of what would later become Universal Microservices Architecture.

Front-End and Edge Evolution

Where the Theory Met Reality

By the late 2000s, cross-platform development had gone mainstream. Mobile adoption was on the rise, browsers were becoming more powerful, and companies were realizing that users expected their products to work seamlessly across different devices. The industry responded with a steady flow of solutions that promised to solve the problem.

Java Applets once led this effort. Flash and Silverlight followed, providing rich experiences abstracted from the underlying runtime. By the time smartphones became popular, frameworks like Cordova, Xamarin, and later React Native and Flutter made similar claims, now targeting mobile devices directly. Each new framework shared the same confident story: write once, run anywhere.

Demos reinforced this vision. A single codebase could generate apps for iOS and Android. Business logic could be written once and deployed across different runtimes. The same API could power multiple interfaces. For executives, it meant lower costs. For developers, it meant less duplication. For users, it meant consistent experiences across devices.

But in reality, it was much more difficult. I led teams building products for iOS, Android, and the web, and I saw firsthand how fragile the promise of portability was once projects moved from slide decks to production.

Four Dimensions of Failure

Performance was the first major issue. A feature that ran smoothly on a high-end iPhone might struggle on a lower-end Android device. Memory limits, CPU differences, and operating system behaviors all combined to make portable logic act differently in real-world use.

Part of this performance gap was structural. Cross-platform frameworks had to support the intersection of capabilities available on all target platforms. If iOS exposed a hardware-accelerated API for a specific operation but Android did not, the framework typically could not use it, because doing so would break portability. The result was a lowest-common-denominator execution model: the system ran at the capability level of its least capable target. Native teams, by contrast, could use every available optimization on their platform. The abstraction layer did not just add overhead; it actively prevented teams from using the hardware strengths that differentiated their platforms.

Debugging was the second challenge. Frameworks were designed to hide platform differences in theory, but in practice, they often added another layer for developers to navigate. When issues arose, the framework rarely offered enough visibility to diagnose the problem. Teams frequently had to bypass the abstraction entirely, diving back into the native platform to understand what was happening.

Some frameworks went further than just sharing business logic and attempted to unify the user interface layer as well. Cordova and Xamarin rendered web-style layouts inside a native shell. Early React Native versions used JavaScript-defined components that mapped to native UI elements, but with gaps in fidelity. The result was that developers spent considerable effort trying to make layouts designed for a browser feel at home on a mobile device, adjusting touch targets, navigation patterns, and animation timing for each platform.

User experience was the third concern. Customers did not care about the behind-the-scenes architecture; they cared about consistency. If a map rendered differently on Android than on iOS, or if a workflow stalled in the browser while running smoothly on mobile, trust in the product declined.

Team coordination was the fourth challenge. Frameworks rarely eliminated the need for specialized platform teams; instead, they created new points of tension. A fix that worked on iOS might cause regressions on Android. A feature that fits neatly into the browser might not translate well to mobile. What was marketed as simplicity often ended up requiring more negotiation.

The Lesson of the Edge

The most important insight I gained during this time was that portability is not about moving code everywhere; it is about delivering consistent results everywhere. The frameworks we relied on promised the former, but they could not ensure the latter.

For me, the evolution of front-end and edge computing was a turning point. It revealed that portability was never just about running the same code everywhere. It was about ensuring consistent results across fundamentally different environments. That insight laid the groundwork for a more profound lesson, one that became clearer in the project described in the next section.

Fragmentation in Practice: The Vector Maps Project

Part 1: The Narrative

Around 2010, I found myself leading a startup project that would influence my perspective on architecture for years. The goal seemed simple when summarized in one sentence: create a system that could deliver offline vector maps across iOS, Android, the web, and a supporting backend. Beneath that simplicity lay a level of complexity that was fully revealed only once we began the work.

At that time, offline mapping was nearly unheard of at scale. Major mapping platforms assumed constant connectivity. To load a map, a network connection was necessary. To search for a location, access to a central service was required. The idea that a phone could store detailed vector data, render it smoothly, and calculate routes without network access was unconventional. For us, it became the product's core promise.

The technological environment made this challenge even more acute. iOS was rapidly maturing, but Android was fragmented across hardware with vastly different performance profiles. Many devices had limited CPU power, modest memory, and screens that made graphics rendering unpredictable. Browsers were improving, but web performance still lagged behind native applications. Each runtime had its own constraints, making a one-size-fits-all approach impossible.

Part 2: Team Setup

Our team structure reflected this reality. We divided into verticals, each responsible for a specific runtime. The iOS team worked in Objective-C, the Android team in Java, the web team focused on browser technologies, and the backend team ensured data pipelines supported the entire ecosystem.

This is a pattern now recognized as a direct expression of Conway's Law: the observation, first made by computer scientist Melvin Conway in 1967, that organizations tend to produce system designs that mirror their own communication structures. Our communication structure was platform-first, so our architecture became platform-first too.

The separation allowed teams to optimize their platforms deeply. iOS engineers focused on maximizing performance from graphics libraries. Android developers battled memory management on lower-end hardware. The web team experimented with rendering techniques that pushed browsers to their limits. The backend team built synchronization logic to enable users to download and refresh data efficiently.

What this also meant, though we did not yet fully appreciate it, was that we were duplicating far more than just code. Every platform team had its own test suite for the same business rules, its own CI/CD pipeline running the same categories of checks, and its own maintenance workload. When a bug appeared in the routing logic, it had to be found, fixed, and verified independently four times. When a new requirement came in, it had to be estimated and staffed four times. The multiplication was invisible in the early days because each team felt productive. The total organizational cost only became visible later.

An obvious question is why we did not write the routing logic once in C or C++ and share it across platforms through a bridge layer. On iOS, C++ can be called directly. On Android, the JNI (Java Native Interface, a mechanism that allows Java code to call functions written in C or C++) provides a path to native code. In theory, a single C++ routing core could have powered all four targets. In practice, the team made a different call. The build complexity of maintaining a C++ core, writing JNI bindings for Android, and managing Objective-C bridges for iOS was considered higher than the cost of duplication at that stage of the startup. It was the right call for speed in the short term. It was the wrong call for long-term consistency. That trade-off, and the pain it caused later, is precisely the problem UMA is designed to prevent.

Part 3: Euphoria

Despite the devices' constraints and the fragmented nature of the work, the project began to take shape faster than any of us expected. Each platform team made meaningful progress in its own area. On iOS, engineers pushed graphics libraries beyond their intended limits, coaxing smooth rendering from hardware that was far from powerful. On Android, the team learned to work within strict memory limits, developing aggressive management strategies that kept the application stable even on lower-end devices.

When we finally assembled the pieces, the product exceeded our expectations. For the first time, users could download an entire city to their phones and navigate freely without relying on a signal. They could pan, zoom, and search offline, with the kind of responsiveness that seemed impossible just months earlier. Travelers described the experience as transformative. I remember watching telemetry streams showing people moving across cities, zooming into neighborhoods, and discovering points of interest, all powered by our work.

In those early months, the issue of fragmentation did not feel urgent. We understood that implementations across iOS, Android, and web were not exactly the same, but the differences seemed manageable. As long as the main features functioned, we tolerated the variations. The excitement of creating something new overshadowed the subtle inconsistencies. We convinced ourselves that alignment could always come later, once the foundation was stable.

Part 4: Collapse

Success fuels ambition. Once the initial versions of the product received overwhelmingly positive feedback, expectations quickly increased. From that energy, we decided to add an intelligent layer to the maps: a system that would suggest points of interest, routes, and contextual information in real time. Some processing would happen in the cloud to leverage more computing power, while other processing would occur on the device to ensure responsiveness and personalization.

Once we started deploying these features, the weaknesses of our fragmented approach became clear. The inconsistencies tolerated in the early stages suddenly became noticeable to users. Different devices started delivering different results. A suggested restaurant might appear on iOS but not on Android. A route calculated on the web might differ from one on mobile. Initially, these discrepancies seemed isolated, but over time, they revealed a pattern. The promise of a seamless experience across platforms started to slip away.

Fixing the problem was a real challenge. Each team dug into its own runtime, convinced the issue was local. The iOS team checked their rendering engine, while the Android team optimized memory. The backend team looked for flaws in their synchronization logic. But no single bug explained the discrepancies. After days of brainstorming, it became clear: the issue was not caused by a single mistake. It was built into the system. Each platform had implemented core parts of the logic in slightly different ways, invisible in isolation. When combined with cloud computation, the inconsistencies are compounded.

The experience was demoralizing. Everyone had worked hard to make their platform as strong as possible, and each implementation looked solid on its own. But when combined, the cracks became obvious. The independence that had once felt empowering became a liability. Instead of a single product with consistent behavior, we had multiple versions stitched together, each pulling in its own direction.

What struck me most was the emotional cost. Developers do not want to spend their days fighting inconsistencies. They want to build. They want to solve meaningful problems and see their work reflected in products that delight users. Instead, they were forced into a defensive posture, patching holes in a leaking boat rather than steering toward new horizons.

This was the moment when I began to question the definition of portability itself. For years, the industry had defined it as the ability to reuse code across environments. But what we learned in practice was that reused code was meaningless if it did not produce consistent outcomes. A map that behaved differently across devices was not truly portable, no matter how much code it shared.

In hindsight, this project taught me more than just about fragmentation. It laid the groundwork for a new perspective on architecture. It demonstrated that abstractions ignoring platform realities will always break down under pressure. It showed that developer effort alone cannot fix flawed foundations. And it revealed that the only way to achieve genuine portability is to design systems where business logic is both portable and consistent from the start. These lessons were tough at the time, but they became priceless later.

The Three Principles Behind UMA

Focus on Business Logic, Not Infrastructure

Looking back at the last 20 years of architectural trends, a clear pattern stands out. Every new wave claimed to simplify things and let developers focus on what truly mattered. But in reality, attention kept shifting toward infrastructure, while the logic that delivered value to users was treated as secondary.

Service-Oriented Architecture encouraged us to think in terms of services, contracts, and schemas. The focus was on reuse, but most of the effort went into managing the complex middleware that connected everything. Microservices shifted the discussion toward agility and independent deployment, but once again, the emphasis was on containers, orchestration tools, and service meshes. Serverless generated excitement by hiding servers entirely, yet most of the conversation centered on triggers, cold starts, and cloud billing models. Even frontend frameworks promised portability, but developers spent more time dealing with abstraction layers than improving the workflows users rely on.

The vector maps project made this painfully clear. As we saw in the section "Fragmentation in Practice: The Vector Maps Project," the routing algorithm should have been the single source of truth, the piece of logic users could trust, regardless of device. Instead, it was rewritten multiple times: once in Objective-C for iOS, once in Java for Android, once in JavaScript for the web, and a server-side version for batch processing. Each version operated in isolation, but slight differences built up over time.

This pattern repeats across industries. An e-commerce pricing engine is often implemented differently in the mobile app, the backend, and the reporting pipeline. A rule that applies a 10% discount for loyalty members might calculate the base price before tax in the mobile version, after tax in the backend API, and use a cached rate in the reporting pipeline. Each version passes its own tests. But a customer who sees three different final prices across channels immediately loses trust in the product.

In healthcare, the stakes are even higher. A clinical decision support rule that recommends a drug dosage based on patient weight might be implemented differently in the hospital workstation, the mobile app used by ward nurses, and the backend that generates prescriptions. A small difference in rounding logic or unit conversion can produce different recommendations. That inconsistency is not just a user experience problem; it is a patient safety issue.

The lesson is that portability must start with business logic. If the logic is not consistent, no amount of containerization, orchestration, or serverless deployment will save the system. Focusing on business logic shifts how teams think and operate. Instead of creating multiple runtime-specific implementations, developers can focus on improving the shared logic itself. Testing becomes easier because the unit under test is portable and stable. Debugging speeds up because discrepancies no longer hide behind runtime differences.

Respect Native APIs Where They Matter

One of the long-standing temptations in software architecture has been the desire to eliminate platform differences. Since the early days of runtime fragmentation, the industry has endeavored to unify diverse environments with a single abstraction. The goal was always the same: write once, run anywhere. However, the reality was that such abstractions worked in slides and demos but not in real-world deployment.

The cycle repeated with Java, Flash, Silverlight, Cordova, Xamarin, React Native, and Flutter. Each offered versions of cross-platform portability. For startups with limited resources, this seemed like salvation. But once applications scaled, the story became familiar. Performance lagged behind native apps. Access to new APIs was delayed because frameworks had to catch up with Apple and Google. Debugging became layered.

The issue with all these approaches was not that they were poorly designed. Many were impressive feats of software engineering. The problem was that they were based on a flawed assumption: that platform differences could be hidden forever. In reality, platforms evolve for valid reasons. iOS adds new APIs to leverage its hardware and ecosystem. Android reveals features that showcase the variety of supported devices. Browsers implement standards that balance innovation and security. Treating these differences as mere annoyances to be hidden ignores the fact that they are part of what makes each platform unique.

As we saw in the section "Fragmentation in Practice: The Vector Maps Project," rendering maps on iOS was different from rendering them on Android. The graphics stacks varied, the memory models differed, and the performance characteristics could not be made identical. A framework that aimed to unify rendering across platforms would have forced a lowest-common-denominator result. The better approach was to respect each environment: let iOS handle rendering with its own APIs, let Android optimize memory in its own way, and focus on keeping the routing and navigation logic portable.

Respecting native APIs is not a compromise; it is a strategy. It recognizes that platforms are not problems to fix but realities to work with. By respecting native APIs, developers can leverage the strengths of each environment while keeping a core of business logic portable. The key insight is that portability and uniformity are not the same. Portability means ensuring that the same business logic yields consistent results across different environments. Uniformity means forcing every environment into the same mold. The former builds resilience, while the latter creates brittleness.

This is why UMA does not try to abstract away everything. It establishes clear boundaries. Business logic is made portable, tested, and trusted to run consistently across different runtimes. Native APIs are respected for all other aspects.

Make Logic Truly Portable Across Environments

At its core, UMA is built around one key principle: business logic must be truly portable. This means more than just moving code from one environment to another. It means ensuring consistent results no matter where it runs.

The truth I have come to understand is that portability without consistency is an illusion. Users do not experience code; they experience outcomes. From their perspective, a system is only portable if it behaves the same way regardless of the environment. Anything else is duplication disguised as reuse.

True portability requires more than just moving code around. It requires designing logic in a way that it can be trusted across environments. That trust comes from three practices: defining logic in a portable format, packaging it so it can run anywhere, and testing it across runtimes to ensure consistency.

Defining logic in a portable format means avoiding the pitfalls of runtime-specific assumptions. A business rule should not rely on a particular API call or memory model. It should be expressed in a form that can run in different environments without changing its meaning.

Packaging logic to run anywhere is the second requirement. Modern tools like WebAssembly provide the missing piece here. By compiling logic into a portable binary format, it becomes possible to run it in browsers, on devices, or within cloud environments with the same guarantees.

The third and most crucial practice is testing across different runtimes. It is not sufficient to run unit tests in a single environment. The same test suite must confirm outcomes in every supported runtime. Only then can consistency be assured.

Just as importantly, true portability changes how organizations approach architecture. Teams stop debating which runtime should own a feature and begin focusing on where it should run to deliver the best experience. They stop duplicating efforts across platforms and start collaborating to improve shared logic. They stop accepting inconsistencies as inevitable and start expecting consistency as the standard.

Reflection and Naming UMA

Why UMA Is Not a Silver Bullet

Every new generation of software architecture has been launched with great excitement. Service-Oriented Architecture was supposed to eliminate duplication by creating shared services across the enterprise. Microservices promised to break the monolith into small, agile units. Serverless claimed to free developers from infrastructure worries. Frameworks like Cordova, Xamarin, React Native, and Flutter suggested we could ignore runtime fragmentation and treat all platforms equally. Each approach delivered real value in its own context. However, none of them lived up to their most ambitious promises.

It is essential to acknowledge this history because it sets the stage for UMA. Universal Microservices Architecture is not a silver bullet that erases complexity. What UMA does is address a persistent problem: the hidden costs of fragmentation. It reframes portability from superficial code reuse to consistent outcomes. UMA exists to protect capability contracts and the boundaries around business logic from being rewritten, duplicated, or allowed to drift apart across environments. Microservices and serverless were agile in deployment, but agility in shipping code is not the same as reliability in outcomes.

When I present UMA, I am careful not to frame it as final or absolute. As an architect, my philosophy is shaped by the awareness that any system we design today will be incomplete tomorrow. Technologies evolve, user expectations shift, and the constraints of one era become irrelevant in the next. UMA is designed with that spirit in mind. It does not promise perfection; it promises resilience.

Adaptability over Perfection

One of the toughest lessons I have learned in architecture is that perfection is not just unachievable; it is also risky. Every time the industry has tried to create the perfect model or framework, it has ended in disappointment. The reason is straightforward: technology keeps evolving. The systems that thrive are not the ones that chase perfection, but the ones that prioritize adaptability.

SOA aimed for perfection, and in doing so it became fragile. Microservices corrected SOA's rigidity but failed to balance it with a commitment to consistency. Serverless delivered agility but did not deliver stability. Through these cycles, I began to notice a pattern. Every model that claimed finality eventually collapsed under the weight of change. The only systems that endured were those that could evolve.

This is also why I resist the idea of UMA as a perfect solution. What I want is an architecture that can adapt smoothly to new runtimes, APIs, and demands while still maintaining the integrity of its business logic. UMA is based on that principle. It does not aim for perfection; it aims for resilience.

Adaptability is not just a technical quality; it is a cultural one. Teams that embrace adaptability are willing to change direction when evidence demands it. By keeping business logic portable and consistent, UMA allows teams to experiment with infrastructure choices without fear of breaking the system.

A New Architectural Direction

As I started to outline the three principles behind UMA, I realized I was no longer talking about technical preferences. I was describing a mindset. The story of SOA, microservices, serverless, and cross-platform frameworks was not just about tools; it was about misplaced focus. Time and again, the industry chased after perfecting infrastructure and ignored what mattered most: the logic that users rely on.

What makes this a philosophy rather than a checklist is its humility. UMA does not claim to solve every problem or replace every model. It accepts that other approaches will still have their place. A monolith can be the right choice in some contexts. Microservices can still provide independence. Serverless can still accelerate experimentation. UMA does not deny their value; it reframes their limitations. It asks us to evaluate them not by how elegantly they move code around but by whether they preserve consistency of outcomes across environments.

Looking Back, Facing Forward

Reflecting on this chapter, the story is one of perseverance and growth. The industry promised reuse with SOA, agility with microservices, and speed with serverless architectures. Frameworks claimed to deliver portability across runtimes. While each of these approaches made progress, they also revealed their limitations. What tied their failures together was not a lack of effort, but a misguided focus: too often, the energy was directed at infrastructure and abstractions rather than the logic that defined the product.

From this pattern emerged three key principles:

1. Business logic should be the primary focus, as it is the only part of the system that delivers direct value to users.

2. Native APIs should be respected, because pretending all platforms are the same leads to brittle abstractions.

3. True portability should be measured by consistent outcomes, not by whether code compiles in multiple environments.

Together, these principles redefine portability in a way that transforms frustration into clarity. What started as lessons from projects and setbacks turned into a philosophy. UMA is not a magic solution, and it does not claim to be one. It serves as a direction: a way of designing systems that value adaptability over perfection and outcomes over abstractions.

This philosophy sets the stage for what comes next. The following chapters will shift from principles to practice, demonstrating how UMA can be implemented through runtime abstraction layers, packaging strategies, and metadata-driven governance. But it is crucial to carry this mindset forward. Without the philosophy, the tools risk becoming another cycle of promises they cannot keep. With it, they can be the foundation of a more resilient approach to software architecture.

PART II

Designing UMA Architectures

CHAPTER 5

Building Universal Services

From Capability to Portability, the Anatomy of UMA Services

Introduction

When I was growing up, I joined the Scouts and stayed with it from elementary school through college. One of the first things I learned was how to pack a backpack. At first, it seemed straightforward: stuff things in, zip it up, and go. Out in the mountains, you learn quickly that packing is not about convenience. It is about survival.

A well-packed bag means you are adaptable. We learned to distribute weight so heavy items sat close to the back and high up, where they would not throw off your balance on a climb. We double-wrapped essentials against sudden rainstorms. We carried layers so the same pack worked in the cold morning, the hot afternoon, and the unexpected storm. Pack in a way that lets you adapt to whatever the day brings.

Before I started a family, I ran a startup in Italy. Every year, I took two weeks to recharge. A rule from growing up near the mountains: pick a random spot on the map and walk there on foot. No shortcuts, no car. Just me, my gear, and the trail. Packing for two weeks of hiking taught me discipline. Every item had to earn its place. Food and water were essential, but too much meant a punishing load. I needed a tent, but it had to be light enough to carry day after day. A first aid kit was non-negotiable, even if I hoped not to use it. And there was always the unknown: a storm the forecast missed, a trail blocked by a rockslide, an ankle twisted in the first hour. My backpack had to be ready for anything, balanced enough to adapt, and not so heavy that it became a burden.

E. Piovesan, *Universal Microservices Architecture*, https://doi.org/10.1007/979-8-8688-2794-5_5

That mindset carried directly into software architecture. Designing services is about the same preparation and balance. Most services today are overstuffed bags. They are packed with everything the developer could think of logic, runtime dependencies, storage options, all bundled into a single heavy unit. They work for a while. As soon as you need to move them from cloud to edge, or from desktop to mobile, you are repacking. Each environment requires its own version, its own assumptions. Over time, the original service splits into multiple codebases. What was one idea becomes fragmented, inconsistent, and hard to maintain.

Antipattern Embedding infrastructure or runtime assumptions directly into core application logic, such as hardcoding database connection details or cloud SDK references without dependency injection, is the architectural equivalent of gluing items inside your pack. You can carry it, but you cannot adapt.

Universal Microservices Architecture takes a different approach. Each service is an atomic unit, meaning self-contained and complete in itself, not related to atomic transactions. It contains only what belongs inside. Business logic stays pure, free from assumptions about runtime or operating system. The contract defines what the service accepts and produces. Metadata describes what the service contains and what it needs. Abstraction layers provide the standardized form that lets the same contents travel across environments.

Done right, you build once and run anywhere. Done wrong, you are stuck endlessly repackaging. A skilled hiker carries the same gear across forests, valleys, and peaks. An architect who knows how to design atomic services applies the same logic across browsers, edge nodes, and cloud environments.

Design-Time Priorities

Portability is not a runtime trick. It begins at design time, before a line of code is written. The sequence matters: contract first, then logic, then abstraction, then metadata. Each layer depends on the clarity of the one before it. A service that starts from a runtime assumption and works backward will carry that assumption forever. A service that starts from a clean contract can travel anywhere the adapter reaches.

Design-time portability means the decisions you make at the drawing board, specifically about what belongs inside the service and what belongs outside it, determine whether the service can move. Runtime portability is the result: the same compiled binary executing in a browser, at the edge, or in the cloud without modification. The two are related but distinct. Compilation portability, the ability to build for multiple targets, is necessary but not sufficient. A binary that compiles to WASM but carries hidden dependencies on a specific file system or network stack is not portable at runtime. The design has to be clean first.

The 90/10 framing is useful but should not be treated as a hard rule. In many services, adapters handle the environmental differences while the core stays unchanged. In some cases, particularly around memory models, numerical encoding, and string handling, the split is less clean. Every programming language carries assumptions about these things. Be aware of them when designing the core, and let the adapter absorb what the core cannot avoid.

Runtime Portability and Adapters

The same service binary can run in different environments through thin adapters. These adapters handle the differences that cannot be standardized: file systems, network stacks, device interfaces, and I/O conventions. The core logic stays unchanged. What changes is the narrow translation layer between the service and the environment in which it runs.

Browsers, edge nodes, and cloud servers are genuinely different environments with different strengths and constraints. The browser is close to the user but resource-limited. The edge sits between user and cloud, offering low latency within tight execution windows. The cloud has scale and power but carries network distance. The goal is one service that spans all three without being rewritten for each. Adapters make that possible.

The Feature Flag Evaluator

To make these ideas concrete, this chapter builds a feature flag evaluator from scratch. Feature flags are a good candidate for demonstrating portability precisely because they appear everywhere: enabling features for a subset of users, managing safe rollbacks, and running A/B experiments. Most teams write this logic multiple times across different clients, services, and environments. Writing it once and running it anywhere is exactly the problem UMA solves.

The evaluator also demonstrates why certain services are well-suited to portability. Its logic is purely computational: given a flag definition and a user context, return a decision. There is no required network call, no file-system dependency, and no environment-specific state. The contract is clean, the logic is deterministic, and the binary compiles to WebAssembly without modification. Those three properties, together, make a service a strong portability candidate.

What This Chapter Covers

The chapter proceeds as follows. First, the three fundamental service types: stateless, stateful, and subscribable. These categories are not arbitrary. They represent the fundamental ways a service handles its relationship with state and time. Choosing the wrong type makes a service harder to test, scale, and port.

Next, the required anatomy of every UMA service: contract, logic, abstraction, and metadata. This is not a suggestion. It is a structural requirement, and each layer has strict rules about what it can and cannot assume.

Then, runtime portability in practice, following a single service across browsers, Edge, and the cloud and showing how each adapter works while the service itself remains unchanged.

Then autonomy and boundaries: a practical checklist covering latency class, trust domain, resource budgets, failure domains, ownership, and change cadence. These dimensions turn portability from a claim into a measurable property.

The feature flag evaluator is built step by step through the chapter. The annotated snippets here highlight the key decisions. The complete runnable implementation is available in the companion repository at

> `https://github.com/enricopiovesan/UMA-code-examples/tree/main/chapter-05-feature-flag-evaluator`

Finally, the anti-patterns: the five most common ways services fail to achieve portability, drawn from real experience, each paired with an explanation of why it fails and how to recognize it early.

Portability is not a promise for the future. It is a choice made at design time, starting with a single service. The mechanism is concrete: a contract that declares what the service does, a WASM binary that carries the logic without runtime assumptions, and adapters that connect that binary to whatever environment needs it. The backpack either travels or it does not. That is decided before you leave the house.

Service Types: Stateless, Stateful, Subscribable

Not all services behave the same way. Some carry no memory of the past, responding only to the input before them. Others retain state across requests, holding information that must be queried, updated, or shared. Still others exist to broadcast events, allowing other services to subscribe and react when something changes. A service can also combine these characteristics: a stateful service that also publishes events, for example, is both stateful and subscribable at the same time.

In Universal Microservices Architecture, these differences matter. Choosing the wrong type makes a service harder to test, scale, and port across environments. Choosing the right type makes boundaries cleaner and implementation simpler. UMA recognizes three fundamental service types: stateless, stateful, and subscribable. They are practical lenses, not abstract categories, and understanding them is the first step in deciding what goes inside a service and what stays outside it.

Stateless Services

A stateless service performs a specific task based solely on the input it receives at that moment and produces an output without retaining anything about the interaction. It does not remember the caller. It does not accumulate history. Each request is fully self-contained.

Consider a train station information kiosk. You ask for the next departure from Milan to Rome. The kiosk returns the schedule. It does not remember that you asked yesterday, does not track how often you travel, and does not adjust its answer based on your history. Each query is independent. That is stateless behavior: input in, output out, nothing retained.

In UMA, stateless services are the simplest and most portable type. They carry no memory and make no assumptions about their runtime environment, which means they can move freely across environments. A stateless service compiled to WebAssembly can run in a browser, on an edge gateway, or in a cloud worker with the same logic and contract. The portability characteristics do vary across WASM execution environments. Browser WASM, edge workers, and cloud WASM runtimes differ in startup behavior, memory limits, and I/O conventions. The core logic stays identical; the adapter absorbs those differences.

Stateless services appear everywhere in technical systems. A matrix multiplication service takes two matrices, returns the product, and forgets everything. An image thumbnail generator accepts an image, resizes it, and returns the result without retaining any memory of the previous task. A currency converter receives a source currency, a target currency, and an amount, applies a rate, and returns the converted value. Even AI inference can operate statelessly: a model processes an input as a single-turn, context-free request, produces a prediction, and discards the context once the output is returned.

The trade-off is predictable. Stateless design can cause repeated work when context must be resent with each request. Serialization and transport costs grow with large inputs. These overheads are generally manageable and, importantly, transparent. There is no hidden coupling to debug when a stateless service misbehaves. The overhead is measurable because the boundary is clean. There are also costs around idempotency and external dependencies. Idempotency, the guarantee that calling a service twice with the same input produces the same result without unintended side effects, must be designed in explicitly when a stateless service touches external state through an adapter. If the service calls an external rate source, that call adds latency and availability risk that the caller cannot see from the contract alone. Keep those calls in the adapter, not the core.

In Practice: A Tiny Stateless Service

The following is a minimal stateless UMA service: a fixed-rate currency converter. The input is a JSON object containing the source currency, target currency, and amount. Output is the same object plus the applied rate and the converted result. No state is maintained between calls. The rate table is embedded in the demo's logic. In a production system, an adapter would refresh rates from an external source without touching the core logic.

Contract shape:

```
Input:
{ "from": "USD", "to": "EUR", "amount": 12.50 }

Output:
{ "from": "USD", "to": "EUR", "amount": 12.50, "rate": 0.92, "result": 11.50 }

Notes:
1. The rate table is embedded. In a production system, an adapter
   refreshes rates without touching the core logic.
```

2. All values are deterministic. There is no clock, no network, no file system inside the logic.

Minimal Rust core (WASI target, stdin/stdout):

```
// Cargo.toml
// [package] name = "fx"  version = "0.1.0"
// [dependencies] serde = { version = "1", features = ["derive"] }
//                serde_json = "1"

use std::io::{Read, Write};
use serde::{Deserialize, Serialize};

// Use descriptive names for clarity
#[derive(Deserialize)]
struct CurrencyConversionInput {
    from: String,
    to: String,
    amount: f64,  // Note: f64 can accumulate rounding errors in financial
}             //  calculations. Use a decimal library in production.

#[derive(Serialize)]
struct CurrencyConversionOutput {
    from: String,
    to: String,
    amount: f64,
    rate: f64,
    result: f64,
}

fn rate(from: &str, to: &str) -> Option<f64> {
    match (from, to) {
        ("USD", "EUR") => Some(0.92),
        ("EUR", "USD") => Some(1.09),
        ("USD", "CAD") => Some(1.35),
        ("CAD", "USD") => Some(0.74),
```

```
        (a, b) if a == b => Some(1.0),
        _ => None,
    }
}

fn main() {
    let mut buf = String::new();
    std::io::stdin().read_to_string(&mut buf).unwrap();
    match serde_json::from_str::<CurrencyConversionInput>(&buf) {
        Ok(inp) => {
            if let Some(exchange_rate) = rate(&inp.from, &inp.to) {
                // Precision is fixed at 2 decimal places in this demo.
                // Production systems should make precision configurable
                // per currency (e.g., JPY uses 0 decimals, KWD uses 3).
                let out = CurrencyConversionOutput {
                    from: inp.from, to: inp.to, amount: inp.amount,
                    rate: exchange_rate,
                    result: (inp.amount * exchange_rate * 100.0).round()
                    / 100.0,
                };
                let json = serde_json::to_string(&out).unwrap();
                let _ = std::io::stdout().write_all(json.as_bytes());
            } else {
                let _ = std::io::stdout()
                    .write_all(br#"{"error":"unsupported pair"}"#);
                std::process::exit(2);
            }
        }
        Err(_) => {
            let _ = std::io::stdout()
                .write_all(br#"{"error":"bad input"}"#);
            std::process::exit(1);
        }
    }
}
```

Build to a portable binary:

```
rustup target add wasm32-wasip1
cargo build --release --target wasm32-wasip1
# artifact: target/wasm32-wasip1/release/fx.wasm
```

Run locally:

```
echo '{"from":"USD","to":"EUR","amount":12.5}' | wasmtime target/wasm32-
wasip1/release/fx.wasm
```

```
Expected output:
{"from":"USD","to":"EUR","amount":12.5,"rate":0.92,"result":11.5}
```

Adapter sketch (the core fx.wasm does not change across environments):

```
Browser:  Load the module with WebAssembly.instantiateStreaming.
          Pass the JSON string via a stdin shim.
          Return the stdout string to the UI.

Edge:     HTTP handler reads the request body.
          Pipes it to the module as stdin.
          Returns stdout as the HTTP response.

Cloud:    Serverless function does the same as Edge.
          Optionally adds audit logging outside the module.
```

The complete, runnable implementation is in the companion repository:

`https://github.com/enricopiovesan/UMA-code-examples/tree/main/chapter-05-feature-flag-evaluator`

Stateful Services

A stateful service keeps information across requests. It stores data that can be queried, updated, or modified over time. Unlike a stateless service, which responds and forgets, a stateful service must answer questions like "What is in this shopping cart right now?" or "What is the current profile for this user?" That memory is what makes the service useful and also makes the design more complex.

The contract for a stateful service must be explicit about how the state is created, read, and modified. Stateful services are not inherently less portable than stateless ones, but they require more deliberate planning. Portability is preserved when the service declares its state requirements in its contract and allows adapters to connect to the underlying persistence layer. It is lost when the core logic is tied to a specific database SDK, a hardcoded file path, or an environment-specific storage API.

A useful rule: make the state explicit and narrow. Define exactly what the service owns. Expose a small set of read and write operations through the contract. Keep the core logic unaware of where bytes are stored between calls. In UMA, the adapter decides how to satisfy persistence in each environment. That separation is what allows the same stateful service to run in a browser with IndexedDB, on an edge node with a local key-value store, or in the cloud with a managed database, without modifying the logic.

Stateful services appear in any domain where continuity matters. A profile service stores and retrieves user information. A shopping cart retains items across sessions. A playlist carries a sequence of media across browser refreshes. A productivity tool saves work-in-progress. What is common across all of these is that the current request depends on what came before it. The service cannot start from scratch each time.

Scale and consistency introduce real trade-offs here. Reads and writes compete for the same records. Throughput depends on how the state is partitioned and how contention is handled. Latency is affected by where the state is stored relative to the runtime. A profile read from a local cache feels instant. A cart write crossing a slow network link does not. These are architectural choices, and UMA does not eliminate them. It makes them visible by forcing the state contract to be declared rather than assumed.

In Practice: A Tiny Stateful Cart

The following sketch shows the separation UMA expects. The contract is JSON in and JSON out. The logic is pure. Storage is a trait that the adapter implements on a per-environment basis.

Contract shape:

```
{
  "op": "add" | "remove" | "get",
  "cartId": "c-123",
  "item": { "sku": "ABC-1", "qty": 1 }
}
```

Rust-like core (pseudocode showing the structural pattern):

```
// Core types
#[derive(Clone)] struct Item { sku: String, qty: i32 }
#[derive(Default, Clone)] struct Cart { items: Vec<Item> }

// Storage interface implemented by each adapter
trait Storage {
    fn load_cart(&self, cart_id: &str) -> Option<Cart>;
    fn save_cart(&self, cart_id: &str, cart: &Cart);
}

// Pure logic, no runtime calls inside
fn apply(cart: &mut Cart, op: &str, item: Option<Item>) {
    match op {
        "add" => if let Some(it) = item {
            if let Some(existing) = cart.items.iter_mut()
                .find(|x| x.sku == it.sku) {
                existing.qty += it.qty;
            } else {
                cart.items.push(it);
            }
        },
        "remove" => if let Some(it) = item {
            cart.items.retain(|x| !(x.sku == it.sku));
        },
        "get" => {}  // read-only, no mutation needed
        _ => {}
    }
}

// Entry point used by adapters
fn handle<S: Storage>(store: &S, cart_id: &str, op: &str,
    item: Option<Item>) -> Cart {
    let mut cart = store.load_cart(cart_id).unwrap_or_default();
    if op != "get" {
        apply(&mut cart, op, item);
```

```
        if op == "add" || op == "remove" {
            store.save_cart(cart_id, &cart);
        }
    }
    cart
}

// Note: concurrent add/remove operations require the adapter to
// implement locking or optimistic concurrency at the storage layer.
// The core logic does not handle contention; that belongs in the adapter.
```

Adapter sketch per environment:

```
Browser:  Implement Storage on top of IndexedDB or localStorage.
Edge:     Implement Storage on a local key-value store or file-
backed store.
Cloud:    Implement Storage on a managed database or durable object.
```

The complete, runnable implementation is in the companion repository:

https://github.com/enricopiovesan/UMA-code-examples/tree/main/chapter-05-feature-flag-evaluator

Subscribable Services

Some services excel when they broadcast a message and move on. A subscribable service shares events or state changes as they occur, and subscribers who are connected at that moment receive them. If a subscriber is absent, the event is missed unless a separate retention mechanism is in place. That is not a flaw in the model. It is the model doing its job.

Subscribable services are the foundation of event-driven architecture. The core pattern is producer/consumer: one service publishes events according to its internal rules, and any number of consumers subscribe and react independently. Neither side needs to know the other exists. A payment system can publish a charge-succeeded event. Fulfillment, analytics, and messaging services can each subscribe and react in their own way, on their own schedule, without the payment service knowing or caring who is listening.

In UMA, a subscribable service treats time as a series of signals. The contract defines the structure of each event and the conditions under which it is published. The logic decides when to emit. The runtime adapter handles transport and distribution. The service itself holds no state about individual subscribers.

Delivery guarantees belong in the adapter or a companion store, not in the subscription service itself. The three standard models are at-most-once, where events may be dropped but are never duplicated; at-least-once, where events are guaranteed to arrive but may arrive more than once; and exactly-once, which requires coordination and is the most expensive to achieve. Choosing the right model depends on the use case. A live sports score update can be tolerated at most once. A financial transaction notification cannot. The subscribable service declares its emission behavior. The adapter selects the delivery model appropriate for the environment.

Adapters play a specific role in addressing delivery and synchronization challenges that vary by environment. In IoT deployments, devices may disconnect and reconnect unpredictably. The adapter is responsible for buffering missed events, replaying them on reconnect, and reconciling state divergence without changing the core service logic. In browser environments, the adapter handles the gap between a tab that goes inactive and a live event stream: it may pause consumption, resume on focus, or delegate to a service worker for background delivery. The core subscribable service emits events according to its contract in all cases. The adapter absorbs the environmental complexity. Technical systems use subscribable services to connect components without tight coupling. An IoT gateway publishes sensor readings at a steady cadence. Consumers watch the stream for anomalies without polling the gateway for each value. A user activity stream aggregates events such as profile updates, purchases, and comments into a single channel that each subscriber processes independently. These patterns shift the load from request-reply to continuous flow. Throughput and latency depend on how events are batched, how backpressure is handled, and where delivery happens.

In UMA, portability comes from keeping the event shape and emission rules inside the service, while the adapter maps the stream to the local transport. In a browser, the adapter might use a MessagePort or EventSource. At the edge, a lightweight pub-sub socket. In the cloud, a managed event bus. The core logic does not change across any of these.

In Practice: A Tiny Subscribable Service

The following is a minimal publisher that streams events as newline-delimited JSON. It publishes a short sequence of weather alerts, one per second, then exits. Connected subscribers receive the events. Subscribers that are not connected when an event is emitted do not receive it.

Event contract (each event is a single JSON object on its own line):

```
{
  "type": "weather.alert",
  "region": "NW-1",
  "severity": "watch",
  "message": "Wind increasing",
  "ts": "2025-09-21T17:00:00Z",
  "seq": 3
}
```

```
Notes:
1. The service does not maintain per-subscriber state.
   Delivery guarantees belong in adapters or companion stores.
2. The event shape is the contract. Adapters translate transport only.
```

Minimal Rust publisher (WASI target):

```
// Cargo.toml
// [package] name = "weather_pub"  version = "0.1.0"
// [dependencies] serde = { version = "1", features = ["derive"] }
//                serde_json = "1"

use serde::Serialize;
use std::{io::Write, thread, time::{Duration, SystemTime, UNIX_EPOCH}};

#[derive(Serialize)]
struct Alert<'a> {
    r#type: &'a str,
    region: &'a str,
    severity: &'a str,
    message: &'a str,
```

```
    ts: String,
    seq: u32,
}

fn iso_now() -> String {
    let now = SystemTime::now()
        .duration_since(UNIX_EPOCH).unwrap();
    format!("{}.{:03}Z", now.as_secs(), now.subsec_millis())
}

fn main() {
    let severities = ["info", "watch", "warning", "warning", "info"];
    let messages  = ["Clear", "Wind increasing", "Heavy rain",
                    "Thunderstorm", "Clearing"];
    for i in 0..severities.len() {
        let event = Alert {
            r#type: "weather.alert",
            region: "NW-1",
            severity: severities[i],
            message:  messages[i],
            ts:  iso_now(),
            seq: i as u32,
        };
        let line = serde_json::to_string(&event).unwrap();
        let mut out = std::io::stdout();
        let _ = out.write_all(line.as_bytes());
        let _ = out.write_all(b"\n");
        let _ = out.flush();
        thread::sleep(Duration::from_secs(1));
        // Note: some edge environments do not support multi-threading
        // or sleep. In those cases, replace the sleep with an
        // event-loop tick provided by the adapter.
    }
}
```

Build and run:

```
rustup target add wasm32-wasip1
cargo build --release --target wasm32-wasip1
wasmtime target/wasm32-wasip1/release/weather_pub.wasm
# Five JSON lines appear, one per second.
```

Adapter sketch:

```
Browser: Wrapper starts the module, exposes a readable stream to the UI.
         Each stdout line becomes an event in a MessageChannel.
         The UI listens and updates a ticker.

Edge:    Worker binds HTTP chunked responses or Server-Sent Events.
         Each stdout line is written to the open connection as it arrives.

Cloud:   Handler reads stdout lines and pushes them to a managed bus.
         Consumers subscribe to the bus per their delivery requirements.
```

The publisher declares the event shape and emits it on a schedule, then exits. It does not track subscribers, does not retry, and does not buffer. If retention or replay is required, pair it with a stateful store through an adapter. The core remains unchanged, preserving portability.

Choosing the Right Type

Stateless, stateful, and subscribable are not mutually exclusive. A service can be both stateful and subscribable: it holds state and publishes events when that state changes. The types are lenses for asking the right question at design time. Does this service need to remember anything between calls? Does it need to broadcast changes to other services? Does it need both?

The answers determine what goes inside the service boundary, what belongs in the adapter, and what belongs in a separate service entirely. Get the type wrong, and you will fight the design at every stage of testing, scaling, and porting. Get it right, and the boundary becomes obvious, and the work of building follows naturally from the shape of the problem.

Required Anatomy of a UMA Service

Every robust system has an internal structure that defines how its parts interact. A bridge is not just stone and steel. It is arches, piers, and spans, each playing a specific role without taking on the work of another. A living cell is not just matter. It is a nucleus, membrane, and cytoplasm, each governed by rules that keep the whole functioning. UMA services are no different. They cannot be treated as shapeless blocks of code. They require a defined internal structure, and that structure is non-negotiable.

Without structure, services become tangled. Logic, runtime details, and metadata blur together. The result is fragile code that is hard to migrate and impossible to reason about at scale. With structure, services stay atomic: small, self-contained, and composable. Each piece has a defined shape, clear connectors, and no hidden surprises inside.

UMA requires four layers for every atomic service, in this order:

1. **Contract**: The explicit declaration of what the service accepts and produces
2. **Logic**: The pure business computation, unaffected by environment
3. **Abstraction**: The thin adapter that bridges logic to a specific runtime
4. **Metadata**: The self-description that makes the service discoverable, testable, and governable

What matters is not just what each layer owns but what it cannot assume. Logic cannot call a database client directly. The contract cannot hide behaviors that affect outputs. Abstraction cannot expose platform details to the logic layer. Metadata cannot drift from reality. These boundaries keep services portable and predictable.

1. The Contract: Defining the Boundaries of Interaction

The contract comes first. Before a line of logic is written, the contract defines what the service accepts, what it produces, and what constraints govern both. It is the service's visible boundary. Clarity or confusion at this boundary determines whether the service is portable or locked in.

A contract is more than a type definition. It is a promise: the service will always interpret inputs in a specific way and return outputs in a specific format. The luggage tag analogy is useful but incomplete. A real UMA contract is richer than a label identifying the owner and destination. It covers input and output schemas, error models, resource budgets, versioning information, and governance constraints. It answers the four questions every caller asks: what this service does, what it needs, what it returns, and what rules both sides must honor.

UMA demands that contracts be explicit and unambiguous. They must not conceal optional behaviors that silently change outputs. They must not change over time without versioning. They must not make assumptions about where the service runs. Including a server timestamp in a response format already implies an environment-specific claim. Declare only what the service controls. Let adapters handle external context.

Versioning deserves particular attention. A contract that changes without a version signal silently breaks every caller. In UMA, contracts carry an explicit version identifier. When a breaking change is required, a new version is published alongside the old one. The old version is deprecated with a documented sunset date. Non-breaking additions, such as optional output fields, can be made to an existing version, but any change that affects existing callers requires a new version. This is not bureaucracy. It is the mechanism that makes contracts durable.

On Backward Compatibility Additive changes to a contract, adding optional fields, and extending enumerations are generally safe. Removing fields, changing types, or altering the semantics of existing fields are breaking changes. When in doubt, version it.

The power of a clean contract becomes clear through contrast. A shopping cart service whose contract accepts item identifiers and quantities and returns a total price can run anywhere. The browser passes items from a client-side form. The edge passes them from a cache. The cloud passes them from a database. Each environment interacts through the same contract, and the service does not care where the items came from.

A cart service whose contract requires primary keys from a specific database schema is already trapped. It cannot run in a browser because the browser cannot provide a database key. It cannot run on a lightweight edge node because the schema is not available there. The contract has embedded a runtime assumption that should have been handled by an adapter. The same failure mode applies to a feature flag evaluator whose contract requires a network token from a specific identity provider. The contract has assumed the presence of infrastructure that may not exist in every environment.

Vague or incomplete contracts cause different but equally serious problems. If the evaluator describes its inputs as simply 'user data' without a schema, consumers must make assumptions. If dependencies are listed incorrectly, orchestration systems connect them in ways that fail at runtime. Sloppy metadata creates friction precisely where clarity is most needed. A solid contract shields the logic from drift and lets adapters handle environmental details. A flawed contract exposes those details upward, making portability an illusion.

2. Logic: The Heart of the Service

Logic is the pure business computation that transforms input into output. It is the reason the service exists. A feature flag evaluator's logic is the evaluation process: a series of comparisons and calculations that yield a decision. A shopping cart's logic totals the items. A currency converter applies a rate. In every case, the logic must behave deterministically, producing the same result for the same input, and operate without hidden dependencies on its runtime environment.

A useful concept here is the pure function. A pure function takes inputs, produces an output, and does nothing else. It reads no global state, writes no side effects, and makes no assumptions about its environment. Given the same inputs, it returns the same output, always. UMA logic is pure in this sense. It does not open sockets, query databases, read files, or call cloud SDKs. Those operations belong in the adapter.

Note on Language Assumptions Every programming language carries assumptions about memory models, numerical encoding, and string handling. Rust and JavaScript, for example, handle integer overflow differently. Unicode normalization varies across runtimes. When compiling to WebAssembly, be explicit about these boundaries. Define the encoding your contract uses, and let the adapter handle any necessary conversion before the data enters the core.

The boundaries of this layer are defined by what is kept out, not just what is inside. Database queries, filesystem access, and network calls have no place here. Neither do environment-specific references, such as cloud SDKs, device APIs, or operating system handles. If these assumptions enter the core, the service becomes tied to its runtime. It cannot be compiled once and run anywhere. The Lego brick has been glued to the table.

Anti-examples make the boundary concrete. A cart service that directly connects to a specific SQL database to fetch prices is no longer portable. It is tied to that storage system. Running it in a browser or on an edge node will fail. A feature flag evaluator that calls an external API during evaluation now depends on network latency, availability, and authentication. It is no longer a self-contained, predictable unit. These are not edge cases. They are the most common way services lose portability, and they almost always happen because the logic layer was not defended at design time.

When logic is kept clean and free of hidden dependencies, it becomes the most portable part of the system. Compile it once and reuse it across environments without changes. That is the core promise of UMA. When logic absorbs infrastructure, that promise is broken at the source.

3. Abstraction: Bridging Logic to Runtime

Clean logic and a precise contract are not enough on their own. They define what a service does and how others call it. They do not show how to make it work in a specific environment. A service compiled to WebAssembly cannot directly interact with a browser storage API, an edge gateway socket, or a cloud provider queue. Something must bridge the gap between the core and the reality of each runtime. That is the abstraction layer.

Three related terms appear in discussions of this layer and warrant distinction. The abstraction is the architectural concept: the boundary between the service core and the runtime. The runtime adapter is the concrete implementation of that boundary for a specific environment: the browser adapter, the edge adapter, and the cloud adapter. The capability envelope is a broader term that encompasses the full set of what a service can do in a given runtime context, including the adapter, resource constraints, and the trust rules that govern access. These terms are related but not interchangeable. In practice, when talking about the code that bridges logic to runtime, the right term is runtime adapter.

Healthy adapters stay thin. They do not define business rules; those belong in the logic layer. They do not dictate the shape of the message, which belongs in the contract. They focus on mapping. In a browser, an adapter might serialize a JavaScript object to JSON and stream it into a WASM module. At the edge, it might convert an HTTP request body into bytes for evaluation. In the cloud, it might connect stdin and stdout to a serverless function handler. The core remains untouched. The adapter does the wiring.

When adapters stay pure, the same binary travels smoothly. When adapters expand to include business rules or runtime assumptions, the core's clarity suffers. A developer who decides the feature flag evaluator should log directly to a cloud database every time a flag is checked has not built a thin adapter. They have embedded storage logic into the translation layer. An adapter that handles retries, rate limiting, and authorization inside the module has become a bloated middleman. Portability breaks because the browser cannot use the same database or retry system as the cloud function.

Think of the abstraction as the narrow part of an hourglass. The wide possibilities of environments meet the steady shape of the service core at that narrow point. If the narrow part stays narrow, the service flows smoothly from one side to the other. If it widens and starts holding more than translation, the flow clogs and the design fails.

In UMA, adapters are designed to be replaceable and lightweight. Multiple implementations can coexist, each tailored to a specific runtime. The browser adapter looks different from the cloud adapter, but both protect the same core logic and contract. This is what enables the same atomic service to run in environments with vastly different resources and assumptions.

4. Metadata: Making Services Self-Describing

A library where every book has a blank cover is not a library. The words inside are intact, but without a title, author, or subject, nobody can find what they need. Services without metadata have the same problem. They may have clean logic, precise contracts, and thin adapters, but without a description, they are invisible and underused.

Metadata gives a UMA service its voice. It answers the basic questions that humans and machines ask of any system component: what is this service, what version am I looking at, what inputs does it expect, what outputs does it produce, where are the examples and documentation, and what policies govern its use. In UMA, metadata is not optional. It is the glue that connects services into a functioning ecosystem. Without it, services exist in theory but cannot be found, validated, or orchestrated in practice.

The feature flag evaluator with metadata tells a developer immediately whether it fits their needs. An automated test harness validates requests against the declared schema before they reach the logic. An AI assistant reads the metadata and correctly routes messages. The evaluator is no longer a black box. It is a self-describing unit that others can rely on.

Weak metadata is almost as damaging as no metadata. If the evaluator describes its inputs as 'user data' without a schema, consumers still have to make assumptions.

If dependencies are listed incorrectly, orchestration fails at runtime. Sloppy metadata creates exactly the friction that clear contracts are supposed to eliminate.

A metadata block for the feature flag evaluator looks like this:

```
{
  "id": "feature-flag-evaluator",
  "version": "1.0.0",
  "description": "Evaluates a feature flag for a given user context.
                  Returns the selected variant and the reason for
                  selection.",
  "contract": {
    "input":  "schema:flag-evaluator-input@1",
    "output": "schema:flag-evaluator-output@1"
  },
  "policy": {
    "qualityTier": { "latencyP50Ms": 1, "deterministic": true },
    "budgets":      { "maxMemMb": 4, "maxCpuMs": 2 }
  },
  "runtime": {
    "format": "wasm32-wasip1",
    "entrypoint": "evaluate"
  },
  "tags": ["feature-flags", "experimentation", "stateless"]
}
```

Metadata is the final layer of the anatomy. With logic at the core, the contract as the handshake, and abstraction as the bridge, metadata turns an isolated unit into a participant in a broader system. It gives each service a name, a version, a description of its behavior, and a way to be cataloged and validated. Without it, even the cleanest services remain invisible. With it, they can be found, trusted, and composed at scale.

A Cutaway View of a UMA Service

The four layers form a concentric structure. At the center is the logic: the smallest and most crucial part, where the computation happens and where purity must be protected. Surrounding it is the contract: it does not affect the logic, but it makes the logic usable by providing a clear interface to the outside world. Outside the contract is the abstraction: a thin shell that connects the core to different runtimes without introducing new business rules. On the outside is metadata: the label and connective tissue that makes the service discoverable, versionable, and governable.

Each layer has its role. Each protects the others. Together, they form a service that is both atomic and universal.

Traditional Service vs. UMA Service

The four layers are easier to understand by comparison. Most teams think of a service as a package of business logic, infrastructure calls, and deployment scripts. UMA separates those concerns deliberately.

Aspect	Traditional Service	UMA Service
Logic	Often mixed with infrastructure code (DB queries, API calls)	Pure computation, environment-agnostic
Contract	Implicit in code or documentation, sometimes leaky	Explicit, unambiguous, versioned, portable
Abstraction	Rarely distinct, runtime assumptions hardcoded	Thin adapter layer, replaces environment-specific details without touching logic
Metadata	Minimal or absent, tied to deployment scripts	First-class makes service discoverable, testable, governable
Deployment	Fixed to a platform or stack	The same binary runs in the browser, Edge, or cloud via WASM
Governance	Manual, tied to runtime monitoring	Built in through metadata and contract validation

Traditionally, logic and environment are intertwined, contracts are incomplete, and metadata is an afterthought. Services are tightly coupled to the conditions under which they were created. In UMA, each layer has a distinct role. The separation transforms a service from a local artifact into a portable unit.

The difference is architectural and cultural. Traditional services are built assuming they will remain in a single environment. UMA services are designed for travel.

Atomic Services and the Lego Analogy

A UMA service is like a Lego brick. Each brick is small, self-contained, and precisely shaped. It makes no assumptions about the structure it will join. Its power comes not from complexity but from its ability to connect cleanly to others in countless arrangements.

The logic is the solid core of the brick. The contract is the set of studs and sockets that make it connectable. The abstraction is the slight variation that lets the same brick snap into different assemblies. The metadata is the label on the box that tells you what kind of brick you are holding and how to use it.

Building services this way changes how systems grow. Instead of connecting large rigid blocks, you combine small, versatile units. A shopping cart calculator connects to a tax calculator, which connects to a currency converter, each service portable and reusable. The system grows by adding more ways to assemble the same lightweight pieces, not by increasing their weight.

The Lego analogy is not about simplicity. It is about durability. Lego bricks have outlasted decades of building fashions because their connectors are consistent and their shapes are well-defined. UMA services aim for the same durability. By staying atomic, they can be recombined in ways their creators never anticipated, outlasting individual runtimes, platforms, and frameworks.

At its core, a UMA service is built on discipline. The contract defines the handshake. The logic provides the function. The abstraction connects the core to real-world environments. The metadata gives the service its identity. Together, these layers represent more than an architectural pattern. They represent a shift in how services are developed: from artifacts tied to a single runtime to portable components that work across platforms, devices, and clouds.

Runtime Portability and Adapters

Users do not think about where code runs. Whether a search box responds instantly in a browser, a notification arrives from the edge, or a recommendation is generated in the cloud, what matters is that the service works. For architects, achieving that seamlessness is the challenge. Browsers, edge nodes, and cloud servers are genuinely different environments with different strengths and constraints. The browser is close to the user but resource-limited. The edge sits between user and cloud, offering low latency within tight execution windows. The cloud has scale and power but carries network distance. The goal is one service that spans all three without being rewritten for each.

UMA addresses this directly. By keeping logic and contracts clean and using thin runtime adapters, the same service can be packaged once and connected to each environment through an adapter tailored to that runtime. To the user, one seamless experience. To the architect, one binary with three distinct interfaces.

The Feature Flag Evaluator Across Three Runtimes

Take the feature flag evaluator. At its core, it accepts a user profile and a flag definition and returns a decision. The logic is purely computational. The contract is a clean input-output definition. Nothing in the binary knows where it will run. That is the point.

In a browser, the evaluator lives inside a single-page application. The adapter is a JavaScript wrapper that serializes a user object to JSON, passes it into the WebAssembly module, and reads back the result. The impact is immediate: a button appears or disappears based on the user profile, with no network round-trip and no cloud waiting time.

At the edge, the evaluator runs inside a worker close to the user. The adapter receives an HTTP request, extracts the necessary context, and passes it into the same binary. The decision happens milliseconds after the client. This reduces latency while allowing the system to enforce global rules without involving the cloud.

In the cloud, the evaluator becomes part of a large-scale experimentation platform. The adapter is a serverless function handler that takes incoming requests, forwards the input to the WebAssembly module, and returns the response. Hundreds of thousands of evaluations per second, distributed across regions.

Across all three environments, the binary is identical. What changes are the adapters, each tailored to the environment's strengths and constraints. The logic and contract stay the same. The abstraction bridges the gap.

One Binary, Three Adapters

The portability model can be visualized as a single binary at the center with three connectors branching outward. Each connector is a runtime adapter translating the clean contract into the expectations of a different environment.

The browser adapter takes JavaScript objects from the application, serializes them to JSON, and streams them into the WASM binary. The service runs on the user's device and returns a result that the UI can apply immediately. The edge adapter reads inputs from HTTP requests, parses them, and pushes them into the same module. The result flows back into the worker's response within a tight execution window. The cloud adapter connects the binary to a serverless handler that reads from an incoming request, calls the binary, and returns the result at scale.

The diagram below shows this structure: three adapters as separate entry points into a single sealed module, each arrow pointing inward to the binary and outward with the response. Not three services. One service with three distinct interfaces.

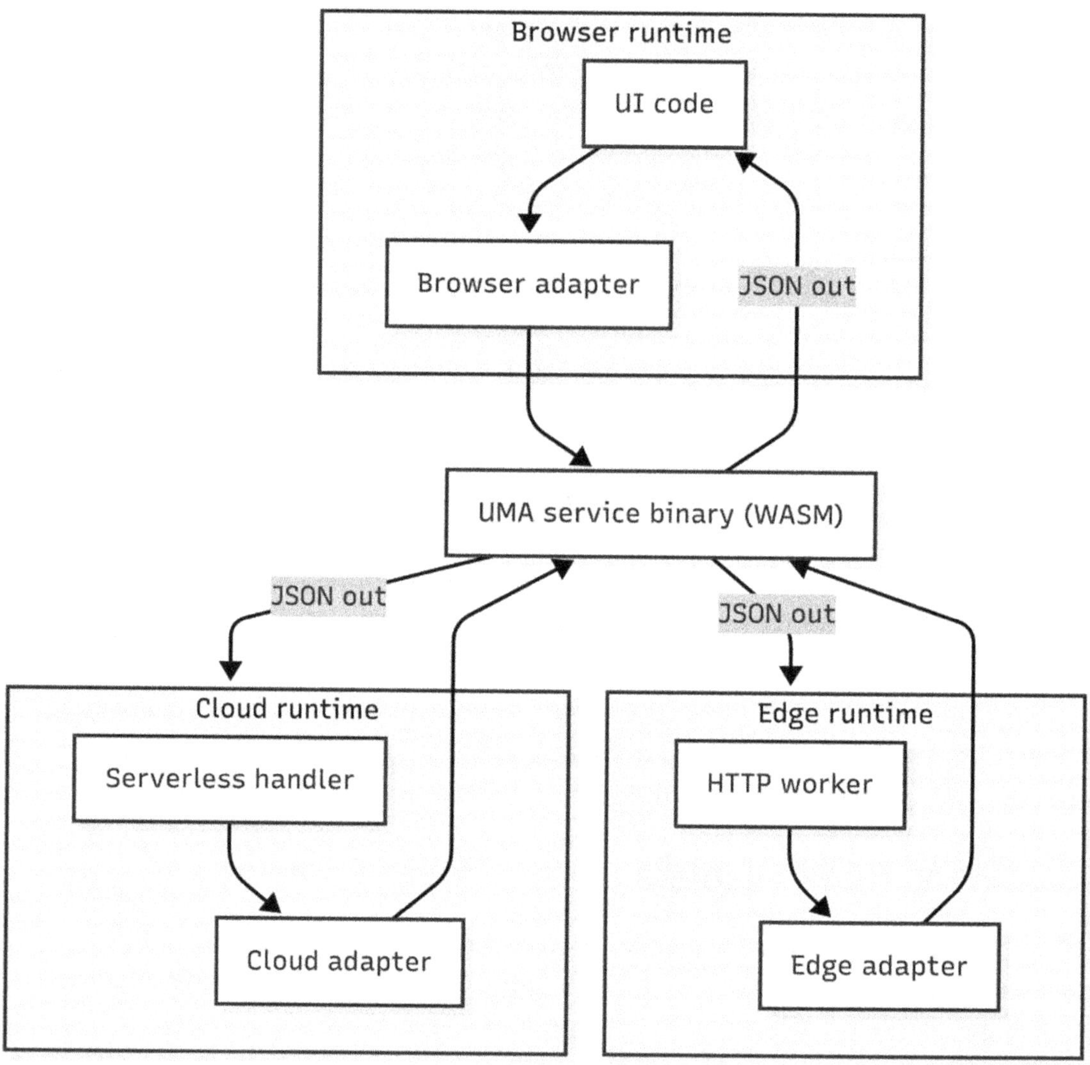

Figure 5-1. *One service binary at the center. Three thin adapters translate inputs and outputs to each runtime. The core does not change*

Cold Starts and Startup Costs

Portability comes with practical considerations. A UMA service compiled to WebAssembly may run in a browser, at the edge, or in the cloud, but the startup profile differs across environments. These differences are real and worth understanding, though they are not flaws in the model.

In a browser, the binary must be fetched and initialized. This adds a small delay the first time a service is used. Modern browsers cache aggressively, so subsequent calls are fast. At the edge, workers have strict execution windows and may be suspended between requests. A worker who initializes the binary from scratch on each request introduces tens of milliseconds of overhead. A warm worker responds instantly. In the cloud, serverless environments amplify this effect. Cold starts can stretch into hundreds of milliseconds if the runtime must load the module, allocate memory, and establish context before the first call returns.

These costs are predictable, which is their most important property. Because the core is sealed and consistent, startup time is stable and measurable across environments. Once loaded, steady-state performance is close to native code. The architect's job is to account for cold paths in the design: keep modules small so they load quickly, reuse warm instances where possible, and push initialization into adapters rather than into the logic itself.

Note on WASM Execution Environments Browser WASM, edge workers, and cloud WASM runtimes differ in more than startup behavior. Memory limits, threading support, available system interfaces, and I/O conventions vary. Wasmtime, Wasmer, and browser engines each implement WASI to different degrees. Test your binary in each target environment, not just in one. Assume the adapter will need to compensate for at least some of these differences.

Autonomy and Boundaries

Every architecture succeeds or fails based on the clarity of its boundaries. Services that try to do too much become overwhelmed. Services that depend too heavily on their neighbors become fragile, breaking when anything around them changes. Autonomy is the answer. A service that owns its work, defines its limits, and clearly declares its dependencies can operate across different environments and integrate into larger systems without risk.

In UMA, autonomy is not a design preference. It is the foundation of portability. A service can only move if its boundaries are strong enough to withstand the change. When a feature flag evaluator runs in a browser or cloud, it does so because the service knows exactly what belongs to it and what belongs to the adapter. The same principle applies to more complex services. Each must own its state and logic, expose it through clear contracts, and avoid leaking assumptions about the environment into its core.

The Autonomy Checklist

Boundaries have concrete, measurable qualities. A complete picture of a service's autonomy covers six dimensions: ownership, change cadence, state scope, team ownership, latency class, trust domain, resource budget, and failure domain. These dimensions turn autonomy from a principle into a checklist.

Ownership and Team Accountability

Every service needs a clear owner: the team or individual accountable for its contract, its logic, and its behavior in production. Without a declared owner, services drift. Contracts go unversioned. Breaking changes appear without notice. Dependencies accumulate without review. Ownership is not just an organizational concern. It is an architectural one. A service without a clear owner cannot be trusted by the services that depend on it.

Change cadence follows from ownership. How often does this service's contract change? How often does its logic change? A service that changes weekly has different governance needs than one that has been stable for two years. Declaring change cadence makes the dependency risk visible to callers before they build against the contract.

State Scope

State scope defines exactly what data the service owns and manages. A profile service owns user attributes. A cart service owns cart items. Neither owns anything outside that boundary. When the state scope is unclear, services start to reach into each other's data, creating hidden coupling that survives even the most careful refactoring.

State scope also determines portability constraints. A service with a narrow state scope, a small amount of structured data with a handful of read and write operations, can run in a browser tab or an edge worker. A service with a wide state scope, large event streams, or historical records belongs in an environment capable of matching.

Latency Class

Every service lives within a tolerance for how quickly it must respond, and that tolerance shapes its boundary. A feature flag evaluator in a browser belongs in the sub-millisecond class: it must answer almost instantly because the user is waiting for a UI element. A shipment tracker that updates a package location can live in a second class. An analytics pipeline may belong to a batch class where delays of hours are acceptable.

Defining a latency class is not about optimization. It is about honesty. A service that promises sub-millisecond responses but depends on a remote database is lying to itself, and the consequences appear as broken expectations in production. Making latency explicit also helps with portability. A service in the seconds class can move between cloud and edge because both environments can meet that requirement. A service in the sub-millisecond class may be limited to browser or edge, but it is still portable within that boundary because the expectation has been declared.

Trust Domain

Every service has a circle of callers it accepts and credentials it recognizes. The trust domain defines who is allowed to access the service and what authentication is required. A profile service might accept only authenticated requests from the application itself. A shipment tracker might accept partner systems with appropriate credentials. Each addition to the trust circle expands the service's responsibility and changes its boundary.

In UMA, the trust domain is declared in the contract and enforced in the adapter. The logic stays clean. The contract states the policy. The abstraction handles runtime enforcement. A service that trusts anyone who can reach its endpoint is not autonomous: it is exposed. A service that embeds cloud-specific identity checks directly into its logic is not portable: it is trapped. The right approach keeps trust explicit and enforcement in the adapter layer.

Clear trust domains make services composable. Without them, orchestration is a guessing game, and migration between environments carries hidden risk. With them, a service can move from browser to edge to cloud without changing who it trusts, only how that trust is enforced technically.

Resource Budget

Every service uses CPU cycles, memory, storage, and sometimes GPU capacity. These budgets are rarely unlimited, and they determine where a service can live. A profile service with a tight budget, storing small amounts of structured data and performing moderate computations, fits easily in a browser tab or edge worker. A shipment tracker handling large event streams and historical records has a larger budget, which draws it toward cloud environments with greater capacity.

Setting a budget is not about constraining creativity. It is about making commitments visible. A service that requires 500 MB of memory cannot claim to run on a lightweight IoT device. One that requires GPU acceleration cannot run everywhere by default. Declared budgets also shield the system from hidden costs. When a service runs beyond its intended budget, it starves other services and undermines resilience. With declared and enforced budgets, orchestration becomes predictable. A scheduler knows where to place the service. Adapters can prepare the right execution environment. Portability becomes measurable rather than aspirational.

Failure Domain

The failure domain defines the scope of damage when a service goes down or misbehaves. When a profile service stops responding, it may block a user from logging in. It should not bring down the payment system. When a shipment tracker updates slowly, customers get frustrated. It should not shut down the logistics platform. By defining its failure domain, a service declares what it owns and, equally importantly, what it does not.

In UMA, narrow failure domains make portability safer. A service with a well-defined failure domain can be moved between environments with less risk because orchestrators know how to contain its faults. If it crashes in a browser tab, only that session is affected. If it stalls at the edge, retries can be isolated. If it goes dark in the cloud, only the workflows that directly depend on it feel the impact.

The mistake is to let failure domains blur. A service that takes on critical responsibilities without declaring them turns small failures into widespread outages. Treating failure domains as part of the service anatomy ensures that each atomic unit is not only functional but also resilient. Autonomy is measurable not just in what the service does but in how it fails.

Worked Example: The Profile Service

The autonomy checklist becomes concrete when applied to a real service. A profile service stores and retrieves user attributes. It is a common service, present in almost every system, and a good test of the checklist because it seems simple on the surface and reveals genuine design decisions under examination.

Ownership is clear: the identity team owns the profile service. Its contract, logic, and production behavior are its accountability. Change cadence is low: the core profile schema changes rarely, with new optional fields added occasionally. Breaking changes require an increment in the version number and a deprecation notice.

State scope is narrow: user name, preferences, and recent activity. The profile service does not own authentication tokens, payment methods, or order history. Those belong to other services, each with its own contracts and adapters.

Latency class is fast but not sub-millisecond. A profile read typically powers a visible feature, such as a personalized dashboard, so it must return within tens of milliseconds. This narrows the design choices. Caching strategies are viable. Heavy queries to remote stores are not.

The trust domain is tight: only authenticated application calls are accepted. The profile service does not respond to anonymous queries from user devices and does not trust external partners directly. Adapters in different runtimes handle token verification, but the service never assumes a particular identity system.

The resource budget is modest: small memory footprint, moderate CPU usage, and no GPU requirements. The service fits comfortably in an edge worker or a lightweight cloud container. This budget prevents it from being pressed into roles it was not designed for, such as analytics processing or large-scale recommendation.

The failure domain is limited: if the profile service fails, users experience degraded personalization. Payment, shipping, and messaging systems continue to operate. Declaring this limit makes the service safer to migrate between runtimes and allows it to fail locally without cascading.

Boundary and Ownership Map

The profile service autonomy can be mapped visually. At the center is the service core: the business logic and the profile state it manages. Surrounding the core is the service boundary, defined by the contract and reinforced by the six autonomy dimensions. Outside the boundary are the adapters, each designed for a specific runtime, each connecting to the same contract without altering the core.

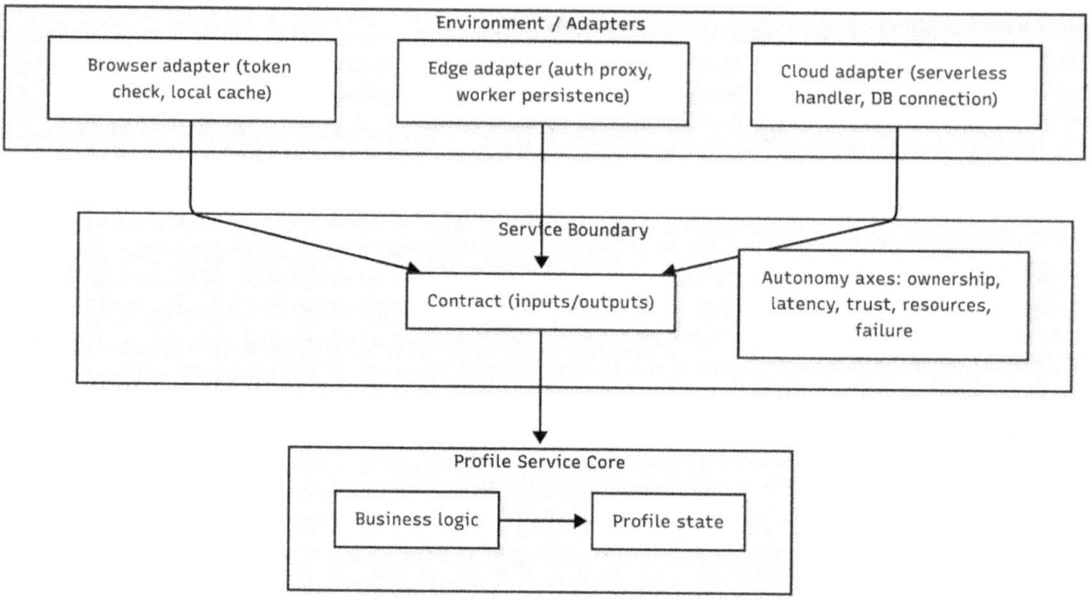

***Figure 5-2.** The profile service manages its logic and state within its boundary. The contract defines the exact point of interaction. The autonomy dimensions outline its obligations. Outside the boundary, adapters in browser, edge, and cloud environments handle runtime concerns without modifying the core*

With this map, ownership is visible. Inside the boundary, the profile service controls its state and logic. The contract is the precise line that defines how it interacts with other services. Outside the boundary, the adapters handle runtime concerns. Each adapter connects through the same contract, keeping the service portable and protected from its environment.

Thinking in terms of autonomy shifts the focus from runtime details to architectural design. A service is no longer just code running somewhere. It is a self-contained unit with clear ownership of its logic and state, explicit interaction contracts, and declared obligations across six dimensions. These boundaries protect the service from the assumptions of any single runtime while giving it the flexibility to operate across many. For the profile service, this means performance issues are addressed within the contract rather than hidden in adapters, trust assumptions are explicit rather than implied, and failure modes are mapped rather than discovered during outages.

Once services respect their own boundaries, they can be composed safely into larger systems without becoming a monolith. Each unit remains accountable for what it owns, and only what it owns, regardless of where it runs.

In Practice: Build One Today

Why a Feature Flag Evaluator

Feature flags are everywhere. Teams use them to enable features for a subset of users, safely roll back changes, and run A/B experiments. Most teams write this logic multiple times across different clients, services, and environments. That duplication is exactly the problem UMA solves, which makes the feature flag evaluator an ideal first service to build the UMA way.

Feature flags also have the right properties for demonstrating portability. The logic is purely computational: given a flag definition and a user context, return a decision. There is no required network call, no file-system dependency, and no environment-specific state. The contract is clean. The logic is deterministic. The binary compiles to WebAssembly without modification. Those three properties, together, make a service a strong portability candidate; not every service has them, but when they are present, the case for UMA is immediate and verifiable.

The evaluator also builds directly on the concepts introduced earlier in this chapter. The "Required Anatomy of a UMA Service" section defined what every UMA service must contain. The "Runtime Portability and Adapters" section showed how the same binary runs across environments with thin adapters. The "Autonomy and Boundaries" section established how to declare what a service owns. The evaluator demonstrates all of it in one concrete, runnable example.

The annotated snippets here highlight the key decisions. The complete runnable project, including all adapter implementations and test vectors, is in the companion repository:

```
https://github.com/enricopiovesan/UMA-code-examples/
tree/main/chapter-05-feature-flag-evaluator
```

Prerequisites Rust toolchain with the wasm32-wasip1 target (rustup target add wasm32-wasip1). Node.js 20 or later. npm. wasmtime on your PATH. Optionally use jq for inspecting JSON output. See the repository README for exact version requirements and installation instructions.

Step 1: Define the Capability

Before writing a line of code, state clearly what the service does. In UMA, this is the first and most important step: defining the capability in a way that is independent of any runtime or implementation detail.

For the feature flag evaluator, the capability is, given a flag definition and a user context, to return a decision. That decision must be deterministic, portable, and bound by clear performance expectations.

Inputs:

- flag: a unique identifier and configuration for the feature flag.
- variants: the possible values the flag can return.
- weights: optional distribution for randomized rollout.
- rules: optional targeting conditions (for example, if country equals CA, serve variant B).
- context: attributes of the current user, device, or environment.

Outputs:

- flag: the same identifier passed in.
- variant: the chosen outcome.
- reason: why the variant was selected: rule match, weighted hash, or default.
- meta: optional telemetry including evaluation duration and matched rule identifier.

Quality tier and resource budget:

- Deterministic hashing, identical results across all runtimes for the same input.
- p50 latency under 1 ms for a single evaluation on commodity hardware, excluding cold start and network round-trip.
- Maximum 4 MB memory per evaluation.
- Maximum 2 ms CPU per evaluation.

These numbers are not aspirational targets. They are commitments that shape every design decision that follows. A service that cannot meet its declared budget in one environment cannot claim to be portable to that environment.

High-level pseudocode for the entry point:

```
// Single entry point, runtime-agnostic
fn evaluate(flag: FlagDefinition, ctx: Context) -> EvaluationResult {
    // 1. Check targeting rules in order
    // 2. If no rule matches, apply weighted hash
    // 3. Return variant + reason + telemetry
}
```

The full runnable implementation is at:

> https://github.com/enricopiovesan/UMA-code-examples/tree/main/chapter-05-feature-flag-evaluator

See core/src/lib.rs for the Rust implementation of eval_flag, and the corresponding TypeScript wrapper in the adapter layer.

Step 2: Write the Contract

With the capability defined, the next step is to express it as a contract. The contract is declarative and runtime-agnostic. The same contract guides adapters across browser, edge, and cloud, and it is the source of truth for schema validation in all three.

The contract for the feature flag evaluator has two parts: a schema defining the structure of inputs and outputs and a policy block making performance and resource expectations explicit. The full contract files are at contracts/input.schema.json and contracts/output.schema.json in the companion repository.

Schema excerpt:

```
{
  "$id": "schema:flag-evaluator@1",
  "type": "object",
  "properties": {
    "flag":     { "type": "string" },
    "variants": {
      "type": "array",
      "items": { "type": "string" },
```

```
      "minItems": 1
    },
    "weights": {
      "type": "array",
      "items": { "type": "number", "minimum": 0 }
    },
    "context": { "type": "object", "additionalProperties": true }
  },
  "required": ["flag", "variants", "context"]
}
```

Policy block:

```
{
  "policy": {
    "qualityTier": {
      "latencyP50Ms": 1,
      "deterministic": true
    },
    "budgets": {
      "maxMemMb": 4,
      "maxCpuMs": 2
    },
    "telemetry": {
      "emit": ["durationNs", "ruleId", "hashInput"]
    }
  }
}
```

The policy block lives alongside the schema in the repository's contract directory. It is not enforced by the runtime in this chapter's example yet. Chapter 5 introduces the runtime layer that validates against declared budgets at execution time.

The schema defines the data contract. The policy sets the operational boundaries. Any adapter can use both to enforce, test, or optimize the service without touching the core logic.

The complete contract files are in the companion repository:

> https://github.com/enricopiovesan/UMA-code-examples/tree/main/chapter-05-feature-flag-evaluator

Step 3: Implement the Core Logic Once

With the capability defined and the contract in place, the logic follows. The principle is simple: write it once, run it anywhere. The implementation avoids all runtime-specific APIs, so it compiles cleanly to a portable WebAssembly binary.

The logic follows three steps: check targeting rules in order, fall back to weighted distribution if no rule matches, return the selected variant with a reason and optional telemetry.

Rust implementation (core/src/lib.rs in the companion repository):

```
pub fn eval_flag(flag: &Flag, ctx: &Context) -> EvalResult {
    // Step 1: Check targeting rules in order
    for rule in &flag.rules {
        if rule.matches(ctx) {
            return EvalResult::new(&flag.key, &rule.variant, "rule_match");
        }
    }

    // Step 2: Weighted hash fallback
    // deterministic_hash produces identical results across all runtimes
    // for the same seed and flag key, which is what makes the evaluator
    // portable. The hash function is pure: no clock, no network, no I/O.
    let idx = deterministic_hash(&ctx.seed, &flag.key) % flag.
    variants.len();
    let variant = &flag.variants[idx];

    // Step 3: Return decision
    EvalResult::new(&flag.key, variant, "weighted_hash")
}
```

On Determinism A deterministic function always produces the same output for the same input, regardless of when or where it runs. The hash function here takes a user seed and a flag key and returns a stable index into the variants list. The same user always gets the same variant for the same flag, in every environment, across every runtime. This is what makes the evaluator trustworthy for experiments: you can verify a result independently of where the evaluation happened.

One anti-pattern to watch for here: if you find yourself adding a conditional that selects a different hash function based on the runtime environment, such as using the Web Crypto API in the browser and a different library on the server, that branch does not belong in the core. It belongs in the adapter. Platform-specific branches inside logic are covered in detail in the section "Anti-patterns to Avoid." The rule is simple: if the hash function must differ by environment, define it as an interface and implement it in each adapter. The core calls the interface and stays identical everywhere. The full implementation, including data structures, the hash function, rule matching, and telemetry, is in the companion repository:

`https://github.com/enricopiovesan/UMA-code-examples/tree/main/chapter-05-feature-flag-evaluator`

Step 4: Add Adapters Around It

The core logic is now a single function that compiles into a portable WebAssembly module. Adapters expose that same function in different environments without modifying anything inside it. The pattern is the same in every case: receive input in the environment's native format, translate it to the contract shape, call the evaluator, and return the result.

The pseudocode below shows the structure of each adapter. The complete, runnable adapter implementations are in the companion repository.

Browser Adapter

Load the WASM module once. Expose an evaluate function whose API matches the contract exactly.

```
// Pseudocode: browser adapter
let module = null

async function init() {
    if module is not loaded:
        fetch evaluator.wasm
        instantiate via WebAssembly.instantiateStreaming
        cache the instance
}

async function evaluate(request) {
    await init()
    serialize request to JSON per contract schema
    pass JSON into the WASM module
    deserialize and return the result
}
```

Complete implementation: adapters/browser/ff.js in the companion repository.

Edge Adapter

Map HTTP requests to the contract, then call the same evaluator module.

```
// Pseudocode: edge adapter
function handle(httpRequest) {
    body = read JSON from request body
    validate body against contract schema
    decision = evaluate(body)   // same binary, same function
    return HTTP 200 with JSON decision
}
```

Complete implementation: adapters/edge/worker.ts in the companion repository.

Cloud Adapter

Receive an HTTP or event payload, validate it against the schema, and forward it to the evaluator.

```
// Pseudocode: cloud adapter
async function handler(event) {
```

```
    input = parse JSON from event body
    validate input against contract schema
    output = await evaluate(input)
    return statusCode 200 with JSON output
}
```

Complete implementation: adapters/cloud/handler.ts in the companion repository.

Notes Applying to All Adapters Schema validation uses the same contract files defined in Step 2. Adapters may add telemetry fields without changing the evaluator logic. Cold starts and the first WASM load are one-time costs per runtime instance. Keep the module initialized between requests where the environment permits.

The complete, runnable adapters are in the companion repository:

https://github.com/enricopiovesan/UMA-code-examples/tree/main/chapter-05-feature-flag-evaluator

Step 5: Run and Verify

One evaluator. Three adapters. The goal now is to prove the binary runs the same way in all three environments, with identical results for identical inputs.

Clone and Build

```
git clone https://github.com/enricopiovesan/UMA-code-examples.git
cd UMA-code-examples/chapter-05-feature-flag-evaluator

# Run the lab script for a guided walkthrough
./scripts/run_lab.sh lab1-country-match

# See the repository README for full build instructions
# and environment-specific run commands.
```

Browser Run

1. Start the dev server from the repository.
2. Load the sample page and open DevTools.
3. Run the provided evaluate(req) call in the console.
4. Verify that output fields match the contract and that identical inputs return the same variant on repeated calls.

Edge Run

1. Launch the edge worker following the repository instructions.
2. Use curl to send the sample request payload.
3. Confirm the response variant and reason match the browser result.

Cloud Run

1. Deploy the serverless function using the provided script.
2. Invoke with the same request payload.
3. Confirm identical decision and reason across all three environments.

Determinism Test

Determinism means the same input always produces the same output, regardless of runtime, timestamp, or execution order. The repository includes test vectors: a set of known inputs with their expected outputs. Run them across all three environments and confirm they match.

```
./scripts/run_vectors.sh
Expected output (verified against the repository):
PASS  lab1-country-match   variant=B  reason=rule_match
PASS  lab2-weighted-hash   variant=A  reason=weighted_hash
PASS  lab3-default         variant=A  reason=weighted_hash
All vectors passed. Determinism confirmed across runtimes.
```

If any environment returns a different variant for the same input, the hash function or rule-matching logic includes a platform-specific branch that should not be in the core. Isolate it and move it to the adapter.

Telemetry and Budgets

- Confirm the evaluator emits durationNs and ruleId in the meta field.
- Inspect logs to verify p50 evaluation time stays within the declared 1 ms budget.
- The first call in each runtime incurs a cold-start cost. Keep the module warm between requests where the environment allows.

Contract Validation

- Each adapter validates the request and response against the same schema from Step 2.
- Run the schema check script to catch any drift between what the adapter sends and what the contract declares.

With the same contract at the center and adapters around it, the evaluator behaves consistently across browsers, Edge, and the cloud. The diagram below shows the final structure:

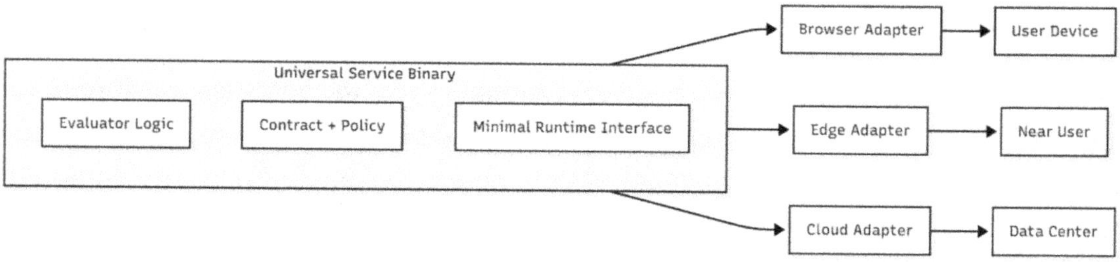

Figure 5-3. *The evaluator contract anchors the service. Thin adapters let it speak to browsers, Edge, and the cloud. One binary. Three interfaces. This is UMA's pattern in its simplest form*

Two anti-patterns surface naturally at this stage of building. If any adapter starts containing business logic, such as rule evaluation or variant selection, that is the over-granularity pattern in reverse: the adapter has absorbed work that belongs in the core. If the binary deployed to the browser differs in version from the binary deployed to the cloud, that is version drift. Both are covered in the section "Anti-patterns to Avoid" with specific remedies. The feature flag evaluator is intentionally small. That is the point. Roll it out today, apply it to a project you already have, and see the contract-first portable approach working in your own environment. Once you have built one service this way, the boundaries, adapters, and governance principles become second nature. The next section covers the anti-patterns that undo this work if left unchecked.

Anti-patterns to Avoid

Anti-patterns are not hypothetical. Every one of these has appeared in production systems built by experienced teams. They share a common root: the core qualities UMA is designed to protect, clean contracts, isolated logic, and consistent binaries and get compromised one small decision at a time. Each compromise seems reasonable in the moment. Collectively, they make the system fragile, hard to migrate, and expensive to maintain.

UMA gives you a vocabulary to recognize these failures early. Once you can name a hidden coupling or a leaky contract as a violation of the model, correcting course is straightforward. The hard part is seeing them before they calcify into assumptions that the whole system depends on.

Hidden Coupling Through Shared Databases

Warning When multiple services share the same database schema, they develop hidden dependencies that make each service's internal structure visible to all others. A single schema change can propagate through unrelated parts of the system, turning a local update into a widespread outage.

Why Teams Fall into This Trap

A shared database appears efficient at first. Everyone queries the same tables, reuses existing joins, and avoids the overhead of designing APIs. Legacy systems make this especially tempting because the database already exists, and connecting another service appears faster than defining a new contract. The problem is that what is efficient today becomes fragile as the system grows. When schemas change, every consumer is at risk.

Example

At a retail platform, the shipment service and the profile service both depended on the same users table. The profile team added a new field for login history, which triggered a schema migration. During the rollout, the ORM for the shipment service failed because it expected the older schema. A profile feature update blocked order processing. Neither team had agreed to that dependency. It had accumulated silently through shared table access.

In a SaaS billing system, multiple services queried the invoices table directly. The finance team added an index to improve reporting performance. A poorly tested trigger slowed all write operations. Billing, customer notifications, and account dashboards all started timing out because they were connected through a schema none of them owned.

How to Recognize It

The signal is a schema change in one service that causes failures in another. If two services share a table and you cannot change that table's structure without coordinating across both teams, the boundary is wrong. The dependency exists; it is just undeclared.

How to Avoid It In UMA, each service owns its persistence and shares information through contracts or events, never through direct table access. If the profile service updates its schema, the shipment service is unaffected because it depends only on the profile contract, not on the underlying storage. The initial design effort is higher. The operational cost of schema migrations drops to near zero because they are contained.

Leaky Contracts That Expose Runtime Details

Warning: Contracts are meant to hide runtime details. When they expose internal information, such as environment identifiers, infrastructure fields, or provider-specific metadata, they bind consumers to an implementation that should be invisible. Every runtime change propagates outward.

Why Teams Fall into This Trap

It starts innocuously. A developer adds a debugging field to a response or exposes a runtime identifier to aid monitoring. Over time, consumers come to rely on these fields. What was diagnostic information becomes an informal contract. Removing or changing those fields breaks callers, and changing runtimes without breaking clients becomes nearly impossible.

Example

An API designed to return feature flag decisions began including the underlying container's podName and clusterRegion in its response, added for logging convenience. Internal monitoring scripts quickly began parsing those values. A third-party integrator cached results keyed on them. When the service migrated from Kubernetes to a serverless environment, the entire downstream broke. The contract had embedded environment-specific details that should never have left the service boundary.

A payment service included the cloud provider's internal request identifier in error payloads. Developers built dashboards and alerting rules around it. Switching providers or renaming internal identifiers became impossible without breaking client error handling.

How to Recognize It

Look for fields in response contracts that describe where the service is running rather than what it produced. Names like podName, functionId, runtimeVersion, clusterRegion, or lambdaRequestId in a response body are immediate signals. If a consumer depends on those fields for anything other than discarding them, the contract is already leaking.

How to Avoid It UMA contracts describe capabilities, not execution environments. Inputs and outputs carry business semantics. Debugging information stays internal or flows through structured telemetry that is explicitly separate from the contract. When you find yourself adding a field that describes the runtime rather than the result, stop. That field belongs in an observability pipeline, not in the response schema.

Over-Granularity That Destroys Coherence

Warning Splitting logic into too many small services creates orchestration overhead, raises latency, and scatters business rules across fragments that must be coordinated to produce any useful result. What appears modular in a diagram often becomes brittle in production.

Why Teams Fall into This Trap

Teams hear 'smaller is better' and apply it without a stopping condition. A checkout flow becomes a dozen microservices: one for promotions, one for taxes, one for receipts, and one for shipping estimates. Each is internally clean. Together, they form a fragile chain where a single failure can block the entire workflow. The pursuit of purity overshadows the need for coherence.

Example

An e-commerce team divided its checkout pipeline into separate services for tax calculation, promotion eligibility, shipping cost estimation, payment routing, and invoice formatting. On paper, it looked clean. In production, what had been a 200 ms synchronous operation stretched to over 1.2 seconds because of network hops between services. A bug in the promotion service blocked the entire checkout flow even for orders with no promotions, because the orchestration assumed all services would respond before proceeding.

A media platform created microservices for string formatting and image resizing as standalone deployable units. Developers spent more time wiring dependencies between them than building features. Outages were harder to diagnose because the logic for a single user action was spread across four services.

What Right Granularity Looks Like

The feature flag evaluator in this chapter is an example of correct granularity. It is a bounded unit of real business value: a service that decides, for a given user, whether a feature is active. That decision is atomic. It does not need to be split into a rulematcher service, a hash-calculator service, and a telemetry-recorder service. Those are implementation details within a single coherent capability.

The test for right granularity is whether the service represents a complete, independently useful capability. A tax calculator that takes a cart and returns a tax amount is a candidate. A service that performs one arithmetic operation and returns the result is not a service; it is a function call. A service that handles the full checkout flow, including payment, is too large because it combines capabilities with different latency classes, trust domains, and failure modes.

How to Avoid It Define services around capabilities, not around code units. A capability is something a caller needs to have done, with a clear input, a clear output, and a meaningful business result. If splitting a service into two pieces means neither piece is useful without the other, the split is wrong. Keep services small enough to be testable and portable in isolation and large enough to be coherent on their own.

Platform-Specific Branches Inside Logic

Warning Embedding runtime checks directly into core logic breaks portability. Conditionals that branch on the execution environment scatter runtime assumptions through the code, making it impossible to guarantee consistent behavior across environments.

Why Teams Fall into This Trap

Developers add these branches to address immediate compatibility issues: handle a file path differently on the server, adjust a browser timeout, or call a platform-specific API at the edge. Each change is small and local. Over time, the core logic becomes a patchwork of environment-specific decisions. What started as a single service is now multiple partial implementations hidden within a single codebase.

Example

A team building a feature flag evaluator added branches to handle hashing differently in browser and server environments. The browser path used the built-in Web Crypto API. The server path used an external hashing package. The change was made to solve a real compatibility problem. When test vectors ran across environments, the evaluator produced different rollout results for the same user. Two users comparing notes would see different experiences. The binary was no longer one service. It was two services sharing a file.

A notification service handled push delivery differently depending on whether it ran in the cloud or on-premises. Those conditionals grew over time into separate code paths inside the same module. Debugging required first establishing which runtime was in use before any meaningful investigation could begin.

How to Recognize It

Search the core logic for any conditional that branches on runtime context: if (isBrowser), if (isCloud), if (process.env.RUNTIME === 'edge'), or any check against environment variables that selects different execution paths. Each one is a runtime assumption that has leaked into the wrong layer.

How to Avoid It Runtime differences belong in adapters, not in core logic. If the hashing algorithm must differ between browser and server, define the hash function as an interface in the contract and implement it separately in each adapter. The core calls the interface. Each adapter provides the implementation appropriate for its environment. The core remains identical across all runtimes, which makes it portable.

Version Drift Between Environments

Warning Running different versions of the same service across environments breaks consistency and erodes trust in the system. Even small version mismatches produce subtly different behaviors that are difficult to detect until they reach users.

Why Teams Fall into This Trap

Version drift accumulates through uneven deployment pipelines. The browser bundle updates first. The edge node lags behind because deployments are staged. The cloud rollout takes two weeks to propagate across regions. Each runtime ultimately runs a slightly different binary. Teams assume the differences are harmless because the changes seemed minor. They are rarely harmless for long.

Example

In one rollout, a feature flag evaluator ran version 1.2 in the browser and version 1.1 at the edge. For most users, this produced no visible difference. Then, a targeting rule was updated in 1.2. Users saw the new variant on the client. The edge still routed traffic based on the older logic. The same user received different experiences depending on which environment handled their request. Engineers spent days tracing reports of inconsistent rollouts before the version mismatch surfaced as the cause.

A payment service updated API error codes in the cloud runtime but not in the embedded mobile SDK. The difference seemed minor. It broke client-side error handling in ways that triggered false retries and, in some cases, duplicate transactions.

How to Recognize It

If different runtimes report different version identifiers for the same service, drift has already occurred. If your deployment pipeline has separate release processes for browser, edge, and cloud builds of the same service, drift is structurally guaranteed over time.

How to Avoid It UMA treats the binary as a single artifact: built once, tested once, and deployed consistently to all runtimes. One build pipeline. One test suite. One artifact version that propagates to the browser, edge, and cloud simultaneously. If your current pipeline cannot enforce this, treating version parity as a contract violation is the right starting point. Early detection of drift through contract validation is a process problem. Drift that surfaces in production is a trust problem.

Anti-patterns at a Glance

Five patterns, one root cause: the core qualities UMA protects get compromised one local decision at a time.

- **Hidden Coupling Through Shared Databases:** Breaks autonomy. Schema changes in one service ripple through all consumers. Fix by sharing contracts and events, not tables.
- **Leaky Contracts That Expose Runtime Details:** Bind consumers to infrastructure. Fix by keeping contracts capability-focused and routing diagnostics through telemetry.
- **Over-Granularity That Destroys Coherence:** Fragments business logic into chains that fail together. Fix by defining services around complete, independently useful capabilities.
- **Platform-Specific Branches Inside Logic:** Hides multiple implementations in one binary. Fix by moving runtime differences into adapters and keeping the core identical.
- **Version Drift Between Environments:** Produces divergent behavior that is invisible until it reaches users. Fix by treating the binary as a single artifact and using a single deployment pipeline.

Takeaways and Bridge to Chapter 5

UMA in Practice

UMA has moved from concept to implementation. The feature flag evaluator is a small service, but it exercises every principle in the model: a capability defined once, a contract that makes assumptions explicit, a portable binary that does not change, and adapters that connect it to different runtimes. The value of UMA is no longer theoretical. The same decision engine produces identical results regardless of where it runs. That is a verifiable property, not a claim.

The "Anti-patterns to Avoid" section matters for the same reason. Most teams have encountered at least one of these. Some will recognize their current system in more than one. The point is not that these mistakes are avoidable in hindsight. The point is that UMA provides a vocabulary to identify them before they solidify. Hidden coupling, leaky contracts, and version drift are not vague issues in code quality. They are specific violations of the model, and each violation has specific remedies.

The Bigger Picture

A single feature flag evaluator demonstrates the idea. It does not address the challenges that appear when you have dozens or hundreds of universal services operating together. At that scale, you need more than contracts and adapters. You need packaging standards, runtime abstraction, and mechanisms to coordinate services across environments without losing the simplicity you started with.

Contracts and adapters provide portability for individual services. Scaling UMA requires runtimes and abstraction layers that can consistently host, discover, and govern services. Chapter 5 examines how those layers work. You will see how packaging turns binaries into portable artifacts, how runtime abstraction hides environmental differences at a system level, and how orchestration allows many services to operate side by side without losing their independence.

The journey moves from one evaluator to a broader landscape where universality is the default, not the exception.

CHAPTER 6

The UMA Runtime Layer

Threads, Events, and Adapters in Harmony

Introduction: The Runtime As the Real Abstraction

Every System Runs Twice

The first version exists in the design: clean contracts, well-named capabilities, and a diagram that makes the architecture legible. The second version exists on the machine, where timing, resource limits, and host differences modify that design in ways no diagram captures. A service can compile cleanly and pass contract validation, then behave differently across environments because background tasks finish in a different order, network calls resolve asynchronously on one host and synchronously on another, or an adapter blocks where the design assumed it would not. These are not syntax errors. They are execution differences, and they are the real portability problem.

Traditional systems address this class of problem through clock synchronization, logical clocks, and distributed event logging and replay algorithms. UMA takes a different position: rather than coordinating across hosts after the fact, it eliminates the source of variance by making the runtime itself the sole scheduler and event sequencer. The UMA Runtime Layer establishes a consistent environment where service logic interacts with its surroundings through a single, controlled path. It does not replace engines like Node, Deno (a secure JavaScript and TypeScript runtime built on V8), or Wasmtime (a fast, standards-compliant WebAssembly runtime designed for server and edge environments). It operates above them, providing a standard framework for loading services, binding adapters, scheduling work, and recording results. That framework transforms runtime behavior from an opaque, host-dependent layer into a predictable, rule-governed system.

Think of it as the stage manager for a distributed performance. The service logic is the script. The adapters are the instruments. The runtime ensures every cue plays in the correct sequence, regardless of where the stage is set. Whether the service runs in

E. Piovesan, *Universal Microservices Architecture*, https://doi.org/10.1007/979-8-8688-2794-5_6

the browser, at the edge, or in the cloud, the execution order is the same, the events are recorded in the same sequence, and the observable outcomes are identical.

The UMA Runtime Layer has four concrete components, each with a defined responsibility. The AdapterManager selects and binds the correct network adapter at startup. The EventBus maintains a logical clock, incrementing a counter with each emitted event, ensuring deterministic, host-clock-independent event order. The ThreadManager schedules execution synchronously within a single logical task. The LifecycleRecord captures the binding decision, the event sequence, and the final state in a persistent metadata document. These four components are not abstractions. They are the actual modules in the runtime crate, and every behavior described in this chapter can be observed directly by running the post-fetcher lab at `https://github.com/enricopiovesan/UMA-code-examples/tree/main/chapter-06-post-fetcher-runtime`.

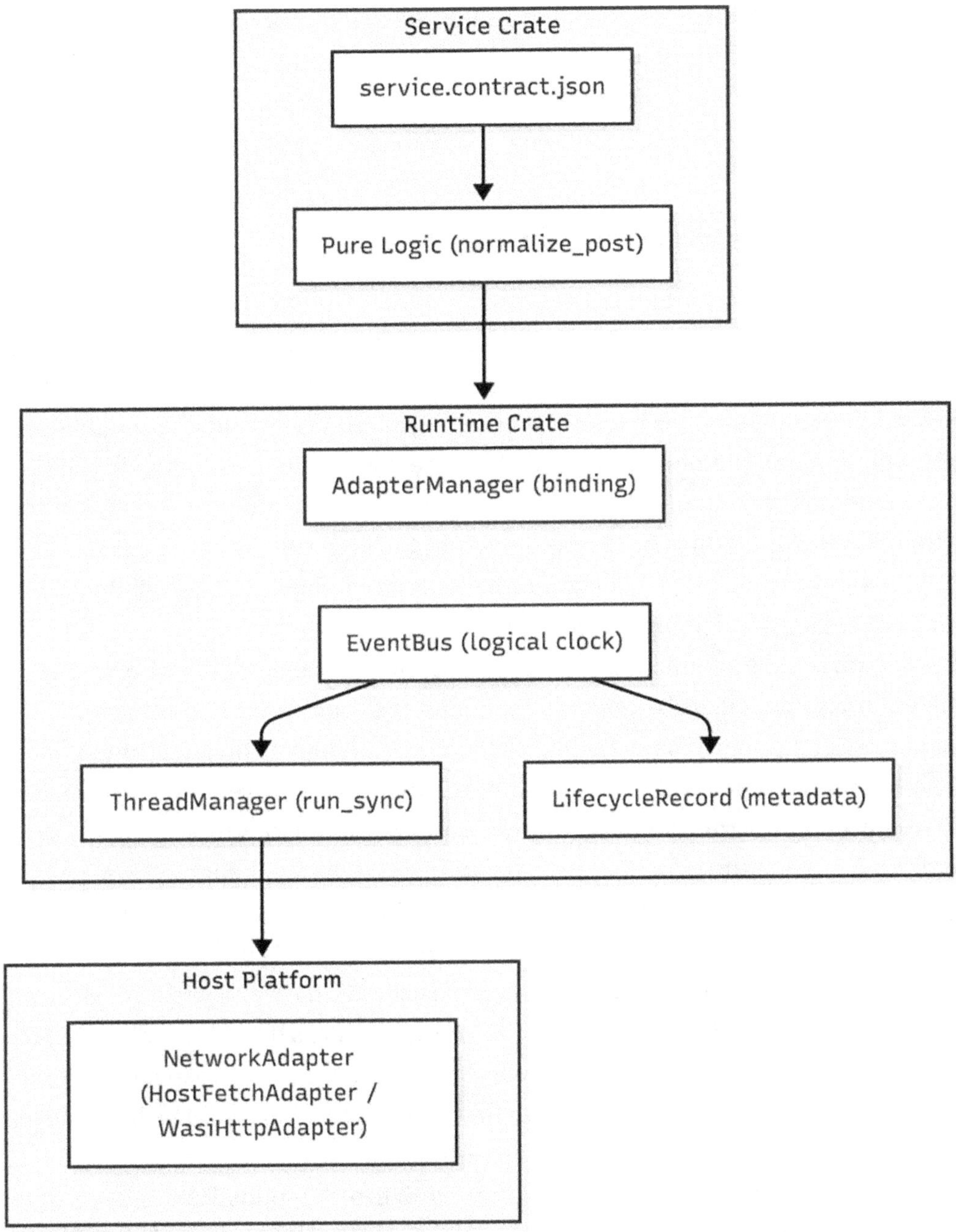

***Figure 6-1.** The UMA runtime links service logic to the host environment through the AdapterManager, EventBus, ThreadManager, and LifecycleRecord. Each component has a defined responsibility. The host provides the adapter implementation; the runtime controls everything else*

Portability, properly understood, is a guarantee of execution, not a compilation property. The same contract and the same logic will always run under the same orchestration rules, producing consistent results across browsers, edges, and clouds. By the end of this chapter, that claim will be measurable, not theoretical.

The Role of the UMA Runtime

A runtime is not neutral infrastructure.

Every runtime makes decisions. When to schedule work, how to handle errors, which resources to expose, and what to record. Traditional runtimes like Node, the JVM, or .NET make those decisions implicitly, driven by platform defaults, host configuration, and the ambient environment. The UMA Runtime makes them explicitly driven by contracts and policy. That distinction is the source of portability.

The UMA Runtime does not compete with platform runtimes. It operates above them, providing a meta-layer that standardizes service behavior across all hosts. Its responsibilities are divided into three areas.

Execution management. The runtime owns the service lifecycle: when a service instance starts, what it does before the first adapter call, and how it terminates. It sequences work through a logical scheduler rather than relying on host thread models. The result is the same regardless of the order of operations on every host.

Environment abstraction. The runtime exposes capabilities through adapters rather than direct platform APIs. When service logic needs a network fetch, it calls a capability. The runtime resolves that capability to the adapter bound at startup. The logic never knows which adapter ran. It never knows which host it is on.

Governance and policy enforcement. Each execution is validated against contracts and policy before any side effects occur. The runtime checks header validity, enforces declared capability constraints, and records lifecycle metadata for inspection or replay. If validation fails, execution stops before the first adapter call is made. The lifecycle state is set to failed, and no network event is ever emitted.

The post-fetcher runtime example illustrates all three responsibilities in a single runnable codebase. Its functional requirements are worth stating directly because they provide a concrete framework for everything that follows in this chapter.

The service accepts a JSON input containing a URL and an optional set of HTTP headers, fetches a JSON document from that URL, and normalizes it into a canonical Post shape with four fields: id, userId, title, and body. The runtime validates request headers before any network call. If an unrecognized header is present, execution stops, the lifecycle state is set to failed, and no fetch event is emitted. The runtime records every step as a deterministic event sequence using a logical clock: each event carries an integer counter as its timestamp, not a wall-clock value, so the sequence is identical across hosts. On completion, the runtime persists a lifecycle record capturing the adapter binding decision, the full event log, the final state, and the logical clock value.

A reader who has built a similar service in a traditional microservices pattern will notice one concrete difference. In the traditional pattern, normalization logic, the HTTP call, error handling, and logging are co-located in a single function. In the UMA pattern, the pure normalization logic lives in the service crate, and the runtime crate owns everything else. That separation is not cosmetic. It is the architectural decision that makes the service portable, testable in isolation, and verifiable across environments.

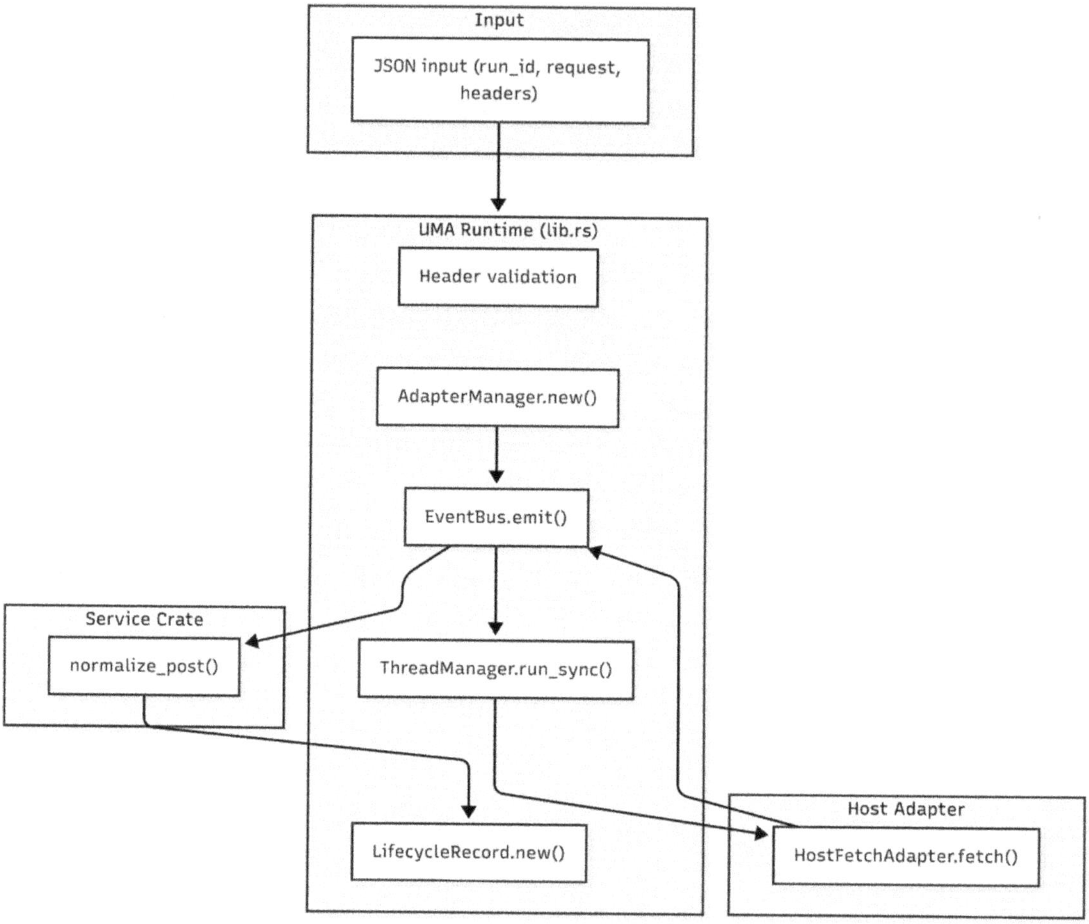

Figure 6-2. *The UMA Runtime sits above the host adapter and below the service logic. It standardizes execution, adapter binding, and policy enforcement without replacing the underlying platform runtime*

The reference implementation is at `https://github.com/enricopiovesan/UMA-code-examples/tree/main/chapter-06-post-fetcher-runtime`. Every behavior described in this chapter can be directly observed by running the labs in that directory. The validated path is the native Rust cloud host smoke flow. The TypeScript runtime is a parity reference for the core scenarios. The browser and Edge host files are illustrative scaffolding, not validated quick-start paths.

When a UMA service runs locally and later on a remote edge node, it behaves consistently in both environments because the runtime is part of the service, not part of the host. Debugging, testing, and deployment all occur under the same orchestration rules. Portability is no longer a property of the infrastructure. It is a property of the runtime.

The Service Loader: From Contracts to Running Instance

A UMA service never starts on its own.

Every execution begins through a loading sequence that reads the declared contracts, validates them against available adapters and runtime policy, binds the correct capability implementation to the service, and initializes the lifecycle record before a single line of business logic runs. That sequence is not a convention. It is a hard boundary. A service that bypasses it is not running under UMA guarantees. It is running as any other process, lacking the portability and verifiability properties described in this chapter.

The loading sequence has three phases: validation, binding, and initialization. Each phase is a gate. Failure at any phase stops execution before side effects occur.

Validation

The runtime reads the service contract, the adapter capability contract, and the runtime policy. It checks that the declared capabilities have corresponding adapter implementations and that the adapter versions are compatible with the service's requirements. Compatibility is evaluated at the major and minor version level: a service declaring a requirement against version 1.0.0 will bind to any adapter implementing 1.0.x. If any declared capability cannot be fulfilled, the runtime sets the lifecycle state to failed and halts before initialization.

In the post-fetcher example, the service contract declares one required capability: network.fetch. The adapter capability contract at contracts/adapter.network.contract.json defines the fetch operation, its request and response shapes, and its semantics. The runtime policy at contracts/policy.runtime.json declares the adapter selection strategy and observability requirements. All three are read at startup. The contracts are compiled into the binary, not loaded dynamically at runtime, which means the validation step is fast and the runtime never depends on file system access to determine whether it can proceed.

Binding

After validation, the runtime selects the adapter implementation and records the binding decision in the lifecycle metadata. The binding is driven by two inputs: the host environment and the operator-supplied environment variables.

On native targets, the default adapter is HostFetchAdapter, which uses reqwest blocking to perform synchronous HTTP GET requests. If the UMA_ENABLE_RETRY environment variable is set, the runtime wraps the selected adapter in a RetryAdapter that retries failed requests up to three times. If UMA_ENABLE_CACHE is set, a CacheAdapter wraps the result, returning cached responses by URL for the lifetime of the adapter instance. The wrappers are composed in a defined order: retry is applied first, then cache. The impl_name field in the binding record reflects the full composition, for example, cache-retry-host-fetch, so the lifecycle record is an exact description of what ran.

The Binding Metadata component in the loading sequence is the AdapterBinding struct. It carries two fields: impl_name, which records the composed adapter name, and host, which records the platform identifier (native for non-wasm targets, wasm32 for WebAssembly). These two fields are the minimum information needed to reconstruct which execution path the runtime chose without re-running the service or inspecting the environment.

On wasm32 targets, the runtime attempts to select a WasiHttpAdapter. The current implementation returns a stable error because outbound WASI HTTP is not wired in this example. If a host provides a working WASI HTTP implementation, the adapter selection path is the same: the AdapterManager reads the target architecture at compile time and returns the appropriate implementation.

Initialization

Once binding is complete, the runtime allocates the EventBus, initializes the ThreadManager, and emits the first lifecycle event. The event type is start, the data payload carries the runId from the input, and the logical clock is set to zero. From this point forward, every step the runtime takes is recorded as an event before execution continues to the next step.

The following Rust code from lib.rs shows the actual initialization sequence. It is not pseudocode. This is the code that runs.

```
// From runtime/src/lib.rs
pub fn run_json(
    input_json: &str,
    adapter: Option<Box<dyn NetworkAdapter>>,
) -> Result<(String, String)> {
    // Parse input against the service contract
    let input: Input = serde_json::from_str(input_json)?;
```

```
    let thread_manager = ThreadManager::new();
    let mut event_bus = EventBus::new();

    // First lifecycle event: logical clock starts at 0
    event_bus.emit("start", json!({ "runId": input.run_id.clone() }));

    // Validate headers before any adapter call
    let allowed_headers = ["accept", "content-type", "authorization"];
    let mut header_validation_failed = false;
    for (key, value) in &input.request.headers {
        let lower = key.to_ascii_lowercase();
        if !allowed_headers.contains(&lower.as_str()) {
            event_bus.emit("error",
                json!({ "error": format!("unexpected header {}", key) }));
            header_validation_failed = true;
        }
    }

    // Bind adapter: selection driven by target arch and env vars
    let adapter_manager = AdapterManager::new(adapter);

    // ... fetch, normalize, persist lifecycle record
}
```

The run_json entry point in lib.rs. Input is parsed, the EventBus is initialized with a logical clock at zero, headers are validated before any adapter call, and the AdapterManager selects the binding. No dynamic contract loading occurs at runtime.

Versioning and Side-by-Side Isolation

When services depend on different versions of the same capability, the runtime does not impose a single global choice. Each service instance carries its own binding record. Two services running concurrently can bind different adapter implementations of the same capability as long as each adapter declares a compatible contract version. The binding record in the lifecycle metadata captures exactly which version each instance used, so a post-run audit can determine whether two runs used the same adapter path or different ones.

To make this concrete: a service compiled against network.fetch version 1.0.0 will bind to any adapter declaring 1.0.x. A second service compiled against version 1.2.0 will bind to any adapter declaring 1.2.x. If the host environment provides both adapter versions, each service binds independently. If only one version is available and it satisfies both requirements, both services bind to it. The runtime checks compatibility at bind time using a major-minor comparison. The patch level is not a constraint.

This mechanism preserves independence without sacrificing determinism. Each run produces a lifecycle record that documents the exact binding decision. A reader can inspect two lifecycle records side by side and determine whether differences in output are attributable to different adapter versions, different environment variables, or differences in the input itself.

How the Loading Sequence Appears in Practice

Running the post-fetcher lab produces a JSON output that contains both the service output and the lifecycle record. The lifecycle record captures the binding decision directly. For the default cloud path, the binding shows impl: "host-fetch" and host: "native". After enabling both wrappers with UMA_ENABLE_RETRY=1 UMA_ENABLE_CACHE=1, the binding shows impl: "cache-retry-host-fetch". The normalized output is identical in both cases. The binding record is the only thing that changes, and it changes in a predictable, documented way.

Run lab3 to observe this directly:

```
# Default binding
./scripts/run_lab.sh lab1-cloud-golden-path

# Composed binding with retry and cache wrappers
./scripts/run_lab.sh lab3-adapter-binding-and-wrappers
```

Lab commands for observing adapter binding in the post-fetcher runtime. The normalized output matches across both runs. The lifecycle binding record differs, reflecting the adapter composition the runtime selected at startup.

A service never starts on its own. The loading sequence is the runtime asserting its role as the single point of control over how a service enters execution. That control is what makes the service portable, the binding auditable, and the execution reproducible on any host that satisfies the declared capability requirements.

The Thread and Event Manager: Determinism Across Environments

Concurrency is where portability breaks.

Two services running identical logic on different machines can produce different results because their events arrive in different orders, their timers fire at different wall-clock times, or their thread schedulers interleave work differently. These differences are not bugs in the traditional sense. They are the expected behavior of systems that let the host decide when things happen. UMA makes a different choice: the runtime is the sole event scheduler. The host never decides the order of execution. The runtime does.

The mechanism is the EventBus. It maintains a single logical clock, an integer counter that starts at zero and increments by one each time an event is emitted. Every event carries its counter value as a string timestamp. The order of events is therefore the order of emission, not the order of wall-clock time. Two runs of the same service with the same input will produce the same event sequence, the same logical timestamps, and the same output, regardless of which host they run on or what load the host is under.

This is not a claim about performance. It is a claim about reproducibility. The runtime does not guarantee that events happen fast. It guarantees that events happen in the same order every time.

The EventBus in the Implementation

The EventBus struct in event_bus.rs is the complete implementation of this idea. It holds a Vec of Event structs and a u64 clock. Each call to emit converts the current clock value to a string, constructs an event with that timestamp, appends it to the vector, and increments the clock. There is no async processing, no sorting, and no concurrency. The bus is append-only and strictly sequential.

```
// From runtime/src/event_bus.rs
pub struct EventBus {
    pub events: Vec<Event>,
    pub clock: u64,
}
```

```
impl EventBus {
    pub fn new() -> Self {
        Self { events: Vec::new(), clock: 0 }
    }

    pub fn emit(&mut self, event_type: &str, data: Value) {
        let t = self.clock.to_string();
        let event = Event {
            t,
            type_: event_type.to_string(),
            data,
        };
        self.events.push(event);
        self.clock += 1;
    }
}
```

The EventBus from event_bus.rs. The logical clock is a u64 counter. Each emitted event receives the current clock value as a string, then the clock increments. There is no wall-clock dependency, no async scheduling, and no sorting. Event order is emission order, always.

The full event sequence for a successful post-fetcher run is start (clock 0), fetch_request (clock 1), fetch_response (clock 2), normalized (clock 3), and end (clock 4). The logical clock value at termination is 5, which matches the logicalClock field in the lifecycle record. If header validation fails, the sequence is: start (clock 0), error (clock 1), end (clock 2). No fetch_request event is ever emitted when validation fails. The lifecycle record captures the exact clock value at which the run ended, making the event count directly verifiable from the metadata alone.

The Thread Manager

The Thread Manager in thread_manager.rs is deliberately minimal. Its run_sync method accepts a closure and executes it on the current thread, returning the result. There is no thread pool, no task queue, and no cooperative scheduling. In this example, there is one logical task per invocation, so the implementation is a direct passthrough.

```
// From runtime/src/thread_manager.rs
pub struct ThreadManager;

impl ThreadManager {
    pub fn new() -> Self { Self }

    pub fn run_sync<F, R>(&self, f: F) -> R
    where
        F: FnOnce() -> R,
    {
        f()
    }
}
```

The ThreadManager from thread_manager.rs. It executes work synchronously on the current thread. The design is intentionally simple: determinism comes from the EventBus, which controls event order, not from thread coordination.

The simplicity of the ThreadManager is a design statement. Determinism in UMA does not come from sophisticated scheduling. It comes from the EventBus owning the sequence. The ThreadManager exists to make the boundary between the runtime and the host explicit: the runtime calls run_sync, the host executes the closure, and control returns to the runtime. If a more complex runtime needed cooperative multitasking or prioritized task queues, those mechanisms would be implemented inside the ThreadManager without touching the EventBus or the event sequence.

How Determinism Appears in Practice

The golden fixture at tests/fixtures/expected_golden.json is the concrete proof of determinism. It captures the exact output and lifecycle record for a run against the hermetic fixture URL uma-fixture://sample-post. The integration test in run_cloud.sh builds the runtime, runs it on that input, and compares the output, byte-for-byte, against the golden fixture using jq. If the event sequence, the logical timestamps, or the normalized output differ in any way, the test fails.

Run lab1 to observe this directly:

```
./scripts/run_lab.sh lab1-cloud-golden-path
```

Lab 1 runs the validated cloud path and compares output against the golden fixture. A passing run proves that the runtime produced the exact event sequence, logical timestamps, and normalized output recorded at authoring time.

The golden fixture shows five events with logical timestamps 0 through 4, a logicalClock of 5, a state of "terminated," and a normalized post matching the fixture data. Every field in that record is the direct output of the EventBus and LifecycleRecord working together. Nothing in the output depends on the system clock, the host load, or the order in which the operating system schedules threads.

Determinism As an Architectural Property

Determinism in UMA is not a constraint imposed on the developer. It is a property that emerges from the design. The developer writes pure service logic and declares capabilities. The runtime controls when those capabilities are called and records what happened. Because the runtime owns the sequence, the developer gets reproducibility for free.

You have probably seen the alternative. A service that passes all its unit tests, deploys cleanly, and then fails intermittently in production because two events arrived in the wrong order on a loaded host. The failure is real, the logs are incomplete, and reproducing it requires either luck or a carefully constructed load test. In a UMA service, that class of failure is structurally prevented. The event sequence is the same on a loaded cloud host as on a developer laptop, because neither the cloud host nor the developer laptop determines the sequence. The EventBus does.

Determinism does not mean rigidity. The service still interacts with the outside world through adapters. Network responses vary. Adapter implementations can change. What stays constant is the structure of the execution: the order of events, the shape of the lifecycle record, and the rules that govern when execution proceeds and when it stops. That constancy is what makes a UMA service testable, verifiable, and trustworthy across the full range of environments it runs in.

Adapters and Capabilities: Extending the Runtime Without Leaking It

A UMA service has no knowledge of its host environment.

It does not call operating system APIs. It does not know whether it is running in a browser tab, an edge worker, or a cloud function. It does not reference an HTTP client library. All of that is intentional. A service that reaches directly into its host environment couples permanently to that environment. Portability ends the moment the first platform-specific call is made.

But all useful logic must eventually touch the outside world. A service that fetches nothing, stores nothing, and emits nothing is not a service. It is a pure function. The question is not whether to cross the boundary between logic and environment. The question is who controls that crossing, how it is recorded, and what guarantees it carries.

The answer is the adapter.

What an Adapter Is

An adapter is the runtime's mediated connection to a host capability. It implements a trait defined in the service crate, exposes that implementation to the runtime through a factory, and handles the translation between the service's capability call and whatever the host environment actually provides. The service never calls the adapter directly. It calls a capability. The runtime resolves that capability to the bound adapter and executes the call through the monitored path.

The NetworkAdapter trait in service/src/api.rs defines the interface every network adapter must implement:

```
// From service/src/api.rs
pub trait NetworkAdapter {
    fn fetch(
        &self,
        url: &str,
        headers: &std::collections::HashMap<String, String>,
    ) -> Result<NetworkResponse>;
}

pub struct NetworkResponse {
    pub status: u16,
```

```
    pub headers: std::collections::HashMap<String, String>,
    pub body: String,
}
```

The NetworkAdapter trait from service/src/api.rs. Every adapter, regardless of host environment, implements this interface. The service logic never sees anything beyond this contract.

The HostFetchAdapter in adapter_manager.rs implements this trait for native targets using reqwest blocking. The WasiHttpAdapter in wasi_http_adapter.rs implements it for wasm32 targets. The CacheAdapter and RetryAdapter in their respective files wrap any existing adapter, composing behavior without modifying the underlying implementation. All four types implement the same trait. From the service logic's perspective, they are indistinguishable.

Adapter Composition and the Binding Record

The AdapterManager selects and composes adapters at startup. The selection logic is straightforward: start with the base adapter for the target platform, then apply wrappers in the order dictated by the environment variables UMA_ENABLE_RETRY and UMA_ENABLE_CACHE. The resulting impl_name is a composed string that documents the full adapter stack. cache-retry-host-fetch means a CacheAdapter wrapping a RetryAdapter wrapping a HostFetchAdapter. The runtime records this string in the lifecycle metadata before the first capability call.

```
// From runtime/src/adapter_manager.rs (native path, simplified)
let mut adapter: Box<dyn NetworkAdapter> = Box::new(HostFetchAdapter {});
let mut impl_name = "host-fetch".to_string();

let enable_retry = std::env::var("UMA_ENABLE_RETRY").is_ok();
let enable_cache = std::env::var("UMA_ENABLE_CACHE").is_ok();

if enable_retry {
    adapter = Box::new(RetryAdapter::new(adapter, 3));
    impl_name = format!("retry-{}", impl_name);
}
```

```
if enable_cache {
    adapter = Box::new(CacheAdapter::new(adapter));
    impl_name = format!("cache-{}", impl_name);
}

let binding = AdapterBinding {
    impl_name,
    host: "native".to_string(),
};
```

Adapter composition in adapter_manager.rs. The base adapter is selected for the target platform. Wrappers are applied in order based on environment variables. The resulting impl_name is a composed string that documents the full adapter stack recorded in the lifecycle metadata.

This design has a direct governance consequence. An operator who wants to add retry behavior to every cloud deployment sets UMA_ENABLE_RETRY=1 at the host level. The service binary does not change. The contracts do not change. The lifecycle record for every subsequent run shows the retry wrapper in the binding field, making the change auditable across the entire fleet without touching a single line of service code.

The Monitored Capability Call

Every adapter call passes through the runtime's event recording path. The runtime emits a fetch_request event before the call and a fetch_response event after it. If the call fails, an error event is emitted instead of fetch_response. The event data captures the URL on the way in and the HTTP status on the way out. The logical clock advances with each event, so the position of every capability call in the execution sequence is recorded precisely.

This is the monitored call path from lib.rs:

```
// From runtime/src/lib.rs
event_bus.emit("fetch_request",
    json!({ "url": input.request.url.clone() }));

let fetch_result = thread_manager
    .run_sync(|| adapter_manager.fetch(
        &input.request.url,
        &input.request.headers,
    ));
```

```
match fetch_result {
    Ok(resp) => {
        event_bus.emit("fetch_response",
            json!({ "status": resp.status }));
        // parse body, normalize post, emit normalized or error
    }
    Err(err) => {
        event_bus.emit("fetch_response", json!({ "status": 0 }));
        event_bus.emit("error", json!({ "error": err.to_string() }));
    }
}
```

The monitored capability call path in lib.rs. A fetch_request event is emitted before the adapter is called. A fetch_response event is emitted after. Every step is recorded in the EventBus before the control moves forward.

The event timestamps in this sequence are logical clock values, not wall-clock readings. A fetch_request event at clock position 1 always precedes a fetch_response at clock position 2, regardless of how long the actual network call took or what the system clock read at either moment. This is the fix for a subtle correctness problem in the original chapter: a timestamp based on performance.now() or any wall-clock source would differ between a fast edge node and a slow cloud function, making the event hashes non-comparable across environments. Logical timestamps eliminate that variance entirely. Two runs of the same service with the same input will produce identical event hashes because the timestamps are counters, not clocks.

Adapter Manifests and Trust Domains

Each adapter carries metadata that the runtime uses during binding: a capability name, a contract version, and a trust domain. The trust domain declares where the adapter is permitted to operate and what privileges it carries. A browser adapter may only access browser fetch APIs. A cloud adapter may extend to persistent storage and tracing backends. The runtime enforces these boundaries at bind time, not at call time.

The adapter capability contract at contracts/adapter.network.contract.json defines the fetch operation, its request and response shapes, and its semantics. The semantics field is set to idempotent, which tells the runtime and any downstream consumers that calling the adapter twice with the same input is safe. The runtime policy in contracts/policy.runtime.json defines the adapter selection strategy, the preferred adapter order, and whether binding decisions should be persisted in the lifecycle record.

These metadata documents are tools of governance, not just technical validation. They make every external dependency of a service explicit, versioned, and auditable. A service cannot quietly acquire new capabilities between deployments. Every capability it uses is declared in a contract, every adapter that fulfills that capability is validated against the contract version, and every binding decision is recorded in the lifecycle metadata before execution begins.

Controlled Extensibility

Adapters evolve independently of the services that use them. A browser adapter that initially wraps the native fetch API can later add a circuit breaker. An edge adapter can incorporate request coalescing to protect upstream services during traffic spikes. A cloud adapter can swap its storage driver or tracing backend. None of these changes requires rebuilding the service binary. The runtime validates compatibility at bind time and enforces it at every capability call.

The RetryAdapter and CacheAdapter in the repository illustrate this directly. Both are wrapper types that implement NetworkAdapter by delegating to an inner adapter. Both can be composed with any base adapter that implements the same trait. Adding retry behavior to the HostFetchAdapter requires one environment variable and produces a new binding record. Removing it requires unsetting that variable. The service binary is untouched in both cases.

This is what controlled extensibility means in practice. The adapter boundary is the point at which the runtime's guarantees end and the host environment begins. Everything inside that boundary is deterministic, recorded, and reproducible. Everything outside it is the host's responsibility. The adapter is the contract between those two worlds, and the runtime enforces it on every call.

Metadata and Lifecycle Governance

A UMA service does not just run. It describes itself while running.

Every instance produces a lifecycle record: a structured document that captures the service identity, the contract version, the adapter binding decision, the full event log, the final state, and the logical clock value at termination. That record is not a log file appended as an afterthought. It is a first-class output of the runtime, constructed from the same data structures that govern execution and validated against the metadata schema before being returned to the caller.

This self-description is what transforms the runtime from an executor into an observable, policy-aware system. The lifecycle record answers four questions any operator, auditor, or downstream agent will ask of a running service: what ran, what decisions it made, what happened during execution, and what state it finished in. No external monitoring system is required to answer those questions. The record carries the answers itself.

The LifecycleRecord Structure

The LifecycleRecord struct in metadata.rs defines the shape of the persisted record. It maps directly to the metadata schema declared in contracts/metadata.schema.json. The fields are service (the service name from the contract), service_version (the contract version), policy_ref (the name of the runtime policy that governed the run), bindings (the adapter binding decision, keyed by capability name), events (the full event log from the EventBus), state (the final lifecycle state), and logicalClock (the clock value at termination).

```
// From runtime/src/metadata.rs
#[derive(Serialize)]
pub struct LifecycleRecord {
    pub service: String,
    pub service_version: String,
    pub policy_ref: String,
    pub bindings: Bindings,
    pub events: Vec<Event>,
    pub state: String,
    #[serde(rename = "logicalClock")]
    pub logical_clock: u64,
}

#[derive(Serialize)]
pub struct Bindings {
    #[serde(rename = "network.fetch")]
    pub network_fetch: BindingImpl,
}
```

```
#[derive(Serialize)]
pub struct BindingImpl {
    #[serde(rename = "impl")]
    pub impl_name: String,
    pub host: String,
}
```

The LifecycleRecord struct from metadata.rs. Every field maps directly to the metadata schema in contracts/metadata.schema.json. The record is constructed at the end of run_json and returned alongside the service output.

The lifecycle states defined in the runtime policy are registered, validated, bound, initialized, running, terminated, and failed. In the current implementation, the runtime transitions directly to terminated on a successful run and to failed if any error event was emitted during execution. The state field in the lifecycle record is set by inspecting the event log: if any event has the type "error," the final state is "failed." Otherwise, it is terminated. This rule is deterministic and requires no external state machine.

Deterministic Replay, Auditability, and Testability

The lifecycle record enables four operational properties that are difficult or impossible to achieve in systems that treat observability as an afterthought.

Deterministic replay. The event log in the lifecycle record is the complete execution trace. Given the same input and adapter binding, the runtime will produce the same event sequence, logical timestamps, and output. A replay is not a rerun against a live environment. It is a verification that the same inputs, fed through the same runtime with the same adapter, produce the same outputs. The golden fixture in tests/fixtures/expected_golden.json is the checked-in proof of this property for the post-fetcher service.

Auditability. The binding field records exactly which adapter implementation ran. The events field records every step the runtime took, in order, with logical timestamps. An auditor reading the lifecycle record can reconstruct the full execution path without access to the service binary, the host environment, or any external logging system. The record is self-contained and self-describing.

Testability. The runtime tests in runtime/src/tests.rs verify the lifecycle record directly. test_run_json_with_dummy_adapter asserts that a successful run produces exactly five events and a logicalClock of 5. test_header_validation_and_final_state asserts that a run with an invalid header produces a failed state. test_header_validation_skips_network_fetch asserts that no fetch_request event is emitted when validation fails. Each test is a direct assertion against the lifecycle record fields, not against log output or side effects.

Recoverability. Because the lifecycle record captures the binding decision alongside the event log, an operator investigating a failed run can determine exactly which adapter path was active at the time of failure. If the failure is adapter-specific, the binding record identifies it. If the failure is input-specific, the event log shows at which step execution stopped. The two pieces of information together are sufficient to diagnose most runtime failures without reproducing the environment.

Policy As a Runtime Concern

The runtime policy at contracts/policy.runtime.json declares three things: the adapter selection strategy for each capability, the binding mode (eager for required capabilities, lazy for optional ones), and the observability requirements (whether binding decisions should be persisted). In the current implementation, the policy file acts as the declared runtime contract rather than a fully interpreted policy engine. Adapter selection and observability behavior are implemented directly in the AdapterManager and the LifecycleRecord. Future iterations can wire the policy parser to drive those decisions dynamically without changing the service binary or the contracts.

The key design principle is that policy lives alongside the service, not in the infrastructure. An operator who deploys this service to a new environment does not need to configure a central policy server or modify a shared registry. The policy reference is embedded in the lifecycle record of every run, so any downstream system reading that record knows which policy governed the execution.

The Circular Dependency in the Governance Loop

The governance diagram for this section shows a loop: the service instance holds a policy reference, the runtime evaluates that policy against the metadata store, the metadata store updates the lifecycle state, and the lifecycle state feeds back into the event stream. This loop is real, and it creates a dependency that deserves explicit acknowledgment.

The practical risk is evaluation order: if the policy evaluator reads the metadata store while the lifecycle record is being written, it may act on a partially complete record. The mitigation is straightforward in the current implementation because the runtime writes the lifecycle record atomically at the end of run_json, after all events have been emitted and the final state has been determined. The policy evaluator never runs concurrently with the write. The loop is sequential, not concurrent, which eliminates the race condition.

In a more complex runtime where policy evaluation runs continuously against a live metadata store, the correct strategy is to treat the lifecycle record as an append-only log and evaluate policy only against complete, immutable snapshots. Each completed run produces a snapshot. Policy evaluation operates on snapshots. The live record is never read while it is being written. This pattern is the same one used in event-sourced systems and distributed ledgers, and it applies directly to UMA lifecycle governance at scale.

In Practice: A Portable Runtime Example

Portability is a property that must be demonstrated, not claimed.

The post-fetcher service is compiled once. It runs across three different host configurations: a native cloud path using HostFetchAdapter, a browser scaffold using the Web Fetch API, and an edge scaffold using a lightweight worker shim. In each case, the service performs the same sequence of operations: validate the input headers, emit a start event, fetch a JSON document, normalize it into a canonical Post shape, emit an end event, and persist the lifecycle record. The core logic and the contracts do not change between hosts. The adapter changes. Everything else stays the same.

The validated path in this example is the native Rust cloud host. The TypeScript runtime is a parity reference that mirrors the runtime's behavior for readers who want to explore its design in a more familiar language. The browser and edge host files are illustrative scaffolding: they show where a JS or Wasm binding layer would attach, but they are not part of the validated quick-start path. A reader who wants to extend the example to a real browser or Edge deployment has a clear starting point in those files.

What the Runtime Does Across All Three Hosts

The following diagram shows the execution path the runtime takes regardless of the host. The binary is the same. The contracts are the same. The event sequence is the same. Only the adapter changes.

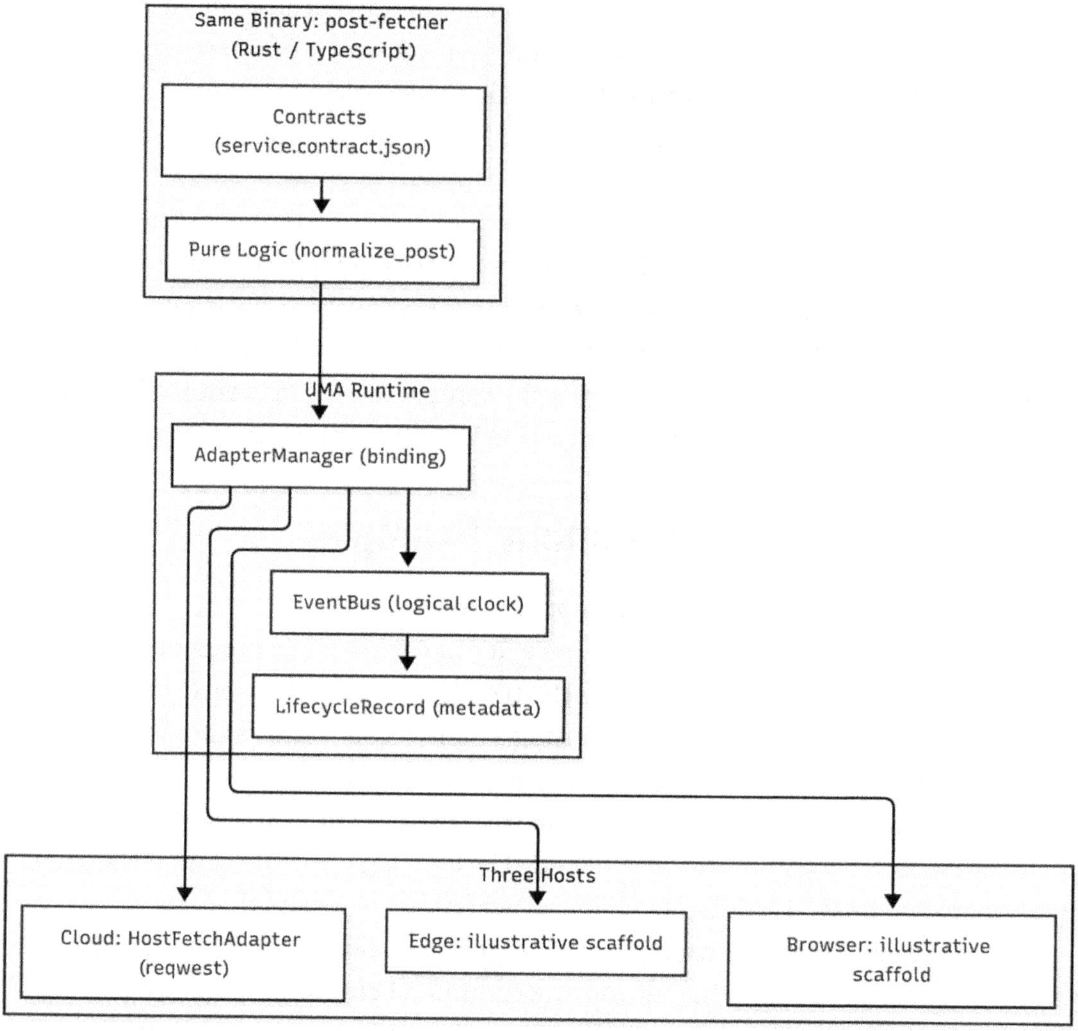

***Figure 6-3.** The runtime binds a host-specific adapter at startup, records the binding decision, and monitors each capability call through the EventBus. The service logic and contracts are unchanged across all three hosts*

The Execution Flow in Code

The runOnce pattern below captures the core of what the runtime does on each host. It is not pseudocode. The Rust version is in runtime/src/lib.rs. The TypeScript version is in ts/src/lib.mjs. Both implementations follow the same structure.

```
// TypeScript reference runtime: ts/src/lib.mjs (simplified)
export async function runJson(inputJson, adapter) {
  const input = JSON.parse(inputJson);
  const eventBus = new EventBus();          // logical clock starts at 0
  eventBus.emit("start", { runId: input.runId });

  // Validate headers before any adapter call
  const allowed = new Set(["accept", "content-type", "authorization"]);
  let validationFailed = false;
  for (const [key] of Object.entries(input.request.headers ?? {})) {
    if (!allowed.has(key.toLowerCase())) {
      eventBus.emit("error", { error: `unexpected header ${key}` });
      validationFailed = true;
    }
  }

  // Select and compose adapter
  const adapterManager = createAdapterManager(adapter);

  if (!validationFailed) {
    eventBus.emit("fetch_request", { url: input.request.url });
    try {
      const resp = await adapterManager.adapter.fetch(
        input.request.url, input.request.headers ?? {});
      eventBus.emit("fetch_response", { status: resp.status });
      const post = normalizePost(JSON.parse(resp.body));
      if (post) eventBus.emit("normalized", { id: post.id });
      else eventBus.emit("error", { error: `status ${resp.status}` });
    } catch (err) {
      eventBus.emit("fetch_response", { status: 0 });
      eventBus.emit("error", { error: err.message });
    }
  }

  eventBus.emit("end", {});

  return {
    output: { normalizedPost, events: eventBus.events },
```

```
    lifecycle: {
      bindings: { "network.fetch": adapterManager.binding },
      events: eventBus.events,
      state: eventBus.events.some(e => e.type === "error")
        ? "failed" : "terminated",
      logicalClock: eventBus.clock,
    },
  };
}
```

The runJson function from the TypeScript reference runtime in ts/src/lib.mjs. The structure mirrors the Rust implementation in runtime/src/lib.rs. Both use a logical clock, validate headers before the adapter call, and return a lifecycle record alongside the service output.

Proving Portability with the Parity Check

Portability is proven by the parity check, not by assertion. The compare_impls.sh script runs both the Rust and TypeScript implementations against the same three lab scenarios and compares their summarized runtime behavior. The comparison covers the adapter binding, the lifecycle state, the logical clock value, the normalized post, and the event type sequence. If any of these differ between implementations, the script fails with an explicit diff.

```
# Run the full parity check across all three lab scenarios
./scripts/run_lab.sh lab4-rust-ts-parity

# Or run individual scenarios
./scripts/compare_impls.sh lab1-cloud-golden-path
./scripts/compare_impls.sh lab2-header-validation-fail-fast
./scripts/compare_impls.sh lab3-adapter-binding-and-wrappers
```

The parity check commands. lab4-rust-ts-parity runs all three scenarios and compares Rust and TypeScript output. A passing run proves that both implementations produce identical binding records, event sequences, and lifecycle states for the same inputs.

Table 6-1 summarizes the observable properties across all three host configurations for a successful run against the hermetic fixture:

Table 6-1. *Observable properties of the post-fetcher service across host configurations. The validated paths (Rust and TypeScript cloud) produce identical output. The browser and Edge paths are illustrative scaffolding with the same structural model*

Property	Cloud (Rust)	Cloud (TypeScript)	Edge (illustrative)	Browser (illustrative)
Binary	post-fetcher (Rust)	post-fetcher (TS)	same model	same model
Adapter bound	host-fetch	host-fetch	edge scaffold	browser scaffold
Input contract	same	same	same	same
Output shape	same	same	same	same
Event sequence	match	match	illustrative	illustrative
Logical clock at the end	5	5	N/A	N/A
Persistence backend	stdout JSON	stdout JSON	not validated	not validated

The validated Rust and TypeScript paths produce matching output and event hashes for the same input. The browser and Edge scaffolding files demonstrate where host-specific adapter wiring would attach for a team that wants to extend the example. The model is the same across all four. The validation coverage is intentionally focused on fully wired paths.

The reviewer's production note is worth stating directly: the post-fetcher runtime is a teaching example, not a production system. It lacks circuit breakers for the HostFetchAdapter, rate limiting, secrets management for the authorization header, and persistent storage for the lifecycle record beyond stdout. A team-building production capability on this model should treat these as the next layer of adapter composition, not as modifications to the service binary or the contracts. The adapter boundary is exactly the right place to add each of those concerns.

Anti-patterns and Common Pitfalls

The patterns that undermine a UMA system are rarely dramatic. They are small acts of convenience: a conditional branch added to handle one edge case, a shared variable introduced to avoid a second initialization, and a version check skipped to ship faster. Each one feels reasonable in isolation. Together, they erode the properties this chapter has described, turning determinism into an assumption and portability into a claim rather than a proof.

Each anti-pattern below maps to a specific boundary in the UMA architecture. Recognizing which boundary is being crossed makes the fix obvious.

Logic Inside an Adapter

Anti-pattern An adapter that makes business or policy decisions has become part of the service. Two environments sharing the same contract now behave differently, without any visible change to the contract.

This anti-pattern starts with a legitimate optimization. A network adapter notices that certain URLs should be retried on a 503 response. The developer adds a conditional inside the adapter's fetch method. Later, someone adds a data transformation for a specific response shape. Then a logging call. Then, a business rule about which status codes constitute success.

The adapter is now making decisions that belong in the service logic or the runtime policy. The two environments that share this adapter will diverge silently: one host may receive responses that trigger the conditional, while another does not. The lifecycle record will show the same binding in both cases, because the adapter name has not changed. But the behavior is different.

The boundary is absolute: adapters translate calls; they do not interpret them. Any condition that changes the intent of a capability call, rather than the mechanics of how it is executed, belongs in the service logic or in a composable wrapper with its own binding record entry. The RetryAdapter in the repository is the correct model: it wraps the base adapter, applies a retry policy, and records its presence in the impl_name field of the binding record, so the behavior is visible in the lifecycle metadata.

Platform Branching Inside Service Logic

Anti-pattern Service logic that checks its host environment has coupled itself to that environment. The runtime can no longer guarantee identical execution across hosts.

The symptom is an environment check inside the service logic: a conditional that reads a platform identifier, an environment variable, or a compile-time flag and branches to different behavior based on the result. The motivation is usually performance or compatibility. The consequence is that the binary no longer behaves consistently across environments, regardless of what the contracts say.

The correct approach is to handle all environmental differences through adapters. If cloud deployments need persistent storage and browser deployments need IndexedDB, those are two different adapter implementations of the same storage capability. The service logic calls the capability. The runtime binds the correct adapter at startup. The service binary stays the same. The binding record shows which adapter ran.

This is not a theoretical constraint. The post-fetcher runtime enforces it structurally: the service crate in service/src/lib.rs has no knowledge of reqwest, no knowledge of the wasm32 target, and no conditional compilation flags. All of that lives in the runtime crate and the adapter implementations. A developer who finds themselves adding a cfg(target_arch) attribute to service logic is crossing the boundary that makes the service portable.

Shared State Outside the Persistence Adapter

Anti-pattern Global variables, static caches, and mutable statics in the runtime layer corrupt the lifecycle record when multiple instances run concurrently or when a module is re-entered during replay.

UMA's determinism depends on immutability between runs. Each invocation of run_json creates a new EventBus, a new ThreadManager, and a new AdapterManager. Nothing carries over from a previous run. If a developer introduces a static variable to cache an expensive initialization, that cache persists across invocations. The second run starts with the state from the first. The lifecycle record for the second run no longer describes a complete, self-contained execution.

The CacheAdapter in the repository illustrates the correct model: the cache is an instance variable on the adapter struct, scoped to the lifetime of a single AdapterManager. It does not persist across run_json invocations. If a team needs cross-invocation caching, the correct place for it is a storage adapter that writes to a declared, versioned, policy-governed backend. The capability call is recorded in the event log. The persistence decision is in the binding record. Nothing is hidden.

Unrecorded Asynchronous Work

Anti-pattern Asynchronous work that is not recorded in the EventBus will not appear in the lifecycle record. The run cannot be verified or replayed.

The EventBus is the single source of truth for what happened during a run. Any work that bypasses it is invisible to the lifecycle record, to the parity check, and to any downstream system that consumes the metadata. This includes fire-and-forget tasks, background threads spawned inside an adapter, and callbacks registered with the host environment outside the ThreadManager.

The correct approach is to let the runtime own all scheduling. Every asynchronous action should produce an event before it executes and another event when it completes or fails. The ThreadManager.run_sync pattern enforces this for the network fetch: the call is wrapped, the event is emitted before the call, and the result event is emitted after. A more complex runtime with multiple concurrent tasks would extend the ThreadManager to coordinate them while preserving the same event-emission contract.

Version Drift Across Environments

Anti-pattern Adapters that evolve independently without a shared contract registry accumulate silent mismatches. A service that passes validation in one environment fails in another without any visible change to the contract.

This anti-pattern appears at the fleet level rather than in a single service. Individual adapters are updated by different teams on different schedules. The contract versions in each adapter's manifest drift apart. A service compiled against network.fetch 1.0.0 binds successfully in the cloud environment, where the adapter declares 1.0.3, but fails in the edge environment, where an older adapter declares 1.1.0 under a different major-minor interpretation.

The mitigation is to treat adapter contracts with the same discipline as service contracts: semantic versioning, a shared registry, and runtime validation before binding. The runtime policy in policy.runtime.json is the right place to declare the preferred adapter selection order and the compatibility rules. Skipping this validation for convenience is how fragmentation begins. The binding record becomes unreliable, and portability becomes something teams believe rather than something the lifecycle record proves.

The Common Thread

Every anti-pattern above has the same root cause: treating the runtime as infrastructure to work around rather than as the authoritative layer that makes the architecture reliable. The runtime succeeds because it replaces implicit platform assumptions with explicit, enforced contracts. Each time a developer bypasses a boundary, adds hidden state, or skips a version check, they are re-introducing exactly the kind of implicit assumption that UMA was designed to eliminate.

The architecture stays clean when discipline is built into the boundaries, not enforced by convention. The runtime provides that discipline through contract validation at binding time, event recording at every capability call, and lifecycle metadata that makes every execution decision visible. When those boundaries are respected, portability is proof. When they are not, it is a story teams tell about their systems rather than something the lifecycle record can demonstrate.

The next chapter applies these runtime principles to a more complex scenario: multiple services composing capabilities across a shared contract graph, with the runtime layer governing interaction boundaries between them.

CHAPTER 7

Portability with WebAssembly and Native Runtimes

From Containers to Components, How WebAssembly Makes Universality Real

Introduction: The Search for a Common Runtime

Every reliable system has a subtle form of bravery: the courage to operate quietly without attracting attention. When a cable car leaves the station and moves into the fog, passengers seldom think about the strength of the steel, the tension in the cable, or the precision of the motor. They trust it because it works the same every time. That sense of unseen safety is the highest praise for an engineered system.

Software has aimed for the same trust for decades. The approaches have varied. The Java Virtual Machine pursued behavioral consistency through a system-independent bytecode format and the "Write Once, Run Anywhere" principle: one source compiles to bytecode, and each platform's JVM generates the native binary at runtime from that common intermediate form. Containers pursued portability through process isolation, packaging an application with its dependencies so that it runs consistently across hosts that share the same kernel. Cross-platform frameworks like React Native and Flutter pursued portability through unified APIs and abstraction layers that translate a single codebase into platform-specific behavior without requiring the developer to target each platform directly.

Each approach solved a real problem. Each also introduced its own constraints. The JVM carries a managed runtime with startup costs and memory overhead that make it a poor fit for edge and embedded environments. Containers depend on a shared

E. Piovesan, *Universal Microservices Architecture*, https://doi.org/10.1007/979-8-8688-2794-5_7

kernel and add significant resource weight for lightweight workloads. Cross-platform frameworks abstract away platform differences but cannot fully escape them: the abstraction layer itself must be maintained across every target, and when platform APIs diverge, the framework diverges with them.

The deeper issue is that all three approaches treat portability as a property of the runtime or the framework, something the infrastructure provides. UMA takes a different position. Portability is a property of the service definition. A service declares what it does, what it requires, and what it guarantees. Runtimes interpret those declarations through adapters and capabilities. When multiple runtimes follow the same contract model, they become interchangeable, connected not by shared syntax or shared binaries but by shared discipline.

WebAssembly currently provides the most effective foundation for this discipline. It is a compact, language-agnostic binary format that separates logic from host-specific details. Its security model enforces containment. The WebAssembly System Interface (WASI) creates a common vocabulary for capabilities. Together, they enable logic compiled once to run safely across native targets and WASI-capable hosts without changes to the service logic or the contract.

UMA's principle extends beyond WebAssembly. If a future technology provides a better foundation for the same guarantees, the model can incorporate it without disrupting existing services or teams. Portability in UMA relies on separating logic, contract, and execution, not on any particular binary format.

This chapter explores how that separation becomes tangible. It explains the layers that enable UMA's runtime portability, discusses the roles of WASI and the Component Model in establishing shared capabilities, and demonstrates that a single service definition can drive both a WASI binary and a native binary with identical observable behavior. The reference implementation for this chapter is at `https://github.com/enricopiovesan/UMA-code-examples/tree/main/chapter-07-portability-lab`.

By the end of this chapter, you will understand: what UMA means by architectural portability versus technological portability; how contracts define behavior that stays stable across runtimes; how the UMA runtime enforces determinism and lifecycle consistency across execution targets; and how portable and native binaries can coexist under one contract with identical observable outcomes.

Trust in software, like trust in a cable car, relies on predictability. No matter the environment, the same inputs should produce the same observable results. UMA formalizes that expectation as an architectural property, not a hope.

WebAssembly As a Cross-Platform Foundation

The Runtime We Did Not Expect

Each generation of developers inherits a runtime it did not choose. Browsers prioritized security but lacked uniformity across vendors. Mobile platforms are optimized for power efficiency but restrict key functionality behind vendor-specific toolchains. Cloud environments offered scalability but blurred the boundaries between client, edge, and server. Each runtime embodied its own model of safety and performance, and teams spent more effort adapting to host conventions than improving their systems.

WebAssembly was not originally designed to solve this fragmentation. Its initial goal was modest: to improve browser performance by providing a low-level compilation target for languages like C and Rust. But in the pursuit of speed and safety, it produced something more: a portable, deterministic, sandboxed environment where precompiled bytecode runs safely and predictably. The same binary can run in a browser, at the edge, on the command line, or in a serverless environment. That was not the original plan. It became the most important consequence.

WebAssembly's strength comes from what it deliberately omits. A module has no implicit access to the operating system, the file system, or the network. It depends on explicit interfaces for all external interactions. Using linear memory and a compact instruction set, it separates behavior from environment. A module's output depends only on its inputs and the permissions it has been explicitly granted. That design makes determinism a practical, verifiable feature rather than an abstract goal.

Within UMA, WebAssembly is not the end goal. It is the current best foundation, carrying service logic in a form that respects the contract model and runs reliably on different compatible hosts. When a more capable format appears and provides the same guarantees, UMA will adopt it. The architecture is defined by contracts, not by binaries.

A Runtime Aligned with UMA's Principles

An architecture that defines behavior through contracts requires the runtime to do more than execute code. It must enforce boundaries, isolate effects, and maintain consistent service behavior across every environment. WebAssembly provides these capabilities by design.

Each module operates in its own isolated memory space and communicates only through declared imports and exports. There is no hidden state, no shared memory between modules, and no implicit access to host resources. External systems such as time, storage, or network are reached only through declared interfaces outside the sandbox. This mirrors UMA's contract model precisely: each service describes what it needs and what it provides, and WebAssembly enforces that discipline at the binary level.

Language neutrality extends this alignment. In UMA, the service definition matters more than the implementation language. WebAssembly strengthens this by allowing code written in many languages to compile to the same binary format. A rule evaluator written in Rust, a report generator in Swift, and a validator in C++ can all compile to WebAssembly modules that run under the same UMA runtime. The contract governs behavior. The language is a compilation detail.

Isolation completes the picture. WebAssembly modules cannot access anything beyond what they have been explicitly granted. This acts as an enforcement layer for UMA's capability model. The runtime maps capabilities declared in a service contract to host functions exposed through adapters. When a service requests file access, the adapter provides it through a declared interface. If that capability is absent or not declared, the runtime prevents the operation. Permission boundaries become verifiable rather than assumed.

Note Browser environments do not natively implement WASI imports. To run a WebAssembly module that depends on WASI in a browser, you must provide a JavaScript-based shim or polyfill that maps WASI calls to browser APIs. The Chapter 7 reference implementation targets native and WASI-capable server environments. Browser execution is outside the scope of the validated lab path in this chapter.

Separating Logic from Binary

In UMA, a service is defined by its intent, not its binary. The contract captures what the service does, what it requires, and how it interacts with its environment. Once that intent is formalized, the runtime can produce any executable form that satisfies the same rules.

Traditional systems bind business logic to their host through build scripts, embedded libraries, and configuration files that mix definition with execution. UMA breaks that dependency. The build pipeline becomes a translation step, while the core logic remains unchanged. The same service can compile to a WASI binary for portable execution or to a native binary for direct hardware access. Each binary conforms to the same declared contract, ensuring consistent behavior across platforms.

The Chapter 7 example makes this concrete. The contract at CONTRACT.json declares two capabilities: analyze.image and read.gpu.frame. It declares two event schemas: image.analyzed and gpu.telemetry.reported. It declares execution constraints that distinguish the portable path (compatible with browser-wasm, edge-wasm, and server-wasm) from the native-gpu path (target-specific, requiring desktop or native-gpu scope). The same CONTRACT.json governs both the WASI runner compiled to wasm32-wasip1 and the native runner compiled for the host architecture. Neither binary has any logic for choosing its own execution path. The contract makes that declaration. The runtime reads it.

```
// From CONTRACT.json (execution constraints)
"execution": {
  "constraints": {
    "portable": {
      "compatibility": "universal",
      "reason": "runs in WASI sandbox without host privileges",
      "scope": ["browser-wasm", "edge-wasm", "server-wasm"]
    },
    "native-gpu": {
      "compatibility": "target-specific",
      "reason": "requires GPU driver access for adapter enumeration",
      "scope": ["desktop", "native-gpu"]
    }
  }
}
```

The execution constraints block from CONTRACT.json. The portable constraint declares universal compatibility for WASI-capable environments. The native-gpu constraint declares target-specific compatibility for desktop hosts. Both constraints are read by the runtime at startup to select the appropriate execution path.

Note The browser-wasm, edge-wasm, and server-wasm scopes in the portable constraint represent potential deployment targets consistent with UMA's architectural principles. The Chapter 7 lab validates only the native and WASI paths. Browser and Edge deployments are outside the scope of this chapter's reference implementation.

When new execution targets appear, only the build pipeline and adapter layer change. The service definition stays intact. Teams do not rewrite logic when new runtimes emerge. They recompile with updated adapters and verify the contract still governs both paths. That separation is what allows UMA to evolve faster than the platforms it runs on.

Inside the WebAssembly Runtime

To understand why WebAssembly provides such a dependable foundation for UMA, it helps to look at what actually happens when a module starts. Unlike conventional processes that rely on implicit assumptions about memory or I/O, a WebAssembly module begins as compact bytecode that expects nothing from its host. The runtime creates a sandbox with linear memory, a stack, and a defined interface for capabilities. Within that boundary, every instruction executes deterministically. Two identical modules with the same input always produce the same output, regardless of where they run.

When a UMA service compiled to WebAssembly starts, the runtime allocates the sandbox, loads the module's declared imports, and binds each adapter to the corresponding host function. The service does not know which adapter implementation it received. It only knows that the declared capability is available. This abstraction allows the same module to run unchanged on any host that satisfies the declared interface.

The following pseudocode captures the core of this pattern. The runtime does not interpret the service. It enforces its boundaries.

```
// Runtime execution pattern (illustrative)
function executeService(module, capabilities) {
  const sandbox = createSandbox();
  const adapters = loadAdapters(capabilities);
  bindAdapters(sandbox, adapters);
```

```
  return sandbox.run(module);
}

// createSandbox: allocates isolated linear memory and stack,
//   returns a context with no host access by default.

// loadAdapters: reads declared capability names from the contract,
//   finds matching host implementations, returns a binding map.

// bindAdapters: injects the adapter implementations as imports
//   into the sandbox so the module can call them by name.
```

The WebAssembly execution pattern. The runtime creates an isolated sandbox, loads adapters for the declared capabilities, binds them as imports, and runs the module. If a module requests a capability that is not declared or not available on the host, execution stops with a clear error rather than undefined behavior.

Note This flowchart represents the adapter-based, WASM-centric architectural pattern. The Chapter 7 implementation uses a dual-target portability model with direct capability access: the contract is read at startup by both runners, and the capability gate is enforced through the execution constraints block rather than through a dynamic adapter registry. The pseudocode above shows the conceptual model. The actual implementation is in runtime/crates/runner_native/src/main.rs and runtime/crates/runner_wasm/src/main.rs.

WebAssembly's precision is its architectural contribution. Safety and reproducibility are default conditions of the execution model, not features added later. UMA builds on this by adding contracts that define service behavior before execution begins. The runtime becomes the bridge between declared intent and controlled operation. The result is a system where predictability is an architectural guarantee, not a configuration choice.

WASI and the Component Model

Capabilities As the Universal Interface

WASI is the bridge between a WebAssembly module and the real world. Traditional runtimes expose files, sockets, and devices through global system calls that depend on operating system permissions set outside the program. A process either has permission or it does not, and the decision is made by the host, not by the program itself. WASI replaces this with capability-based access. A module can use only the resources it has been explicitly granted. There are no hidden permissions, no ambient state, and no implicit trust in the host.

This aligns directly with UMA's contract model. Every service declares what it provides and what it requires. Those declarations form a contract that defines how the service interacts with its environment. When the service starts, the runtime interprets the declarations and binds them to host adapters. A service that reads configuration receives a read_config capability. A service that emits telemetry receives a log_event capability. Nothing else is accessible.

In WASI Preview 2, capabilities are expressed as named interfaces in the WebAssembly Interface Type (WIT) format. Each interface defines the function signatures, input types, and output types that a module can call. The host provides implementations of those interfaces. The module calls them by name. At no point does the module reach past the interface into the host environment directly.

The correct WASI Preview 2 interface for logging is wasi:logging/logging. A UMA capability mapped to that interface declares both the capability name and the WASI interface it resolves to:

```
// UMA capability declaration (conceptual)
{
  "capabilities": {
    "log_event": {
      "wasi_interface": "wasi:logging/logging",
      "quality_tier": "high",
      "resource_budget": "low"
    }
  }
}
```

A UMA capability mapped to the correct WASI Preview 2 logging interface. The capability name is the service-facing identifier. The wasi_interface field names the WASI interface that the runtime resolves to at bind time.

When execution begins, the runtime reads the capability declarations and binds the correct adapters for the current host. The same capability name can resolve to a WASI adapter on a WASI-capable host or to a native adapter on a desktop host. The binding decision is recorded in the lifecycle metadata. The service sees no difference.

This is where adapter behavior leakage becomes a real risk. A logging adapter that timestamps messages using the host clock rather than the runtime's logical clock will produce different timestamps across runs, altering event ordering and invalidating deterministic logs. UMA detects such leakage by comparing event sequences across runs. If the output hashes diverge between a WASI run and a native run on the same input, the adapter is the first place to investigate. The contract declares the expected behavior. The adapter must honor it.

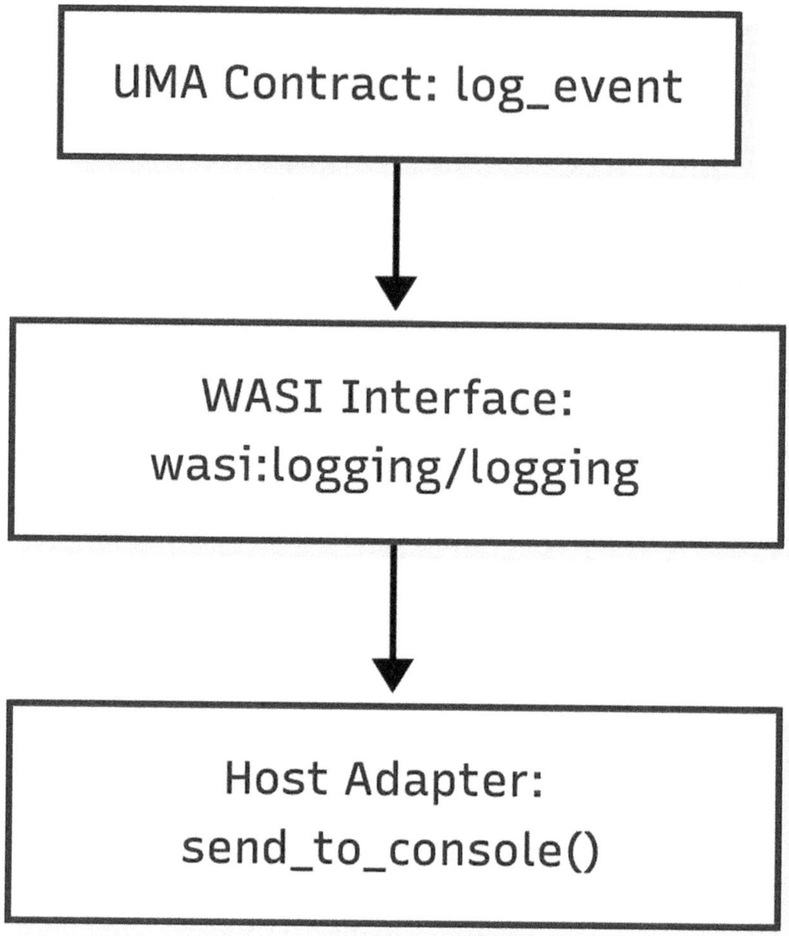

Figure 7-1. *Mapping a UMA capability to a WASI interface. Each UMA capability resolves to a specific WASI interface, which the runtime maps to a host function. The service never calls the host directly. All access is declared, verified, and controlled*

From UMA Capability to WASI Component

WASI specifies how a single module interacts with its host system. The Component Model extends this by managing communication between multiple modules. While WASI sets the boundary between a sandbox and its host, the Component Model establishes boundaries between modules that may originate from different languages, runtimes, or vendors.

In UMA, those boundaries are already established as contracts. Each service specifies its capabilities and requirements. The Component Model converts those declarations into portable, machine-readable interfaces expressed as WIT files. Instead of using hand-written language bindings, each capability is represented by a WIT definition that specifies inputs, outputs, and permitted operations. This turns UMA's metadata into an executable format that the runtime can validate and compose automatically.

When a UMA service is compiled to WebAssembly, the runtime generates WIT files that serve as translation layers between the service and its adapters. Modules written in Rust, Swift, or C++ can then interact through shared WIT definitions rather than through shared libraries or hand-written glue code. The WIT file is the contract made executable.

```
// UMA capability definition
"log_event": {
  "inputs": { "message": "string", "level": "string" },
  "outputs": { "status": "ok" }
}

// Generated WIT interface (WASI Preview 2 format)
package example:logging;

interface log-event {
  log: func(message: string, level: string) -> result<_, string>;
}
```

From UMA capability to WIT interface. The capability declaration defines the service-facing contract. The generated WIT interface expresses that contract in the WASI Component Model format, allowing modules written in different languages to compose through shared definitions.

The Component Model guarantees that both sides of a capability boundary communicate through structured data, not through code. When the runtime compiles a service, it uses the generated WIT to connect the service module either to its host adapter or to another module that provides the same capability. The interface is generated once, validated by the runtime, and reused across different components.

Auto-Generated Adapters, Not Hand-Written Bindings

Traditional systems rely on manually created bindings to connect different languages and runtimes. Developers translate interface definitions into code for each language, adjust signatures and conventions by hand, and maintain those bindings as the interface evolves. Over time, bindings drift from their original specifications, leading to subtle inconsistencies and broken contracts.

UMA addresses this by generating adapters automatically from service metadata. When a capability is declared in a contract, the UMA toolchain creates both the WIT interface and the adapter code from that declaration. The adapter correctly exposes functions, types, and capability checks without manual translation. When the contract changes, the toolchain regenerates the relevant adapters, keeping every runtime instance aligned with the current metadata.

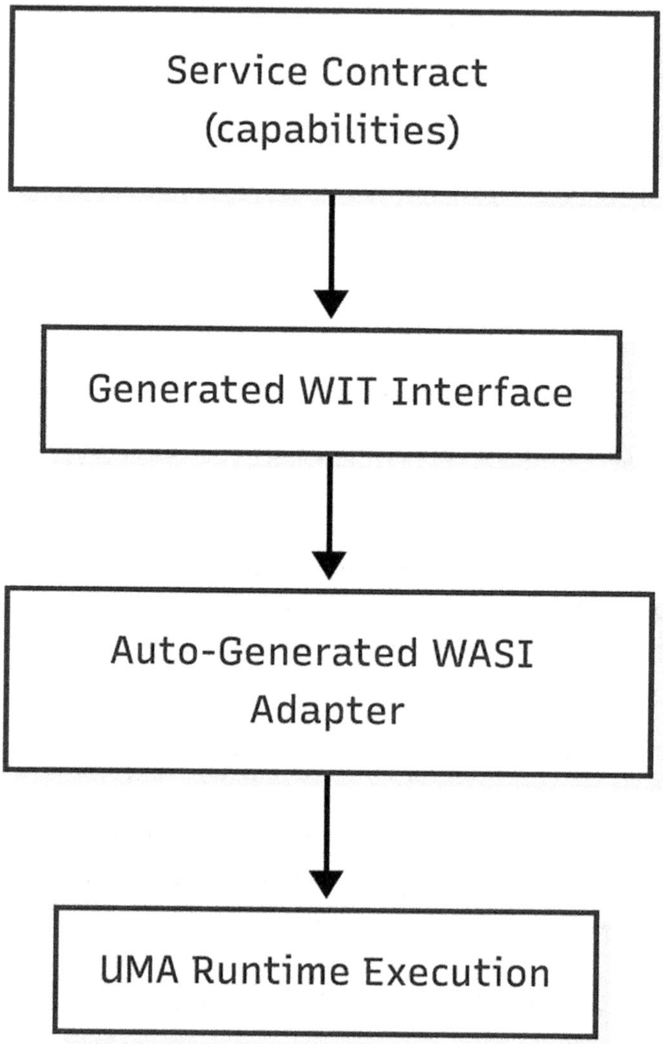

Figure 7-2. *From capability contract to WASI adapter. The UMA toolchain transforms declared capabilities into generated adapters that connect the service to the runtime. No manual bindings are written, and adapter logic stays synchronized with the source contract*

Automation here reduces effort and enforces consistency. When a developer updates a contract, the CI pipeline regenerates adapters, checks interface compatibility, and rejects the deployment if any mismatches are detected. The validation step makes adapter verification part of the runtime lifecycle rather than a separate manual review:

```
// CI validation pattern
if (!verifyGeneratedAdapters(contract, generated)) {
  fail("Adapter mismatch: regenerate bindings before deployment");
}
```

> *Adapter verification in the CI pipeline. The validation step confirms that each capability matches its adapter and WIT definition before execution begins. Adapters are compiled expressions of the contract, not interpretations of it.*

UMA services communicate across languages and runtimes because the shared contract makes the interaction model explicit, versioned, and machine-verifiable. The interface is generated once and reused. Portability extends across the full lifecycle: building, deploying, and integrating while maintaining consistent confidence in interface validity at every stage.

Forward Compatibility by Design

Lasting architectures achieve durability by distinguishing foundational principles from temporary implementations. UMA separates what services declare from how runtimes execute those declarations. The technology used for execution is an implementation detail, not a dependency.

Today, WebAssembly is the most effective foundation for UMA's objectives. Its sandboxed execution, deterministic behavior, and capability-based security align with UMA's design principles. But UMA is not bound to it. If a future platform provides the same isolation, determinism, and contract enforcement, UMA can integrate it without changing service definitions. The only adjustment needed is in the adapter layer, which links contracts to the host environment.

This adaptability stems from UMA's layered architecture. At the top is the service layer: portable logic and declarative contracts. Below is the runtime layer: execution, orchestration, and capability binding. These layers interact only through declared capabilities. Whether those capabilities connect to WASI, a native API, or a future runtime, the interaction model stays consistent.

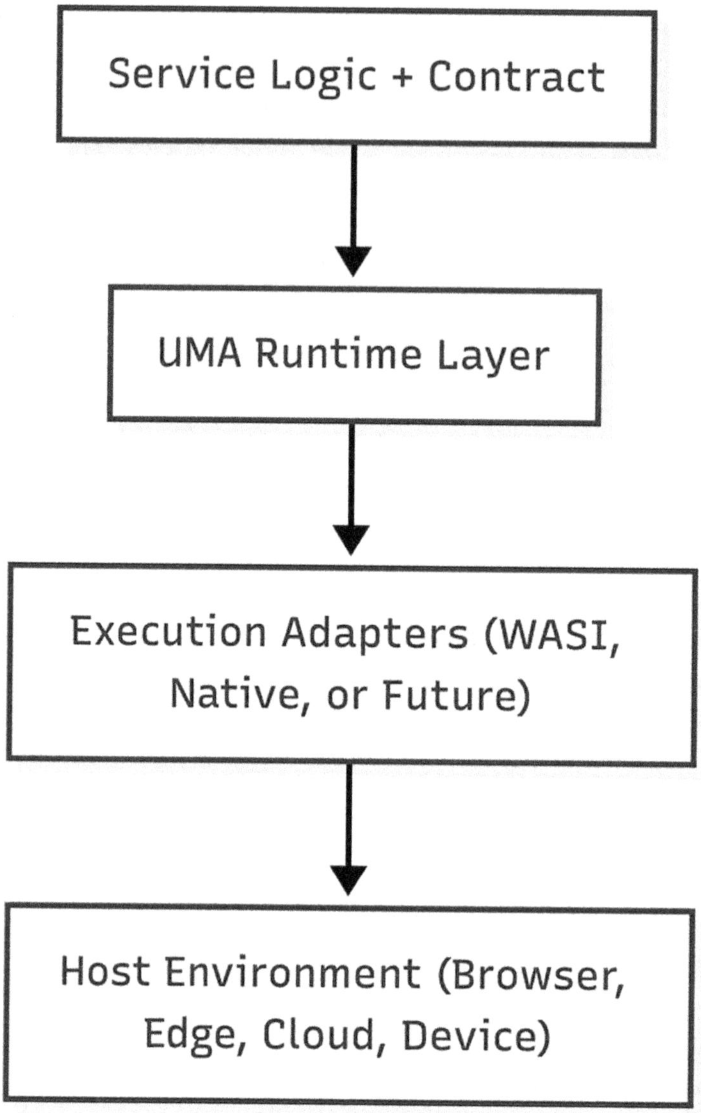

Figure 7-3. *UMA layering for forward compatibility. Services interact only through contracts and capabilities. The runtime interprets those definitions through adapters that can target WebAssembly, native binaries, or any future runtime that supports the same model*

This design enables UMA to evolve alongside the execution ecosystem. New runtimes can be integrated by compiling new adapters and verifying capability mappings against host APIs. Service definitions, metadata, and behavior stay unchanged. Modernization becomes a pipeline-and-adapter concern, not a service rewrite.

Forward compatibility in UMA is intentional, not accidental. By decoupling definition from execution, UMA ensures that technological advancement enhances the platform rather than fragmenting it. The contract is the constant. The runtime is the variable. As long as that separation holds, the architecture outlives any particular execution technology.

Determinism You Can Measure

Scope and Metrics

When comparing runtimes, UMA prioritizes measurable consistency over raw speed or language features. Determinism is not a theoretical ideal. It is an observable, logged, and verifiable property. A runtime is considered deterministic under UMA's model if it can run the same service twice with the same input and produce identical lifecycle event sequences, identical event IDs, and identical state hashes. That definition makes reproducibility a quantifiable metric for runtime quality, not a claim teams make about their systems.

The scope of determinism in UMA is specific. It applies to the ordering of events within a single service invocation. It does not require wall-clock timestamps to match across runs. Wall-clock time is permitted in adapter telemetry but must never influence control flow within the service. Only logical sequence IDs determine event ordering. This separation ensures that execution order is independent of host time, enabling accurate replay, debugging, and cross-environment validation.

The following illustrative pseudocode shows how the UMA runtime handles events deterministically. Each event receives a logical sequence ID that increments with each step. No wall-clock values influence the sequence.

```
// Deterministic event loop (illustrative)
function executeService(service, events) {
  const sandbox = createSandbox();
  let seq = 0;
  for (const event of events) {
```

```
    seq++;
    const context = { seq, timestamp: logicalClock(seq) };
    sandbox.handle(event, context);
    recordLifecycle(service, event.type, seq);
  }
  return verifyDeterminism(service);
}
```

Deterministic event loop pattern. Each event receives a logical sequence ID rather than a wall-clock timestamp. The runtime tracks event order and state hashes to verify consistent behavior across runs and environments.

Accepted Time Sources

UMA distinguishes strictly between time sources that may influence control flow and those that may not. The rule is simple: only logical clocks govern execution. Wall-clock data may appear in telemetry but cannot affect decisions.

Table 7-1. *Accepted time sources in UMA. Only logical clocks may determine control flow within a service. Wall-clock data is permitted in adapter telemetry but must not influence event ordering or state transitions*

Source	Allowed In	Purpose	Controls Execution
Logical Clock	Service Logic	Event ordering and replayability	Yes
Wall Clock	Adapters Only	Telemetry and user-facing timestamps	No
System Clock Offset	Runtime Metadata	Environment diagnostics only	No

Detecting hidden clocks is a practical concern when onboarding existing code into UMA. Static analysis of the service crate for direct time or randomness calls is the first line of defense:

```
# Static analysis patterns for non-deterministic sources
grep -R "SystemTime::now" src/
grep -R "Instant::now" src/
grep -R "rand::" src/
```

Static analysis patterns for detecting non-deterministic sources in Rust service code. Any direct call to system time or random number generation inside the service crate is a determinism violation. These belong in adapters, not in core logic

Runtime Comparison

The table below compares measurable characteristics across four key execution models. Its purpose is not to declare a winner but to show how each model balances startup predictability, resource footprint, and isolation. UMA's abstraction layer manages these trade-offs through contract metadata and runtime enforcement rather than by mandating a single platform.

Table 7-2. *Runtime characteristics across four execution models. Figures are indicative benchmarks from UMA internal testing and public sources, including the Wasm vs. Containers comparison. Relative ratios remain consistent across environments even when absolute values differ*

Metric	WebAssembly	Containers	JVM	Native
Startup latency	15–40 ms	450–900 ms	300–700 ms	5–30 ms
Memory footprint	6–20 MB	150–400 MB	120–250 MB	10–40 MB
Cold start variance	±5%	±25%	±15%	±10%
Isolation level	Strong sandbox, deterministic	Process isolation, shared kernel	Managed memory, moderate isolation	OS-level only
I/O model	Capability-based (WASI)	System calls and network namespaces	Managed abstractions (JVM I/O)	Direct OS and driver access
Best suited for	Portable, low-latency, safe workloads	Cloud-native services and orchestration	Enterprise systems with JVM languages	Performance-critical or hardware-specific logic

All runtimes discussed here can behave deterministically under UMA's abstraction layer when they follow the same contracts and lifecycle rules. UMA does not view these results as a competition. It integrates runtimes. Since services in UMA are defined by contracts rather than by specific execution environments, all four models are viable options within a unified architecture. The runtime is chosen based on capability requirements, resource budgets, and trust domains declared in metadata, not based on developer preference or platform convention.

A compute-heavy service may run natively to access GPUs or vector instructions. A lightweight edge worker may run as a WebAssembly module for faster startup and stronger isolation. Both follow the same contract, lifecycle model, and event semantics. The runtime difference is an implementation detail. The behavioral contract is the constant.

Running UMA on Native Runtimes

Beyond WebAssembly: UMA's Dual Runtime Model

UMA was never intended to depend on a single execution technology. WebAssembly made UMA's portability model practical, but it does not define its limits. The core principle is the separation of architectural intent from runtime implementation. A service specifies its behavior through contracts. The runtime guarantees that behavior is carried out safely within the stated capabilities.

The UMA runtime supports two service types. Sandboxed modules, typically compiled to WebAssembly, run in a deterministic environment with limited privileges and communicate via adapters for all input and output. Native binaries interact directly with the operating system to access hardware unavailable within a sandbox: GPUs, local drivers, specialized peripherals. Both types are managed by the same orchestration layer, use the same event system, and follow identical lifecycle policies.

The distinction between the two paths is declared in the contract, not embedded in the code. The Chapter 7 CONTRACT.json illustrates this directly. The portable constraint declares universal compatibility for WASI-capable targets. The native-gpu constraint declares target-specific compatibility requiring a desktop or native-gpu scope. The runner reads those constraints at startup and selects the appropriate execution path. Neither binary contains branching logic for host detection. The contract does that work.

```
// From runner_native/src/main.rs
// Capability gate enforced by contract scope
let allow_gpu =
    contract.execution.constraints["native-gpu"]["compatibility"]
        == "target-specific";

let telemetry = if allow_gpu {
    pollster::block_on(gpu_info())?
} else {
    None
};
```

The capability gate from runner_native/src/main.rs. The native runner reads the execution constraints from the contract at startup and decides whether to invoke the GPU telemetry path. No host-detection logic lives in the service. The contract makes the declaration.

The Image Tagger and GPU Telemetry Example

The Chapter 7 reference implementation pairs two services that demonstrate UMA's dual execution model in practice. The first is the image analyzer, a portable service that processes grayscale PGM images using deterministic rules. It reads pixel data, computes brightness and contrast metrics, and classifies the result using thresholds loaded from the contract parameters. Because it relies only on file access and pure computation, it compiles cleanly to WebAssembly targeting wasm32-wasip1 and runs identically in a WASI sandbox or natively.

The second path is the GPU telemetry extension. When the native runner starts and the contract declares the native-gpu capability as target-specific, the runner attempts to enumerate the available GPU adapters using wgpu. If an adapter is found, it emits a gpu.telemetry.reported event with the adapter name, backend, and a wall-clock timestamp. If no adapter is found or the GPU feature is not enabled at compile time, it emits the same event with a fallback reason. In both cases, the event passes schema validation against the contract before it is published to the bus.

The pairing demonstrates UMA's core claim: that portability and specialization coexist under a single contract. The portable path proves deterministic analysis is achievable without host privileges. The native path shows that target-specific capabilities can extend behavior without contaminating the portable core.

Shared Events Across Runtimes

In UMA, interoperability is based on shared contracts rather than shared binaries. Whether a service runs in a WebAssembly sandbox or as a native binary, communication happens through events that conform to the schema declared in the contract. The runtime is the neutral intermediary: it validates each event payload against the contract schema before publishing it to the bus.

The bus implementation in bus/src/lib.rs makes this concrete. The publish_validated function serializes the payload, retrieves the schema for the named event from the contract, and calls jsonschema::is_valid on native targets before printing the JSONL line. On WASI targets, the schema lookup still occurs to confirm the event is declared, but full JSON Schema validation is omitted because the jsonschema crate targets native builds. The WASI runner relies on the shared core logic producing structurally correct payloads.

```
// From bus/src/lib.rs
pub fn publish_validated<T: Serialize>(
    c: &contract::Contract,
    event: &str,
    payload: &T,
) -> Result<()> {
    let json = serde_json::to_value(payload)?;
    validate_payload(c, event, &json)?;
    let line = format_event(event, &payload)?;
    println!("{}", line);
    Ok(())
}

// On native targets: calls jsonschema::is_valid against the
contract schema.
// On wasm32 targets: confirms the event is declared, skips full
validation.
```

The publish_validated function from bus/src/lib.rs. Every event passes through this function before reaching stdout. On native targets, JSON Schema validation runs against the contract. On WASI targets, event declaration is confirmed. Schema enforcement is real, not aspirational.

The event schemas in CONTRACT.json define the minimum required fields for each event. The image.analyzed event requires service, path, and tags. The gpu.telemetry.reported event requires timestamp. Both the native and WASI runners produce payloads that satisfy these constraints because they call the same publish_validated function with the same contract. The schema check is the enforcement layer. The shared core logic is the source of behavioral consistency.

Dual Paths Under One Runtime

The UMA runtime handles WebAssembly modules and native binaries through the same orchestration layer. Both are managed entities connected via a shared event contract and governed by the same lifecycle rules. The main difference is in how they interact with the host environment. The WASM runner accesses files only through WASI preopens. The native runner uses the OS file API directly and can optionally invoke GPU hardware.

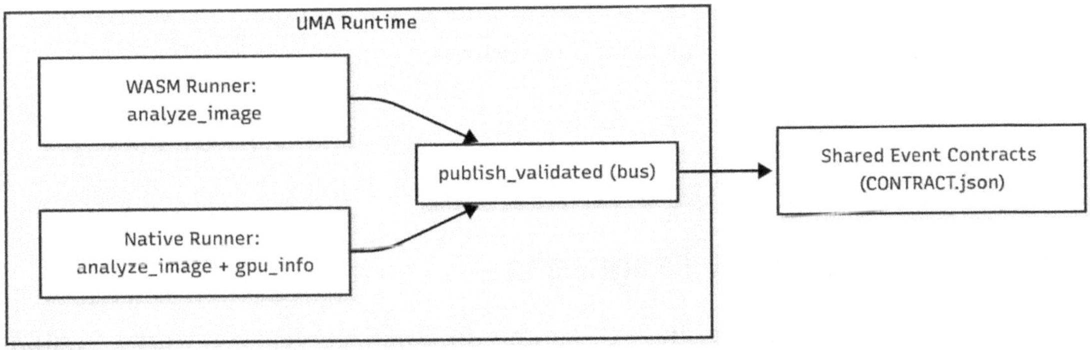

Figure 7-4. *Dual paths under one UMA runtime. Both the WASM and native runners call the same analyze_image function from core_service and publish through the same publish_validated bus. The native runner additionally invokes gpu_info when the contract permits it. Both paths produce events validated against the same contract schema*

This model demonstrates that portability and performance are not competing concerns. A WebAssembly module delivers security, isolation, and consistent behavior across WASI-capable hosts. A native binary delivers hardware access and OS-level performance. UMA combines both within a single architectural framework. Developers choose the execution path based on capability requirements, not on platform constraints. The runtime handles the differences, and the contract enforces consistency across both.

Why It Matters

Portability is often framed as a trade-off against performance. Systems designed to run everywhere tend to sacrifice fine control. Systems optimized for speed tend to bind tightly to a single platform. UMA reframes that tension. The runtime is a flexible layer governed by a shared contract model. Portability and capability coexist because they are defined at different layers: the contract defines what the service does, and the execution path defines how it is done in a specific environment.

In practice, teams no longer need to fragment their architectures to serve different targets. A UMA platform can incorporate WASI modules for portable analysis workloads and native binaries for GPU-intensive tasks. All components share the same metadata format, lifecycle hooks, and event schema. They work together because the contract makes the interaction model explicit. When a new runtime appears, such as a GPU engine, a secure enclave, or an AI accelerator, UMA requires only a new adapter that translates existing capabilities to the new environment. The contracts do not change. The services do not change. The architecture absorbs the new runtime without fragmentation.

Bridging Languages and Toolchains

One Architecture, Many Languages

Modern systems rarely rely on a single programming language. Teams integrate multiple ecosystems to balance performance, safety, and expressiveness. A machine learning pipeline might use Rust for the core inference logic, Swift for a native macOS companion, and TypeScript for browser-facing orchestration. Each language brings its own build tools, dependency management, and deployment conventions. Without a unifying layer, those differences accumulate into friction: mismatched interfaces, duplicated logic, and fragile integration points that break when any one component changes.

UMA resolves this by treating the contract as the single source of truth and the programming language as a compilation detail. The contract specifies what a service does, what capabilities it requires, and what events it emits. Once that intent is formalized, any language that can produce a binary satisfying the contract is a valid implementation. The runtime reads the contract and enforces the interface. It does not care which compiler produced the binary.

The Chapter 7 implementation demonstrates this concretely. The core analysis logic lives in a Rust crate, core_service, which compiles to both a native binary and a WASI binary targeting wasm32-wasip1. A TypeScript reference implementation in ts/src/lib.mjs mirrors the same analysis logic for readers who want to inspect the behavior in a familiar language. Both implementations are governed by the same CONTRACT.json. The Rust implementations produce identical image.analyzed payloads regardless of target. The TypeScript reference produces the same payload for the same input, as verified by the compare_impls.sh parity check.

Multi-language Build Pipeline

In UMA, the build process is orchestration, not translation. The developer defines the service once in the contract. The pipeline generates the binaries for each declared target. Language-specific details are contained within each build step. The contract and metadata remain unchanged across all of them.

The Chapter 7 Makefile captures the two validated build targets:

```
# From chapter-07-portability-lab/Makefile

# Build the Rust workspace (native + WASI)
build:
cd runtime && cargo build --all \
  && cargo build -p runner_wasm --target wasm32-wasip1

# Build only the WASI target
wasm:
cd runtime && rustup target add wasm32-wasip1 \
  && cargo build -p runner_wasm --target wasm32-wasip1

# Run the native binary
run-native:
cd runtime && cargo run -p runner_native \
  -- ../sample-data/sample.pgm

# Run the WASI binary via Wasmtime
run-wasm:
wasmtime run --dir=. \
  runtime/target/wasm32-wasip1/debug/runner_wasm.wasm \
  sample-data/sample.pgm
```

The Chapter 7 Makefile build targets. The native runner compiles for the host architecture. The WASI runner targets wasm32-wasip1. Both share the same CONTRACT.json and the same core_service crate. The TypeScript reference implementation runs separately via Node.

The build pipeline produces three executables from one contract: a native binary for the host platform, a WASI binary for wasm32-wasip1-compatible runtimes, and a TypeScript module for Node. Each conforms to the same declared contract. The runtime validates each binary against its declared capabilities and event schemas before execution begins.

The metadata governing all three is the same: CONTRACT.json. Adding a new language to this pipeline requires three things: a build step that compiles to a target the runtime recognizes, a validation step that verifies the binary against the contract, and the contract itself, which already exists. No changes to the service definition are needed.

Language As a Compilation Detail

Programming languages influence how developers think, but they should not dictate how systems interact. UMA enforces this distinction. The contract outlines the interface, the declared capabilities, and the events a service can emit or receive. Developers implement that behavior in whatever language fits their environment. The runtime ensures that all implementations behave consistently, provided they satisfy the same contract.

The Chapter 7 image analyzer makes this visible. The core analysis function, analyze_image_data in core_service/src/lib.rs, is a pure function: it takes a file path and a contract, reads pixel data, applies thresholds loaded from the contract parameters, and returns tags and metrics. The TypeScript equivalent in ts/src/lib.mjs implements the same logic: it reads the same CONTRACT.json, applies the same threshold logic, and produces the same output for the same input. The syntax differs. The behavior is identical. The parity check in compare_impls.sh verifies this for every built-in sample image.

```
// Rust: core_service/src/lib.rs
pub fn analyze_image_data(
    path: &str,
    contract: &contract::Contract,
) -> Result<AnalysisResult> {
```

```
    let (w, h, px, maxval) = load_pgm_ascii(path)?;
    let avg_norm = sum / pixels as f32 / maxval as f32;
    let contrast = (max - min) as f32 / maxval as f32;
    let (dark_t, bright_t) = thresholds_from_contract(contract);
    // apply thresholds, return tags and metrics
}

// TypeScript: ts/src/lib.mjs
export function analyzeImageData(pgmSource, contract) {
  const { width, height, pixels, maxVal } = parsePgmAscii(pgmSource);
  const avgNorm = maxVal > 0 ? avg / maxVal : 0;
  const contrast = maxVal > 0 ? (max - min) / maxVal : 0;
  const thresholds = thresholdsFromContract(contract);
  // apply thresholds, return tags and metrics
}
```

The same analysis logic in Rust and TypeScript. Both functions read thresholds from the contract, compute the same metrics from pixel data, and apply the same tagging rules. The parity check in compare_impls.sh verifies that the output is identical for the same input across both implementations.

This approach eliminates language-level coupling at the integration boundary. Services interact through verifiable contracts. When a service changes, the runtime checks compatibility at the contract level, not at the code level. A new language or execution format can join the architecture as long as it can describe its behavior through metadata and produce a binary that satisfies the declared interface. The contract is the constant that holds the system together.

Extending UMA to New Languages and Runtimes

A universal architecture must evolve alongside its ecosystem. UMA was designed with this in mind. It does not depend on specific compilers or language bindings. It establishes a clear contract between intent and execution. As long as a new language or runtime can satisfy that contract, it becomes a first-class participant.

Integrating a new language requires three integration points. The first is a schema compatible with UMA's metadata format: the new language's build output must produce a binary that matches the declared capabilities and event schemas. The second is a build adapter for the CI pipeline: a build step that compiles the new language to a recognized target. The third is a validation step that verifies the binary against its declared capabilities before deployment.

```
# Illustrative build configuration for future language targets
build:
  zig:
    target: wasm32-wasip1
    output: dist/zig-module.wasm
  mojo:
    target: ai-accelerator
    output: dist/mojo-service.bin
```

Illustrative build configuration for future language targets. Zig targeting wasm32-wasip1 and Mojo targeting an AI accelerator both integrate through the same three-step pattern: schema compatibility, build adapter, and contract validation. The existing CONTRACT.json does not change.

This flexibility also positions UMA for AI-assisted development. As code generation models improve, the focus shifts from producing logic to verifying that the generated behavior adheres to architectural rules. UMA already provides that verification layer. Generated services can be validated, versioned, and governed using the same contract mechanism as hand-written modules. The runtime enforces compliance. The contract is the guardrail that lets automation operate safely alongside traditional development.

By treating language as a compilation detail, UMA shifts the architectural focus from tooling to behavior. New languages, new runtimes, and new automation methods can integrate as long as they respect the contract model. The contract remains the constant. Everything else is a variable the architecture is designed to absorb.

In Practice: A Portable Runtime Example

Portability is not proven by architecture diagrams. It is proven by running the same service in two environments and comparing the output.

The Chapter 7 portability lab does exactly that. One contract, one shared Rust crate, two runners. The native runner compiles for the host architecture and can optionally access GPU hardware. The WASI runner compiles to wasm32-wasip1 and runs in a Wasmtime sandbox with access only to explicitly pre-opened directories. Both runners call the same analyze_image function from core_service. Both publish events through the same publish_validated bus. Neither runner contains conditional logic for host detection. The contract makes all execution decisions.

The lab is at `https://github.com/enricopiovesan/UMA-code-examples/tree/main/chapter-07-portability-lab`. Every behavior described in this section can be observed by running the labs directly.

From Contract to Execution

When either runner starts, it loads CONTRACT.json from the repository root and constructs a Contract struct from it. The contract includes the service identity, capability declarations, event schemas, and execution constraints. The runner uses the contract in three ways: it reads the execution constraints to determine whether the GPU capability is permitted on the current host, it passes the contract to analyze_image so that tagging thresholds come from contract parameters rather than hardcoded values, and it passes the contract to publish_validated so that every emitted event is checked against the declared schema before reaching stdout.

The runtime selection logic in the native runner reads the execution constraints directly:

```
// From runtime/crates/runner_native/src/main.rs
fn main() -> Result<()> {
    let contract = contract::Contract::load_from(contract_path)?;
    let svc = format!("{}:{}", contract.service.name,
                               contract.service.version);

    // Shared portable path: same as WASM runner
    core_service::analyze_image(&path, &svc, &contract)?;

    // Capability gate: read from contract, not from env vars
    let allow_gpu = contract.execution.constraints
        ["native-gpu"]["compatibility"] == "target-specific";

    let telemetry = if allow_gpu {
        pollster::block_on(gpu_info())?
    } else {
        None
    };
```

```
    // Always emit gpu.telemetry.reported, fallback if no adapter
    match telemetry {
        Some(t) => bus::publish_validated(&contract,
                          "gpu.telemetry.reported", &t)?,
        None    => bus::publish_validated(&contract,
                          "gpu.telemetry.reported", &fallback)?,
    }
    Ok(())
}
```

The native runner entry point from runner_native/src/main.rs. The portable analysis path is identical to the WASM runner. The GPU capability gate is read from the contract execution constraints. Both telemetry success and fallback paths publish through the same schema-validated bus.

The WASM runner entry point is simpler. It loads the same contract, calls the same analyze_image function, and exits. It does not attempt the GPU path because that capability is not declared as compatible with WASI targets in the contract. The WASI binary is shorter not because it is less capable in its intended domain but because the contract correctly limits what it can do.

```
// From runtime/crates/runner_wasm/src/main.rs
fn main() -> Result<()> {
    let contract = contract::Contract::load_from(contract_path)?;
    let svc = format!("{}:{}", contract.service.name,
                               contract.service.version);
    core_service::analyze_image(&path, &svc, &contract)?;
    Ok(())
}
```

The WASM runner entry point from runner_wasm/src/main.rs. It is the portable path in full: load contract, call shared logic, exit. The GPU path is absent because the contract does not declare it as compatible with WASI targets.

The Shared Core Logic

The analyze_image_data function in core_service/src/lib.rs is the deterministic core of both runners. It is a pure function: its output depends only on its inputs and the contract parameters. It contains no hidden clocks, no random number generation, and no host calls outside the declared file access. Every input path and calculation is reproducible. Run it twice with the same PGM file and the same contract, and it produces the same tags and metrics both times.

The function reads tagging thresholds from the contract parameters block:

```
// From runtime/crates/core_service/src/lib.rs
pub fn analyze_image_data(
    path: &str,
    contract: &contract::Contract,
) -> Result<AnalysisResult> {
    let (w, h, px, maxval) = load_pgm_ascii(path)?;
    let avg_norm = sum as f32 / (px.len() as f32 * maxval as f32);
    let contrast = (max - min) as f32 / maxval as f32;
    let (dark_t, bright_t) = thresholds_from_contract(contract);

    let mut tags = Vec::new();
    if avg_norm < dark_t  { tags.push("mostly_dark".into()); }
    if avg_norm > bright_t { tags.push("mostly_bright".into()); }
    if contrast > 0.8      { tags.push("high_contrast".into()); }
    if tags.is_empty()     { tags.push("neutral".into()); }

    Ok(AnalysisResult { tags, metrics: ImageMetrics { w, h,
        avg: avg_norm, contrast } })
}
```

The analyze_image_data function from core_service/src/lib.rs. Thresholds are read from the contract parameters. The tagging logic is purely deterministic: no clocks, no randomness, no host calls. The same function runs in both the native and WASI runners.

The thresholds default to 0.4 for dark and 0.6 for bright if not specified in the contract. Edit CONTRACT.json to change those values and rerun either runner: the output changes without touching the Rust code. This is UMA's declarative strength in its most direct form. The logic is stable. The decision boundaries are configurable through the contract.

Schema enforcement is handled by publish_validated in bus/src/lib.rs. Before any event reaches stdout, the function serializes the payload, retrieves the schema for that event name from the contract, and calls jsonschema::is_valid on native targets. If the payload fails schema validation, the function returns an error, and the event is never published. The test rejects_payload_that_does_not_match_schema in bus/src/lib.rs verifies this directly: it passes a malformed image.analyzed payload with tags as a string rather than an array and asserts that publish_validated returns an error containing "payload failed schema validation." Schema enforcement is not aspirational. It is tested.

Running the Labs

The lab scripts in the scripts/ directory provide the validated execution paths. Start with the full lab sequence:

```
# List available labs
./scripts/list_labs.sh

# Lab 1: prove native and WASM produce identical image.analyzed events
./scripts/run_lab.sh lab1-native-wasm-parity

# Lab 2: compute SHA-256 digests of the shared payloads
./scripts/run_lab.sh lab2-shared-payload-digest

# Lab 3: exercise failure paths and capability gates
./scripts/run_lab.sh lab3-failure-paths-and-capability-gates

# Lab 4: verify Rust and TypeScript parity for shared analysis logic
./scripts/run_lab.sh lab4-rust-ts-reference-parity

# Run the full smoke suite
./scripts/smoke_portability_labs.sh
```

The Chapter 7 lab commands. Lab 1 is the primary proof of portability. Lab 2 reduces the proof to payload digests. Lab 3 exercises failure behavior. Lab 4 verifies the TypeScript reference implementation matches the Rust implementation for shared analysis logic.

Lab 1: Native and WASM Parity

Lab 1 is the core portability proof. The lab_parity.sh script builds the WASI runner, runs both the native and WASI runners against the same sample image, captures their JSONL output, and filters the image.analyzed events from both and diffs them line by line. A passing run produces output like this:

```
# Expected output from lab1-native-wasm-parity
Comparing shared image.analyzed events between native and WASM
Parity check passed: shared events are identical.

# The shared image.analyzed event (identical from both runners)
{"event":"image.analyzed","payload":{"service":
  "uma.image-analyzer:1.0.0","path":"../sample-data/sample.pgm",
  "tags":["high_contrast"],"metrics":{"width":8,"height":8,
  "avg":0.5,"contrast":1.0}}}

# The native runner also emits this (absent from WASM output)
{"event":"gpu.telemetry.reported","payload":{"timestamp":
  "2025-10-11T12:00:00Z","reason":
  "gpu feature not enabled or adapter not found"}}
```

Expected output from lab1-native-wasm-parity. The shared image.analyzed event is identical across both runners. The native runner additionally emits gpu.telemetry.reported, which is outside the shared parity check by design. The WASM runner does not emit it because the contract does not permit that capability on WASI targets.

The native runner emits gpu.telemetry.reported even when no GPU adapter is found. This is intentional: the fallback event uses the same schema and passes the same validation as a successful telemetry event. The capability boundary is explicit regardless of hardware availability.

Lab 2: Payload Digest

Lab 2 extends the parity proof to a SHA-256 digest of the shared payloads. The digest_shared.sh script extracts the image.analyzed payload from both output files and pipes them through shasum. A passing run shows matching hashes:

```
# Expected output from lab2-shared-payload-digest
Native digest
a3f8c2...  -
WASM digest
a3f8c2...  -
```

Matching SHA-256 digests from lab2-shared-payload-digest. The digest proves payload-level parity independent of JSONL formatting differences. Identical hashes mean identical behavior.

Matching digests prove payload-level parity independent of any formatting differences in the JSONL output. If the digests ever diverge, the analysis logic has drifted between the native and WASM paths, and the lab flags it immediately. This is portability as a measurable property, not a claim.

Lab 3: Failure Paths and Capability Gates

Lab 3 verifies that the system fails correctly. The break_trust.sh script exercises three failure scenarios:

The first scenario feeds a malformed PGM file to the native runner. The load_pgm_ascii function in core_service rejects it immediately with a "Only P2 PGM is supported" error before any event is published. The runner exits with a non-zero status. No schema-invalid event is ever emitted.

The second scenario runs the WASM runner against the malformed file without the required directory preopen. Wasmtime denies file access because the directory was not granted as a preopen capability. The runner fails to open the file and exits with an error. This is WASI's capability model working as designed: the module cannot access a resource it was not explicitly granted.

The third scenario verifies that the native runner always emits gpu.telemetry.reported, even without a real GPU adapter. The fallback payload contains a timestamp and a reason field, both of which are required by the contract schema. The event passes validation and is written to stdout. The capability boundary is explicit regardless of hardware.

```
# Expected output from lab3-failure-paths-and-capability-gates
Corrupted image run: expect native validation failure
  [error] Only P2 PGM is supported
```

```
WASM runner without repo preopen: expect access denial
  [error] failed to open file

Native GPU telemetry fallback still emits gpu.telemetry.reported
  {"event":"gpu.telemetry.reported","payload":{...}}

Failure-path lab completed successfully.
```

Expected output from lab3-failure-paths-and-capability-gates. Malformed input is rejected before any event is published. WASI preopen enforcement prevents unauthorized file access. The GPU telemetry fallback emits a valid, schema-compliant event even without hardware. Each failure mode is deterministic and observable.

Portability Matrix

The following table summarizes what is portable, what is target-specific, and where to look in the implementation for each concern:

Table 7-3. *Chapter 7 portability matrix. The portable concerns are identical across both runners. The target-specific concerns are isolated to the native runner and gated by the contract execution constraints*

Concern	WASM Runner	Native Runner	Where to Look
Contract loading	Yes	Yes	contract::Contract::load_from
File access	Via WASI preopens	OS file API	scripts/break_trust.sh
GPU access	No	Optional (GPU feature flag)	runtime/crates/runner_native
Event schema check	Declaration only	Full JSON Schema validation	bus::publish_validated
Deterministic analysis	Yes	Yes	core_service::analyze_image_data
Time source	None in a portable path	Used for telemetry only	runner_native/src/main.rs
Parity verification	Yes	Yes	scripts/lab_parity.sh

The portability matrix makes the architectural boundary visible. Everything above the GPU access row is shared. Everything below it is either target-specific or a runtime difference in how the same guarantee is implemented. The contract governs both columns. The lab scripts verify both columns. Nothing in this table is taken on trust.

One Runtime, Many Paths, Same Behavior

When both runners are executed against the same input and their image.analyzed events are compared, what emerges is not two implementations of the same idea but one behavior observed from two different execution environments. The contract defined what the service does. The runners implemented it in their respective environments. The parity check proved they arrived at the same result.

The native runner adds GPU telemetry. The WASM runner does not. That difference is not a portability failure. It is a capability boundary, declared in the contract, enforced by the runners, and verified by the labs. The portable behavior is preserved exactly. The target-specific behavior is isolated exactly. There is no conditional branching in the shared logic, no environment detection in the core service, and no coordination required between the two runners beyond sharing a contract file.

That is UMA's architectural insight expressed as a running experiment. Portability is not a feature of the runtime. It is a consequence of making the contract the single source of truth for what a service does and where it is permitted to do it.

Anti-patterns and Common Pitfalls

The patterns that undermine a UMA portability model are rarely dramatic. They are small acts of convenience that feel reasonable in isolation and accumulate into systems that behave differently across environments without any obvious reason why. Each anti-pattern below maps to a specific boundary in the UMA architecture. Recognizing which boundary is being crossed makes the fix clear.

Technical Pitfalls

Host-Specific Imports in Core Logic

Anti-pattern Service logic that calls host APIs directly has coupled itself permanently to that host. The same binary cannot run on a different target without modification.

A UMA service must never depend directly on host APIs. When core logic includes OS calls, SDK imports, or framework-specific objects, it binds itself to that environment. Those dependencies belong in adapters, not in service logic.

The Chapter 7 core_service crate demonstrates the correct approach. The analyze_image_data function in core_service/src/lib.rs reads a file using Rust's standard fs::read_to_string. On native targets, this resolves through the OS file API. On WASI targets, the same call resolves through the WASI filesystem interface, using only the directories that Wasmtime preopened. The function itself contains no conditional compilation and no platform detection. The execution environment handles the translation. The service logic stays pure.

The boundary is absolute: all external dependencies are expressed through capability declarations in the contract, not through direct library imports in the service code. Any import that ties the logic to a specific runtime belongs in an adapter.

Hidden Clocks or Non-deterministic Randomness

Anti-pattern Determinism is one of UMA's core guarantees. Any hidden source of time or randomness in service logic breaks it. Two identical runs with the same input will no longer produce the same output.

Service logic must not call the system clock or any random number source directly. UMA provides time and randomness through declared capabilities so that the values are controlled, auditable, and replaceable for testing. The core_service crate enforces this: analyze_image_data contains no time calls and no random number generation. The only time value in the Chapter 7 codebase appears in runner_native/src/main.rs, where

Utc::now() is used exclusively for the gpu.telemetry.reported timestamp. That value is emitted in the telemetry event payload for observability purposes. It does not influence any decision in the analysis path.

The distinction matters for replay. If a timestamp influences which tag is applied to an image, two runs of the same service at different times will produce different results. That is not a deterministic service. Static analysis of the service crate for SystemTime::now, Instant::now, and rand::calls is the first check when onboarding existing logic into a UMA architecture.

Filesystem or Network Access Outside Declared Capabilities

Anti-pattern Bypassing declared capabilities by calling the filesystem or network stack directly defeats UMA's security model, which relies on explicit permissions enforced at the boundary.

All I/O must flow through the capability boundary. In the Chapter 7 implementation, file access in the WASI runner is gated by Wasmtime preopens. If the directory containing the sample image is not passed via --dir=, the runner fails immediately with a file access error. This is not a bug. It is the security model working correctly. The service cannot access a resource it was not explicitly granted.

The break_trust.sh script in the labs exercises this boundary deliberately: it runs the WASI runner without the required preopen and verifies that the runner exits with an error rather than silently accessing a resource outside its declared scope. Routing I/O through capabilities enables this kind of verification. Direct filesystem or network calls from inside the service crate would bypass it entirely.

Organizational Pitfalls

Declaring Universal Without Cross-Runtime Validation

Anti-pattern A service can be called universal only after it has been compiled and tested across more than one runtime. Declaring it universal after it runs only locally defeats UMA's purpose.

The Chapter 7 smoke script enforces this directly. The smoke_portability_labs.sh script runs cargo test across the full workspace, verifies the TypeScript reference implementation, and then runs all four labs, including the native-WASM parity check and the digest comparison. A service that passes these checks has been proven portable through observable output, not by assumption.

Teams that skip cross-runtime validation before shipping rely on the contract declaration rather than behavioral proof. The contract says the service is compatible with browser-wasm, edge-wasm, and server-wasm targets. The smoke tests prove that the shared analysis behavior holds for the native and WASI targets that are currently validated. Any claim of portability beyond those validated targets requires additional evidence.

Skipping Adapter Contracts

Anti-pattern Adapters written without contract validation introduce drift between declared behavior and actual execution. Small inconsistencies produce mismatched types, broken bindings, and security gaps that are difficult to trace.

The bus crate in Chapter 7 implementation enforces adapter contract compliance through the publish_validated function. Every event emitted by either runner passes through this function before reaching stdout. On native targets, the payload is validated against the JSON Schema declared in CONTRACT.json. If the schema check fails, the function returns an error, and no event is published. The adapter cannot silently emit a malformed event.

The test suite in bus/src/lib.rs includes rejects_payload_that_does_not_match_schema, which directly verifies this enforcement path. Manual adapter implementations that bypass this function trade schema compliance for convenience. Over time, those shortcuts lead to integration failures that are expensive to diagnose because the violation is not visible at the boundary where it occurs.

Copy-Pasting Metadata Instead of Generating It

Anti-pattern Duplicated metadata disconnects the copy from its source contract. When the original evolves, the copy falls out of sync and validation fails silently.

The Chapter 7 codebase uses a single CONTRACT.json as the authoritative source for all three implementations: the native runner, the WASM runner, and the TypeScript reference. All three load the file at runtime using the same relative path. There is no copy. When the contract changes, for example, when a threshold is adjusted in the parameters block, all three implementations pick up the change on the next run without any manual synchronization.

In distributed systems where teams maintain separate service repositories, the temptation is to copy the contract file and modify it locally. Once the original evolves, the copies diverge. Validation passes locally but fails at integration. The correct approach is to treat the contract as a versioned artifact distributed through a shared registry, with each consumer declaring a dependency on a specific contract version rather than maintaining its own copy.

Why Governance Matters

Governance in UMA is not a process layer added on top of the architecture. It is embedded in the execution path. Every rule described in this chapter is enforced through automated validation rather than team discipline. The runtime reads the contract, the bus validates every event, and the CI pipeline verifies parity across targets before any deployment proceeds.

This model replaces periodic reviews with continuous verification. Problems surface at the moment they are introduced, not after deployment. Teams can iterate confidently because the contract and the validation suite together form a safety net that is always active. Governance is not a constraint on development velocity. It is what makes high velocity sustainable over time.

The Architecture That Outlives Its Runtimes

UMA's real achievement is not in running services inside a browser, a desktop, or the cloud. It is in making those services behave the same everywhere. Portability in UMA is not a technological feature. It is an architectural discipline.

Each service defines its behavior once through a contract, and every runtime interprets that contract in precisely the same way. The binary format, the language, and the compiler are details. The behavior is invariant. That separation allows UMA to survive the evolution of runtimes. WebAssembly may dominate today, but new formats will appear. UMA's structure ensures that none of them redefine the system's principles.

Services continue to declare capabilities, lifecycles, and events. The runtime continues to enforce them. The contract stays constant while execution adapts.

The Chapter 7 lab demonstrates this in the most direct way possible. One CONTRACT.json. One analyze_image_data function. Two runners producing identical image.analyzed payloads. The parity check proves it. The digest check reduces it to a hash. The failure-path lab shows what the boundaries look like when they are tested. None of this requires trust. All of it is verifiable.

When teams know that their services will run identically across hosts, they stop fearing change. When systems can be recompiled for a new target without touching the core logic, modernization becomes routine. UMA achieves this not through abstraction layers that hide complexity but through explicit boundaries that prevent drift. The contract is visible. The capability gates are visible. The event schemas are visible. Every decision the architecture makes is expressed in metadata that any developer can read.

The UMA runtime layer enforces a consistent contract, lifecycle, and observability model across all targets. As described in the section "Determinism You Can Measure," the runtime selects the appropriate execution path for each host while preserving deterministic behavior and verifiable outcomes. That model spans browsers, mobile devices, desktops, and cloud services: the same contracts, the same capability boundaries, and the same event schemas, wherever the service runs.

We learn to trust a system not because it is simple, but because it behaves the same wherever it runs. UMA's portability turns that trust into an architectural property. The next chapter applies this foundation to a more complex scenario: multiple services composing capabilities across a shared metadata graph, with the runtime layer governing the interaction boundaries between them.

CHAPTER 8

Contracts, Events, and Orchestration

How Metadata Becomes Execution Logic in UMA

Introduction: When Definition Becomes Orchestration

A system that can describe itself can also direct itself.

Most distributed systems maintain two separate layers: one that describes what should happen and one that executes it. Configuration files, workflow scripts, and orchestration frameworks all exist to translate human plans into runtime actions. The translation step is where things go wrong. Specifications drift from implementations. Orchestration logic becomes a second codebase that no one fully owns. The gap between intent and behavior widens every time a service changes while the surrounding wiring remains the same.

UMA removes that translation step. The runtime interprets metadata, analyses relationships, and produces behavior directly from the definitions encoded in service contracts. Services connect according to their declared contracts, not to external wiring. Control logic is replaced by a shared understanding of what each service is, what it emits, and what it expects.

The GitHub companion for this chapter is available at `https://github.com/enricopiovesan/UMA-code-examples/tree/main/chapter-08-metadata-orchestration` and demonstrates this concretely. Run ./scripts/run_lab.sh lab1-baseline-cloud-flow to execute the full pipeline and see the output referenced throughout this chapter. Four services, image.tagger, telemetry.logger, edge.cache, and ai.model.evaluator are each described by a contract. No orchestration code connects them. The runtime reads the contracts, discovers which services subscribe to which events, enforces policy, and dispatches execution. The full orchestration emerges from the metadata.

E. Piovesan, *Universal Microservices Architecture*, https://doi.org/10.1007/979-8-8688-2794-5_8

This chapter traces that shift from static descriptions to dynamic behaviors. It starts with the service contract, showing how structure and semantics define both a service's functional role and its boundaries. Those declarations extend into events, which serve as verifiable evidence that behavior occurred. The runtime links these elements by interpreting metadata to generate flows that align with architectural goals.

The middle sections show how orchestration arises naturally from this model. Discovery, scheduling, and adaptation are not externally programmed. They are identified through metadata evaluation. When two contracts declare compatible capabilities, the runtime establishes a connection. When constraints differ, interaction is blocked. Performance and scalability follow the same logic. Because each service specifies its quality of service, resource limits, and placement policies, the runtime automatically monitors and upholds those expectations. Scaling decisions use the same reasoning that guides orchestration: when demand grows, the runtime creates additional instances that satisfy the declared constraints.

Security follows the same pattern. Each contract carries its own identity, classification, and policy references. The runtime automatically enforces isolation and access controls, without additional frameworks. The same metadata that guides orchestration defines the conditions under which service interactions are permitted. Safety is continuous, not a separate audit step.

The result is a system that self-organizes through its own descriptive language. Contracts specify not only what exists but also how it behaves. Events capture those behaviors as structured evidence. The runtime maintains alignment between the two. What emerges is an architecture that manages, scales, and protects itself through understanding rather than control.

From Interfaces to Contracts

The Limits of Interfaces

Interfaces were designed to specify how software components interact, not how they behave. That distinction did not matter much when execution environments were predictable. A backend service deployed on a known stack could depend on shared infrastructure and consistent assumptions. As systems moved closer to users, into browsers, mobile devices, and edge nodes, those assumptions broke down. The same code now runs in dozens of different contexts, each with its own performance profile, connectivity characteristics, and policy requirements.

An interface, whether expressed through REST, gRPC, or a typed SDK, describes a function's signature and the shape of its inputs and outputs. It shows that a call to analyzeImage() expects a file and returns a set of tags. It does not explain how that operation performs under load, what constraints govern it, or what guarantees it provides in exchange for trust. The interface defines the form of the exchange. It says nothing about the contract with the runtime.

Some existing formats have moved in this direction. OpenAPI x-extensions allow authors to annotate retry policies, timeouts, and rate limits alongside method definitions. gRPC service configuration supports load-balancing directives and per-method deadline settings. These additions acknowledge that behavioral constraints are a recognized need. UMA builds on that instinct by making such constraints a first-class, runtime-enforced element of every service definition, not an optional documentation layer.

Consider a simple image analysis service running across three environments: a browser, an edge node, and a cloud host. The interface is identical in all three. The behavior is not.

Table 8-1. *Interface behavior differences across browser, edge, and cloud environments for the same image analysis service*

Environment	Behavior	Hidden Difference
Browser	Performs lightweight analysis locally using WebAssembly.	Skips GPU telemetry and runs without attestation.
Edge	Executes full model with cached weights, emits results over WebSocket.	Adds latency and omits full tracing.
Cloud	Runs high-precision analysis on GPU and publishes metrics to a monitoring system.	Produces extra telemetry not defined in the interface.

From the outside, all three services look compatible. They respond to the same method call, return the same schema, and follow the same API. Their actual operational behaviors diverge in ways the interface cannot capture because it was not designed to capture them. It assumes uniform conditions. Modern distributed systems rarely provide them.

UMA addresses this disconnect through contracts. An interface describes what functions are available. A contract specifies how those functions behave, what resources they require, and what events they must emit to demonstrate compliance. It adds a layer of intent. A UMA contract covers not just syntax but also latency targets, environmental requirements, policies, and observability metrics. These become part of the runtime verification process, not conventions that developers are expected to remember.

When the browser skips GPU telemetry or the edge node delays event publication, a system built on interfaces has no mechanism to detect or explain the discrepancy. In UMA, these are immediately identified as validation failures or policy exceptions. The runtime does not assume consistent behavior. It checks for it. The contract does not replace the interface. It completes it.

The Contract As a Behavioral Boundary

A UMA contract is a living description of what a service can do, under what conditions, and how that behavior is verified at runtime. It is not a static document. It is a binding agreement between the code and its environment, and it travels with the executable rather than sitting in a separate repository.

Each UMA service includes a uma.contract.yaml file. The contract declares the service's capabilities, input and output schemas, latency expectations, placement rules, required policies, and emitted events. Each element becomes part of the runtime's validation process. The image.tagger service used throughout this chapter and the companion code illustrates the structure:

```
name: image.tagger
version: 1.1.0
capabilities:
  - media.tagging
inputs:
  - image/jpeg
outputs:
  - tags: [string]
constraints:
  latency_ms_p99: 50
  placement: [browser, edge, cloud]
events:
```

```yaml
  emits:
    - name: image.analyzed.v1
      schema: contracts/schemas/image.analyzed.v1.json
  subscribes:
    - pattern: image.received.v1
      schema: contracts/schemas/image.analyzed.v1.json
policies:
  requires:
    - org.telemetry.standard
observability:
  traces: required
  metrics: required
```

The image.tagger service contract showing capabilities, constraints, events, and policies

The contract specifies behavioral boundaries, not just a technical signature. The service can only run in the declared placements. It must emit image.analyzed.v1 after execution. It must satisfy the latency constraint and the attestation requirement, or the runtime marks it non-compliant. The rules are explicit and verifiable.

The runtime's role shifts as a result. At startup, it reads the contract, validates it against known schemas, and evaluates constraints. During execution, it monitors emitted events for compliance. After completion, it logs validation results and policy decisions. The runtime does not automatically trust the service. It observes, measures, and records whether the service behaved as declared.

This elevates behavior to a primary architectural property. Developers no longer need to scatter guarantees across configuration files and environment-specific scripts. The contract is a single source of truth, consistent wherever the service runs. The same service transitions from browser to cloud without rewriting logic, because the contract specifies what must be true rather than how to achieve it in each context. Consumers can read the contract to understand the service's promises and the conditions for safe integration. Policy systems can use this metadata to enforce organizational standards automatically. Observability tooling can trace events against declared schemas without additional instrumentation.

One Service, Three Runtimes

The contract becomes meaningful when the same service runs in different environments. The image.tagger example demonstrates how UMA maintains consistent behavior across browsers, Edge, and cloud without altering the core logic. Each environment interprets the same contract. The runtime enforces it using local capabilities and limitations.

When the browser loads image.tagger, the UMA client runtime reads uma.contract.yaml and evaluates each declared rule. It confirms that placement includes a browser and that no external GPU requirement is specified. The service runs inside a WebAssembly sandbox with restricted access to local resources. Telemetry collection is marked as required, so metrics are recorded. After completing analysis, the runtime emits image.analyzed.v1, validates it against the declared schema, and logs the result.

On the edge node, the same service and contract are deployed unchanged. The UMA edge runtime performs the same validation sequence but extends execution using the host's available hardware. The latency constraint remains at 50 milliseconds at the 99th percentile. The runtime measures and enforces it. If observed latency exceeds the target, the runtime emits a validation.failed event with a reason code, giving monitoring systems early visibility of performance drift.

In the cloud, the same binary runs again under the same contract. The UMA cloud runtime validates the service's digital signature before execution, checks the attestation policy in the registry, and confirms that GPU telemetry and performance data are published to the monitoring system. After execution, it emits the same image.analyzed.v1 event as the browser and Edge, validated against the same schema. Despite running on different infrastructure, all three executions produce equivalent observable outputs.

Table 8-2. *Runtime validation lifecycle results across three deployment environments*

Stage	Browser	Edge	Cloud
Contract loaded	Valid	Valid	Valid
Policy evaluation	Local	Cached	From registry
Execution	Sandbox	Hardware GPU	Full GPU
Event validation	OK	OK	OK
Telemetry scope	Basic	Extended	Full
Overall status	Compliant	Compliant	Compliant

The runtime enforces consistency through validation, not through identical infrastructure. The contract specifies what must remain unchanged. Each runtime adjusts its execution while ensuring that the essential outcomes match the declared schema, latency target, and policy requirements. Developers write one service, define one contract, and rely on the UMA runtime to enforce compatibility and trust. Portability becomes an architectural property, not a feature that needs to be re-engineered for each deployment target.

Validation and Lifecycle Trace

Every UMA service follows a lifecycle that begins when its contract is loaded and ends when its events are validated. The process turns a static declaration into measurable evidence. Unlike traditional runtime models, UMA validation is continuous, not a one-time startup check. Each execution stage produces proof that the service adhered to its contract.

The runtime begins by loading the service manifest and verifying its integrity. It confirms the contract file exists, complies with the current schema, and matches the version registered in the registry. If validation passes, the runtime computes a digest of the contract and records it alongside the service ID. That digest serves as the reference for all subsequent checks.

Next, the runtime evaluates environmental constraints: placement rules, latency targets, and declared capabilities. For image.tagger, it confirms that GPU telemetry is required and that latency must not exceed 50 milliseconds at the 99th percentile. It maps these requirements to available local resources. If the environment cannot satisfy them, the runtime marks the service as degraded and emits a warning event before execution begins.

The multi-contract fan-out that the Chapter 8 companion code demonstrates follows this pattern across all four services simultaneously. The conceptual sequence is:

```
contracts = load_all_contracts(manifest)
validated = []

for contract in contracts:
    validate_schema(contract)
    constraints = evaluate_constraints(contract)
    validated.append((contract, constraints))

binding_graph = discover_bindings(validated)

results = parallel_execute([
    (contract, prepare_runtime_context(constraints))
    for contract, constraints in validated
    if binding_graph.is_reachable(contract)
])

for contract, result in results:
    validate_event(result, contract.events)
    emit_telemetry(result, contract)
    emit_event("validation.passed", contract_version=contract.version)
```

Multi-contract fan-out pseudocode showing parallel execution across discovered bindings

Each function in this sequence performs validation or enforcement based on metadata, not on logic embedded in the service itself. The four supporting functions do the following work. validate_schema loads the UMA contract schema, runs a JSON Schema check against the contract file, and records a digest on success. evaluate_constraints reads the placement, latency, and resource fields and maps them to available environment capabilities, emitting a service.degraded event if the environment cannot satisfy them. prepare_runtime_context creates an isolated sandbox, binds the appropriate transport adapters for the declared placement, and initializes the telemetry pipeline. execute_service runs the service binary inside the sandbox, records latency and output hash, and returns the result for event validation.

After execution, the runtime carries out a lifecycle closure step. It compares observed behavior against declared targets. If latency, schema, and policies all match the contract, the runtime emits a validation.passed event. These events follow the UMA CloudEvents profile, described in full in the section "Event Envelope and Transport Mapping," which ensures they can be correlated across environments. The runtime updates its telemetry registry with an immutable record of the validation outcome.

Operators reason about services based on their behavior, not their location. The same logs, events, and metrics are available across all environments, standardized through metadata. When a browser service emits a validation event, it is schema-identical and semantics-identical to one from the edge or cloud. Debugging is simplified because failures trace directly to the contract rule that caused them. Over time, these traces build a behavioral history that reveals not only what was executed but also whether it met its declared obligations.

Determinism As Design

Determinism in UMA is an explicit architectural decision, not a byproduct of careful engineering.

A deterministic system produces the same observable output for identical inputs and contexts, regardless of where it executes. Traditional distributed systems assume that identical code yields identical results. That assumption fails regularly. Timing differences, resource contention, and environmental variation cause divergence that interfaces cannot detect. UMA does not rely on the assumption of sameness. It verifies sameness through contract evaluation and runtime validation.

Determinism starts with metadata. Each service specifies the conditions under which its actions are valid. The runtime reads this metadata before executing and adjusts its behavior to reflect the declared intent. When two runtimes evaluate the same contract, they validate and execute within the same logical constraints. Their performance or hardware usage may differ. Their events, schema hashes, and validation results will not.

During execution, the runtime enforces determinism through sandboxing, schema validation, and telemetry normalization. Services run in isolated environments. Interactions are confined to event exchanges defined by a schema. Every emitted event is validated before publication. The runtime records the contract version and hash in each event header, allowing downstream systems to verify the exact contract version that produced a specific result.

The companion code for this chapter demonstrates this directly. When image.tagger completes analysis in both edge and cloud environments, it emits image.analyzed.v1 with an identical payload hash. The cloud instance may include additional telemetry events. The analytical output is unchanged. Both are accepted by the UMA event validator because they share the same contract reference, schema validation result, and lifecycle phase.

The actual runtime log output from the Chapter 8 companion code looks like this:

```
[info] policy.digest <sha256>
[warn] policy.violation policy.deny forbid_evaluator_in_browser continuing
due to fail-open
[info] binding.created image.analyzed.v1 → telemetry.logger
[info] binding.created image.analyzed.v1 → edge.cache
[info] binding.created image.analyzed.v1 → ai.model.evaluator
[info] validation.passed event_schema=image.analyzed.v1
[info] telemetry.ok {"source":"telemetry.logger","event":"image.analyzed.
v1","status":"passed"}
[info] cache.ok {"source":"edge.cache","event":"image.analyzed.
v1","status":"passed"}
[info] evaluator.ok {"id":"img-001","score":0.7}
```

Runtime log output from lab1-baseline-cloud-flow showing policy check, binding discovery, and event validation

Three contracts are loaded and validated. Policy is checked before any binding is created, and the violation is surfaced explicitly rather than silently skipped. Bindings are discovered from the contract declarations, not from hardcoded routing. Each subscriber receives the same event and emits its own validation record. The orchestration is the direct product of the metadata, not of any workflow engine.

Determinism as a design principle also makes trust an architectural property. When every runtime produces the same observable outcome for the same contract, reliability is no longer tied to infrastructure alignment. Errors remain possible, but their origins are no longer hidden inside the environment. They appear as breaches of declared rules. The transparency enables UMA to scale across diverse infrastructures while maintaining consistent, predictable results.

The UMA Service Contract and Behavior Definition

A contract is the unit of truth in a UMA system.

The preceding section "From Interfaces to Contracts" established why interfaces are insufficient: they describe the shape of an exchange but not how that exchange behaves across environments. This section examines what a contract actually contains, how it is validated, and what architectural properties it enables. The contract is not an extension of the interface. It is a separate artifact with a different purpose. An interface describes what functions exist. A contract specifies how those functions behave, the conditions they require, and the evidence they must produce.

Structure and Semantics of a UMA Contract

A UMA contract specifies behavior through metadata. It does not describe how a service is built. It describes how the service operates within the UMA runtime. Every field in the contract corresponds to a runtime property that can be validated, monitored, or enforced. The goal is a self-describing service: one that communicates its purpose and capabilities before execution begins.

The canonical format is YAML, organized into five sections. The image.tagger contract from the Chapter 8 companion code represents the full structure:

```
name: image.tagger
version: 1.1.0
capabilities:
  - media.tagging
inputs:
  - image/jpeg
outputs:
  - tags: [string]
constraints:
  latency_ms_p99: 50
  placement: [browser, edge, cloud]
  resources:
    cpu: 0.2
    memory_mb: 64
events:
  emits:
```

```
    - name: image.analyzed.v1
      schema: contracts/schemas/image.analyzed.v1.json
  subscribes:
    - pattern: image.received.v1
      schema: contracts/schemas/image.analyzed.v1.json
policies:
  requires:
    - org.telemetry.standard
observability:
  traces: required
  metrics: required
```

The image.tagger service contract showing the full five-section structure including events and policies

Each section describes a specific aspect of behavior. The metadata block identifies the service, its version lineage, and its domain, linking it to discovery and audit processes. Capabilities detail what the service consumes and produces, expressing intent without depending on code-level APIs. Constraints specify where and how the service can operate, defining the resource boundaries the runtime uses for scheduling decisions. The events section declares what the service emits and what it subscribes to: these declarations are the foundation of contract-driven orchestration, because the runtime discovers bindings by matching emits against subscribes across contracts. Policies list the organizational rules that must be satisfied before execution is permitted. Observability defines the signals the service will emit, giving monitoring systems a predictable map of what to measure and when.

During execution, the UMA runtime reads, validates, and connects this metadata to the appropriate adapters and policies. Validation happens before any service logic runs. The service's capabilities, constraints, and obligations are verified upfront, making the contract both a declaration and a guarantee. After publication, the contract is stored in a registry that tracks versions, ownership, and policy references, forming the basis for orchestration and trust across the system.

A contract moves through five stages: declaration, validation, execution, observation, and evolution. At declaration, the author defines the uma.contract.yaml. At validation, schema and policy checks confirm the definitions are accurate and internally consistent. At execution, the runtime binds adapters and runs the service within the verified constraints. At observation, metrics and events are emitted as evidence of compliance. At evolution, a new version is published to the registry, retaining lineage with its predecessors. Each stage connects intent with evidence, ensuring that service behavior remains consistent, measurable, and discoverable across environments.

Schema and Validation Rules

Every UMA contract begins as a schema validation problem. The schema does not constrain what a service can do. It ensures that the contract's definitions are precise enough to be acted on. When a new contract is introduced, the runtime runs three checks in sequence: structural validation confirms the contract is well-formed YAML that conforms to the UMA contract schema; semantic validation inspects the declared capabilities and constraints for internal consistency; policy validation checks that all referenced policies exist in the registry and that the service's classification satisfies the governance rules that apply to it.

The ordering matters. Structural validation comes first because an invalid schema cannot be safely parsed for semantic content. Policy validation comes last because it reasons about an already-verified definition. Evaluating policies against a structurally broken contract would produce unreliable results. The flow proceeds from structure outward: each stage adds context and confidence before the next begins.

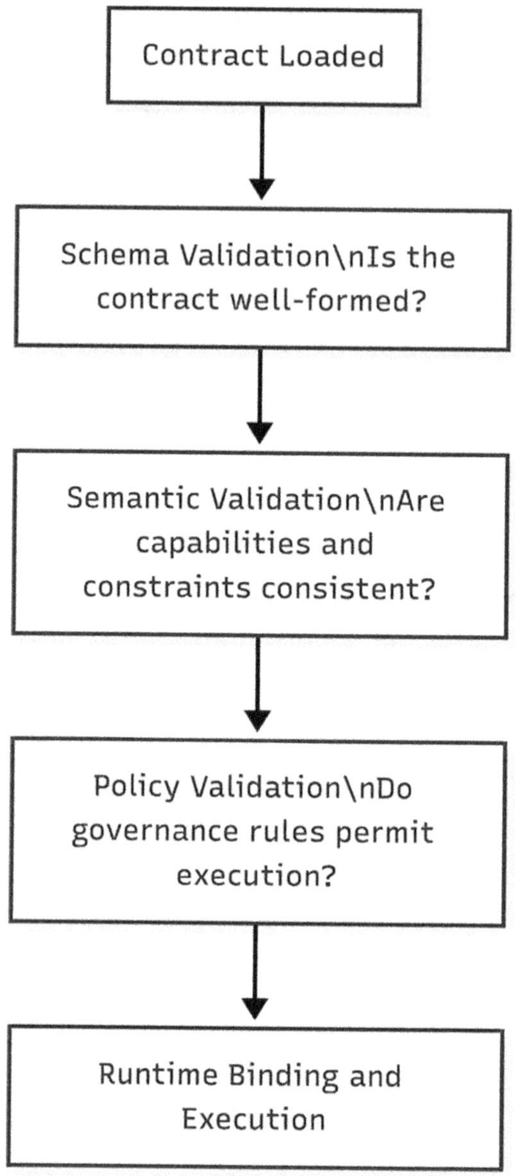

Figure 8-1. *Validation in UMA proceeds from structure outward. Schema validation confirms the contract is well-formed before semantic checks inspect its content, and policy validation runs last against an already-verified definition*

Validation is continuous, not a one-time startup gate. Each contract is rechecked whenever its environment, dependencies, or version changes. The registry records the latest digest of each contract and detects any divergence between declared and actual behavior. If a service relies on a deprecated or incompatible contract, the registry flags it and blocks execution until the dependency is resolved. Compatibility is managed through declarative rules, so the system's evolution does not depend on manual coordination between teams.

Once a contract passes validation, it becomes a verified unit of intent: a piece of metadata that the runtime can execute and the registry can preserve as a stable reference point. Validation is therefore not an administrative concern. It is the mechanism that gives the contract its credibility.

Capabilities and Constraints

Capabilities and constraints are the operational boundaries of every UMA service. They are not configuration entries. They are the active interface through which a service declares what it can do and the conditions under which it can do it safely.

When the runtime loads a service, it interprets capabilities as declared needs and constraints and treats situational limits as constraints. A capability like media.tagging indicates that the service requires access to image processing primitives. A constraint like placement: [browser, edge, cloud] restricts the acceptable execution environments, ensuring the service runs only where its requirements can be met. These two categories work in opposite directions: capabilities expand what the service can do and constraints narrow where it can do it.

This balance makes UMA self-regulating. Services declare both their capabilities and their limits. The runtime interprets those declarations, checks compatibility with available adapters, and determines placement. If the host cannot satisfy a declared capability or violates a constraint, the service does not start. All decisions are logged in metadata and added to the lifecycle trace, ensuring that orchestration remains auditable.

At runtime, capabilities define what a service may perform. Constraints define where it may operate. The UMA runtime interprets both declarations together to build a validated execution context. This mechanism replaces rigid environment checks with declarative reasoning. A service that states its goals through capabilities and its limits through constraints can operate in any compatible runtime without modification. Each execution becomes a consistent decision rather than a conditional assumption.

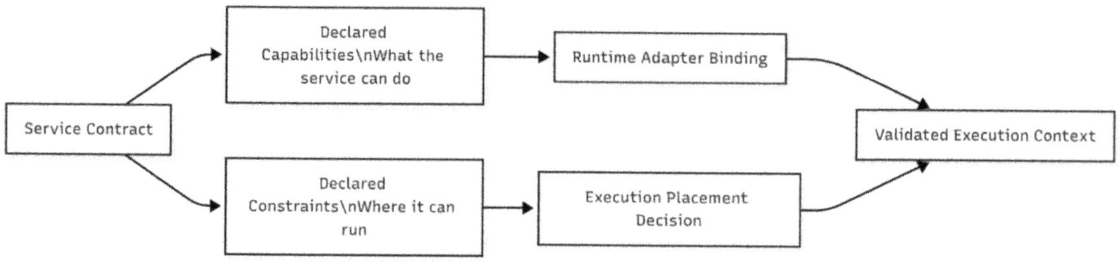

Figure 8-2. *At runtime, capabilities define what a service may perform, and constraints define where it may operate. The UMA runtime evaluates both declarations together to produce a validated execution context*

Events As Behavioral Contracts

Events are how a UMA service proves it behaved as declared.

The contract specifies the service's promises. Events provide verifiable proof that those promises were kept. Every event a service emits is a structured record of fulfilled obligations, not a simple notification. UMA standardizes this approach using the CloudEvents specification maintained by the Cloud Native Computing Foundation (CNCF). CloudEvents defines a common envelope format for event data, standardizing fields such as id, source, type, and time. This allows events from different systems to be processed and routed by shared tooling regardless of transport or platform. UMA adopts CloudEvents as its base format and extends it with additional attributes to support contract traceability and runtime determinism.

The event envelope is produced by the image.tagger service in the Chapter 8 companion code demonstrates the structure:

```
{
  "specversion": "1.0",
  "id": "a4e31b21-92e0-4f35-a88b-91d8b613fe7d",
  "source": "image.tagger",
  "type": "image.analyzed.v1",
  "time": "2025-10-25T11:32:00Z",
  "datacontenttype": "application/json",
  "data": { "id": "img-001", "tags": ["even", "low-entropy"] },
  "umaserviceid": "image.tagger",
  "umacontractversion": "1.1.0",
  "umaruntimeid": "cloud-runner",
```

```
  "traceparent": "00-5e7b13c9a5d22f34b6a6b4d9fcb501a2c3d4e5f600000001-
  a1b2c3d4e5f60001-01",
  "phase": "normal",
  "reasonCode": "OK"
}
```

UMA CloudEvents event envelope with standard fields and UMA extension attributes

The standard CloudEvents fields carry the event's identity and payload. The UMA extension attributes add the traceability layer. umaserviceid identifies the source service. umacontractversion links the event to the exact contract version that governed the execution, allowing downstream systems to verify that the behavior matched a known, approved definition. umaruntimeid records which runtime instance produced the event.

The time field records the moment of emission in UTC ISO 8601 format. In UMA, it serves two purposes: it provides the ordering anchor for event correlation across runtimes, and it forms part of the signed payload used to detect replay or tampering during cross-domain validation.

The traceparent field is defined by the W3C Trace Context specification, which provides a standard header format for propagating trace identity across service boundaries. It encodes four values: a version byte, a globally unique 32-character trace identifier, a 16-character parent span identifier representing the immediate caller, and a flags byte that controls sampling behavior. By including traceparent in every event envelope, UMA ensures that a single logical operation spanning browser, edge, and cloud can be reconstructed as a unified trace in any OpenTelemetry-compatible observability platform, regardless of which runtime produced each span. The format follows the W3C specification precisely: two hex characters for the version, followed by 32 hex characters for the trace ID, 16 hex characters for the parent ID, and two hex characters for the trace flags, each segment separated by a hyphen.

CloudEvents extension attribute names follow a strict convention: lowercase alphanumeric characters only, no dots, no hyphens. The UMA extension attributes in the envelope above, umaserviceid, umacontractversion, and umaruntimeid, conform to this rule. Any reference to these attributes in code, contracts, or schemas should use this naming form consistently.

The runtime adds these extensions automatically as the service emits the event, creating a consistent behavioral record. The same envelope format is used regardless of whether the event travels through WebSocket, gRPC, or a message broker. The runtime does not modify the payload. It enforces the contract surrounding it. When a service declares that it emits image.analyzed.v1, the runtime validates that the emitted event conforms to the schema and carries the required metadata. Validation occurs at emission time, not during development, so every observable action can be verified against the contract that produced it.

Policies and Governance

Policy is the link between intent and control.

A contract specifies what a service does. Policies specify what the system must verify before that behavior is permitted. Governance in UMA is not an added management layer. It is built into the runtime's interpretation of contracts. Each policy encodes a rule that can be checked automatically: which classifications can access certain capabilities, how data flows across tenants, and when deprecated contracts must be blocked. The org.telemetry.standard policy used in the Chapter 8 companion code is a concrete example. It contains a deny rule that prevents ai.model.evaluator from running in a browser context. The runtime evaluates that rule before creating any bindings and surfaces the violation explicitly in the execution log.

Policies are both local and global. Local policies apply to a single service and travel with its contract. Global policies are stored in a shared catalog and referenced by identifier. The runtime fetches the relevant definitions, validates the service against them, and logs the result in its lifecycle record. Every decision leaves an auditable trail: which rule permitted or denied execution, at what time, and against which contract version.

The combination of contracts and policies forms a verifiable chain from declaration to enforcement. Organizational standards are maintained even as services evolve independently. Local innovation cannot override shared policy, because the boundary between them is explicit and enforced at runtime. Policy is not an afterthought applied to a finished system. It is a property of the architecture from the first execution.

Observability Declarations

Observability in UMA begins at design time.

Each service declares what it will report and how those signals should be interpreted. This information becomes part of the contract, allowing the runtime to build a predictable map of what will be measured and when. Instead of instrumenting code after deployment, observability is treated as a first-class concern that can be validated, versioned, and audited alongside every other behavioral property.

When the runtime loads a contract, it registers the declared telemetry fields and sets up adapters for metrics, traces, and logs. The service does not know which monitoring system will receive those signals. It only guarantees their existence. A declaration like traces: required tells the runtime that trace data will be emitted during every execution. The latency constraint in the contract creates the quality-of-service expectation that the runtime later verifies against actual measurements.

Observability declarations serve two goals. They enable runtime behavior to be measured without host-specific instrumentation, and they give governance systems a basis for detecting deviations between declared and actual performance. The registry stores these declarations alongside the contract, enabling automated comparison of historical data and rapid identification of services that fail to meet their promises. Every metric becomes an assertion of trust, proving that the system behaves as it was designed to.

Versioning and Evolution

Versioning in UMA is a structural property of the architecture, not a release management convention.

Each contract, adapter, and policy carries its own version. When the runtime loads a contract, it compares the version against related components to confirm they can coexist safely. Two services can implement the same capability with different contract versions, provided their schemas are semantically compatible. The runtime verifies these relationships automatically. If a service depends on a deprecated or incompatible contract, the registry flags it and blocks execution until the dependency is resolved or explicitly approved by policy.

The registry maintains the full history of each contract: creation dates, supersession events, and dependent services. This lineage supports safe rollbacks, reproducible environments, and incremental upgrades. New versions can be deployed while older ones remain active until all consumers have migrated. The architecture evolves without forcing coordinated cutover across the system.

Contract Lifecycle

A UMA contract is a dynamic artifact, not a static document. It progresses through distinct stages that indicate its maturity relative to its environment.

At the design stage, behaviors, constraints, and telemetry are defined. At validation, schema and policy checks confirm the definitions are accurate. At runtime, the contract becomes active, producing evidence of compliance through events and metrics. Over time, contracts are revalidated periodically against their environment and dependencies. Drift detection in the registry confirms that implementations remain aligned with declared behavior. When a contract is updated, the new version retains its lineage and undergoes the same cycle. Deprecated versions remain visible until all dependent services have migrated, preserving observability and governance records.

The lifecycle continues after a service stops running. UMA maintains a comprehensive record of all executed contracts, including validation results, event summaries, and policy decisions. This creates an immutable trace of architectural intent over time, providing reliable evidence for audits and future assessments.

Ownership and Scope of Authority

Every UMA contract has a specific owner, and that ownership carries operational weight.

Ownership designates who have the authority to modify the contract, approve changes, and accept its obligations. When a service publishes a contract, the registry records the owner and links it to an organizational domain or team identifier. Any update to that contract must come from an authorized identity within that domain. The registry verifies the signer of new versions. The runtime confirms that deployed instances match the owner metadata. Unverified changes are blocked.

Authority in UMA is intentionally scoped. A contract owner manages a single service or capability. They cannot override shared policies or cross-domain agreements, which are governed by higher-level entries in the global policy catalog. Local teams can iterate on their contracts freely. Organizational policies remain consistently enforced regardless of what any individual contract declares.

Every behavioral change in a UMA system can be traced back to the specific individual or team responsible for creating, approving, and deploying it. Ownership is not a procedural formality. It is an architectural boundary that makes accountability concrete and auditable.

Event Envelope and Transport Mapping

Every UMA service speaks the same event language.

UMA CloudEvents Profile

At the core of UMA's communication model is a single universal event envelope based on the CloudEvents standard. Every message a UMA service sends or receives uses this format. The envelope is the connection between intent and observation, carrying both the data payload and the metadata that define context, version, and traceability.

UMA extends the standard CloudEvents fields with reserved attributes that ensure determinism and provenance. umaserviceid identifies the source service. umacontractversion links the event to its originating contract. umaruntimeid records the runtime instance that produced it. traceparent, defined by the W3C Trace Context specification, propagates distributed trace identity across service boundaries. By encoding a globally unique trace ID, a parent span ID, and sampling flags in a standardized format, traceparent allows any OpenTelemetry-compatible platform to reconstruct the full execution path of a request that spans multiple runtimes and transports. Additional optional attributes, such as phase and reasonCode, describe the current execution stage and the result of each operation. Together, these extensions make every envelope self-explanatory: any UMA runtime can determine where an event originated, which contract produced it, and why it was allowed to exist.

What distinguishes the UMA CloudEvents profile is not its syntax but the discipline behind it. Every runtime adds the same extensions to every event before emission, creating a consistent behavioral record. A completed phase in the browser and one in the cloud mean the same thing and are validated against the same schema. The envelope becomes a guarantee of semantic parity, not just a container for data. Communication in UMA depends not on shared code or shared infrastructure but on a common behavioral language. Services emit and consume events whose shape, metadata, and intent remain consistent across all execution paths.

Binding Across Transports

The UMA envelope travels through multiple transports without changing its meaning.

Whether the runtime delivers an event via WebSocket, a gRPC stream, or a message broker, the structure and metadata remain identical. The only thing that changes is the adapter responsible for transmitting the envelope. Each adapter applies a standard binding that maps CloudEvents fields to the native headers or message formats of the underlying protocol. This separation allows UMA to support any transport without altering the event itself.

A service emitting image.analyzed.v1 in a browser might send it over WebSocket. The same service running in a cloud worker might use gRPC. The event's metadata, schema, and validation rules are unchanged in both cases. The runtime selects the appropriate adapter based on declared constraints, policy, and environment capabilities. The developer does not make that choice at the service level.

Transport is a technical detail in UMA, not an architectural dependency. The integrity of the envelope defines the interaction. The chosen path determines only how that integrity reaches its destination.

Operational Signals

Every UMA runtime produces its own operational signals in addition to service events. These signals record state changes that affect the system's health or configuration. They are not part of service logic. They are a structured feedback mechanism that keeps orchestration predictable and auditable.

Signals such as contract.drift.detected or transport.binding.changed are generated automatically when a contract deviates from its declared metadata or when a new binding is applied at runtime. Each signal uses the same CloudEvents envelope as all other UMA events, so monitoring tools and governance systems can subscribe to them without special integration. When a runtime adjusts to a new environment or recovers from failure, those changes are visible as structured events rather than log noise. Design, execution, and observation remain connected. Every architectural change that the runtime makes is recorded in a form that both humans and automated policies can act on.

One Envelope, Many Paths

A single UMA event can traverse multiple environments while remaining structurally and semantically identical throughout.

Consider the image processing pipeline in the Chapter 8 companion code. The image.tagger service produces an image.analyzed.v1 event. The runtime dispatches it to three subscribers: telemetry.logger, edge.cache, and ai.model.evaluator. Each subscriber receives the same envelope with the same metadata, validates it against its declared schema, and emits its own response event. The transport differs for each subscriber. The envelope does not.

When the registry records the event sequence, it shows perfect alignment across all three dispatch paths. Each runtime recorded the same payload hash and the same contract version reference. What differs is the path the event took to reach each subscriber and the response each subscriber produced. The behavioral outcome, the log structure, and the validation results are identical for the core event. This uniformity is the practical expression of UMA's consistency model. Consistency does not depend on where an event travels. It depends on how faithfully the runtime enforces the contract that governs it.

The Runtime That Orchestrates Itself

Orchestration in UMA is not programmed. It is discovered.

Traditional orchestration systems require someone to define the wiring: which service calls which, in what order, under what conditions. That definition becomes a second codebase. It drifts from the services it coordinates. When services change, the orchestration logic has to change too, and it rarely does on the same schedule. UMA takes a different position. The contracts themselves contain everything the runtime needs to connect services. No workflow code is required. No external coordinator is needed.

Service Registration and Discovery

A UMA runtime operates without configuration files or manual service lists. Each service registers itself by publishing its contract to the registry. Registration is declarative, not procedural. When a service starts, the runtime reads its own contract, verifies it against local policies, and submits it as an active entry in the registry. The registry becomes a live catalog of all active capabilities: what each service can do, which version it runs, and which dependencies it satisfies.

Discovery is the reverse of registration. Services locate other services by querying the registry for a declared capability rather than a specific address. The registry resolves the query through metadata, returning only services that satisfy the specified constraints and policies. Services connect through contracts rather than configuration. Their relationships are transparent and reproducible.

The process is inherently cyclical. As services evolve, new contracts replace old ones and the registry updates to reflect the current system topology. Each change triggers a validation cycle. References stay consistent. Outdated versions are not silently retained. The result is a dynamic architecture where each runtime observes, logs, and adapts to changes independently, without central coordination. The registry is the system's shared memory and its ultimate source of truth.

Runtime Topology and Coordination

After registration, the UMA runtime constructs a dynamic system topology. The topology is not fixed. It is an evolving graph derived entirely from contracts and events. Each node represents a service. Each edge represents a declared capability or dependency. As contracts change, the topology updates automatically.

Coordination arises from this topology rather than from a centralized scheduler. When a service emits an event, the runtime queries the graph to identify services that have declared themselves as consumers of that event type. It routes the message through the appropriate transport, enforcing policies and constraints along the way. New services can join the topology and participate immediately without redeployment or manual configuration.

The Chapter 8 companion code demonstrates this directly. The image.tagger contract declares that it emits image.analyzed.v1. The contracts for telemetry.logger and edge.cache both declare subscribe patterns that match that event. The ai.model.evaluator contract subscribes to the same pattern. The runtime discovers all three bindings by reading the contracts. No routing table exists in any service. No workflow script defines the dispatch sequence. The runtime log confirms the result:

```
[info] binding.created image.analyzed.v1 → telemetry.logger
[info] binding.created image.analyzed.v1 → edge.cache
[info] binding.created image.analyzed.v1 → ai.model.evaluator
```

The binding discovery log output shows three contracts resolved to three subscribers from metadata alone

Three bindings, created from three contract declarations, with no orchestration code. The topology reflects both structure and behavior, forming the basis for observability and governance.

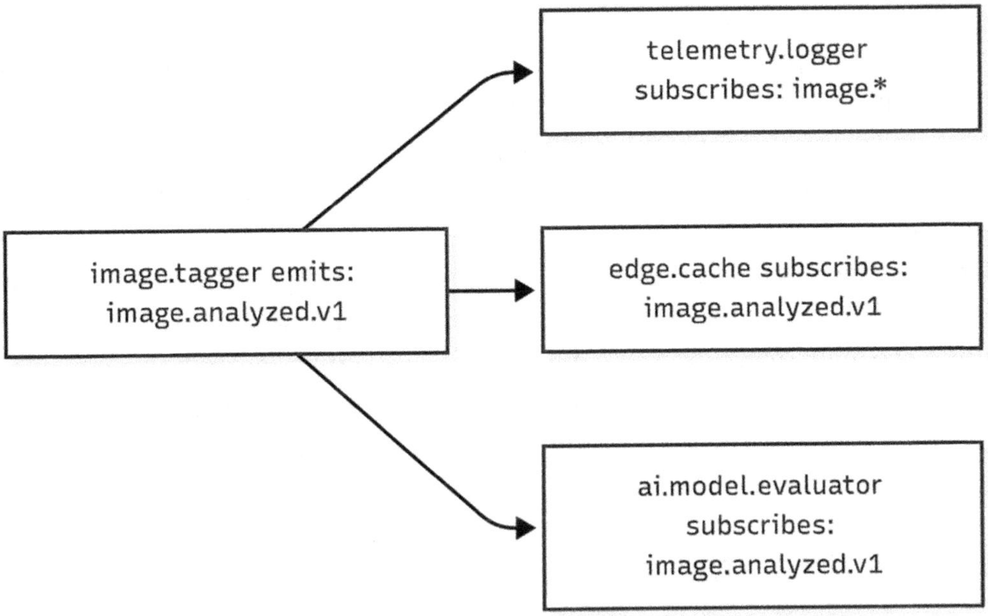

Figure 8-3. *The Chapter 8 orchestration binding graph generated from contract declarations by tools/graph.js. No routing code exists in any service. All three bindings are discovered at runtime from the emits and subscribes fields in the contracts*

Each runtime periodically syncs its local graph view with the registry to detect changes in version, ownership, or capabilities. The system adapts quickly, redirecting requests, retiring outdated paths, and activating new ones as contracts change.

Policies and Selection Rules

When multiple services can satisfy the same request, the runtime chooses among them based on policy and metadata, not on fixed routing logic.

Selection rules express preferences and constraints, such as latency limits, trust levels, regions, or offline tolerance. The runtime uses these factors to prioritize availability, cost, and security while maintaining consistent results. The process begins when a service emits an event that requires a response. The runtime queries the registry for candidates matching the declared capability and contract version, then filters them against active policies. A service flagged as experimental may only qualify for use in a development environment. A service with a high-trust classification may be preferred in production contexts.

The Chapter 8 companion code illustrates one concrete policy decision: ai.model.evaluator is denied placement in the browser by the org.telemetry.standard policy. In the default fail-open mode, the runtime surfaces the violation and continues. In fail-closed mode, execution stops. The policy is evaluated before any binding is created, and the decision is recorded in the execution log. Changing the policy changes the runtime behavior without touching any service code.

Because selection rules are declarative, they can be updated without redeployment. Modifying a policy or a constraint immediately affects runtime decision-making. Over time, the interplay of contracts, metrics, and selection rules forms a feedback loop that makes orchestration both predictable and adaptive. Selection in UMA is not optimization. It is trust. The runtime's goal is not the fastest implementation but the one that most faithfully satisfies the declared intent within the applicable constraints.

Declarative Orchestration

In UMA, orchestration is not embedded in a controller or a workflow engine. It emerges from contracts.

Each contract declares the events a service emits and consumes, the capabilities it requires, and the guarantees it provides. The runtime interprets these declarations and connects services into flows that reflect the system's intended behavior. No developer writes choreography code. The runtime does the reasoning.

The orchestration patterns that emerge from this model are recognizable. A direct pattern connects a producer and a consumer through a shared event type. A choreography pattern arises when multiple consumers react independently to the same event, producing distributed behavior without central control. A compensation pattern occurs when a service emits corrective events to undo or modify earlier actions. These flows are not defined in advance. They develop dynamically as the runtime evaluates current contracts, capabilities, and policies.

Declarative orchestration allows UMA to adapt while maintaining consistency. When a new service publishes a compatible contract, it automatically joins the workflow. When a service is retired or updated, the change is detected, and event routes are adjusted without manual intervention. The architecture appears centrally managed, yet the coordination is entirely distributed. At runtime, UMA interprets intent from metadata, evaluates potential connections, and executes them within policy boundaries. Control through explicit logic is replaced by coordination through shared understanding of contracts.

The Chapter 8 Pipeline in Practice

Consider a document intelligence pipeline where images are tagged, results validated, and a model evaluates confidence. Four services participate: image.tagger produces the analysis, telemetry.logger validates and records the event, edge.cache persists the result locally, and ai.model.evaluator scores the output. None of these services reference any other directly. None contains routing code. Each declares only what it emits and what it subscribes to.

When image.tagger emits image.analyzed.v1, the runtime checks the registry and finds every service that has declared a matching subscribe pattern. All three subscribers qualify. The runtime routes the event to each in turn using the appropriate transport for the execution environment. After each subscriber completes, it emits its own response event: telemetry.validation.v1, cache.persisted.v1, and inference.completed.v1, respectively. Each response event is validated against its declared schema before the runtime records it.

Running lab1-baseline-cloud-flow from the Chapter 8 companion code produces the full sequence:

```
[info] policy.digest <sha256>
[warn] policy.violation policy.deny forbid_evaluator_in_browser continuing
due to fail-open
[info] binding.created image.analyzed.v1 → telemetry.logger
[info] binding.created image.analyzed.v1 → edge.cache
[info] binding.created image.analyzed.v1 → ai.model.evaluator
[info] validation.passed event_schema=image.analyzed.v1
[info] telemetry.ok {"source":"telemetry.logger","event":"image.analyzed.
v1","status":"passed"}
[info] cache.ok {"source":"edge.cache","event":"image.analyzed.
v1","status":"passed"}
[info] evaluator.ok {"id":"img-001","score":0.7}
```

Full lab1-baseline-cloud-flow output showing policy evaluation, binding creation, and per-subscriber validation

Every line in this output is a direct product of contract declarations. The policy digest is computed from the policy schema file and logged before any binding is created. The policy violation surfaced and is attributed to the specific deny rule. The three bindings are discovered from the subscribers' declarations in each subscriber contract. The validation result is checked against the image.analyzed.v1 JSON schema. Each subscriber's response is logged with its source and status. The entire orchestration is traceable back to the metadata that produced it.

If a fifth service is introduced with a subscribe pattern-matching image.analyzed.v1, the runtime adds it to the topology on its next registry sync. No existing service is modified. No routing configuration is updated. The new service declares its intent, and the runtime acts on it. The pipeline extends itself.

Where Metadata Becomes Behavior

The execution graph is the program. Metadata is the instruction set.

Execution Graphs

In UMA, behavior is derived from structure. Each contract specifies inputs, outputs, and dependencies. The runtime constructs an execution graph from those declarations. The graph is not manually designed or pre-configured. It is inferred automatically from the metadata. Each node represents a service. Each edge represents an event or capability. Links form when two contracts declare compatible intent.

When a service emits an event, the runtime queries the graph to identify which other services can respond. It checks constraints, enforces policies, and schedules execution along the matching edges. The flow reflects architectural intent without any imperative orchestration code. The graph is the program. The metadata is the instruction set.

Each node executes within an isolated environment that upholds its declared capabilities and constraints. UMA enforces this through sandboxed runtimes that prevent one service from affecting another beyond its designated scope. Isolation is not just a safety feature. It is part of the behavioral model, ensuring that contracts remain pure, deterministic, and unaffected by host-specific interactions.

The graph changes as services are added, removed, or updated. New nodes are created when contracts are registered. Outdated nodes are retired when contracts are deprecated. The runtime maintains a live view of the current system state. Execution paths adjust automatically, ensuring all active interactions remain valid under the most recent definitions. Behavior is not coded explicitly. It emerges from the graph's structure.

Concurrency and Scheduling

Concurrency in UMA is governed by metadata rather than by explicit thread management.

Each contract specifies which operations are independent, which require sequencing, and which can run in parallel across environments. The runtime interprets these declarations to enable safe concurrency without requiring developers to manage locks, queues, or synchronization primitives. When multiple services respond to the same event, the runtime executes them concurrently, provided their constraints and dependencies do not conflict. If two services share an input and modify a shared resource, UMA identifies the conflict through capability metadata and enforces serialization.

Scheduling follows the same declarative principle. The runtime arranges tasks based on policy and resource constraints, not arbitrary priority assignments. A contract that declares high latency tolerance and low resource allocation will produce different scheduling decisions than one demanding immediate response or GPU access. The scheduling engine evaluates these declarations against current system conditions and determines execution order in real time.

Because scheduling is driven by metadata, it adapts continuously. Changes in load, resource availability, or policy automatically affect task dispatching without modifying the service code. The concurrency model is dynamic in practice but predictable in principle. UMA achieves parallelism through shared understanding of declared intent, not through procedural control.

Lifecycle Events and State Transitions

Every UMA service announces its own progress through observable state transitions.

States are not assumed by the runtime. They are declared as metadata-driven events that specify the exact execution phase. The typical flow moves from initialized through running to either completed or failed. Each transition is tracked by the runtime and emitted as a CloudEvent that external systems can observe and verify. When a service moves from initialized to running, the runtime emits a service.started event carrying the contract version, placement, and active constraints. When execution is completed, a service.completed event captures the outcome, latency, and relevant telemetry. When a failure occurs, a service.failed event records the cause and the recovery policy that was applied.

Error handling uses the same declarative approach. A contract specifies the behavior to invoke when a failure occurs: retry, escalate, or compensate. The runtime interprets these instructions, executes the appropriate response, and records the result as part of the lifecycle trace. Recovery is predictable, repeatable, and auditable across all environments.

These lifecycle transitions collectively form a dynamic record of system behavior. Progress, success, and failure are all represented as consistent, structured events that monitoring tools, auditors, and other services can consume. The runtime's actions are always visible. Every state change is part of the architecture's observable record.

End-to-End Execution Trace

An end-to-end execution trace is where UMA's metadata model proves its value most concretely.

When a request enters the system, the runtime logs every stage of its journey, from the initial event emission to the final state transition. Each service contributes its own lifecycle events, telemetry entries, and trace identifiers, all linked through metadata rather than through code. The result is a continuous, self-describing chain of evidence that can be reconstructed at any time without additional instrumentation.

The Chapter 8 pipeline demonstrates this. A run beginning with image.tagger involves the runtime identifying all services that handle image.analyzed.v1, dispatching to each in order of the binding graph, and collecting telemetry at every step. The telemetry.logger service validates the event schema and records telemetry.validation.v1 result. The edge.cache service persists the payload and records a cache.persisted.v1 result. The ai.model.evaluator service scores the output and records an inference.completed.v1 result. Every action carries the same traceparent identifier and the same contract version reference, so the entire flow can be replayed or audited as a single coherent unit.

The trace also records policy and selection decisions: which runtime executed each service, why a specific candidate was chosen, what policy rules were evaluated, and what they produced. If a failure occurs, the trace shows the recovery path and the compensating events that restored system integrity. End-to-end tracing eliminates the separation between logging and behavior. Execution generates its own record. The architecture remains both observable and reproducible as a direct consequence of being metadata-driven.

Performance and Scalability

Performance in UMA is declared before it is measured.

Performance Boundaries and Constraints

Each service contract sets explicit performance boundaries that the runtime monitors and enforces continuously. These are not targets expressed in documentation that someone hopes to meet. They are commitments that the runtime verifies against observed behavior during every execution cycle.

Common parameters include latency targets, throughput limits, and resource ceilings for CPU and memory. The image.tagger contract in the Chapter 8 companion code declares a latency_ms_p99 of 50 milliseconds. The runtime measures actual execution time on every call. If the observed latency drifts above the declared target, the runtime logs the variance, and the telemetry audit tool surfaces it explicitly:

```
node tools/validator.js audit
```

```
[info] drift.latency within 47ms ≤ 50ms target
```

Telemetry audit output from tools/validator.js showing latency drift check against declared contract target

If the latency exceeds the threshold, the output changes to a warn-level drift event, giving operators early visibility before performance degrades further. Because these boundaries are contractual, they apply uniformly across all deployment environments. The same latency rule governs image.tagger whether it runs in a browser sandbox, on an edge node, or in a cloud instance. The runtime is the enforcement mechanism in all three cases.

UMA treats performance constraints as architectural properties, not operational concerns. They specify not only the expected response time of a service but also its behavior under stress. By encoding these limits in metadata, the system elevates quality of service from a configuration concern to a verifiable design commitment. Performance can be reasoned about and upheld with the same precision as functionality.

Execution Metrics

Performance in UMA is measurable because every runtime action produces structured evidence.

Metrics are not assembled after deployment. They are generated during normal operation and drawn directly from lifecycle and telemetry events. The runtime tracks latency, throughput, and resource usage for each contract version, linking measurements to the declared boundaries that govern them. The Chapter 8 companion code writes latency measurements to logs/telemetry.jsonl as uma.qos.latency.ms entries on every execution. The report script aggregates them:

```
./scripts/report.sh
```

```
Telemetry entries: 4
Latency p99: 47 ms
```

Report script output from scripts/report.sh showing aggregated latency metrics from the telemetry log

Observability declarations in the contract specify what the runtime should monitor. Execution metrics record how those measurements perform in practice. When the runtime detects that latency or throughput has drifted outside declared limits, it logs the deviation and reports it to the registry. The feedback loop ensures that performance decisions are based on actual data rather than assumptions.

Because metrics are linked to contract metadata, they remain structurally consistent across environments. A service running in the browser and the same service running in the cloud produce the same telemetry shape, which makes cross-runtime comparisons straightforward. Over time, this consistency enables the system to establish performance baselines, automatically identify anomalies, and track improvements across contract versions. Execution metrics make performance a shared fact rather than a per-environment anecdote.

Load Balancing and Distribution

Load distribution in UMA is driven by metadata and policy, not by infrastructure configuration.

Each service contract gives the runtime the information it needs for placement and routing decisions. Capabilities, constraints, and resource declarations specify where and how a service can operate. Policies encode organizational rules around trust level, regional preferences, and latency goals. The runtime evaluates these elements in real time and selects the best execution path when an event arrives.

When demand increases, UMA does not simply replicate services. It examines contract metadata to determine which instances can safely scale and which must remain localized. A service with a tenant_scope: isolated constraint can only scale within its own domain. A service with placement [browser, edge, cloud] can be distributed across multiple runtimes. This approach allows UMA to balance workloads predictably without breaching security or compliance boundaries defined in the contracts.

Load balancing decisions are continuously refined through runtime feedback. As telemetry reveals actual latency or resource usage, the runtime adjusts distribution to maintain declared quality of service. Each adjustment is recorded in the lifecycle log, so every routing decision remains traceable and explainable. Distribution is not a deployment concern in UMA. It is an architectural behavior that emerges from metadata.

Cost Efficiency and Optimization

UMA treats efficiency as a consequence of good architecture, not a separate operational activity.

Because each service declares its performance limits and resource requirements, the runtime can reason about efficiency rather than react to problems. The same metadata that governs placement and policy also informs cost management, enabling the system to automatically balance performance against resource consumption. When underutilization or repeated idle cycles are detected, workloads can be consolidated without violating quality-of-service guarantees. When latency exceeds acceptable levels, the runtime can scale horizontally or migrate execution to a faster environment. All adjustments are governed by the same lifecycle events and policies that govern normal orchestration.

No tuning scripts or deployment-specific configuration files are required. Metadata declares the intent. The runtime converts that intent into adaptive action. Efficiency is not a byproduct of execution in UMA. It is a measurable outcome of architecture that was designed to be explicit about its own constraints from the start.

Scaling Scenarios

Scalability in UMA is not an infrastructure problem. It is a metadata problem, and metadata already has the answer.

As workloads grow, the runtime evaluates contract constraints, assesses available runtimes, and decides how to expand execution capacity within the declared rules. The scaling process uses the same reasoning as orchestration and load balancing. Growth is controlled and predictable because the rules governing it are explicit.

Consider the Chapter 8 pipeline under increasing load. As input volume grows, the runtime monitors latency measurements from the telemetry log. When edge nodes approach their declared latency ceiling, the runtime retrieves the image.tagger contract from the registry, confirms that placement includes the cloud, and launches additional instances there. No configuration files are modified. No human intervention is required. The decision follows directly from the contract metadata. When the workload drops, idle metrics trigger consolidation. The entire cycle, expansion, redistribution, and reduction, is recorded as lifecycle events, producing a transparent audit trail of every scaling decision.

Scaling in UMA is a natural extension of its declarative model. The system expands and contracts following the same rules that govern its logic. Scalability is not an afterthought. It is an inherent outcome of architecture that treats its own constraints as first-class data.

Security Considerations

Security in UMA is not an additional layer on top of the architecture. It is a property of the architecture itself.

That claim deserves an honest qualification before elaboration. UMA's security model derives trust from metadata: from contracts, registry entries, and policy references. That is a powerful approach when the metadata is fresh, the registry is reachable, and the contracts are authentic. In real distributed systems, none of those conditions is guaranteed at all times. The sections below describe both what UMA's declarative model provides and where it requires additional controls.

Declarative Trust and Identity

Trust in UMA begins with metadata. Each service contract declares not just behavior but also who can invoke it, what data it can handle, and its operational classification. Identity is built into the structural design rather than managed as a separate operational concern.

When a service registers, its contract includes ownership, domain, and classification fields. The runtime uses these to build a trust boundary around the service. A contract classified as internal cannot interact with one classified as confidential unless a policy explicitly permits the exchange. A service with a restricted tenant_scope is isolated from other tenants even when they share the same runtime infrastructure. Access decisions are based on metadata evaluation, not on runtime exceptions or informal permissions accumulated over time.

Traditional security models treat trust as something established externally: through certificates, roles, or runtime tokens managed outside the application. UMA tightens that relationship. The same metadata that describes what a service does also defines what it is permitted to do. When a contract is updated to declare new capabilities, those capabilities inherit the same trust classification. Unauthorized services cannot access them unless a new policy version explicitly grants permission.

Consider a multi-tenant invoicing pipeline. Each service instance declares its tenant_scope and classification in its contract. When a request arrives, the runtime checks both the caller's registered identity and the callee's contract metadata. If one tenant's invoice processor attempts to consume events from another tenant's workflow, the registry blocks the interaction before any code executes. The enforcement is declarative, not conditional logic written into each service.

In UMA, a service authenticates itself not through embedded credentials but through registered metadata that the runtime verifies against the registry and applicable policies. The registry is the authoritative source for ownership, access, and classification. Any UMA runtime can establish consistent trust relationships without local reconfiguration. Every authorization decision can be traced to a specific contract field and verified at execution time.

Capability Isolation

UMA enforces isolation through the same metadata that defines functionality.

Each contract declares which capabilities the service can access: file input/output, network, GPU compute, or event emission. These declarations establish a capability boundary that the runtime enforces during execution. If a capability is not declared, the service cannot exercise it, regardless of what the host environment permits.

This collapses the usual separation between permission and intent. In most systems, security permissions are managed outside the application, in configuration files, infrastructure policies, or runtime tokens. UMA binds permissions directly to the contract. A service's capabilities and its permissions are the same declaration. Capability isolation is a consequence of the definition itself, not an additional control layer applied after the fact.

The Chapter 8 pipeline illustrates this with three services operating in strict isolation. The image.tagger service declares media.tagging as its only capability. The edge.cache service declares storage.kv. The telemetry.logger service declares telemetry.ingest. Each runs in its own sandbox. Each is restricted to its declared scope. Any attempt to exercise an undeclared capability produces an immediate runtime rejection. That boundary holds whether the runtime is a browser sandbox, an edge node, or a cloud server, because it is enforced by the contract, not by the host.

Policy Enforcement and Auditability

Every action in a UMA system undergoes policy evaluation, and every policy decision is recorded.

Policies declare which contract interactions are permitted, which data exchanges are allowed given classification boundaries, and which runtime conditions must be satisfied before execution proceeds. The runtime evaluates these rules during normal operation. Enforcement is continuous and automatic. When a service emits an event, the runtime checks whether both the emitter and the intended receivers comply with current policy. If a rule blocks the communication, the runtime stops the transmission and logs the violation before execution occurs. Policy acts as a preventative guarantee, not a reactive control.

Auditability is built into the same process. Every approval and every denial is recorded alongside its policy reference, timestamp, and result. These records accumulate in the registry as a comprehensive compliance history. In the event of an incident, the trace identifies precisely which contract, policy, and runtime instance were involved and what reasoning produced the decision. In traditional architectures, enforcement and logging are often handled separately, which creates gaps between what was permitted and what was recorded. UMA integrates them. The runtime enforces and records in a single operation. Compliance is a continuous architectural property that can be verified at any moment, not a periodic manual audit.

Secure Event Flow

Security in UMA extends to the movement of data between services.

Every event envelope carries metadata that enables the receiver to verify its source, authenticity, and integrity. The umacontractversion field links the event to the exact contract version that governed its production. The traceparent field connects it to the distributed trace that spans the full execution path. Before processing an event, the receiver validates this information against the registry to confirm that the source and schema are trusted. No custom middleware is required. The runtime performs the check as part of standard event processing.

Events that cross environment boundaries remain cryptographically linked to their original context through the traceparent and umacontractversion fields. These attributes make tampering detectable even when the event passes through intermediaries. The runtime appends its own signature at each hop and records the transfer in the lifecycle log. The result is a chain of custody that tracks every step from emission to final consumption. Each event becomes a self-contained record of trust, carrying the proof of how and why it was permitted to exist.

Cross-Domain Execution

UMA enables services to interact across organizational domains. Each cross-domain exchange is governed by explicit metadata rather than informal trust.

Contracts declare not only what data a service handles but also the conditions under which that data can leave its domain. When a service from one domain attempts to emit an event for a receiver in another, the runtime verifies both contracts and the trust settings in the registry. If the recipient domain has not approved the sender's classification, or if a policy prohibits the data transfer, the exchange is blocked before it occurs.

Cross-domain coordination relies on federated registries that synchronize trust metadata without sharing the underlying data. Each domain manages its own contracts and policies but can access verified metadata from partner domains. A service from one organization can consume another's event only if both registries confirm the interaction and the contract versions are compatible. All cross-domain actions are logged in lifecycle records and policy audits alongside local events.

Three failure modes require explicit attention in any cross-domain deployment. First, network partitions can prevent a runtime from reaching the registry, forcing a choice between failing closed, blocking all execution until connectivity is restored, and failing open, proceeding on cached metadata at the risk of acting on stale policy. UMA recommends configuring a maximum staleness window, after which the cached policy must be treated as unverified. Second, stale metadata can cause enforcement drift: a service whose classification has been updated in the registry may continue operating under its prior trust level until its local cache refreshes. Registry sync lag should be monitored as a security metric, not just an operational one. Third, registry compromise is the highest-severity threat to this model, because the registry is the root of trust for ownership, classification, and policy references. Registry infrastructure must be hardened, access-controlled, and backed by append-only audit logs that can detect and recover from tampering.

It is also worth stating clearly what metadata enforcement does not replace. Firewalls, network segmentation, and mutual TLS remain essential layers of defense in cross-domain communication. UMA adds a declarative, auditable enforcement layer on top of the network. It does not substitute for the network controls beneath it. The two layers work together. Removing either weakens the overall posture.

Security As a Consequence of Architecture

The strongest security claim UMA makes is also the one that requires the most careful qualification.

Because every action, dependency, and permission is described through metadata, the runtime has a complete and verifiable picture of its boundaries at any given moment. Trust, identity, isolation, and policy enforcement all derive from the same declarative foundation. When a service declares what it does, it simultaneously declares what it is permitted to do. The runtime enforces those declarations and logs every decision. The alignment between intent and protection is continuous, not periodic.

That model holds when the metadata is current, the registry is reachable, and no external process has modified the service state between validation and execution. In real distributed systems, all three of those conditions can fail. A partial network failure may leave a runtime operating on a cached contract version that no longer reflects the current policy. A dynamic configuration change pushed outside the contract lifecycle can introduce behavior that the governance layer cannot detect. An external integration that bypasses the event envelope, such as a direct database write or a sidecar process operating outside the UMA boundary, can create observable side effects that the declarative model cannot observe. Architects adopting UMA should explicitly map these boundaries, instrument them for observability, and treat them as trust gaps that require additional controls beyond what the contract model provides.

Metadata integrity is the single most critical security property in a UMA system. If contracts or registry entries can be tampered with, every guarantee described in this section is undermined without touching any application code. Three controls address this risk directly. First, each contract should be signed by its owner at the time of publication, and the runtime should verify that signature before loading the contract, rejecting any version whose signature does not match the registered public key. Second, the registry should store contracts in an append-only log with cryptographic chaining so that any modification to a historical entry produces a detectable inconsistency. Third, the runtime should compute and compare the digest of the loaded contract against the digest recorded at registration. Any mismatch is a critical policy violation that halts execution until the discrepancy is resolved. These controls ensure that the declarative trust model remains trustworthy even when the metadata infrastructure itself is the target.

Security in UMA is a quality of structure. The architecture defends itself by following its own specifications precisely. That is a genuine property and a meaningful one. It is also bounded by the integrity of the metadata that the specifications are written in, the reachability of the registry that stores them, and the completeness of the boundary that the contract model draws around the system. Design for all three, and the security model is as strong as the architecture it describes.

PART III

Deploying, Securing, and Scaling

CHAPTER 9

From Services to Systems

How UMA Service Graphs Emerge

Introduction: From Independent Services to Composed Systems

A UMA system is not designed. It is declared into existence.

The companion code for this chapter is available at `https://github.com/enricopiovesan/UMA-code-examples/tree/main/chapter-09-service-graph`. Run ./scripts/run_graph_demo.sh lab1-upload-only to see the starting state and work through the five labs as the chapter progresses.

In the context of UMA, a system is a set of independently deployed services that cooperate through declared events and capabilities. No service knows the full topology. Each knows only its own contracts. The system's structure is the sum of those declarations as interpreted and maintained by the runtime. A service graph is the directed graph that the runtime constructs and maintains from those declarations: each service is a node, and each event-driven relationship between a producer and a consumer is an edge.

Traditional distributed architectures approach composition in several ways, each solving part of the problem. Service meshes manage traffic and observability at the network layer, but they do not describe what a service does or what it depends on. Event-driven architectures decouple producers from consumers through message brokers, but the relationships between services are still defined outside the services themselves, in broker configuration or consumer group assignments. Declarative orchestration tools define relationships in configuration files, but those files must be written and maintained separately from the services they connect. UMA adds what all three lack: each service carries its own declaration of what it provides and what it expects, and the runtime derives the system topology from those declarations rather than from external configuration.

E. Piovesan, *Universal Microservices Architecture*, https://doi.org/10.1007/979-8-8688-2794-5_9

This difference matters because it changes what the runtime can do. When every capability, constraint, and event is represented as data within the service contract, the runtime can automatically discover compatible services, route events without being told where to send them, detect when compatibility breaks, and reconstruct the architecture's structure at any moment from the live contracts.

This chapter builds that system from a single service. Starting with one service is a simplification for teaching purposes, not a constraint of the model. In practice, UMA systems begin with multiple services already present, and the runtime evaluates all declared contracts simultaneously. The single-service starting point makes each architectural property visible in isolation before the system grows.

The chapter follows the system step by step. A single upload service starts the graph. A compatible tagging service joins it. A metadata indexer extends it further. Along the way, the chapter examines what makes compatibility work, what happens when it breaks, and how the runtime maintains the graph as the architecture evolves. The final sections examine what becomes possible when the graph's structure is machine-readable: architectural observability, gap detection, and AI-assisted extension proposals.

The First Service: Starting the System

Every UMA system begins with a single observable fact.

The Upload Service

The system begins with one service that receives images. From the user's perspective, it is the only visible component: a client sends an image, and the upload service accepts it. At this stage the architecture is intentionally minimal. The upload service does not know how the image will be processed, which services will analyze it, or where results will be stored. Its responsibility is limited to receiving input and announcing that a meaningful event has occurred.

An observable action is a fact the service reports about its own behavior in a form that other components of the system can detect. Storing a file is an internal operation. Emitting image.uploaded is an observable action: it is structured, named, and visible to the runtime and to any service that has declared interest in it. This distinction is what allows UMA services to remain independent. A service does not orchestrate what happens next. It reports what it did, and the runtime handles the rest.

The upload service declares its behavior in a JSON contract. The companion code for this chapter stores these contracts in the scenarios/ folder, one JSON file per service. The full contract for the upload service in lab1-upload-only looks like this:

```
{
  "kind": "uma.service-contract",
  "specVersion": "1.0",
  "service": {
    "id": "upload-service",
    "version": "1.0.0",
    "summary": "Accepts an image upload and emits a discovery event.",
    "placements": ["cloud", "edge"]
  },
  "capabilities": [
    { "id": "media.ingest", "version": "1.0" }
  ],
  "events": {
    "consumes": [],
    "emits": [
      {
        "name": "image.uploaded",
        "schema": "contracts/schemas/image-uploaded.event.v1.json"
      }
    ]
  },
  "io": {
    "inputSchema": "contracts/schemas/image-upload.request.v1.json",
    "outputSchema": "contracts/schemas/image-upload.response.v1.json"
  }
}
```

The upload-service contract from lab1-upload-only. The events.emits declaration is what the runtime uses to build the service graph. The io section declares the request and response schemas that validate the service's inputs and outputs.

Two properties in this contract matter architecturally. First, the events.consumes array is empty. The upload service reacts to nothing. It only produces. Second, the events.emits entry declares image.uploaded with a schema reference. A service declares interest in an event by adding a matching entry to its own events.consumes array. The runtime reads both declarations, finds the match, and creates an edge. No service needs to know the address or identity of any other service.

In production deployments, the upload service must handle two failure modes. First, storage may fail before the event is emitted. In this case, the event must not be emitted, since downstream services would attempt to process a file that does not exist. Second, the event delivery mechanism may be unavailable at the moment of emission. UMA runtimes address this through at-least-once delivery backed by a persistent event log. If the runtime cannot confirm delivery, the service retries emission using an idempotency key derived from the file identifier, ensuring that duplicate emissions produce a single downstream effect.

The runtime's event routing layer also warrants scrutiny as a potential single point of failure. A single runtime instance that becomes unavailable takes all event routing with it. UMA addresses this in two ways. The runtime is stateless with respect to service logic: it routes events based on contract metadata stored in the registry, so any runtime instance can resume routing after a restart. The event log provides durability: events emitted before a runtime failure are retained and replayed once the runtime recovers. In large deployments, multiple runtime instances read from the same contract registry and event log, providing horizontal scalability and eliminating the single point of failure at the routing layer.

Emitting the First Event

The upload service's primary responsibility is not to store the file but to announce that a meaningful event has occurred. When an image arrives, the service stores the file and emits image.uploaded. This event represents an observable fact: a new image has entered the system. The upload service does not attempt to determine what should happen next. It reports the upload and stops.

The contrast with direct-call architectures is instructive. In many distributed systems, it would seem natural for the upload service to immediately call another service to process the image. One service invokes the next, waits for a response, and continues. In this model, every service must know which component runs after it. If the processing pipeline changes, the upstream service must be updated. Over time, these dependencies accumulate, making the architecture harder to change.

UMA separates observable actions from service execution. Instead of invoking another service directly, the upload service emits an event describing what has occurred. This event is written to the runtime's event log. The runtime reads from the log and routes the event to every registered subscriber. Any service that has declared interest in image.uploaded by listing it in its events.consumes array will receive the event. The upload service does not know how many such services exist, where they run, or what they do with the image.

The Rust implementation of this pattern in the Chapter 9 companion code concretely shows the structure. The upload service is represented as a contract file that the runtime reads at startup. The runtime's Rust library in src/lib.rs builds the graph by iterating over every service's emits and consumes declarations and creating edges wherever a match is found. The service itself contains no routing logic. All coordination is derived from the metadata.

Because services communicate through observable events rather than direct calls, new services can be added without modifying existing ones. A new component declares that it consumes image.uploaded and the runtime connects it automatically. The upload service continues operating unchanged. The architecture grows by addition, not by rewiring.

Run lab1-upload-only to see the starting state:

```
./scripts/run_graph_demo.sh lab1-upload-only
```

```
Scenario: lab1-upload-only

Services
- upload-service v1.0.0
  summary: Accepts an image upload and emits a discovery event.
  placements: cloud, edge
  capability: media.ingest@1.0
  emits: image.uploaded (contracts/schemas/image-uploaded.event.v1.json)

Edges
- none

Waiting Consumers
- none
```

Output from lab1-upload-only. One service, one emitted event, no edges yet. The system is ready to grow the moment a compatible consumer registers.

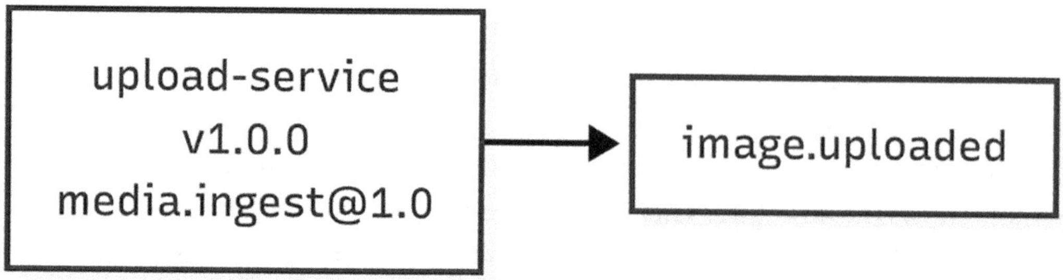

Figure 9-1. *The system begins with a single service and a single observable event. No edges exist yet. The architecture is ready to grow the moment a compatible consumer registers*

The resource profile of the upload service is worth considering. Because its responsibility is limited to accepting input and emitting a single event, its compute requirements are low. The dominant costs are I/O: writing the file to storage and writing the event to the log. For large files, streaming writes avoid buffering the entire payload in memory. The service contract declares a placement constraint of cloud and edge, which the runtime uses to schedule execution on hosts with appropriate I/O capacity. A latency_ms_p99 constraint in the contract, if declared, would allow the runtime to monitor upload throughput and trigger scaling decisions automatically when it drifts above the target.

Capability Discovery: Finding Compatible Services

The runtime does not wait to be told which services belong together.

At this point in the system, the upload service has completed its work. An image has been received, and the image.uploaded has been emitted. The runtime can observe that a new image has entered the system, but no other service has yet responded to this event. The architecture faces a simple question: what should happen next?

In many traditional systems, the answer would already be embedded in the upload service. After storing the file, the service would call another component to analyze the image. The pipeline would be predetermined. UMA avoids this. The upload service does not decide how the system evolves. It exposes an observable event and allows other services to react if their contracts indicate compatibility.

Declaring Capabilities

For the runtime to discover compatible services, each service must describe what it can provide. In UMA this is done through capability declarations. A capability represents a well-defined type of functionality that a service offers. Instead of exposing an implementation detail or API endpoint, the service declares the functional role it can perform within the system.

A natural candidate to process uploaded images is a tagging service. The image-tagger consumes image.uploaded, analyzes the image content, and emits image.tagged with descriptive labels. Its contract declares the media.tagging capability with a version, lists image.uploaded as a consumed event, and declares image.tagged as an emitted event. The relevant fields from the image-tagger contract in lab2-image-tagger are the following:

```
{
  "kind": "uma.service-contract",
  "specVersion": "1.0",
  "service": {
    "id": "image-tagger",
    "version": "1.0.0",
    "summary": "Consumes uploaded images and emits semantic tags.",
    "placements": ["cloud"]
  },
  "capabilities": [
    { "id": "media.tagging", "version": "1.0" }
  ],
  "events": {
    "consumes": [
      {
        "name": "image.uploaded",
        "schema": "contracts/schemas/image-uploaded.event.v1.json"
      }
    ],
```

```
    "emits": [
      {
        "name": "image.tagged",
        "schema": "contracts/schemas/image-tagged.event.v1.json"
      }
    ]
  },
  "io": { ... }
}
```

The image-tagger contract from lab2-image-tagger. The io section is unchanged from the upload service example and is omitted for brevity. The events.consumes entry for image.uploaded is the declaration that creates the edge to the upload service when the runtime evaluates both contracts.

The capability declaration does not specify how tagging works internally. The service might rely on machine learning models, computer vision libraries, or specialized hardware. None of those implementation details is visible to other services. The capability identifier is a stable reference that persists through internal changes, as long as the declared behavior remains consistent.

In practice, a capability declaration also carries non-functional properties that constrain how the runtime uses it. A media.tagging capability might declare a p99 latency target of 200 milliseconds and a maximum throughput of 50 requests per second. These constraints become part of the runtime's selection logic. When multiple providers offer the same capability, the runtime can prefer the one whose declared properties best match the current system conditions.

Stability across changes requires versioning. UMA contracts include a version field following semantic versioning conventions, defined at semver.org as a three-part MAJOR.MINOR.PATCH number. A PATCH increment signals a bug fix. A MINOR increment signals new capabilities that are backward compatible. A MAJOR increment signals a breaking change that existing consumers must explicitly adopt. The runtime treats different major versions as distinct capabilities and will not route events from a v1 consumer to a v2 provider without an explicit compatibility declaration. This versioning discipline allows the architecture to evolve without surprise failures.

Runtime Discovery

Once services declare their capabilities, the runtime evaluates possible relationships between them. Capability discovery is the process by which the runtime identifies compatible services and establishes connections based on their declared metadata.

The runtime maintains a registry of all active service contracts. Capability identifiers, event declarations, and schema references are stored in this registry and continuously evaluated as services appear or change. The matching algorithm is an inverted index lookup. At registration time, each event type a service declares in its emits array is added as a key in the index, with the service as the value. When another service registers with a matching entry in its consumes array, the runtime finds the match in constant time and creates an edge. This approach scales to tens of thousands of services because the lookup cost does not grow with the total number of services. It grows only with the number of subscribers for a specific event type, which is typically small. A runtime that restarts and rebuilds its in-memory routing tables from the registry in a single sequential scan.

When an event is emitted, the runtime does not recompute all relationships from scratch. It queries the index for the event type and retrieves the registered subscriber list immediately. Between emission and delivery, the event passes through three stages. First, the emitting service writes the event to the runtime's local event log, a persistent append-only structure. Second, the runtime reads from the log and routes the event to each registered subscriber. Third, each subscriber acknowledges receipt. Until acknowledgement is received, the runtime retains the event in the log and will redeliver it after a configurable timeout. This at-least-once delivery model means consumers must be idempotent: receiving the same event twice must produce the same result as receiving it once. If a subscriber remains unavailable beyond the configured retention window, the event is moved to a dead-letter queue, and an operational alert is raised.

The runtime recognizes that the image-tagger declares image.uploaded in its consumer array and that the upload service declares image.uploaded in its emits array. Their relationship emerges from the compatibility of their metadata. Neither service explicitly references the other. The upload service is unaware that the image-tagger exists. The image-tagger does not need to know which service uploaded the image.

Connecting the Services

Once the runtime identifies a compatible producer and consumer, it establishes the edge between them. This connection does not require modifying either service. The upload service continues to emit image.uploaded and the image-tagger reacts when that event arrives. The runtime interprets the metadata and routes the event accordingly.

Run lab2-image-tagger and then use contract_diff.sh to inspect exactly what changed in the contracts between lab1 and lab2:

```
{
  "kind": "uma.service-contract",
  "specVersion": "1.0",
  "service": {
    "id": "image-tagger",
    "version": "1.0.0",
    "summary": "Consumes uploaded images and emits semantic tags.",
    "placements": ["cloud"]
  },
  "capabilities": [
    { "id": "media.tagging", "version": "1.0" }
  ],
  "events": {
    "consumes": [
      {
        "name": "image.uploaded",
        "schema": "contracts/schemas/image-uploaded.event.v1.json"
      }
    ],
    "emits": [
      {
        "name": "image.tagged",
        "schema": "contracts/schemas/image-tagged.event.v1.json"
      }
    ]
  },
  "io": { ... }
}
```

Output from lab2-image-tagger. The first edge in the system has appeared. Neither service was modified. The runtime created the edge by matching the upload service's emits declaration against the image-tagger's consumes declaration.

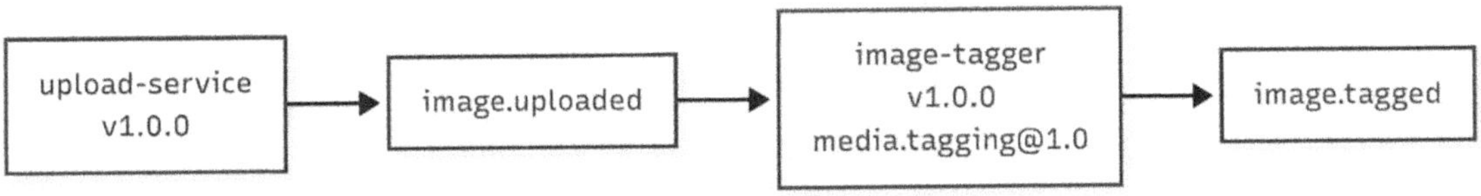

***Figure 9-2.** The first edge in the system appears when image-tagger registers its contract declaring image.uploaded as a consumed event. Neither service was modified. The edge emerged from metadata compatibility*

The connection was not designed explicitly in code. It emerged from the compatibility of two contract declarations. This is the first structural connection in the system, and it illustrates the central property of UMA: architecture emerges from metadata, not from wiring.

Event Interaction: How Services Begin to Collaborate

Two services connected through an event are not a pipeline. They are the beginning of a graph.

The Image Tagger Reacts

Once the runtime connects the upload service and the image-tagger, the system contains its first functional interaction between two independent services. The upload service emits image.uploaded whenever a new image arrives. The image-tagger, having declared that it consumes that event, receives it and begins analyzing the image content. The image-tagger produces descriptive tags: labels that characterize what appears in the image.

From the image-tagger's perspective, the interaction is simple. Whenever a compatible event appears, the service processes the image and produces output. The service may rely on machine learning models, computer vision libraries, or specialized hardware. None of those implementation details affects how the service participates in the system. What matters architecturally is that the service reacts to a known event type and performs its responsibility when that event arrives.

Emitting the Analysis Result

After the image-tagger completes its work, the result must become visible to the rest of the system. Just as the upload service announced that an image had been received, the image-tagger announces that tagging is complete. The relevant emits declaration from its contract is:

```
"emits": [
  {
    "name": "image.tagged",
    "schema": "contracts/schemas/image-tagged.event.v1.json"
  }
]
```

The emits declaration from the image-tagger contract. The schema reference points to the JSON Schema file that validates the event payload structure before any subscriber receives it.

The image.tagged event indicates that an image has been analyzed and that descriptive tags are now available. The event does not dictate what should happen next. It exposes the result so that other services can respond if their responsibilities depend on this information. At this stage the system produces two observable events: image.uploaded emitted by the upload service and image.tagged emitted by the image-tagger. Each represents a meaningful step. Additional services can react to either without modifying the services already running.

Why Events Enable Collaboration

Event-driven interaction is a pattern in which services communicate by emitting and consuming named, structured messages rather than by calling each other directly. The emitter does not wait for a response. The consumer acts when the message arrives. The runtime mediates the exchange.

In many distributed systems, services coordinate through direct calls. One service invokes another, waits for a response, and continues execution. In this model, every service must know which component runs after it completes its work. If the pipeline changes, the services involved must be modified to reflect the new sequence. As systems grow, these dependencies accumulate.

Event-driven interaction avoids this problem. Services expose what has happened and allow other services to respond when appropriate. The upload service does not know which service will tag the image. The image-tagger does not know which service uploaded the file or which services may use the tagging results. Each service reacts to the events it understands and emits new events when it completes its work.

It is important to acknowledge the tradeoffs this pattern introduces. First, eventual consistency: when multiple services react to the same event, their local state updates are not atomic. A consumer that crashes mid-processing leaves the system in a partially updated state. UMA addresses this through idempotent consumers and compensating events. Each consumer tracks which event identifiers it has successfully processed. Before processing any event, the consumer checks whether its id is already in its processed-events store. If it is, the consumer discards the event and acknowledges delivery without repeating the work. In Rust, this store can be as simple as a HashSet written to a local file between runs. In production, a shared store with a unique constraint on the event id provides the same guarantee across multiple consumer instances.

Second, observability complexity: in a direct-call system, a request trace is linear. In an event-driven system, a single upload can trigger a fan-out to many consumers, making correlation across the trace harder. UMA uses the traceparent field in the CloudEvents envelope to propagate trace identity through every consumer, allowing the full fan-out to be reconstructed as a single trace in any OpenTelemetry-compatible platform.

Third, ordering guarantees: if two events concerning the same resource are emitted in quick succession, consumers may receive them out of order depending on the delivery mechanism. Services that require ordered processing should declare a partition key in their contract, allowing the runtime to route events for the same resource to the same consumer instance in sequence.

These tradeoffs are manageable. They are also the cost of the property that makes the architecture extensible: because services do not call each other directly, new services can join the architecture by reacting to existing events without requiring changes to already running services.

The System Is Ready to Grow

At this stage, the system contains two collaborating services connected through events. The upload service announces that an image has been received. The image-tagger reacts to the image, analyzes it, and emits image.tagged. The runtime has produced a new observable signal that describes the tagging result. This signal is now available for additional services to consume.

A service responsible for storing searchable metadata, for example, could declare that it consumes image.tagged. When the runtime detects this compatibility, it connects the new service automatically. The existing services require no modification. The architecture grows by extending the existing event flow, not by rewiring what already exists.

The Service Graph: When Architecture Emerges

Three services connected through events are no longer just a pipeline. They are a graph.

A New Requirement Appears

At this point, the upload service receives images and emits image.uploaded. The image-tagger reacts to that event, analyzes the image, and emits image.tagged. The system recognizes what appears in an image, but the tags produced by the analysis exist only as an event flowing through the runtime. If the system is expected to support image content-based search, the analysis results must be stored in a form that can be queried later.

A natural candidate for this responsibility is a metadata indexer. Its purpose is to take the tags generated by the image-tagger and store them in an index that allows images to be retrieved based on their content. The metadata-indexer does not need to know which component produced the tags it receives. Its responsibility is simply to process the tagging results and maintain a searchable representation of the metadata.

Consuming the Analysis Event

For the metadata-indexer to participate in the system, it must declare that it reacts to the results produced by the image-tagger. The relevant section of its contract in lab3-indexer is the following:

```
"events": {
  "consumes": [
    {
      "name": "image.tagged",
      "schema": "contracts/schemas/image-tagged.event.v1.json"
    }
  ],
  "emits": [
    {
      "name": "metadata.indexed",
      "schema": "contracts/schemas/metadata-indexed.event.v1.json"
    }
  ]
}
```

The events section from the metadata-indexer contract. It declares image.tagged as a consumed event, which matches the image-tagger's emitted event, and metadata.indexed as its own emitted event, which future services can consume in turn.

Once this declaration is available, the runtime detects that the image-tagger produces exactly the event required by the metadata-indexer. Through this compatibility, the runtime establishes the interaction between the two services without requiring either component to know about the other.

The Service Graph Emerges

With the metadata-indexer added to the architecture, the system now includes three services that communicate through events. The upload service emits image.uploaded when a new image arrives. The image-tagger consumes that event, analyzes the image, and emits image.tagged. The metadata-indexer consumes the tagging result and stores it in a searchable form.

A service graph is the directed graph that the UMA runtime constructs and maintains from registered contract metadata. Each service is a node. Each event-driven relationship between a producer and a consumer is a directed edge. The runtime builds this graph automatically from the emits and consumes declarations in each contract.

No architect draws it manually. It is a live representation of the current system topology, derived from the same metadata that governs execution.

Run lab3-indexer to see the three-service graph:

```
./scripts/run_graph_demo.sh lab3-indexer
```

```
Scenario: lab3-indexer

Services
- image-tagger v1.0.0
  capability: media.tagging@1.0
  consumes: image.uploaded (contracts/schemas/image-uploaded.event.v1.json)
  emits: image.tagged (contracts/schemas/image-tagged.event.v1.json)
- metadata-indexer v1.0.0
  capability: media.search-indexing@1.0
  consumes: image.tagged (contracts/schemas/image-tagged.event.v1.json)
  emits: metadata.indexed (contracts/schemas/metadata-indexed.event.
  v1.json)
- upload-service v1.0.0
  capability: media.ingest@1.0
  emits: image.uploaded (contracts/schemas/image-uploaded.event.v1.json)

Edges
- image-tagger -> image.tagged -> metadata-indexer
- upload-service -> image.uploaded -> image-tagger

Waiting Consumers
- none
```

Output from lab3-indexer. Three services, two edges, no waiting consumers. The architecture has formed a complete chain from image receipt through tagging to indexing, entirely from contract declarations.

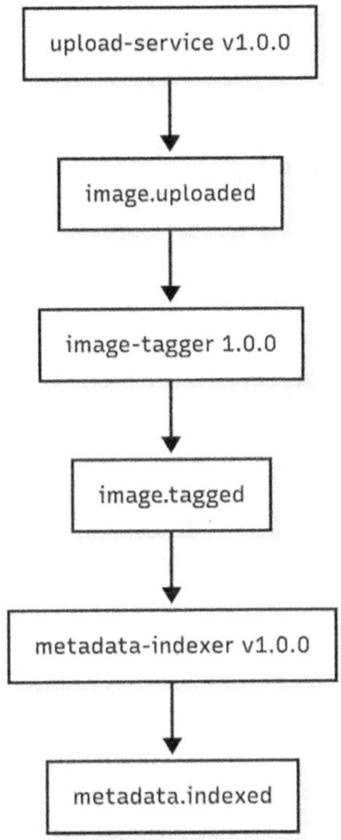

Figure 9-3. *The three-service graph after lab3-indexer. Each service contributes one responsibility and exposes its results through a named event. The runtime maintains all three edges solely from contract declarations*

This is an important shift in how the architecture should be understood. Earlier in the chapter, the system could still be interpreted as a simple sequence of reactions. Now the relationships between services are becoming part of the architecture itself. The runtime is no longer coordinating isolated interactions. It is maintaining an emerging topology of cooperating components.

What makes this structure significant is that it was not wired together manually. The upload service did not need to know that an indexing service would eventually exist. The image-tagger did not need to be modified when the metadata-indexer was introduced. The relationships emerged from compatible event declarations and runtime interpretation. In real-world systems, legacy or non-UMA services that do not declare their capabilities can be integrated through adapters or gateways: specialized components that emit UMA events in response to actions from a legacy service or consume UMA events and translate them into API calls suitable for external systems.

This allows mixed environments in which legacy and UMA-native services coexist without requiring immediate, large-scale refactoring.

Graph Evolution: A Living Architecture

A service graph is not a fixed artifact. It is a live representation of the current contracts in the environment.

How the Graph Stays Current

The system now consists of three cooperating services. This structure should not be interpreted as a finished pipeline. In traditional systems, once a sequence of services has been defined, the architecture tends to remain static. Changes to the workflow often require modifying existing services or introducing new orchestration logic. UMA systems evolve differently.

Because the relationships between services are defined through metadata and events rather than explicit calls, the architecture remains open to change. New services can appear, existing services can scale or evolve, and the runtime can adjust the connections between them without requiring modifications to services already running. The service graph behaves like a living architecture: it reflects the current set of services available in the environment and the relationships that exist between their declared capabilities and events.

The runtime continuously evaluates service metadata and maintains the relationships that form the graph. When new services join the environment, the runtime determines whether their declared capabilities or event requirements match the events already present. If a compatible relationship exists, the runtime automatically establishes the interaction. In some environments, multiple services may declare compatible capabilities or react to the same event. Event-driven architectures often allow several services to respond independently to the same signal. When multiple providers offer the same capability, the runtime may apply selection policies such as priority rules or load balancing defined in service contracts.

Runtime Adaptation and Versioning

Services may evolve through new versions while maintaining compatibility with existing events. To support safe evolution, UMA contracts include a version field following semantic versioning conventions. A change that preserves the existing interface increments the minor version. A change that breaks consumers increments the major version and changes the capability identifier, for example, from media.tagging@1.0 to media.tagging@2.0. The runtime treats different major versions as distinct capabilities and will not route events between incompatible versions without an explicit compatibility declaration.

When introducing updates, compatibility can be managed by supporting both old and new versions simultaneously or by following versioning strategies that minimize breaking changes. If a new service version introduces a change that is not backward compatible, the version number in the capability or event declaration changes, so that dependent services and the runtime can detect incompatibility before attempting to connect them. Managed versioning allows architects to plan incremental upgrades and phased rollouts without unexpected service failures.

Idempotency is the property that processing the same event more than once produces the same result as processing it once. Every CloudEvents envelope carries an id field that is unique per emission. Consumers implement idempotency by maintaining a processed-events store: a key-value structure that records the event identifiers they have successfully handled. Before processing any event, the consumer checks whether its id is already in the store. If it is, the consumer discards the event and acknowledges delivery without repeating the work. If it is not, the consumer processes the event and records the id on completion. In Rust, this store can be as simple as a HashSet written to a local file between runs. In production, a shared store with a unique constraint on the event ID column provides the same guarantee across multiple consumer instances.

When Compatibility Breaks

The companion code for this chapter includes a deliberate compatibility break that demonstrates one of UMA's most important properties: metadata mismatches produce visible, recoverable failures rather than silent behavioral drift.

In lab4-broken-compat, the image-tagger is updated to version 1.1.0, and its emitted event is renamed from image.tagged to image-tagged-renamed. The metadata-indexer contract is not updated. It still declares image.tagged as its consumed event. The result is immediate and explicit:

```
./scripts/run_graph_demo.sh lab4-broken-compat

Scenario: lab4-broken-compat

Services
```

```
- image-tagger v1.1.0
  capability: media.tagging@1.1
  consumes: image.uploaded (contracts/schemas/image-uploaded.event.v1.json)
  emits: image-tagged-renamed (contracts/schemas/image-tagged-renamed.
  event.v1.json)
- metadata-indexer v1.0.0
  capability: media.search-indexing@1.0
  consumes: image.tagged (contracts/schemas/image-tagged.event.v1.json)
  emits: metadata.indexed (contracts/schemas/metadata-indexed.event.
  v1.json)
- upload-service v1.0.0
  capability: media.ingest@1.0
```

Output from lab4-broken-compat. The edge from image-tagger to metadata-indexer has disappeared. The metadata-indexer appears in the Waiting Consumers section because it declares a dependency on image. tagged, but no service currently emits that event. The graph fracture is visible, named, and localized.

Run graph_diff.sh to see exactly what changed between the stable and broken states:

```
./scripts/graph_diff.sh lab3-indexer lab4-broken-compat
```

```
Graph diff: lab3-indexer -> lab4-broken-compat

Added services
- none

Removed services
- none

Added edges
- none

Removed edges
- image-tagger -> image.tagged -> metadata-indexer

Added waiting consumers
```

```
- metadata-indexer waiting for image.tagged

Removed waiting consumers
- none
```

Output from graph_diff.sh comparing lab3-indexer to lab4-broken-compat. One edge removed, one waiting consumer added. The diff is precise, machine-readable, and can be caught in CI before the change reaches production.

Lab5-fixed-compat restores the original event name in the image-tagger contract. The runtime reconnects the services automatically. No code changes are required in the metadata-indexer. The graph returns to its three-service, two-edge state the moment the corrected contract is registered. This is what metadata-driven architecture makes possible: system recovery comes from restoring declarative consistency, not from rewriting orchestration logic.

An Expanding Graph

The service graph continues to evolve as new services appear. A service responsible for generating image thumbnails, for example, could declare that it consumes image.uploaded and emits thumbnail.generated. When the runtime detects this compatibility, it adds the new node and edge without touching the existing services. The upload service continues emitting the same event. Two services now react to it: the image-tagger and the thumbnail generator. The graph has grown a branch.

Use contract_diff.sh between any two labs to inspect exactly which contract fields changed and use graph_diff.sh to see how those changes affected the graph topology. These two tools together provide the Git-style architectural diff that makes UMA evolution auditable and reversible.

The graph is therefore not a fixed structure but a representation of the current relationships between services in the environment. As services declare compatible capabilities and events, the architecture expands organically while preserving the independence of each component.

Observing the System

The architecture is legible because the contracts are readable.

Seeing the System

Once several services are participating in the architecture, engineers need to understand how the system works. In many distributed systems, this is difficult. Services interact through APIs, message queues, or internal orchestration logic, and understanding how the system behaves often requires examining logs, tracing requests, or reading the source code of multiple components.

UMA systems provide a different perspective. Because services explicitly declare their capabilities and events, the runtime maintains a representation of the relationships between them. From the operator's point of view, the architecture becomes visible as a service graph. Each service appears as a node. The events exchanged between services form the connections that describe how information flows through the system.

The Chapter 9 companion code demonstrates this directly. The Rust CLI and its TypeScript parity implementation both render the graph from the same contract metadata. The graph_snapshot.sh script produces a machine-readable JSON export of the current graph state:

```
./scripts/graph_snapshot.sh lab3-indexer
```

```
{
  "scenario": "lab3-indexer",
  "services": [...],
  "edges": [
    { "from": "image-tagger", "event": "image.tagged", "to": "metadata-
    indexer" },
    { "from": "upload-service", "event": "image.uploaded", "to": "image-
    tagger" }
  ],
  "waiting": []
}
```

JSON output from graph_snapshot.sh for lab3-indexer. The edges array captures the full topology in a form that monitoring tools, CI pipelines, and AI analysis tools can process without parsing log files or reading source code.

This view makes the architecture easier to reason about. Instead of tracing individual requests across multiple services, engineers can inspect the graph and immediately understand how data moves through the system. More importantly, this representation reflects the actual runtime relationships between services. As the system evolves and new services appear, the graph changes accordingly, providing a continuously updated picture of the architecture.

Lifecycle Events

To maintain an accurate view of the system, the runtime must track more than just the events exchanged between services. It must also track the lifecycle of the services themselves. Whenever a service becomes available, its contract and metadata are registered with the runtime. This registration allows the runtime to evaluate the capabilities and events declared by the service and determine whether it can participate in the existing architecture. When a service is updated, replaced, or removed, the runtime updates its internal representation accordingly.

These changes are described through lifecycle events that capture the moments when services appear, evolve, or disappear within the environment. service.registered fires when a new service becomes available. service.updated fires when a contract or capability declaration changes. service.removed fires when a service is no longer available. By observing these lifecycle events, the runtime continuously adjusts the service graph to reflect the system's current state.

If the metadata-indexer were removed, the runtime would detect the change and update the graph immediately. The image-tagger would continue emitting image.tagged, but the edge to the metadata-indexer would disappear and that event type would have no subscriber. The graph makes this visible as a structural gap rather than a silent failure.

Reconstructing the Graph

Because services describe their behavior through metadata and events, the runtime can determine the system's structure without inspecting any application code.

In practice, the runtime constructs the service graph in three steps. First, at service registration, it adds the service's emits and consumes entries to the routing index and inserts a node into the graph with edges for each declared relationship. Second, at runtime, every lifecycle event triggers a graph update: service.registered adds a node, service.updated re-evaluates its edges, and service.removed removes its node and all associated edges. Third, the runtime periodically computes derived graph properties: reachability, which services can be reached from a given source event; depth, how many hops separate two services; and fan-out, how many subscribers react to a given event. These properties are cached and exposed through the runtime's administrative API, allowing monitoring tools and CI pipelines to query the current graph state without reconstructing it from scratch each time.

The Chapter 9 Rust implementation in src/lib.rs exposes this structure through the load_scenario_graph and build_graph functions. The buildGraph function in the TypeScript parity implementation in ts/src/lib.mjs performs the same construction. Both produce identical output, verified by compare_impls.sh on every lab. Engineers working with either implementation see the same graph, because the graph is derived from the same contract metadata.

As services evolve and new components appear, the same metadata-driven analysis continues to update the graph. Engineers no longer need to infer the system's architecture by tracing requests or reviewing source code. The runtime already maintains the information required to understand how services interact.

Architectural Observability

Observability in distributed systems traditionally focuses on metrics, logs, and traces. These signals help engineers understand what the system is doing internally, but they do not always reveal how the architecture itself is structured. UMA introduces an additional perspective: architectural observability.

Because the runtime maintains relationships between services based on declared events and capabilities, it also maintains an explicit representation of the system's organization. Engineers can therefore observe not only the internal behavior of services but also the structure of the architecture that connects them.

A representative architectural observability dashboard for a UMA system shows three panels. The left panel renders the service graph as a directed node-link diagram, with nodes colored by health status and edges weighted by event throughput. Clicking a node reveals its contract metadata, current version, and declared constraints. The center panel shows a live event stream filtered by event type, with each row displaying the event identifier, source service, timestamp, and delivery status for each subscriber. The right panel shows drift alerts: services whose observed latency or error rate deviates from their declared contract targets. Grafana with a graph plugin, such as Apache ECharts, can render the node-link view using data from the runtime administrative API that exposes the graph in JSON format. Backstage can surface the same contract metadata through its software catalog plugin.

In production environments, these interactions are governed by security and policy controls enforced by the runtime. Service contracts may include authentication requirements, authorization rules, or policy constraints that determine which services are allowed to emit or consume particular events. By associating security policies with contracts and capabilities, UMA environments ensure that event interactions remain controlled while preserving the architectural flexibility of metadata-driven discovery.

AI-Assisted Architecture Discovery

A machine-readable graph is also a machine-analyzable graph.

Analyzing the Architecture

At this stage the system contains three cooperating services. The upload service receives images, the image-tagger analyzes them, and the metadata-indexer stores searchable metadata. Together these components form a service graph that describes how information flows through the architecture.

What makes this structure particularly interesting is that the relationships between services are not hidden inside application code. They are described explicitly through service metadata, event declarations, and capability identifiers. Because this information is machine-readable, any tool that can read the contract files can reconstruct the system's behavior. By observing which events are emitted and which services react to them, a tool can understand how images enter the system, how they are tagged, and how their metadata is stored and made searchable.

The graph_snapshot.sh script in the companion code exports the current graph as JSON with a single command. This JSON output is the starting point for any analysis. A developer can pipe it directly to an LLM API, post it to a monitoring endpoint, or process it with a script that checks for structural properties. The JSON format is simple enough that no preprocessing is required: the edges array contains every relationship in the system, and the waiting array contains every broken dependency.

Discovering Missing Capabilities

Once the architecture can be analyzed programmatically, the next step is recognizing what may be missing. When a tool examines the service graph, it can observe how information flows through the architecture and which events exist at different stages of processing.

In the current example, the system receives images, tags their content, and stores searchable metadata. From the graph's perspective, several processing stages are visible. Images enter the system through image.uploaded. Analysis results flow through image.tagged. Indexed metadata flows through metadata.indexed. Examining the graph also reveals that image.uploaded has only one subscriber: the image-tagger. No service currently reacts to produce visual previews, such as thumbnails.

From an architectural perspective, this observation suggests a potential capability gap. A thumbnail generator service could react to image.uploaded and produce smaller preview versions of the image. These previews could be used in user interfaces, galleries, or search results. The important aspect of this suggestion is that it emerges from analyzing the graph structure, not from reading the application code. Because the service graph exposes how data flows through the system, automated tools can reason about which capabilities are present and which opportunities for additional functionality remain unexplored.

AI Techniques for Graph Analysis

Three AI techniques are applicable to service graph analysis, each suited to a different type of question.

The most immediately demonstrable approach uses large language models. The JSON output from graph_snapshot.sh can be sent directly to any LLM API as context for architectural review. Given the graph JSON, an LLM can describe what the system does in plain language, identify event types that have no subscribers, propose new services that would extend the system logically, and flag structural patterns that typically indicate missing redundancy or tight coupling. This approach requires no training and no additional tooling beyond the graph export command already present in the companion code. A developer can run graph_snapshot.sh lab3-indexer, copy the output, and ask any capable LLM to identify architectural gaps and suggest extensions.

A more advanced approach uses embedding-based similarity to match event names and capability identifiers against a knowledge base of known architectural patterns.

When the system emits image.uploaded but has no subscriber producing thumbnails, a similarity search over a catalog of common image processing pipelines surfaces the thumbnail generation pattern as a likely missing capability. This approach does not require training data from the current system. It works by comparing the current graph structure against a curated library of architectural patterns, making it useful for teams building a new system who want to cross-check their design against established practice.

The most sophisticated approach uses graph neural networks trained on a corpus of service graphs from multiple systems. A GNN can learn structural patterns that historically correlate with production incidents, missing redundancy, or high coupling and apply that learning to a new graph. This approach requires a substantial corpus of labeled graphs for training, which makes it more appropriate for platform teams operating at scale than for individual development teams. As UMA adoption grows and organizations share anonymized graph data, this class of analysis becomes increasingly practical.

In all three cases, the AI analysis provides guidance rather than decisions. Architectural choices remain the responsibility of human engineers who understand the domain, the operational constraints, and the system's long-term direction. What AI analysis adds is the ability to surface patterns and gaps that may not be immediately visible when a system has grown to tens or hundreds of services.

Human-Guided Evolution

Although automated tools can analyze the service graph and suggest potential extensions, architectural decisions ultimately remain the responsibility of human engineers. The role of AI in this context is not to redesign the system automatically but to assist architects by highlighting opportunities that may not be immediately visible.

What makes this collaboration between human architects and automated analysis possible is the explicit nature of UMA systems. Because services describe their behavior through contracts and metadata, the structure of the architecture becomes visible not only to people but also to machines. Architects can rely on tools to explore the architecture, analyze its evolution, and surface potential improvements. Instead of manually inspecting large collections of services, they can observe the service graph and evaluate suggestions generated from its structure.

The architecture becomes easier to understand and easier to evolve. Human architects continue to guide the system's design, while automated analysis helps reveal how the architecture might grow.

Key Takeaways

What began as a single service receiving images became a system of three cooperating components, connected without a single line of orchestration code.

The upload service reports an observable event. The image-tagger declares that it consumes that event and emits a new one. The metadata-indexer declares that it consumes the tagging result. The runtime reads these declarations, builds the routing index, creates the edges, and maintains the graph as the environment changes. No service knows the full topology. Each knows only its own contracts. The system's structure is a consequence of those declarations, not something designed separately from them.

The broken compatibility demonstration makes this concrete in the other direction. When the image-tagger renames its emitted event, the edge to the metadata-indexer disappears and a waiting consumer appears. The graph fracture is visible, named, and localized. The fix is to restore the declaration. The runtime reconnects the services automatically. Architecture recovery comes from restoring declarative consistency, not from rewriting orchestration logic.

Because this structure is defined through metadata, it is also observable. The graph_snapshot.sh command exports the current topology as JSON. The graph_diff.sh command shows exactly what changed between two states. These outputs can drive monitoring dashboards, CI gate checks, and AI-assisted gap analysis, all from the same contract files that govern execution.

The service graph reveals that architecture does not need to be predefined as a rigid pipeline. It can emerge as services declare their capabilities and events, grow as compatible services join, fracture visibly when compatibility breaks, and heal when consistency is restored. Each component remains independent, yet together they form a structure that describes how information moves through the system and proves it through observable evidence.

Services become systems. And systems that describe themselves through metadata can also explain themselves to the tools that help us understand and evolve them.

CHAPTER 10

Security and Trust Boundaries in UMA

Trust and Security in Portable Service Architectures

Introduction: Why Trust Matters in Device-Independent Systems

Modern software systems have outgrown the infrastructure boundaries that once made trust implicit. For most of software history, the question of whether a component could be trusted was answered by where it ran. Applications deployed inside a controlled network, protected by firewalls and managed by a single organization, inherited trust from their environment. Security teams concentrated their efforts on the perimeter. Services communicating within the same operational domain were treated as implicitly safe. Deployment pipelines, network segmentation, and centralized identity systems reinforced these assumptions, and for a long time, the model held.

These conditions shaped an entire generation of architectural decisions. Developers relied on deployment pipelines to guarantee code provenance. Security teams relied on firewalls and network segmentation to regulate access. Platforms assumed that most components running within their boundaries had already passed a controlled validation and review process. In such a context, architecture did not need to explicitly describe trust relationships between services. The infrastructure provided them implicitly.

Over time, software systems have increasingly operated beyond these established boundaries. The rise of mobile computing, edge platforms, and browser-based execution models gradually shifted where code could run. A service that once existed exclusively inside a server cluster might now execute inside a browser runtime compiled to WebAssembly. A component designed for a cloud platform might later be deployed inside an edge node to reduce latency for users in distant regions. In other situations,

E. Piovesan, *Universal Microservices Architecture*, https://doi.org/10.1007/979-8-8688-2794-5_10

components of a system may execute on personal devices or within sandboxed environments belonging to entirely different organizations. As these patterns emerged, one limitation of traditional architecture became increasingly visible. When software moves across environments, the guarantees once provided by infrastructure begin to weaken.

Network boundaries no longer guarantee trust when services operate outside those networks. Deployment pipelines cannot ensure integrity if portable services are executed across multiple runtimes. Platforms cannot assume that all loaded services were developed under consistent operational assumptions. Although portability increases flexibility, it also removes many of the implicit guarantees upon which traditional software systems have depended.

This realization echoes a broader shift across many areas of distributed computing. Systems that scale across organizations, platforms, and geographic boundaries rarely rely on implicit trust. Instead, they rely on explicit descriptions of identity, capability, and behavior. Modern security architectures describe this shift as Zero Trust. This model, formally defined in NIST Special Publication 800-207, holds that no user, device, or service is implicitly trusted based on its network position. Every request must be authenticated, authorized, and continuously validated, regardless of its origin. In distributed protocols, similar principles manifest as capability negotiation, identity verification, and contract validation among participants.

Universal Microservices Architecture applies these principles directly to portable services. Rather than assuming that trust emerges from infrastructure, UMA treats trust as something that must be described and verified through the architecture itself. Each service includes machine-readable metadata that describes who the service is, what it can do, which dependencies it requires, and under which conditions it can safely operate.

The following example shows the structure of this metadata, drawn from the Chapter 10 companion implementation:

```
{
  "kind": "uma.trusted-service-contract",
  "specVersion": "1.0",
  "service": {
    "id": "case-redactor",
    "version": "1.0.0",
    "publisher": "uma.book.team",
```

```
    "trustTier": "internal",
    "placements": ["cloud", "edge"]
  },
  "capabilities": [
    { "id": "case.redaction", "version": "1.0" }
  ],
  "permissions": [
    "storage.read",
    "storage.write",
    "events.publish"
  ],
  "dependencies": [
    {
      "name": "safe-redaction-kit",
      "version": "4.2.0",
      "provenance": "verified",
      "checksum": "sha256-safe-redaction-kit-4.2.0"
    }
  ]
}
```

Service metadata declaring identity, capabilities, permissions, and dependency provenance.

This metadata enables execution environments to evaluate services before execution begins. When a runtime encounters a service, it does not simply load its code and begin execution. Instead, it evaluates the service metadata, verifies declared dependencies, examines capability requirements, and determines how the service may interact with other components in the system. The runtime then decides whether the service can execute in that environment and what constraints must be applied. In the Chapter 10 companion implementation, this decision is governed by a runtime-policy.json file that declares trusted publishers, allowed trust tiers, placement-level permissions, and event routing rules. The runtime evaluates each incoming service contract against this policy before allowing execution to proceed. A service is blocked if its publisher is not on the trusted list, its trust tier is not permitted, or its requested permissions exceed those declared in its contract.

Communication between services follows a similar principle. Interactions are governed by explicit contracts that define the structure of messages, the capabilities that can be invoked, and the conditions under which services may react to events produced by others. In this model, services are no longer isolated pieces of code that happen to run on a platform. They become participants in a structured ecosystem in which identity, capabilities, and constraints are explicitly declared and continuously evaluated.

This approach is particularly important in environments where services may execute across multiple runtimes. A service might run in a browser today, inside an edge runtime tomorrow, and inside a cloud platform the following week. The surrounding infrastructure may change, but the architectural guarantees that govern how the service behaves remain attached to the service itself.

The UMA trust model arises from the necessity to make trust portable. Runtimes interpret service metadata, enforce execution boundaries, regulate inter-service communication, and validate dependencies before integrating a service into a running system. These mechanisms enable systems to evolve dynamically while maintaining the reliability and safety previously ensured by tightly controlled environments.

The following diagram illustrates how the three layers of the UMA trust model relate to one another:

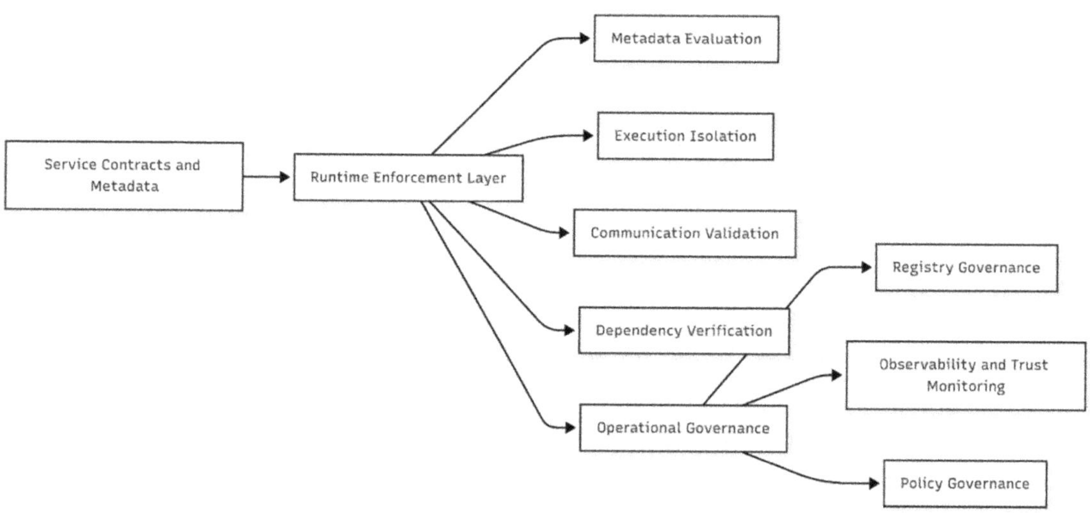

Figure 10-1. *Service metadata declaring identity, capabilities, permissions, and dependency provenance*

Subsequent sections analyze the architectural mechanisms supporting this model and detail how UMA runtimes interpret service metadata, validate dependencies, and regulate service interactions across heterogeneous execution environments.

Understanding the Risk Landscape

Risks in Portable Execution Environments

Software architectures have traditionally been designed around relatively stable execution environments. Applications were deployed within controlled infrastructure, protected by network boundaries, and governed by centralized operational processes. These conditions created implicit assumptions about trust. Services were expected to run within known environments, communicate with systems managed by the same organization, and depend on libraries that had passed through controlled development pipelines. As software systems evolved toward distributed architectures, some of these assumptions began to weaken. Microservices, cloud platforms, and event-driven systems have increased the number of independent components participating in a running system. Even so, most services still operated within a shared operational domain, usually inside a cloud platform or enterprise infrastructure where trust relationships could be managed centrally.

Portable architectures accelerate this transition by enabling services to operate across a broader range of environments. In a portable system, services may execute across browsers, edge nodes, mobile devices, and cloud platforms. A service that originates in one environment may later run in another without modification. Components that interact at runtime may have been developed by different teams, deployed through different processes, or executed under different security policies. This mobility introduces risks that traditional architectural models were not designed to address.

In many real-world systems, UMA services are introduced gradually rather than replacing existing systems immediately. Legacy services can be wrapped with lightweight adapter components that expose UMA-compatible capability metadata while delegating execution to the original implementation. This approach allows the runtime to discover and interact with legacy functionality through the same metadata-driven mechanisms used by native UMA services, enabling incremental adoption without requiring large-scale rewrites.

A trust boundary is the point at which a system transitions from one security domain to another. It is typically where data, identity claims, or execution authority move between components operating at different levels of trust. Security and access control are enforced at these boundaries through service metadata and runtime policies. Each service declares the resources it requires, such as data access, external APIs, or system capabilities, and the runtime validates these permissions before execution. This approach allows UMA environments to enforce consistent trust boundaries across client, edge, and cloud runtimes while preventing services from accessing capabilities that were not explicitly declared.

To analyze these risks systematically, this chapter applies the STRIDE threat model as a classification framework. STRIDE was developed at Microsoft as a structured method for identifying security threats across distributed systems. It identifies six categories of threat: Spoofing, Tampering, Repudiation, Information Disclosure, Denial of Service, and Elevation of Privilege. Each risk category described in this section maps to one or more of these threat types, making the analysis applicable to standard security reviews and threat modeling exercises. The table below summarizes these mappings before each risk is examined in detail.

Table 10-1. *UMA portable architecture risk categories mapped to STRIDE threat types*

Risk Category	STRIDE Threat Types	Primary Concern
Loss of Infrastructure Trust Boundaries	Spoofing, Elevation of Privilege	Services impersonate trusted components when infrastructure verification is absent
Runtime Heterogeneity	Tampering, Denial of Service	Inconsistent runtime constraints alter service behavior or prevent execution
Supply Chain and Dependency Risks	Tampering, Elevation of Privilege	Compromised or unverified dependencies introduce malicious or unstable behavior
Capability Abuse and Event Cascades	Elevation of Privilege, Denial of Service	Unrestricted capability access or unbounded event reactions destabilize the system
Execution Environment Drift	Tampering, Repudiation	Services behave differently across environments, making behavior difficult to verify or audit

Understanding these risks is essential before introducing the architectural mechanisms that address them. The following subsections examine the primary threats that arise when services become portable and execute across heterogeneous environments.

Loss of Infrastructure Trust Boundaries

Traditional software systems rely heavily on the stability of the infrastructure in which they run. Applications are typically deployed inside environments controlled by a single organization, where network topology, runtime configuration, and operational policies are well understood. These conditions allow architects to make assumptions about trust. Services inside the same environment are often treated as implicitly trustworthy, and security controls focus primarily on protecting the boundaries between internal systems and external actors. This model works reasonably well when systems operate within a clearly defined infrastructure perimeter. Network segmentation, access control policies, and deployment pipelines provide layers of protection that help maintain system integrity. Services running inside the same operational domain benefit from shared identity systems, centralized monitoring, and consistent security enforcement.

Portable architectures fundamentally challenge these assumptions. A service may be executed in environments that were not originally designed to host it. It may run inside a browser sandbox, an edge runtime, or a lightweight execution environment embedded within another application. In some cases, services may move across multiple environments during their lifecycle. Under these conditions, the traditional notion of an internal system boundary becomes difficult to maintain. The environment executing a service may not share the same identity infrastructure, security policies, or operational controls as the environment where the service was originally developed.

This shift weakens several assumptions on which traditional architectures depend. The location of a service no longer guarantees that it is part of a trusted system. The infrastructure may not consistently enforce security policies. Components that interact at runtime may originate from different deployment pipelines and may be governed by different operational practices. Trust cannot be inferred from infrastructure alone. Systems must rely on mechanisms that allow services to describe their identity, capabilities, and dependencies independently of the environment in which they run.

The diagram below contrasts the traditional trust model, where services operate within a shared network boundary, with the portable architecture model, where services execute across heterogeneous runtimes with no shared perimeter:

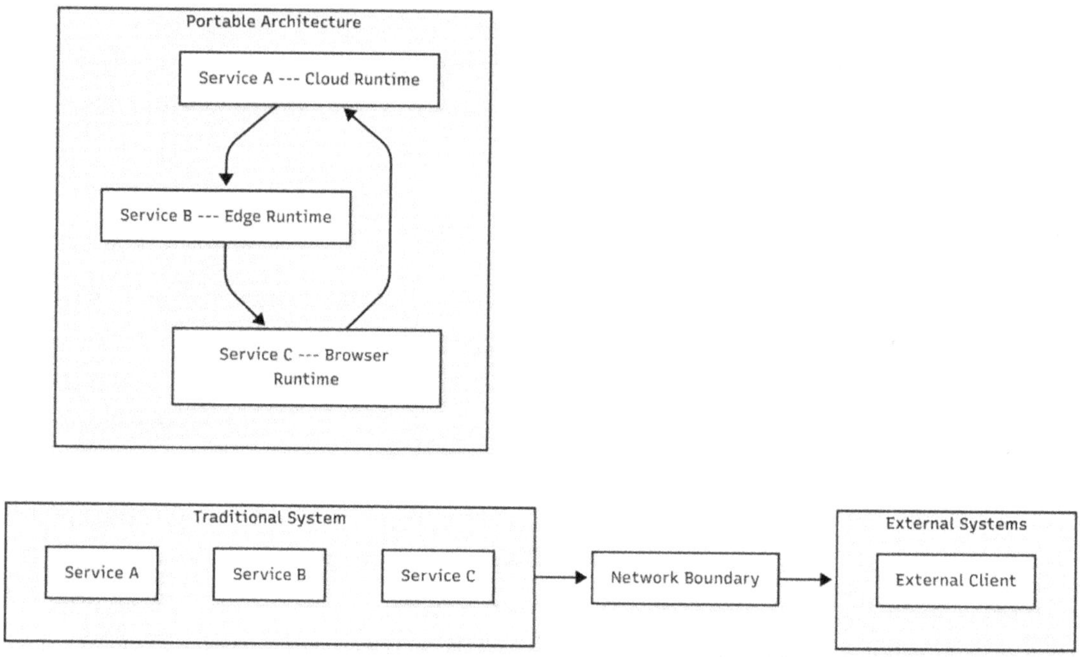

***Figure 10-2.** Traditional infrastructure trust boundaries compared with portable service execution across heterogeneous runtimes. In the traditional model, network position establishes trust. In a portable architecture, each service must carry and declare its own trust credentials.*

Runtime Heterogeneity

For many years, architects could assume that most services in a system would execute within a small and predictable set of environments. Applications typically ran on application servers, inside containers, or within virtual machines hosted on controlled infrastructure. Although these environments differed in implementation, they shared many of the same underlying assumptions. Processes ran on an operating system, networking behaved as expected, and security controls were enforced through well-understood mechanisms. This relative uniformity simplified architectural reasoning. When a service was designed and deployed, its behavior could be evaluated within the context of a known runtime environment.

Today, a single service may execute across a wide variety of runtimes. It may run in a container in a cloud environment, on a lightweight edge runtime near users, or in a browser sandbox compiled to WebAssembly. In some systems, parts of the same application may operate simultaneously across several of these environments. Although these runtimes may support similar programming languages and frameworks, they are not architecturally equivalent. Each environment exposes different capabilities and enforces different constraints. Browser environments restrict access to the file system and operating system. Edge runtimes often impose strict limits on execution time and resource usage. Serverless platforms introduce their own lifecycle and scaling behaviors. Even WebAssembly runtimes, designed to provide a consistent execution model, may expose different host interfaces across platforms.

A service designed with the assumptions of one runtime may behave unpredictably in another. Dependencies that function correctly within a containerized environment may rely on features that are unavailable or restricted in a browser sandbox. Security guarantees may vary depending on the strength of the runtime's isolation model or the policies enforced by the host environment. In such conditions, the runtime environment itself becomes a variable that influences a system's behavior and safety. Architects can no longer assume that a service will operate under identical conditions wherever it runs. Instead, systems must account for the diversity of execution environments and evaluate whether a service can safely operate within the capabilities and constraints of the runtime that hosts it.

Supply Chain and Dependency Risks

Software systems rarely exist as isolated units of code. Even relatively small services rely on a wide range of external components, including libraries, frameworks, runtime interfaces, and other services. Over time, modern development practices have made this reliance more pronounced. Package managers, shared frameworks, and open-source ecosystems allow developers to assemble complex systems quickly by integrating components from many different contributors.

In traditional architectures, these dependencies are typically managed within a controlled development and deployment environment. Build pipelines, validate dependencies before software is released, and provision runtime environments with carefully curated libraries and system components. Although supply chain risks have always existed, the infrastructure surrounding the system often provides mechanisms to review and control which dependencies are included in the production environment.

Portable architectures introduce additional complexity in dependency management. When services are designed to execute across multiple environments, their dependency surface expands. A portable service may rely not only on application libraries but also on runtime-specific interfaces, host capabilities, and external modules that vary by execution environment. Components compiled for environments such as WebAssembly may depend on host functions provided by the runtime, while services operating at the edge may rely on platform-specific APIs for storage, networking, or event processing.

These layers of dependency create additional pathways through which vulnerabilities or malicious code can enter a system. A library introduced during development may contain vulnerabilities that only appear under certain runtime conditions. A runtime extension or plugin may expose capabilities that allow unintended access to system resources. In distributed systems where services interact dynamically, one compromised component can propagate unexpected behavior across multiple parts of the system. The challenge is not limited to malicious actors. Dependency complexity can also introduce operational risks. Version incompatibilities, inconsistent runtime interfaces, and unexpected interactions between components can cause services to behave differently depending on where they execute.

As services become more portable and ecosystems become more interconnected, the integrity of the software supply chain becomes a central architectural concern. Systems must be able to understand the dependencies a service relies on, evaluate their provenance, and verify that they are compatible with the runtime environment in which the service will execute.

To operationalize supply chain trust, architects should adopt concrete verification techniques across five areas.

Signature-based verification uses cryptographic signatures to confirm that a dependency was published by a trusted party. Tools such as Sigstore allow publishers to sign artifacts and consumers to verify those signatures at download time, ensuring a library has not been swapped or injected with malicious code after publication.

Hash-based integrity checks compare a dependency's cryptographic hash against a known-good value published by the maintainer. If the hashes differ, the dependency has been modified and should be rejected. In the Chapter 10 companion implementation, every declared dependency includes a checksum field that the runtime evaluates before allowing execution to proceed.

Provenance attestation standards such as in-toto and SLSA (Supply-chain Levels for Software Artifacts) provide a framework for recording and verifying the full build lineage of an artifact, from source commit through packaging and distribution. These standards allow a runtime or deployment pipeline to confirm not only that a dependency is intact but also that it was produced through a verifiable process.

Automated compatibility checks, implemented through tools such as OWASP Dependency-Check and Syft, scan declared dependencies for known vulnerabilities and version conflicts. Integrating these checks into CI/CD pipelines catches issues before services reach production environments.

Policy enforcement tools such as Open Policy Agent allow organizations to define machine-readable rules governing which dependency sources and versions are permitted. The runtime evaluates each dependency declaration against these rules before execution begins, blocking services that rely on disallowed or unverified components.

However, operationalizing these techniques introduces its own set of challenges. Integrating new verification tools with existing CI/CD pipelines may require custom adapters and ongoing maintenance, especially in organizations with heterogeneous technology stacks or legacy deployment practices. Automated checks sometimes produce false positives or block legitimate deployments, leading to delayed releases and operational friction. As systems scale, the volume of artifacts and dependency verifications can strain build infrastructure or overwhelm monitoring systems. To mitigate these challenges, teams should invest in careful tool selection and phased rollout, set clear escalation paths for handling blocking issues, and regularly review verification rules for accuracy and relevance. Establishing feedback loops between development, security, and operations teams helps identify recurring issues and continuously adapt the supply chain trust model to real-world conditions.

Capability Abuse and Event Cascades

Distributed systems rely heavily on communication between independent components. Services exchange messages, respond to events, and expose capabilities that other parts of the system may invoke. These patterns allow systems to evolve in a modular way, enabling independent services to collaborate without requiring tight coupling between their implementations. In traditional architectures, the scope of these interactions is often constrained by infrastructure boundaries and predefined service interfaces. Services typically communicate with a known set of counterparts, and the pathways through which messages travel are relatively predictable. Even in microservice architectures, service discovery mechanisms and API gateways often help regulate how services interact.

Portable architectures create a more dynamic and variable operational environment. When services are designed to execute across heterogeneous runtimes, they may interact with components that were not originally anticipated during development. Event-driven systems amplify this effect. A service may subscribe to events produced by other services, react to signals emitted by the runtime environment, or invoke capabilities exposed by newly deployed components.

A service reacting to an event may trigger a cascade of additional actions across multiple parts of the system. Under certain conditions, these reactions may produce behaviors that were never explicitly designed. Other services may invoke a capability in ways that exceed the expectations of its original developers. In complex distributed systems, such interactions can propagate quickly, making it difficult to predict how the system will respond to certain stimuli. If services are allowed to invoke capabilities without clear restrictions, a compromised component may exploit those capabilities to influence other parts of the system. Poorly governed event subscriptions may allow services to react to signals that expose sensitive information or trigger unintended operations.

These challenges highlight the importance of controlling how services communicate and which capabilities they can access. In portable architectures, the interaction surface between services must be carefully defined and monitored to prevent unintended behaviors from spreading across the system.

Execution Environment Drift

Even when a service is designed to be portable, the environment in which it executes continues to influence its behavior. Portable architectures allow services to move across platforms, but the characteristics of each runtime environment still shape how those services interact with the surrounding system. In traditional deployments, execution environments tend to remain relatively stable. A service deployed within a container platform or application server usually runs under consistent operating system assumptions, resource limits, and security policies. When behavior changes, those changes are often tied to explicit updates in configuration or software versions.

Portable systems introduce greater variability in execution environments. A service may execute within a cloud runtime during development, later run inside an edge environment to reduce latency for users, and eventually operate within a browser sandbox compiled to WebAssembly. Each of these environments may impose different limits on memory usage, networking capabilities, file system access, and execution time. Even when the underlying code remains unchanged, the surrounding runtime can alter the conditions under which the service operates.

Such differences can lead to subtle behavioral drift. A dependency that performs reliably within a server environment may fail when executed in a restricted sandbox. A service designed to process events in a long-running process may behave differently when deployed in a serverless environment where execution lifecycles are short-lived. Differences in host capabilities, configuration defaults, or available system interfaces may cause a service to produce different results depending on where it runs. Such variations can be difficult to detect during development. A system that appears stable in one environment may exhibit unexpected behavior once deployed into another runtime.

Consider a financial service originally developed and thoroughly tested in a containerized cloud environment, later deployed to edge devices at retail locations. In the new environment, subtle differences in supported cryptographic libraries and restricted file system access resulted in authentication failures that went undetected during initial testing. Transactions began to fail intermittently, causing operational disruption and loss of business confidence. Had UMA principles been in place, the deployment process would have included explicit, machine-readable metadata detailing the service's cryptographic requirements and storage expectations. The edge runtime could have blocked the incompatible deployment by evaluating this metadata before execution and signaling the need for environment adjustments or service adaptation.

A similar pattern emerges in other domains. In an IoT deployment for smart healthcare facilities, a patient monitoring service might be designed and tested in a hospital data center, then later deployed to run on embedded gateways within the healthcare facility. If runtime memory constraints or differences in supported sensor interfaces are not clearly declared and validated, this migration can result in dropped data, delayed alerts, or device integration failures. By applying UMA's metadata-driven verification, these issues can be detected before rollout, allowing the runtime to flag incompatible deployments and prompting corrective action.

For portable architectures to remain reliable, systems must be able to understand a service's requirements and evaluate whether a given runtime environment can safely support them. Without mechanisms that allow runtimes to interpret service expectations and enforce compatibility constraints, execution environment drift can undermine both reliability and security. The next section introduces the architectural principles that address these challenges and explains how Universal Microservices Architecture uses service metadata and runtime validation to maintain trust across heterogeneous environments.

The UMA Trust Model

Trust As an Architectural Property

For much of the history of distributed systems, trust has been closely tied to infrastructure. Services were considered trustworthy because of where they ran. If a component executed within the boundaries of a controlled network, it was generally assumed to belong to the system and to operate under the same operational policies as the rest of the application. This assumption shaped many architectural decisions. Security controls were concentrated at the system's perimeter. Internal services often communicated freely with one another because the environment itself was considered trustworthy. Deployment pipelines, network segmentation, and centralized identity systems helped reinforce these boundaries.

As shown earlier, portable architectures challenge these assumptions. When services transition across diverse runtimes, infrastructure boundaries alone can't determine trustworthiness. A service might run in environments not initially intended for it and interact with components from various teams, deployment processes, or operational areas. In such scenarios, location isn't a reliable trust indicator. Consequently, architectures that depend solely on infrastructure boundaries find it difficult to provide consistent security assurances.

A different approach is required. Instead of inferring trust from the environment in which a service runs, portable architectures must express trust through the architecture itself. Services must provide verifiable information that allows the system to evaluate their identity, capabilities, and the conditions under which they can safely participate in the running system.

In this model, trust is established as an architectural property rather than as an environmental assumption. A service is not trusted simply because it is present within a runtime environment. Instead, it must present the information necessary for the runtime to evaluate whether it can safely execute and interact with other components. This information includes the service's identity, the capabilities it exposes, the dependencies it requires, and the constraints under which it is intended to operate. Execution environments then use this information to determine how a service may participate in the system. Runtimes evaluate service metadata before execution begins, verify compatibility with the current environment, and regulate how services communicate with one another. Trust emerges from the continuous validation of these architectural declarations rather than from implicit assumptions about infrastructure.

This shift mirrors broader trends in modern distributed systems. Security architectures increasingly rely on continuous verification rather than perimeter-based trust. Software supply chains emphasize provenance and transparency into dependencies. Distributed protocols depend on explicit contracts that define how independent components interact. Portable service architectures follow the same principle. When services carry the information required to evaluate their identity, capabilities, and dependencies, systems can maintain reliable trust relationships even as services move across heterogeneous environments.

The following subsections examine the architectural mechanisms that enable this model, beginning with the role of service identity and provenance in establishing the origin and authenticity of portable services.

Service Identity and Provenance

In any distributed system, the first step in establishing trust is understanding where a component comes from. When services operate inside a controlled infrastructure, this question is often answered indirectly through the deployment process. Components that reach a production environment have typically passed through internal build pipelines, version control systems, and operational reviews. The infrastructure itself becomes the mechanism for establishing provenance.

Portable architectures complicate this process. A service designed to execute across multiple environments may not always be deployed through a single centralized pipeline. It may be discovered dynamically through a registry, distributed as a portable module, or executed within runtimes that operate outside the direct control of the organization that produced the service. Under these conditions, infrastructure alone cannot guarantee that a service originates from a trusted source. For portable systems to remain trustworthy, services must carry verifiable identity information that allows runtimes to evaluate their provenance.

Service identity establishes a stable reference that uniquely identifies a component within the system. This identity includes the service name, version, publisher, and trust tier. These attributes allow the runtime and other services to recognize the component and evaluate whether it meets the requirements for participation. Identity alone, however, is not sufficient. Systems must also verify that the service being executed genuinely originates from the declared source.

Provenance mechanisms provide this verification. Through signatures, artifact validation, or trusted registries, runtimes can confirm that a service has not been altered since it was produced and that a recognized entity published it. In practice, service identity is established through asymmetric cryptography. A publisher signs a service artifact using a private key, typically with an Ed25519 or ECDSA P-256 algorithm. The runtime holds or retrieves the corresponding public key, either from a trusted certificate authority or from a pinned key registry, and uses it to verify the signature before execution.

In the Chapter 10 companion implementation, publisher trust is declared explicitly in the runtime-policy.json file under the trustedPublishers field. This mirrors a certificate authority model where the policy file acts as the trust anchor: only services whose publisher identity matches an entry in the trusted list are permitted to execute. The following excerpt shows how this is expressed:

```
{
  "trustedPublishers": [
    "uma.book.team",
    "uma.platform.ops"
  ]
}
```

Publisher trust declarations from runtime-policy.json. Only services whose publisher field matches one of these values are permitted to execute.

Private keys used for signing must be stored in hardware security modules or secrets management systems such as HashiCorp Vault or cloud-provider key management services. They must never be embedded in service artifacts or committed to source control. The public key or certificate used for verification should be distributed through a controlled registry or embedded in the runtime policy, not retrieved dynamically from an untrusted source at execution time.

Establishing identity and provenance becomes especially important in portable architectures where services may be discovered and executed dynamically. A runtime may encounter a service for the first time during execution and must decide whether to allow that service to participate in the system. Without a mechanism to verify the component's origin and authenticity, the runtime has little basis for making that decision. By embedding identity and provenance information directly within service metadata, portable architectures enable runtimes to evaluate service authenticity before execution. This verification step ensures that components participating in the system originate from trusted sources and have not been modified in ways that could compromise their behavior.

Once the origin of a service has been established, the system can move to the next dimension of trust: understanding what the service is allowed to do.

Capability Declarations

Once the origin of a service has been established, the system must determine what that service is allowed to do. In portable architectures, this question cannot be answered solely by examining the service's code or relying on assumptions about the environment in which it runs. Instead, services must explicitly describe the capabilities they expose and the operations they are intended to perform.

A capability represents an operation or function that a service offers to the rest of the system. Examples include evaluating a feature flag, retrieving configuration data, processing an event, or transforming input data into a new representation. By explicitly declaring these capabilities, a service allows the runtime and other system components to understand how it is intended to participate in the architecture. In traditional systems, such behavior is often inferred through API definitions or service interfaces. Portable architectures require a more explicit approach. Because services may be discovered and executed dynamically across heterogeneous environments, the runtime must interpret service behavior without relying on assumptions about the surrounding infrastructure.

Capability declarations fulfill this requirement by making a service's behavior visible through its metadata. When a service is published or registered, it declares the capabilities it exposes and provides information on how to invoke them. This information includes the structure of inputs and outputs, the events a service may emit or consume, and any constraints governing the use of the capability.

The following diagram shows how capability declarations flow from a portable service through its metadata to the execution runtime and onward to other services:

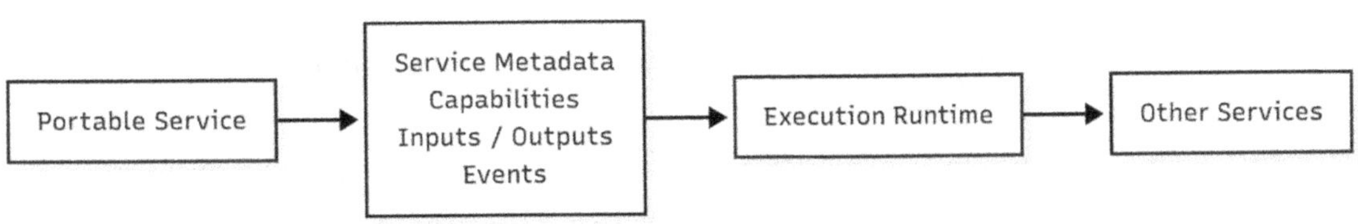

***Figure 10-3.** Capability declarations allow runtimes to understand how portable services interact with the system. Service metadata describes the capabilities exposed by a service, enabling execution environments to validate interactions and regulate communication between components*

Execution environments use these declarations to regulate how services interact. Before allowing a capability to be invoked, the runtime can verify that the caller is permitted to access it and that the interaction complies with the system's architectural contracts. In practice, enforcement is achieved through runtime checks and integration with policy engines. When a capability invocation is requested, the runtime evaluates the service metadata and contract using policy evaluation tools such as Open Policy Agent or custom rule engines to determine whether the operation is allowed by defined security and operational rules. These engines act as enforcement points within the execution flow, automatically rejecting or permitting requests based on organizational policy and contract compliance. Runtime checks validate constraints such as input structure, access rights, and invocation context before allowing the operation to proceed.

By evaluating capabilities in this manner, the runtime reduces the risk of unintended interactions among loosely coupled services. Capability declarations also facilitate system extensibility. New services can introduce additional capabilities without requiring existing components to be tightly integrated with their internal implementations. Provided that capability definitions remain consistent, services can evolve independently while still participating in the broader system architecture.

In portable architectures, these declarations become a key mechanism for controlling how services interact across heterogeneous runtimes. By making capabilities explicit and verifiable, the architecture can regulate interactions between services even when they execute in different environments.

Dependency Transparency

Portable services rarely operate in isolation. A service that exposes capabilities typically relies on other components to perform its work. These components may include supporting services, runtime features, external modules, or libraries that provide essential functionality. In conventional architectures, many of these dependencies remain implicit. Build systems declare some of them through package managers or dependency manifests, while others are assumed to exist within the runtime environment. Application servers, container images, and operating systems often provide libraries and interfaces that services rely on without explicitly declaring them at the architectural level.

These assumptions become problematic when services are expected to execute across heterogeneous environments. Portable architectures allow the same service artifact to run within multiple runtimes. A component may execute in a containerized cloud environment, on an edge runtime, or in a WebAssembly sandbox embedded in a host application. Each of these environments provides different capabilities and exposes different runtime interfaces. Dependencies that exist in one environment may be unavailable or restricted in another.

Dependency transparency refers to the practice of declaring the external components and runtime capabilities required by a service in its architectural description. These declarations allow execution environments to evaluate whether a service can operate safely within the current runtime context. A service may depend on other services that provide supporting functionality such as configuration management, authentication, or data access. It may require runtime capabilities such as networking, time sources, or persistent storage interfaces. It may also rely on external modules, libraries, or plugins that extend its behavior.

By explicitly declaring these dependencies, the system can reason about service compatibility before execution begins. A runtime can verify that the required dependencies are available, confirm that their versions are compatible, and determine whether the current environment exposes the capabilities the service requires. The following example shows how a service declares its dependencies in the companion implementation:

```
{
  "service": "feature-flag-evaluator",
  "version": "1.0.0",
  "capabilities": ["evaluate-flag"],
  "dependencies": [
    {
      "service": "flag-config",
      "version": ">=1.2.0"
    }
  ],
  "runtimeRequirements": [
    "network",
    "clock"
  ]
}
```

Service metadata declaring dependencies and runtime requirements. The runtime evaluates these declarations before execution to verify compatibility with the current environment.

Such declarations allow the runtime to evaluate compatibility between services and their execution environment. If a required dependency is unavailable or incompatible, the runtime can prevent the service from starting or restrict its participation in the system. Dependency transparency, therefore, enables portable services to be evaluated and integrated safely across heterogeneous environments. By exposing the relationships between services, runtime capabilities, and external modules, the architecture provides the information necessary for runtimes to enforce compatibility and maintain system integrity.

Contract-Based Interaction

In portable architectures, service interactions cannot depend on implicit assumptions about implementation details or runtime environments. A service may execute in a browser, at the network edge, or within a cloud platform. The language used to implement the service, the runtime in which it executes, and the infrastructure surrounding it may all differ. Under these conditions, traditional integration patterns that rely on shared libraries or tightly coupled APIs quickly become fragile. Reliable interoperability requires a different foundation. That foundation is the service contract.

A contract defines the formal interface through which a service exposes its capabilities. It specifies the operations that can be invoked, the structure of the data exchanged, and the conditions under which those operations are considered valid. Unlike conventional interface definitions embedded within source code, contracts in portable architectures are expressed as machine-readable artifacts that exist independently of the service implementation. This separation allows the system's interaction model to be reasoned about, validated, and enforced without requiring access to the internal logic of the participating services.

The contract establishes a clear boundary between provider and consumer. A consumer interacts with the service exclusively through the interface described by the contract. The service guarantees that requests conforming to the contract will be processed according to the defined semantics. Because the contract is independent of implementation, the service's internal structure can evolve without affecting external components, provided the contract remains stable. This principle is particularly important in systems designed for portability. When services move across execution environments, assumptions about serialization formats, network protocols, or runtime capabilities cannot be taken for granted. The contract, therefore, becomes the authoritative description of the interaction model. It describes not only the shape of requests and responses, but also the expectations that govern their use, including validation constraints, versioning information, and compatibility guarantees.

The following example demonstrates the structure of a contract describing a single operation exposed by a service:

```
    {
  "service": "feature-flag-evaluator",
  "version": "1.0.0",
  "operations": {
    "evaluateFlag": {
      "inputs": {
        "userId": "string",
        "flagKey": "string"
      },
      "outputs": {
        "enabled": "boolean"
      }
    }
  }
```

A contract describing the evaluateFlag operation. The inputs and outputs are defined explicitly, allowing callers to construct valid requests and interpret responses without knowledge of the service's internal implementation.

The architectural value of contracts extends beyond documentation. Because contracts are expressed in a structured and machine-readable form, they can be interpreted by tooling and runtime platforms. Validation can occur before the service logic is executed, ensuring that requests conform to the expected schema. Version compatibility can be verified automatically, preventing incompatible components from interacting. In systems that support capability discovery, contracts may also serve as the mechanism through which services advertise their available functionality.

In practice, metadata validation and capability matching incur minimal overhead because they rely on lightweight structured-data comparisons rather than on dynamic code inspection. In most deployments, discovery and validation occur during service initialization or capability registration, keeping runtime execution paths efficient.

This shift from implicit integration to explicit agreement has important consequences for system design. Instead of binding components together through shared code or informal API conventions, the architecture treats service interactions as verifiable relationships defined by contracts. In portable architectures such as Universal Microservices Architecture, this principle allows services to remain interoperable across heterogeneous runtimes. A service compiled to WebAssembly and executed in a browser can interact with another service running in a cloud environment as long as both sides adhere to the same contract definition. The portability of the service does not compromise the predictability of its interactions because the contract preserves the system's structural and behavioral expectations.

Contract-based interaction functions as a fundamental mechanism for maintaining architectural integrity in portable systems. By replacing implicit coupling with explicit agreements, services can evolve independently while ensuring reliable collaboration across diverse environments.

Enforcement at Runtime

In portable systems, where services may run across multiple environments and interact dynamically, relying solely on design-time guarantees is insufficient. The runtime system must ensure that the interactions and behaviors defined by the architecture are respected during system operation. Rather than acting only as an execution host, the runtime becomes an enforcement layer that evaluates services and their interactions before execution occurs. This evaluation ensures that services conform to the constraints defined by their contracts, that their dependencies are valid and trustworthy, and that communication between components follows the system's established rules.

This enforcement role is particularly important in architectures where services can be deployed or executed in different contexts. A service that runs safely in one environment may behave differently when executed elsewhere if assumptions about dependencies, communication channels, or execution boundaries are not verified. The runtime provides the mechanism that removes these uncertainties by validating the conditions required for safe execution.

Enforcing these rules introduces additional validation steps during service invocation. Although these checks add modest runtime overhead, they provide the guarantees required for services to operate safely across heterogeneous environments. The following diagram shows where each enforcement mechanism operates within the service invocation lifecycle:

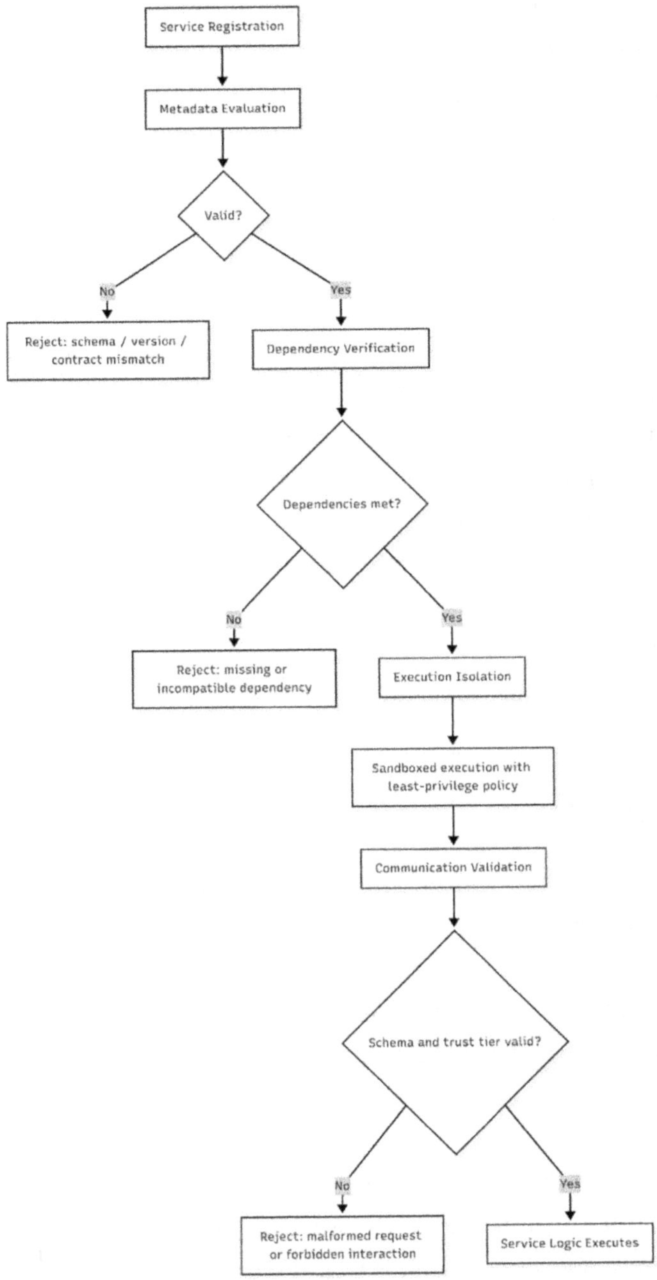

Figure 10-4. *Runtime enforcement pipeline. Each gate must pass before execution proceeds to the next stage. A rejection at any point prevents the service from reaching execution*

In this model, enforcement occurs at four points in the service invocation lifecycle. Before a service is executed, the runtime evaluates the service's metadata and verifies that the request matches the contract defined for that capability. The runtime also ensures that execution boundaries are respected, preventing services from exceeding their intended privileges or accessing restricted resources. Communication between services is validated to guarantee that messages conform to the expected structure and security constraints. The service's declared dependencies are verified to ensure that the components required for execution are present and trustworthy.

In the Chapter 10 companion implementation, these checks are performed against uma.trusted-service-contract artifacts. Every service in the system declares its identity, trust tier, publisher, permissions, dependencies, and event contracts using this structure. The runtime evaluates each field before allowing execution to proceed. A service that omits a required field, declares an untrusted publisher, or requests a permission not listed in its contract is rejected before its logic is ever reached. Together, these enforcement mechanisms transform architectural definitions into operational guarantees. The runtime does not simply execute services. It evaluates each interaction to ensure that it conforms to the architectural rules defined for the system.

The following subsections examine each enforcement mechanism in detail.

Metadata Evaluation

In portable architectures, the runtime must interpret capabilities and requirements without relying on implementation details. This interpretation is made possible through service metadata. Metadata provides the structured description of a service's identity, capabilities, inputs, outputs, dependencies, and execution requirements. Before a service is executed, the runtime evaluates this metadata to determine whether the invocation is valid and whether the environment satisfies the conditions required for safe execution.

When a request is made to invoke a service capability, the runtime inspects the service's metadata. The runtime verifies that the requested operation exists, that the provided inputs match the schema defined by the contract, and that any declared constraints are satisfied. If the request does not conform to these conditions, the invocation is rejected before the service logic is executed. This validation step protects the system from a range of potential failures. Invalid input structures, incompatible contract versions, and unsupported capabilities can be detected immediately. By performing this verification before execution, the runtime prevents malformed interactions from propagating through the system and producing unpredictable behavior.

Metadata evaluation also enables runtime environments to interpret services consistently across different execution contexts. Because the metadata describes the service in a machine-readable form, the runtime can apply the same validation logic regardless of where the service is deployed. A service executed in a browser environment, at the network edge, or within a cloud runtime can be validated using the same metadata rules.

The following example shows the metadata structure that the runtime evaluates during invocation in the companion implementation:

```
  {
 "kind": "uma.trusted-service-contract",
 "specVersion": "1.0",
 "service": {
   "id": "feature-flag-evaluator",
   "version": "1.0.0",
   "publisher": "uma.book.team",
   "trustTier": "internal",
   "placements": ["cloud", "edge"]
 },
 "operations": {
   "evaluateFlag": {
     "inputs": {
       "userId": "string",
       "flagKey": "string"
     },
     "outputs": {
       "enabled": "boolean"
     }
   }
 },
 "dependencies": [
   "user-context-service"
 ]
}
```

A uma.trusted-service-contract evaluated by the runtime before execution. The runtime verifies the operation exists, the input schema matches the request payload, and all declared dependencies are available.

When a request is received, the runtime reviews the associated metadata to verify that the operation exists and that the request payload matches the predefined input schema. If these conditions are met, the runtime advances to the next enforcement stage. If not, the request is rejected, and an error is returned to the caller. This metadata assessment offers a reliable method for validating service interactions prior to execution. By analyzing the metadata linked to each service, the runtime guarantees that interactions comply with the system's architectural rules. This strategy minimizes dependence on implicit assumptions and ensures that portable services function consistently across different environments.

Execution Isolation

Execution isolation ensures that services operate within clearly defined boundaries, preventing them from interfering with other system components. In portable architectures, where services may execute across heterogeneous environments, maintaining these boundaries is essential for preserving system stability and security. Without isolation, a faulty or malicious service could access resources beyond its intended scope, modify shared state, or disrupt the execution of other services.

The runtime enforces isolation by restricting the capabilities available to each service during execution. A service receives access only to the resources explicitly granted to it, such as memory regions, network interfaces, or external capabilities. Any attempt to access resources outside these boundaries is blocked by the runtime environment. This approach follows the principle of least privilege, ensuring that services operate with only the permissions required to perform their intended functions.

In portable systems, isolation is often implemented through sandboxed execution environments. Sandboxes restrict how a service interacts with the underlying system by limiting access to the host environment. The runtime mediates all interactions between the service and external resources, preventing unauthorized operations. This mediation allows services compiled for one environment to execute safely in another without exposing the host system to unintended behavior.

Isolation mechanisms must also ensure that services cannot interfere with each other's execution state. Memory isolation prevents a service from reading or modifying another component's memory. Execution boundaries ensure that failures in one service do not propagate into unrelated parts of the system. These guarantees are particularly important in systems where services may be dynamically discovered or loaded at runtime.

In environments that support portable execution formats such as WebAssembly, isolation is reinforced by the execution model's design. The runtime provides a controlled environment where services operate within a constrained memory space and interact with the external world only through explicitly defined interfaces. These interfaces are mediated by the runtime, which can enforce policies governing access to system capabilities.

The following example illustrates how a runtime restricts a service's capabilities during execution:

```
    {
  "execution": {
    "memoryLimitMB": 64,
    "allowedCapabilities": [
      "http-client",
      "time-access"
    ],
    "filesystemAccess": "none"
  }
}
```

Runtime execution constraints applied to a service. The service is limited to a specific memory allocation and may only access the capabilities explicitly listed. Attempts to use unsupported capabilities or exceed defined resource limits are rejected by the runtime.

Execution isolation ensures that services remain within their designated operational boundaries. This containment preserves system integrity and prevents services from affecting the execution state or resources of other components. In portable architectures, where services may operate across heterogeneous environments, isolation serves as a foundational safeguard, enabling independent services to execute safely without compromising overall system stability.

Communication Validation

Services in a distributed architecture interact through messages, requests, and events. These interactions represent one of the most sensitive points in the system because they form the boundaries through which services exchange information and invoke capabilities. If communication is not validated, incorrect or malicious messages can propagate through the system, leading to failures, inconsistent behavior, or unintended access to functionality.

Communication validation ensures that interactions between services conform to the contracts defined by the architecture. Before a message reaches the service's logic, the runtime verifies that the message's structure and content match the expectations described in the service contract. This verification prevents malformed requests, incompatible versions, or unexpected data from entering the execution flow.

The validation process begins with schema verification. Each operation defined by a contract specifies the structure of the input data it accepts. The runtime evaluates incoming requests against this schema, ensuring that required fields are present and that data types match the expected definitions. Requests that fail this validation step are rejected before execution proceeds.

Version compatibility is another important aspect of communication validation. As services evolve, contracts may introduce new fields or modify existing structures. The runtime must determine whether a request corresponds to a compatible contract version. When incompatibilities are detected, the interaction can be rejected or routed through system-defined compatibility mechanisms.

Communication validation also plays a role in preserving the integrity of the interaction model. Services should be able to invoke only operations explicitly declared in the contract. If a request attempts to call an undefined operation or includes parameters that violate the defined schema, the runtime prevents the request from reaching the service logic.

The following example illustrates a schema that the runtime uses to validate a request to a service operation:

```
{
  "operation": "evaluateFlag",
  "inputSchema": {
    "type": "object",
    "required": ["userId", "flagKey"],
```

```
    "properties": {
      "userId": { "type": "string" },
      "flagKey": { "type": "string" }
    }
  }
}
```

Input schema used by the runtime to validate a service invocation request. If the payload does not include all required fields with the correct types, the request is rejected before execution begins.

When a request is received, the runtime evaluates the payload against the schema defined for the operation. If the request includes all required fields and the data types match the expected definitions, the invocation proceeds. If the structure does not conform to the schema, the runtime rejects the request and returns an error to the caller.

In the Chapter 10 companion implementation, communication validation also enforces trust tier rules across service boundaries. Two services that are individually permitted to execute may still be denied communication if the consumer's trust tier is not listed as an allowed receiver for the event in question. This is demonstrated in lab4-forbidden-communication, where an upload-bridge service and a partner-audit-sink service both pass their individual execution checks, but the communication between them is blocked because the partner trust tier is not permitted to receive case.redacted events. The policy that governs this decision is declared explicitly in runtime-policy.json under the eventRules field.

Communication validation, therefore, acts as a protective boundary between services. By ensuring that every interaction conforms to the defined contract and trust rules, the runtime preserves the integrity of service communication and reduces the risk of errors or unauthorized access propagating through the system.

Dependency Verification

Portable architectures assume that services may execute across different environments, often with different infrastructure, libraries, or runtime capabilities available. Under these conditions, implicit assumptions about dependencies can quickly become a source of instability. A service that depends on a specific library, capability, or external component may behave correctly in one environment but fail in another if those dependencies are missing or incompatible.

Dependency verification addresses this problem by ensuring that all required components declared by a service are present and compatible before execution begins. Instead of discovering missing dependencies at runtime, the runtime evaluates the service's dependency declarations and verifies that the required resources are available in the execution environment. These dependency declarations are defined in the service metadata. The metadata describes the external services, libraries, or capabilities required by the service to operate correctly. When the runtime prepares to execute a service invocation, it evaluates these declarations and compares them against the capabilities available in the current environment.

If the runtime detects that a required dependency is unavailable or incompatible, the service invocation is prevented from proceeding. This early validation prevents failures that would otherwise occur during execution and provides clear feedback about the missing or incompatible component. The following example shows how a service declares its dependencies in the companion implementation:

```
    {
  "service": "feature-flag-evaluator",
  "dependencies": [
    {
      "name": "user-context-service",
      "version": ">=2.0.0"
    },
    {
      "name": "feature-store",
      "version": "1.x"
    }
  ]
}
```

Dependency declarations evaluated by the runtime before execution. If compatible versions of the required components are not available, the invocation is rejected, and the specific missing dependency is reported.

Before executing the service, the runtime evaluates these dependency requirements. It determines whether compatible versions of the required components are available and accessible within the current environment. If the conditions are satisfied, execution proceeds. If not, the invocation is rejected, and the system reports the specific dependency that could not be resolved.

In the Chapter 10 companion implementation, dependency provenance is also evaluated as part of this check. Each dependency declaration includes a provenance field and a checksum. The runtime rejects any service whose dependencies have untrusted provenance values or empty checksums, regardless of whether the dependencies are otherwise available. This is demonstrated in lab3-untrusted-dependency, where the case-redactor service is denied execution because one of its declared dependencies carries a provenance value of untrusted rather than verified.

Dependency verification also contributes to supply chain trust. By declaring dependencies explicitly and validating them before execution, the system reduces the risk of unintentionally executing code that relies on unverified or incompatible components. This verification step helps maintain consistency across environments and supports the reliable portability of services. Dependency verification ensures that services execute only when their declared requirements are satisfied, protecting the system from hidden assumptions and reinforcing the architectural principle that service behavior must be governed by explicit, verifiable declarations rather than implicit environmental conditions.

Operational Considerations

Runtime enforcement mechanisms are only as reliable as the operational practices that keep them accurate, visible, and current. The mechanisms described in the previous section establish how trust is enforced within the architecture. Metadata evaluation, execution isolation, communication validation, and dependency verification ensure that service interactions conform to the system's rules. These mechanisms operate automatically at runtime, but their effectiveness depends on how the architecture is governed and observed in practice.

Organizations adopting portable architectures rarely begin with completely new systems. In practice, UMA capabilities such as service metadata, contracts, and runtime validation are introduced incrementally alongside existing services, allowing legacy services and UMA services to coexist during the transition. Services may be executed across multiple environments, evolve independently, and interact dynamically through contracts and metadata. Under these conditions, operational practices must ensure that the information used by the runtime remains accurate, that violations of architectural rules are detected, and that policies governing service behavior are managed consistently across the system.

Operational governance is therefore an essential complement to runtime enforcement. The architecture must maintain reliable metadata sources describing services and their capabilities. Operators must be able to observe how services interact and detect deviations from expected behavior. Policies governing execution, communication, and dependency usage must be defined and maintained to ensure consistent enforcement across environments.

These operational responsibilities form the control layer of the architecture. While the runtime enforces rules during execution, operational practices ensure that these rules remain accurate, transparent, and trustworthy. The following subsections examine three operational concerns that support the system's trust model: registry governance, observability and trust monitoring, and policy governance.

Registry Governance

The registry is the source of truth for service metadata. If the registry drifts, the runtime drifts with it. In portable architectures, service metadata and contracts are central elements of the system's operation. The runtime relies on these artifacts to evaluate service capabilities, validate interactions, and verify dependencies. For this reason, the metadata that describes services must be maintained in a reliable and authoritative location. Registry governance addresses the operational practices required to manage this information and ensure that it remains trustworthy over time.

A registry serves as the catalog of services and capabilities available within the architecture. It stores the metadata that defines each service, including its contract, version, declared dependencies, and execution requirements. When a service is discovered or invoked, the runtime may consult the registry to retrieve the information necessary to evaluate whether the interaction is valid.

Since the registry is the primary source of service metadata, maintaining its integrity is vital for system stability. If the registry's metadata becomes inconsistent, outdated, or unverified, the runtime could misinterpret services or enable incompatible interactions. Therefore, strong governance practices are essential to ensure that metadata is accurate, properly versioned, and validated prior to being accessed by the runtime.

One aspect of registry governance involves managing the lifecycle of service definitions. When a new service capability is introduced, its metadata must be reviewed and registered so that other system components can discover it. As services evolve, updated versions of their contracts must be recorded while maintaining compatibility with existing consumers. The registry must also track the status of deprecated capabilities and ensure that obsolete entries are eventually removed.

Version management plays a central role in this process. A registry must maintain clear associations between service versions and their corresponding contracts. When multiple versions of a service are available, the runtime must determine which version satisfies the compatibility requirements for a particular interaction. Governance practices should therefore ensure that versioning policies are applied consistently and that contract changes are documented and traceable.

Access control is another important element of registry governance. Because the registry defines how services interact within the system, unauthorized modifications could introduce incorrect metadata or malicious capabilities. Operational policies must therefore restrict who can publish or modify registry entries and ensure that all updates are validated before they are accepted.

Registries may also expose discovery interfaces, allowing services or runtime environments to query available capabilities. This discovery process enables dynamic service composition and supports architectures in which components can be integrated without prior configuration. Governance policies and validation rules must ensure that discovery mechanisms expose accurate, well-structured metadata so that the runtime can reliably interpret service capabilities.

In some cases, multiple services may declare the same capability. UMA runtimes resolve this situation through deterministic metadata rules defined by the service declarations. Services may specify priority, compatibility attributes, filtering constraints, or execution ordering to guide routing decisions. When multiple services remain valid candidates, the runtime may treat them as independent consumers, allowing them to react in parallel without introducing hidden coupling between implementations.

When a service starts, it loads its contract and capability metadata. The runtime validates this metadata and registers the service with the capability registry. Once registered, other services can discover the capability through the registry and interact with it according to the declared metadata. This lifecycle allows new services to appear dynamically while preserving deterministic discovery and execution behavior. As services evolve, new versions of capabilities or contracts may appear in the registry while older versions remain in use. UMA registries should allow services to declare compatibility ranges for their capabilities so that consumers can discover implementations that match their expectations. This approach allows services to evolve independently while maintaining interoperability across the system.

Operational deployments introduce additional requirements beyond discovery and capability matching. Registries must remain highly available, metadata validation should be enforced during service registration, and monitoring systems should track capability usage and dependency relationships across services. These practices allow teams to detect incompatible changes early, understand how capabilities propagate through the architecture, and maintain confidence that the system can evolve safely as new services are introduced.

Through these practices, registry governance ensures that the metadata used by the runtime remains authoritative and consistent. By maintaining a reliable catalog of service definitions and contracts, the architecture preserves the foundation on which runtime enforcement and service interoperability depend.

Observability and Trust Monitoring

Enforcement tells the system what is allowed. Observability tells operators whether enforcement is working as intended. Runtime enforcement mechanisms provide strong guarantees that service interactions conform to architectural rules. However, enforcement alone is not sufficient to operate a portable system effectively. Operators and architects must also be able to observe how the system behaves in practice and detect when interactions approach or violate the boundaries defined by the architecture. Observability and trust monitoring provide the visibility required to understand how enforcement mechanisms function in a running system.

In portable architectures, services can be deployed across various environments and evolve separately over time. In these scenarios, operational teams need to understand how services interact, which contracts they call, and if runtime validation mechanisms work correctly. Observability goes beyond traditional metrics like latency or throughput; it must also include signals that indicate architectural correctness.

One category of signals concerns contract validation events. When the runtime evaluates service metadata and verifies communication schemas, the results of these checks provide valuable information about the system's health. Rejected requests, schema mismatches, or version incompatibilities indicate that components may be interacting in unexpected ways. Monitoring these events allows operators to identify integration problems early and address them before they propagate through the system.

Another important category of signals relates to dependency resolution. When a service is executed, the runtime verifies that its declared dependencies are present and compatible. Failures in dependency verification may indicate configuration drift between environments or incomplete deployments. Observing these events helps operators ensure that services remain portable and that the execution environment satisfies the requirements declared by each component.

Execution boundaries also generate observable signals. Isolation mechanisms may detect attempts by a service to access unauthorized resources or exceed defined execution limits. Such events may indicate programming errors, misconfigured capabilities, or malicious behavior. Recording and analyzing these signals allows the system to maintain visibility into the enforcement of execution policies.

Trust monitoring aggregates these signals to provide a broader view of system integrity. Instead of focusing solely on performance metrics, trust monitoring evaluates whether the system continues to operate within the architectural constraints that define it. Metrics such as contract validation failures, dependency mismatches, and policy violations provide insight into how well the architecture is being respected during operation.

Effective observability practices treat enforcement mechanisms as sources of operational intelligence. Logs, metrics, and tracing data generated by the runtime can reveal patterns of service interaction and highlight areas where architectural assumptions may no longer hold. By analyzing these signals, operators can detect emerging issues and maintain confidence that the system continues to behave as designed.

In this way, observability and trust monitoring extend the architectural model into the operational domain. While the runtime enforces the system's rules, monitoring mechanisms ensure that those rules remain visible and verifiable as the system evolves.

A concrete monitoring example illustrates how these signals appear in practice. When the runtime rejects a service invocation due to a contract validation failure, it emits a structured log entry recording the service identifier, the operation that was attempted, the specific field that failed validation, and the timestamp. An operator monitoring this stream can immediately identify which service sent a malformed request, which contract version was expected, and whether the failure is an isolated incident or a pattern indicating a broader integration problem. The same approach applies to dependency verification failures: the log entry names the missing or incompatible dependency, the version that was declared, and the version that was found, giving the operator everything needed to diagnose and resolve the issue without examining the service code directly.

Incident response in a UMA system follows the same metadata-driven approach that governs execution. When a trust violation is detected, whether a publisher identity mismatch, an undeclared permission request, or a forbidden cross-boundary communication, the runtime blocks the interaction and records the denial with full context in the audit log. The first response step is to query the audit log for the affected service identifier and retrieve the full denial reason and the policy rule that triggered it. If the violation indicates a misconfiguration, the service contract or runtime policy can be corrected and the service re-registered without affecting other services in the system. If the violation indicates a compromised or tampered artifact, the service can be removed from the registry immediately, which prevents all further discovery and execution of that service across all runtimes consulting the same registry. Because trust decisions are explicit and logged, the response process is deterministic rather than investigative.

A concrete monitoring example illustrates how these signals appear in practice. When the runtime rejects a service invocation due to a contract validation failure, it emits a structured log entry that records the service identifier, the attempted operation, the specific field that failed validation, and the timestamp. An operator monitoring this stream can immediately identify which service sent a malformed request, which contract version was expected, and whether the failure is an isolated incident or a pattern indicating a broader integration problem. The same approach applies to dependency verification failures: the log entry names the missing or incompatible dependency, the version declared, and the version found, giving the operator everything needed to diagnose and resolve the issue without examining the service code directly.

Incident response in a UMA system follows the same metadata-driven approach that governs execution. When a trust violation is detected, whether a publisher identity mismatch, an undeclared permission request, or a forbidden cross-boundary communication, the runtime blocks the interaction and records the denial with full context in the audit log. The first response step is to query the audit log for the affected service identifier and retrieve the full denial reason and the policy rule that triggered it. If the violation indicates a misconfiguration, the service contract or runtime policy can be corrected and the service re-registered without affecting other services in the system. If the violation indicates a compromised or tampered artifact, the service can be removed from the registry immediately, preventing further discovery and execution of that service across all runtimes consulting the same registry. Because trust decisions are explicit and logged, the response process is deterministic rather than investigative.

Policy Governance

Runtime enforcement applies the rules. Policy governance ensures those rules remain correct, current, and consistently distributed. Runtime enforcement mechanisms apply the rules that define how services may execute, interact, and depend on external components. These rules are expressed as policies that govern the runtime's behavior. Policy governance addresses how these rules are defined, managed, and evolved to ensure that the system continues to operate within its intended architectural boundaries.

Policies define the constraints under which services operate. These constraints may include restrictions on resource usage, permitted communication channels, acceptable dependency sources, or allowed execution capabilities. While the runtime is responsible for enforcing these policies during execution, the policies themselves must be maintained through operational processes that ensure their correctness and consistency.

In portable architectures, policy governance is crucial because services often operate across different environments and administrative domains. Policies regulating execution in one environment must be compatible with those in others. Operational governance ensures that policies are clearly defined and interpreted consistently across various runtime environments.

The following example shows the runtime policy used in the Chapter 10 companion implementation. It declares which publishers are trusted, which trust tiers are permitted to execute, which permissions are available per placement, and which event consumer tiers are allowed per event type:

```
{
  "kind": "uma.runtime-trust-policy",
  "specVersion": "1.0",
  "trustedPublishers": [
    "uma.book.team",
    "uma.platform.ops"
  ],
  "allowedTrustTiers": [
    "internal",
    "partner"
  ],
  "placementRules": {
```

```
    "cloud": {
      "allowedPermissions": [
        "storage.read",
        "storage.write",
        "events.publish",
        "events.subscribe"
      ]
    },
    "edge": {
      "allowedPermissions": [
        "storage.read",
        "events.publish",
        "events.subscribe"
      ]
    }
  },
  "eventRules": {
    "image.uploaded": {
      "allowedConsumerTiers": ["internal", "partner"]
    },
    "case.redacted": {
      "allowedConsumerTiers": ["internal"]
    }
  }
}
```

The runtime-policy.json from the Chapter 10 *companion implementation. This policy is evaluated for every service invocation. A service published by an unlisted publisher is denied before execution begins. A service requesting a permission not listed under its placement is denied, even if the permission is declared in its contract. An event consumer whose trust tier is not listed under the relevant event rule is denied communication, even if both services individually pass their execution checks.*

Policy definitions are often expressed as structured configuration artifacts that the runtime can evaluate during service invocation. These artifacts define which capabilities a service may access, which external services are permitted as dependencies, or what limits apply to resource consumption. Because policies influence the runtime's behavior, changes to policy definitions must be carefully controlled and reviewed before deployment.

Versioning and change management are key elements of policy governance. As the architecture evolves, new policies may be introduced and existing ones refined. Governance processes must ensure that policy changes do not unintentionally disrupt service interactions or invalidate existing contracts. Maintaining versioned policy definitions allows the system to apply appropriate rules while preserving compatibility with services that depend on earlier policy configurations.

Policy governance also includes the mechanisms for distributing policies across the system. Runtime environments must receive updated policy definitions in a controlled and consistent manner so that enforcement behavior remains predictable. This distribution process may rely on centralized configuration systems, policy registries, or deployment pipelines that propagate policy updates to all relevant runtimes.

Deployment pipelines play an important role in this process. Integrating automated policy checks into the pipeline allows teams to verify compliance with operational and security requirements before promoting changes to production. Services that fail policy validation are blocked at the pipeline stage rather than discovered at runtime. Similarly, dependency reviews conducted before deployment validate the provenance and compatibility of third-party components, reducing the risk of supply chain issues reaching production.

Runtime enforcement introduces measurable but manageable overhead. Metadata evaluation and schema validation operate on structured JSON documents and typically complete in under one millisecond for well-formed service contracts. Dependency verification adds a lookup against a local or cached registry, which can be optimized by preloading dependency manifests at service registration time rather than at each invocation. Execution isolation in WebAssembly environments imposes a one-time sandbox initialization cost at module load, not per invocation, making the amortized impact negligible for long-running services. Communication validation performs schema matching against pre-compiled validators, keeping per-request overhead low. The most significant mitigation strategy is to move enforcement earlier in the lifecycle: validating metadata and dependencies at registration time rather than at invocation time, eliminating repeated checks on the hot path. Teams operating at scale should also consider caching policy evaluation results for stable service versions and invalidating the cache only when policy definitions change.

Another aspect of governance involves auditing and review. Because policies determine how services are allowed to behave, organizations must verify that these rules align with security, operational, and architectural objectives. Regular review of policy definitions helps ensure that the runtime's constraints continue to reflect the system's intended design. Scheduling periodic access reviews for service registries and policy configurations limits unauthorized modifications and surfaces stale or overly permissive rules before they affect production.

Through policy governance, the architecture maintains control over the rules that guide service behavior. While runtime enforcement ensures that policies are applied during execution, governance practices ensure that those policies remain accurate, transparent, and aligned with the system's evolving needs.

Preserving Trust in Portable Systems

Portability and trust are not in conflict. They require the same thing: explicit declarations, consistent enforcement, and continuous visibility. Portability allows software systems to operate across environments that differ in infrastructure, runtime capabilities, and operational constraints. A service may execute in a browser, within an edge runtime, or in a cloud platform, and may move between these contexts over time as systems evolve. This flexibility expands the reach of software systems and enables new architectural patterns, but it also introduces new risks. Assumptions that once remained stable within a single deployment environment can no longer be relied upon when services interact dynamically across heterogeneous execution contexts.

Traditional systems often rely on environmental stability to maintain trust. Services run within a known infrastructure, dependencies are installed and managed within a controlled environment, and interactions occur between components that share common assumptions about configuration and execution. In portable architectures, these assumptions become fragile. Differences in runtime capabilities, dependency availability, and communication boundaries can cause services to behave differently depending on where they execute. Without architectural safeguards, these differences can lead to unpredictable behavior and operational instability.

The challenges described in this chapter illustrate how portability alters a system's trust model. Execution environment drift can cause a service to behave differently across environments. Communication boundaries introduce opportunities for invalid or malicious interactions. Dependency uncertainty can expose systems to incompatibilities or supply chain risks. Each of these concerns reflects a broader architectural reality: when systems become portable, trust cannot rely on the stability of the surrounding infrastructure.

Addressing these challenges requires treating trust as a deliberate architectural property rather than an implicit assumption. The architecture must define how services establish identity, how they interact safely, and how their dependencies are declared and verified. Identity and attestation provide the mechanisms through which services establish authenticity. Execution isolation ensures that components operate within clearly defined boundaries, preventing interference with other services or with the underlying runtime environment. Dependency transparency allows the system to understand which external components a service relies on and to verify that those dependencies are available and trustworthy.

Contract-based interaction further strengthens this model by defining how services communicate through explicit agreements. Contracts describe the structure of inputs and outputs, the operations a service exposes, and the constraints that govern those operations. By expressing these agreements as machine-readable artifacts, the architecture enables runtimes and tooling to validate interactions before execution. Services no longer rely on implicit knowledge of each other's behavior. Instead, interactions are guided by verifiable definitions that remain consistent across environments.

The effectiveness of these architectural mechanisms depends on their enforcement during execution. Runtime environments evaluate service metadata, validate requests against contract definitions, verify declared dependencies, and maintain isolation boundaries between services. This enforcement ensures that architectural constraints remain active during system operation. Interactions that violate the rules defined by the architecture are detected and rejected before they can affect the system's behavior.

Operational practices extend these guarantees beyond the runtime itself. Service registries maintain authoritative records of contracts, metadata, and capabilities, allowing runtimes and other services to discover and interpret components consistently. Observability mechanisms provide visibility into how services interact and whether runtime validation mechanisms are functioning correctly. Trust monitoring enables operators to detect contract mismatches, dependency failures, or policy violations as they occur. Governance processes ensure that the policies guiding execution remain consistent and aligned with the system's evolving needs.

To operationalize these principles, architects should adopt governance practices that reinforce trust and stability as the system evolves. Several are especially critical for effective early adoption. Instituting regular audits of service contracts and metadata identifies inconsistencies or outdated definitions before they affect production. Integrating automated policy checks into deployment pipelines verifies compliance with operational and security requirements before changes are promoted. Establishing a routine for dependency reviews validates the provenance and compatibility of third-party components. Scheduling periodic access reviews for service registries and policy configurations limits unauthorized modifications. Encouraging cross-team reviews of contract changes reveals integration risks before they reach production and supports architectural consistency.

Portable architectures require a layered approach to trust. Architectural design establishes the rules governing service behavior, runtime systems enforce these rules during execution, and operational governance maintains the information and policies necessary for reliable system operation. Each layer reinforces the others, creating an environment in which services can evolve independently while maintaining predictable, secure interactions. As software systems increasingly depend on portability to support diverse execution environments, these architectural principles become essential. Sustaining trust in such systems relies on clear definitions of service behavior, robust enforcement mechanisms, and operational practices that ensure ongoing observability and governance.

CHAPTER 11

Architecting with UMA: Decisions, Patterns, and Tradeoffs

How Architects Design, Evaluate, and Evolve UMA Systems in Real-World Environments

Introduction: From Structure to Interaction

Every system eventually reaches a point where structure alone is insufficient. Early in design, architecture is controlled and predictable. Capabilities are well defined, contracts explicit, and capability boundaries clear. Each component has a specific purpose, and interfaces are intentional. As systems evolve, clarity diminishes. Teams add new capabilities with limited knowledge of the existing system. Services respond to external events, extensions alter behavior, and components may interpret the same signals differently. Overlapping responsibilities increase the dynamism of service relationships. UMA addresses these challenges by making interactions explicit and governable, enabling architects to manage complexity and maintain coherence as boundaries shift.

Complexity grows when interaction is treated as an implementation detail rather than an architectural concern. Decisions about ownership, event semantics, extension mechanisms, and runtime behavior often remain implicit, embedded in code or conventions instead of being formally expressed. This makes systems harder to reason about, less predictable, and more prone to unintended consequences as they evolve. UMA addresses this by making interactions explicit and governed. Capabilities are defined independently, but their relationships are formalized through contracts and

E. Piovesan, *Universal Microservices Architecture*, https://doi.org/10.1007/979-8-8688-2794-5_11

interpreted via metadata. Events convey structured meaning, extensions follow defined mechanisms, and declarative rules govern runtime behavior.

This chapter examines how these mechanisms affect real-world systems. It covers the following areas in order: how architecture shifts from static design to observable system behavior, how the architect's role changes in a behavior-driven model, the core decision axes that shape every UMA system, the architectural patterns that emerge from applying those decisions consistently, how systems are designed to evolve without fragmentation, the anti-patterns and failure modes that arise when decisions are made poorly, practical guidelines for making these decisions under real constraints, and the principles that tie the model together. The ski patrol incident workflow introduced below serves as the running reference example throughout. The companion implementation uses a media upload workflow to demonstrate the same architectural principles across six runnable labs.

To address these complexities, UMA systems rely on several key mechanisms that become central as architectures grow. Metadata provides a structured, machine-readable description of capabilities and system elements. Contracts formally govern the expectations between capabilities. Event semantics define the meaning and structure of interactions between services. Extension points and runtime rules make system adaptation explicit and controlled. These mechanisms turn implicit interactions into explicit, governable processes.

At this stage, architecture must be understood in terms of both structure and interaction. Consider a capability that reports a ski patrol incident. Structurally, it is a single, well-defined service with a clear contract and a stable output event. But its behavior differs depending on where it executes. On a mobile device with no connectivity, it stores the event locally and propagates it when a signal becomes available. At the edge, it enriches the event with contextual signals. In the cloud, it feeds into classification and dispatch workflows. The structure does not change across these contexts, but the interaction model does. Understanding both dimensions is what allows the system to remain coherent as the same capability moves across environments. This example recurs throughout the chapter as a reference point for the decisions and tradeoffs described in each section. The companion implementation at chapter-11-architectural-tradeoffs demonstrates the same architectural principles using a media upload workflow across six runnable labs.

System behavior is determined by how capabilities communicate, extend, and coexist within a shared runtime. Within this model, the architect's role shifts accordingly.

The definition of individual capabilities remains important, but it is no longer sufficient to ensure system coherence. Equal, if not greater, importance is placed on the decisions that govern how those capabilities are organized, how ownership is established and extended, how events are modeled and interpreted across boundaries, how metadata defines and constrains behavior, and how the system maintains consistency as it evolves across teams and environments with different runtime conditions.

These decisions form the operational foundation of a UMA system, affecting composability, observability, and safe change management. The following sections examine these decisions in detail, focusing on their application in real-world environments where systems grow incrementally, contributors have varying context, and runtime constraints differ across client, edge, and cloud. Later sections offer concrete examples, real-world scenarios, and common anti-patterns, connecting theoretical models and decision points to real cases and challenges.

The following sections address the core dimensions of UMA system design: capability structure, event modeling, metadata design, runtime placement, and state management. Each dimension requires explicit choices and tradeoffs that shape system behavior. Together, these dimensions determine whether a UMA system can manage complexity while maintaining coherence.

From Architecture As Design to Architecture As System Behavior

The Limits of Static Architecture and Metadata-Driven Behavior

Traditional architecture describes what a system is made of. UMA requires architecture to also describe how a system behaves. Traditional software architecture has largely been defined in terms of structure. Systems are decomposed into components or services, responsibilities are assigned, and interfaces are specified to control interaction. This structural perspective has been effective in environments where system boundaries remain relatively stable and where interactions between components are predictable and limited in scope. As systems evolve, however, the assumptions that support this model begin to weaken. This challenge was introduced in Chapter 9 in the context of portable execution environments and runtime heterogeneity, where static deployment assumptions broke down as services moved across browsers, edge nodes, and cloud platforms. Chapter 11 extends that analysis from the deployment level to the architectural design level.

Static architecture models are not designed to capture this level of variability. They describe the components and how they are connected, but they do not fully capture how the system behaves as those components interact over time. Important aspects such as event semantics, execution ordering, conflict resolution, and runtime decision-making remain outside the architectural model. As a result, they are often addressed implicitly through implementation logic or operational conventions rather than being expressed explicitly as part of the architecture. This creates a divergence between the architecture as defined and the system's behavior in practice.

In UMA, this extension is realized through metadata, treated not as auxiliary information or documentation but as a formal, machine-readable layer that defines the properties of capabilities, the semantics of their interactions, and the constraints that govern execution. This layer includes the description of capability intent, input and output contracts, dependency relationships, event semantics, and the rules that regulate extension, coordination, and conflict resolution. By elevating metadata to this role, architectural definition is no longer limited to the arrangement of components. It also includes the information required to interpret how those components behave when composed and executed within a system.

This introduces a form of constrained emergence. Behavior is not arbitrary, nor is it entirely predetermined. It is governed by explicit rules encoded in metadata and interpreted consistently by the runtime. Predictability is achieved not by eliminating variability, but by ensuring that the rules governing interaction are complete, unambiguous, and uniformly applied across the system. Deficiencies in metadata, whether through omission, inconsistency, or ambiguity, directly affect system behavior, as the runtime depends on this layer to resolve decisions that are not captured in structure alone. The metadata-first service design pattern translates this principle into a concrete design approach, showing how capabilities are defined through structured metadata before any implementation is written.

Observability, Design Implications, and the Shift to Behavioral Architecture

When behavior is determined by metadata and runtime interpretation, observability must extend to the architectural layer, not just the infrastructure layer. Traditional observability practices focus on signals such as logs, metrics, and traces, which provide visibility into system execution. While these signals are essential, they are typically tied to implementation details and operational state. They describe what the system is doing, but not necessarily why it is behaving in a particular way, nor how that behavior relates to architectural intent. Chapter 9 introduced observability as a trust mechanism, focusing on contract validation events and dependency verification signals. Chapter 11 extends this to architectural observability, where the signals of interest are capability interactions, event semantics, and metadata usage patterns.

To effectively implement observability in UMA systems, architects should apply concrete practices that expose these dimensions in actionable ways. This starts with providing interfaces for metadata inspection, enabling developers and operators to review the current definitions in use, including capability contracts, event types, supported extensions, and relevant constraints. Implementing event tracing is equally important: services should emit trace information whenever significant events are processed, capturing which capabilities responded, which metadata rules were applied, and the resulting decisions. Correlating these traces with metadata enables direct analysis of how architectural intent affects actual runtime behavior. Additionally, implementing metrics on metadata usage, such as the number of capability invocations per metadata version, the frequency of extension point invocations, or the rates of conflict resolution events, can illuminate how the system is functioning and evolving. These practices not only improve visibility but also provide early signals for detecting inconsistencies, ambiguities, or emerging failure modes.

This approach shifts observability from a reactive activity to a structural property of the system. Instead of reconstructing behavior after the fact through logs and traces, the system exposes the information required to understand its behavior as it occurs. Architectural intent, expressed through metadata, becomes directly observable alongside execution. The same metadata that defines behavior also provides the context needed to interpret it during runtime.

The transition from architecture as structural design to architecture as system behavior introduces a change not only in how systems are described but also in how they must be designed. When behavior is no longer fully determined by static composition, design decisions can no longer focus exclusively on decomposition, interface definition, and dependency management. They must also account for how behavior is expressed, interpreted, and governed at runtime. This affects the role of boundaries within the system. In traditional models, boundaries are defined to isolate responsibilities and control dependencies between components. In a behavior-driven system, boundaries must also define how capabilities participate in interaction, how they interpret shared events, and how they can be extended without compromising system coherence. A boundary that is structurally correct but behaviorally ambiguous introduces uncertainty that cannot be resolved through structure alone.

These factors change how architecture is evaluated. Structural correctness is necessary but not sufficient. A well-designed system must also ensure consistent behavior interpretation, stable interaction resolution, and clear runtime decision-making. Systems that meet structural requirements but lack behavioral governance will degrade as complexity grows. The shift to behavior-driven architecture requires a broader design perspective, extending responsibility from defining components to establishing conditions for predictable system behavior as it evolves. This perspective provides the foundation for the following sections, where these considerations are translated into concrete design dimensions and decision points for UMA systems.

The Architect's New Responsibility in UMA

The shift from architecture as structural design to architecture as system behavior requires a corresponding shift in how design decisions are framed. Rather than focusing solely on the decomposition of systems into components and the definition of their interfaces, architectural design must address the conditions under which behavior remains consistent, interpretable, and governable as the system evolves. In UMA, these conditions are expressed through a set of design dimensions that define how capabilities are structured, how interactions are modeled, how metadata governs behavior, and how execution is managed across different runtime environments. Each dimension represents a space of possible choices, where different approaches lead to different trade-offs among composability, predictability, and operational complexity. The following sections examine these dimensions as interdependent aspects of a system, with behavior emerging from their combined effect. The goal is not to prescribe a single solution but to outline the constraints and considerations that help UMA systems remain coherent as they scale and evolve.

Defining Constraints in Architecture

In UMA, design extends beyond structural definition and includes the conditions under which behavior remains consistent as the system evolves. These conditions are expressed as constraints that define how capabilities interact, how events are interpreted, and how behavior can be extended or modified. Structural elements describe what exists in the system, while constraints define how the system is allowed to behave under varying conditions. Architectural design, therefore, involves defining a space of valid interactions rather than fully determining behavior through static composition. Capabilities can evolve independently, and new behaviors can be introduced, but only within the limits established by these constraints. The system is not a fixed arrangement of components but a bounded environment in which behavior emerges without violating consistency.

Constraints operate across multiple dimensions of the system. They govern ownership by defining responsibility boundaries and extension points. They define event semantics to ensure that interactions remain interpretable across different consumers. They regulate execution by specifying how and when behaviors are applied and how conflicts are resolved when multiple capabilities respond to the same conditions. They also define the structure and interpretation of metadata, ensuring that runtime decisions remain predictable. By making these constraints explicit, architecture shifts from prescribing structure to governing behavior. Structural design remains necessary, but it no longer guarantees correctness on its own. Correctness now depends on the consistency with which behavior is defined, interpreted, and coordinated across the system.

In traditional architectures, ownership is used to establish clear boundaries of responsibility. Each component or service is assigned control over a specific domain, including its data, behavior, and lifecycle. Interaction between components is coordinated either through direct invocation or through centralized orchestration mechanisms that define the sequence and conditions under which operations are executed. In UMA, ownership remains necessary but is no longer sufficient to describe how behavior is coordinated across the system. Capabilities retain responsibility for their domain, but they do not operate within a single, predefined orchestration flow. Instead, they participate in a shared interaction model where coordination is achieved through event exchange and metadata interpretation, allowing execution paths to be determined at runtime rather than prescribed at design time.

Under these conditions, ownership defines responsibility, but not control over system behavior. A capability governs its own logic and data, but it does not determine how other capabilities will respond to the events it produces. Multiple capabilities may react to the same event, and the resulting behavior depends on the set of participants and the rules that govern their coordination. Coordination is therefore distributed rather than centralized and requires explicit mechanisms to remain consistent. Event semantics must ensure that interactions are interpreted uniformly across capabilities. Metadata must define how multiple responses are combined, ordered, or constrained. Conflict resolution rules must determine how competing behaviors are reconciled when multiple capabilities act on the same conditions. Without these constraints, distributed coordination would introduce ambiguity and reduce predictability.

In traditional architectures, control over system behavior is achieved through direct invocation, centralized orchestration, and tightly defined execution paths. In UMA, behavior is not governed by direct control of execution paths but rather by rules that influence how capabilities interact. These rules are expressed through metadata, which defines how events are interpreted, how capabilities participate in interactions, and how multiple contributions are combined at runtime. Rather than prescribing a fixed sequence of operations, the architecture defines the conditions under which different behaviors are permitted. This model replaces direct control with a form of constrained influence. Metadata does not execute behavior, but it defines the boundaries within which behavior can emerge. It specifies which capabilities are eligible to respond to a given event, under what conditions they may do so, how their responses are ordered or combined, and how conflicts are resolved when multiple behaviors compete. The runtime applies these rules to determine the resulting system behavior. The system remains governable because the rules shaping behavior are visible, structured, and enforceable.

This approach allows systems to accommodate change without continuous restructuring. As capabilities are introduced or evolve, constraints ensure their interactions remain coherent with the system. The architecture does not need to be redefined for each change, as long as changes operate within established boundaries. In this context, design requires defining boundaries precisely enough for the system to evolve without losing coherence.

Designing for AI Interpretation

UMA systems are not only executed by machines but are also interpreted, extended, and in some cases partially constructed by automated agents. Architectural design must account for both human and machine interpretation. This requirement affects how capabilities are described. Descriptions must be explicit, unambiguous, and structured so that automated systems can reason about them. Capability intent, inputs, outputs, constraints, and dependencies must be encoded in machine-readable formats to enable discovery and composition without manual interpretation. In practice, this often takes the form of widely adopted metadata standards such as JSON Schema, OpenAPI, or domain-specific languages tailored for capability modeling. For example, a capability may be described using an OpenAPI document that details endpoints, input and output schemas, and supported operations or a custom JSON Schema that captures the structure and constraints for event payloads. Choosing a format depends on integration requirements and the level of expressiveness needed, but the essential property is that metadata is accessible and interpretable by automated tooling. Human-readable documentation may complement this information, but it cannot serve as the primary source of truth.

Interaction design is similarly affected. Events must carry well-defined semantics that can be interpreted consistently across both human-developed and machine-driven components. Ambiguity that might be resolved informally by developers becomes a source of inconsistency when interpreted by automated systems. Designing events, therefore, requires precision in meaning, structure, and expected behavior across different consumers.

In the ski patrol workflow, an agent operating at the edge receives an Incident Reported event and queries the capability registry to discover what capabilities are available and compatible with the current runtime context. It evaluates the metadata of candidate capabilities, including their trust tier, placement constraints, and required permissions, and proposes an execution path: triage assistance locally, classification at the edge if connectivity allows, and dispatch coordination in the cloud. The agent does not execute these capabilities directly. It submits a proposal to the UMA runtime, which validates the plan against the system contracts and policies before approving or modifying it. The agent then observes the resulting events to confirm progress and adjusts its next proposal accordingly. This interaction model keeps the agent's authority bounded by the same metadata and policy rules that govern human-initiated workflows, preventing agent-driven execution from bypassing architectural constraints.

Metadata plays an expanded role in this context. It governs runtime behavior and enables automated reasoning about the system. Agents use metadata to discover capabilities, determine compatibility, infer interactions, and evaluate the impact of changes. This requires metadata to be complete, consistent, and structured to support both execution and interpretation. The presence of automated agents also affects how systems evolve. Changes to capabilities, contracts, or metadata can be analyzed and acted upon by machine-driven processes, including validation, refactoring, and composition of new behaviors. This introduces new requirements for consistency and versioning, as ambiguities or inconsistencies in metadata can propagate through automated workflows more rapidly than through human-driven processes.

Designing for both humans and AI systems, therefore, requires a dual perspective. The system must remain understandable and operable by developers while also being interpretable and usable by automated agents. This is achieved not by duplicating representations, but by ensuring that the primary representation of the system, expressed through contracts and metadata, is sufficiently precise and structured to serve both purposes. In UMA, this dual interpretability comes from treating metadata as a first-class architectural element. Systems that meet this requirement support both human reasoning and automated interaction without separate models. Systems relying on implicit knowledge or informal descriptions cannot be reliably interpreted beyond their original implementation context.

Core Architectural Decision Axes in UMA

What defines the architecture is not only how services are organized, but also how they declare capabilities, expose intent through metadata, and participate in a shared event space. The transition from structure-based architecture to behavior-driven systems introduces a different category of design decisions. In traditional systems, architectural choices are often expressed through topology, layering, and ownership boundaries. In UMA, these concerns are not removed, but they are no longer sufficient to explain how a system behaves in practice. The system's behavior emerges from capability interactions, and as a result, architectural decisions must be evaluated in terms of their impact on composition, evolution, and runtime coherence. This section examines the primary axes along which these decisions are made. Each axis represents a tension that cannot be resolved through a single best practice but must instead be balanced based on context, constraints, and desired system properties. The goal is not to prescribe fixed rules but to provide a framework for evaluating trade-offs in systems where behavior is defined by metadata and interaction rather than static design.

Service Granularity: How Small Is Too Small?

A service should be as small as possible while still expressing a complete and stable unit of behavior. Service granularity has always been a central concern in distributed system design. In UMA, the question is reframed but not eliminated. The issue is no longer only about deployability or team ownership but about how effectively a service can express a capability through its contract and participate in a broader system of interactions. A service that is too coarse tends to aggregate multiple capabilities under a single contract. This reduces clarity, limits reuse, and makes it more difficult for other services to discover and compose functionality. It also increases the likelihood that unrelated changes will affect the same service, reducing the system's ability to evolve incrementally.

A service that is too fine-grained introduces a different set of problems. When capabilities are decomposed excessively, the system becomes dependent on a high volume of interactions. This increases coordination overhead, amplifies the number of events in circulation, and can make the system's behavior harder to reason about. In such cases, the cost of composition begins to outweigh its benefits. In UMA, granularity is best understood in terms of capability boundaries rather than technical boundaries. A service should represent a single, coherent capability that can be described, discovered, and invoked independently. This capability must be meaningful both to developers and to automated systems that rely on metadata for orchestration and reasoning.

The definition of appropriate granularity depends on how capabilities are modeled, how often they change, and how they are composed at runtime. In systems where metadata drives discovery and interaction, the clarity and stability of the capability contract are the main indicators of appropriate granularity. Architectural discipline in UMA comes from consistently aligning service boundaries with well-defined capabilities and validating those boundaries through observed interaction patterns at runtime. The following decision tree provides a practical tool for evaluating whether a capability boundary is appropriately scoped:

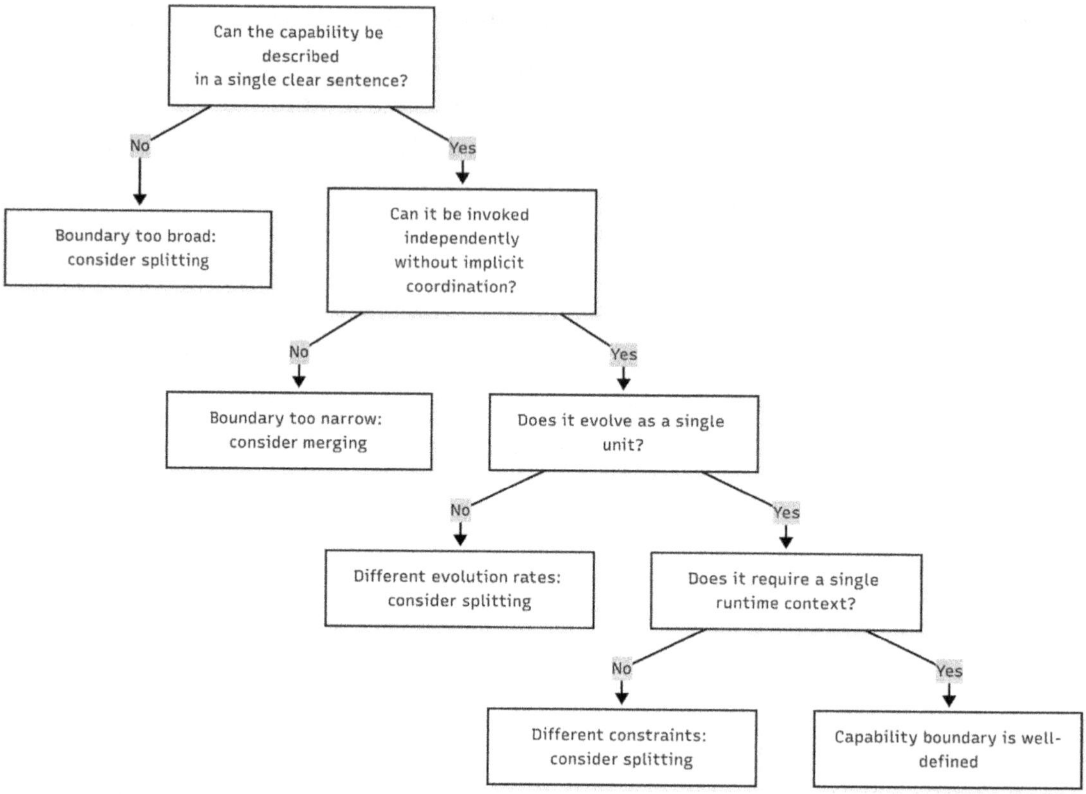

Figure 11-1. *UMA portable architecture risk categories mapped to STRIDE threat types*

Capability Boundaries and Service Responsibility

A capability boundary must be semantically coherent and operationally complete. Without both conditions, the system cannot compose reliably. Defining capability boundaries is one of the most consequential decisions in UMA. A capability is not simply a function or an API surface. It represents a unit of behavior that the system can rely on, describe through metadata, and compose with other capabilities at runtime. A service is responsible for implementing exactly one such capability or a tightly cohesive set of behaviors that together form a single, meaningful unit. Technical constraints do not define this responsibility. They determine the clarity and stability of the capability being exposed. When boundaries are well defined, services can evolve independently without introducing ambiguity into the system.

Poorly defined capability boundaries lead to two common failure modes. In the first, a service attempts to encapsulate multiple unrelated concerns. This results in contracts that are difficult to interpret and reuse and in metadata that does not clearly communicate intent. In the second, a capability is fragmented across multiple services, requiring coordination to achieve even simple outcomes. This increases coupling at the interaction level, even if services appear independent at the implementation level. In UMA, responsibility is expressed through the contract and its associated metadata. The contract defines what the service does, while metadata defines how it behaves within the system. This includes the events it emits, the conditions under which it reacts, and the constraints that govern its execution. Together, these elements establish a clear boundary that other services can depend on without knowledge of internal implementation.

A capability boundary must therefore satisfy two conditions. It must be semantically coherent, meaning it represents a single, well-understood concept within the domain. It must also be operationally complete, meaning it can be invoked and produce meaningful results without requiring implicit coordination with unrelated services. In systems where behavior emerges from interaction, precise capability boundaries directly influence the system's ability to evolve. Clear boundaries reduce ambiguity, improve discoverability, and enable reliable composition. Ambiguous boundaries introduce hidden dependencies that only become visible at runtime, making them harder to detect and resolve.

Event Design: Signals, Noise, and Coupling

Events describe facts, not intentions. Their usefulness depends on how clearly those facts are expressed. Events are the primary mechanism through which services interact in UMA. They are not auxiliary constructs used for integration, but fundamental elements that define how behavior propagates across the system. An event represents the occurrence of something meaningful within the system. Its purpose is to communicate that a state transition or outcome has taken place, without prescribing how other services should respond. Poorly designed events introduce ambiguity. When event names are vague, when payloads mix unrelated concerns, or when the meaning of an event depends on implicit context, services that consume these events must rely on assumptions. Over time, these assumptions become hidden dependencies, increasing coupling and making the system more difficult to reason about.

A well-designed event acts as a clear signal. It communicates a single, well-defined occurrence, expressed in terms that are stable and meaningful within the domain. The structure of the event reflects this clarity. Its payload contains only the data necessary to describe what happened, without embedding logic or anticipating specific consumers. The distinction between signal and noise becomes important as the number of services and interactions grows. Emitting too many events, or emitting events that do not represent meaningful changes, creates noise within the system. Emitting too few events limits extensibility, as services are not given sufficient information to react independently.

In UMA, event design is guided by the principle that events should be stable representations of domain facts. They should not encode workflow steps, internal states, or transient processing details. Instead, they should capture outcomes that are meaningful beyond the scope of a single service, allowing other services to interpret and act on them independently. This approach requires discipline in how events are named, structured, and versioned. Names must reflect domain concepts rather than implementation details. Payloads must remain consistent over time, with changes introduced in a way that preserves backward compatibility. Metadata plays a role in this process by providing additional context about event semantics, enabling services to discover and interpret events without relying on external documentation.

Metadata Design: Expressiveness vs. Simplicity

Metadata must be expressive enough to capture capability nuances and simple enough to be understood, validated, and maintained across teams over time. Metadata is the mechanism through which services in UMA describe their capabilities, constraints, and participation in the system. It enables discovery, guides interaction, and provides the information required for both humans and automated systems to reason about behavior. A key tension in metadata design lies between expressiveness and simplicity. Excessively expressive metadata tends to become difficult to manage. When schemas attempt to encode every possible detail, they grow in complexity and lose clarity. This makes them harder to interpret, increases the likelihood of inconsistent usage, and introduces friction in both development and evolution. Conversely, metadata that is too minimal fails to provide the information required for meaningful interaction. If key aspects of behavior are omitted or left implicit, services must rely on external knowledge or assumptions to operate correctly.

In UMA, metadata should be designed to express what is necessary for correct and reliable interaction and nothing more. These dimensions typically include the capability's semantics, the events it produces or consumes, the conditions under which it operates, and the constraints that govern its execution. Simplicity does not imply lack of structure. Well-designed metadata is often highly structured but organized to emphasize clarity and consistency. A small number of well-defined fields, used consistently across services, is generally more effective than a large number of optional or loosely defined attributes. The balance between expressiveness and simplicity must also be maintained over time. Changes to metadata should, therefore, be evaluated not only in terms of immediate utility but also in terms of their impact on long-term comprehensibility and stability. Versioning plays a critical role in managing this evolution. Metadata must be able to change without breaking existing consumers, and services must be able to operate with multiple versions when necessary.

Runtime Placement: Client, Edge, or Cloud?

In UMA, runtime placement is an architectural aspect, not merely a deployment detail. It illustrates how capabilities interact with their environment and how the system adjusts to evolving conditions. Services in UMA are not confined to a single execution environment; a capability can run on the client, at the edge, or in the cloud, as long as dependencies and constraints are met. This flexibility creates a new kind of architectural decision, where placement depends on behavior rather than being a fixed system property. Selecting runtime placement influences latency, scalability, cost, data locality, and security. These considerations are interconnected, and decisions in one area often lead to trade-offs in others. Consequently, placement should not be fixed at design time but guided by metadata constraints and characteristics.

Executing a service on the client offers advantages in terms of responsiveness and reduced network dependency. It enables interactions with minimal latency and supports operation in disconnected or constrained environments. However, client-side execution is limited by device capabilities, resource availability, and security considerations. Edge execution provides a balance between proximity and capability. By placing services closer to the point of interaction, latency can be reduced while still leveraging more controlled, scalable infrastructure than the client can provide. Cloud execution remains the most flexible in terms of computational power, storage, and centralized control. It is well-suited for heavy processing, aggregation, and coordination across large datasets or multiple services. However, reliance on cloud execution increases latency for end users and introduces dependencies on network availability.

The following matrix provides a systematic comparison of placement options across six decision dimensions:

Table 11-1. *Runtime Placement Decision Matrix. Use this to compare placement options against the capability's constraints before committing to an execution context*

Dimension	Client	Edge	Cloud
Latency	Lowest: no network hop	Low: near point of interaction	Higher: depends on network distance
Data Locality	Highest: data stays on the device	Medium: regional data access	Lower: data moves to the central store
Resource Availability	Limited: constrained by the device	Moderate: controlled infrastructure	High: scalable on demand
Connectivity Dependency	None: operates offline	Low: tolerates intermittent connectivity	High: requires a stable network
Cost Profile	Low marginal cost	Moderate: infrastructure and distribution	Variable: scales with usage
Security Boundary	Device-level: harder to enforce centrally	Controlled: organizational boundary	Strongest: centralized policy enforcement

In UMA, runtime placement is not encoded in the service implementation but expressed through metadata that defines requirements, constraints, and preferred execution contexts. This allows the system to reason about where a service should run based on current conditions and available environments. Metadata fields might explicitly specify minimum CPU or memory requirements, acceptable latency thresholds, preferred or required regions, and whether certain security certifications are necessary. The ability to move capabilities across runtimes introduces additional considerations for consistency and observability. Services must behave predictably regardless of where they are executed, and their behavior must be observable across environments. This reinforces the importance of clear contracts and stable metadata, as they provide the foundation for portability.

State Management Across Distributed Services

In UMA, state is not a centralized asset. It is the result of how capabilities interpret and react to events over time, guided by the contracts and metadata that define their behavior. Each service maintains its own local representation of state, derived from the events it produces and consumes. This representation is not authoritative for the entire system but is sufficient for the capability the service provides. The state is therefore inherently distributed, with no single service responsible for maintaining a complete and unified view. The meaning of that state is defined by the capability contract and its associated metadata. A service does not simply store data. It interprets events according to declared semantics. Two services may consume the same event and derive different state representations, each valid within the context of their respective capabilities. This is not an inconsistency, but a reflection of how responsibilities are separated across the system.

UMA systems implement state management through three complementary approaches. Event sourcing is the foundation: each service persists the sequence of events it has consumed rather than a snapshot of derived state. This allows the service to rebuild its internal view by replaying those events, which is essential for resilience and debugging. Local state projection means each service maintains only the state required by its own contract, derived from the events it declares as inputs. It does not replicate broader system state. When a capability needs context it does not own, it obtains it by subscribing to the relevant event or invoking the capability that owns that data. Synchronization across environments is handled through event propagation rather than direct state replication. A capability running on a mobile device records events locally and propagates them to edge or cloud capabilities when connectivity is available. The receiving capability processes those events in sequence, applying the same contract-defined semantics regardless of when they arrive. This tolerates partial connectivity without requiring distributed transactions or global locks.

This model introduces a different approach to consistency. Rather than enforcing immediate synchronization across services, UMA systems accept that state may temporarily diverge. Consistency is achieved over time as events propagate and are interpreted in accordance with stable contracts. Because the state is derived, its quality is directly tied to the quality of event design and metadata definition. The boundary of state responsibility is therefore aligned with the boundary of the capability. A service maintains only the state required to fulfill its contract and avoids replicating broader system state without a clear purpose. When additional context is required, it is obtained through interaction rather than duplication. Observability becomes essential in this model. Since the state is distributed and derived, understanding the current condition of the system requires visibility into both the events being processed and the state maintained by individual services.

The Ski Patrol Workflow: Decision Axes in Practice

The ski patrol incident workflow demonstrates how all six decision axes work together within a unified system that functions across mobile, edge, and cloud environments. When a patroller spots an injured skier in a remote part of the mountain and logs the incident on a mobile device, the system must still operate despite potentially limited or no connectivity. This scenario encompasses every decision axis discussed in this section. The system's granularity includes six capabilities, each representing a complete domain action: Incident Reporting, Triage Assistance, Incident Classification, Dispatch Coordination, Response Management, and Incident Closure. Each capability has a single, well-defined responsibility that can be described in one sentence and activated independently. Event design: each capability emits a stable domain fact. Incident Reported, Incident Triaged, Incident Classified, Patrol Assigned, Response Started, and Incident Closed each description of what occurred without prescribing how other capabilities should respond. Metadata design: each capability declares its placement constraints, required permissions, and event contracts in structured metadata. The triage capability on the mobile device declares that it can operate without connectivity. The dispatch capability declares that it requires cloud placement and system-wide visibility. Runtime placement: each capability executes where its constraints are met. Incident Reporting runs on the mobile device. Triage Assistance runs locally or at the edge. Classification and Dispatch run in the cloud. Response Management is distributed across field devices. State management: each capability maintains only the state required by its contract. The mobile device records events locally and propagates them when connectivity is available. The cloud capabilities process these events in sequence when they arrive, applying consistent semantics regardless of the delay.

The companion implementation at chapter-11-architectural-tradeoffs uses a media upload workflow to demonstrate the same decision axes across six runnable labs. The baseline scenario in lab1-baseline shows all six axes in a coherent state: three services, stable domain events, concise metadata, distributed event progression, constraint-driven placement, and local state projections. Each subsequent lab degrades one or more axes to demonstrate the failure modes described in the section "Anti-patterns and Failure Modes." The recovered architecture in lab6-recovered-architecture returns all axes to coherent values, showing that recovery comes from disciplined choices rather than from adding more services or more orchestration.

The decision axes in this chapter are interdependent, and their combined effect determines system behavior. Service granularity shapes how capabilities are defined. Capability boundaries determine how responsibilities are expressed and how services interact. Event design governs how information flows across the system, while metadata provides the structure through which these interactions are described and interpreted. Runtime placement defines where capabilities execute and under what constraints, and state emerges from how events are processed across these distributed components. A change in one dimension, such as refining capability boundaries or adjusting event structure, affects how the state is derived, how services are composed, and how the system evolves. The architect's role is to ensure these dimensions remain aligned. Coherence in UMA results from the consistent application of principles across these interconnected areas, not from rigid structure.

Architectural Patterns for UMA Systems

Architectural patterns in UMA connect decision axes to practical implementation. They are common solutions that arise when decision axes are applied consistently. The earlier outlined decision axes define UMA systems at a conceptual level by setting capability boundaries, service interactions, metadata-driven behavior, and distributed execution. While these provide a framework for understanding system behavior, they do not specify how to build systems in practice. Architectural patterns fill this gap by illustrating recurring solutions that naturally emerge from consistent application of decision axes. In UMA, these patterns are a result of designing around capabilities, events, and metadata, demonstrating how services are broken down, interactions coordinated, and behavior assembled into higher-level workflows.

Unlike traditional architectural patterns that focus on structure or deployment, UMA patterns center on interaction and interpretation. They describe how capabilities are discovered and combined, how events drive coordination without central control, and how metadata enables adaptation and evolution. The patterns in this chapter are reference models, not prescriptive rules. They illustrate how UMA principles can be applied to achieve coherent, scalable, and adaptable systems, making implicit design decisions explicit and supporting effective reasoning about trade-offs and system behavior.

Capability-based Decomposition

Decomposition in UMA starts by identifying capabilities and defining their boundaries based on responsibility, semantics, and interaction, rather than layers, components, or data ownership. A capability is a meaningful unit of behavior within the domain that remains stable over time. It includes not only what a service does but also how other services interpret and utilize that behavior. This method contrasts with traditional service decomposition, where boundaries are often set by system layers, database partitions, or organizational structures. Although these factors may influence design, they are secondary to the definition of capabilities. A service is considered well-designed when its capability can be understood independently of its implementation and can engage in the system through clear contracts and metadata.

Capability-based decomposition requires discipline in separating concerns. Each service should represent a cohesive unit of behavior that does not depend on implicit coordination with unrelated services. When multiple capabilities are grouped without a clear unifying concept, the result is a service that is difficult to interpret and reuse. Conversely, when a capability is fragmented across services, the system becomes dependent on coordination patterns that increase runtime complexity. In UMA, decomposition is closely tied to how services interact through events and how their behavior is described through metadata. A capability is not defined in isolation but in relation to the events it produces and consumes and the metadata that expresses its role within the system. This ensures that decomposition supports composition, allowing services to be combined into larger behaviors without tight coupling.

The process of identifying capabilities is iterative. Initial boundaries are often refined as the system evolves and interaction patterns become clearer. Observing how services are composed at runtime provides valuable feedback on whether capabilities are appropriately defined. A frequent need for coordination among the same set of services may indicate that a boundary is too narrow. Repeated changes affecting multiple concerns within a single service may suggest that a boundary is too broad. Capability-based decomposition also supports portability across execution environments. Because capabilities are defined independently of runtime placement, the same service can be executed in different contexts, provided its constraints are satisfied.

Event-Driven Orchestration Patterns

In UMA, services coordinate through events instead of direct control flow. Orchestration arises from distributed capability responses rather than from a centralized component guiding each step. This doesn't eliminate orchestration but shifts its nature. It's no longer a central process owning the workflow; instead, it becomes a distributed pattern of reactions, where each service contributes to a broader outcome without needing full knowledge of the sequence. Commonly, UMA uses event-driven progression, where domain events implicitly define the process flow. Each service listens for specific events, assesses them against its capability contract and metadata, and generates new events once conditions are met. The entire workflow isn't stored in a single location but results from these interactions.

However, fully distributed orchestration introduces its own challenges. Without clear boundaries, workflows can become difficult to reason about, especially as the number of participating services grows. Events may be emitted without a clear understanding of how they contribute to a broader outcome, leading to fragmented or unintended behavior. To address this, UMA systems often rely on implicit orchestration contracts expressed through metadata. These contracts do not define a rigid workflow but establish expectations about how events relate, what conditions must be met, and how services should interpret specific signals. In some cases, a more explicit coordination mechanism is required. UMA supports patterns in which a service acts as a coordinator for a specific outcome, not by directly controlling execution, but by observing events and emitting new ones that guide the system toward a desired state.

The balance between distributed and coordinated orchestration depends on the workflow. Simple, well-defined processes can often be handled through fully distributed event progression. More complex scenarios, especially those involving long-running interactions or conditional branching, may benefit from introducing coordinating services that provide structure without centralizing control. The effectiveness of event-driven orchestration in UMA depends on clear event design and precise metadata. Events must represent meaningful transitions, and metadata must provide sufficient context for correct interpretation.

The following diagrams illustrate both orchestration patterns:

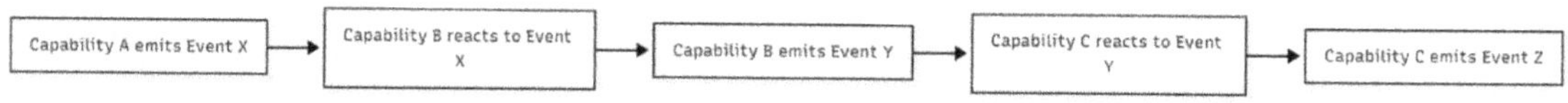

***Figure 11-2.** Event-driven progression through distributed capability reactions. Each service reacts to events based on its own contract and metadata, producing new events that advance the system behavior without centralized control*

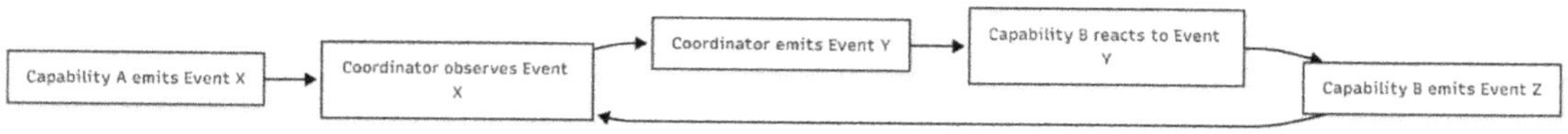

***Figure 11-3.** Coordinated orchestration through event observation and emission. A coordinating service influences the progression of a workflow by observing events and emitting new ones, providing structure while preserving loose coupling between participating services*

Metadata-First Service Design

In UMA, metadata-first design begins by defining the capability in a structured, machine-readable form before introducing any implementation details. Implementation then becomes a realization of that definition, rather than the origin of it. Traditional service design begins with code. Interfaces and documentation are derived from implementation, and any descriptive artifacts are often incomplete or inconsistent. Metadata-first design changes the service contract's role. The contract is no longer limited to input and output definitions. It now includes semantics, event interactions, constraints, and execution characteristics. Metadata becomes the authoritative source of truth for how both humans and automated systems should interpret a service. Designing services in this way requires a shift in process. Architects and developers define the capability using metadata first, establishing clear expectations for behavior and interactions. This enables greater consistency across services. When metadata follows shared structures and conventions, services can be discovered, composed, and analyzed uniformly. Automated tools can reason about capabilities, validate interactions, and assist in composing workflows without relying on implicit knowledge or external documentation.

Metadata-first design also supports portability and adaptability. Because behavior is described independently of implementation, services can be executed in different environments or replaced with alternative implementations without changing how the system understands them. This aligns with the broader goal of separating capability definition from runtime concerns. However, this approach introduces new responsibilities. Metadata must be precise, stable, and maintained with the same rigor as code. Inaccurate or outdated metadata undermines the system's ability to reason about behavior and can lead to incorrect composition or execution. Governance mechanisms are therefore required to validate metadata and ensure consistency across services. In UMA, metadata-first design enables systems to describe and adapt themselves. Services become self-describing units of behavior, supporting dynamic composition and execution.

Runtime-Aware Service Design

In UMA, services are designed with the expectation that they may execute in different environments. Runtime constraints are not implementation details, but integral aspects of the capability definition. Traditional service design often assumes a stable execution environment. Dependencies, performance characteristics, and resource availability are treated as implicit conditions. In UMA, these factors must be made explicit. A service must define not only what it does but also under what conditions it can operate effectively. This information is expressed through metadata, allowing the system to determine where and how a capability should be executed. Runtime-aware design begins by identifying the constraints associated with a capability. These include resource requirements, latency sensitivity, data access needs, and security considerations. When these constraints are explicit, services become portable across environments. The same capability can be executed across different runtimes, provided its requirements are met. This decouples service design from deployment decisions, enabling more flexible system behavior.

This approach also necessitates designing for variability. A service may behave differently depending on where it is executed. Latency, data availability, and resource limits can affect performance and responsiveness. Runtime-aware design requires anticipating these differences and ensuring that behavior remains consistent within acceptable bounds. This may involve defining fallback strategies, degraded modes of operation, or alternative execution paths. Another consideration is the interaction between services operating in different environments. When capabilities are distributed across client, edge, and cloud, coordination must account for differences in availability and communication latency. Event-driven interaction supports this model, but only if services are designed to tolerate delays, retries, and partial failures. Metadata plays a central role in enabling runtime awareness, providing the information required to evaluate whether a service can be executed in a given environment and how it should behave under specific conditions.

Composing Services into Workflows

In UMA, workflows are not predefined as fixed step sequences. Instead, they develop from combining capabilities that interact via events, guided by contracts and metadata. Unlike traditional workflow systems where the operation sequence is explicitly designed and centrally managed, UMA's workflow is implicit. It is shaped by the relationships between events, the conditions for service reactions, and the capabilities offered. The process starts by identifying the desired outcome and the necessary capabilities. Each capability adds a specific behavior, and their interactions create the overall workflow. These interactions occur through events signaling progress and triggering subsequent actions, rather than through direct calls. Metadata plays a crucial role by providing information on how capabilities can be combined, the events they generate and handle, and the conditions they require.

A key characteristic of UMA workflows is their open-ended nature. New capabilities can be introduced that respond to existing events, extending or modifying the system's behavior without requiring changes to existing services. However, implicit composition introduces challenges in visibility and control. Because workflows are not centrally defined, it can be difficult to understand how a particular outcome is achieved or to predict how changes will affect system behavior. This reinforces the importance of observability and metadata, which provide the means to trace interactions and reason about workflows at runtime.

***Figure 11-4.** Workflow composition through event-driven capability interaction. A workflow emerges from a sequence of events produced and consumed by independent capabilities, each contributing to the overall outcome without centralized control*

Example: Ski Patrol Incident Workflow

This is the workflow first introduced in the section "Introduction: From Structure to Interaction." The following describes it in full detail, showing how the decisions and patterns discussed in Sections II through V are expressed in a single, coherent system that operates across mobile, edge, and cloud runtimes.

On a winter morning, a patroller identifies an injured skier on a remote section of the mountain. Using a mobile device, the patroller records the incident, including location, observed condition, and initial notes. At this point, connectivity may be limited or unavailable, yet the system must still respond. The reporting capability executes directly on the mobile device. It captures the input and produces an Incident Reported event, which is stored locally and propagated when connectivity allows. The system does not depend on immediate access to a central service. The capability operates within the device's constraints while preserving the same contract and behavior.

A triage capability then evaluates the reported information. In this context, it may execute on the same device or on a nearby dispatch machine, depending on availability. This capability incorporates contextual signals such as location, historical incident patterns, and environmental conditions and produces an Incident Triaged event. The analysis is assisted by a local or edge-deployed AI model, allowing initial assessment without requiring cloud connectivity. The classification capability consumes both the reported data and the triage output. When connectivity is available, this capability may execute at the edge or in the cloud, where additional data and broader system context can be accessed. It produces an Incident Classified event that represents a more stable and consistent interpretation of severity and type.

Dispatch coordination follows. This capability typically operates in a more connected environment, such as a dispatch station or cloud service, where visibility into patroller availability and system-wide conditions is required. It consumes the classification event and emits a Patrol Assigned event, assigning resources to the incident. As the response progresses, a response management capability tracks updates through events such as Response Started and Response Completed. These updates may originate from mobile devices used by patrollers in the field, with events synchronized as connectivity permits. The system tolerates partial connectivity, allowing local actions to be recorded and later integrated into the broader workflow. Finally, the closure capability emits an Incident Closed event, completing the observable sequence. This capability may execute in the cloud, where incident data is consolidated, persisted, and made available for reporting and analysis.

At no point is the workflow tied to a single runtime. Each capability executes where its constraints are met, while maintaining a consistent behavioral model defined through contracts and metadata.

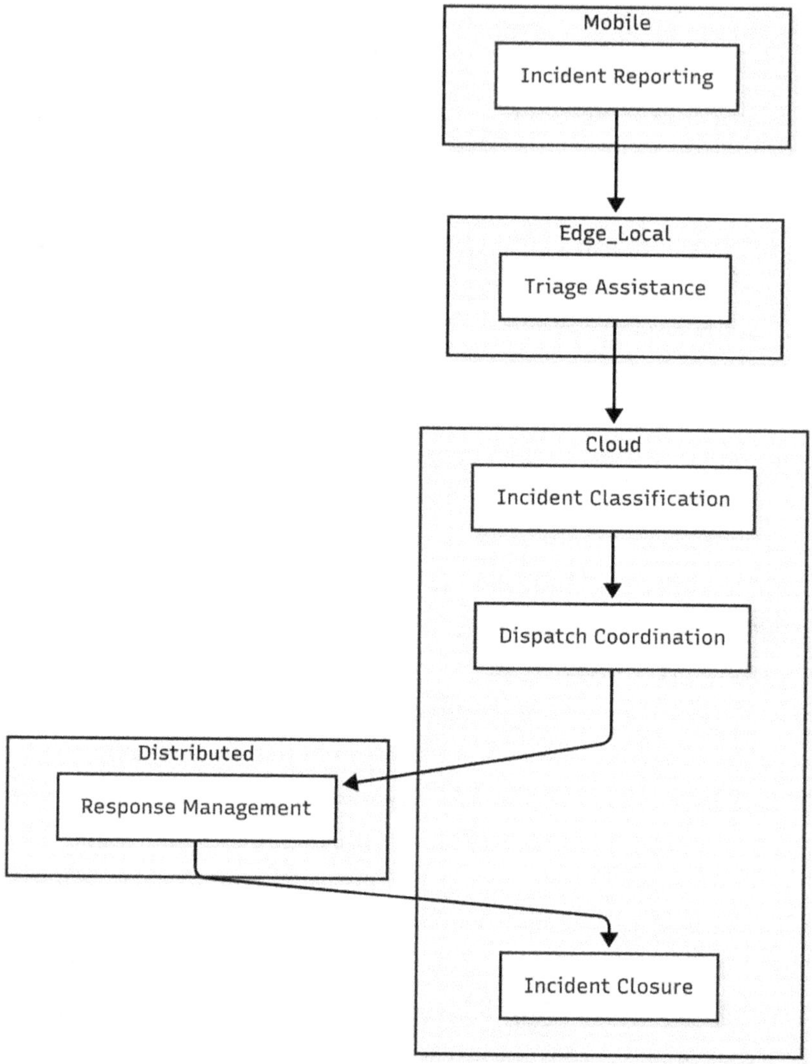

***Figure 11-5.** Capability-driven ski patrol workflow in a UMA system. Each capability executes in the most appropriate runtime, mobile, edge, or cloud, enabling flexible orchestration and independent evolution while preserving a consistent event-driven flow*

This workflow is supported by six capabilities, each defined independently of where it executes: Incident Reporting running on the mobile device; Incident Triage Assistance, optionally AI-assisted, running locally or at the edge; Incident Classification leveraging broader context in edge or cloud environments; Dispatch Coordination operating where system-wide visibility is available; Response Management distributed across field devices; and Incident Closure consolidating results in the cloud. Each capability is described through metadata that defines its behavior, constraints, and preferred execution contexts.

This example illustrates a key property of UMA systems: behavior is defined independently of execution. The same capability can operate on a mobile device, a local machine, or in the cloud, provided its constraints are satisfied. Execution placement becomes a function of context rather than a fixed architectural decision. AI is integrated as a capability rather than a separate layer. The triage capability uses AI to enrich event interpretation, but it participates in the system in the same way as any other service, consuming and producing events in accordance with its contract. The workflow is therefore not tied to a centralized control plane or a single deployment environment. It progresses across disconnected, local, and cloud contexts, maintaining coherence through shared event semantics and metadata. This distinguishes UMA from conventional microservices architectures, where services are typically bound to stable, server-side environments. In UMA, portability and adaptability are inherent system properties, rather than extensions.

Designing for Evolution and Change

In traditional architectures, evolution is managed as a constraint, one that slows change as much as it enables it. UMA addresses this challenge by treating evolution as a core architectural property. In UMA systems, evolution is not treated as an afterthought or a maintenance concern. Capabilities are defined through metadata, and their behavior is resolved at runtime based on context, constraints, and compatibility. This allows multiple versions of a capability to coexist and enables systems to adapt without requiring coordinated changes across all consumers. Compatibility is no longer enforced solely through rigid versioning strategies. Instead, it is expressed through contracts that describe behavior, expectations, and constraints. These contracts allow consumers and providers to evolve independently, while the runtime ensures that interactions remain valid. The following sections explore how versioning, compatibility, and incremental evolution are handled in UMA systems and how these mechanisms enable continuous change without sacrificing stability. The examples in this section extend the ski patrol workflow introduced in the section "Introduction: From Structure to Interaction" and developed in the section "Core Architectural Decision Axes in UMA."

Versioning Strategies for Services and Metadata

In UMA, versioning describes change rather than enforcing it. Version information is expressed through metadata at the capability level, not through deployment artifacts or naming conventions. Versioning is often treated as a property of deployed services. A service exposes an interface, a version is assigned, and consumers are expected to align with that version as it evolves. This approach introduces coordination overhead as systems grow. In UMA systems, a capability represents behavior, not an implementation, and its version reflects the evolution of its contract, including inputs, outputs, constraints, and semantics. This information is not implicit in code or endpoints. It is explicitly described and made available to the runtime. Instead of binding consumers to a specific service version, the system resolves the most appropriate capability version at runtime. Multiple versions of the same capability can coexist, each describing a valid contract. Consumers express their requirements through constraints, and the runtime selects a compatible provider based on those constraints and the current execution context.

Consider the Incident Triage capability in the ski patrol workflow. Its initial version, v1.0, accepts location and observed condition as inputs and produces an Incident Triaged event as output. A second version, v2.0, extends this contract by adding an optional AI confidence score field to the output and declaring a new runtime requirement for an edge-deployed inference model. Both versions remain registered in the capability registry. A mobile client built against v1.0 continues to consume the original event structure without modification. A new dispatch coordination capability built after v2.0 was released can take advantage of the confidence score to prioritize resource allocation. The runtime selects the appropriate version based on each consumer's declared requirements and the constraints of the current execution environment. No coordinated migration is required. This scenario corresponds to lab7-versioned-capability in the companion implementation, where the same pattern is demonstrated using a media upload workflow with two coexisting triage capability versions.

A key property of UMA systems is the coexistence of multiple versions of a capability. When a capability evolves, older versions do not need to be immediately removed. They remain available for consumers who depend on them, while newer versions can be introduced for consumers who require additional functionality or improved behavior. This enables gradual adoption and reduces the risk associated with change. Version selection is performed dynamically. When a capability is required, the runtime evaluates the consumer's requirements, the available capability versions, and the constraints of the current environment. These constraints may include latency, data locality, resource availability, or execution context. Based on this evaluation, the system selects the most appropriate version. This process extends beyond simple version matching. It allows the system to prefer implementations that are better suited to the context, including those that incorporate AI or enhanced logic. Versioning becomes part of the system's adaptive behavior rather than a static contract between components.

Migrating Legacy Services to Metadata-Based Versioning

Organizations adopting UMA versioning from a legacy system can follow an incremental migration path. The process typically follows four key phases. Assessment involves identifying critical service interfaces and evaluating their current versioning approaches and dependencies. This establishes a baseline understanding of which services are most tightly coupled to specific version conventions and which carry the highest migration risk. Metadata enrichment involves representing version information explicitly in metadata alongside existing deployment artifacts. Contract changes, inputs, outputs, and compatibility expectations are added to the metadata layer without disrupting existing consumers. This phase extends the metadata schema rather than replacing the existing versioning mechanism. Parallel operation introduces metadata-based versioning while maintaining support for existing versioning strategies. Both legacy and new consumers operate without disruption during this phase. Compatibility is maintained by running the metadata-driven selection logic alongside the existing resolution mechanism. Runtime integration gradually shifts responsibility for version selection and compatibility checks from manual processes to automated runtime resolution. Legacy systems transition at their own pace, and the metadata layer becomes the authoritative source of truth as adoption increases. By following these phases, architects can introduce metadata-based versioning step by step, reducing risk and ensuring a smooth transition.

Backward Compatibility in Distributed Systems

In UMA systems, backward compatibility is expressed through contracts and evaluated at runtime. Compatibility is determined by the alignment between what a consumer requires and what a capability provides. Backward compatibility is often treated as a constraint imposed on service evolution. In traditional distributed systems, once an interface is exposed, it must be preserved to avoid breaking consumers. This leads to conservative design choices, accumulation of legacy behavior, and increasing complexity over time. When a capability evolves in UMA, it can introduce new fields, extend behavior, or improve internal logic without invalidating existing consumers, as long as the declared contract remains compatible. Compatibility is defined by required and optional elements, supported structures, and behavioral expectations, rather than by a fixed interface tied to a specific deployment. The system does not assume synchronized upgrades. Different consumers may have different expectations, and multiple versions of a capability can coexist. The runtime evaluates these differences by comparing consumer requirements with the metadata of available capability versions, selecting a provider that satisfies the declared constraints.

Consider the Incident Classification capability in the ski patrol workflow. Its initial version produces an Incident Classified event containing category and location fields. A new version of this capability adds a severity field to support improved dispatch prioritization. The existing Dispatch Coordination capability, which was built against the original contract, declares only category and location as inputs. The new severity field is defined as optional in the updated contract. When the runtime evaluates compatibility between the updated Classification capability and the existing Dispatch consumer, it confirms that all required fields are satisfied and permits the interaction. The Dispatch capability continues to operate unchanged. A new version of Dispatch that wants to use severity can declare it as a required input, which causes the runtime to select only the updated Classification capability for that consumer. Both consumers coexist without disruption, and no coordinated migration is required. This scenario corresponds to lab8-backward-compatible-extension in the companion implementation.

Metadata enables more expressive compatibility rules than those typically found in static interface definitions. It can describe optional fields, supported ranges, conditional behavior, and deprecation signals. It can distinguish between stable elements and those that may evolve. This allows compatibility to be evaluated with precision rather than through binary matching. Older versions of a capability can remain available as long as they are required, supporting consumers who depend on them. As usage decreases, these versions can be deprecated and eventually removed without disrupting the system. In UMA systems, backward compatibility is not achieved by freezing interfaces. It is achieved by making compatibility explicit, machine-readable, and resolvable at runtime. This allows systems to evolve continuously while maintaining stable interactions across independently changing components.

Evolving Capabilities Without Breaking Consumers

In UMA systems, capabilities evolve independently of their consumers. Consumers are not bound to static interfaces. They are bound to contracts that can be satisfied by multiple implementations over time. In traditional systems, evolving a service without breaking consumers requires careful coordination. Changes are introduced through new versions, existing interfaces are preserved, and migration paths are defined. Even with these practices, evolution remains constrained by the need to maintain compatibility with all existing consumers. In UMA systems, a capability represents behavior described through metadata, and its evolution is reflected in changes to that metadata rather than in tightly coupled interfaces. Consumers do not bind to a specific implementation or version. They declare their requirements, and the system resolves a compatible capability at runtime. This decoupling fundamentally changes how evolution is managed.

In the ski patrol workflow, the Response Management capability begins as a simple event tracker that records Response Started and Response Completed events from field devices. As operational needs grow, a second version is introduced that incorporates an edge-deployed AI model to predict response times and flag at-risk situations. This version runs at the edge rather than on mobile devices and produces an enriched event with additional fields. The original mobile-based version continues to run for devices that cannot meet the edge runtime requirements. The runtime selects between the two versions based on the declared constraints of each device context. Field patrollers using older devices experience no disruption, while dispatch coordinators with access to edge infrastructure benefit from the enhanced capability automatically. This scenario corresponds to lab9-capability-coexistence in the companion implementation.

When a capability is extended, new inputs, outputs, or behaviors can be introduced without requiring existing consumers to change. These additions are expressed as optional elements or extended constraints within the metadata. Consumers who are unaware of these extensions continue to operate against the subset of the contract they require, while newer consumers can take advantage of the enhanced functionality. When a capability changes in a way that is not backward compatible, a new version is introduced alongside the existing one. Both versions remain available, each describing a valid contract. The runtime selects the appropriate version based on the consumer's declared requirements and the current execution context. This allows evolution to occur without forcing immediate migration. A key aspect of this model is late binding. The relationship between a consumer and a capability is not fixed at design time. It is established dynamically at runtime based on metadata, constraints, and availability. This allows the system to adapt as capabilities evolve, without requiring changes to the consumer. Deprecation becomes a managed process rather than a disruptive event. Metadata can signal deprecation status and guide the runtime away from outdated versions while still allowing them to be used when necessary.

Managing Incremental System Evolution

In UMA systems, incremental evolution is the default mode of operation, not a compromise between stability and progress. Systems do not evolve in discrete steps. Change is introduced continuously, often across components operating in different environments and following different release cycles. In UMA systems, evolution is managed incrementally through the capability model and metadata. Capabilities can be introduced, extended, or replaced without requiring a system-wide transition. Each change is localized, described explicitly, and resolved at runtime. This allows the system to evolve as a collection of independent changes rather than as a sequence of coordinated releases. New capabilities can be added alongside existing ones without disrupting current workflows. Because capabilities are discovered and selected dynamically, the system can incorporate new behavior as soon as it becomes available. Existing consumers continue to operate against the contracts they depend on, while new consumers can take advantage of additional capabilities.

This incremental model is particularly important in environments where different runtimes evolve at different speeds. Mobile devices may not update frequently, edge systems may operate under constrained conditions, and cloud services may evolve rapidly. UMA accommodates these differences by allowing capabilities to exist across multiple runtimes and versions simultaneously, with the runtime selecting appropriate combinations based on context. Deployment is no longer the primary mechanism for coordinating change. Instead, evolution is driven by the introduction and resolution of capabilities. As new metadata becomes available, the system can adapt its behavior without requiring synchronized releases. This reduces the need for large-scale migrations and enables continuous delivery of incremental improvements.

Observability plays a critical role in this process. Because interactions are mediated through capabilities and events, the system can track which versions are used, how often they are invoked, and under which conditions they succeed or fail. This information supports decisions about when to promote new capabilities, when to deprecate older ones, and how to guide the system toward more efficient or reliable configurations. AI can participate in this feedback loop by analyzing usage patterns, identifying inefficiencies, and suggesting adjustments to capability selection or deployment. In this context, evolution is managed by both developers and system behavior. Change is introduced gradually, validated through runtime behavior, and integrated without disrupting existing functionality. This enables systems to grow and adapt over time while maintaining coherence across independently evolving components.

Anti-patterns and Failure Modes

Most failure modes in UMA systems arise not from incorrect implementations but from incorrect boundaries, excessive flexibility, or lack of discipline in how capabilities and metadata are defined. Every architectural model introduces new trade-offs. UMA reduces coupling between services and enables systems to evolve independently, but it also shifts complexity into metadata, runtime resolution, and capability composition. When these elements are misapplied, the system does not fail immediately. It degrades over time, often in ways that are difficult to detect. These issues tend to emerge gradually, as the number of capabilities increases and the system evolves across multiple runtimes. Unlike traditional architectures, where failures are often tied to specific components or interfaces, UMA failures are systemic. They appear as loss of clarity, unpredictable behavior, or increasing difficulty in reasoning about the system. Because behavior is resolved at runtime, these problems can remain hidden until they reach a level where they affect reliability or performance.

The following sections describe common anti-patterns and failure modes observed in UMA systems. Each one represents a deviation from the model's intended use and underscores the importance of maintaining clear capability boundaries, disciplined metadata design, and controlled runtime behavior. The companion implementation at chapter-11-architectural-tradeoffs demonstrates each failure mode as a runnable lab scenario. Lab 2 through Lab 5 each isolate one anti-pattern. Lab 6 shows the recovered architecture. Understanding these failure modes is essential for building systems that remain adaptable and stable.

Over-granular Service Decomposition

Over-granular decomposition results in a large number of narrowly scoped capabilities that collectively create a system that is difficult to reason about, even though each capability behaves correctly in isolation. Because UMA encourages defining behavior as independent capabilities, there is a natural inclination to make those capabilities as small and specific as possible. While this can increase reuse in theory, in practice, it often leads to fragmentation. Workflows become chains of fine-grained interactions, increasing the number of events, the volume of metadata, and the overall coordination required at runtime. This issue is not immediately visible. The system continues to function, and each capability behaves correctly in isolation. The problem emerges as the system grows. Small changes require orchestrating multiple capabilities, latency increases due to additional hops, and the runtime must resolve an expanding set of possible combinations.

In UMA, capabilities are intended to represent meaningful units of behavior rather than arbitrary fragments of logic. A capability should encapsulate a complete responsibility that can be understood and reused independently. When capabilities are defined too narrowly, they lose this property and become implementation details exposed at the architectural level. A practical indicator of over-granular decomposition is the shape of workflows. If a simple operation requires a long sequence of capability interactions, or if capabilities exist primarily to pass data from one step to another without adding meaningful behavior, the system is likely over-decomposed. Another indicator is duplication of orchestration logic, where similar sequences of capabilities are repeatedly composed to achieve slightly different outcomes.

This failure mode often originates from applying microservice principles without adapting them to the UMA model. In traditional systems, smaller services can improve isolation. In UMA, excessive granularity increases runtime complexity because composition is dynamic and resolved at execution time. Correcting this requires redefining capability boundaries. Capabilities should be coarse enough to represent a complete action or decision while remaining independent and composable. In practice, this means grouping related logic into a single capability when it forms a cohesive unit, even if further splitting is possible.

Detection: workflows requiring more than four capability hops for a simple operation, or capabilities that exist solely to pass data between steps without adding behavior. In the companion implementation, lab2-over-granular shows this pattern directly: the image analysis flow is split into five services across four interactions, including a byte loader and a validator that add coordination overhead without contributing meaningful domain behavior. Running the diff between lab1-baseline and lab2-over-granular isolates the exact axis change. Prevention: define capability boundaries around complete domain actions before decomposing further, and validate boundaries by asking whether the capability can be described in a single clear sentence. Resolution: identify clusters of capabilities that are always composed together and merge them into a single capability with a unified contract. The lab1-baseline scenario shows the coherent version of the same workflow using three services.

Metadata Bloat and Loss of Clarity

Metadata bloat does not appear as a failure at first. Each addition is justified in isolation. Over time, the metadata loses coherence, and the system becomes harder to reason about. Metadata is central to UMA systems. It defines capabilities, describes their behavior, and enables runtime resolution. As the system evolves, metadata grows to capture additional constraints, variations, and operational details. Without discipline, this growth leads to bloat, where metadata becomes dense, inconsistent, and difficult to interpret. New fields are added to support new requirements, optional attributes accumulate to preserve compatibility, and annotations are introduced to guide runtime decisions. Over time, however, the metadata loses coherence. It becomes harder to determine which fields are essential, which are optional, and which are no longer relevant.

As clarity decreases, the system becomes harder to reason about. Developers struggle to understand how capabilities are defined and how to use them. The runtime must process increasingly complex metadata, making resolution more expensive and less predictable. Small inconsistencies in how metadata is structured or interpreted can lead to divergent behavior across environments. A common indicator of metadata bloat is the presence of fields that are rarely used or poorly understood. Another is the duplication of similar concepts expressed in slightly different ways across capabilities. The root cause is often the absence of clear boundaries and governance. Without a consistent schema and a disciplined approach to evolution, metadata expands to accommodate every new use case.

Addressing this requires treating metadata as a first-class design artifact. Schemas must be defined, versioned, and enforced. Each field should have a clear purpose, and additions should be evaluated for their impact on the overall model. It is also important to distinguish between descriptive metadata and operational hints. Mixing these concerns leads to confusion, as fields intended for human understanding become entangled with those used for runtime decision-making.

Detection: fields that are rarely used in runtime decisions, duplicate concepts expressed differently across capabilities, or metadata that requires explanation before it can be interpreted. In the companion implementation, lab5-over-orchestrated shows this pattern through the workflow-coordinator service, whose metadata declares eight fields, including workflowTable, branchRules, retryRules, manualOverrides, observabilityHooks, and priorityRules. This level of detail belongs in orchestration logic, not in capability metadata. Prevention: establish a shared schema with mandatory review for new fields and separate descriptive metadata from operational attributes. Resolution: audit all metadata fields against actual runtime usage, deprecate unused fields, and consolidate duplicate concepts into a single canonical representation. The lab6-recovered-architecture shows the same coordinator capability with focused, concise metadata.

Hidden Coupling Through Events

The absence of explicit connections does not eliminate coupling in event-driven systems. It changes its form. Coupling becomes implicit and difficult to detect until a change to an event breaks multiple consumers in unexpected ways. Event-driven interaction is a core aspect of UMA systems. Capabilities communicate by emitting and consuming events, allowing workflows to emerge without predefined control flow. This reduces direct dependencies between components and enables flexible composition across runtimes. However, a capability emits an event based on its internal logic, and multiple other capabilities react to that event. Over time, assumptions form around the structure, timing, and meaning of that event. These assumptions are rarely centralized or explicitly documented. They are embedded in the behavior of the consuming capabilities. As the system evolves, this implicit coupling becomes problematic. A change to an event, even a small one, can affect multiple consumers in unexpected ways. Because the relationships are not explicitly declared, it is difficult to identify all affected components.

This issue is often introduced gradually. Initially, events are defined with a clear purpose, and a small number of consumers rely on them. As new capabilities are added, they begin to subscribe to existing events to avoid duplicating logic. Over time, events become shared integration points, and their meaning expands beyond their original intent. A common indicator of hidden coupling is when a single event is consumed by many unrelated capabilities, each interpreting it slightly differently. Another is when changes to an event require extensive testing across the system to ensure that no unintended side effects occur. In UMA, events should represent well-defined facts about the system, not generalized triggers for arbitrary behavior.

Metadata plays a critical role in addressing this issue. Events and their semantics should be explicitly described, including their structure, intent, and expected usage. Capabilities that consume events should declare their dependencies in a way that can be analyzed and validated. Another important practice is to limit the scope of events. Instead of creating broad, generic events that serve multiple purposes, events should be specific and aligned with clear domain concepts.

Detection: a single event consumed by more than three unrelated capabilities, or changes to an event requiring testing across a large portion of the system. In the companion implementation, lab3-hidden-event-coupling shows this pattern through the processing.ready event, which both the image-analyzer and the metadata-indexer consume with different interpretations. The event name is vague, and its consumers depend on implied semantics rather than explicit domain facts. Running the diff between lab2-over-granular and lab3-hidden-event-coupling isolates the exact event semantics axis change. Prevention: define events narrowly around single-domain facts and declare consumer dependencies explicitly in metadata. Resolution: introduce more specific event types to replace overloaded ones, and update consuming capabilities to declare their dependencies against the new types. The lab1-baseline scenario shows image.uploaded and image.analyzed as stable domain facts with clear, non-overlapping consumers.

Runtime Ambiguity and Unpredictable Behavior

Runtime ambiguity occurs when multiple capabilities satisfy the same requirements, but there is no clear, deterministic way to choose among them. The system continues to operate, but its behavior becomes difficult to predict and harder to validate. UMA systems rely on runtime resolution to select capabilities based on metadata, constraints, and context. This flexibility allows the system to adapt across environments and evolve without centralized coordination. However, when resolution criteria are unclear or inconsistent, the system can exhibit ambiguous or unpredictable behavior. This issue often emerges as the number of capabilities increases. Different teams introduce alternative implementations, each valid in isolation, but overlapping in scope. Without clear prioritization or selection rules, the runtime must choose between equivalent options. Small differences in metadata, such as latency hints or optional constraints, can influence the outcome in ways that are not immediately visible.

Another source of ambiguity is inconsistent metadata. If capabilities describe similar properties using different conventions, the runtime may interpret them differently. This leads to situations where capability selection appears arbitrary, even though it follows internal logic that is not transparent to developers or operators. The impact of this failure mode is not always immediate. The system may function correctly in most scenarios but produce unexpected results in edge cases. These inconsistencies erode confidence in the system and complicate debugging, as behavior depends on runtime conditions that are difficult to reproduce. A common indicator of runtime ambiguity is non-deterministic behavior across environments. The same request may resolve to different capabilities in different contexts, even when the intended outcome is identical.

Addressing this requires introducing clear resolution strategies. Metadata should include explicit signals for prioritization, such as preferred execution contexts, performance characteristics, or capability rankings. When multiple capabilities are valid, the system should apply deterministic rules to ensure consistent selection. It is also important to standardize how metadata is defined and interpreted. Consistent schemas and naming conventions reduce ambiguity and allow the runtime to reason about capabilities more reliably.

Detection: non-deterministic capability selection across environments, or inability to explain why a specific capability was chosen when multiple candidates exist. In the companion implementation, lab4-runtime-ambiguity shows this pattern through two overlapping media.analyze capabilities, image-analyzer-edge and image-analyzer-cloud, neither of which declares a selection_rank. The runtime has no deterministic way to choose between them. Running the diff between lab3-hidden-event-coupling and lab4-runtime-ambiguity isolates the runtime placement axis change. Prevention: include explicit selection_rank values or placement constraints in capability metadata from the start, and define deterministic selection rules in the runtime policy. Resolution: audit overlapping capability definitions, narrow their scope, and add explicit selection criteria. The lab6-recovered-architecture shows image-analyzer-edge with a clear selection_rank of 40 and an explicit latencyTargetMs field, making selection deterministic.

Over-orchestration and System Fragility

Over-orchestration occurs when workflows are explicitly defined in detail through centralized coordinators, reintroducing the same coupling that UMA is designed to avoid.

UMA systems enable workflows to emerge from the interaction of independent capabilities. This reduces the need for centralized control and enables behavior to adapt dynamically to context. A common failure mode arises when this flexibility is constrained by excessive orchestration. Instead of allowing capabilities to react to events and resolve interactions at runtime, the system begins to enforce predefined sequences. Each step is tightly controlled, and dependencies between capabilities become explicit and fixed. This approach can appear beneficial in the short term. It provides a clear view of the workflow and makes behavior easier to trace. However, it gradually reintroduces the same coupling that UMA is designed to avoid. Capabilities become dependent on specific execution paths, and changes to one part of the workflow require updates to the orchestration logic.

As the system evolves, orchestration layers tend to become more complex. New conditions, exceptions, and variations are added to handle different scenarios. The orchestration logic becomes a central point of control, and any change to it carries a high risk of unintended side effects. The system becomes more fragile, as failures in the orchestration layer can disrupt entire workflows. A common indicator of over-orchestration is the presence of large, centralized components that coordinate multiple capabilities. Another is when workflows are defined as fixed sequences rather than as reactions to events. If adding or modifying a capability requires changes in a central orchestrator, the system is likely over-orchestrated.

The root cause is a shift from declarative to imperative control. Instead of describing what capabilities can do and allowing the system to resolve interactions, the architecture dictates how interactions must occur. Addressing this requires reestablishing the balance between orchestration and choreography. Capabilities should communicate through events and metadata, allowing workflows to emerge naturally. Orchestration should be used selectively, for example, when enforcing global constraints or coordinating critical operations, but not as the default mechanism for composing behavior.

Detection: a central component coordinating more than three capabilities, or workflows defined as fixed sequences rather than event reactions. In the companion implementation, lab5-over-orchestrated shows this pattern through a workflow-coordinator service that consumes image.uploaded and image.analyzed and emits analyze.now and index.now as instruction events. Both downstream capabilities, image-analyzer and metadata-indexer, run only when told to by the coordinator. The verdict changes to fragile, and three warnings appear: over_orchestrated, metadata_bloat, and state_drift. Running the diff between lab4-runtime-ambiguity and lab5-over-orchestrated isolates the orchestration, event semantics, metadata quality, and state model axes, all changing simultaneously, which is itself a signal that the anti-pattern is systemic rather than isolated. Prevention: prefer choreography over orchestration as the default coordination model, introducing centralized coordination only for global constraints. Resolution: decompose the orchestration logic into event-driven capability reactions, retaining a coordinator only for the minimal set of cross-cutting decisions that cannot be expressed through metadata alone. The lab6-recovered-architecture removes the coordinator entirely and returns to stable domain events, recovering the coherent verdict.

Practical Guidelines for Architects

UMA does not remove architectural trade-offs. It changes how they are managed.

The concepts introduced in the previous sections describe how UMA systems are structured, how they evolve, and where they can fail. Applying these ideas in real systems requires a different level of precision. Architectural decisions are made under constraints, with incomplete information, and often under pressure to deliver incrementally. In this context, there is no single correct way to design a system. The same capability can be decomposed in different ways, deployed across different runtimes, or expressed through different contracts. Each choice introduces trade-offs that affect performance, maintainability, and the ability to evolve. Instead of relying on fixed boundaries and predefined integration points, UMA provides a model in which behavior is described through capabilities, interactions are defined through contracts and events, and execution is resolved at runtime. This increases flexibility, but it also requires discipline. Poor decisions in capability design, metadata structure, or runtime placement can degrade the system even if each component is implemented correctly. The following sections provide criteria for evaluating options, identifying risks, and understanding the consequences of different design choices.

When to Split or Merge a Service

Deciding whether to split or merge a service is one of the most frequent and most impactful decisions in a UMA system. The capability model encourages decomposition, but it does not prescribe how far that decomposition should go.

Splitting too early or too aggressively introduces fragmentation. Merging too much creates rigid components that are difficult to evolve. A capability should represent a coherent unit of behavior that can be understood and reused independently. When a service contains multiple responsibilities that evolve at different rates, require different execution contexts, or serve distinct consumers, it becomes a candidate for decomposition. However, decomposition introduces cost. Each additional capability increases the number of interactions, the volume of metadata, and the complexity of runtime resolution. If splitting results in capabilities that exist primarily to pass data between steps without adding meaningful behavior, the system is likely over-decomposed.

In UMA, boundaries are defined at the capability level and are expected to evolve. Because behavior is described through metadata and contracts rather than fixed service interfaces, capabilities can be split, merged, or reassigned across runtimes with less friction. This allows architects to optimize for change over time, not just initial decomposition. A practical way to evaluate this decision is to consider how the capability is used. If it is always invoked as part of a larger sequence and never independently, merging may be more appropriate. If it is reused across different workflows or requires distinct execution contexts, splitting provides more flexibility. Evolution patterns also provide a strong signal. If changes to one part of a service frequently require changes to another, they likely belong to the same capability. If they evolve independently, separating them reduces coupling and simplifies maintenance.

A common mistake is to split capabilities too early based on anticipated scaling or ownership concerns. For example, separating Incident Classification and Dispatch Coordination in the ski patrol workflow into distinct capabilities before the system requires it can introduce unnecessary coordination overhead. Events must be passed between capabilities, additional contracts must be maintained, and failure scenarios become more complex. A more effective approach is to keep these responsibilities within a single capability until there is clear evidence of independent evolution, such as different scaling requirements, ownership boundaries, or runtime constraints. At that point, the capability can be split with well-defined contracts and minimal disruption to the overall system. The objective is not to maximize decomposition but to maintain clarity and adaptability. Capabilities should be large enough to represent meaningful behavior and small enough to evolve independently.

How to Define Clear Capability Boundaries

A capability should represent a complete and meaningful action or decision within the system. It is not a fragment of implementation logic, nor a thin wrapper around a data transformation.

Clear capability boundaries are essential to maintaining coherence in a UMA system. When boundaries are unclear, the system becomes difficult to reason about, even if each capability functions correctly. A capability encapsulates behavior that can be understood independently, including its inputs, outputs, and constraints. When a capability is well-defined, its purpose is clear without requiring knowledge of how it is used in a specific workflow. Ambiguity often arises when capabilities are defined in terms of technical layers rather than domain responsibilities. For example, separating data retrieval, validation, and processing into distinct capabilities may reflect internal implementation details, but it exposes unnecessary architectural-level detail. In UMA, these concerns should be grouped when they form a cohesive unit of behavior. The boundary should align with what the system does, not how it is implemented.

Another source of unclear boundaries is overlapping responsibility. When multiple capabilities perform similar functions with slight variations, the system introduces redundancy and confusion. This often leads to inconsistent behavior and makes it difficult for the runtime to determine which capability to use. A practical way to evaluate a boundary is to consider whether the capability can be described in a single, unambiguous sentence. If its purpose requires multiple conditions or exceptions to explain, the boundary is likely unclear. Execution context provides another dimension for defining boundaries. Capabilities that require different runtime environments should be separated if their constraints differ significantly. This allows the system to place them appropriately and avoids embedding environment-specific logic within a single capability. Capability boundaries are not static. As the system evolves, new requirements may reveal that a capability is too broad or too narrow. Adjusting boundaries is part of ongoing maintenance.

Designing Effective Events and Contracts

Events and contracts define how capabilities interact in a UMA system. When designed well, they enable flexibility and independent evolution. When designed poorly, they introduce ambiguity, hidden coupling, and inconsistent behavior.

A contract describes what a capability expects and what it provides. An effective contract is precise enough to be validated but not overly restrictive. It should capture the essential aspects of the interaction without embedding assumptions about a specific implementation or workflow. Clarity in contracts begins with structure. Inputs and outputs should be well-defined, with clear distinctions between required and optional elements. Optional fields allow capabilities to evolve without breaking existing consumers, while required fields establish a stable foundation for interaction. Semantics are equally important. A contract should describe not only the shape of the data but also what that data represents. Two capabilities may accept the same structure but interpret it differently, leading to inconsistent outcomes.

Events represent facts that occur within the system. They are not commands or instructions, but descriptions of state changes or outcomes. Designing effective events requires discipline in naming, structuring, and using them. An event should convey a clear and specific meaning, aligned with a domain concept, rather than acting as a generic trigger for multiple behaviors. Ambiguity in events leads to unintended coupling. When multiple capabilities use an event for different purposes, its meaning becomes diluted. Changes to the event can have unpredictable effects across the system. To avoid this, events should be narrowly scoped and tied to a single, well-defined concept. Contracts and events should be aligned. Events often carry data between capabilities, and their structure should be compatible with the contracts of both producers and consumers. Metadata plays a central role in making contracts and events explicit, allowing the runtime to validate compatibility and resolve interactions dynamically.

Another important consideration is evolution. Contracts and events must be designed to accommodate change. This involves allowing extensions through optional fields, avoiding breaking changes where possible, and introducing new versions when necessary. The system should support the coexistence of multiple versions, with the runtime selecting compatible combinations. In event-driven UMA systems, multiple capabilities may react to the same event, which can lead to conflicting actions or duplicated processing if not controlled. To ensure safe evolution, coordination rules must be defined at the contract level, including idempotency, clear ownership of decisions, and priority where needed.

Ensuring Metadata Quality and Consistency

Metadata is the foundation of UMA systems. When metadata is inconsistent or unclear, the system's behavior becomes difficult to predict, even if the underlying capabilities are correct.

Ensuring metadata quality begins with structure. All capabilities should follow a shared schema that defines how inputs, outputs, constraints, and behavioral attributes are expressed. This schema must be explicit and consistently applied. Variations in how similar concepts are represented introduce ambiguity and reduce the system's ability to reason about capabilities consistently. Clarity is as important as structure. Each field in the metadata should have a well-defined purpose. Fields that serve multiple meanings or depend on implicit context create confusion and lead to inconsistent interpretation. Consistency must be enforced across teams. In distributed environments, different teams will independently define capabilities. Without shared conventions and validation mechanisms, metadata evolves in multiple directions. Establishing guidelines for naming, structuring, and describing capabilities helps maintain a coherent model. Automated validation can ensure that new or updated metadata conforms to these expectations before it is introduced into the system.

Another important aspect is managing the metadata lifecycle. As capabilities evolve, metadata must be updated to reflect changes in behavior, constraints, or compatibility. Obsolete fields should be deprecated and eventually removed. Allowing outdated or unused metadata to persist increases complexity and makes the current state of the system harder to understand. Separation of concerns within metadata is also critical. Descriptive elements, such as inputs and outputs, should be clearly distinguished from operational attributes, such as performance constraints or preferred execution environments. Mixing these concerns leads to metadata that is harder to interpret and more difficult to evolve. Observability supports metadata quality by providing insight into how capabilities are used. By tracking which metadata fields are actively used in runtime decisions and which are ignored, the system can identify areas where metadata is redundant or misaligned with actual behavior.

Choosing the Right Runtime for Each Service

The choice of runtime should not be driven by where a capability was implemented but by the constraints under which it operates.

Unlike traditional architectures, in which services are typically bound to a fixed environment, UMA allows capabilities to run across mobile devices, local machines, edge nodes, and cloud infrastructure. This flexibility enables powerful optimizations, but it also introduces a new dimension of architectural decision-making. Latency is often the most visible factor. Capabilities involved in user interaction or real-time decision-making must execute near the interaction. Introducing unnecessary network hops in these scenarios degrades responsiveness and user experience. Data locality is equally important. Moving data across environments introduces overhead in both performance and security. Connectivity and reliability must also be considered. Mobile and edge environments are often subject to intermittent connectivity. Capabilities that are critical to core workflows should not depend entirely on constant network access.

Resource constraints vary significantly across environments. Mobile devices have limited compute and memory, while edge nodes provide moderate capacity, and cloud environments offer scalable resources. This introduces an important pattern in UMA systems: the coexistence of multiple implementations of the same capability across different runtimes. A lightweight version may execute on the device to provide immediate feedback, while a more advanced version runs in the cloud to refine or validate results. The system can select between these implementations based on context or combine them as part of a broader workflow. Execution placement is therefore not a one-time decision. Metadata plays a central role in expressing these preferences and constraints, enabling the runtime to select the most appropriate execution environment dynamically. A common mistake is to treat runtime selection as an optimization step applied after the system is designed. In UMA, runtime is part of the capability definition. Constraints related to execution should be expressed explicitly from the beginning.

Evaluating Trade-Offs in Real-World Scenarios

Architectural decisions are not made in isolation. Constraints, priorities, and incomplete information shape them. Evaluating trade-offs requires understanding the context in which the system operates.

In UMA systems, the model provides flexibility in how capabilities are defined, composed, and executed, but that flexibility introduces multiple valid options for any given problem. These trade-offs often span multiple dimensions. A capability can be decomposed further to increase reuse, but doing so may introduce additional latency and coordination overhead. Executing a capability locally can improve responsiveness and resilience but may limit access to data or computational resources. Expanding a contract can enable new functionality but may increase complexity and reduce clarity. Each decision affects other parts of the system.

One effective approach is to evaluate decisions along a small set of consistent dimensions. Latency, data locality, coupling, evolvability, and operational complexity provide a useful framework for comparison. When considering alternatives, examining how each option impacts these dimensions helps reveal the consequences of the decision beyond its immediate effect. Trade-offs should also be evaluated over time. A decision that simplifies initial development may create constraints as the system grows. Conversely, introducing flexibility too early may add unnecessary complexity before it is needed. UMA supports incremental evolution, allowing decisions to be revisited as requirements change.

Observability plays a key role in this process. By monitoring how capabilities are used, where they execute, and how they perform, the system provides feedback that can inform future decisions. Patterns such as frequent retries, high latency, or uneven load distribution can indicate that a different configuration would be more effective. This allows architecture to be guided by evidence rather than assumption. AI can further assist in evaluating trade-offs by analyzing system behavior, identifying inefficiencies, and suggesting alternative configurations. In this role, AI does not replace architectural judgment but supports it by providing insights derived from data that would be difficult to process manually. A well-designed UMA system reflects informed decisions that balance competing concerns. It remains flexible enough to adapt as conditions change while maintaining sufficient structure for consistent, predictable behavior.

Principles for Designing UMA Systems

UMA systems are defined by how they structure behavior, manage change, and resolve interactions at runtime. The following principles summarize the core ideas that guide these systems.

They are not rules to be applied mechanically, but criteria for evaluating design decisions as systems evolve.

Behavior should be defined independently of execution. Capabilities represent what the system does, not where it runs. This separation enables the same capability to operate across client, edge, and cloud environments, with execution determined by context and constraints.

Capabilities should represent meaningful units of behavior. They must be large enough to encapsulate a complete action or decision and small enough to evolve independently. Overly granular decomposition increases coordination overhead, while overly broad capabilities reduce adaptability.

Contracts should define interactions precisely. Inputs, outputs, and semantics must be explicit and consistent. A contract should describe what is required and what is provided without embedding assumptions about a specific implementation or workflow.

Events should represent facts, not instructions. They describe what has occurred within the system and enable capabilities to react without introducing hidden control flow. Clear, domain-aligned events reduce ambiguity and prevent unintended coupling.

Metadata should be treated as a first-class design artifact. It defines capabilities, expresses constraints, and enables runtime resolution. Its structure, clarity, and consistency directly influence the system's behavior.

Versioning and compatibility should be resolved at runtime. Multiple versions of a capability can coexist, and compatibility is determined through contracts rather than fixed interfaces. This allows systems to evolve without requiring coordinated changes across all components.

Execution placement should be driven by context. Latency, data locality, resource availability, and connectivity determine where a capability should run. The system should adapt dynamically, selecting the most appropriate environment based on current conditions.

Workflows should emerge from capability interaction. Behavior is not defined by rigid orchestration but by the composition of capabilities that react to events and contracts. Centralized control should be minimized to preserve flexibility and resilience.

Evolution should be continuous and incremental. Capabilities can be introduced, extended, or replaced without disrupting the system. Change is managed through metadata and runtime resolution rather than through synchronized deployments.

Clarity should be preserved as the system grows. Capability boundaries, metadata definitions, and event semantics must remain understandable and consistent. Without clarity, flexibility turns into ambiguity, and the system becomes difficult to maintain.

These principles provide a foundation for designing systems that remain adaptable over time. They reflect a shift from static structure to dynamic composition, where behavior is defined declaratively and resolved in context. A UMA system is defined not by specific technologies, but by how it manages behavior, interaction, and change.

Conclusion: Key Learnings

Architecture in UMA is not a static artifact. It is an active system that governs behavior, manages interaction, and evolves in response to context.

This chapter has examined how UMA systems shift from structure-based design to behavior-driven architecture and what that shift demands of architects in practice. The key learnings from this chapter are the following.

Architecture must describe behavior, not only structure. Static models are insufficient once systems operate across heterogeneous runtimes, asynchronous interactions, and independently evolving capabilities. The metadata layer fills the gap between what is built and how it behaves.

The six decision axes are interdependent. Granularity, event semantics, metadata quality, orchestration, runtime placement, and state management cannot be optimized in isolation. A change in one axis affects the others. Coherence comes from keeping all six axes aligned, not from optimizing any single one.

Anti-patterns degrade systems gradually, not suddenly. Over-granularity, metadata bloat, hidden event coupling, runtime ambiguity, and over-orchestration each begin as a reasonable response to real pressures. They become problems when applied without discipline. The companion labs make this degradation visible and reversible.

Recovery comes from clearer constraints, not more complexity. Lab6 in the companion implementation recovers a fragile, ambiguous architecture by removing the coordinator, restoring stable domain events, and adding explicit selection metadata. No new services are added. Clarity is restored through better decisions, not additional components.

Evolution is a system property, not a migration event. Versioning, backward compatibility, and capability coexistence are built into the UMA model. The three new labs, lab7 through lab9, demonstrate that capabilities can coexist across versions, that optional fields extend behavior without breaking consumers, and that AI-enhanced implementations can be introduced alongside basic ones without disruption.

The ski patrol workflow demonstrates all of these properties together in a single system that operates across mobile, edge, and cloud runtimes without a centralized control plane, maintaining coherence through shared event semantics and metadata.

Chapter 11 builds on this foundation by examining how systems evolve without fragmentation. It focuses on how drift, coexistence, and version sprawl can stay governed rather than becoming chaos and introduces the patterns and practices that keep architecturally coherent systems coherent as they grow across teams, runtimes, and time.

PART IV

Operating and Evolving UMA Systems

CHAPTER 12

Evolving and Adapting UMA Systems

WebAssembly Maintaining Coherence in Systems That Continuously Change

Introduction: Architecture After Deployment

Even though most systems are carefully planned, their behavior can become hard to grasp right after deployment. During the design phase, the architecture seems well-controlled, with clearly defined capabilities, explicit contracts, and intentional system boundaries. Interactions are depicted through clear relationships, and diagrams offer a cohesive view of the system. At this point, behavior is mostly predictable because it is confined by what has been explicitly modeled. While complexity is present, it is limited by design choices and the scope of implementation.

After deployment, the controlled conditions established during design are no longer present.

New capabilities are introduced incrementally, often by teams operating with partial knowledge of the system as a whole. Services begin to react to events in ways that were not fully anticipated, and multiple components may interpret the same signal differently depending on their responsibilities and context. Runtime environments evolve, constraints change, and the system begins to exhibit behaviors that were not explicitly designed. Over time, the gap between the architectural model and the system's actual behavior increases. The structure remains documented, but the system itself becomes dynamic, shaped by ongoing interactions rather than fixed composition.

This divergence is not the result of poor design alone. It reflects a limitation in the traditional definition of architecture. Most architectural models focus on structure: components, interfaces, and dependencies. These models assume that if the structure

E. Piovesan, *Universal Microservices Architecture*, https://doi.org/10.1007/979-8-8688-2794-5_12

is correct, the resulting behavior will remain consistent. This assumption weakens as systems grow in scale and become more variable. When multiple services interact asynchronously, when behavior is extended without modifying existing components, and when execution spans heterogeneous environments, system behavior can no longer be fully derived from structure alone.

To compensate, organizations introduce coordination mechanisms intended to preserve consistency. Documentation, governance processes, and review cycles attempt to align teams and control change. Versioning strategies are introduced to manage compatibility, and operational procedures attempt to mitigate unintended interactions. These mechanisms provide temporary stability, but they rely heavily on discipline and shared understanding. As the number of services, teams, and interactions increases, coordination becomes more difficult to sustain. In practice, inconsistencies accumulate, behavior diverges across environments, and architectural intent becomes progressively harder to enforce.

A different approach is required, one that does not rely solely on static structure or human coordination to maintain system integrity. Architectural definition must extend beyond describing components to include the rules that govern how those components interact and evolve over time. Contracts define expected behavior, metadata describes capabilities and constraints, and execution environments continuously evaluate compatibility and enforce interaction rules. Under these conditions, behavior remains explicit even as the system changes, and consistency is maintained through enforcement rather than assumption.

Architecture, in this context, is not limited to design-time decisions. It defines the conditions under which change can occur without introducing inconsistency. Stability is achieved by ensuring that evolution remains controlled, interpretable, and observable, rather than by attempting to prevent change altogether. Deployment, therefore, marks the point at which architecture begins to operate under real conditions. From that moment onward, the system is no longer defined only by its structure but by how its components are interpreted, combined, and constrained during execution.

This chapter examines the following areas in order. The section "The Myth of Finished Architecture" addresses why systems are never architecturally complete and how structural correctness diverges from behavioral reality over time. The section "Systems As Continuously Interpreted Structures" reframes architecture as a continuously interpreted structure rather than a fixed composition. The section "Evolution Without Fragmentation" examines how evolution produces fragmentation and how contracts anchor behavior as systems change. The section "Runtime-Governed

Evolution" explains how runtime governance becomes the enforcement layer when manual coordination reaches its limits. The section "Observability As Architectural Validation" covers observability as a mechanism for architectural validation, not just operational monitoring. The section "Coordinating Change Across Teams" addresses how coordination across teams changes when contracts replace communication as the primary alignment mechanism. The section "Anti-patterns in System Evolution" catalogs the anti-patterns that cause evolution to become fragmentation. The section "A Practical Evolution Scenario" covers adoption in brownfield systems, including incremental strategies and why full rewrites fail. The section "Adopting UMA in Practice: From Fragmentation to Controlled Evolution" describes the conditions under which UMA adoption becomes necessary. The companion implementation at chapter-12-evolution-without-fragmentation provides six runnable labs that demonstrate the full arc from contract anchor baseline through behavioral drift, duplication, version sprawl, runtime-governed coexistence, and hybrid adoption.

The Myth of Finished Architecture

Why Systems Are Never Complete

Architectural design typically presumes a point of completion, but in reality, systems never truly reach a final state. Capabilities are set, contracts are made, and the system is seen as stable once it meets its initial requirements. Delivery milestones emphasize this view by signaling the shift from design to implementation. At this stage, the architecture is regarded as a finished product, and any subsequent modifications are seen as extensions rather than integral parts of the architecture.

In practice, systems continue to evolve under the influence of forces intrinsic to their operation. New capabilities are introduced as requirements emerge from real usage. Existing capabilities are extended to support additional consumers with different expectations. Event flows expand as more services begin to react to previously isolated signals. Over time, the number of interactions increases, and the system's behavior becomes shaped by these interactions rather than by its original design. Consider a customer profile normalization capability that begins with two consumers. As the system grows, a third consumer arrives with slightly different expectations about what a normalized profile contains. The capability adapts incrementally. Each adaptation is locally valid, but collectively they shift the capability away from its original definition without any single change appearing to cause a problem.

Changes in runtime conditions further prevent architectural closure. Execution environments evolve, introducing new constraints related to performance, security, or resource availability. Capabilities designed for one environment may be executed in another, requiring adaptation without altering their declared behavior. These variations are not exceptional cases. They are a normal consequence of systems that operate across multiple environments.

Organizational factors also contribute to continuous change. Systems are extended by teams that were not involved in their original design. Each addition is locally consistent, but globally the system becomes more complex. Assumptions implicit in the initial architecture are no longer shared, and new capabilities are introduced based on a partial understanding of existing behavior. The result is not immediate failure, but gradual divergence between the original architectural intent and the actual system behavior.

Under these conditions, architecture cannot be treated as a completed structure. It represents a bounded description of the system at a given point in time, while the system itself continues to evolve through the accumulation of new capabilities, interactions, and execution contexts. Treating architecture as complete leads to a false sense of stability, in which change is managed as a deviation from the design rather than as an expected, continuous process. A more accurate perspective considers architecture as something that remains active throughout the system's lifecycle. Instead of defining a fixed arrangement of components, it defines the conditions under which change can occur without introducing inconsistency. Completion is replaced by continuity, and stability is achieved by ensuring that ongoing evolution remains interpretable and constrained.

Structural Correctness vs. Behavioral Reality

A system can remain structurally correct while its behavior becomes inconsistent. The gap between what is declared and what actually happens is where fragmentation begins. Architectural models traditionally treat structural correctness as the primary indicator of system validity. Capabilities are defined with clear responsibilities, interfaces regulate interaction, and dependencies are explicitly managed. When each capability adheres to its contract, and all connections are properly defined, the system is considered correct. This perspective assumes that behavior is a direct and stable consequence of structure.

In practice, structural models offer only a partial perspective on the system. Behavior emerges from how independent capabilities react to shared signals over time. Multiple consumers may respond to the same event, each applying their own interpretation and producing distinct side effects. These interactions are not centrally coordinated, and their outcomes depend on factors such as execution timing, ordering, and runtime context. As a result, the same structural configuration can produce different behaviors without any change in its defined components or interfaces.

This creates a critical distinction. Structural definitions describe what the system is allowed to do, while behavior reflects what the system actually does under real conditions. The two can diverge without any structural violation. Returning to the profile normalization example: the customer.profile.normalize capability may expose a structurally valid contract while three different consumers each rely on different interpretations of what a normalized profile means. The structure has not changed. The behavior has fragmented.

The introduction of new capabilities amplifies this effect. Additional consumers can react to existing events without modifying the original producers. From a structural perspective, the system remains unchanged: contracts are respected and interfaces are stable. From a behavioral perspective, the system has evolved. New side effects are introduced, interactions become denser, and outcomes depend on combinations of capabilities that were not considered during initial design.

Variability in runtime environments further increases this gap. Capabilities may execute under different constraints depending on where they are deployed. Differences in resource availability, security policies, or execution models influence how interactions occur and how results are produced. A capability that behaves consistently in one environment may produce different outcomes in another, even when its contract remains unchanged.

These conditions reveal the limits of relying solely on structure. Structural correctness ensures interface compatibility, but it does not guarantee consistent outcomes. A complete architectural perspective must therefore extend beyond structure. Contracts define expected behavior at capability boundaries, while metadata provides the context required to interpret interactions consistently across consumers and environments. Execution environments enforce these constraints, ensuring that interactions remain valid as the system evolves.

How Systems Degrade over Time

System degradation occurs gradually as valid changes accumulate over time, rather than from poor design or single failures. Each update targets a particular requirement: expanding capabilities for new use cases, responding to new consumers, or adapting to different environments. These modifications ensure compatibility, uphold existing agreements, and retain local correctness. On an individual decision level, the system stays consistent. The overall impact of these changes only becomes clear when assessed together.

As capabilities evolve to support additional consumers, their behavior begins to shift. Extensions are introduced incrementally, often without redefining the original intent of the capability. Over time, the same contract is relied upon by consumers with different expectations, and the capability adapts to satisfy them all. The result is behavioral drift. The capability no longer represents a single, clearly defined function but a set of context-dependent behaviors that vary based on input patterns, execution conditions, or the consuming service. In the companion implementation, lab2-behavioral-drift shows this directly: the profile-normalizer capability at version 1.1.0 has adapted to serve legacy-sync with older semantics while simultaneously serving profile-indexer with newer ones. The contract remains structurally stable. Its meaning has become imprecise.

When further extension becomes difficult without affecting existing consumers, duplication emerges as a practical alternative. Similar logic is reimplemented in a separate capability or adapted independently for a different execution environment. Lab3-duplicate-implementations shows this progression: profile-normalizer-cloud and profile-normalizer-edge exist as separate services, each evolving under different constraints. What was once a single conceptual behavior becomes multiple inconsistent representations.

At the same time, the system's interaction surface expands. Existing events attract additional consumers, each of whom introduces new processing logic. These consumers operate independently and are unaware of each other. The outcome of a single event becomes the result of multiple concurrent reactions, influenced by execution order, timing, and partial failures.

These patterns reinforce each other. Behavioral drift makes capabilities harder to extend safely, encouraging duplication. Duplication introduces divergence, which increases the complexity of interactions. As interaction complexity grows, the impact of implicit assumptions becomes more pronounced. The system continues to operate, and its structure remains valid, but its behavior becomes progressively more difficult to predict, reason about, and control.

To achieve alignment as systems evolve, organizations can employ concrete mechanisms. Contract testing verifies that capabilities continue to adhere to their declared behavior as changes are introduced, preventing undetected drift. Runtime policy engines enforce interaction rules and compatibility constraints dynamically. Automated schema validation, capability discovery services, and continuous integration checks further reinforce behavioral consistency. These mechanisms make evolution a managed and observable process.

The Limits of Coordination

Coordination is frequently presented as the main method for ensuring consistency in evolving systems, but its effectiveness wanes as systems expand in size and complexity. Teams coordinate through documentation, shared guidelines, design reviews, and communication channels aimed at maintaining architectural integrity. Changes undergo assessment prior to implementation, dependencies are coordinated among teams, and versioning strategies are employed to handle compatibility issues. When managed carefully, these mechanisms can slow divergence and offer some stability.

Coordination operates on shared understanding, but large systems are composed of many capabilities developed and maintained by different teams with varying contexts. No single participant maintains a complete view of all interactions, dependencies, and execution paths. As new capabilities are introduced and existing ones evolve, the number of relationships requiring alignment increases. Communication must scale with the number of interactions, not just the number of components, making it progressively more difficult to ensure that all relevant considerations are understood and addressed.

Even when coordination is effective at the design level, it cannot fully account for runtime behavior. Interactions between capabilities are influenced by execution timing, concurrency, partial failures, and variations in runtime environments. These factors are not visible during design discussions and cannot be fully captured in documentation or review processes. A change that appears correct when evaluated in isolation may produce unintended effects when combined with other capabilities during execution. Coordination can align intentions, but it cannot guarantee outcomes.

Versioning strategies are often used to mitigate these limitations by allowing multiple representations of a capability to coexist. While this reduces the immediate impact of breaking changes, it introduces additional complexity. Multiple versions must be maintained, consumers must choose between them, and compatibility must be managed across an increasing number of combinations. Coordination shifts from preventing inconsistency to managing it without eliminating the underlying divergence.

The limitation is not organizational, but structural. Coordination relies on human interpretation of system behavior, while the system itself operates through interactions that are resolved at runtime. Without mechanisms that define and enforce how capabilities interact under real conditions, consistency depends on assumptions that cannot be maintained as the system evolves. Alignment must therefore be supported by the architecture itself, through explicit definitions of behavior and constraints that can be validated at execution time.

Systems As Continuously Interpreted Structures

Architectural models traditionally describe systems as compositions of components connected through well-defined interfaces. This view is insufficient for systems where behavior emerges from independent capabilities interacting under varying conditions. Once these structures are established, behavior is assumed to follow from their arrangement. This treats execution as the realization of a predefined design, where the role of the runtime is limited to carrying out interactions that have already been determined. The same structural composition can produce different outcomes depending on how interactions are interpreted at runtime. Execution is influenced by context, constraints, and the presence of additional capabilities that were not part of the original design. Under these conditions, behavior cannot be fully derived from structure alone.

A more accurate model considers systems as continuously interpreted structures. Capabilities define the boundaries of responsibility, but behavior is shaped by how their contracts are understood, by how metadata provides context, and by how execution environments enforce constraints. Architecture, therefore, extends beyond composition, defining not only how capabilities are connected but also how their interactions are interpreted and governed during execution.

From Static Composition to Runtime Interpretation

Architectural composition lays out which capabilities exist and how they connect, but it doesn't completely determine the system's behavior during operation. In traditional models, once components and interfaces are set, behavior is seen as a predictable result of that structure. This assumes interactions are static and that execution follows predetermined paths. However, in distributed systems, interactions are more dynamic. Capabilities respond to events, handle requests, and engage in flows that are not strictly linear or centrally managed. Multiple capabilities can react to the same signal, each applying its own logic and producing varied effects.

The same structural composition can therefore produce different outcomes without any change to its defined components or interfaces. A new consumer may introduce additional processing in response to an existing event. A capability may interpret input differently based on context or metadata. Execution paths may vary depending on runtime conditions such as ordering, concurrency, or partial failure. In the profile normalization domain, the profile.normalized event is consumed by both profile-indexer and profile-audit. Both consumers share the same structural connection to the same event. Their behavior at runtime, however, is shaped by how each interprets the event's semantics within its own contract context.

Understanding systems as interpreted rather than executed shifts the focus of architecture. Instead of assuming that behavior is fully determined at design time, architecture must define how interactions are understood and validated as they occur. This requires making the conditions that influence behavior explicit, ensuring that interactions remain consistent even as the system evolves.

Contracts and Metadata As Behavioral Definitions

A contract encompasses more than just the structure of an interaction. It sets the expected behaviors at the boundary of a capability, including the semantics of inputs and outputs, the significance of events, and the conditions that make interactions valid. Architectural models often view contracts as interface definitions, detailing inputs, outputs, and interaction patterns between capabilities. Metadata usually acts as supplementary, offering descriptive information about capabilities without directly affecting behavior. However, this separation is not maintained in systems where behavior must be consistent across independent capabilities and different execution contexts.

Without semantic definition, compatibility is reduced to structural matching, where capabilities can connect but may not interpret interactions consistently. Metadata provides the context required to interpret contracts. It describes constraints, capabilities, and conditions that influence how interactions should be understood and executed. This includes information on execution requirements, compatibility rules, data semantics, and other factors not captured by the contract alone. While contracts define what is expected, metadata defines how those expectations should be interpreted in different contexts.

Behavior emerges from the combination of these two elements. A contract without metadata lacks the context needed for consistent interpretation across consumers. Metadata without a contract lacks a defined boundary for interaction. Together, they establish a complete definition of behavior that can be understood independently of implementation.

This relationship becomes critical as systems evolve. New capabilities may interact with existing ones without prior coordination, relying on contracts and metadata to determine compatibility. Treating contracts and metadata as behavioral definitions allows architecture to extend beyond static structure. Behavior is no longer inferred from implementation or assumed through coordination. It is explicitly defined, context-aware, and interpretable at runtime.

Stability Through Explicit Rules

Stability in systems where behavior arises from independent capabilities cannot depend solely on prediction. Instead, it must be ensured by mechanisms active during execution. Explicit rules specify how interactions are allowed, managing compatibility among capabilities, constraining contract use, and validating interactions under certain conditions. These rules go beyond checking inputs and outputs to interpret behavior and maintain interaction consistency, even as capabilities evolve independently.

These rules are applied at runtime, where interactions are resolved. When a capability attempts to interact with another, the rules determine whether the interaction is compatible, how the contract should be interpreted in the current context, and what constraints must be enforced. This allows the system to evaluate interactions based on actual conditions rather than relying on assumptions made at design time. By governing interactions in this way, rules actively shape system behavior. They prevent invalid combinations of capabilities, constrain how events are interpreted, and ensure that extensions do not introduce unintended side effects. Instead of attempting to predict all possible behaviors, the system enforces boundaries within which behavior can safely emerge. Stability is no longer derived from a fixed and fully understood structure but from the continuous enforcement of rules that maintain consistency across interactions.

Controlled Emergence

Behavior in UMA systems arises within set boundaries rather than from rigid definitions. The system remains adaptable while maintaining coherence because its environment for behavior to develop is clearly defined and managed. In contrast, traditional architectures assume behavior is entirely predetermined during design, with variability seen as an exception brought in through configurations or conditional logic. When systems comprise independent capabilities, outcomes are produced by the interaction of multiple capabilities responding to common signals, rather than a single linear process.

This does not mean system behavior becomes arbitrary. Interactions are bounded by contracts, interpreted through metadata, and governed by explicit rules applied during execution. A new capability can introduce additional processing in response to an existing event, extending system behavior without modifying existing components. At the same time, rules ensure that this extension remains compatible with existing contracts and does not violate established constraints.

Controlled emergence provides a balance between rigidity and unpredictability. Behavior is not fixed, and the system can evolve in response to new requirements and contexts. At the same time, this evolution remains bounded, interpretable, and aligned with architectural intent. The system does not need to be fully specified to remain consistent. It needs to be governed to ensure consistency as it changes.

Evolution Without Fragmentation

Change is inevitable in distributed systems. The key issue is how to implement change without sacrificing coherence. As new features are added, existing ones develop, and more consumers join, inconsistencies start to surface. Similar functionalities may yield varying results, consumers may interpret the same contract differently, and multiple versions of behavior may exist side by side without clear boundaries. These issues are not due to poor design but stem from a lack of mechanisms to keep the system aligned during changes. To avoid fragmentation, evolution must be treated as a core architectural concern.

Why Change Introduces Fragmentation

Fragmentation doesn't stem from a single design decision; instead, it results from the evolution of systems through a series of locally valid changes that are not aligned at the overall system level. This process typically starts with behavioral divergence. A capability that initially defines a clear and consistent function is extended to support additional use cases. New consumers introduce requirements that reinterpret the original contract, and the capability adapts incrementally to satisfy them. Over time, the same contract comes to be associated with multiple behavioral expectations. Different consumers rely on different aspects of the capability, and its behavior becomes dependent on context rather than on a single, well-defined purpose.

As divergence increases, duplication becomes a practical response. When extending an existing capability introduces risk for current consumers, similar functionality is implemented separately. This duplication may occur within the same environment or across different execution contexts, where the same conceptual behavior is adapted independently in each context. Parallel versions emerge as a way to manage these differences. Instead of replacing existing behavior, new versions are introduced to support updated requirements while preserving compatibility for existing consumers. While this avoids immediate breakage, it introduces coexistence without alignment.

These conditions lead to inconsistent consumption. Consumers interacting with different versions or implementations of a capability experience different outcomes for what is conceptually the same operation. Fragmentation is the result of this progression: behavioral divergence leads to duplication, duplication leads to parallel versions, and parallel versions lead to inconsistent consumption. The system continues to function, but coherence is lost. The companion labs make this arc visible: lab1 shows the coherent anchor, lab2 shows drift beginning, lab3 shows duplication across environments, and lab4 shows the fragmented state where version proliferation is no longer governed.

Contracts As the Anchor of Evolution

A contract specifies the expected behavior at a capability boundary, ensuring consistency for all consumers regardless of implementation details. To maintain alignment as capabilities evolve, a stable reference point is essential. This clear definition allows behaviors to stay stable even when the implementation changes. Capabilities can be expanded, optimized, or adapted for different environments without changing their external understanding. Rather than deducing behavior from innermost implementation details, consumers depend on the contract as the definitive source.

The separation between contract and implementation is critical. When behavior is implicitly tied to implementation, any modification can alter how a capability is interpreted by its consumers. By isolating behavior at the contract level, implementation becomes evolvable without affecting external interactions.

Consider the customer profile normalization capability. Its initial contract defines a single stable boundary:

```
capability: customer.profile.normalize
version: 1.0.0
inputs:
  profile_id: string
  raw_fields: object
outputs:
  normalized_profile: object
  normalization_version: string
constraints:
  idempotent: true
  max_latency_ms: 200
  placements: [cloud, edge]
```

> *This contract is the authoritative definition for all consumers. The profile-indexer and profile-audit capabilities both consume the normalized_profile output, and neither requires knowledge of how normalization is implemented internally. When the implementation is updated to support additional field formats, the contract remains unchanged. Consumers continue to operate without modification. The lab1-contract-anchor scenario in the companion implementation shows this baseline in its coherent state, where the runtime validates both consumers against the same contract version and records compatibility evidence*

Contracts also provide the basis for managing coexistence between different versions of a capability. When new versions are introduced, their compatibility is determined by their alignment with existing contracts. Instead of relying on coordination to ensure consistent interpretation, the contract defines the criteria that govern whether multiple versions can operate within the same system.

Versioning As Controlled Coexistence

Multiple behavior versions are inevitable in evolving systems. The main difficulty lies not in their presence but in how they coexist. Versioning is typically seen as a way to manage change, used when existing behaviors cannot be altered without impacting current users. In reality, various consumers rely on different interpretations of functionality, influenced by their needs, constraints, and adoption timing. Therefore, versioning is not merely an optional approach but an essential requirement for ongoing system evolution.

Uncontrolled versioning leads to fragmentation. When versions are introduced without clear compatibility criteria, consumers must choose between alternatives that may differ in subtle or significant ways. Over time, the system accumulates versions that overlap in functionality but differ in behavior, increasing interaction complexity and reducing consistency across consumers. Lab4-version-sprawl demonstrates this condition: profile-normalizer-v1 and profile-normalizer-v2 coexist, but version selection depends on consumer-specific conventions rather than explicit compatibility rules. The verdict is fragmented.

Controlled coexistence requires that versions are not treated as independent implementations but as variations governed by the same behavioral definitions. Compatibility must be explicitly defined to allow different versions to operate within a shared framework of expectations. Backward compatibility ensures that existing consumers can continue to function without modification, while forward compatibility allows newer capabilities to interact with earlier versions without requiring immediate alignment. When versioning is governed in this way, multiple versions can coexist without introducing ambiguity. Lab5-runtime-governed-coexistence shows the recovery: profile-normalizer-v2 carries a backward_compatible_from declaration, and the runtime uses this to route legacy-sync to v1 and newer consumers to v2 without consumer involvement.

Evolving Capabilities Without Breaking Consumers

Changes to a capability seldom stay limited to just its implementation. To prevent these changes from spreading, it's essential to isolate modifications within the capability itself while keeping the external behavior stable. This requires a clear distinction between the guarantees a capability offers and how it accomplishes them. The external contract specifies the expected behavior for all users, whereas the internal implementation can change to address new needs, improve performance, or adapt to different environments. As long as the contract stays the same, users can interact with the capability without needing to change, even if the internal details do.

Achieving this separation requires that changes be evaluated against the contract rather than against existing implementations. When new functionality is introduced, it must be expressed in a way that either preserves the current contract or extends it without altering its existing meaning. Changes that would modify the interpretation of existing interactions must be isolated through new contracts or controlled versioning, ensuring that existing consumers remain unaffected.

Isolation of change also requires controlling how dependencies between capabilities are expressed. When capabilities rely on implicit assumptions about each other's behavior, changes in one capability can propagate unpredictably to others. By constraining interactions to explicitly defined contracts and avoiding reliance on implementation details, dependencies remain stable even as capabilities evolve independently.

Event Evolution and Semantic Stability

An event can remain valid at the schema level even as its meaning shifts over time. Just because the structure stays compatible doesn't mean behavior will be consistent across all consumers. Events describe how capabilities exchange information and trigger system actions. As new consumers are added and existing ones change, events are expanded to meet new needs. This can include adding new fields, reinterpreting existing ones, or updating processing assumptions. Different consumers might depend on various parts of the event, and new consumers might interpret it in unexpected ways.

Maintaining semantic stability requires that the meaning of an event remains consistent as it evolves. Changes must preserve the original interpretation of existing data, ensuring that current consumers continue to process the event in the same way. Extensions should be additive, introducing new information without altering the semantics of existing content. This allows new consumers to derive additional behavior while existing ones remain unaffected.

Semantic stability also depends on how events are interpreted in different contexts. Consumers must rely on the event's defined meaning rather than on implicit assumptions about its use. When interpretation is based on shared semantics rather than on implementation-specific logic, events can be extended without introducing divergence. In the profile normalization domain, the profile.normalized event must carry a stable meaning for both profile-indexer and profile-audit even as new fields are added for newer consumers. Lab3-duplicate-implementations shows what happens when this stability breaks: the profile.normalized event produced by the cloud copy carries different semantics than the one produced by the edge copy, and the runtime cannot prove they mean the same thing.

Runtime-Governed Evolution

Mechanisms like contracts, versioning, and explicit rules guide system evolution without causing fragmentation. Their success depends on proper application during execution. In distributed systems, behavior is shaped at runtime, with capabilities interacting under different conditions. Variations in context, timing, and system state influence these interactions and their outcomes. Design-time validation and coordination alone cannot fully address these factors. To keep evolution controlled, architectural rules must be enforced where interactions occur. The runtime layer enforces and interprets these rules, assessing interactions through contracts, metadata, and governing principles to ensure compatibility and adherence to constraints as capabilities develop.

The Limits of Manual Governance

As systems grow, the coordination mechanisms described in the section "The Myth of Finished Architecture" reach their limits for the same reasons: interaction count scales faster than communication can manage it, and runtime behavior cannot be fully captured in design discussions. A change that appears correct in isolation may produce unintended outcomes when combined with other capabilities during execution.

As systems evolve, coordination becomes reactive. Effort shifts toward identifying inconsistencies after they occur, resolving conflicts between capabilities, and managing divergence that has already been introduced. The cost of maintaining alignment increases, while the ability to prevent misalignment through communication decreases. Coordination remains necessary, but it is no longer sufficient to preserve consistency in a system where behavior is determined by interactions resolved at runtime.

The limitation is inherent to the approach. Coordination depends on human interpretation of system behavior, while the system itself operates through interactions resolved dynamically under conditions that cannot be fully anticipated. Without mechanisms to enforce alignment during execution, consistency relies on assumptions that degrade over time.

Runtime As the Enforcement and Resolution Layer

The runtime doesn't just route requests or events; it assesses whether each interaction is valid, interprets its meaning, and applies relevant constraints. When capabilities interact, the runtime evaluates their actions based on the defined contract, contextual metadata, and compatibility and execution rules. As a result, the outcome of an interaction depends not only on the capabilities involved but also on how the interaction is resolved during runtime.

Compatibility is not assumed. It is determined dynamically. A capability may expose a contract that is structurally compatible with another, yet differences in version, context, or constraints may affect whether the interaction is valid. The runtime evaluates these conditions before allowing the interaction to proceed, ensuring that behavior remains consistent with defined expectations.

Resolution extends beyond validation. When multiple versions of a capability or multiple interpretations of an interaction are possible, the runtime determines which path is appropriate under the current conditions. This may involve selecting a compatible version, adapting the interaction within defined constraints, or enforcing specific rules that guide how the interaction should be executed. These decisions are not embedded within individual capabilities but are derived from the system's governing definitions.

The following diagram shows how the runtime enforcement layer is structured internally:

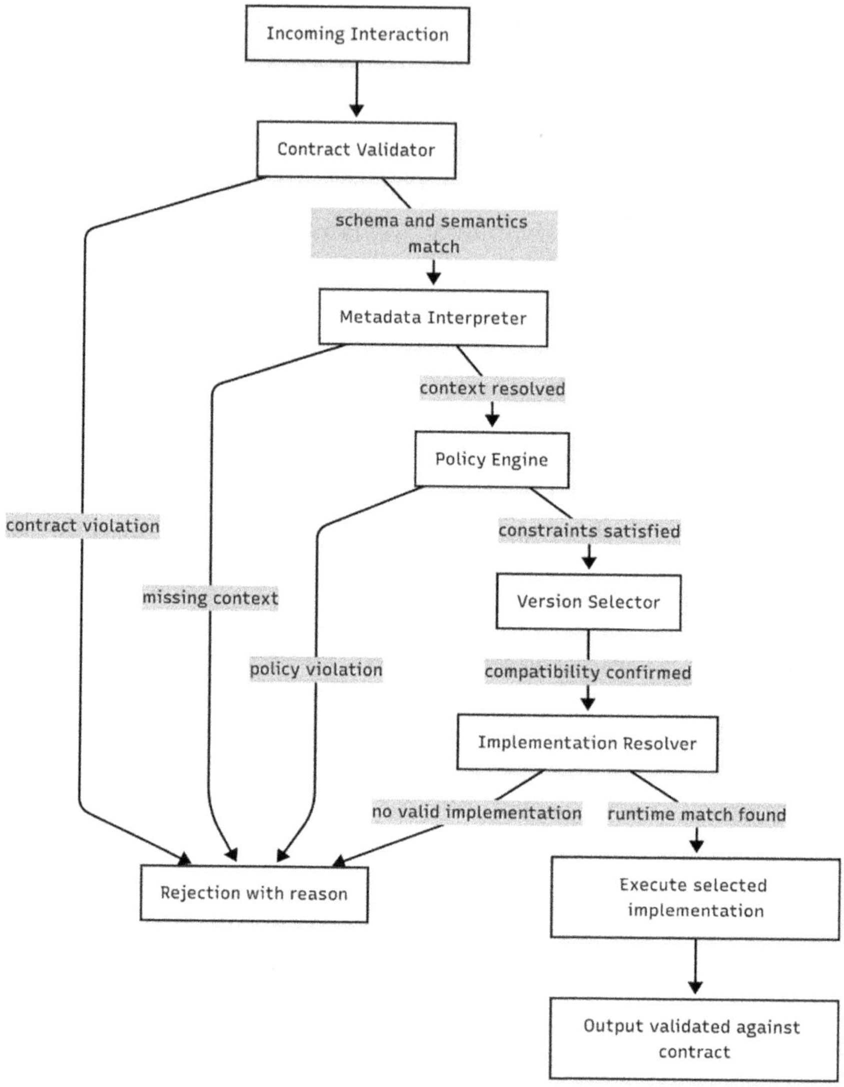

Figure 12-1. *Runtime enforcement layer. An incoming interaction passes through contract validation, metadata interpretation, and policy evaluation before the runtime selects and executes a compatible implementation. Each sub-component can independently reject the interaction, preventing invalid combinations from reaching execution*

By conducting these evaluations, the runtime actively influences system behavior. It governs how capabilities interact, prevents invalid combinations from occurring, and keeps the actual execution aligned with the declared behavior. Rather than depending on static assumptions or external coordination, the system enforces consistency during interactions. This transforms the architecture's role from establishing a fixed structure to setting the rules for resolving behavior. The runtime applies these rules, enabling the system to evolve while maintaining coherence.

Managing Coexistence Through Runtime Resolution

Multiple versions of a capability arise naturally from ongoing development. Managing their coexistence involves resolving interactions dynamically, rather than assuming compatibility. When two capabilities interact, the runtime assesses the available versions considering compatibility, constraints, and rules. The choice of version is not predetermined during design but is a resolution process occurring at runtime based on current conditions. For example, Lab5-runtime-governed-coexistence demonstrates this: it directs legacy-sync to profile-normalizer-v1 and newer consumers to profile-normalizer-v2, guided by the backward_compatible_from declaration and the consumer's contract requirements. Importantly, neither consumer needs to be aware of the other version.

This resolution ensures that interactions remain consistent even when multiple versions are present. Consumers are not required to manage all possible compatibility combinations explicitly, and capabilities do not need to embed logic to handle every version they may encounter. Instead, the runtime applies the same set of governing definitions to determine which interactions are valid and how they should proceed.

Dynamic resolution also allows systems to evolve incrementally. New versions can be introduced alongside existing ones, and their adoption can occur gradually without requiring immediate alignment across all consumers. As long as compatibility is defined and enforced, different versions can coexist without introducing ambiguity or behavioral inconsistency. Versioning becomes a controlled aspect of system behavior rather than a source of fragmentation.

Preventing Invalid System States

Preventing inconsistency involves ensuring that the system cannot reach states that contradict its defined behavior. This is enforced during runtime. As systems grow and evolve, the possible interactions between capabilities increase, as do the conditions under which these interactions occur. Without constraints, different combinations of capabilities, versions, and execution contexts could lead to outcomes that do not align with the system's intended behavior. These inconsistencies do not always manifest as immediate failures. They often appear as subtle deviations, where interactions remain structurally valid but lead to results that violate expected semantics or constraints.

Each interaction is evaluated not only for structural compatibility but also for alignment with the rules and constraints that define valid system behavior. When an interaction would introduce a state that violates these constraints, it is rejected or constrained before it can affect the system. This evaluation accounts for contract compatibility, version alignment, execution context, and defined policies governing interaction.

Invalid system states often emerge from combinations of individually valid interactions. A capability may behave correctly in isolation, and each interaction may appear valid when considered independently, yet their combination can produce outcomes that violate system-level expectations. Detecting these conditions requires evaluating interactions in context rather than in isolation and applying rules that reflect the system's overall behavior. Preventing invalid states at the point of execution, the system maintains coherence as it evolves.

Observability As Architectural Validation

Observability in UMA systems should go beyond just execution details to include understanding how interactions are interpreted, how decisions are made, and whether behavior aligns with established contracts, metadata, and rules. Typically, observability is seen as a way to grasp system behavior through logs, metrics, and traces, which reveal what the system is doing by capturing execution details from various components and interactions. Although this visibility helps diagnose failures and monitor performance, it does not guarantee that the system adheres to its architectural design. Therefore, observability also serves as a means to verify that the system functions within its specified constraints, not merely as a way to observe its activities.

The Limits of Traditional Observability

Traditional observability gathers execution data but does not clarify why specific interactions happen or if they are valid within the system architecture. Logs and traces detail what occurs during execution but do not show if interactions adhere to the intended contract semantics or if a different approach might have been better. Metrics can highlight performance traits but do not indicate whether the behavior complies with established constraints.

As systems evolve, this lack of context becomes more significant. Multiple versions of capabilities may coexist, events may trigger different sets of consumers, and runtime conditions may influence how interactions are resolved. Traditional observability captures these variations as execution data, but it does not provide a consistent framework for interpreting them. The same sequence of events may represent correct behavior in one context and misalignment in another, yet logs and traces alone do not distinguish between these cases. The result is visibility without interpretive value.

Addressing this limitation requires shifting the focus of observability from execution to interpretation. Observability must provide insight into how interactions are evaluated against architectural definitions, enabling behavior to be understood in terms of contracts, metadata, and governing rules.

Observing Behavior Through Architectural Definitions

Interactions should be understood based on contracts that specify expected behaviors and metadata that offer context. This approach moves the focus from merely recording events to assessing whether those events align with the intended system operation. In this framework, interactions are viewed at the capability level rather than by infrastructure. Instead of just tracing a request or event across services, it is evaluated based on which capabilities are involved, how their contracts are interpreted, and the conditions under which the interaction is deemed valid.

Consider a scenario where the profile.normalized event is produced by profile-normalizer and consumed by both profile-indexer and profile-audit. Traditional observability captures the propagation of this event, showing which services receive it and how they process it. From this perspective, the system appears to be functioning correctly as long as each consumer responds without error. From an architectural perspective, additional questions arise. Each consumer may interpret the same event differently based on its contract and associated metadata. One capability may treat the event as a trigger for enrichment and another as a signal for validation. Observing the interaction therefore requires visibility into how each capability interprets the event, not just that it received it.

This distinction becomes more important as the system evolves. New consumers may be introduced, existing ones may change their behavior, and events may be extended to include additional information. Without observing how these changes affect interpretation, it is not possible to determine whether the system remains aligned with its architectural definitions.

Grounding observability in contracts and metadata, behavior can be evaluated against defined expectations rather than inferred from execution. Architectural observability requires instrumentation at three levels. The first is runtime decision tracing, which captures which contract version was evaluated, which constraints were checked, and which implementation was selected for each interaction:

```
{
  "trace_id": "t-9f3a",
  "capability": "customer.profile.normalize",
  "contract_version": "2.0.0",
  "consumer": "profile-indexer",
  "constraints_evaluated": ["idempotent", "max_latency_ms", "placement"],
  "implementation_selected": "profile-normalizer-v2",
  "resolution_reason": "version 2.0.0 satisfies consumer contract
  declaration",
  "outcome": "allowed"
}
```

The second is metadata usage metrics, which reveal how the system is actually being governed versus how it was intended to be governed. Key metrics include contract_version_invocation_count by capability and version, constraint_evaluation_failures by constraint type, version_selection_distribution showing which implementations are selected per consumer, and semantic_drift_score derived from the proportion of interactions resolved through legacy compatibility paths versus governed paths.

The third is drift detection queries. A basic architectural health check compares the number of interactions resolved via governed paths to the total interaction count for a capability. When the governed path ratio drops below a defined threshold, it signals that drift is accumulating. A dashboard monitoring the customer.profile.normalize capability would alert when version_fragmentation warnings exceed zero or when more than 20 percent of interactions are resolved through legacy compatibility paths rather than the primary governed contract line.

Understanding Decisions, Not Just Execution

Observing execution creates a record of what happened but doesn't reveal how those outcomes were reached. To truly understand system behavior, it's essential to see how decisions are made. Every interaction between capabilities involves a series of evaluations. When a capability either produces or consumes an event or calls another capability, this interaction is checked against established contracts, metadata, and rules. These checks help determine if the interaction is valid, whether a specific capability version is compatible, and how factors like execution context or policies should shape the results. Without insight into these decision processes, execution traces remain incomplete.

Decision visibility requires that the factors influencing interactions are observable. This includes evaluating contract compatibility, resolving version coexistence, and enforcing constraints that govern how capabilities interact. Observability must expose not only the results of these evaluations but also the reasoning that led to them, allowing behavior to be understood as the outcome of defined rules rather than as an emergent property of execution alone.

Understanding decisions also provides a basis for validating architectural intent. If behavior is defined through contracts, metadata, and rules, then observing how decisions are made allows verification that these definitions are being applied correctly.

Detecting Drift and Inconsistency

Drift happens when the system's actions diverge from its original design. This divergence isn't always apparent through failures or errors. One type of drift occurs when contracts are applied consistently in structure but not in meaning. Different users might depend on various parts of the same contract or interpret its semantics slightly differently. These variations often develop gradually as capabilities evolve separately. From an execution standpoint, interactions still seem valid, but the system no longer functions under a shared understanding of behavior.

Another form emerges through changes in runtime conditions. Variations in execution context, version coexistence, or constraint enforcement can alter how interactions are resolved. The same interaction may produce different outcomes depending on these conditions, without any explicit change in the participating capabilities. Traditional observability does not reliably expose these conditions.

When observability is grounded in architectural definitions, divergence can be identified earlier. Differences in how contracts are interpreted, how rules are applied, or how versions are resolved become visible as deviations from expected behavior. Instead of waiting for failures, the system can be evaluated continuously for alignment between its definitions and its execution. Early detection of drift allows corrective action before inconsistencies become embedded in the system. Observability, in this context, is not a reactive tool for diagnosing issues but an active mechanism for ensuring that the system continues to operate according to its architectural principles.

Coordinating Change Across Teams

As systems expand, multiple teams implement changes within diverse contexts and priorities. In systems where behavior is explicitly defined and enforced during runtime, the importance of coordination evolves. Consistency no longer hinges on all participants sharing a complete understanding of every interaction. Instead, the architecture sets boundaries that allow teams to work independently, decreasing the need for ongoing alignment. While coordination remains essential, its focus shifts from controlling behavior to establishing conditions that permit independent development without causing inconsistencies.

The Scaling Problem of Coordination

As systems grow, coordination becomes increasingly complex, driven not just by the number of teams but by the multitude of interactions and dependencies that develop between capabilities. Each new capability creates additional relationships that need understanding and management, with changes potentially impacting various parts of the system in ways that are not immediately obvious. As the interactions multiply, maintaining alignment demands more effort, often disproportionately. Teams must consider how their modifications influence existing capabilities, how others utilize those capabilities, and how interactions fluctuate under different conditions. This necessitates knowledge beyond local ownership, making it challenging for any single team to fully grasp the effects of their changes.

Partial knowledge becomes the default condition. Teams operate with an understanding of their own capabilities and immediate dependencies but lack visibility into the broader system. Changes are introduced based on this limited perspective, and alignment depends on assumptions about how other parts of the system behave. The cost of coordination increases as systems evolve. More time is spent in discussions, reviews, and validation processes intended to reduce uncertainty. Despite this effort, complete alignment cannot be achieved, as the number of possible interactions exceeds what can be fully understood through communication alone.

Why Communication Does Not Preserve Consistency

Communication can align intentions but cannot ensure consistent interpretation or execution of behavior. The challenge lies in how behavior is defined and applied. In distributed systems, behavior is shaped not just by design choices but also by how interactions are understood during runtime. Even if teams agree on the purpose of a contract or event, each capability interprets that purpose independently. Small differences in assumptions, context, or constraints can cause behavior variations that go unnoticed during design discussions. Over time, as capabilities develop, these differences build up, leading to divergence that cannot be fixed by communication alone.

Even when communication is frequent and detailed, it cannot capture all the conditions under which interactions occur. Runtime factors such as execution context, concurrency, and partial failures influence behavior in ways not fully captured in design artifacts. As a result, behavior diverges not because teams fail to communicate, but because communication cannot fully represent how interactions are resolved in practice. Consistency requires more than shared understanding. It requires that behavior be defined in a way that can be interpreted uniformly across capabilities and enforced at execution time.

Contracts As Coordination Boundaries

When a contract specifies the guaranteed behavior of a capability, teams can function independently within that scope. Interaction relies on shared definitions instead of assumptions, creating a clear boundary for coordination. Teams don't need to know how other capabilities are built nor coordinate changes beyond those outlined in the contract. This boundary limits both parties in an interaction: producers must keep their behavior aligned with the contract, while consumers depend on the contract rather than inferred or internal details. This mutual understanding fosters a stable and predictable interaction, where expectations are clear and verifiable.

The difference between coordination through communication and coordination through contracts becomes concrete when multiple teams interact around the same capability. In a traditional system with four consumer teams and one provider team, each consumer team must communicate its requirements directly to the provider and to every other team whose behavior might affect the interaction. This produces n-squared coordination channels: four consumers interacting with the provider, plus cross-consumer alignment, produces twenty or more communication paths that must remain active as the system evolves.

In a UMA system, this is replaced by a single contract boundary. The team responsible for the customer.profile.normalize capability publishes a versioned contract:

```
capability: customer.profile.normalize
version: 2.0.0
inputs:
  profile_id: string
  raw_fields: object
outputs:
  normalized_profile: object
  normalization_version: string
constraints:
  idempotent: true
  placements: [cloud, edge]
compatibility:
  backward_compatible_from: 1.0.0
```

The profile-indexer team reads this contract and declares a dependency on it. They do not need to contact the normalizer team to understand the implementation, discuss field naming, or coordinate rollout timing. The runtime validates their interaction against the contract at execution time. If the interaction is compatible, it proceeds. If not, the rejection includes the specific constraint that failed, giving the consuming team precise information to resolve the incompatibility without a meeting.

When the normalizer team introduces version 2.1.0 with an additional optional output field, they publish the new contract version alongside the existing one. The backward_compatible_from declaration allows the runtime to route older consumers to the original contract behavior without any involvement from the consumer team. New consumers can declare against 2.1.0 independently. No cross-team synchronization meeting is required. The contract replaced the coordination channel.

Contracts, therefore, redefine how coordination is achieved. Instead of aligning teams through communication about behavior, alignment is established through shared definitions that govern interactions. Coordination shifts from managing dependencies between teams to managing the boundaries that define how capabilities interact, enabling independent evolution without relying on continuous synchronization.

Independent Evolution with Shared Guarantees

Sustainable independence relies on shared guarantees. It's not about removing constraints but making sure they are explicit, consistent, and enforced throughout the system. These guarantees are established through contracts, metadata, and rules that govern how capabilities behave and interact. They define what remains constant as the system evolves, providing a stable foundation for cross-team collaboration. When these guarantees are well-defined, teams can develop their capabilities within those boundaries without impacting others. Internal modifications stay local if they maintain the expected boundary behavior. Consumers depend on these guarantees rather than implementation details, enabling them to operate independently of specific changes.

This model also clarifies when coordination is required. Changes that preserve existing guarantees can be introduced independently, while changes that alter those guarantees must be managed explicitly. Instead of coordinating all changes, teams focus on the specific points where behavior is defined and shared. This reduces the scope of coordination while ensuring that critical changes are visible and controlled. Independent evolution, therefore, emerges from constraint rather than from isolation.

Anti-patterns in System Evolution

Evolution without clear governance tends to develop distinct failure patterns. Each anti-pattern starts as a logical local response to specific pressures but becomes a source of fragmentation over time as it accumulates. The accompanying implementation helps identify and reverse these patterns. Labs 2 to 4 focus on isolating different degradation modes. Lab 5 demonstrates the recovery process, while Lab 6 shows that recovery can happen without a complete rewrite.

Silent Contract Drift

Declared behavior and actual behavior often differ when contracts aren't regarded as the definitive source of interaction. As capabilities evolve internally, they introduce changes that affect how behavior is understood, without updating the contract itself. Users rely on the original declaration, while the real outcomes are shaped by implementation. This divergence typically happens gradually. Small internal adjustments seem safe alone, but over time, they alter the effective behavior of the capability. Since the contract stays the same, these differences aren't immediately obvious and are rarely checked explicitly. The system still works, but interactions lose a shared understanding, causing subtle inconsistencies that are hard to trace back to their root cause.

In the companion implementation, lab2-behavioral-drift shows this pattern: the profile-normalizer at version 1.1.0 has adapted its behavior to serve legacy-sync with older semantics while simultaneously serving profile-indexer with newer ones. The contract anchor axis changes from stable to drifting. The behavioral_drift and manual_governance_limit warnings appear. Detection: the verdict changes to at-risk, and the contract anchor axis value shifts in the diff output. Prevention: treat the contract as the authoritative definition and evaluate all internal changes against it before deployment. Resolution: restore the contract to match actual behavior, then introduce a new version for the diverging interpretation rather than continuing to stretch the existing one.

Metadata Treated As Documentation

Metadata is collected but not enforced, making it a mere descriptive tool rather than an active system component. It may include details about context, constraints, or intent, but these are not reliably used during operation. Consequently, capabilities interpret or overlook metadata inconsistently, creating a disconnect between expected and actual behavior. While metadata seems to offer structure and alignment, without enforcement, it cannot ensure uniform understanding. Over time, teams may treat metadata as the ultimate truth, even though the system relies on implicit assumptions built into its design, leading to unnoticed divergence.

Detection: runtime decision traces show constraints listed in metadata that are never evaluated, or constraint_evaluation_failures at zero despite known boundary conditions. Prevention: treat metadata fields as executable constraints from the moment they are defined and include them in contract validation. Resolution: audit metadata fields against actual runtime behavior and remove or enforce any field that is not actively used in resolution decisions.

Event Overloading

An event is expanded to fulfill multiple roles, gathering various fields and interpretations that exceed its initial intent. Rather than acting as a precise, targeted behavioral indicator, it transforms into a versatile structure utilized by different users for diverse objectives. As more consumers depend on the event, its semantics become increasingly ambiguous. Changes introduced for one use case may affect others in unintended ways, and consumers begin to rely on specific subsets of the event that are not consistently defined. In the profile normalization domain, this is what lab3-duplicate-implementations begins to show: the profile.normalized event produced by the cloud copy carries different semantics than the one produced by the edge copy. The semantic_instability warning appears when event semantics shift to an unstable state.

Detection: a single event consumed by more than three unrelated capabilities, or semantic_instability warnings in the runtime assessment. Prevention: define events narrowly around single-domain facts and explicitly declare consumer dependencies in metadata. Resolution: introduce more specific event types to replace the overloaded one, and update consuming capabilities to declare their dependencies against the new types.

Bypassing Architectural Constraints

Direct interactions occur outside the established contracts and rules to quickly meet immediate needs. These shortcuts typically involve direct calls, shared data access, or implicit agreements between capabilities that are not part of the formal architectural model. While they can speed up short-term development, they create dependencies that are uncontrolled by the system's constraints. These dependencies are hard to monitor and are not subject to the same validation and enforcement as standard interactions. Over time, as these shortcuts multiply, they weaken architectural boundaries and raise the risk of unintended side effects.

Detection: interactions that do not appear in the capability's declared contract surface or runtime traces that bypass the contract validator entirely. Prevention: require all capability interactions to be declared through contracts before implementation begins. Resolution: identify each direct dependency, wrap it in an explicit contract, and route the interaction through the runtime enforcement layer.

Uncontrolled Version Proliferation

New versions are released without explicit compatibility guidelines or lifecycle management, leading to fragmentation instead of structured development. Instead of establishing how different versions connect, each new release is considered an independent implementation. Over time, multiple versions coexist without a clear strategy for compatibility or deprecation. Lab4-version-sprawl demonstrates this directly: profile-normalizer-v1 and profile-normalizer-v2 coexist, but version selection depends on consumer-specific conventions rather than explicit compatibility rules. The verdict becomes fragmented, and the version_fragmentation warning appears.

Detection: version_fragmentation warning in the runtime assessment, or version selection that depends on consumer-side conventions rather than runtime-enforced compatibility rules. Prevention: define backward_compatible_from declarations for every new version when it is introduced, and enforce version selection through the runtime policy. Resolution: introduce explicit compatibility rules between existing versions and migrate version selection to the runtime. Lab5-runtime-governed-coexistence shows the recovered state.

Hidden Coupling Through Adaptation Layers

Adaptation layers are used to bridge gaps between capabilities, but they rely on assumptions about how these capabilities behave that aren't documented in contracts or metadata. Although they can lessen immediate friction, they also introduce hidden dependencies. Changes in one capability may require updates to multiple adaptation layers, and inconsistencies can emerge when these layers evolve independently. Because the coupling is indirect, it is difficult to detect and reason about. Over time, the system accumulates layers of implicit logic that obscure the original architectural intent and make evolution more fragile.

Detection: changes to a single capability requiring updates across multiple adaptation layers, or runtime traces that pass through translation components not declared in any capability contract. Prevention: express all behavioral differences between capabilities through contracts and metadata rather than through intermediary translation logic. Resolution: replace adaptation layers with explicit versioned contracts that define the expected behavior at each boundary, and route interactions through the runtime enforcement layer.

A Practical Evolution Scenario

This scenario illustrates how a single capability can degrade from a coherent, well-defined baseline into a fragmented state and then recover through runtime governance. It aligns with the companion labs. A team develops a customer profile normalization capability for two internal users: a profile indexer and an audit service. The capability is clearly defined, its contract is explicit, and both users share the same understanding of its output. This is demonstrated in lab1-contract-anchor: with one contract lineage, stable event semantics, active runtime enforcement, and no warnings.

Over the following months, a third consumer arrives: a legacy batch synchronization service that expects an older representation of a normalized profile. Rather than introducing a new version, the team adapts the existing capability to handle both interpretations. The contract remains structurally unchanged. Internally, however, the capability now produces different outputs depending on which consumer is calling it. The contract anchor has moved from stable to drifting. This is lab2-behavioral-drift.

To avoid further risk to the existing consumers, a different team creates a separate edge-optimized copy of the normalization capability for low-latency scenarios. Both implementations share the same capability name and event name, but they evolve under different constraints. Small differences accumulate. The profile.normalized event now means something slightly different depending on which environment produced it. Semantic instability and duplicate behavior warnings appear. This is lab3-duplicate-implementations.

Version 2.0.0 is introduced to address the growing divergence. But no compatibility rules are defined between v1.0.0 and v2.0.0. Consumers select versions based on internal conventions rather than runtime-enforced rules. The system is now fragmented. This is lab4-version-sprawl, where the verdict changes to fragmented.

Recovery does not require replacing the existing implementations. The team introduces explicit compatibility declarations: profile-normalizer-v2 carries backward_compatible_from: 1.0.0. The runtime now resolves version selection based on these declarations, routing legacy-sync to v1 and newer consumers to v2. The fragmentation warnings disappear. The verdict becomes governed. This is lab5-runtime-governed-coexistence.

The legacy core is never rewritten. Instead, a governed facade wraps it. New consumers interact with the facade through an explicit contract. The legacy internals remain in place behind it, isolated from new interactions. This is lab6-hybrid-adoption. The verdict remains governed, and the system continues to evolve without requiring a full redesign.

Adopting UMA in Practice: From Fragmentation to Controlled Evolution

Adoption is not simply switching from one system to another. Systems keep evolving as changes are made, so assuming a stable starting point is impractical. The goal is not to replace the system but to influence its evolution by adding mechanisms that gradually align behaviors with clear definitions and enforceable rules.

Brownfield Systems

Most systems that require this architectural model are the result of long periods of incremental change. What appears as a set of defined interfaces often conceals a layer of implicit dependencies and interpretations that are not formally captured. Capabilities have been introduced, extended, and interconnected over time, often by different teams operating under varying assumptions. In these systems, contracts are rarely the true source of behavioral definition. While interfaces or schemas may exist, they do not fully describe how interactions are interpreted. Behavior is distributed across implementation logic, conditional handling, data transformations, and ordering assumptions that have evolved over time. Consumers depend not only on what is declared but also on how providers behave in practice. This creates implicit contracts that are enforced through usage rather than through explicit definition.

These implicit contracts are difficult to identify. They are embedded in code paths, operational expectations, and historical decisions that are no longer visible in documentation. A capability may appear to expose a stable interface, while its correct usage depends on assumptions about timing, data completeness, or side effects that are not expressed at the boundary.

Coupling extends beyond direct dependencies and becomes systemic. Capabilities may depend on shared data representations, coordinated execution flows, or specific interpretations of events that are not governed by explicit definitions. Adopting an architectural model based on explicit contracts and runtime enforcement in this context requires acknowledging that the existing system cannot be fully understood or redefined in a single step. The objective is to progressively make implicit behavior explicit at the boundaries of interactions.

Why Full Rewrites Fail

Rewriting a system from scratch presumes that the system can be stabilized long enough to define and develop its replacement. In practice, the system continues to evolve during the rewrite process. A complete rewrite assumes stability for the new system's development, but new requirements emerge, existing behaviors change, and integrations expand. Consequently, the new system is built against a moving target, and by the time it's finished, it may only represent a snapshot of a system that has already changed. The complexity of the current system further complicates accurate reproduction, as much of its behavior is implicit, embedded in implementation details, operational practices, and evolving contracts.

Even after a rewrite is complete, the system can revert to a similar state if the underlying model for defining and enforcing behavior does not change. The initial clarity achieved through redesign gradually erodes as new requirements are incorporated without mechanisms to maintain alignment. A more effective approach is to change how the system evolves rather than attempting to replace it entirely.

Incremental Adoption Strategy

Adoption proceeds through a consistent process of clarifying and controlling behavior, even when different system components develop at varying speeds. It begins with recognizing actual capability boundaries in practice. Since these boundaries are often ambiguous, establishing them doesn't require immediate overhauls but involves identifying where interactions happen and considering those points for explicit definition. Afterward, contracts can be created to specify the true nature of these interactions. These contracts should mirror real-world capabilities rather than idealized expectations. Basing contracts on observed behaviors ensures they serve as a trustworthy foundation for alignment.

With contracts in place, enforcement can be introduced progressively. Initially, enforcement may be limited to validation and observability, providing visibility into how interactions align with defined contracts. As confidence increases, enforcement can be extended to influence how interactions are resolved, preventing incompatible behavior and constraining execution within defined rules.

As behavior becomes explicit and enforced at capability boundaries, internal implementation can begin to evolve independently. Logic previously intertwined with other parts of the system can be isolated, and dependencies on implicit assumptions can be reduced. This enables the gradual extraction of behavior into more clearly defined capabilities, without requiring a full redesign.

Deployment Strategies for UMA Migration

Incremental adoption requires deployment strategies that enable UMA-governed capabilities to coexist with ungoverned legacy behavior during the transition. Three common patterns are used in brownfield systems. The strangler fig pattern creates a governed facade in front of an existing capability. New consumers connect through this facade via a clear contract, while the legacy system remains behind it. The facade manages behavior definition and enforces it externally, isolating legacy internals from new consumers. This approach is shown in lab6-hybrid-adoption, where profile-normalizer-v2 wraps legacy-profile-core without replacing it. The legacy system continues to operate as before, while the governed boundary expands. For teams adopting UMA, this pattern enables migration to start at the highest-value capability boundary without initially altering the internals.

Parallel operation with runtime routing keeps two versions of a capability active simultaneously, with the runtime directing consumers to the appropriate version based on declared compatibility constraints. This avoids the coordination cost of a synchronized cutover and allows consumers to migrate at their own pace. Lab5-runtime-governed-coexistence shows this pattern: profile-normalizer-v1 serves legacy-sync, while profile-normalizer-v2 serves newer consumers, with the runtime selecting the correct version for each interaction based on the backward_compatible_from declaration. No consumer requires awareness of the other version. For the full production runtime model showing how WASM modules execute across browser, edge, and cloud environments with event-driven coordination, see Chapter 13.

Contract-first extraction reverses the usual sequence of migration. Instead of rewriting an existing capability and then defining its contract, the contract is written first to reflect the actual behavior of the existing implementation. Enforcement is introduced gradually, beginning with validation and observability, and extended to constraint enforcement as confidence increases. This grounding in observed rather than intended behavior prevents the discrepancies that arise when contracts are written against an idealized model and then reconciled with a system that behaves differently in practice.

Hybrid Systems

Adoption does not create a uniform system where all capabilities operate under the same model. Some areas are managed through implicit behavior, while others rely on explicit contracts and enforcement mechanisms. Achieving complete consistency across all capabilities is rarely possible in practice. Certain parts remain unchanged due to stability concerns, external dependencies, or minimal impact, whereas others are gradually adapted. When designing new capabilities, these principles are often incorporated from the beginning, while existing components typically only reveal defined behaviors at their boundaries. As a result, the system evolves unevenly, influenced by differences in context, ownership, and constraints.

Managing a system with mixed behavior requires clear boundaries. Contracts define how capabilities interact, regardless of whether their internal behavior is explicit or implicit. Runtime enforcement ensures that interactions across these boundaries remain consistent with defined expectations, even when one side relies on legacy assumptions. Over time, the portion of the system governed by explicit definitions can expand, but variation in how capabilities are implemented remains a characteristic of real systems.

When to Adopt UMA

Adoption is relevant when the expenses of maintaining consistency through coordination, interpretation, and correction surpass the costs of implementing clear definitions and enforcement mechanisms. A key sign is rising coordination costs, as changes involve multiple teams, and even well-defined modifications rely on shared understanding across capabilities. This indicates a system where behavior at boundaries is not consistently defined, and alignment depends more on communication than on enforceable rules.

Another signal is inconsistency in behavior across consumers. The same interaction produces different outcomes depending on context, version, or interpretation. Diagnosing these inconsistencies requires reconstructing intent from execution, indicating that behavior is not explicitly defined or uniformly interpreted.

Versioning complexity also points to the need for adoption. Multiple versions of capabilities coexist without clear compatibility rules, and consumers must navigate differences that are not governed by a consistent model. Limited visibility into system behavior provides another indication. Observability may capture detailed execution data, but it does not explain how interactions are interpreted or why specific decisions are made.

These signals do not require immediate or complete transformation. Systems with high interaction density, frequent change, and multiple independent teams benefit most from explicit contracts and runtime governance. Smaller systems with limited interactions and stable requirements may not justify the overhead of introducing these mechanisms.

The Nature of Evolving Systems

Systems do not stay in the original state they were designed for. To keep alignment, behavior must be explicitly defined so it can be consistently interpreted as the system changes. Stability is achieved not by maintaining structure itself but by controlling how changes occur and how interactions are managed. Mechanisms like contracts, metadata, and runtime enforcement help keep behavior consistent, decreasing the need for extensive coordination and shared understanding. Observability ensures these mechanisms are correctly applied, allowing ongoing assessment of the system against its architectural plans.

Adoption of this model does not occur as a single transition but as an incremental, ongoing process. As systems evolve, explicit definitions expand, implicit assumptions are reduced, and behavior becomes increasingly governed rather than inferred. Architecture, in this form, is not a fixed design but a continuously applied framework that enables systems to adapt while preserving coherence.

Conclusion: Key Takeaways

This chapter explores how systems continue to evolve after deployment and why achieving coherence requires more than just careful initial planning. Systems never truly reach a final state. The architecture established at deployment is just a snapshot within an ongoing process influenced by emerging capabilities, new users, changing execution environments, and expanding team expertise. Viewing architecture as complete can create a misleading sense of stability.

Structural correctness does not guarantee behavioral consistency. A system can remain structurally valid while its behavior becomes inconsistent across consumers, environments, and versions. The gap between what is declared and what actually happens is where fragmentation begins.

Fragmentation follows a predictable arc. Behavioral drift leads to duplication, duplication leads to version sprawl, and version sprawl leads to consumers experiencing different outcomes from what is conceptually the same operation. Each step is locally valid. The cumulative effect is incoherence. The companion labs at chapter-12-evolution-without-fragmentation make this arc visible and reversible across six runnable scenarios.

Contracts are the anchor of evolution. A stable contract allows implementations to change, environments to vary, and versions to coexist without forcing consumers to adapt. Without an explicit contract as the authoritative behavioral definition, changes propagate unpredictably.

Runtime governance is what makes coexistence safe. Versioning without runtime enforcement is a source of fragmentation rather than a mechanism for controlled evolution. When the runtime resolves version selection, validates compatibility, and enforces constraints, multiple versions can coexist without ambiguity.

Adoption does not require a rewrite. Lab 6 in the companion implementation demonstrates that a legacy core can remain in place when explicit contracts and runtime enforcement govern its boundaries. The objective is not to replace the system, but to change how it evolves.

Chapter 12 builds on this foundation by examining how decisions made during evolution, including capability proposals, runtime approvals, and version selections, can become queryable system artifacts rather than transient events.

CHAPTER 13

Agents, MCP, and the Runtime of Reasoning

From Capabilities to Decisions

Introduction: From Services to Decisions

Earlier chapters examined what services are, how they run across environments, and how systems form through contracts, events, and metadata. The central challenge that emerges from that foundation is not running a service but deciding which services to run, in what order, and in which environment to reach a goal.

Traditional systems address this with fixed execution paths: a request arrives and triggers a sequence of steps defined during development. This works when capabilities are few, environments are stable, and all possible execution paths can be anticipated at design time. As systems grow and capabilities multiply across environments, that assumption breaks down. The same goal may be reachable through several paths, and the right path depends on factors only known at runtime: where data lives, what latency constraints apply, what trust policies are in force, and what the results of earlier steps reveal.

In these conditions, a request is no longer a trigger for a fixed sequence. It becomes a goal that the system must achieve using whatever capabilities are available at runtime. The system must discover what it can do, evaluate possible paths, select appropriate capabilities, and adjust based on each result. This changes the system's role from executing fixed sequences to constructing execution flows dynamically.

To make this work, three concerns that are typically combined in older architectures must be separated. The system needs to run capabilities reliably across environments. It needs to describe and expose what capabilities are available so they can be discovered and understood. And it needs to decide which capabilities to use to reach a specific goal.

E. Piovesan, *Universal Microservices Architecture*, https://doi.org/10.1007/979-8-8688-2794-5_13

Each of these concerns operates under different constraints and evolves at a different pace. Combining them creates rigidity. Separating them creates the conditions for runtime composition.

In the architecture described in this chapter, each concern is handled by a distinct layer. The UMA runtime executes capabilities according to their contracts, keeping behavior consistent across environments. The Model Context Protocol (MCP) exposes and describes capabilities in a structured, discoverable way. Agents handle reasoning about goals, selecting capabilities, and constructing execution flows. WebAssembly enables these components to operate across browser, edge, and cloud environments using a consistent execution model.

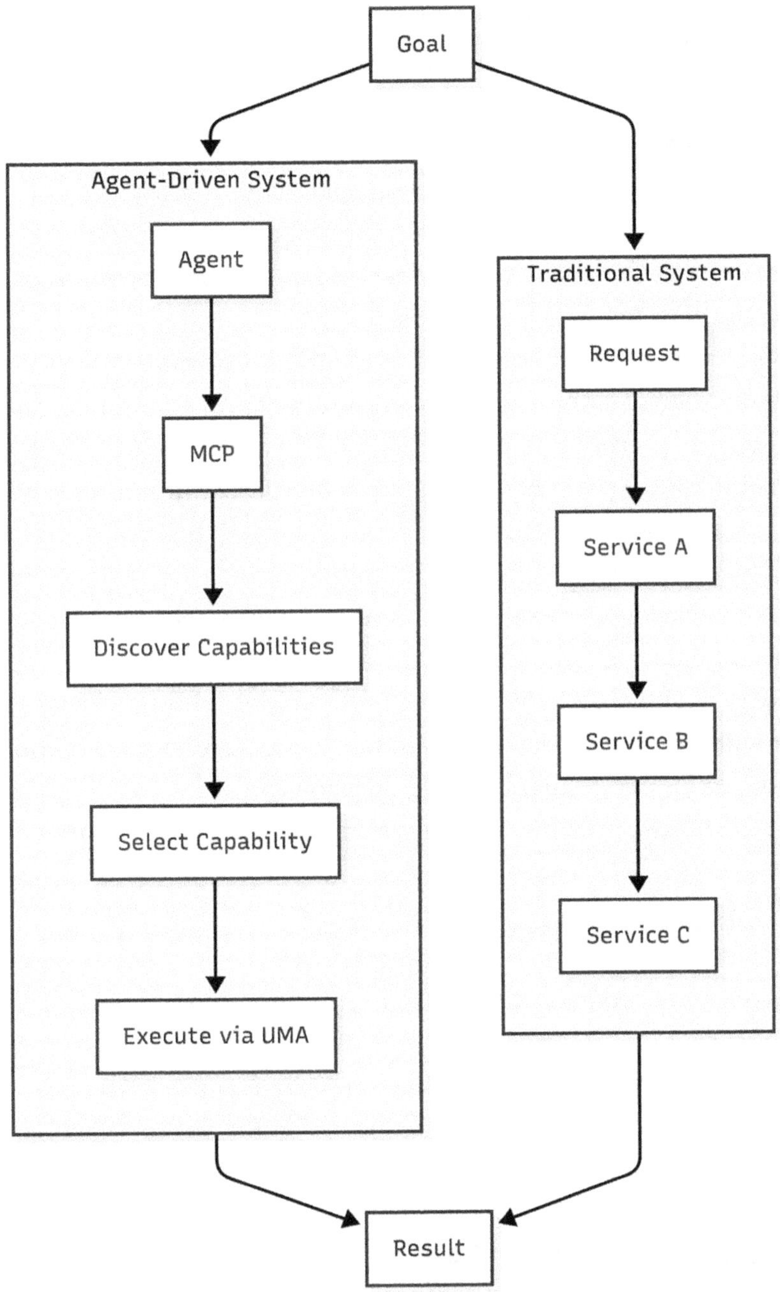

***Figure 13-1.** Fixed execution versus runtime-constructed execution. Traditional systems execute a fixed sequence of services determined at design time. Agent-driven systems receive a goal, discover available capabilities at runtime, select and execute them, and use each result to determine the next step*

Throughout this chapter, a latency-sensitive routing decision serves as the running example. The system must decide whether to compute a route hint at the edge or defer the full authorization decision to the cloud, depending on trust constraints, compliance policies, and data locality. This is the same scenario demonstrated in the companion implementation at chapter-13-discoverable-decisions, where six labs trace the decision from opaque execution through structured proposals, authority feedback, bounded revision, approved execution, and a full queryable trace. Each section that introduces a new concept grounds it in this routing scenario.

This chapter examines the following areas in order. "The Three-Layer Model" section introduces the three-layer architecture separating agents, MCP, and UMA execution and explains why these responsibilities must remain distinct. The section "What MCP Really Is (and Is Not)" defines MCP precisely, including its protocol structure, capability description format, and what it is not. The section "Agents As a Reasoning Layer" describes agents as the reasoning layer and the decision loop through which execution flows are constructed at runtime. "The Decision Lifecycle" section traces the full decision lifecycle from capability projection through proposal, authority validation, bounded revision, approved execution, and queryable trace. The section "From Model to Running System" bridges the architectural model to the running system demonstrated in Chapter 13. The companion implementation at chapter-13-discoverable-decisions provides six runnable labs demonstrating the full arc from opaque execution through governed, queryable decisions.

The Three-Layer Model

As systems move from fixed execution paths to runtime-constructed processes, the architecture must separate concerns that were traditionally combined. Discovery, decision-making, and execution operate under different constraints and evolve at different speeds. Treating them as a single concern produces rigid systems that cannot adapt when capabilities change or execution conditions vary across environments.

Why Responsibilities Must Be Separated

In traditional systems, discovery, decision-making, and execution are combined within the same services or orchestration layers. An API endpoint may validate a request, decide which services to call, execute business logic, and return a result, all within a single logical boundary. This works when execution paths are known in advance and the set of available capabilities changes slowly.

As systems become more distributed and capabilities more portable, this model breaks down. Services may run in different environments, new capabilities may appear without redeploying the entire system, and execution constraints such as latency, cost, and data locality may vary across requests. Under these conditions, the correct execution path cannot be assumed in advance.

Discovery is concerned with describing what exists. Decision-making concerns selecting what should happen. Execution concerns performing the selected operation reliably and consistently. Combining these concerns into a single layer creates tight coupling among what the system can do, what it decides to do, and where it runs. A change in one area affects all others. Separating them allows each part of the system to evolve independently. New capabilities can be added and exposed through the discovery layer without changing the decision logic. Decision strategies can evolve without modifying how services execute. Execution environments can change without requiring the system to redefine how capabilities are described or how decisions are made.

In the routing scenario, this separation is visible from the first lab. The edge surface exposes route_hint.lookup through MCP. The agent queries that surface and forms a proposal. The cloud validates the proposal against compliance policy. Each layer does exactly one thing. The edge MCP node does not decide whether the route hint is compliant. The agent does not execute the authorization check. The cloud runtime does not invent a new plan. The system functions because each responsibility stays in its correct layer.

The Three-Layer Architecture

Once discovery, decision-making, and execution are treated as separate responsibilities, the system organizes into distinct architectural layers. Each layer has a specific role, a clear boundary, and a defined relationship with the others.

Layer	Responsibility
Agents	Reasoning and decision-making
MCP	Discovery and capability exposure
UMA	Execution
WASM	Portability across environments

The UMA runtime forms the execution layer. It runs services according to their contracts, manages lifecycle, handles adapters, and ensures execution remains consistent regardless of where the services run. UMA is where behavior is performed.

Above the execution layer is the discovery layer, implemented through MCP. This layer exposes capabilities, describes their interfaces and constraints, and provides a structured way to query what the system can do. MCP does not execute services and does not decide which services should be used. It makes capabilities visible and understandable so that other parts of the system can use them.

Above the discovery layer is the reasoning layer, implemented by agents. Agents interpret goals, query the discovery layer to understand what capabilities are available, select appropriate capabilities, and construct execution flows dynamically. Agents do not execute services directly. They rely on the execution layer to perform the work.

WebAssembly supports these layers by enabling both discovery components and execution components to run across different environments without requiring separate implementations for each location.

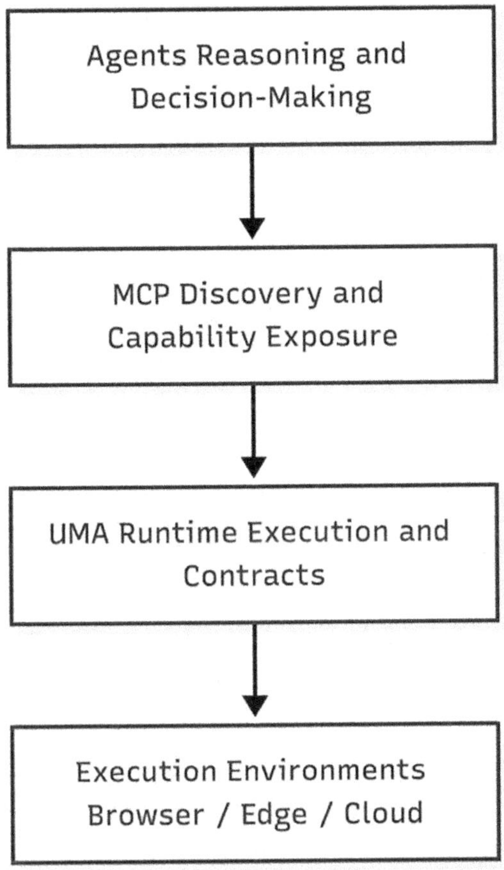

Figure 13-2. *The layered architecture. Agents reason and decide. MCP exposes and describes capabilities. The UMA runtime executes services according to their contracts. WebAssembly enables consistent operation across browsers, Edge, and cloud environments*

Layer Responsibilities in Detail

Agents receive an objective, evaluate the current context, query the discovery layer to determine which capabilities are available, and select which capabilities to use and in what order. After each step is executed, the agent evaluates the result and determines the next action. Execution becomes an iterative process guided by decisions rather than a fixed sequence. Two executions of the same goal may follow different paths if the environment or available capabilities differ.

MCP exposes what the system can do, how capabilities can be invoked, what inputs they require, what outputs they produce, and under what constraints they operate. It provides a structured interface for describing and querying capabilities, organizing information about available services, their contracts, their location, and their execution constraints. MCP does not execute services or decide which services to use. Its role is to describe and expose capabilities so that other parts of the system can discover and use them.

UMA ensures that when a capability is selected, it can be executed reliably and consistently, respecting its defined inputs, outputs, constraints, and lifecycle. The execution layer focuses on performing the work defined by a capability, not on deciding when or why to perform it. Because execution is separated from discovery and decision-making, the same capability can execute in different environments without changing how it is described or how decisions are made about its use.

Why This Model Matters

Separating discovery, decision-making, and execution changes how systems are designed, evolve, and operate at runtime.

System behavior is no longer fully defined at design time. Instead of encoding execution paths as fixed workflows, the system defines capabilities and exposes them through the discovery layer. Agents construct execution flows at runtime based on objectives, available capabilities, and the current execution context. Behavior emerges from the interaction between layers rather than being entirely predefined.

A new capability can be added to the execution layer and exposed through the discovery layer without changing the decision layer. The agent can discover the new capability and incorporate it into its decision process when appropriate. The system evolves by adding capabilities rather than by rewriting workflows.

Execution is no longer tied to a single environment. Because execution is handled by a dedicated runtime and capabilities are described independently of where they run, the system can choose where to execute a capability based on latency, cost, data locality, or resource availability. The same capability may run in a browser in one scenario, at the edge in another, and in the cloud in a third, without changing how it is described or how the agent uses it.

Deterministic execution and probabilistic decision-making can coexist within the same system without being tightly coupled. The execution layer remains deterministic and contract-driven, ensuring reliability and consistency. The decision layer can use adaptive or probabilistic methods to determine which capabilities to use. Separating these concerns allows the system to incorporate reasoning and adaptation without compromising execution reliability.

What MCP Really Is (and Is Not)

MCP is one of the most easily misunderstood parts of this architecture because it does not fit cleanly into traditional categories. It is not a runtime, not an orchestrator, not a service registry, and not an agent. Understanding what it actually is requires setting aside these familiar comparisons.

MCP As a Protocol

MCP is a protocol. It defines a standard way to describe, expose, and query capabilities so they can be discovered and used by agents or other systems at runtime. It is not a product, not a runtime, and not a service implementation.

The protocol defines how a capability is represented, including its inputs, outputs, constraints, and context. It defines how this information can be queried, how a system can discover available capabilities, and how they can be used. By defining a common structure for describing capabilities and a common interface for querying them, MCP standardizes the interaction between reasoning components and executable capabilities.

Agents do not need to know how a capability is implemented internally or where it runs. They only need to understand how to query MCP and how to interpret the capability descriptors it returns. MCP defines how systems describe what they can do in a way that machines can understand and query. It provides a shared language between the decision layer and the execution layer, allowing capabilities to be discovered and used without tightly coupling agents to specific service implementations or execution environments.

A capability is registered with an MCP node using a structured descriptor that defines its identity, interface, constraints, and execution context. The following shows the registration format for the route_hint.lookup capability from the companion implementation:

```
    {
  "capability": "route_hint.lookup",
  "version": "1.0.0",
  "description": "Computes a routing hint from locally visible inputs
  without requiring authoritative policy evaluation.",
  "inputs": {
    "tenant_id": { "type": "string", "required": true },
```

```
    "request_context": { "type": "object", "required": true }
  },
  "outputs": {
    "route_hint": { "type": "string" },
    "confidence": { "type": "number" }
  },
  "constraints": {
    "authoritative": false,
    "requires_trust_validation": true,
    "max_latency_ms": 50,
    "placements": ["edge"]
  }
}
```

An agent queries a local MCP node to discover available capabilities using a structured query:

```
GET /capabilities?input_type=routing_request&placement=edge
```

The MCP node returns a list of capability descriptors matching the query. The agent evaluates the descriptors, selects route_hint.lookup based on the placement constraint and latency budget, and submits a proposal naming the capability, its inputs, and the constraints it cannot validate locally. The MCP node does not validate the proposal itself. Its role ends when the capability descriptor is returned to the agent.

Two additional techniques reduce the operational cost of runtime discovery. Capability caching stores recently queried MCP descriptors in the agent's local context for the duration of a session or request. When an agent has already discovered that route_hint.lookup is available at the edge with a 50ms latency budget, it does not need to query the MCP node again for subsequent steps in the same execution flow. The cache is invalidated when a new session begins or when the MCP node signals a capability update. This reduces discovery round-trips from one per step to one per session for stable capability sets. Cost optimization requires that cost signals be part of the capability descriptor returned by MCP. When a capability declares its expected resource usage, data transfer cost, and execution environment, the agent can evaluate cost as a first-class selection criterion alongside latency and data locality. The route_hint.lookup capability at the edge avoids a cloud round-trip at low cost, deferring the expensive authoritative resolution to route_selector.resolve only when the proposal requires it.

This cost-aware selection is only possible when capability descriptors expose cost signals through MCP.

MCP As a Discovery Interface

Within the layered architecture, MCP serves as the discovery layer. While the protocol defines how capabilities are described and queried, the architectural role of MCP is to expose those capabilities so they can be discovered and understood at runtime.

The discovery layer makes the system's capabilities visible. It provides structured information about what the system can do and how each capability can be used, including the capability name, required inputs, produced outputs, constraints, location, execution environment, and other relevant metadata. This information allows agents to evaluate which capabilities are suitable for a given objective and under what conditions they can be executed.

Agents interact with the system through this discovery interface. Instead of calling specific services directly, an agent queries MCP to determine what capabilities are available and how they can be used. The agent then selects a capability and requests its execution through the execution layer. MCP acts as the interface that allows reasoning components to discover and understand execution capabilities without being tightly coupled to specific services or environments.

MCP As a Capability Graph

Capabilities in a system are not simply a list of independent functions. Each capability has relationships with other capabilities, with data, and with the environments in which it can run. MCP should not be understood as a flat registry of services but as a structured representation of capabilities and their relationships.

Each capability is associated with inputs and outputs, which determine how it can be connected to other capabilities. Some capabilities depend on the results of others. Some capabilities can be composed together to form higher-level operations. Capabilities may exist in multiple versions, run in different environments, and be subject to constraints related to performance, cost, security, or data locality.

MCP organizes this information so that capabilities can be discovered not only individually but also in terms of how they can be combined. Agents can query MCP to find capabilities that produce a specific output, accept a specific input, run in a specific environment, or satisfy certain constraints. In the routing scenario, the agent queries for capabilities with placement=edge and finds route_hint.lookup. It then queries for capabilities that accept a route_hint input and finds route_selector.resolve in the cloud. The composition path emerges from the capability graph, not from hardcoded integration logic.

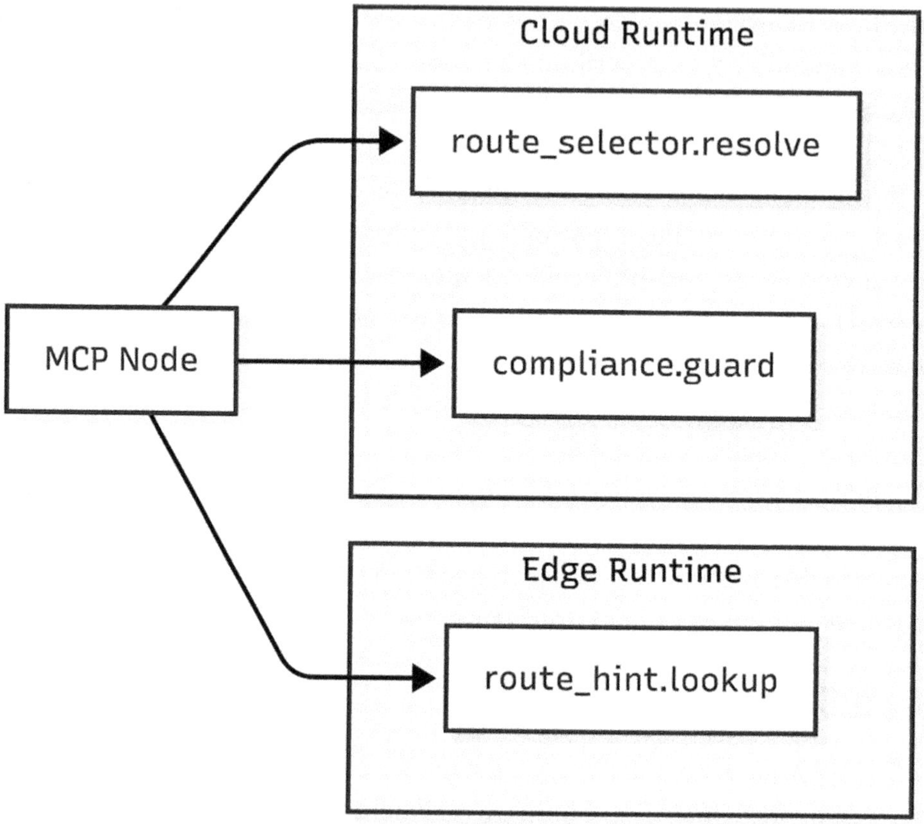

Figure 13-3. *MCP as a capability graph. An MCP node exposes available capabilities and the runtimes in which they execute. route_hint.lookup runs at the edge. route_selector.resolve, and compliance.guard run in the cloud. Agents query the MCP to discover what is available and where it can be executed without directly invoking any service*

What MCP Is Not

MCP is not the runtime. It does not execute services, run business logic, or manage service lifecycles. Execution is the responsibility of the UMA runtime. When a capability is selected, MCP does not run it. It only provides the information required to understand how that capability can be invoked.

MCP is not the orchestrator. It does not determine the sequence of operations required to complete a task, nor does it control the flow of execution. The responsibility for selecting capabilities and determining the order in which they are executed belongs to the agent. MCP provides information about available capabilities, but it does not decide how they are used.

MCP is not the agent. It does not interpret goals, evaluate results, or make decisions. It does not plan or construct execution flows. MCP responds to queries by describing capabilities and their constraints, but it does not initiate actions on its own.

MCP is not the service. It does not implement business functionality and does not contain the logic that performs the work associated with a capability. The implementation of capabilities is performed by services executed by the UMA runtime.

These distinctions matter because MCP can appear to be part of the runtime or part of the orchestration layer if its role is not clearly defined. MCP exposes and describes capabilities. Agents decide which capabilities to use. UMA executes the selected capabilities. MCP therefore acts as the interface that connects reasoning to execution without becoming part of either layer.

Agents As a Reasoning Layer

In the layered model, the execution layer runs capabilities, and the discovery layer exposes them. Once these two layers are separated, a third responsibility becomes necessary: determining which capabilities to use, in what sequence, and under what conditions to achieve a specific objective. This responsibility belongs to the reasoning layer, implemented by agents.

From Requests to Goals

Traditional software systems are typically designed around requests that map directly to operations. A request enters the system, the system determines which service or workflow corresponds to it, and execution follows a fixed sequence of steps. In this model, a request effectively defines what should be executed. The system does not need to determine how to achieve the outcome because the steps have already been defined during development.

In agent-driven systems, the system receives a goal rather than a fully specified request. A goal defines the desired outcome but does not specify the exact sequence of steps required to achieve it. The system must determine which capabilities are available, which ones are appropriate for the current context, and in what order they should be executed. This distinction matters. When the system operates on goals, the steps required to reach the outcome may vary depending on available capabilities, data location, execution constraints, and intermediate results. The system must be able to determine the steps required to achieve the goal at runtime, which requires a component that can interpret the goal, discover available capabilities, select appropriate ones, and dynamically construct an execution flow.

What an Agent Is (Architecturally)

An agent is a component responsible for constructing execution flows at runtime by selecting and composing capabilities in order to achieve a goal. This definition is architectural rather than technological. It does not depend on a specific model, framework, or implementation. What defines an agent in this architecture is its responsibility within the system.

An agent receives a goal and interprets it in the context of the current system state. To determine what actions are possible, the agent queries the discovery layer through MCP. MCP returns descriptions of available capabilities, including their inputs, outputs, constraints, and execution environments. Based on this information, the agent selects one or more capabilities that can move the system closer to the desired outcome. Once a capability is selected, the agent triggers its execution through the UMA runtime. After execution, the result is returned to the agent. The agent evaluates the result against the original goal and determines the next step.

This process is iterative. The agent does not define the entire execution flow in advance. Instead, it constructs the flow step by step, using the results of each execution to inform the next decision. An agent is not defined by a particular type of model or algorithm. It is defined by its role: interpreting goals, discovering capabilities, selecting actions, triggering execution, evaluating results, and continuing this process until the goal is achieved.

The Agent Decision Loop

The behavior of an agent-driven system can be understood as a decision loop that connects goals, discovery, execution, and evaluation. Instead of following a fixed workflow, the system moves through a repeated sequence of discovery, selection, execution, and evaluation steps.

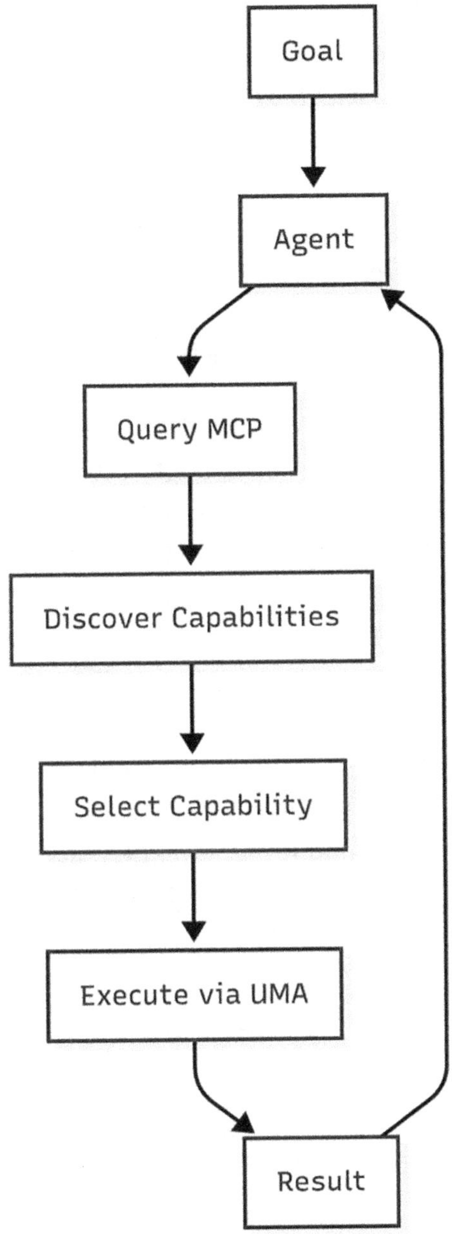

Figure 13-4. *Agent decision loop. An agent receives a goal, queries the discovery layer to identify available capabilities, selects a capability, and triggers execution through the UMA runtime. After execution, the agent evaluates the result and determines the next step. This loop continues until the objective is satisfied*

In the routing scenario, the agent receives the goal of producing a compliant route selection for a tenant request. It queries the edge MCP node and discovers route_hint.lookup. It selects that capability, triggers execution, and receives a route hint with a confidence score. It then queries the cloud MCP node, discovers route_selector.resolve and compliance.guard, and determines that both are needed to produce the final authorized route. The loop runs twice before the goal is satisfied. The execution path is not defined in advance. It emerges from the two iterations.

Deterministic Execution vs. Probabilistic Reasoning

An important architectural distinction in this model is the separation between deterministic execution and probabilistic or adaptive reasoning. These two types of behavior operate under different constraints and serve different purposes.

The execution layer, implemented through UMA services, must be deterministic and contract-driven. A capability defines its inputs, outputs, and constraints, and when executed with a given input, it is expected to behave consistently with its contract. Deterministic behavior is necessary for reliability, testing, observability, and governance.

The reasoning layer, implemented through agents, operates differently. Agents receive goals, evaluate available capabilities, and decide which actions to take. This decision process may be adaptive and may involve probabilistic methods, heuristics, or models that operate on incomplete information. The role of the agent is not to perform deterministic computation but to decide which capabilities should be executed and in what sequence in order to achieve a goal.

Layer	Type
Agents	Probabilistic or adaptive reasoning
MCP	Descriptive
UMA services	Deterministic execution
WASM	Execution portability

Maintaining this separation is important. Agents decide what should happen. MCP describes what is possible. UMA executes what has been selected. When these responsibilities are kept separate, the system can combine adaptive decision-making with reliable execution without mixing concerns or compromising system reliability.

Agents and Services Are Not the Same

Agents and services may be implemented using similar technologies and may even run within the same execution environment, but they represent different architectural roles.

A service implements a capability. It defines a contract, accepts inputs, produces outputs, and performs a specific task. Services belong to the execution layer and are responsible for deterministic behavior. Their purpose is to perform well-defined operations reliably and consistently.

An agent does not primarily implement a single capability. Its role is to select and compose capabilities in order to achieve a goal. An agent interprets objectives, queries the discovery layer, selects services to execute, evaluates results, and determines the next step. An agent can be understood as both a consumer and a composer of capabilities, whereas a service is an implementation of a capability.

This distinction is architectural. It is possible to implement an agent as a UMA service so that it can run within the same runtime and use the same lifecycle and portability mechanisms. However, even when implemented this way, the agent's responsibility remains different. The agent is responsible for decision-making and flow construction, while other services execute specific capabilities. Maintaining this distinction prevents decision-making logic from becoming mixed with execution logic, keeping the system easier to reason about and evolve.

When Not to Use Agents

The architectural model described in this chapter is designed for systems that must discover capabilities at runtime, dynamically construct execution flows, and operate across multiple environments. This model is not appropriate for every type of system.

If a system follows a fixed and well-understood workflow that does not change frequently, fixed orchestration is often simpler, more predictable, and easier to maintain. The overhead of runtime discovery and decision-making does not provide significant benefits because the execution path is already known and unlikely to change. Systems with hard real-time requirements are also not well-suited to multi-step decision loops. When strict and predictable latency is required, execution paths must be tightly controlled and optimized. Very simple CRUD systems are another case where this model is usually unnecessary. Highly regulated or strictly deterministic environments may also limit the usefulness of agent-driven execution, where execution paths must be fully auditable, predictable, and approved in advance.

The following decision tree provides a systematic way to evaluate whether agent-driven execution is appropriate for a given scenario:

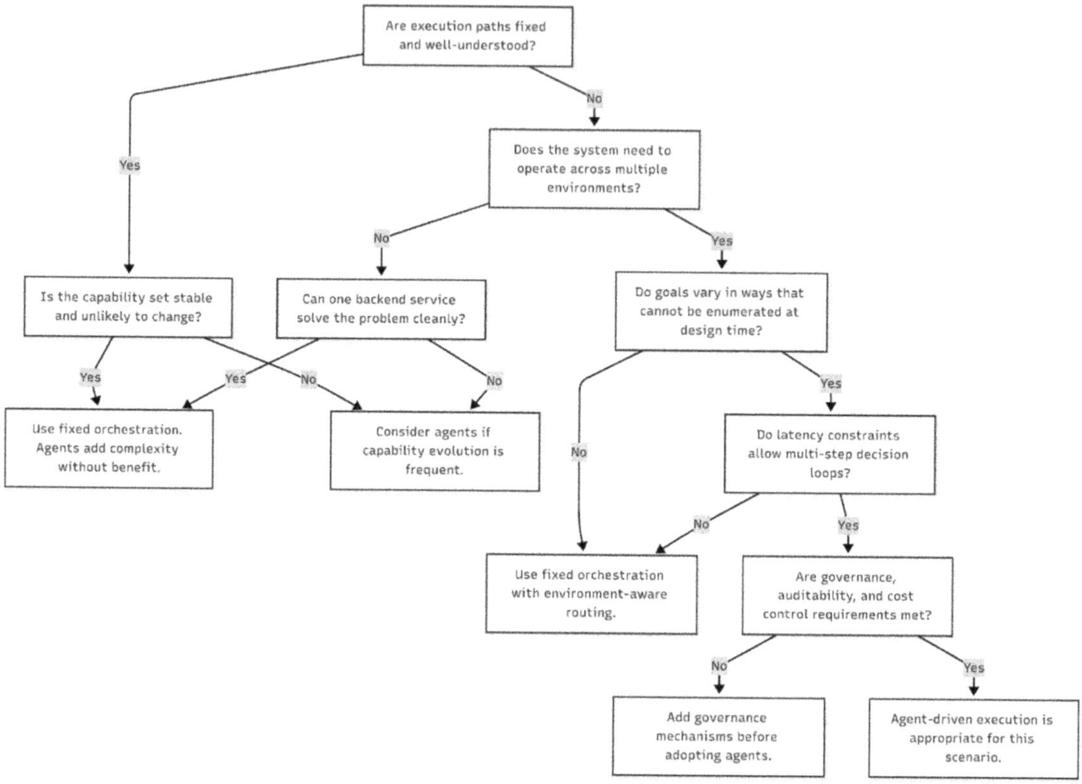

***Figure 13-5.** Decision tree for evaluating whether agent-driven execution is appropriate. Start at the top and follow the path that matches the system's characteristics. Use agents only when the bottom-right path is reached with all conditions satisfied*

The Decision Lifecycle

A decision becomes visible when it is expressed as a proposal artifact, not when it produces a result. The routing scenario demonstrates five stages through which a decision moves from opaque execution to a governed, queryable outcome.

The companion implementation at chapter-13-discoverable-decisions makes each stage runnable. The six labs trace the same routing decision as it gains visibility at each step. Running the diff between labs is the fastest way to see exactly which axis changed and what that change produced.

Stage 1: Capability Projection (lab1-capability-projection)

The system successfully executes a latency-sensitive routing step. The cloud runtime shifts the routing step under load and produces the correct route selection result. From an execution perspective, everything works. From an architectural perspective, the decision is opaque.

The edge surface exposes route_hint.lookup, tenant_profile.read, and latency_budget.observe as locally visible capabilities. The cloud holds the authoritative capabilities: route_selector.resolve, compliance.guard, and trace_artifact.write. Both surfaces exist, and both can be queried. The problem is that the reasoning that led to the routing outcome is not emitted as an inspectable artifact. The system knows what it did. It cannot explain why.

The verdict at this stage is opaque. Two warnings appear: proposal_hidden and authority_gap. The edge is acting on local context without any authoritative validation, and the decision is buried inside execution rather than expressed as a first-class artifact. Execution success is not the same as architectural transparency. The gap between the two is what this chapter addresses.

Stage 2: Explicit Proposal (lab2-edge-proposal)

The edge now emits a structured proposal that names the desired change, states its assumptions, and explicitly identifies the constraints it cannot validate locally. The proposal names proposal.route_shift.write as a new capability on the edge surface and declares two unresolved questions: whether edge placement satisfies the trust policy and whether the move remains auditable under compliance requirements.

This is the key architectural shift. The system is not yet executing differently. It is describing its intent before acting. A proposal that admits what it cannot validate locally is more trustworthy than one that guesses. The agent now has something to submit to the authoritative layer rather than an implicit assumption to act on.

The verdict changes to discoverable. The proposal is now visible and structured, even though it has not yet been evaluated. The proposal_hidden warning disappears. The authority_gap warning remains because the edge is still acting as a planning authority only, which is correct. The edge should propose, not approve.

Stage 3: Authority Feedback (lab3-authority-feedback)

The authoritative cloud layer evaluates the edge proposal, rejects the initial move, and returns violations plus remediation guidance. The rejection is not silent. It explains exactly what failed and what bounded change would make the proposal acceptable.

The two violations are route authorization depends on policy metadata not replicated at the edge, and the proposed path would weaken the audit story for sensitive tenants. The guidance that follows is equally specific: keep edge planning focused on route hint generation, not final authorization, and defer the compliance-sensitive branch resolution to the authoritative cloud path.

This is what validation contributes beyond a gate. A silent rejection forces the planner to guess what changed. An actionable rejection gives the planner exactly what it needs to revise. The trace artifacts at this stage include initial-proposal.json and validation-response.json. The system now has a record of what was proposed and why it was rejected. The verdict remains discoverable, and the authority_gap warning is gone because the authority model has shifted to authoritative-validation.

Stage 4: Bounded Revision (lab4-single-revision)

The planner revises the proposal once, preserving the latency objective while deferring the trust-sensitive decision to the authoritative layer. The revised proposal keeps route hint generation at the edge but leaves final authorization and tenant-sensitive branching in the cloud.

The revision model is single-revision. This is not an implementation detail. It is an architectural property. Bounded revision is what keeps discoverability from collapsing into endless negotiation between planner and validator. If the planner and validator can keep negotiating indefinitely, the decision lifecycle becomes difficult to reason about, and the unbounded_revision warning appears. One revision cycle is enough. The planner narrows the problem. The validator approves or rejects with guidance. The planner revises once again that guidance. Authority then approves, or the process terminates.

The trace at this stage captures initial-proposal.json, validation-response.json, revised-proposal.json, and approval-summary.json. The full reasoning path is now queryable even before execution begins.

Stage 5: Approved Execution (lab5-approved-execution)

The system resolves the approved proposal into concrete capability selection and final placement under authoritative control. The selected capabilities are route_hint.lookup at the edge, route_selector.resolve in the cloud, and compliance.guard in the cloud. Execution honors the approved proposal rather than silently improvising a different composition.

This distinction matters. Execution that resolves an approved plan is architecturally different from execution that replans on the fly. When execution resolves an approved plan, the decision and the execution remain traceable to the same artifact. When execution replans silently, the approved decision and the actual execution diverge. The implicit_replanning warning captures this failure mode and changes the verdict to unstable.

The verdict at this stage is discoverable. A partial_trace warning appears because the system records planning artifacts but not yet the full path from approved proposal to concrete execution. The next stage closes that gap.

Stage 6: Queryable Trace (lab6-queryable-trace)

The full decision lifecycle is now exposed through discoverable surfaces. The trace is a first-class output that captures proposal, feedback, revision, approval, execution, and artifact identifiers in one queryable chain. The six artifacts are initial-proposal.json, validation-response.json, revised-proposal.json, approval-summary.json, execution-summary.json, and decision-trace.json.

The trace can be queried from both the edge and the cloud. The edge exposes decision_trace.query as a surface capability. The cloud exposes the full artifact chain through trace_artifact.write and decision_trace.query. A reader can inspect the full decision lifecycle without having to read hidden runtime code paths.

The verdict changes to governed. All warnings disappear. This is the Chapter 13 payoff: the system is executable, discoverable, and explainable simultaneously.

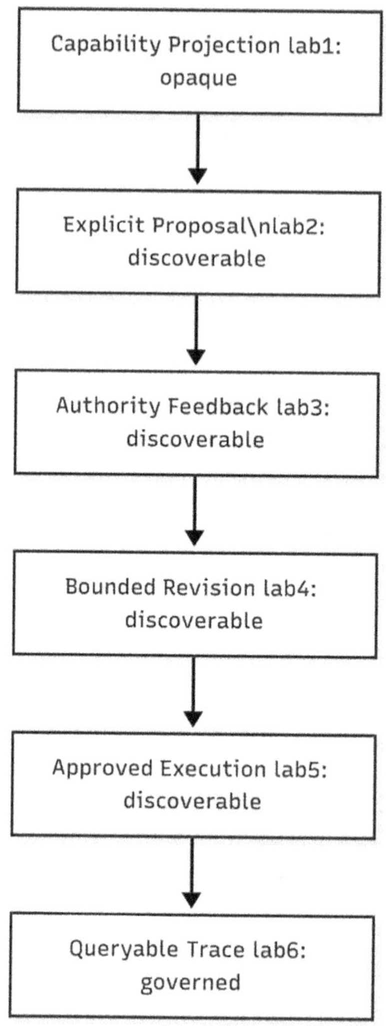

Figure 13-6. *The decision lifecycle across six labs. Each stage adds a layer of visibility. The system moves from opaque execution to governed, queryable decisions without changing the underlying routing logic*

From Model to Running System

The three-layer model, the MCP protocol, the agent decision loop, and the decision lifecycle together define how a UMA system makes decisions that are both executable and explainable. What remains is to see how these elements operate together as a complete system running across browser, edge, and cloud environments.

Chapter 13 provides that demonstration. It follows a single request as it moves through capability discovery, agent-driven reasoning, service execution, and result composition across multiple runtimes. The focus is on observing how the concepts established in this chapter combine to produce a coherent and adaptable execution model, rather than introducing new ones.

When reading Chapter 13, the aspects that connect most directly to this chapter are the following. The separation of discovery, decision-making, and execution established in "The Three-Layer Model" section is visible in how MCP nodes, agents, and UMA services each play a distinct role without overlapping. The capability descriptor format from the section "What MCP Really Is (and Is Not)" is what agents use to query available capabilities before constructing a plan. The agent decision loop from the section "Agents As a Reasoning Layer" is the runtime behavior that drives each step from intent to result. The proposal and trace artifacts from "The Decision Lifecycle" section are what make the system's decisions inspectable after execution completes.

The routing scenario in this chapter and the report generation scenario in Chapter 13 demonstrate the same architectural properties in different domains. Both systems begin with a goal. Both discover capabilities through MCP. Both construct execution paths at runtime. Both produce results that can be traced back to the decisions that shaped them. The difference is scale and narrative depth. Chapter 13 establishes the model. Chapter 13 runs it.

Conclusion: Key Learnings

This chapter has established the architectural foundation for systems that construct execution flows at runtime rather than following fixed execution paths.

Discovery, decision-making, and execution are distinct responsibilities. MCP exposes capabilities. Agents construct execution paths. UMA executes selected capabilities. Combining these concerns creates rigid systems that are difficult to evolve. Separating them allows each layer to change independently.

MCP is a protocol, not a runtime. It defines how capabilities are described, registered, and queried. It does not execute services and does not decide which services to use. Its role is to make the system queryable without collapsing into either execution or orchestration.

A decision becomes visible when it is expressed as a proposal artifact, not when it produces a result. The six labs at chapter-13-discoverable-decisions demonstrate that a system can execute correctly while remaining opaque and that opacity is an architectural property, not an operational one.

Authority and discoverability strengthen each other. A proposal that admits what it cannot validate locally is more trustworthy than one that guesses. Validation that returns actionable guidance is more useful than a silent rejection.

Bounded revision is what keeps discoverability from collapsing into endless negotiation. The decision lifecycle must be finite: one revision cycle, one approval, one execution, one trace.

The queryable trace is the payoff. When the full artifact chain from proposal to execution is preserved, the system can be inspected, audited, and replayed without reading hidden runtime code paths.

Chapter 13 brings these elements together in a complete reference system running across browser, edge, and cloud environments, showing how proposal, validation, execution, and trace operate as a continuous flow rather than as isolated architectural concepts.

PART V

Realizing UMA Systems

CHAPTER 14

The Reference Experience

A Living UMA System, Running Across Browser, Mobile, and Runtime Boundaries

Introduction: Bringing the System to Life

Until now, each system component has been introduced and examined individually to develop the underlying ideas with clarity and precision.

UMA defines how services execute, focusing on the structure, behavior, and constraints that govern runtime execution. MCP defines how capabilities are exposed, described, and discovered, providing a consistent interface for locating and understanding services. Agents introduce a layer of reasoning, enabling decisions to be formed dynamically based on available capabilities and contextual information. WASM provides the foundation for portability, allowing the same components to operate consistently across browser, edge, and cloud environments.

Each of these elements addresses a specific concern in modern distributed systems. Together, they form a system that behaves differently from traditional architectures, in which integration is typically fixed, and execution paths are established before the system runs.

How these elements interact as part of a single, continuous flow has not yet been demonstrated. While understanding each component in isolation is necessary, it does not fully capture the system's behavior as a whole.

This chapter addresses that gap by tracing a complete system from start to finish. A single request moves through capability discovery, agent-driven reasoning, service execution, and result composition across multiple runtimes. The focus is on observing how existing concepts combine to produce a coherent and adaptable execution model, rather than introducing new ones.

Throughout this process, the separation of responsibilities remains explicit and unchanged. UMA is responsible for execution, ensuring that services perform their

E. Piovesan, *Universal Microservices Architecture*, https://doi.org/10.1007/979-8-8688-2794-5_14

defined behavior within the constraints specified by their contracts. MCP is responsible for exposing and organizing capabilities, making them discoverable without embedding execution logic. Agents are responsible for reasoning and decision-making, selecting which capabilities to use and in what sequence. WASM enables these components to operate across environments without requiring changes to their core behavior.

The system described here is constructed through the interaction of these layers at runtime, rather than through fixed integration paths.

What This Chapter Covers

This chapter begins by introducing the report generation scenario and the distributed data sources the system must work with. It then describes the three-layer architecture, MCP nodes, UMA services, and agents, as it operates across runtimes. From there it traces the full runtime flow step by step: entering the system, agent reasoning, execution through UMA, crossing runtimes with WASM, and composing the result. The second half examines what actually changed in the architecture, the design principles the system proves, and what the model enables next. The chapter closes with a retrospective on architecture as a living system.

The System We Will Follow

The system examined in this chapter is centered on a single, concrete task: generating a report from distributed data sources, enriching it through analysis, and producing a structured summary that can be consumed by a user or another system.

At first glance, this task appears straightforward: data is collected, processed, and presented. In practice, each step involves multiple capabilities, diverse execution environments, and varying constraints related to performance, availability, and access.

Data Sources and Their Distribution

The data required to generate the report does not reside in a single location. It is distributed across local datasets available in the browser, edge services that provide aggregated or pre-processed information, and cloud-based systems responsible for heavy computation or long-term storage. Each source exposes different interfaces, operates under different constraints, and evolves independently.

Some data is available locally, such as within the browser, where recent user interactions, cached datasets, or session-specific information can be accessed with minimal latency. This data is typically small, immediately available, and closely tied to the current request context.

Other data is exposed through edge services, which often provide aggregated or pre-processed information, reducing the need to access raw datasets repeatedly. These services operate closer to the user, offering lower latency and improved responsiveness, but may have limited computational capacity and only partial visibility of the overall data landscape.

Additional data resides in cloud-based systems, where larger datasets are stored, and more intensive processing can be performed. These systems support complex computations, analytical models, and historical records. Accessing them introduces higher latency and may require additional considerations for cost, security, and data transfer.

The distribution of data across these environments presents a fundamental challenge. Generating a report requires identifying relevant data, determining its location, understanding access methods, and deciding how to combine it with data from other sources. The distributed nature of the data is not an implementation detail, and it directly shapes how requests are interpreted and how execution is structured.

The Expected Output

Generating a report in this context involves more than collecting raw data. The expected result is a structured output that combines retrieved information, derived insights, and a concise summary suitable for direct consumption or integration with other systems.

Clearly defined data elements, including metrics, records, and aggregated values from underlying sources, form the factual basis of the report and must remain consistent with the data retrieved during execution. In addition to raw and aggregated data, the system generates derived insights such as trends, comparisons, or computed indicators that require processing beyond simple retrieval. A summary layer captures the most relevant aspects of the report in a compact form, enabling interpretation without reviewing every data element.

The final output remains consistent even as data sources, processing steps, or execution environments vary. Consumers interact with a stable representation, independent of how the result is produced.

Why a Fixed Workflow Does Not Fit

A system for generating reports from distributed data sources could be implemented as a fixed workflow, with each step explicitly defined in advance. At a small scale, this approach can be effective. When data sources are stable, processing requirements are well understood, and execution environments are consistent, a fixed workflow offers predictability and ease of implementation.

The scenario in this chapter introduces conditions that make this approach difficult to sustain. Data sources are distributed and may change over time in structure and availability. Some sources may become temporarily inaccessible, while others may introduce new capabilities or interfaces. Execution environments vary in latency, computational capacity, and access constraints across browser, edge, and cloud. Processing requirements are not uniform; some reports require only basic aggregation, while others depend on advanced analysis or additional enrichment.

Fixing all possible execution paths in advance increases complexity rapidly. Each variation in data source, processing requirement, or execution environment adds branches to the workflow. Maintaining such a system requires continuous updates for new combinations, making evolution difficult without risking inconsistencies or errors.

Under these conditions, a system built on fixed execution paths becomes rigid. It can handle known scenarios but struggles to adapt when available capabilities or execution context changes. Generating a report becomes a process that unfolds at runtime, where each stage depends on the capabilities that are available and the conditions under which they operate.

The request to generate a report defines an objective, not a fixed procedure. It specifies the desired outcome but does not determine how to achieve it. The system must interpret the request, identify relevant data sources, select processing steps, and determine how to combine intermediate results. Report generation becomes a sequence of decisions made at runtime, each determining which capability to use, where to execute it, and how its output contributes to the overall result.

The Architecture

The system comprises three primary layers. MCP nodes are responsible for exposing and organizing capabilities deployed across browser, edge, and cloud environments. UMA services provide the execution layer, implementing the behavior associated with each capability and operating within the constraints defined by their contracts. Agents interact with the system through MCP, using the exposed capabilities to construct and execute a process that satisfies the request's objective.

> *These components are distributed rather than centralized. MCP nodes can run in different runtimes while maintaining a consistent interface, enabled by WASM. UMA services may also be distributed, with certain capabilities executing closer to the user and others delegated to environments with greater computational capacity.*

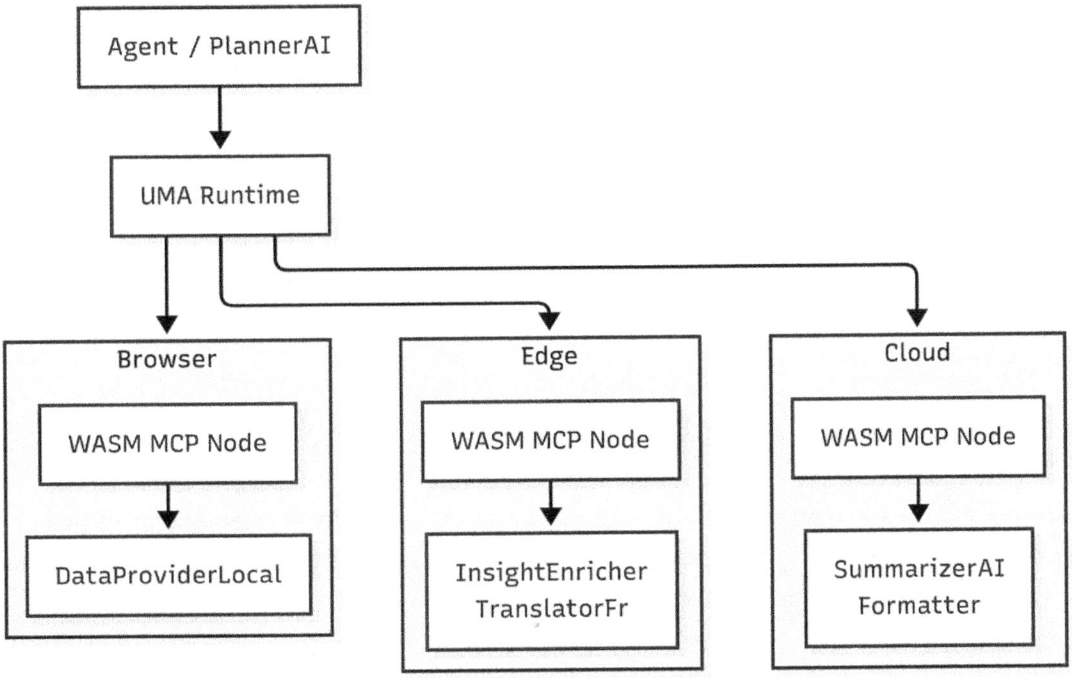

Figure 14-1. *Shows how the three layers relate to each other across browser, edge, and cloud runtimes*

MCP Nodes Across Runtimes

MCP nodes are deployed across multiple environments, forming the entry points through which capabilities are exposed and discovered. Each node provides a consistent interface for interacting with capabilities, regardless of its location. It supports querying available capabilities, retrieving their descriptors, and understanding how they can be used within the context of a request.

The placement of MCP nodes influences how and where capabilities are discovered. A node running in the browser can expose capabilities that depend on local context. An edge node can provide access to services that aggregate or preprocess information closer to the user. A cloud-based node can expose capabilities that rely on large datasets or computationally intensive operations. Despite being distributed, these nodes participate in a shared model of capability exposure, allowing discovery to extend across runtime boundaries while presenting a consistent interface.

UMA Services Across Runtimes

UMA services form the execution layer of the system. Each service implements a specific capability, defined through a contract that describes its behavior, inputs, outputs, and constraints. Services are distributed across browser, edge, and cloud runtimes, with placement influenced by the capabilities they provide and the constraints they carry.

Execution is always driven through the contract associated with a capability. The system does not interact directly with service implementations but with the defined interface that describes how a capability can be invoked and what it produces. This allows services to evolve independently, as long as they continue to satisfy their contracts.

Agents Interacting Through MCP

Agents interact with the system through MCP nodes, using the exposed capabilities to construct and execute a process that satisfies the objective of a request. Their role is not to directly invoke services but to reason about available capabilities and determine how to combine them to produce the desired result.

Interaction begins when the agent queries MCP to discover available capabilities in the current context. Based on the descriptors returned, the agent evaluates possible approaches and constructs a sequence of steps. Execution does not occur directly through the agent; it proceeds through MCP, which provides the interface for invoking capabilities and ensures that interaction with the system remains consistent. The role of the agent remains distinct from both MCP and UMA: It does not expose capabilities, and it does not implement execution logic.

Step 1: Entering the System

A request enters the system with an objective. The objective for this chapter is concrete: generate a structured report in French from distributed data sources. The request does not prescribe how to achieve that objective. It carries the information needed to describe the desired outcome, along with contextual data that may influence how the system responds.

In practice, a request is not a free-form instruction. It carries a structured representation of intent that the runtime can evaluate. For the primary scenario in this chapter, the request structure looks like this:

```
{
  "target": "report",
  "targetLanguage": "fr",
  "preferAI": true,
  "allowDegraded": false,
  "localOnly": false
}
```

The runtime uses each field during discovery. The `targetLanguage` field signals that a translation step will be required, making `TranslatorFr` a candidate. The `preferAI` field indicates that `SummarizerAI` should be ranked above `SummarizerBasic` when both are available. The `localOnly` flag, when true, excludes any capability whose contract carries an `excludes: local-only` constraint, which eliminates `SummarizerAI` and `PlannerAI` from consideration. The `allowDegraded` flag governs what the runtime does when a required capability is unavailable.

An MCP node acts as the entry point for the request. A request initiated by a user interface is typically sent to a node running in the browser. A request generated by an external system or service may enter through a node deployed at the edge or in the cloud. Regardless of its origin, the request is handled through the same interface, ensuring a consistent starting point for processing. The MCP node does not execute business logic and does not determine how the request will be fulfilled. Its responsibility is to prepare the request, attach context, and expose it to the runtime for discovery.

Once the request is received, the MCP node associates it with the relevant context. Context includes information about the execution environment, such as available runtimes, access permissions, and proximity to specific data sources. It may also include request-specific parameters that define the scope of the report or constraints that govern how results are produced. This context is not an auxiliary detail. It directly influences which capabilities are considered valid and how they can be executed.

With the request and its context established, the MCP node initiates capability discovery. Discovery operates through contract-based matching. The system queries available capability contracts and evaluates them against the request's objective and context. This evaluation considers the intent expressed by each capability, the inputs it requires, the outputs it produces, and any execution constraints defined in the contract.

The outcome of this process is a set of candidate capabilities, represented as capability descriptors derived from their contracts. For the report generation scenario, the initial discovery pass identifies `DataProviderLocal` as the only candidate for the `provide-source-fragments` need because it is the only contract whose intent matches and whose constraints are satisfied under the current context. At this stage, no decisions have been made about which capabilities will be used or how they will be combined. The system has established the objective, attached the relevant context, and exposed the available options.

Step 2: Agent Reasoning

Following capability discovery, the system has access to a set of candidate capabilities that can help fulfill the request. No execution has taken place, and no specific sequence of operations has been established. The responsibility shifts to the agent, which interprets the request's objective and evaluates how the available capabilities can be used to achieve it.

The Agent's Role

The agent represents the system's reasoning component. It neither executes capabilities nor exposes them. Its role is to analyze the request, evaluate available options, and determine a viable approach to fulfill the objective. All interaction with the system occurs through MCP, which provides access to capabilities without exposing implementation details or triggering execution.

Through MCP, the agent explicitly queries the available capabilities and retrieves their descriptors. A capability descriptor for `DataProviderLocal` looks like this:

```
{
  "name": "DataProviderLocal",
  "version": "1.0.0",
  "intent": "provide-source-fragments",
```

```
  "inputs": [],
  "outputs": ["source_fragments"],
  "constraints": {
    "runtime": ["browser-wasm", "edge-wasm"],
    "requires": ["local"],
    "excludes": []
  },
  "emitsEvents": ["CapabilityExecuted", "ContextUpdated"],
  "metadata": {
    "description": "Exposes local project source fragments to the
    runtime.",
    "tags": ["source", "local", "input"]
  }
}
```

This is the form WASM MCP returns to the agent when it queries available capabilities. The agent uses the `intent` field to determine whether the capability contributes to the current unmet need and the `constraints` field to evaluate whether it can execute under the current conditions. MCP provides these options but does not participate in decision-making. It exposes what is available in the system, while the agent determines how those capabilities should be used.

How the Agent Constructs a Plan

Using the retrieved capability descriptors, the agent evaluates how capabilities can be combined. This evaluation is based on contract compatibility: the outputs of one capability must satisfy the input requirements of another, and execution constraints must remain valid within the context of the request. The agent does not rely on fixed workflows. It constructs a plan dynamically based on what is available at runtime.

For the French AI report scenario, the agent evaluates the full set of available capabilities and constructs the following sequence: `DataProviderLocal` to load source fragments, `InsightEnricher` to derive structured facts, `SummarizerAI` to generate a richer summary (selected over `SummarizerBasic` because `preferAI` is true and AI is available), `TranslatorFr` to translate the output to French, and `Formatter` to produce the final structured report.

The plan is expressed as a sequence of steps. Each step references a capability, defines how its inputs are derived from the request or from previous results, and specifies the expected output. Decision-making at this stage involves evaluating trade-offs between available options. Some capabilities may offer lower latency but limited functionality, while others may deliver more comprehensive results but require higher resources. The agent evaluates these trade-offs in the context of the request and selects a combination of capabilities that aligns with both the objective and the environment's constraints.

Agent State Model

The agent does not move through a single linear pass. It cycles through a set of states as it queries, evaluates, proposes, and responds to validation outcomes. Figure 14-2 shows the agent state transitions from capability query through proposal, validation, and optional replanning.

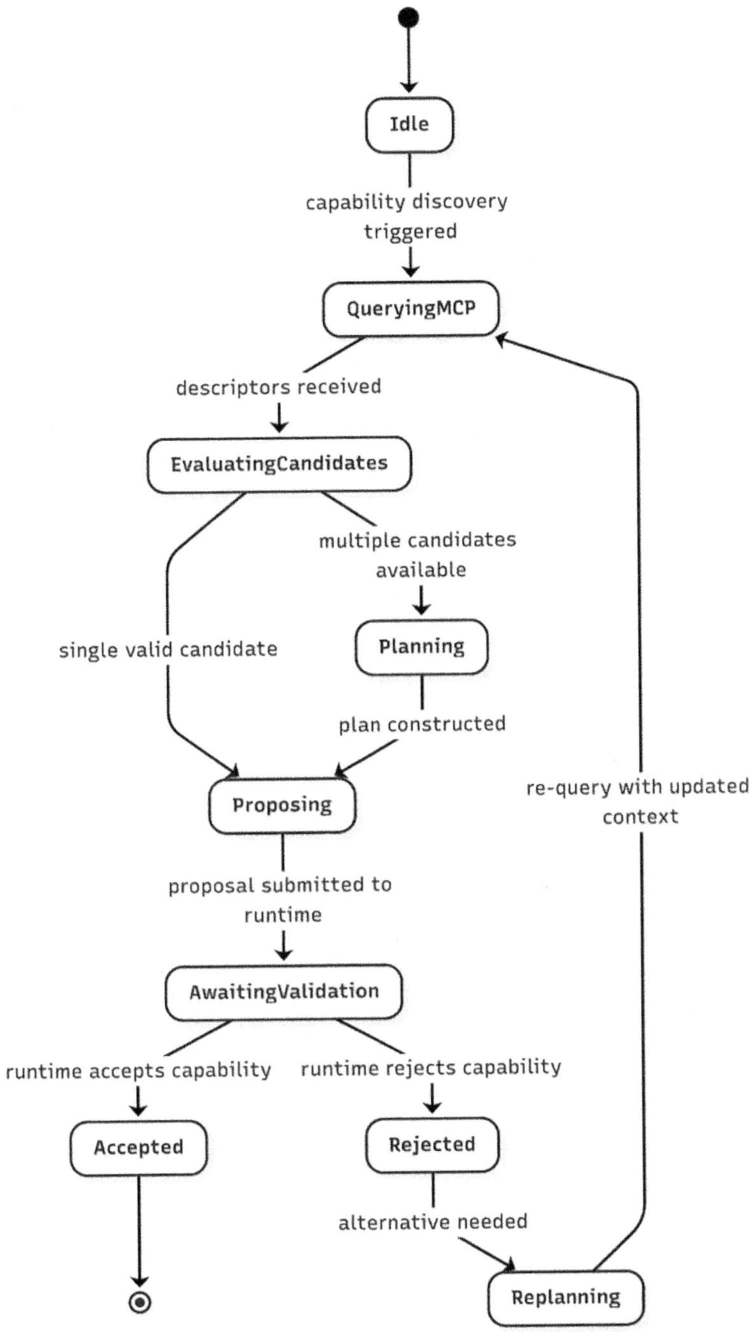

***Figure 14-2.** Agent state transitions from capability query through proposal, validation, and optional replanning*

The `Replanning` state is significant. When the runtime rejects a proposed capability, the agent does not fail. It returns to `QueryingMCP` with updated context reflecting the rejection, re-evaluates the remaining candidates, and proposes an alternative. This is exactly what happens in the runtime override scenario: the agent proposes `SummarizerAI`, the runtime rejects it because `localOnly` is true and `SummarizerAI` excludes `local-only` execution, and the agent reselects `SummarizerBasic` as the valid alternative.

How Contract Compatibility Is Evaluated

Before the runtime accepts any capability the agent proposes, it performs a three-step compatibility check.

Step one: the runtime checks whether all inputs declared in the contract are present in the current execution context. `SummarizerAI` declares `structured_facts` as a required input. If `InsightEnricher` has not yet executed and populated structured facts in the context, `SummarizerAI` is rejected with the reason: `missing input: structured_facts`.

Step two: the runtime checks whether any `excludes` constraint in the contract conflicts with the current goal. `SummarizerAI` excludes `local-only`. If the request has `localOnly: true`, the capability is rejected with the reason: `capability violates local-only execution constraints`. This is the rejection that occurs in the `use-case-5-agent-validation` scenario.

Step three: the runtime checks whether the `requires` fields are satisfied. `SummarizerAI` requires `ai`. If AI is unavailable in the current context, the capability is rejected with the reason: `AI capability is unavailable in the current context`.

Only when all three checks pass is the capability accepted. The contract in `contracts/summarizer-ai.json` encodes all three constraints explicitly, making the validation outcome inspectable and reproducible.

The plan constructed by the agent remains abstract until execution begins. It defines the structure of the solution without invoking any underlying services. All reasoning remains isolated from execution, and all capability interactions continue to occur through MCP.

As execution progresses, the agent may revisit its decisions. Intermediate results can introduce new information, affect the availability of capabilities, or reveal constraints that were not initially visible. In response, the agent can refine the plan, adjust the sequence of steps, or select alternative capabilities. This iterative behavior allows the system to adapt without relying on fixed workflows.

Step 3: Executing Through UMA

Once the agent has constructed a plan, execution begins by invoking the capabilities identified in that plan. Each step in the plan references a capability rather than a specific service. The agent selects capabilities based on their contracts, without binding those selections to a particular implementation.

Mediated Execution

Execution is always mediated through MCP. The agent does not directly invoke a service implementation. Instead, it requests the execution of a capability by interacting with MCP, which resolves that capability to a suitable UMA service based on its contract and the current execution context. This resolution is not based on service identity but on contract compatibility and runtime constraints, including availability, location, and policy requirements.

A capability does not correspond to a single service implementation. It represents a contract that may be fulfilled by one or more UMA services. At runtime, MCP evaluates the available services that satisfy the contract and selects one that can execute under the current conditions. This allows the system to adapt dynamically, selecting between multiple valid implementations without modifying the plan constructed by the agent.

When a capability is invoked, MCP forwards the request to the selected UMA service along with the inputs required by its contract. These inputs are derived from the plan, either originating from the initial request or produced by previous execution steps. The service executes the behavior defined by the contract and produces an output that conforms to the expected structure.

Event Log and Execution Determinism

Each capability invocation emits a sequence of events that forms the execution record for that step. For the French AI report scenario, the events emitted during the `SummarizerAI` step look like this:

```
[
  {
    "type": "CapabilityDiscovered",
    "capability": "SummarizerAI",
    "status": "candidate"
  },
```

```
  {
    "type": "CapabilityDiscovered",
    "capability": "SummarizerBasic",
    "status": "candidate"
  },
  {
    "type": "CapabilityProposed",
    "capability": "SummarizerAI",
    "status": "proposed"
  },
  {
    "type": "CapabilityValidated",
    "capability": "SummarizerAI",
    "status": "accepted"
  },
  {
    "type": "CapabilityExecuted",
    "capability": "SummarizerAI",
    "status": "success"
  }
]
```

This event log is the verification record for execution determinism. The sequence of `CapabilityDiscovered`, `CapabilityValidated`, and `CapabilityExecuted` events for each step can be replayed or inspected to confirm that the same path would be selected under the same inputs and constraints. For AI-assisted steps like `PlannerAI` and `SummarizerAI`, the event log records the proposal and the validation outcome, making the runtime decision traceable even when the model's internal output varies between runs. The JSON report produced by `cargo run --manifest-path rust/Cargo.toml --render use-case-2-ai-report json` exposes the full event log for every step, providing a concrete artifact for verification.

Error Handling and Degraded Execution

During execution, results are validated against the contracts that define them before they can be used as inputs for subsequent steps. If a capability cannot execute or produce an invalid result, the runtime responds through a defined three-step process.

Consider the case where `TranslatorFr` fails to execute within its timeout constraint. First, a `CapabilityRejected` event is emitted with the failure reason recorded in the event log. Second, the runtime checks whether a fallback is available or whether the goal allows degraded mode via the `allowDegraded` flag. Third, if `allowDegraded` is true, execution continues without translation, and the final report is marked with status `degraded` and `final_language: "en (degraded)"`. The `use-case-4-runtime-adapts` scenario in the repo demonstrates this path in full: the translator is unavailable, the runtime detects this during discovery, and the execution completes with an English report rather than failing silently.

This approach ensures that error conditions are explicit, inspectable, and recoverable without modifying the plan or the underlying capabilities.

Execution Scope

The UMA service operates within a strict boundary. It does not interpret the broader objective of the request or determine how its output will be used. Its responsibility is limited to executing the behavior defined by the contract and returning a result that satisfies that contract. This ensures that services remain focused, composable, and independent of the overall execution flow.

Execution may involve multiple services, each corresponding to a different capability within the plan. The output of one service becomes the input of another, forming a sequence of operations that collectively contribute to the final result. This chaining is not embedded within the services themselves. It is defined by the plan and enforced through contract compatibility between steps.

Because services are distributed across environments, execution may occur in different runtimes. A capability invoked through MCP may be resolved to a service running in the browser, at the edge, or in the cloud. The selection of the execution environment is influenced by the nature of the capability, the availability of resources, and any constraints defined in the contract or context.

Each component in this process operates within a clearly defined boundary. The agent selects capabilities but does not execute them. MCP resolves and routes capability invocations but does not define the execution plan. UMA services execute the behavior defined by their contracts but do not participate in reasoning or coordination.

Step 4: Crossing Runtimes with WASM

Execution in a UMA system is not bound to a single environment. Once capabilities are selected and invoked, their execution can occur across different runtimes, including the browser, edge nodes, and cloud infrastructure. This movement is determined at runtime based on the capability's nature, the request's context, and the constraints defined in the contract.

Portability Through WASM

An MCP node can operate in any of these environments while maintaining the same interface and behavior. Whether running in the browser, at the edge, or in the cloud, the MCP node exposes capabilities, accepts capability invocations, and resolves them to suitable UMA services. This consistency ensures that the system behaves as a unified runtime, even though execution is distributed.

WebAssembly plays the key role in enabling this model. By packaging service logic into a portable and consistent execution format, WASM allows the same capability implementation to run across browsers, edge, and cloud environments without modification. In this chapter, the three AI capability modules are each compiled to WASM and executed via wasmtime. Building the summarizer module is a single command:

```
./scripts/build_summarizer_ai_wasi.sh
```

This compiles the Rust summarizer to the `wasm32-wasip1` target, producing a `.wasm` artifact that the runtime invokes via wasmtime. Running the full French AI report workflow is equally direct:

```
./scripts/run_lab.sh use-case-2-ai-report
```

The same `.wasm` binary runs whether wasmtime is invoked from a server, an edge node, or a browser shell, because the contract defines the interface and wasmtime provides the execution surface. This eliminates the need to rewrite or adapt logic at runtime and ensures consistent behavior regardless of where execution occurs.

Runtime Selection

As a result, execution can span environments throughout the lifecycle of a single request. `DataProviderLocal` executes in the browser when low latency or direct access to session data is required. `InsightEnricher` may execute at the edge to take advantage of proximity to aggregated data sources. `SummarizerAI` and `TranslatorFr` execute in the cloud, where the AI models and compute resources they require are available.

The flow of execution is not tied to a fixed location. It adapts dynamically to the conditions of each step. This is possible because capabilities are defined through contracts and are not bound to a specific implementation or runtime. The same capability can be fulfilled by different UMA services deployed in different environments, as long as they satisfy the contract. MCP resolves each invocation independently, selecting an appropriate service based on availability, constraints, and context.

Because execution is both contract-driven and runtime-resolved, the system can optimize dynamically. Capabilities can be executed closer to the user to reduce latency, near data sources to minimize data transfer, or in the cloud to leverage computational resources. The system can also adapt to failures or resource constraints by resolving capabilities to alternative environments without changing the overall plan.

Mobile Execution Constraints

Mobile environments introduce a distinct set of constraints that the contract model handles without special-casing. A mobile browser is a valid execution target for WASM, and any capability whose contract does not restrict its runtime can execute there. The constraints arise from the environment itself: available memory is limited compared to cloud infrastructure, battery consumption is a concern for long-running operations, and network connectivity may be variable or metered.

The contract model addresses these constraints directly. A capability that requires substantial compute or persistent network access carries `excludes` or `runtime` constraints that prevent the runtime from resolving it to a mobile browser environment. `SummarizerAI`, for example, specifies `runtime: ["edge-wasm", "cloud-wasm"]`, which means it is never resolved to a browser runtime, mobile or otherwise. `TranslatorFr`, by contrast, specifies `runtime: ["browser-wasm", "edge-wasm", "cloud-wasm"]`, making it eligible for mobile browser execution when its inputs are available and its other constraints are satisfied.

This means a mobile user requesting the same French report would receive a workflow where `DataProviderLocal` and `TranslatorFr` execute in the browser, while `SummarizerAI` is resolved to an edge or cloud runtime. The capability definitions remain unchanged. The runtime resolves each step to the most suitable available environment, and the contract constraints ensure that mobile-incompatible capabilities are never placed where they cannot reliably execute.

The result is a system that does not require separate mobile logic or platform-specific adaptations. The same contracts, the same WASM modules, and the same runtime resolution process govern execution across desktop browsers, mobile browsers, edge nodes, and cloud infrastructure.

Crossing Runtimes As a Structural Property

Crossing runtimes is not an implementation detail. It is a direct consequence of how capabilities are defined and resolved. By combining contract-based capability selection with portable execution via WASM, UMA enables a system in which behavior is independent of location and execution can move freely across environments while maintaining consistency and control.

Step 5: Composing the Result

As execution progresses, multiple UMA services produce outputs corresponding to the capabilities defined in the agent's plan. Each output represents the result of a specific operation, performed independently within its execution context and validated against its contract.

Composition Through Contract Alignment

These outputs do not remain isolated. They are passed forward through the sequence of steps defined by the plan, where the result of one capability becomes the input of another. This chaining of results creates a progressive transformation of data, where each step contributes to fulfilling part of the overall objective.

Composition in this model is not performed by a dedicated aggregation layer or a centralized component. There is no separate structure that assembles results independently of execution. Instead, composition is a direct consequence of how capabilities are connected through their contracts. Each capability produces outputs shaped for subsequent steps, and the final result emerges from this sequence of interactions.

The structure of the final output is determined by the plan constructed during the reasoning phase. The agent defines what needs to be produced and how intermediate results should be combined, but it does not execute this combination directly. Execution enforces this structure through contract compatibility, where each step produces outputs that align with the expected inputs of the next.

For the French AI report scenario, this composition unfolds across five steps. `DataProviderLocal` loads three source fragments and places them in the execution context. `InsightEnricher` reads those fragments and derives three structured facts. `SummarizerAI` reads the structured facts and produces a summary, selecting the two most relevant facts through extractive ranking. `TranslatorFr` reads the summary and the structured facts and translates both to French. `Formatter` reads the translated content and assembles the final structured report with project name, language, summary, and highlights fields.

What appears as aggregation is in fact the cumulative effect of multiple capability executions. There is no separate phase where data is gathered and assembled outside the execution flow. The final report is the natural outcome of the sequence of transformations applied to the initial inputs.

Consistency Through Contracts

This approach ensures that composition remains flexible and adaptable. Because it is not hardcoded, the structure of the result can change as the set of available capabilities evolves or as different execution paths are selected. The system does not rely on fixed integration logic but on the alignment of contracts between independently defined services.

From the consumer's perspective, the system produces a single, coherent output. Internally, this output is the result of a distributed process where each capability contributes a portion of the final structure. The consistency of the result is maintained through contracts, not through centralized coordination.

Composition, therefore, reflects the cumulative behavior of the system rather than a separate operation. It emerges from the interaction of capabilities, guided by the plan and enforced through contract compatibility, without requiring a dedicated component to assemble the result.

The Full Runtime Flow

A UMA system does not execute a request through a fixed pipeline or a fixed integration path. Instead, it constructs the execution dynamically based on the objective expressed by the request, the capabilities available at runtime, and the constraints defined by the context. The full runtime flow is not a collection of independent steps but a continuous transformation where each phase builds directly on the outcome of the previous one.

From Intent to Result

The process begins with a request entering the system through an MCP node. The request defines an objective and provides the initial context required for evaluation. At this point, the system has intent, but no knowledge of how that intent will be fulfilled. There is no selected service, no fixed route, and no execution plan.

From this initial state, the system moves into discovery. The MCP node queries available capability contracts and evaluates them against the request's objective and context. The result of discovery is a set of candidate capabilities, represented as capability descriptors. These descriptors define what can be done, but not yet what will be done.

These candidates form the input to the reasoning phase. The agent retrieves the available capability descriptors from MCP and evaluates how they can be combined to achieve the objective. This evaluation is driven by contract compatibility, where the output of one capability must satisfy the input requirements of another, and by constraints that must remain valid across the entire sequence. The agent constructs a plan, expressed as a sequence of steps, where each step references a capability and defines how data will flow between them.

Execution begins when the agent requests the invocation of capabilities defined in the plan. Each invocation is mediated through MCP, which resolves the capability to a suitable UMA service based on contract compatibility and execution context. The selected service executes the behavior defined by the contract and produces an output that conforms to its expected structure. Execution is inherently distributed. Different steps in the plan may be executed in different environments, including the browser, edge runtimes, and cloud infrastructure. The system determines where each capability executes at runtime, based on constraints such as latency, resource availability, and data locality.

As execution progresses, outputs are produced and passed forward through the sequence of steps. Each output is validated against the contract that defines it before being used as input for subsequent capabilities. The system does not rely on shared internal models or tightly coupled integrations. Continuity is maintained through the consistent use of contracts.

The final phase is composition. The system does not invoke a separate aggregation component to assemble results. Instead, the final output emerges from the sequence of transformations defined in the plan. Each capability contributes to shaping the result, and the structure of the output reflects the cumulative effect of all executed steps.

The Flow As a Chain

The entire process can be understood as a continuous chain:

- The request defines intent
- Discovery exposes possibilities
- Reasoning selects a path
- Execution performs the operations
- Composition produces the result

Each phase depends on the previous one and feeds directly into the next. There is no central orchestrator enforcing the flow, and no fixed pipeline dictating execution. The system operates by aligning contracts, context, and runtime decisions.

For the French AI report scenario, this chain runs as follows. The request arrives with `targetLanguage: "fr"` and `preferAI: true`. Discovery surfaces five candidates across three needs. The agent constructs the path `DataProviderLocal, InsightEnricher, SummarizerAI, TranslatorFr, Formatter`. The runtime validates each capability before execution. Each step emits events and updates the shared context. The final output is a structured French report assembled by `Formatter` from the translated content produced by `TranslatorFr`.

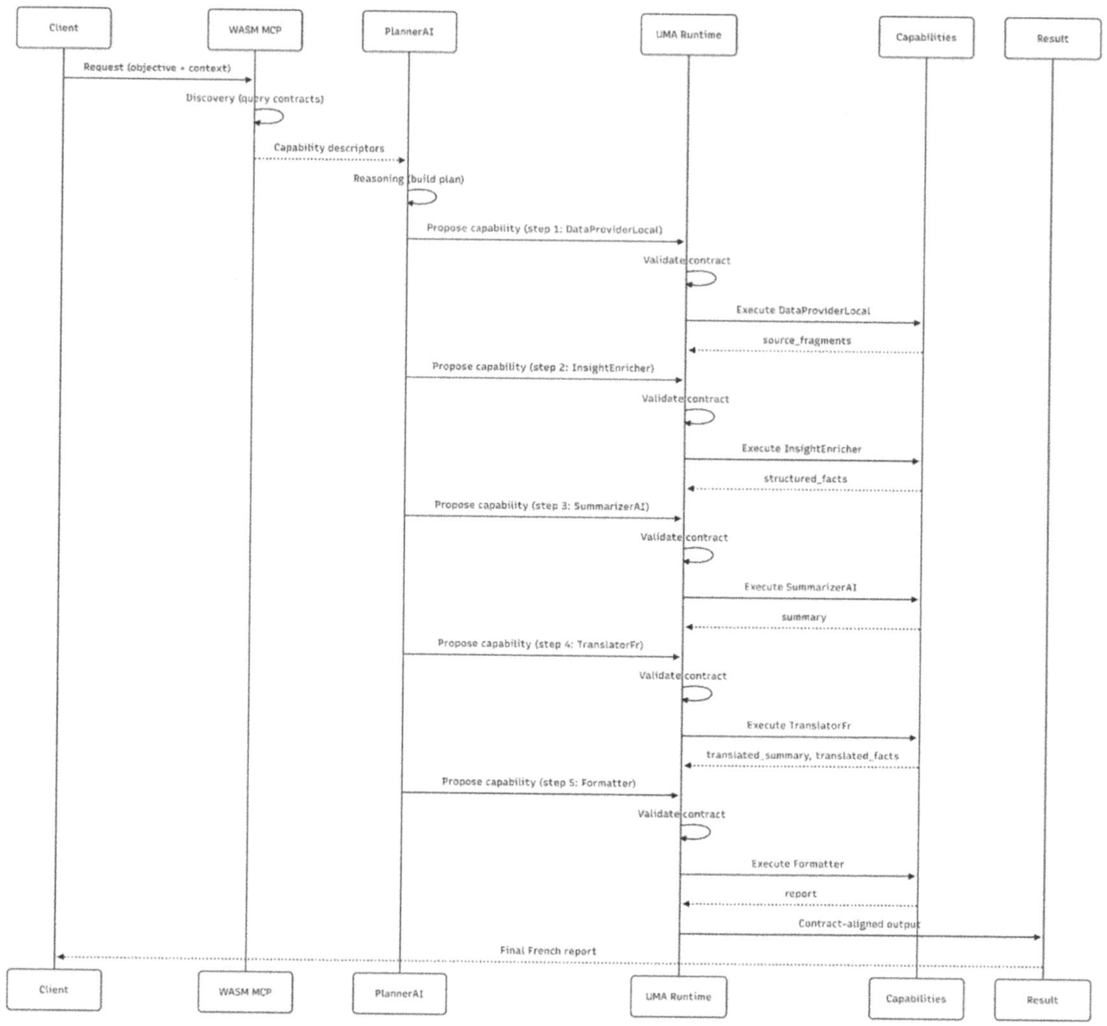

***Figure 14-3.** The full runtime flow from intent to result, including the discovery, reasoning, execution, and composition phases*

What the Consumer Sees

From the consumer's perspective, the system appears simple. A request is issued, and a response is returned. Internally, the system continuously evaluates available capabilities, constructs execution paths, resolves services across environments, and transforms data through contract-aligned interactions. The complexity is not exposed through rigid structure but managed through consistent principles.

This is the core of the UMA model. A system where behavior is not fixed in advance but emerges at runtime from the interaction of independently defined capabilities.

A system where execution is not bound to a single environment but can move across browsers, Edge, and cloud without changing the logic of the system. A system where contracts provide the foundation for both flexibility and control.

When viewed as a whole, the runtime flow is not a sequence of disconnected steps but a unified process. Intent becomes possibility, possibility becomes structure, structure becomes execution, and execution becomes result. That continuity is what allows UMA systems to remain adaptable, portable, and resilient as they evolve.

What Actually Changed

Up to this point, the runtime flow has been described step by step, from request to final result. Each phase has shown how capabilities are discovered, selected, and executed without relying on fixed integration paths. Taken individually, these steps can appear familiar. Systems have always processed requests, invoked services, and combined results.

What has changed is not the presence of these steps, but how they are connected and where decisions are made.

In traditional architectures, the system's structure is defined in advance. Services are wired together through explicit integrations, workflows are encoded in orchestration layers, and execution paths are determined at design time. Even in distributed systems, the flow of data and control is largely established ahead of time, and flexibility is achieved by adding more configuration or more coordination logic.

In a UMA system, this model is reversed. The system does not begin with a structure that dictates execution. Instead, it begins with intent and derives the execution path at runtime. Capabilities are not hardwired together. They are exposed through contracts and discovered dynamically. Decisions about how to fulfill a request are not embedded in the system's structure but are made during execution by evaluating available options.

This shift changes the role of every component. MCP no longer acts as a gateway to a fixed set of services but as an interface for exposing capabilities. The agent no longer follows an established workflow but constructs one dynamically based on what is available. Services no longer participate in coordinated flows but operate independently, bound only by the contracts they satisfy.

No Static Orchestration

Traditional systems rely on orchestration to define how work is performed. A workflow is designed in advance, encoded into the system, and executed step by step. Each service call, each dependency, and each transition is explicitly defined. Whether implemented through orchestration engines, backend services, or frontend logic, the sequence of operations is established before the system runs.

This approach provides control, but at the cost of rigidity. Any change in behavior requires modifying the orchestration logic. Adding a new capability, replacing a service, or adjusting the execution path often involves updating multiple parts of the system. Over time, orchestration layers become complex, tightly coupled to specific services, and difficult to evolve without introducing risk.

In a UMA system, this layer does not exist.

There is no workflow that dictates how a request is fulfilled. The system does not rely on a central component to coordinate execution or enforce a sequence of operations. Instead, the sequence is constructed at runtime based on available capabilities and the objective defined by the request.

The agent replaces orchestration, but not as a static controller. It does not execute a fixed flow. It evaluates the current state of the system, selects capabilities based on their contracts, and constructs a plan dynamically. This plan is specific to the request and can vary between executions, even for similar inputs. When `preferAI` is true and AI is available, the plan includes `SummarizerAI`. When it is false or AI is unavailable, `SummarizerBasic` fills the same role. The plan changes. The orchestration layer does not need to.

Because the plan is not embedded in the system, it does not need to be maintained as part of the codebase. There is no workflow to update when a new capability is introduced or when an existing one changes. As long as capabilities continue to satisfy their contracts, they can be discovered and used without modifying a centralized orchestration layer.

No Hardwired Integrations

In traditional architectures, services are connected through explicit integrations. A service calls another service through a defined endpoint, often relying on specific request and response structures. These connections are established at design time and encoded directly into the system. Even when abstractions are introduced, the underlying relationships between services remain fixed.

This creates a network of dependencies that becomes increasingly difficult to manage as the system grows. Each integration represents a point of coupling. When one service changes, all dependent services must be reviewed and, if necessary, updated. Over time, these connections form a rigid structure in which behavior is determined not only by individual services but also by how they are wired together.

In a UMA system, these direct integrations do not exist.

Services are not connected to each other. They are connected to contracts. A capability is defined by its contract, and any service that satisfies that contract can fulfill it. Services do not call each other directly. They do not reference specific endpoints or rely on knowledge of other services. Instead, they operate independently, exposing their behavior through contracts that can be discovered and used at runtime.

The flow of data between services is defined by the plan constructed during the reasoning phase. Outputs produced by one capability are passed forward as inputs to another, but this relationship is not embedded in the services themselves. It is defined externally, through contract compatibility and runtime decision-making.

Because integrations are not hardwired, the system can evolve without requiring coordinated changes across multiple services. A service can be replaced, moved, or replicated in a different environment as long as it continues to satisfy its contract. New capabilities can be introduced without modifying existing services, and existing capabilities can be composed in new ways without altering their implementation.

Contracts As the System Backbone

In traditional architectures, the system structure is encoded through integrations. Services expose APIs, and relationships are established through direct calls, shared schemas, and orchestration logic. The architecture is not represented explicitly as a single coherent model. It is distributed across implementations, configuration files, and implicit assumptions about how components interact. Understanding system behavior requires reconstructing these relationships from code, tracing execution paths, and interpreting intent after the fact.

UMA introduces a different foundation where structure is expressed explicitly through contracts.

A contract defines a capability in a complete and machine-readable form. It includes the capability's intent, the shape and semantics of its inputs, the structure of its outputs, execution constraints, and any contextual requirements that determine its validity. The contract is not documentation attached to a service. It is the artifact that represents the capability itself.

This separation isolates what a capability is from how it is implemented. Multiple services can satisfy the same contract, and a single service can expose multiple contracts. The system does not rely on specific endpoints or fixed integrations. It evaluates capabilities through their contracts and determines how they can be composed based on compatibility.

Compatibility becomes the system's organizing principle. Outputs produced by one contract can satisfy the inputs of another when their structures and constraints align. Sequences of capabilities emerge from these alignments rather than from hardcoded call graphs. The system forms execution paths by resolving which contracts can be combined to fulfill a given objective.

Because contracts are explicit and standardized, the system's full capability surface can be inspected without executing any service. This enables analysis of what the system can do, identification of overlapping capabilities, and detection of gaps or inconsistencies. The architecture becomes observable as a set of defined capabilities rather than inferred behavior.

Portability follows directly from this model. Contracts are independent of runtime, which allows the same capability definition to be fulfilled by implementations running in different environments. A contract satisfied in the browser can also be satisfied at the edge or in the cloud, provided the execution constraints are met.

Agent-Driven Execution

Traditional systems execute through established paths. Orchestration layers, workflow engines, and service call chains encode in advance how requests are processed. Even in event-driven architectures, reactions are determined by subscriptions configured ahead of time. Execution follows explicitly designed structures, and every valid path must exist before the system runs.

This approach depends on the assumption that meaningful execution paths can be enumerated during development. As systems grow, that assumption becomes increasingly fragile. The number of possible combinations of capabilities expands, and capturing all valid flows requires either complex orchestration logic or repeated changes to existing workflows. Each new requirement often introduces additional coordination points, reinforcing coupling between components.

UMA introduces an execution model constructed at runtime rather than established in advance. An agent operates as a decision-making component that evaluates available capabilities and determines how to compose them to achieve a given objective. Instead of traversing a fixed workflow, the agent interprets intent, inspects the current set of contracts, and derives an execution plan based on compatibility and constraints. The plan is not stored as a static artifact. It reflects the current state of the system, including available capabilities, constraints, and contextual conditions.

Execution proceeds as a sequence of validated steps. Each capability invocation is checked against its contract to ensure that inputs, outputs, and constraints are respected. After each step, the agent reassesses the system's state and determines the next action. The execution path can evolve as new information becomes available or conditions change.

The role of orchestration shifts from defining flows to enabling reasoning. Instead of encoding every possible path, the system encodes the rules that govern valid composition. Contracts define what is possible, and the agent determines what is appropriate under current conditions. Reliability is maintained through validation at each step of execution. Invalid combinations are rejected before invocation, and constraints defined in contracts ensure that capabilities are used within their intended scope.

Design Principles Proven by the System

The system described in this chapter was not constructed to illustrate principles decided in advance. The principles emerge from what was required for the system to function under the constraints imposed by UMA. Each of them can be traced directly to a structural or operational necessity observed in the implementation.

The absence of static orchestration required an alternative mechanism for defining behavior. The need to operate across multiple runtimes required a consistent abstraction independent of the environment. The ability to compose capabilities dynamically required a clear separation between what is exposed and how it is executed. The introduction of runtime decision-making required compatibility with agent-driven execution.

These conditions did not allow for optional design choices. They imposed constraints that shaped the system in specific ways. The resulting principles are not recommendations. They are properties of a system that must operate without fixed flows, without hardwired integrations, and across heterogeneous execution environments.

Contract-First Design

The system defines capabilities before any implementation is introduced. Each capability exists first as a contract that specifies its intent, the structure and semantics of its inputs, the shape of its outputs, and the constraints that govern its execution. Implementation follows the contract and must conform to it, rather than defining it implicitly through code.

This ordering is required for the system to function without fixed orchestration or fixed integrations. In the absence of static execution paths, the system must determine at runtime which capabilities are available and how they can be composed. That determination depends on having explicit, machine-readable definitions that can be evaluated without invoking the underlying services.

Defining capabilities after implementation would prevent this form of reasoning. Service-specific interfaces would become the source of truth, and capability boundaries would be inferred rather than declared. Discovery would require interpreting implementation details, and composition would depend on fixed mappings between services.

A contract-first definition also establishes stability in the presence of change. Implementations can evolve, be replaced, or be distributed across different runtimes as long as they continue to satisfy the contract. The rest of the system does not depend on internal details of any service. It depends only on the validity of the contract.

Separation of Exposure and Execution

The system maintains a strict distinction between capability definition and capability execution. Contracts represent the exposure layer, describing intent, inputs, outputs, and constraints in a form that can be inspected and reasoned about. Implementations operate in a separate layer, providing the concrete behavior required to satisfy those contracts. No implementation detail is embedded in the contract itself.

A unified layer combining definition and execution would prevent the system from evaluating capabilities independently. Discovery requires a representation that is stable, comparable, and free of environment-specific details. Composition requires the ability to match capabilities to structure and constraints rather than to implementation characteristics.

Separation allows the system to treat contracts as the source of truth for capability identity. Implementations become interchangeable as long as they satisfy the contract.

Multiple implementations can exist for the same capability, each optimized for a different environment or operational constraint, while presenting the same exposure. This is visible in the chapter's scenario: `SummarizerBasic` and `SummarizerAI` satisfy the same `generate-summary` intent under different constraints, and the runtime selects between them without the rest of the system knowing or caring which one ran.

Portable Runtime Model

The system operates across multiple execution environments without redefining capabilities or altering their structure. Capabilities are expressed through contracts that remain independent of any specific runtime, while implementations are responsible for satisfying those contracts within the constraints of their environment.

Portability is not achieved through duplication or adaptation layers added after the fact. It is enabled by a consistent abstraction that separates capability definition from execution context. Contracts describe what must be done, and implementations determine how and where it is executed. The system resolves capabilities based on contract validity and compatibility, not on the location of execution.

A runtime-specific model would embed assumptions about environment, dependencies, and execution constraints directly into capability definitions. Such an approach would require rewriting or adapting capabilities for each environment, leading to fragmentation and inconsistency.

Execution selection incorporates runtime awareness without altering capability definitions. When multiple implementations are available, the system evaluates which one satisfies both the contract and the constraints of the current environment. Consistency across environments depends on contract-level validation. Inputs and outputs are checked against contract definitions regardless of where execution occurs.

Agent Compatibility

The system is structured to allow agents to operate directly on its capabilities without requiring fixed workflows or service-specific knowledge. Capabilities are exposed through contracts that provide complete, machine-readable definitions. These definitions include intent, inputs, outputs, and constraints, forming a representation that can be interpreted and evaluated at runtime.

Agent compatibility depends on the ability to reason about capabilities using a consistent, explicit model. Contracts provide that model. Each capability can be discovered, compared, and selected based on its definition rather than on its implementation. The agent evaluates available contracts, determines which ones satisfy the current objective, and constructs an execution plan based on compatibility and constraints.

A system that relies on implicit structure or hardcoded integrations would not support this form of interaction. Agents would need prior knowledge of service interfaces, fixed workflows, or custom integration logic to operate. Execution would be limited to explicitly designed paths, preventing dynamic composition and reducing adaptability.

Execution proceeds through a cycle of evaluation and validation. The agent selects a capability, verifies that its inputs can be satisfied, executes it, and then reassesses the system's state before selecting the next step. Decisions are made incrementally, allowing the execution path to adapt to changing conditions, available capabilities, and intermediate results.

The system's structure does not privilege human-defined workflows over agent-driven execution. Both operate on the same set of contracts, using the same rules of compatibility and validation. This allows agents to participate as first-class actors in the system, capable of constructing and executing plans without requiring separate integration layers.

What This Enables Next

The system described in this chapter establishes a structural foundation that supports forms of behavior that are difficult to achieve with traditional architectures. These behaviors are not speculative extensions. They follow directly from the properties already demonstrated: contract-defined capabilities, separation of exposure and execution, runtime composition, and agent-driven execution.

Each of these properties removes a specific limitation present in conventional systems. Static orchestration is no longer required to define execution paths. Integrations are no longer bound to specific services. Capabilities are no longer tied to a single runtime. Execution decisions are no longer locked at design time.

The result is a system that can be extended without requiring any restructuring of its core. New capabilities can be introduced without redefining workflows. Execution strategies can adapt to context without modifying integrations. Multiple decision-making components can operate on the same set of capabilities without requiring separate coordination layers.

AI-Native Systems

The system exposes capabilities through contracts that define intent, inputs, outputs, and constraints in a consistent and machine-readable form. These contracts are used for discovery, composition, and validation, and they represent the system's complete capability surface, independent of any specific implementation.

Execution is not tied to fixed workflows or hardcoded integrations. Capabilities are selected and composed at runtime based on compatibility and constraints. This establishes a model where behavior is derived from evaluation rather than from fixed control structures.

Within this model, AI-based components do not require a separate integration layer to interact with the system. In traditional architectures, AI systems operate through interfaces designed for human-driven or service-to-service interaction. APIs expose functions, documentation provides context, and workflows define allowed sequences of operations. The AI component is constrained by these structures and cannot reason over the full capability surface.

The system described in this chapter removes that dependency. Contracts provide a complete and uniform representation of capabilities that can be evaluated programmatically. Each contract describes not only the shape of a capability, but also its intent and constraints. This allows an AI component to interpret capabilities as composable units of behavior rather than as isolated endpoints.

Reasoning occurs over the contract layer. The AI component evaluates which capabilities satisfy a given objective, how outputs from one capability can satisfy the inputs of another, and which combinations remain valid under the defined constraints. The same compatibility rules used by the runtime are available to the AI component, allowing it to construct execution sequences without requiring fixed workflows.

Control is maintained without restricting flexibility. The system does not need to anticipate every possible sequence of operations. It defines what is valid, and the AI component determines what is relevant under current conditions. Invalid compositions are rejected through validation, while valid ones are allowed to proceed regardless of whether they were anticipated during design.

Adaptive Workflows

The system does not encode workflows as fixed sequences of steps. Execution paths are formed at runtime through the evaluation of available capabilities, contract compatibility, and current system conditions. Each step is selected based on what can be satisfied at that moment, not based on a path defined in advance.

Traditional workflow systems rely on explicit control structures to handle variability. Conditional branches, fallback paths, retries, and exception handling logic are introduced to account for different scenarios. As the number of possible conditions increases, workflows become more complex. Maintaining correctness requires anticipating combinations of states and encoding them into the workflow definition.

This approach introduces a structural limitation. Every possible variation must be represented explicitly. When new capabilities are added or existing ones change, workflows must be updated to incorporate them.

The model described in this chapter removes the need to represent variability as explicit branches. Capability selection is driven by compatibility and constraints. At each step, the system evaluates which contracts can be satisfied given the current state. Multiple candidates may exist, or none may satisfy the requirements. Selection is resolved through evaluation rather than by traversing fixed alternatives.

Execution proceeds incrementally. After each capability is invoked, the resulting state is evaluated again. Outputs become inputs for subsequent steps, and constraints are rechecked. The next capability is selected based on the updated state, allowing the execution path to evolve as the system progresses. This model handles variability that cannot be fully enumerated in advance, including differences in input data, partial availability of capabilities, changes in execution context, or the introduction of new capabilities.

Runtime Evolution

The system supports changes to its capability set without requiring coordinated updates to integrations or execution logic. Capabilities are defined through contracts, and execution paths are constructed dynamically. These two properties allow the system to evolve while remaining operational.

In traditional architectures, introducing a new capability or modifying an existing one requires updating the components that depend on it. Integrations must be revised, workflows must be adjusted, and compatibility must be validated manually across all affected paths. This creates a dependency between evolution and coordination. Even small changes can require synchronized updates across multiple services, increasing the risk of inconsistency and failure.

The model described in this chapter removes this dependency. Capabilities are introduced as new contracts. Once a contract is defined and an implementation satisfies it, the capability becomes part of the system's available set. No existing capability needs to be modified for the new one to be discovered or used. When contract definitions change, evolution is managed at the contract layer rather than through integration updates. New versions of a contract can coexist alongside existing ones, allowing gradual transition without breaking existing compositions.

Removal of capabilities is also handled without restructuring the system. When a capability is no longer available, it is excluded from the set of valid contracts during evaluation. Execution paths that depended on it are recomposed dynamically using alternative capabilities when available.

Multi-agent Systems

The system exposes capabilities through a shared contract layer that is independent of any single execution path or orchestrator. Capabilities are defined in a uniform, machine-readable form, and execution is determined through runtime evaluation. These properties allow multiple agents to operate on the same system without requiring fixed coordination mechanisms.

In traditional architectures, supporting multiple decision-making components requires explicit coordination. Responsibilities are assigned, interaction patterns are defined, and conflicts are managed through centralized logic or fixed workflows. Each additional participant increases the number of integration points, and coordination becomes a system of its own that must be designed, implemented, and maintained.

The system described in this chapter does not encode coordination as an explicit layer. Agents operate against the same capability surface, defined through contracts. Each agent evaluates available contracts, determines which capabilities satisfy its objective, and constructs execution steps based on compatibility and constraints. No agent requires knowledge of other agents, and no fixed interaction patterns are necessary.

Interaction occurs indirectly through shared state and contract validation. Each capability invocation produces outputs that become part of the system state. Other agents can observe or consume these outputs when they satisfy the input requirements of their own selected capabilities. Coordination emerges from how capabilities connect through their inputs and outputs, not from direct communication between agents.

Conflict is constrained at the contract level. Contracts define what is valid, including input requirements, state constraints, and execution conditions. When an agent attempts to invoke a capability, the invocation is validated against these constraints. If the operation conflicts with another operation or violates the current state, it is rejected before execution.

Conclusion

The system described in this chapter demonstrates what becomes possible when capabilities are defined through contracts, execution is resolved at runtime, and agents participate without becoming authoritative. Six key learnings follow directly from what the system proved.

- **Contract-defined capabilities make the system inspectable without running it.** The full capability surface, including what each capability requires, produces, and constrains, is readable from the contract files alone. Discovery, planning, and validation all operate on this layer without touching service implementations.
- **Runtime validation is what keeps agent participation safe.** The agent proposes. The runtime decides. When `SummarizerAI` is proposed under `localOnly: true`, the runtime rejects it, and the agent reselects. The agent's authority ends at the boundary of the proposal.
- **The event log is the proof of execution.** Every capability invocation emits a traceable sequence of events. For AI-assisted steps, this record makes the runtime decision inspectable even when the model's output varies. The JSON report from `use-case-2-ai-report` is the artifact that proves the system ran the path it claimed to run.
- **WASM portability is not a claim; it is a constraint the contract enforces.** Capabilities specify which runtimes they can execute in. The runtime resolves each step to the appropriate environment based on those constraints. The same `.wasm` binary runs in the browser, at the edge, and in the cloud because the contract defines the interface, and wasmtime provides the surface.

- **Degraded execution is a first-class outcome, not a failure.** When `TranslatorFr` is unavailable and `allowDegraded` is true, the system completes with an English report and marks the result explicitly. Nothing fails silently. The event log records what happened and why.
- **The architecture is defined by what capabilities can be combined, not by how services are wired.** Adding a new capability requires a new contract and an implementation that satisfies it. Nothing else changes. Removing a capability removes it from the discovery set. The rest of the system adapts at the next evaluation.

This chapter closes the demonstrated learning path. The reference application at `chapter-14-portable-mcp-runtime` remains the runnable proof of everything described here. The acknowledgements and closing notes appear in the back matter.

Closing: Architecture As a Living System

What We Used to Believe

Software architecture has traditionally been treated as a design-time activity. Systems are defined by diagrams, service boundaries, and integration paths established before execution begins. The structure of the system is determined by how components are connected, and behavior is encoded through workflows, orchestration logic, and fixed interactions.

This model assumes that the system can be fully described before it runs. Capabilities are implemented within services, relationships are established through APIs, and execution paths are defined in advance. Once deployed, the system follows these structures, and any meaningful change requires revisiting the design, updating integrations, and redeploying components.

Control is achieved through explicit coordination. Workflows define how operations are sequenced, orchestration layers determine which services are invoked, and integration logic ensures that data flows between components in a predictable way. Stability depends on the correctness of these paths and the consistency of the connections between services.

As systems grow, this approach introduces increasing rigidity. The number of integrations expands, dependencies accumulate, and changes require coordination across multiple components. The architecture becomes harder to reason about, not because the system lacks structure, but because the structure is distributed across implementations and encoded in the relationships between them.

This way of thinking treats architecture as something that is designed, implemented, and then executed. The system reflects the decisions made during design, and its ability to evolve depends on how easily those decisions can be revisited and modified.

What the System Proved

The system described in this chapter operates without relying on the structural assumptions outlined above. Execution paths are not fixed, integrations are not hardwired, and capabilities are not bound to specific implementations. Behavior is constructed at runtime through the evaluation of contracts, compatibility, and constraints.

This is not a variation of traditional orchestration. There is no central workflow that determines how requests are processed. Each execution step is selected dynamically based on the current state of the system and the set of available capabilities. The system does not traverse a fixed path. It resolves one.

Integrations are not encoded as direct connections between services. Capabilities are defined independently through contracts, and relationships are determined through compatibility. A capability becomes part of the system not because it is wired into a flow, but because its contract can be satisfied and composed with others.

Execution is not tied to a specific runtime or location. Capabilities can be implemented in different environments and selected at runtime based on constraints. The system does not depend on where execution occurs, only on whether the contract is valid and can be satisfied under current conditions.

Decision-making is not fixed at design time. Agents evaluate available capabilities, construct execution sequences, and adapt those sequences as the system evolves. Behavior is not encoded in advance. It is determined continuously during execution.

These characteristics were not introduced as extensions to an existing model. They were required for the system to function without fixed workflows or fixed integrations. Removing any of them would reintroduce the limitations of traditional architectures: rigid execution paths, tight coupling between components, and dependence on static design-time decisions.

Architecture Moves to Runtime

The system described in this chapter does not treat architecture as a fixed structure established before execution. The relationships between capabilities are not encoded in integrations, and execution paths are not defined as static workflows. Structure is not embedded in how components are wired. It is determined by evaluating contracts and constraints during operation.

In this model, architecture is not a representation of how components are connected. It is the result of how capabilities can be composed at any given moment. The system continuously evaluates which capabilities are available, which constraints are satisfied, and which compositions are valid. Execution paths are formed during this evaluation and exist only as long as they remain valid under current conditions.

Decisions that were traditionally made during design are resolved at runtime. Selection of capabilities, ordering of execution steps, and choice of implementation are determined dynamically. The system does not depend on fixed coordination logic to guide behavior. It depends on the ability to continuously evaluate and validate compositions.

This shifts the role of architecture from defining structure to defining rules. Contracts establish what capabilities exist and how they can be used. Constraints define what combinations are valid. Validation ensures that execution remains consistent with these definitions. The system operates within these boundaries, but it is not constrained to a fixed set of paths.

Stability is no longer derived from static structure. It is derived from the consistency of contracts and the correctness of validation. The system remains reliable not because every path is known in advance, but because every step is evaluated against explicit definitions before it is executed.

Contracts As the Foundation

The system relies on contracts as the primary structural element that defines capabilities, governs composition, and enforces correctness. Every behavior observed in the system depends on the presence of explicit, machine-readable definitions that describe what a capability does, what it requires, and under which conditions it can be executed.

Contracts replace the implicit structure that traditionally exists in integrations and workflows. Instead of deriving behavior from how services are connected, the system derives behavior from how capabilities are defined. Each contract establishes a boundary that is independent of implementation and stable across environments.

This boundary enables consistent evaluation. Capabilities can be discovered, compared, and composed without inspecting service-specific details. The system determines which capabilities are relevant based on contract definitions and forms execution paths by resolving compatibility among inputs, outputs, and constraints.

Validation is anchored in the same layer. Every step in execution is checked against contract definitions before it proceeds. Inputs must conform to expected structures, constraints must be satisfied, and outputs must align with declared schemas. This ensures that dynamically constructed execution paths remain consistent, even when they were not anticipated during design.

The separation between contract and implementation allows capabilities to evolve without affecting the rest of the system. Implementations can change, move across runtimes, or be replaced entirely as long as they continue to satisfy the contract. The system depends on the definition of the capability, not on how it is realized.

Portability, adaptability, and agent-driven execution all rely on this foundation. Without contracts, capabilities could not be evaluated independently, execution could not be constructed dynamically, and validation would depend on implementation-level checks.

Systems That Continue to Become

The system does not reach a final, fixed state after deployment. Its structure is not defined once and then executed indefinitely. Capabilities can be introduced, modified, or removed, and execution adapts to reflect these changes without requiring redefinition of integrations or workflows.

This behavior is a direct consequence of the system's structure. Capabilities are defined through contracts, and execution paths are constructed dynamically. When the set of available capabilities changes, the system does not require a redesign. It evaluates the updated set of contracts and resolves new compositions based on compatibility and constraints.

Evolution occurs through changes in the capability layer, not through changes in integrations. A new capability becomes part of the system as soon as its contract is defined and satisfied. Existing capabilities remain unaffected unless their contracts change. Removal of a capability reduces the available set, and execution paths are recomposed accordingly.

Adaptation is continuous. Each execution reflects the current state of the system, including available capabilities, constraints, and context. There is no assumption that the system will behave the same way across executions. Behavior is determined by evaluation, not by fixed structure.

The absence of a fixed structure does not imply a lack of control. Contracts define boundaries, constraints define validity, and validation ensures that execution remains consistent. Evolution does not introduce instability as long as these definitions remain correct and enforced.

Closing

The model presented throughout this book does not extend traditional architecture. It replaces its underlying assumptions.

Structure is no longer defined through integrations between services. Behavior is no longer encoded in workflows. Execution is no longer constrained to paths determined at design time. The system operates through capabilities defined by contracts, composed through compatibility, and validated continuously during execution.

Architecture does not exist as a fixed artifact that is implemented and then executed. It exists as a set of definitions that are evaluated continuously. Relationships between capabilities are not established once. They are resolved repeatedly based on current conditions and constraints.

Control is not achieved through fixed coordination. It is achieved through explicit definitions and validation. Contracts define what is possible, constraints define what is valid, and execution proceeds only when both are satisfied. Stability emerges from consistency of definitions, not from rigidity of structure.

The system is not shaped by how components are connected but by how capabilities can be composed. It does not depend on knowing all possible execution paths in advance. It depends on the ability to evaluate and validate each step as it occurs.

This shifts the role of architecture from designing structures to defining systems that can resolve themselves. The focus moves from specifying interactions to defining capabilities and the conditions under which they can be combined.

The result is a system that does not remain as it was designed. It reflects the current state of its capabilities, constraints, and context, and it continues to adapt as these elements evolve.

If a system cannot describe itself, it cannot evolve.

APPENDIX A

Reference Tables

UMA Capability Contract Schema

The following table defines the fields of a UMA capability contract. Every capability in a UMA system is described by a contract that conforms to this schema. Fields marked as required must be present for the contract to be valid. Optional fields extend the contract with additional governance, placement, and observability declarations.

Table A-1. *UMA capability contract schema*

Field	Type	Required	Description
name	string	Yes	Unique identifier for the capability. Use dot notation (e.g., image.tagger).
version	semver string	Yes	Semantic version of the contract. Breaking changes increment the major version.
description	string	Yes	Human-readable statement of the capability's single outcome.
inputs	object (JSON Schema)	Yes	Defines the structure, types, and constraints of accepted inputs.
outputs	object (JSON Schema)	Yes	Defines all possible outputs, including degraded responses.

(*continued*)

E. Piovesan, *Universal Microservices Architecture*, https://doi.org/10.1007/979-8-8688-2794-5

Table A-1. (*continued*)

Field	Type	Required	Description
errors	array of error objects	Yes	Lists all declared error conditions, recoverability, and recommended retry behavior.
events.emits	array of event refs	No	Events this capability produces. Each entry references a versioned event contract.
events.consumes	array of event refs	No	Events this capability subscribes to. The runtime uses these to automatically build the service graph.
quality_tier	object	Yes	Declares accuracy, availability, latency, and throughput expectations.
resource_budget	object	Yes	Declares CPU, memory, execution time, and concurrency limits enforced across all runtimes.
placement	array of strings	No	Runtimes where this capability may be deployed. Omitting implies no restriction.
trust_tier	string	Yes	Classifies the execution context. Used for placement decisions and policy enforcement.
policy_refs	array of strings	No	References to governance policies that apply to this capability at runtime.
observability	object	No	Declares signals, formats, and emission points for metrics, traces, and logs.
compatibility	object	No	Declares version ranges compatible with this contract for consumers and adapters.

UMA Runtime Behavior by Environment

The following table summarizes how key UMA behaviors are expressed across the four primary runtime environments. Use this table when designing a capability for multi-environment deployment, selecting enforcement mechanisms for a specific runtime, or evaluating whether a capability's contract declarations translate correctly to a target environment. The capability contract defines behavior once; each runtime enforces it using mechanisms appropriate to its context. Where the native column notes that behavior depends on the deployment context, the contract remains the authoritative source of intent, and the native adapter is responsible for mapping it to the appropriate platform mechanism.

Table A-2. *UMA runtime behavior by environment*

Behavior	Browser	Edge	Cloud	Native
Execution model	Web Assembly module via JS adapter	WASM or native binary via WASI	Container or serverless function	Native binary compiled for the host OS or architecture; WASM is also supported where a compliant runtime is available
Contract validation	At load time via runtime adapter	At registration time	At deployment time via the orchestrator	At startup, the runtime reads and validates the contract before any business logic executes
Event dispatch	Via WebSocket or HTTP adapter	Via MQTT, NATS, or local broker	Via Kafka, EventBridge, or equivalent	Direct in-process dispatch or via a local broker; adapter selection is declared in the contract
Resource budget enforcement	requestIdleCallback, heap tracking via Performance API	Fuel counters, lightweight semaphores	cgroup quotas, container limits	OS-level process controls, such as ulimit or cgroup, are selected by the native adapter
Connectivity model	Variable; offline-first required for resilience	Variable; offline-first required	Assumed available; degraded mode optional	Depends on deployment context; on-device deployments should be treated as edge for connectivity planning purposes

(continued)

Table A-2. *(continued)*

Behavior	Browser	Edge	Cloud	Native
State scope	Short-lived, in-memory, or IndexedDB	Short-lived, local storage or edge cache	Long-lived, managed by cloud storage	Determined by the host application, long-lived state is possible and common in server-side native deployments
Policy enforcement	Enforced by envelope via same-origin and contract rules	Enforced by envelope via local policy store	Enforced by the orchestrator reading contract metadata	Enforced by the native runtime adapter, reading policy references from the contract at startup
Observability	Performance API, console traces	Local telemetry, forwarded on connectivity	Centralized logging and tracing platforms	Stdout, local logging agents, or platform-native observability tooling; signals are declared in the contract regardless of sink
Degraded execution	Progressive fidelity reduction, cached results	Offline queue, lower-fidelity fallback	Regional failover, redundant instances	Fallback to cached results or a lower-fidelity execution path; degraded modes must be declared in the contract to be activated
Agent interaction (MCP)	Supported via HTTP or WebSocket	Supported via the local MCP surface	Supported via a full MCP surface	Supported via MCP over a local Unix socket or loopback interface; the discovery surface is the same regardless of transport

APPENDIX B

Glossary

This glossary defines terms used throughout the book. Entries are organized into two groups: terms specific to Universal Microservices Architecture and foundational terms from the broader distributed systems and web platform space that are referenced in the context of UMA. Where a UMA-specific term differs from its common industry usage, that distinction is noted in the definition.

UMA-Specific Terms

Agent

In UMA, an agent is an architectural component responsible for constructing execution flows at runtime. An agent interprets a goal, queries the discovery layer to understand which capabilities are available, selects appropriate capabilities based on their contracts, and composes them into a plan. Agents do not execute services directly. They rely on the UMA runtime to perform execution. This definition is architectural, not technological: what makes a component an agent in UMA is its responsibility within the system, not the model or framework it uses. In the broader industry, the term "agent" is often used more loosely to refer to any autonomous or AI-driven process.

Backpressure

In UMA, backpressure is the mechanism by which a capability signals to upstream producers that it cannot keep pace with incoming load, prompting them to slow down, queue, or shed requests. Backpressure rules are declared in the capability contract and enforced consistently across all runtimes, whether via token-bucket schedulers in cloud adapters, fairness delays at the edge, or deferred execution in browser runtimes. In general, distributed systems use the same concept, but it is typically implemented ad hoc rather than declared in a contract.

E. Piovesan, *Universal Microservices Architecture*, https://doi.org/10.1007/979-8-8688-2794-5

Capability

The fundamental unit of UMA. A capability is a self-contained, portable piece of business logic that delivers a single, clearly defined, verifiable outcome. It is defined by three elements: an outcome (what it does), a quality tier (how well it must do it), and a resource budget (the limits within which it must operate). A capability is independent of the runtime that executes it. Portability is achieved by separating the pure business logic (the Capability Core) from the runtime-specific bindings (the Capability Envelope) so that the core can be compiled and deployed to any compliant environment without modification. In general, in software engineering, the term "capability" is used informally to refer to any feature or function a system can perform. In UMA, it is a first-class architectural artifact with a formal contract. See also: Capability Core, Capability Envelope, Capability Contract.

Capability Contract

A machine-readable, runtime-verified agreement that specifies how a capability must behave across any compliant runtime. A contract goes beyond an API definition: it includes input and output schemas, error models, event declarations, quality-tier expectations, resource budgets, trust-tier classification, placement constraints, policy references, and observability declarations. The contract is the single source of truth for all parties interacting with the capability, enforced at runtime and not merely at design time.

Capability Core

The pure functional logic of a capability, containing no runtime-specific calls, no direct operating system dependencies, and no hard-coded integrations. The core is expressed entirely in terms of the contract and can be compiled and executed in any compliant runtime without modification.

Capability Envelope

The runtime-specific wrapper surrounding the capability core. The envelope handles input and output binding, platform API integration, hardware access, security enforcement, and orchestration hooks for a specific deployment target. When a capability is moved to a new runtime, the envelope is replaced or recompiled while the core remains unchanged.

Capability Registry

A queryable index of all active capability contracts within a UMA system or federation. The runtime uses the registry to discover capabilities, validate contracts at registration time, match event producers to consumers, and enforce policy. Registries may be centralized, federated, or hybrid. In all configurations, the registry is the authoritative source of truth for contract definitions within its domain.

Event Contract

A versioned, machine-readable definition of a specific event type, including its schema, ownership, delivery guarantees, and governance rules. In UMA, events are not informal messages but governed assets with explicit contracts. Any runtime that can interpret an event contract can safely consume the event, regardless of the broker or transport layer in use.

Event Contract Catalog Architecture (ECCA)

A reference design for managing event contracts with the same rigor applied to service contracts. ECCA treats events as owned, discoverable, and versioned assets with clear governance. It is not the only way to implement event governance in UMA, but it illustrates the core principle: events are portable, governed artifacts with explicit contracts, independent of any specific broker or runtime.

Lifecycle Record

A structured artifact produced by the UMA runtime at the conclusion of every capability execution. It captures the adapter binding decision, the full event log with logical clock values, the final execution state, and any policy evaluations performed during the run. The lifecycle record makes every execution traceable and verifiable without requiring access to source code or re-running the capability.

Metadata Layer

The formal, machine-readable layer in a UMA system that defines the properties of capabilities, the semantics of their interactions, and the constraints that govern execution. The metadata layer includes capability contracts, event contracts, policy references, dependency relationships, and version compatibility declarations. It is not auxiliary documentation; it is the authoritative source of architectural intent that the runtime uses to make execution decisions.

Policy Profile

A named set of governance rules that applies to a capability at runtime. Policy profiles encode organizational requirements such as encryption standards, data residency restrictions, logging mandates, trust tier requirements, and placement constraints. A capability references the applicable policy profiles in its contract, and the runtime automatically enforces them across all environments.

Portability Candidate

A capability whose logic, contract, and runtime requirements make it suitable for compilation and execution across multiple runtimes without modification to its core. A strong portability candidate has purely computational logic, a clean input-output contract, no environment-specific dependencies, and deterministic behavior. Identifying portability candidates early is a key step in UMA system design.

Quality Tier

An explicit declaration within a capability contract that defines how well the capability must deliver its outcome. A quality tier may include accuracy thresholds, availability targets, latency guarantees, and throughput expectations. Because quality tiers are declared in the contract rather than assumed, the same capability can operate across environments with different performance profiles while remaining identifiable as the same logical service.

Resource Budget

An explicit declaration within a capability contract that sets the operational limits within which the capability must function. Resource budgets cover CPU time, memory allocation, execution duration, and maximum concurrency. The runtime enforces these limits using mechanisms appropriate to each environment: fuel counters in Web Assembly runtimes, cgroup quotas in cloud containers, and idle-period scheduling in browsers. The contract defines the budget once; each runtime enforces it according to its own mechanisms.

Runtime Independence

The architectural property of a UMA capability that allows it to execute in any compliant runtime without modification to its core logic. Runtime independence is achieved by separating the capability core from the capability envelope, expressing all behavior through the contract, and ensuring that the runtime adapter handles all environment-specific concerns.

Shadow Mode

A testing and validation pattern in UMA eventing in which a producer emits events to both production consumers and a parallel set of shadow consumers simultaneously. Shadow consumer outputs are discarded rather than acted upon. Shadow mode allows teams to validate schema changes, new adapter versions, or broker migrations under real production traffic conditions before committing to a live switch. Telemetry from shadow consumers feeds back into the event catalog to support evidence-based release decisions.

Trust Tier

A classification assigned to a capability in its contract that describes the security context required for its execution. Trust tiers inform the runtime about placement eligibility, for example, whether a capability may run in an untrusted browser environment or requires a secure enclave, and govern cross-domain interactions by determining which capabilities may interact with which others. Trust tier is a runtime-enforced property, not merely a documentation label.

Universal Microservices Architecture (UMA)

An architectural framework for designing and deploying services across heterogeneous runtime environments, including browsers, edge devices, cloud infrastructure, and native systems, without modifying core business logic. UMA is built on three foundational principles: separating capability logic from runtime execution, expressing all behavior and constraints through machine-readable contracts, and treating portability as a property of the service definition rather than a property of the runtime or framework. UMA addresses the fragmentation problem that arises when the same business logic must run across environments with different APIs, constraints, and execution models. By making contracts the stable center of the architecture, UMA allows teams to build once, govern consistently, and deploy anywhere without forking logic or accumulating runtime-specific debt.

Foundational Terms

Edge Computing

A deployment model in which computation is performed close to the source of data, such as on devices, local gateways, or regional nodes, rather than in centralized cloud infrastructure. Edge environments are characterized by constrained resources, variable or intermittent connectivity, heterogeneous hardware, and stricter latency requirements than cloud environments. In UMA, edge-native design requires capabilities to operate reliably under these constraints, including offline-first execution, progressive fidelity reduction, and deterministic resource budgets.

Event-Driven Architecture

A system design approach in which components communicate by producing and consuming events rather than through direct synchronous calls. Events represent facts that have occurred. Producers emit events without knowledge of who will consume them. Consumers subscribe to events without knowledge of who produced them.

This decoupling allows components to evolve independently and operate across environments with variable connectivity. In UMA, event-driven coordination is a first-class pattern, with events defined as versioned contracts and governed through the event catalog.

MCP (Model Context Protocol)

An open protocol for exposing and describing capabilities in a structured, discoverable way so that agents and other components can query what a system can do without needing to know how it does it. In UMA, MCP serves as the discovery layer between agents and the execution layer. MCP does not execute services or make decisions about which services should be used. It makes capabilities visible and understandable, enabling reasoning components to compose them into execution flows at runtime.

Service-Oriented Architecture (SOA)

An architectural style, prominent in the early 2000s, in which software is structured as a set of modular services communicating through standard protocols. SOA introduced the concept of service contracts as a shared language across teams and contributed foundational ideas around reuse, modularity, and explicit boundaries. UMA builds on these concepts while addressing SOA's limitations, particularly its reliance on centralized integration infrastructure and the absence of runtime-enforced portability.

WASI (Web Assembly System Interface)

A standardized interface that defines how Web Assembly modules interact with operating system resources such as files, network sockets, and clocks in a portable, capability-based way. WASI allows Web Assembly modules to access system resources without being tied to a specific operating system or runtime environment. In UMA, WASI enables the same capability binary to execute in cloud and edge environments that provide WASI-compliant runtimes.

Web Assembly (WASM)

A binary instruction format designed for portable, safe, and efficient execution across different environments, including browsers, edge runtimes, cloud functions, and native systems. Web Assembly modules are compiled from source languages such as Rust, C, or Swift and execute within a sandboxed environment that enforces strict isolation from the host. In UMA, Web Assembly is the primary mechanism for achieving runtime independence: a capability compiled to a Web Assembly module can be deployed to any runtime that provides a compliant execution environment without recompiling its core logic.

Index

A

E. Piovesan, *Universal Microservices Architecture*, https://doi.org/10.1007/979-8-8688-2794-5

B

C

F

G

H

I

J, K

L

M

N

O

P

Q

R

S

V

W, X, Y

Z

GPSR Compliance
The European Union's (EU) General Product Safety Regulation (GPSR) is a set of rules that requires consumer products to be safe and our obligations to ensure this.

If you have any concerns about our products, you can contact us on

ProductSafety@springernature.com

In case Publisher is established outside the EU, the EU authorized representative is:

Springer Nature Customer Service Center GmbH
Europaplatz 3
69115 Heidelberg, Germany

www.ingramcontent.com/pod-product-compliance
Lightning Source LLC
Chambersburg PA
CBHW080253250826
50385CB00022B/593
9798868827938